GENERAL CUSTER'S LIBBIE

GENERAL CUSTER'S LIBBIE

Lawrence A. Frost

ILLUSTRATIONS—E. LISLE REEDSTROM

SUPERIOR PUBLISHING COMPANY-SEATTLE

Library of Congress Card Number 76-2682

Library of Congress Cataloging in Publication Data

Frost, Lawrence A.
General Custer's Libbie.

Bibliography: p.
Includes index.
1. Custer, Elizabeth Bacon, 1842-1933. I. Title.
E467.1.C99F76 973.8′092′4 76-2682 ISBN 0-87564-806-1

FIRST EDITION

Printed in The United States of America

Dedication

Dedicated to Lenore Custer and her husband, the late Colonel Brice C. W. Custer. Like his great-uncle General George Armstrong Custer, he too left a commendable military record.

JUDGE DANIEL STANTON BACON, ELEANOR SOPHIA BACON, ELIZABETH BACON, left to right. Ca. 1854. From a Daguerreotype in author's collection.

CONTENTS

Acknowledgements

There are many people, both living and dead, to whom I would like to express my gratitude for their assistance in preparing this volume. First, of course, is the late Colonel Brice Calhoun Ward Custer, and his two sisters, the late Margaret Elizabeth and Miriam Irene Custer. No less thanks can I offer Mrs. Brice C. W. Custer of Carmel, California, her son Colonel George A. Custer III of Yuma, Arizona, and her husband's brother, Colonel Charles Custer of Las Cruces, New Mexico. Each offered me encouragement and materials without which this volume would be incomplete.

Dr. and Mrs. James H. Flynn of Verona, New Jersey, like true friends, went on lengthy searches for information. Lisle Reedstrom of Cedar Lake, Indiana, Frank Mercatante of Grand Rapids, Michigan, William A. Graf of Iowa City, Iowa, Richard G. Case of Cazenovia, New York, E. B. (Jack) Cooper of Jersey City, New Jersey, Mrs. David Bartlett of Bronxville, New York, Ruth B. Mitchell of the Connecticut Mutual Life Insurance Co. of Hartford, Connecticut permitted me the use of material they owned or had access to.

Jack Manion of Camillus, New York and Gordon Corbett of Waldwick, New Jersey, drove many miles to obtain photographs and information that filled in what would have been a void.

Mrs. Robert Gray of Ridgewood, New Jersey, grand-daughter of Captain George Yates, permitted me to read and use correspondence that gave me an insight into Libbie's last years.

Major Theodore J. Crackel, United States Military Academy, West Point, New York, graciously permitted me to read and quote from his fine unpublished manuscript on the Custers in Kentucky.

John M. Carroll of New Brunswick, the king of researchers, for I know of no one who can top him when it comes to a knowledge of Custer source material, frequently surprised me with information about Libbie I was unaware of.

Then there is that Custer expert of experts, Hugh W. Shick of North Hollywood, California. Hugh and I fell in love with Libbie about the same time. I had several advantages. I live closer to the Custers and Libbie. We both knew that Libbie preferred older men, so I had Hugh on that point too. But true to the cause, Hugh has straightened me out from time to time over the years, and though we do not agree upon every point, we both agree that there was only one Libbie.

The many others to whom I am indebted and most grateful to are: **Monroe, Michigan:** Mrs. Vernon Clark, Monroe County Libarary; Mrs. Marie McNairn, Dorsch Memorial Library; Hugh Winkworth; Charles Verhoeven; Arthur Lesow; Norris Spainhower; Everette Payette; Reverend William N. Mertz, First United Methodist Church; Reverend Paul Markham, Presbyterian Church; Warren Labeau, Monroe County Clerk; Monroe *Evening News;* Mrs. Arvin Phillipart, Mrs. Raymond Pyle, Matthew Switlik, Mrs. Helen Dusseau, Monroe County Historical Museum; Carl Cousino, Monroe County Registrar of Deeds; Harry Seitz Jr., Monroe County Judge of Probate; Mrs John Weaver; Mrs. Martha Barker; The late Miss Lelia Nelson; Mrs. Robert Gustafson, Monroe Historical Commission; Mrs. Janet Cawood; Kathleen Moore; Kathleen Lohr; staff members of Dorsch Memorial Library and Monroe County Library.

MICHIGAN: Lila Colby, Michigan State Library, Lansing; Alvin Skelly, Detroit Public Schools; Mrs. Jill Merke, Detroit; Constance Cooper, Detroit Public Schools; Congressman Marvin Esch, Ann Arbor; Merrill Murphy, Tecumseh; Tecumseh Public Library staff; Detroit Public Schools staff; Dennis R. Bodem, Michigan State Historical Collections, Ann Arbor; Dr. Edward Willoughby, Lansing; Dr. Harold Cummings, Central Michigan University, Mount Pleasant; Howard Berry, Milan; U.S. Senator Philip Hart; Mrs. Ida Brown, Michigan Historical Collections, Ann Arbor; University of Michigan Library, Ann Arbor.

NEW YORK: Mrs. William H. Briggs, Cosmopolitan Club, New York City; Dr. Edward M. Winant, Mrs. Phylis Knowles, Mrs. David Bartlett, Mrs. Donald K. Clifford, Bronxville; Margaret Stearns, Museum of the City of New York; Mrs. Mildred Dillenbeck, Remington Art Memorial Museum, Ogdenburg; Douglas A. Bakken, Cornell University, Ithaca; James J. Heslin, New York Historical Society, New York City; George F. McAdams, Southold; Frances Goudy, Vassar College Library, Poughkeepsie; Josena R. Foley, Canandaigua; Donald D. Robinson, Camillus; Blackburn Hughes Jr., Onteora Park, Tannersville; Gerald J. Parsons, Syracuse Public Libarary; Mrs. Leo Pinckney, Cayuga County Historical Center, Auburn; Mrs. Frederick T. Cummerford, Onteora Park, Tannersville; Richard N. Wright, Onondaga Historical Association, Syracuse; Dr. Sidney Forman, Mrs. Leona P. Patten, West Point Library; Richard E. Kuehne, Kenneth W. Rapp, West Point Museum; Mrs. Gladys R. Connor, Bronxville Public Library; United States Military Academy Library staff; Haines Falls Free Library.

NEW JERSEY: James Horan, Weehawken; Thaddeus J. From, New Jersey Historical Society, Newark; W. Donald Horn, West Orange; Melvin Nichols, Summit.

CALIFORNIA: Mrs. Evelyn Luce, San Diego; Mrs. Margaret Leighton, Santa Monica; Elizabeth S. Wrigley, Francis Bacon Foundation, Claremont; Edward Staples, University of California, Granada Hills; Dick Upton, Play Del Rey; Dr. Jay Monaghan, Santa Barbara; Christian F. Brun, University of California, Santa Barbara.

KANSAS: Tal N. Luther, Shawnee Mission; Mary Allyn, Hays; Mrs. Minnie Millbrook, Topeka; Myrl V. Walker, Sternburg Memorial Museum, Hays; Marc T. Campbell, Forsyth Library, Hays; Nyle H. Miller, Kansas Historical Society, Topeka.

OHIO: Toledo Public Library.

COLORADO: Mrs. Alice L. Sharp, Colorado State Historical Society, Denver; Mrs. Marion Murra, Pueblo Regional Library, Pueblo; Mrs. Alys Freeze, Western History Department, Denver Public Library; Jerome A. Greene, L. Clifford Soubier, Robert Palmer, Denver.

MONTANA: Janet Clayton, Billings Public Library; Hardin Public Library; J. D. Young, Custer Battlefield National Monument, Crow Agency; Superintendent Eldon G. Reyer, Custer Battlefield National Monument, Crow Agency; former superintendent, Custer Battlefield National Monument, William A. Harris.

WYOMING: Gene M. Gressley, Western History Center, University of Wyoming, Laramie; Doug Younkin, Laramie; William Henry Jr., Fort Laramie National Monument; Mrs. Nadya Henry, Torrington; Jack D. Hughes, Cheyenne; Owen B. Williams, Sheridan.

KENTUCKY: James R. Bentley, The Filsom Club, Louisville; John C. Larsen, University of Kentucky; Louise Wallace, U.S. Army Armor School Library, Fort Knox.

ONTARIO, CANADA: Katherine Greenfield, Hamilton Public Library; Dr. Robert Smith, Hamilton.

LOUISIANA: Dr. Frank Hall, Gretna.

TEXAS: Ben Mayfield, El Paso.

CONNECTICUT: Ruth Mitchell, Librarian, Connecticut Mutual Life Insurance Company, Hartford; Mrs. Linda W. Winters, Connecticut State Library, Hartford.

VIRGINIA: Kurt Brandenburg, Mrs. Cheryl Chambers, Museum of the Confederacy, Richmond; Mrs. Frances N. Shively, Alexandria.

DISTRICT OF COLUMBIA: Robert M. Utley, U.S. Park Service, Washington; James B. Rhoads, U.S. Archivist, Washington; Eileen M. Mabry, Roy P. Basler, George W. Shipman, Library of Congress, Washington; Photo and Print Division, Library of Congress; Mark G. Eckhoff, Civil Archives Division, National Archives; Elmer O. Parker, Victor Gondos Jr., Mrs. Sarah Jackson, Old Army Branch, National Archives.

WASHINGTON: Mrs. Jane R. Stewart, Cheney.

NEW MEXICO: Mr. and Mrs. Archie T. Carothers, Santa Fe.

NORTH DAKOTA: James E. Sperry, State Historical Society of North Dakota, Bismarck.

IOWA: William A. Graf, Iowa City; Dr. Stewart E. Reed, Des Moines.

MASSACHUSETTS: Mrs. Lawrence W. Churchill Jr., West Chatham; Yale University Library, Manuscript Division, Cambridge; Enfried Larson, Worcester; Berkshire Athenaeum, Pittsfield.

PENNSYLVANIA: Fred Hummelbaugh, Gettysburg; George Rummell, Gettysburg.

OKLAHOMA: Dean Krakel, Esther Long, National Cowboy Hall of Fame, Oklahoma City; Dr. Ralph E. Owens, Oklahoma City.

MINNESOTA: Minnesota Historical Society, St. Paul.

MISSOURI: Shirley Lacey, Independence; Edward F. Dolan Jr., State Division of Insurance, Jefferson City; Roy E. Schumacher, Missouri Bankers Assn., Jefferson City.

GEORGIA: Captain Charles Merkel Jr., Fort Benning.

Roy Hamlin of Monroe, fine editor that he is, has combed this material free of my most consistent errors of composition and punctuation. In no way is he responsible for those that remain.

And finally, I am indebted to Mrs. Jack Jennette for typing the entire manuscript in conjunction with her many other duties as my office assistant, and to my wife Ethel who proofread the final copy.

L.A.F.

FOREWORD

Elizabeth Bacon Custer—Libbie to all who knew her then and of her today—was truly a heroine in her own right. She shared her husband's triumphs and misfortunes with equal perception and tact. But above all Libbie was a lady in the grand old style so sadly in disrepair today.

Libbie lived through a turbulent period in our history, the Civil War in particular and the frontier of the American West in general. Although she did not share her husband's discomforts during the War Between The States, she was nearby in Washington, D.C., and because of this she did experience his frequent visits and shared a lack of privacy, for both were celebrities of a sort. The newspapers of the day extolled the heroism of her husband, and she was received in the best homes in Washington, including the White House. Any lesser disciplined young lady could easily have experienced the heady, intoxicating exaltation of adoration—even if by reflection or osmosis—and suffered at the least a turned head. Such was not the case. Oh, sure, she felt the impact of such popularity, but she had what was then known as breeding. Libbie knew the gentle art of feminism without a need of any of the organized political and economic activities believed to be necessary today. She knew how to use her status, and how to use it well, and that was all she was ever guilty of during those exciting days. This was certainly to her credit.

After the Civil War while on the first of several difficult assignments she was to share on the frontier with her husband she proved her strength and wherewithal, especially on the march to Austin, Texas. She may even have been one of the first truly "liberated" women when she—as she later humorously recalled—accidentally left her stays dangling from the limb of a pine tree after having spent the night sleeping in a wagon. She exhibited a marvelous sense of humor and a guarded sense of history when she wrote of the incident and wondered what would be thought by future discoverers of her oversight. The success of her husband's tenure in that wonderful State of Texas was due as much to her efforts as to the General's. Every military wife—then and now—knows this responsibility.

Although there were many army wives who preceded her on the untamed western frontier, Libbie's exposure was to be the most noteworthy in terms of presence and literature. In my opinion, the closest to share this distinction would be the two Mrs. General Carringtons. It would be the leveling influence of these military wives who bumped and jostled in military transports and inadequate public transportation from post to post who are most responsible for bringing "civilization" to the frontier, a recognition shared with the wives of pioneers who settled the areas. Certainly their lives were no easier than their husbands' lives, and most certainly they had as few comforts both in terms of diet and environment and attire. They had to prove to be strong-willed and resourceful. Libbie even recorded her efforts to utilize everything and throw away nothing when she told of stripping her husband's old uniforms and making hook rugs for the floors of their quarters. This was a time when fresh onions in their diet was a luxury, not an everyday occurrence.

Of all her heroic deeds—heroic when compared to today's easy life—none can surpass her absolute performance when at Fort Abraham Lincoln she learned of her husband's death at the Little Big Horn. It *was* a performance, for she maintained a soldierly facade all the while her heart and soul must have been suffering the agonies of a too-soon arrived widowhood. But she showed the stuff she was made of when she quietly and quickly vacated her military quarters as she knew she was no longer a part of the military forces. Her quarters were needed for the next official inhabitants. What a woman! What steel!

After a while it was quite obvious to her, I believe, what she was to do with the rest of her life. Many claim she spent the next fifty-seven years indulging in efforts to perpetuate her husband's memory, deserved or not; to this I object, and most violently. Libbie wrote her memoirs. It is that simple. True, they are qualified histories in that she was not always privy to all the major events and decisions on the frontier which eventually shaped the destiny of this country, but she reported what she observed and heard, and that was a lot. As for perpetuating her husband's memory, I can only say that the events at the Little Big Horn had already prescribed that fate for the General. His life and accomplishments, the Little Big Horn, all facets of the battle and all opinions by arm-chair historians in the future would do more to perpetuate a memory than anything Libbie would write. Libbie's only difference was that her memoirs were written by a woman in love.

Libbie's remaining years were ones often spent in small conflicts. There were the several moves of the statue in Monroe, Michigan, for one thing. The apparent insensitivity of the townsmen in making the moves evidently angered Libbie to such a degree that she never returned to her home. She entered into a campaign of letter writing which resolved nothing. And then there was the statue at West Point which angered her even more, and rightly so. Libbie was unhappy with the inexpertness of the sculptor to capture accurately the dress and mood of the General. Libbie was much more successful with her campaign to have it removed. Today, only a shaft stands where the offensive statue once stood, and the whereabouts of the statue is still in question.

But these, after all, were trivial matters, and fortunately were examples of the most of her problems. Her last remaining years were spent in writing and travelling, both lady-like activities for a famous widow. She often received visitors, and was especially fond of General E. S. Godfrey as Godfrey became more pro-Custer and more anti-Reno. She received lady visitors, most often wives of her husband's comrades and her friends as well. Liza, the black maid who shared so much of the Custers' lives, also visited. Whenever necessary, Libbie could take pen in hand and write a letter to the most influential military officers in Washington and get results, for these were the days when gallantry had not yet been pre-empted by "modern times."

Libbie's death tolled the beginning of the end of an era. The Order of Indian Wars, an organization which met once a year in Washington, D.C., and whose membership was comprised of officers who had been engaged in Indian warfare on the frontier—and much of the membership was related to the 7th U.S. Cavalry in one way or another—expired in 1942. This was truly the end of that era.

Dr. Lawrence Frost, a good friend of mine, has written the first, and I am certain the definitive biography of this remarkable lady. He probably would be the most qualified as well for he has been a friend of the Custer family for many years and has been the recipient of many personal documents from both families in Monroe. I am only grateful the biography has finally been written, and it should become the standard for all biographies of this kind.

For those who are interested in these things, I am including a bibliographic checklist of Libbie's writings. They include:

BOOKS

Tenting On The Plains, or General Custer In Texas and Kansas, New York, Harper Brothers, 1887

Boots And Saddles, New York, Harper Brothers, 1885

Following The Guidon, New York, Harper Brothers, 1890

MAGAZINES

"A New Reno Inquiry," Chicago Westerners Brand Book, July 1967

"An Out-Of-The-Way Meeting," Harper's Weekly, July 18, 1891

"Where Grant Wrote Peace," Harper's Weekly, June 24, 1911

"Where The Heart Is," Lippincott Magazine, February 1900

"Custer's Favorite Photo Of Himself," Teepee Book, July 1916

PAMPHLET

"Custer's Last Battle," General Edward S. Godfrey. Libbie wrote the foreword to this reprint in pamphlet form of the famous Century magazine article.

JOHN M. CARROLL
New Brunswick, N.J.

LIBBIE BACON. Ca. 1855. Author's collection.

PREFACE

Elizabeth Bacon was a most unusual woman. Born in Monroe, Michigan, as the only daughter of a judge — the forebears on each side of her family reaching back to the Mayflower and to English royalty — she was pampered, petted and permitted more than usual liberties, all because her mother had died when she was a young girl.

It must not be construed that care was lacking in her upbringing. Judge Bacon was a cautious man. He loved his daughter dearly, moreso because she was the lone survivor of four children.

Libbie, as everyone called her, in retrospect considered herself a bit of a tomboy, or as near to one as a girl could be in those days. Though a lonely child in the first few years following her mother's death, she was given ample opportunity to obtain a fine though impractical education.

After being exposed to a number of teenage love affairs, she finally succumbed to the vigorous and well-planned campaign of the Boy General, but only after the approval of her father and stepmother had been obtained.

Literally torn from a life of tranquility and comfort and thrust into one of anxiety and turmoil, the transition was one that few women would have endured. With no precedent to guide her, Libbie joined the Army of the Potomac at Winchester, Virginia, in February, 1864, as George Armstrong Custer's bride.

That she adapted to this rough life is attested to by the cordial acceptance of her by Chief of Cavalry General Phil Sheridan. Prior to her arrival, he had vehemently disapproved of officers' wives because they interfered. Later he asked that she remain in camp with his cavalry during the winter season. He had observed that she brought out the best in his officers. Her presence had a salutary effect.

Rougher still was her transition to the Western frontier. Life on the plains was almost a complete reversal of the comforts offered in the East. Frontier life was a continuation of the anxieties and nightmares she had experienced during the Civil War, yet she would't think of going back to the comforts of home. She had married for love. There was nothing else to marry a soldier for.

Women's record on the plains is filled with stories of hardships, perils, kindness, bravery and love for men seeking the end of a rainbow. Like most army women she felt privileged to keep the home fires burning while her husband was making history protecting the frontiers so railroads could be built coast to coast, and the intervening country could be opened to civilization. These were pioneer army women, sharing the danger and hardships of their soldier-husbands.

History is mainly the story of man's achievements. Rarely is the role of woman mentioned unless to star her in the role of queen or as a great beauty. These officers' wives who followed their husbands from post to post are the unsung heroines of western history.

Presented here is the life of this unusual woman through unusual times and conditions. At the time she became attached to the Union's fighting force in Virginia most women there were either laundresses or camp followers; there were a very few nurses. No official provision or recognition was given to the wife of an officer. The recognition and standing of officers' wives in today's army well might have had their origin in Libbie's time because of her deportment and that of her contemporaries.

A rational judgment of George Armstrong Custer can never be attained through the eyes of his detractors alone. To know him well enough to reach a sound and just conclusion as to his character one must see his other side — through the eyes of his wife and friends.

An intelligent woman — and Libbie was that — can see all sides of her husband. Libbie had every opportunity to observe his character under every sort of condition for his life in the military service had been a series of tests and successes that would have turned the heads of older men who were his peers.

Libble was quite critical of men, even more than she was of women. The men she criticized were her husband's fellow officers though they were not his rivals, for the seniority system prevailed. Many were severely critical of him though never openly. To Libbie's way of thinking these associates were officers but not gentlemen since the latter would not criticize their commanding officer behind his back.

Her husband carried no grudges or resentments. He was aware of this failing of some of his officers but preferred that it not be a matter of garrison gossip or comment. He had asked Libbie not to take any side in such matters and invited her not to display in any manner any feeling of resentment or dislike toward an officer or the regiment who had voiced some opinion against him.

Though General Custer had been charged with nepotism, it should be remembered that he was the commander of the Seventh Cavalry first, last and always. He displayed no favoritism for he was as tough with his brother Tom as he was with any other officer serving under him, placing Tom under arrest several times. Custer didn't require, and didn't want, close friends among the officers. Tom Custer had two Medals of Honor; Custer had his Libbie. On this is hinged the rare story of an unbroken devotion.

When she returned to Monroe to repair her shattered life after that terrible tragedy in 1876, she and the widows who suffered with her received no official communication of any kind from President Grant. It was as though he ignored the catastrophe to shut it out of his mind.

This he might do, for some men can close their ears to the anguished cries of the widows. Libbie could not. Their tearful letters tore her apart. She became a sister to the young widows and a mother to the orphans of the Seventh until the end of her days. Always thereafter she maintained a steadfast interest in the welfare of the wives of the officers in her husband's command, doing everything in her power to bolster their morale or aid them in their pension claims.

There was no room in her life for any other man after the General's death. There might have been had his brother Tom survived, so members of the Custer family have told me. She was destined to live alone.

An early interest in women's liberation was inspired by the need for economic independence. She had become the sole support of her husband's aged parents, an obligation requiring more income than she had available. In order to bolster her slender income, she accepted a secretarial position with a New York organization that assisted widows in obtaining some degree of financial security.

Some writers have claimed that out of respect for her no one, during her lifetime, would write or say anything disparaging or detrimental about her husband. Others have said that she spent the balance of her 92 years refuting all statements not complimentary to her husband's memory. Such thoughts are in conflict with each other. If none spoke out then why would it be necessary for her to refute them? These writers either have not seen, or chose to ignore, the Goldin-Benteen letters, Reverend Cyrus T. Brady's book, "Indian Fights and Fighters," or Colonel Robert P. Hughes' article, "The Campaign Against the Sioux in 1876." The letters, book and article, written during her lifetime, villified the hero after he was dead and could not respond. It took the great Indian fighter General Nelson Miles to classify these authors and many to come by saying that it didn't take much courage to kick a dead lion.

Defensively, and well-armed with facts, Libbie responded to the many false statements issued by the character assassins.

What she said and wrote and did was not out of hate for her husband's enemies but for love of him.

Military men of rank, such as Generals Edward S. Godfrey and Nelson Miles, quickly came to her assistance. One by one they shot down the dissidents. None could stand up to the truth.

Once Libbie had died, a new era of disparagement began. Writers like Van de Water, Dustin and Brininstool applied their talents to belittle General Custer. None knew Custer; none had ever fought Indians; none evidenced any interest in the truth.

In her later years Libbie considered the Cosmopolitan Club of New York City her intellectual home. The excitement of the contacts there with the leaders of her sex was a special delight to her. It provided the opportunity of meeting women who had achieved something on their own. A women's libber at heart, she knew the value of equality and independence and had done much in her representative way to obtain it for herself and others.

One would think she might end her days with some feeling of disappointment. But long before the end she said: "I have but two regrets — my husband's death and the fact that I have no son to bear his honored name."

Lawrence A. Frost
Monroe, Michigan

LIBBIE BACON. Ca. 1856. From a Daguerreotype, courtesy of her cousin, Bronson Case, Kansas City, Mo.

CHAPTER 1
DANIEL BACON MOVED WEST

Motionless she sat, like Whistler's mother, looking straight ahead. Her petite figure leaned forward ever so slightly, giving an impression of rapt attention. Before her was a fumed oak library table which held a small steeple-shaped radio placed there earlier by a kindly bellhop. The room was the unoccupied sun parlor of a hotel a short distance from the gray-haired woman's Fifth Avenue apartment. Not having a radio of her own, the thoughtful hotel manager had placed both radio and room at her disposal. He knew how important this June 25th day of 1926 was to this 84-year-old lady.

The faint sounds emanating from the radio gave an illusion of distance which was augmented by the quiet of the room. The deep, almost ominous tones of the narrator sketched an event that had occurred 50 years ago that very day. Voices had been dubbed in to assume the roles of leading participants, and sound effects had been added to create a martial atmosphere.

Officers barked orders as horses' hoofs beat the ground in a passing charge. The thuds of body impact, sounds of gunfire and intermittent cries of men and animals in pain could be as clearly heard as the frequent war whoops of Indians.

Occasionally the gray-haired figure would lean forward as if trying to hear something in the background of this melee of sounds. The soft curls on her forehead would fall back in place as she resumed her erect position though her eyes would not leave the radio nor would she accept the backrest support of her wicker armchair.

At one point the weak tones of the radio grew louder as a clear voice rang out, "Colonel Cooke, send your orderly to Captain Benteen with this message: 'Come on — Big Village — Be quick — Bring packs!' "

The voice was that of General George Armstrong Custer giving his last known order at the battle of the Little Big Horn 50 years ago, the role being taken by an actor for this re-enactment of Custer's Last Stand.

Near the end of the half-hour program, several carbine volleys were fired in the distance, simulating the vain effort of Custer's command in a call for help from his other detachments who were with Major Reno and Captain Benteen. Following this came the fearful sounds of hand-to-hand combat on Custer Hill. Then — silence.

The small figure sat transfixed for a full minute, her expression unchanged. Finally, she said, "Yes, that is how it would have been." This was the widow of General Custer.

She stood up as if to leave. There were no tears, for those had dried up some 50 years ago. Ever so slightly her shoulders sagged as she moved toward the door. She had heard what she had come to hear; there was nothing more to stay for.

Mrs. Elizabeth Bacon Custer had been invited to participate in the semi-centennial anniversary celebration in Montana that day. Wisely, she had declined. Though her health had been failing, it had not been to an extent that it would have interfered. She realized that the participants in the re-enactment would be young. The battle and the story now were legendary. Her presence would have been inexpedient. With the aid of a cane Mrs. Custer slowly made her way back to her apartment with her companion. There her friend politely refused to accept the invitation to share the evening meal with her, for fear of breaking the spell.[1]

Elizabeth Clift Bacon was born on the shores of Lake Erie, April 8, 1842, in the village of Monroe.[2] This fourth oldest community in Michigan[3] had been settled by French voyageurs and fur traders well before 1785.[4] They were the first to recognize the advantages of establishing themselves near the mouth of the River Raisin. Game was abundant, Indians were friendly and transporting fish, furs or trade goods in a canoe was more practical than packing them.

The first settlers called the settlement *Riviere au Raisin.* The English arrived soon after, applying their well-developed commercial instincts to the business advantages of the outpost. In honor of their predecessors they called it Frenchtown. One suspects they found the word Frenchtown easier to say than *Riviere au Raisin.*[5] Soon after President

ELIZABETH CLIFT BACON. Ca. 1852. Oil on canvas in Monroe County Historical Museum.

James Monroe's visit to Michigan in 1817, the village was renamed Monroe.

The slow growing settlement, lining both sides of the River Raisin, gradually lost its frontierlike atmosphere, adopting many of the ways of the newly arriving English.

The War of 1812 had left its scars. The site of a battle and a massacre in 1813, it became the source of the rallying battlecry, "Remember the Raisin,"[6] westerners used so effectively for the remainder of the war.[7]

A Kentucky contingent commanded by General Winchester had marched up from Ohio to repel the British and protect the inhabitants of Frenchtown. On January 22, 1813, it was surprised and overpowered by a superior British force under General Proctor. The Indians, enraged by their losses, brutally butchered wounded Kentucky soldiers the following day. Their treacherous actions were carried out contrary to an agreement with the British Colonel Proctor to protect the wounded.[8]

It was to this war-charred frontier outpost the youthful Daniel Bacon headed. When he arrived in the fall of 1822 the log cabins burned down by the depredating Indians had been replaced by buildings of wood siding or brick. The influx of new people had made it necessary to cut down the many trees that covered the land, a monumental task when one considers that the tools were crude and the labor hard. These were a sturdy people, these pioneers, and ever willing to help a neighbor.

When it came time to build a house or barn, a "bee" was organized. Everyone dropped his work to pitch in and assist the neighbor. Trees were leveled and structures raised in an air of harmony and fellowship. The occasion was accompanied by humor, music and plenty of food. It was not unusual to find a jug over by the well.

The river was the center of all activity. Its water was the source of power for the grist and saw mills, and supplied the tanneries, distilleries and breweries. Every farmer recognized the value of having water close at hand, for his stock, his crops and his family, so he built his home on its banks.

There were other uses for the river too. Ice was cut each winter for the storage of fresh meat throughout the year. A frozen river provided a surface for winter sports, for some enjoyed skating. Everyone enjoyed the horse racing on the river ice. The French would pit their small Canadian horses against those of their neighbors, creating excitement and amusement for all.

A trail had developed between the frontier settlements of Detroit and Toledo. Where it crossed the River Raisin a business center appeared. Stores spread out along the south bank and houses appeared around the courthouse nearby.[9]

Names like Joliet, Father Marquette, Count Frontenac, Robert LaSalle, Jacques Cartier, Champlain and Count Ponchartrain were household words when Daniel Stanton Bacon first reached Monroe. The village had recovered from the ravages of the British and their Indian allies and had entered into an era of trade and farming. Bacon, now 24, foreseeing the need for his fine educational background, offered his services as a teacher.[10]

He had traveled by stage from Rochester to Buffalo, New York, as comfortably as the rough roads would permit. The passage from Buffalo to Cleveland on the *Red Jacket* was exceedingly rough even for this hardy soul. Unable to find employment as a schoolteacher in Ohio, he had boarded the *Prudence* at Sandusky for Detroit.[11] In the vicinity of Monroe he filled the vacancy of a small district school. The pay was small and the pupils few but this didn't deprive him of his urge to obtain security. His years had been spent on the farm of his father so it was natural to turn to the soil for additional income and contentment.

A land office opened in Monroe in early 1823 and young Bacon was one of the first to apply for a land title along the River Raisin.[12] Unafraid of hard labor, for he had received a solid background on his father's farm at Howlett Hill, Onondaga County, New York, he soon cleared ten acres of land,[13] replanting it with nursery stock of peach, apple and plum. Happily repaid for his efforts, for lumber was bringing $12 a thousand, he became concerned over the possibility of falling a victim to the prevalent ague and fever.

Leonard Bacon, the father of Daniel, was a farmer of moderate circumstances.[14] He had been born in

Woodstock, Connecticut, in 1771 where he met and married Elizabeth Clift, January 4, 1798. Their first child, Daniel Stanton, was born in Onondaga County, New York, December 12, 1798. Lydia arrived in 1800. Eliza in 1803, Leonard Clift in 1803, George Washington in 1807, Miriam in 1809, Elihue in 1812 and Charity in 1814.[15]

Many years later, Elizabeth Clift Bacon's granddaughter Libbie Bacon would pencil in her notebook pridefully, "Samuel Clift landed at Plymouth Rock, December 21, 1620 — that makes us Mayflower descendants on both Clift and Bacon sides."[16] Libbie was proud of her ancestry for the Bacons could trace their family back to Alfred the Great of England. In later life she had filled out an application for membership in the Daughters of the American Revolution.[17] A search indicates there is no record in the Washington office of the DAR that she ever had completed her application.[18] Leonard Bacon had been referred to as a "skillful physician and prosperous farmer."[19] Earlier it was stated that he was a farmer. A study of the correspondence to his son makes no mention of other than his ability and interest in farming.[20]

Having lost his wife in the spring of 1823, Leonard found Howlett Hill a constantly painful reminder of happier days. Young in spirit, for he was only 51, he expressed a wish to Daniel to sell out and move to the Michigan frontier. As an on-the-spot observer Daniel was quick to advise Father Bacon the farm he had should be retained for "where could you ever get so good a farm as that you now possess . . . ?" In utter candor, he mentioned that he thought his father too old a man to remove his worldly goods to Monroe, then ended his letter by inviting him to come and see for himself.[21]

Leonard did not have to be asked twice. Lonesome and disconsolate, he yearned for a change and so made the tedious trip. The settlement on the River Raisin did not meet his expectations. The strenuous life of a farmer had toughened him but not enough for the rough way of life he had to endure with his eldest son. There were 26 years difference in their ages. He discovered that the 25 year-old Daniel suffered as much, but tolerated inconveniences with greater fortitude, then recovered more quickly than he from physical discomforts.

Muddy trails instead of roads, plank bottomed beds, Indian scares and the ever present dread of contracting ague and fever (malaria) from the mosquito infested marshlands bordering Lake Erie, hurried his decision.

Soon he had his fill for there was little adventure and an overabundance of hard work. Quite likely he found females too few in number for he soon returned to Howlett Hill in Onondaga County where his fancy turned to lighter things. In a short time he had remarried, his selection being a young woman named Elizabeth.[22]

Howlett Hill was first settled in 1803. At the time of its settlement, Syracuse, just a few miles to the northeast, was a swamp. Everyone predicted the Hill would be the center of a great city. Instead, the swampy valley nurtured the city of Syracuse.[23]

Several years after its founding, John Case built a large frame house[24] there in which Libbie lived for a time in the 1850s and which she visited on her honeymoon. This was a full two-story, white-sided house with green shutters. It featured hand hewn joists, mortise and beam joints secured with wooden pegs, and a casket door three feet wide, permitting easy access into the parlor.[25]

Avid student that he was, Daniel Bacon read law evenings, applying himself to his teaching and farming during the day. The village properties were being purchased and developed by an influx of Eastern folk of English background. Their need for legal assistance was supplied by the youthful but prudent Bacon. The community began to thrive under the guidance of this new blood and there were dreams of a huge lake port and a shipping complex for the resources this verdant territory could supply through its waterways.

Though the French, many of whom were of illustrious parentage, had first occupied the land, they had little drive or desire for worldly possessions. Content with a leisurely existence, many of them married Indians and slipped into an informal and somewhat passive life. Not so the Yankees. They saw opportunity, for the lush, fertile valley of the Raisin offered land that could be developed for profit. The woodlands supplied the lumber so sorely needed in this wild country. The waterways offered cheap transportation into the country's interior. It was their oyster.

Desiring the finer things of life, they built roads and boats, established a newspaper and schools, built churches and mills. A bank was an important by-product, and with it law and order in the form of a courthouse and jail and its all-important whipping post. In this atmosphere of expansion and improvement, Daniel aided the thrifty and energetic emigrants from New York and other eastern states. By the time the Monroe township election rolled around in 1832 he was established and respected to the point of being elected one of three school inspectors.[26] He had been elected a county supervisor just the year before, and again the same year.[27] One month after first elected a school inspector he was elected representative to the Fifth Territorial Legislature, an office he held through the Sixth Legislature.[28] Sentiment favoring him continued to grow.

There was considerable dissent in Michigan Territory over which boundary lines would delineate the proposed State of Michigan. As a result of the dispute, Monroe County refused to send delegates to either of the conventions held to approve the new boundaries. Without hesitation President Andrew Jackson signed the bill making the territory a state and admitting Michigan into the Union.[29]

Daniel had enjoyed his political successes. His desire to serve had been sincere and he knew he had applied himself. His many friends had told him he had done well and were encouraging him to run for higher office. The infant state of Michigan was readying its first election. While the parties were lining up their candidates an advertisement in the first issue of the new weekly, the Monroe *Gazette*, announced, "Republican Whig Nominations For Governor — Charles C. Trowbridge of Wayne — For Lieutenant Governor, Daniel S. Bacon of Monroe."[30]

Though politics occupied the center of conversation, Surveyor Henry Disbrow's announcement in the same issue of the *Gazette* that he would "be under the disagreeable necessity of putting the collection of the subscription—for the building of a bridge over the River Raisin at Macomb Street — into the hand of an officer for collection or the work must be abandoned," must have caused considerable comment.

Daniel's supporters must have concluded they had people thinking their way when the *Gazette* reprinted the brainchild of the Ann Arbor *State Journal*, "The NEXT LIEUTENANT GOVERNOR — The people in the West speaking of the merits of Messrs. Mundy and Bacon for the office of Lieutenant Governor, facetiously say, that *Mundy* (Monday) comes but *once a week*, but they want *BACON every day!* We guess their wants will be supplied in November."

The November 11th issue of the *Gazette* announced that the election of November 6-7, 1837, was a Democratic victory. Monroe, being a Democratic stronghold, giving Acting Governor Steven T. Mason the plurality. Bacon was defeated by Mundy but made a better showing in the final count than Trowbridge, the gubernatorial aspirant.

Monroe was prospering. It had become a conspicuous rival to Detroit. Its water power supplied two flour mills, a woolen mill and three sawmills. An iron foundry, a tannery, three banks, six churches and two printing offices were established. The *Gazette* was one of the latter. It folded several years later and on its ruins was started the Monroe *Sentinel*. Its lifespan was shorter than that of the *Gazette*.[31]

The sale of public lands, beginning in 1835, played a large part in Monroe County's growth. With a population of 3,187 in 1830, it jumped to 10,611 in 1837 — more than 300 per cent. In the same period, the Village of Monroe leaped from 478 to nearly 1,500.[32]

The influx of people brought many of unusual ability: Isaac P. Christiancy, who began as a clerk in the land office and later became a justice of the Michigan Supreme Court and United States senator; Alpheus Felch, governor of Michigan, 1846-1847, and United States senator; Robert McClelland, governor of Michigan, 1852-1853, Congressman, then Secretary of the Interior under President Franklin K. Pierce.[33] They and many others provided leadership and new ideas for this land of opportunity. An aggregate of thirty merchants, six physicians and thirteen lawyers provided impetus and stability.

Bacon and his compatriots saw opportunity in the banking business. In November of 1837, the Merchants and Mechanics Bank announced its opening. Daniel S. Bacon was its president.[34] Several months earlier his name had appeared in the city business directory as the "Assistant Judge of the Circuit Court."[35] Daniel had established himself as a man of stability and importance.

A surprise to many was an annoucement in January of 1838 that a branch of the University of Michigan had been established in Monroe. Local reaction commended the zeal "manifested to establish an institution of higher learning" but deplored the fact that "nothing has been said or done towards the establishment of common schools, which certainly are far more important to the community at large."[36] This had the desired effect for public and private schools soon became a reality.

Efforts were made to expand Monroe's shipping facilities. The Army Engineers had convinced the Government of the value in straightening its river channel into the lake. Several wharves had been built on the river front, and warehouses had been erected nearby. In May of 1838, the steampacket *Rhode Island* began a regular run between Cleveland and Detroit, touching at Monroe on her upward and downward passages. Another packet, the *Gen. Brady*, began a regular run between Monroe and Detrout,[37] touching on intermediate ports and carrying both passengers and freight. Both boats were competing with the steamboat *Monroe* which advertised that it was "of the largest class of steamboats and has a spacious cabin sufficient to accommodate 150 passengers all taking their meals at the same time." It left the Monroe pier each Monday morning for Buffalo, touching at all intermediate ports. Previously, passengers from the East would be required to take a boat from Buffalo to Detroit, then make a wearisome eight hour trip by stage to Monroe.

Daniel watched this progress with great interest for he could not forget the tedious trip he had made a few short years before. He read of other boats vying for the lucrative passenger and freight business: the *Erie*; a 100 ton craft described as the "saucy" *Vance*; the *Newberry*; and the *Macomb*, which would meet the *River Raisin & Lake Erie Rail Road* when it touched at Monroe.

A Young Men's Literary Society was organized at the Court House, and Alpheus Felch, who was destined to be governor in less than ten years, became its first president. For those who had an interest in the healing arts, a continuous ad in the *Gazette* presented an appealing four-month course of medical lectures in the Willoughby Medical College at Willoughby, Ohio, all for $55 "with board offered at reasonable terms." There was a growing need for doctors and there were no problems in taking medical board examinations for there were no boards.

Judge Bacon maintained an active interest in politics and the Whig party. In the spring city election of 1840 he was elected Assessor of his ward, and in November general election he was elected an associate judge of the Circuit Court.[38] The year prior, he had been elected to the Michigan Senate.[39]

Judge Bacon received his early education at a district school in Onondaga County, New York, walking the four miles to it each day. For a short time he had attended an academy in Onondaga Valley.[40] Friendly to everyone, he maintained a lifelong friendship with Levi S. Humphrey beginning soon after he reached Monroe. Bacon was neither conceited nor arrogant. He was realistic. He saw in Humphrey a man of inherent honesty and great business capacity. Humphrey, who could only sign his name, had come to him for aid in transacting all business requiring writing or arithmetic. They became immediate friends and business partners in many ventures.

Levi Humphrey was from Vermont. He was register of the land office in Monroe, and had managed stage coach lines between Toledo and Detroit with considerable success. In his commercial activities he was known as:

Talleyrand the great and grand,
Talleyrand the Dickerer.[41]

In speaking of his partner, Judge Bacon would say, "I have the advantage of Levi in book knowledge but he excels me in his power of observation and his storing away of facts for future reference."[42]

At the age of 38, Daniel remained single. Honors and position he had, and he was propertied though not wealthy. He had worked hard, both physically and mentally. His work, like that of a priest had received his sole application and attention. He had discarded all thought of marriage and had told his parents he would not marry until he was in a position to offer his wife every comfort. Too much suffering had he seen where wives had been forced to accept the hardships and drudgery of a rough frontier life.[43]

Then he met Eleanor. It is said she was teaching district school in Monroe but there are no records to prove this statement.[44] Eleanor Sophia Page with her parents had moved from Rutland, Vermont, to Grand Rapids. Her father, Abel Page, feeling the need for a change, had sold his tavern in 1835 and moved his family to Michigan to establish a nursery.

Abel and his wife Zilphia were of English stock, a characteristic pleasing to Judge Bacon. They were people of integrity with high moral and cultural standards, the sort of people Daniel would be proud to present to his own family.

That they were religious is attested to by Libbie's memories of visits to her grandparents. They had prayers in the morning and in the evening—and then prayers again in between. A return to Monroe was, ofttimes, a respite.

The Page girls had been educated in the East in one of its fine seminaries. The eldest, Eleanor Sophia, was intelligent, a characteristic that appealed to a man 16 years her senior. Her retiring disposition and her self possession were traits that captivated this mature professional man.

Daniel Bacon had pursued a course of propriety and honesty through all of his 38 years. His courtship was carried on in the same vein. There was formality, respect, but never the word "love" in their interchange of letters.[45] That his visit to her home in Grand Rapids was well-received by her gave him considerable satisfaction. He continued to woo her with all of the dignity and formality expected of any man who merited the title "Judge."

The panic of 1837, having had an unwholesome effect upon the business centers of the East, began to curb transportation on Lake Erie. Daniel and his partner had noticed it in there joint enterprises. It would affect his income that year but he decided it should not interfere with his plans. He had made his business forecast in the spring. By June he had firmed his decision to ask the Pages for their daughter's hand in marriage. He had assured Eleanor — he called her Sophia — that the economic conditions in the East had no bearing on his friendship and affection for her. With that he took the big step and petitioned her parents.

The Pages had been impressed with his sincerity and stability. They consented to the union, and the date was set for the second Tuesday in September, 1837.[46]

Daniel's friends, to his embarrassment, made a point of supplying the Pages with letters of extravagant praise. Basically he was a modest man and he made it evident in his letters to Sophia that he was "a plain man without pretension beyond being a good member of society."[47] No endearing terms, no evidences of pent-up emotion were permitted to enter his letters to her. References to himself were made as "your intended" or "your friend." He did permit himself the break in formality by addressing her as "dear Sophia," but this extravagance was not as daring as it might appear since he indulged in a similar style when heading his business letters.

The honeymooning couple left Grand Rapids for Onondaga County, New York. There was some question as the the "uncertainty of steam boats" and Sophia's natural fear of a form of transportation she had never experienced. Daniel suggested that traveling by land might be more desirable. To this she agreed.

Housekeeping was a new experience for both of them. Domesticity, Daniel discovered, was a bit difficult to accede to for a man of 38. Sophia, now 23, found it more agreeable. And it was just a matter of time before evidence of the union made its appearance.

Edward Augustus was born on June 9, 1839. A mischievous child, as an ungovernable first child tends to be, he was his father's pride and joy. When Mrs. Bacon took him to visit his grandparents in Grand Rapids his father, recognizing his wildness and his irrepressible behavior, expressed the faint hope that the boy would meet the expectations of his relatives.[48]

Young Ed was big for his age, and gave evidence of being tall like his father. Daniel was taller than average though somewhat portly now that his heaviest physical endeavor consisted of a short walk to and from his law office.

Young Ed attracted misfortune. When nearly eight year of age he was the victim of a fall induced by an unrepaired back door step, resulting in a spinal injury. After a year of convalescence an unthinking nurse exposed him to a victim of a contagious disease. Contracting the disease, young Ed soon expired.

NOTES — CHAPTER 1

[1]Marguerite Merington in Monroe *Evening News,* February 11, 1950.

[2]Bacon Family Bible, Monroe County Historical Museum.

[3]F. Clever Bald: *Michigan in Four Centuries,* New York, 1954, p. 165.

[4]Talcott E. Wing: *History of Monroe County, Michigan,* New York, 1890, p. 45.

[5]*Ibid,* p. 66.

[6]John M. Bulkley: *History of Monroe County, Michigan,* New York, 1913, Vol. I, p. 105.

[7]George May: *Pictorial History of Michigan: The Early Years,* Grand Rapids, 1967, p. 67.

[8]Wing, p. 59.

[9]Karl Zeisler: *A Child's History of Monroe,* Monroe, 1948.

[10]He had displayed his proficiency by being examined by the Onondaga County (N.Y.) School Inspectors. Col B.C.W. Custer Collection. March 12, 1819.
That he had some thoughts of military service is evidenced by a certificate signed by Capt. Abel Crane and John M. Stewart, on October 7, 1817, at Onondaga, N.Y., indicating he was unfit for military duty, "by having a fractured leg. The leg is split the whole length." BCWC collection.

[11]Marguerite Merington: *The Custer Story,* N.Y., 1950, p. 15.

[12]E. Gray and Ethel W. Williams: *First Land Owners of Monroe County, Michigan,* Kalamazoo, 1968. The earliest patent listed for Daniel S. Bacon was 80 acres in Erie Township, October 10, 1829, p. 56.
Most of the other acquisitions listed were in the year 1835 and in the townships of Whiteford, LaSalle, Ash and Berlin. Purchases in Dundee and Milan soon followed. At a dollar and a quarter an acre he couldn't be too wrong.

[13]Merington, p. 16.

[14]Bulkley, p. 531, states that Daniel S. Bacon came to Michigan Territory in 1835 and that "His first occupation in this sphere of action was a school teacher, for some time conducting a private school in the village of Frenchtown."
In a letter dated November, 1822, (see Merington, p. 15) he refers to a small school he was operating. There is additional evidence he was in Michigan in 1822. See *Michigan Biographies,* Lansing, 1924, Vol. I, p. 37.

[15]Elizabeth (Libbie) Custer's notes, author's collection.

[16]Libbie's notes.

[17]Application blanks were filled for the Abilene, Kansas branch but not signed. Author's collection.

[18]Letter to Mrs. John F. Weaver, Monroe, Michigan, November 30, 1971.

[19]Merington: *The Custer Story,* New York, 1950, p. 14.

[20]Richard Case, of Cazenovia, N.Y., in his letter of September, 1970, stated: "I can confirm that Leonard Case was a farmer but not that he was a physician."

[21]Merington, p. 17.

[22]Elizabeth G., d. September, 1871.

[23]Syracuse (N.Y.) *Herald Journal,* September 8, 1963.

[24]About 1815.

[25]Syracuse (N.Y.) *Post Standard,* September 8, 1963. John Manion of Camillus, N.Y. supplied excellent photos of this fine old structure as well as background information.

[26]Wing, p. 140. Harry Conant and Phanuel W. Warriner were the others. D.S. Bacon was re-elected in April, 1834.

[27]*Ibid,* p. 267.

[28]*Ibid,* p. 256.

[29]Bald, p. 202. January 26, 1837. The Toledo-Michigan War — a bloodless one — was a stormy protest from Monroe County residents over the removal of Toledo from its confines. Aroused to a point of physical dissent, they raised a militia that marched toward Lucas County, Ohio to settle the matter by force. A series of political and legal maneuvers frustrated the Michigan effort. In the end, Toledo became a part of Ohio, and the Upper Peninsula a part of Michigan. Michiganders have long contended they came out the better. Some controversy remains over the "Lost Peninsula," a piece of land extending into Ohion waters but attached to the Michigan mainland. For additional information see Bald, pp. 194-202.

[30]September 2, 1837.

[31]Bald, p. 165; Bulkley, Vol. I, p. 539.

[32]Wing, p. 141.

[33]Bald, p. 165; F. A. Barnard, *American Biographical History,* Cincinnati, 1898, pp. 2-35, 1-103.

[34]Monroe *Gazette,* November 25, 1837.

[35]Monroe *Gazette,* September 16, 1837.

[36]Monroe *Gazette,* January 27, 1838.

[37]Monroe *Gazette,* May 1, 1838.

[38]Monroe *Gazette,* November 24, 1840.

[39]Wing, p. 257.
In 1841 he was re-elected Assessor of the 4th Ward and elected Alderman on the four-man City council. His friend and business partner Levi Humphrey was elected Mayor in 1844. Wing, p. 258. In 1848, Bacon was elected City Treasurer, Wing, p. 259, and then went on to be elected Judge of Probate that year, Wing, p. 277, an office he held through 1852. Monroe County Probate Court records.

[40]Libbie's penciled notes, author's collection.

[41]Wing, p. 477.

[42]Libbie's notes.

[43]Merington, p. 18.

[44]The Monroe *Commercial,* August 12, 1854, stated that Mrs. Eleanor S. Bacon settled at Grand Rapids in 1835, becoming a resident of Monroe in 1837.

[45]Merington, p. 21.

[46]Bacon Family Bible in Monroe County Historical Museum. The Rev. Mr. McKay officiated on September 12, 1837.

[47]B.C.W. Custer family papers.

[48]Merington, p. 22.

CHAPTER 2
THEN CAME LIBBIE

The Bacon home was a gracious structure. It presented an imposing picture at the southerly edge of the business sector. Surrounded by stately elm trees, its white siding and bottle green shutters gave mute evidence of the calm dignity that prevailed within.[1] A well-kept lawn extended to the neat white picket fence that skirted the sidewalk on the Monroe and Second Street sides of the corner lot.

A high board fence enclosed the back yard which, presumably, was intended to be a deterrent to those boys who looked with covetous eyes upon the heavily laden apple, pear and cherry trees they surrounded.

The south lawn sported a four-seated lawn swing the judge had a Mr. Doty place there several days after his daughter Elizabeth's birthday. In no time at all the yard had filled with boys and girls of every age and size, each eager to try Libbie's (her parents rarely called her Elizabeth) new swing.[2]

The noise emanating from this youthful group seemed not to disturb the Bacons. They could sit in their front porch rocking chairs, well out of the afternoon sun, while the youngsters took their turns on the side lot swing. Perhaps they were thinking of little Eddie who had died just four years earlier,[3] and baby Harriet[4] who succumbed one year afterward. Then there was poor little Sophia[5] who had been the first to go some six years back, holding on to life for three short months.

Libbie, now ten years old,[6] was a healthy, vigorous child. She was an only child now, but not a spoiled one, she insisted years later.[7] Her mother and father were indulgent though firm in matters of propriety. When an order was given it was expected that it was to be obeyed. Obedience was a prime objective. Truthfulness was of even greater importance. And above all respect — respect for God, for Country, for her family and for the elderly.

Libbie showed signs of being a bit capricious. She did not always stay home when told to. When questioned about it, there were times she avoided the truth. Judge Bacon concluded that she should be punished. Several times little Libbie was deposited in a clothes closet for a period of repentance. On one such occasion the confinement made her drowsy. A wicker clothes basket seemed to be just the thing in which to take a nap. She availed herself of the opportunity, for there had been no restrictions prescribed when she was placed in the closet. Her parents soon discovered that the punishment they had imposed was having little effect.

Taking away a privilege seemed to be the obvious next step; there would be no play for Libbie that day. To bed she must go while it was light outside and

while other children were playing. Libbie responded by taking a nap, an unsought reaction that came as a surprise to her parents.

Sophia, kneeling by the side of the small bed, offered prayers for the unpredictable youngster.[8] Roused by the low voice in her room, Libbie listened while pretending to sleep. Touched by her mother's obvious concern, she offered to improve her conduct and, at the same time, indicated that she regretted her actions. Deep within she knew she had no regrets for she had enjoyed every minute of her disregard for family orders. She could not tell her mother how she really felt for she knew it would hurt her deeply. It would be as well to say what her mother expected her to say. Yes, she had to admit to herself, it had been fun to cast off the yoke of her father's commands.

The white picket fence that bordered the Bacon front lawn gave the property an air of dignity. But the pickets were an attractive nuisance. Small boys would hold a stick against them as they ran the length of the fence, producing a spine-tingling sound much like that of a machine gun.

The fence gate held a greater attraction for seven-year old Libbie. Her petite figure could be seen using it to swing back and forth as she watched each passer-by. According to the Custer family she was amusing herself in this manner one day when the tow-headed George Armstrong Custer strode by. In a sudden burst of familiarity she called out, "Hello, you Custer boy." Surprised at her own impertinence, she blushed and ran into the house.

Armstrong Custer was living with his half-sister Lydia Ann at the time, a half mile south of the Bacons. Her husband, David Reed, maintained a drayage business, adding considerably to his income by loaning money on real estate.

Young Armstrong, now ten years old, had been summoned from their family home in New Rumley, Ohio, for Lydia Ann — who now preferred being called Ann—had just given birth to a daughter. Armstrong was useful in many ways since there

LIBBIE BACON. Ca. 1857. Author's collection.

LIBBIE BACON at age 17. Ca. 1859. Author's collection.

LIBBIE BACON. Ca. 1860. Author's collection.

LIBBIE BACON. Ca. 1862. Author's collection.

LIBBIE at age 20. Ca. 1862. Author's collection.

PORTRAIT OF LIBBLE. Ca. 1864. Daguerreotype in author's collection.

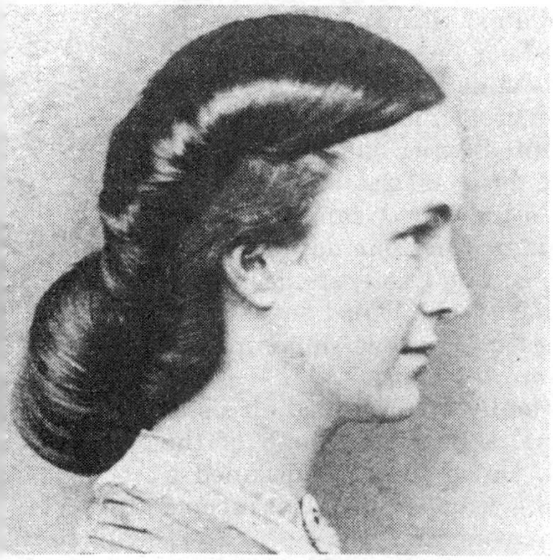

LIBBIE IN PROFILE, carried in a small carte-de-visite size album containing 22 other photographs of her. Ca. 1864. Author's collection.

ANOTHER PROFILE OF LIBBIE. Ca. 1964. Author's collection.

LIBBIE. Ca. 1864. Author's collection.

were horses to care for while her husband was traveling, and the baby to watch while she was doing her housework. He was reliable and handy around the house and was the very one to keep her company during a period of homesickness she was undergoing. He had but several blocks to walk to the New Dublin School which he attended for the next two years.[9]

Mrs. Bacon had been in ill health for some time. The Judge had taken her to several different doctors but they seemed unable to arrive at a diagnosis. During her last pregnancy her health reached its lowest point. She never seemed to regain her health after the delivery of their last child, Harriet, who died in June of 1849.

About this time a group of progressive citizens interested in bettering the education of their offsprings organized the *YOUNG LADIES' SEMINARY AND COLLEGIATE INSTITUTE.*[10] Though not one of the initiators, Judge Bacon did become a Trustee in 1860.[11]

Erasmus J. Boyd, an ordained minister and educator, was selected to direct the institution as its principal, serving 29 years in that capacity. So widespread was his reputation he drew students from coast to coast. In consequence the institution was soon known as the *Boyd Seminary.*

The school year was divided into three terms of 13 weeks each. Most of the students were boarders. The catalogue indicated:

"Although it is expected that Woman will fill the learned professions, yet is she not gifted with a mind that is immortal, and is she not destined to fill stations demanding as thorough discipline and as fine developments, as man?

"We do not wish to see her marshalled in the battle-field, lifting up the sword against her fellow-man, nor mingling in political strife at the ballot box, nor gathering legal honors in the Court House or Congressional Hall. We believe that God made her for other scenes of usefulness and honor. She is the presiding genius of love in the charmed circle of social and literary life.

"Do some ask, do we think of giving girls a College Course of study? You answer, ours is a four years' course of study, equal to that of a college, yet very materially modified, and differing in many respects, adapted, as we think to the specific wants of Woman.

"Our design is to cultivate, not only the mind, but the taste and heart—to make Woman what she should be, not *masculine,* coarse and unlovely, but *educated,* and at the same time refined, and ready for every good work that becomes her."[12]

Libbie was entered as a day student, the Seminary being two short blocks from the Bacon residence. It was an imposing structure from its opening day. This three-story brick mansion facing Cass Street, between Third and Fourth streets, centered on an area of an entire city block.[13] It was blessed with eight teachers and 112 pupils from the very start.

On Libbie's ninth birthday her father had given her a beautifully bound diary on the flyleaf of which he inscribed instruction that it was "to be used by her in keeping a journal of events from this day (April 8, 1851) forward. . . ."[14] Verbally he requested that she make a brief record of her daily activities, keeping the book neat and clean, and preserving it for future reference. Her mother, fearful that she would not be able to write clearly enough, advised her to wait. She did. She waited one year.

For nine years Libbie managed to maintain a sporadic account of her observations and experiences. For a time she made her daily entries religiously, following that period with one of long silence. Recalling her pledge to her father, she would fairly burst into a freshet of explanation and observation. It is from this intermittent daily log we obtain an insight of her development. Her respect for her father and her love for her mother are evident. Their inspiration and guidance along her pathway to womanhood are displayed at every turn. Mother Bacon instilled a religious background, and Father Bacon was the one to emphasize purity of character and the value of high ideals.

Under the date of Thursday, April 8, 1852, she began in ink: "This is my birthday. I am ten years old. Father bought this book one year ago . . . so I begin today." Her present for that birthday was a French book.

On the following day after school, Libbie and her good friend Mary Disbrow went to one of the Catholic churches. Someone had told them they would "see the Catolics (sic) crack eggs." In this they were disappointed though they did stay for the religious services.

Saturday morning was spent in bathing and in studying her Sunday School lesson. The afternoon was devoted to the Singing School. That evening the Wadsworth girls, Harriet and Margaret, arrived with sufficient clothing to be house guests for two weeks. Their young brother James was to join them a few days later. Their parents, going to California, were entrusting them to the Bacons until an aunt and uncle could call and take them to Connecticut.

Several days later, the Judge and Sophia took the Wadsworth girls down to the railroad depot to see their parents off to California. Sophia, noting James Wadsworth's dejection when the train pulled out with his parents aboard, placed him in the lawn swing as soon as they reached home. He soon lost all semblance of his depression, the rhythmic movement of the swing acting as a tranquilizer.

During the time that the Wadsworth girls were house guests, Libbie attended school each day, carefully noting her thoughts in her diary every evening. An addition to the household — six kittens, two of whom were Maltese — was cause for some excitement. Attendance at the Singing School one afternoon resulted in the entry, "I think I have learned a little."

The following morning was reserved for attendance at the Presbyterian Church around the corner where she listened to Reverend Montgomery preach "an excellent sermon." That afternoon provided an incident of greater interest. From her front porch, she could watch a funeral procession at the Methodist Church across the street. No ordinary funeral, it was a military service honoring a veteran of the Revolutionary War, a Mr. Alfred, who had reached the age of 90.

With Monroe a village of 4,800 souls, news traveled fast. Infant mortality was high and life expectancy was short. With the birth rate and the infant mortality extremely high it was a rare family that could count over fifty per cent of its members living past the age of 21. The commonest cause of death was disease, mostly of a communicable nature. Injury ran second. When one departed this life by one's own hand this was a subject of considerable discussion. Libbie, hearing of such an incident, wrote, "A dissipated German by the name of Mr. Aulweingler, living near the depot, committed suicide by hanging himself this afternoon near tea time."

It appears that Libbie was a victim of a commonplace trait—race discrimination, a prevalent characteristic among the English of that period. The village land owners, attorneys, doctors, bankers, merchants and developers were, principally, of English descent. Germans were beginning to move into the county, purchasing farms and evidencing their abilities at blacksmithing, raising nursery stock and other skills useful to a growing community. On the property just north of the Bacons an enterprising German family had opened a wagon and buggy works. The Germans were low on the Monroe social scale[15] but they soon proved to be sound and solid citizens.

One day Margaret Wadsworth was too ill to get out of bed. It was learned that she had a severe chill—ague they called it—a malarial infection common in Monroe County. Judge Bacon had recurrent attacks of it from the time he first lived along the River Raisin. Because of the large marsh lands bordering the shores of Lake Erie, residents thought a malignant marsh air the cause of the intermittent chills and fever.[16] Quinine was the most effective treatment.

The Wadsworths continued as guests. Libbie enjoyed their society and did everything she could to make their stay pleasant. On occasion, Harriet would go to classes with Libbie.

Sunday turned out to be a very unpleasant, rainy day. Church service was attended as usual, followed by Sabbath School, then prayer meeting that evening with the Wadsworth girls. Not very exciting for girls that age who were forced by the inclement weather to remain house bound. And during that night all were awakened by lightning and heavy peals of thunder. Libbie was forced to admit that she was in great fear.

Several days later Maggie Wadsworth left for an overnight visit with Mary Bates after which she planned to spend three days with Mrs. Gale. Jimmy Wadsworth dropped in with a mess of fish that day, staying long enough to help eat them.

There was no singing school on Saturday, May 1st. Mrs. Pierce, the singing instructor, had a very sick baby, inflammation of the brain, Libbie had learned. Maggie Wadsworth offered to stay up with the baby that night. As a result she had to spend the following day in bed in an attempt to catch up with her sleep. Harriet took her turn that night. The Pierce baby had shown no signs of improvement. Several days later the baby died, Harriet staying with Mrs. Pierce for several days following the funeral.

Several mad dogs have been seen around town. As a result a number of little girls who had been using Libbie's swing left for their homes earlier than usual.

Sophia Bacon had been making plans to visit relatives in the East. She had intended leaving on May 16th but the Wadsworths, who had been house guests since April 10th with all intentions of staying but two weeks, had made no move to leave. On the 18th the house was cleared of the Wadsworths, the cat, her kittens and Libbie, the last-named being sent over to the Seminary to stay while the house was shut up during Sophia's absence. The Judge stayed at the Exchange House,[17] managed by his friend Levi Humphrey.

Other than the daily visitations from her father, life went on tranquilly enough. At first Libbie experienced some lonesomeness for her mother but she quickly adapted to the new situation. Mary, the hired girl, picked up her laundry at regular intervals, and Father Bacon took her shopping occasionally.

In one spell of loneliness, the Judge took Libbie to their home where both wrote letters to Sophia. In mid-June Libbie made the admission in her diary that she was not used to being without her mother or father. As the days passed, her loneliness for her mother increased. Then one day a letter arrived which she and her father hungrily devoured. No more than it was read both sat down to answer it for it was decided that Libbie was to meet her mother at Howlett Hill, New York. She would be going to her Aunt Mary's[18] home to be met there by her mother and her Aunt Harriet.[19] There would be no side trip to New York City as she had hoped.

At Howlett Hill she met all of her aunts, uncles and cousins; Bacons, every one. Two weeks later they returned to Monroe by way of Niagara Falls.

After a day of rearranging their home, Libbie went over to visit Mrs. St. John, who was greatly amused at Libbie's new crying doll. The baby doll had been a present from Aunt Harriet's girl Susan.

The Fourth of July, having been on a Sunday, was celebrated on Monday. Libbie made note of the great many firecrackers that were fired and that the Catholics had a celebration (she now spells Catholic with an h) and the English children as well.

Near the end of July, Mrs. Boyd held examinations for the Seminary students in such subjects as the instructors thought necessary. Libbie passed her French examination with little difficulty. Her other subjects had been graded sufficiently high to eliminate the need for examination in each of them. In a sort of celebration she played Jack Straws with Libbie Thurber. On July 29th, diplomas were given to Mary Baker of Jackson, Mary Clark of Detroit, Louise Pictin of Chicago and Elizabeth Wing of Monroe.

On July 31st, Libbie Stone came to stay with the Bacons for two weeks. Since there would be a vacation period of eight weeks, the two girls were looking forward to a pleasant time together. The following afternoon the two girls went to the Daguerrian Room with Mrs. Stone and her children where they had their miniatures taken.

One day Mary Lewis and the two Libbies accompanied Mrs. Stone to the lake. Free from the social restraints of the village, they took off their shoes and stockings and waded along the shore in the cool, clean water. At the mouth of the river the tired trio obtained passage on the steamer *Swan* which took them to the Front Street docks. From there they walked home. Several days later they learned that the *Swan* had burned at the Toledo wharf, apparently the subject of arson.

An object of unusual interest and amusement was the appearance in town of a man with a hand organ and a small monkey. The children soon discovered that both the man and his monkey found their crackers, cookies and flowers acceptable, and their pennies even more so. All were amused when the monkey would reach for a penny, then store it in his mouth with his tiny paw until his master asked for it.

Most Sunday attendances at Sabbath School were uneventful but there was one in early August that was particularly impressive. Some of the small boys present had been observed stoning a squirrel in an elm tree in front of church that day. Since these boys were in the audience along with a number of other boys, Mr. Boyd told them a little story that illustrated the wickedness of killing anything for the mere sport of it. Mr. Foster followed by relating an incident in which two young men saw some wild turkeys fly past them as they sat in front of their home one Sunday. Deciding to hunt them, they obtained their guns, then set out in search for them. After they were found, one of the young men crept in the high grass until he saw one. In attempting to attract its attention he imitated a turkey call. His companion heard it and thinking it was a turkey, shot and killed him. "Mr. Foster was called a few days after to attend the funeral of the young man."

Though aiding in household chores, knitting, sewing and shopping with her mother, Libbie spent a part of each day in reading and studying. Mother Bacon would often read sketches to her and suggest that she read various subjects and topics. Under her direction, Libbie would read the Bible each day.

On one occasion the Judge permitted Libbie and the Stone girl to accompany him to the meadow to observe their source of milk and cream. They met the cow as it was heading for home. Once before they had been allowed to go with him on this chore, the meadow being but a short distance to the west of their house.

Some of the villagers grazed their cows on the village square, an act that was not without its hazards. Presbyterians had voiced some objections to the mess-making pigeons that roosted over the doorway of their sanctuary. When the neighborhood cows obstructed their admission to a Sunday service, and supplied other more objectionable obstructions, the congregation vigorously voiced their objections to the village council. Like politicians universally the Aldermen yielded to the pressure by ordering a discontinuance of grazing in Loranger Square. The square consisted of four large segments of land which comprised the four corners of the intersection of Washington and First Streets. The Court House faced one such segment and the Presbyterian Church another.

On August 20th, P. T. Barnum visited Monroe with his traveling museum which included Tom Thumb. The attendance was heavy, perhaps too heavy, for the stage caved in. One woman suffered a leg fracture and another a broken jaw.

Libbie entered a note that news had come by telegraph that "a propeller ran into the steamboat *Atlantic* and it instantly sunk. It was said there were 500 people on board and that the propeller saved 200."

On the 1st of September there was considerable excitement over the news that a bridge near Adrian had collapsed when a locomotive, drawing coaches loaded with emigrants, passed over it. Several of the passengers were killed.

Cholera had been evident in Toledo for some time. It had been reported that as many as 14 or 15 had been dying from it each day. The latest news was that of the death of Reverend Wright, a Presbyterian minister, and of Dr. Smith, who was known to many Monroe people.

The summer had been unusually arid, most of the wells around the Bacon residence having been dry for some time. The Bacon well seemed to stem from a living spring, a supply adequate for all of the neighbors. Charles Noble's well, which had been dug prior to 1832, had never been dry until that season. But fall brought with it the much needed rains and the reopening of school. On Spetember 22nd, Mother and Father Bacon reminded Libbie she would start school at the Seminary on the next day.

YOUNG LADIES SEMINARY AND COLLEGIATE INSTITUTE, Monroe, Michigan. "Boyd's Seminary" was considered the finest girls' school west of the Hudson River. General Custer encouraged his family to move to Monroe from Tontogony, Ohio, so that his sister Margaret could take advantage of its facilities. Courtesy of Everette Payette.

On the morning of February 27th, 1853, Mr. Wells took Libbie 30 miles west to Tecumseh, where he visited Judge Stillman Blanchard.[20] Mrs. Blanchard served them a lunch after which they returned to Monroe.

Two days later, at the invitation of Fannie Fifield, she visited her home where a seance was being conducted. Through the use of "spiritual knockings" their questions were answered. Libbie retired that evening somewhat in a quandary and lost several hours sleep in thinking about the events she had observed at the Fifields that afternoon. She concluded that she "did not believe in them for they are nothing but a humbug."

Frances Blanchard, daughter of Judge Blanchard, arrived in Monroe the next day to attend the Seminary. This was cause for rejoicing since Frances would be pleasant company.

In the intervening five months since her last entry, Libbie's handwriting had greatly improved. She now wrote more boldly, with greater clarity, better spacing and larger letters.

Uncle Albert Bacon took Libbie with him to attend the services at the Methodist Church that Sunday evening. Libbie's exposure to churches other than her own included attendance at a Catholic Church, the Episcopal Church and at the German Lutheran Church recently dedicated.

For some time now, Libbie had taken music lessons at the Seminary. As a present on March 14th, she was given a piano purchased from Monsieur Ricqueles for $275, the stool costing $10, a gift from her mother.

The establishment of a prestigious girls school stimulated interest in the establishment of a similar institution for educating males. Accordingly, the Monroe *Commercial* of August 25, 1853, printed an editorial announcing the organization of an "Academy for Boys and Young Men" whose first term would commence on the 20th of September. An impressive group of political and business leaders, acting as the Board of Trustees, obtained the old Macomb Street House, formerly a prominent Monroe hotel on the east side of Macomb Street between Front and First Streets. The large, two-story, colonial structure, lemon yellow in color, sat well back from the street. To its rear, facing Scott Street, they added a commodious study hall and a spacious gymnasium. Alfred Stebbins became its principal. On opening day the attendance was large, four boys coming from as far away as Chicago. It was not long before the institution became known unofficially as Stebbins' Academy.[21]

On January 1, 1854, Libbie resumed writing in her diary, at the request of her parents. On the following day her mother told her they were to go to Tecumseh on the train that day. At the depot they found Mr. and Mrs. Cole, Mr. and Mrs. Sterling, Mr. and Mrs. Taylor and Mr. Ward, among others, preparing to make the same trip. In spite of a fatiguing journey all had a lot of fun. When they arrived, the Bacons visited Judge Blanchard who was almost blind.

Small pox had broken out in a number of places in town. One of the Seminary students, Sarah Powell, after being exposed to the disease came back to the Seminary and exposed all the girls. Mr. Boyd sent her home. Libbie was promptly vaccinated.

Several days later one of the girls became ill. The doctor's diagnosis was small pox. As a result the school was closed. In the interval that followed, Libbie spent her time each day in cleaning her room, making her bed, sewing on a shirt for her father, making clothes for her largest doll and playing telegraph with Mary Disbrow — Libbie advises one to take "a long string double and put a little round basket on them to two chairs, and write what you wish to the one on the other chair and put the piece of paper in the basket, draw the string toward the other chair and then the girl or boy will answer it."

Mr. Sarton, the French instructor at the Seminary, called the day after the school closed to tell Sophia he would spend one half hour each day for the next ten days giving Libbie French instructions. It was his opinion that this would enable her to keep pace with the rest of the class, all of whom were more advanced and older than she.

The year 1854 was an incomparable one in Monroe when it came to trouble. Many families were leaving as a result of the discontinuance of service of a major steamship line from Buffalo. Consequently the Michigan Southern Railroad took up its tracks leading to the wharf where these ships had docked.

Small pox had been bad enough but another epidemic of cholera swept through the town; it too was no respecter of persons. At times there were scarecely enough people present at a funeral to bury the dead. On one occasion the undertaker had to solicit help. Fear and rising unemployment caused many to seek a livelihood elsewhere. An exodus resulted. By removal and death the Methodist Church lost 64 members in two years.[22]

For five months there were no entries in Libbie's diary; then, on August 27, 1854, she wrote:

"Alas, my poor diary, you have been sadly neglected. When I last wrote, my Mother sat comfortably in her dear rocking chair by the fire. My dear Mother is sleeping her last great sleep from which she never will awake, no never! No not even to correct my numerous mistakes in this diary. Two weeks ago my Mother was laid in the cold, cold ground and as I stood by that open grave and felt— Oh! God only knows what anguish filled my heart. Oh! Why did they put my mother in that great black coffin and screw the lid down so tight?"

Sophia Bacon had died of "bloody dysentery," the second case in town.[23] She had lapsed into a coma at the last, following a lengthy illness. The Judge had written details to her sister Harriet in Grand Rapids at the very beginning of the illness. She arrived just two hours after Sophia's death.

Sophia's health had been at a low point prior to her last pregnancy, and was not bettered by it. Because of her failing health she had kept to her home more than usual. She was uncomplaining, even reticent, when questioned about her health.[24] Exceedingly religious, a characteristic deeply implanted in Libbie, she leaned heavily on her belief in Christian principles, maintaining a tranquil spirit to the very end.

On the day of Sophia's death, Daniel wrote to his family at Howlett Hill, "My poor wife is no more. Her physicians were unacquainted with the nature of her disease. She bore her sufferings with great composure and Christian fortitude. . . . No lady in Monroe was so universally regretted. . . . Elizabeth bears her affliction well, but the poor girl does not realize the overdevotion of her mother."[25]

Libbie's concern now was for her father. She hoped the Lord would spare her for she knew she was the only comfort he had left. She and her Aunt Harriet planned to go to Grand Rapids the following week. It already had been decided that she could board at the Seminary on her return if she wished, and her father would stay at the Exchange Hotel. In any event, their home was to be broken up.

There is no mention in the diary as to when she returned to Monroe. Her first entry following her return was dated November 12, 1854. The first term of the Seminary had started on the 20th of September. She shared a room on the third floor with one of the teachers, a Miss Thompson who hailed from Heath, Massachusetts. They had a parlor and a bedroom which they had to furnish. From one of the windows there was a picturesque view of the town and Lake Erie, the latter some two miles to the east.

Just the week before, while Libbie was seated in church listening to the sermon, there was a cry of fire. To this was added the news that it was the Seminary. Mr. Boyd led all the rest in covering the four blocks to it. Though the roof at one end of the main building was in flames, the volunteer fire fighters managed to extinguish them.

In evaluating their loss, which was found to be minimal, Mrs. Boyd missed her gold watch, several rings and two bracelets. Suspicion rested on Mrs. Boyd's nurse, Jane. In searching her, the housekeeper and Mrs. Boyd found several articles on her belonging to some of the girls. The suspect declared she was innocent of wrongdoing, that there was nothing else in her possession. In searching her trunk, other articles were found that belonged to the students. Mr. Boyd discovered a dress in her closet in which a dollar bill had been pinned which he had missed.

The girl refused to admit she had taken the watch and jewelry and denied knowing of their whereabouts. The search continued and they were found between her feather and her straw beds with some "lost" wearing apparel.

Disregarding her pleading, Mr. Boyd sent for a magistrate. When it was learned that all of them were attending a public meeting out of town, he

REVEREND ERASMUS J. BOYD, the Principal of the Young Ladies Seminary. Author's collection.

released her. Shortly afterward it was determined that the Seminary building could not have taken fire without some assistance. All evidence pointed to Jane. A magistrate picked her up and lodged her in the county jail. Libbie's reaction penned in her diary was, "Poor girl! How sad she must feel."

Libbie was unable to sleep past five o'clock on Christmas morning of 1854. After she awakened Laura Noble and wished her a Merry Christmas, the two of them went from room to room awakening students and instructors with the same greeting.

Following a visit from her father, she went over to the Fifields to spend the day. On her arrival there, Mrs. Fifield displayed her enthusiasm with, "Well, I ain't going to have any dinner for you." To which Libbie responded,"Well, that is not what I came for." Fannie Fifield had invited Libbie over for dinner and Libbie assumed Mrs. Fifield had originated the invitation. This was a low blow on Christmas day to the motherless young lady. Her first reaction was to feel chagrined but after a little reflection she concluded that both Fannie and her mother were very unladylike. Feeling unwelcome, she left at 3 o'clock, arriving at the Seminary in time for a delicious Christmas dinner.

In the middle of January, 1855, the Exchange Hotel burned down. Several store buildings were destroyed in the blaze, one of them owned by Judge Bacon. The Judge lost a few things out of the room he was staying in at the Exchange including his bed and a stove.

On Libbie's thirteenth birthday her Aunt Harriet sent her a bracelet of her mother's hair with her father's hair in the clasp; her aunt's hair was braided into the shape of a heart with a small chain attached to it and to her mother's wedding ring.

On her own admission, Libbie was quite happy at the Seminary. She was grateful for the privilege of attending such a fine school. Having learned a lot there, she had progressed satisfactorily in music; and she loved all of her teachers. Miss Thompson in particular was appreciated. She summed it up by writing, "I can well say I am happy. I have made up my mind that the Seminary is entirely the best place for me."

In a footnote she admonished her journal not to expect that she would always tell the same story "for my mind, I am afraid, is quite changeable. I declare, who's isn't?"

Mr. Boyd had given her a small area in the garden where she could tend to the flowers she so dearly loved. Each time she took a drawing lesson from Mr. Zeus she would take him a small bouquet of flowers.

During study hour one morning late in April a school chimney caught fire. In fear and trembling, Libbie ran up the stairs to her room for her locket and chain. Though nearly out of breath from the exertion, she had to laugh when she returned to find the fire nearly out.

A tooth seemed to have given her considerable trouble at this time. The day following her session with the dentist she arose with a toothache, stomachache and headache, which made her think "perhaps" she had gotten out of the wrong side of the bed. By that afternoon her discomfort worsened to the point she had to be excused from classes. There being no further reference to this disorder in the days that followed, one concludes that the aches and pains were psychosomatic, other interests soon substituting for them.

Accompanied by Jennie Shelhous and Lizzie Deyer several days later, she went to the farm to pick spring wild flowers—adder tongues, blue violets, butter cups and moss. At the farmhouse they had a drink of milk and were given a pailful to take home.

While gathering sap from some wild grape vines they met several town boys — Jimmie Fifield and the two Hall boys. Willie Hall was Jennie's beau, John was Lizzie's and Jimmie was Libbie's. The boys had a hatchet with them to be used in obtaining slippery elm and sassafras roots. Somehow they never quite reached their objectives. The girls inveigled them into picking bouquets, cutting grape vines and digging roots for them. The boys being bruised and tired from the tasks imposed on them and the girls equally tired from ordering them around, everyone sat down on a large log in the shade. Libbie broke out enough crackers to provide each with two, a welcome repast at that point. It provided the energy needed to make their way home.

LIBBIE'S PENCIL SKETCH made at the Seminary. Author's collection.

EXERCISES WITH A PENCIL made by Libbie at the Seminary. Author's collection.

NOTES — CHAPTER 2

[1]Formerly at the site of the Monroe County Historical Museum, it may now be seen on the southeast corner of Cass and West Seventh streets.

[2]Elizabeth Clift Bacon Diary, No. 1, (1852-1860), manuscript collection, Yale University Library, April 12, 1852, hereinafter called Libbie's Diary.

[3]Bacon Family Bible, Monroe County Historical Museum. Edward Augustus, born June 9, 1839; died April 11, 1848.

[4]*Ibid*; Harriet Duane, born Dec. 20, 1848; died June 27, 1849.

[5]*Ibid*; Sophia, born Oct. 5, 1845; died Jan. 2, 1846.

[6]*Ibid*; Elizabeth Clift, born April 8, 1842.

[7]Merington, p. 23.

[8]*Ibid.*

[9]E. H. Merrill: *Auld Lang Syne.*

The New Dublin School stood on the northwest quarter of the block bounded by Sixth and Seventh and Cass and Harrison streets.

The David Reed residence was located on the east side of Monroe Street near Jones Avenue. In 1874 the Reeds moved one-half mile north, into an impressive new house on the northeast corner of Monroe and Fourth streets.

Both the late James C. Custer and his sister, the late Mrs. Clarabel Vivian, told me that Emanuel Custer had rented a farm one mile south of Monroe on the Dixie Highway. Finding the farm unproductive he moved his family back to New Rumley, Ohio. They were uncertain as to the year.

Wing, p. 318: Emanuel H. Custer moved to Monroe in May, 1842. Soon after his arrival his horses were stolen. He remained only six months, just long enough to make good his losses. Eliz. H. Hanley: *Pageant of Historic Monroe,* Monroe, 1926, p. 35, states that the Emanuel Custer family moved to Monroe in 1842, remaining but a short time before returning to their former place of residence. No source is given. George Armstrong Custer would have been three at the time, whereas his half-sister Lydia Kirkpatrick would have been 18. Since David Reed was then 19, it is quite probable both began their romance that year.

[10]Monroe *Commercial,* Sept. 21, 1854, states that this was its fifth year and the second year of the Young Men's Academy. George A. Custer attended the latter during the years 1853 and 1854, while living with his half-sister, Mrs. David Reed.

[11]Seminary catalogue of 1860, Monroe County Historical Museum Library.

Hanley, p. 40. It has not been determined where Libbie attended school prior to entering the Seminary. The "Dame School" was a characteristic institution for elementary schooling at that time since there were no public schools. A friend or neighbor might offer to teach the rudiments of reading and writing, receiving help with her housework in return. The Dame School nearest the Bacon's would have been Mrs. Keiser's on Second Street between Macomb and Scott streets.

[12]*Ibid.*

[13]*Ibid*; Zaida E. Beck: *Reminiscences of Old Monroe,* (unpublished manuscripts in Monroe County Historical Museum Library).

Formerly it had been a private residence. Soon after the school was organized a large north wing was added for use as a study hall. Its many plant-filled windows provided a cheerful atmosphere.

The second and third floors of the main section were divided into rooms for the boarders, a hall running through the center.

On the main floor there was a platform at the north end on which stood a pipe organ and a teacher's desk. The south end had a higher platform that held a grand piano. Lighting was provided by gas.

A long veranda extended along the east side. On rainy days the girls could be seen walking back and forth on it, arm-in-arm.

The class rooms were furnished with slant-topped, walnut desks large enough to seat two girls. The top could be raised to store their books underneath.

The many vocal and instrumental concerts were given in the south end. Its platform was enlarged and dark green cambric curtains on rings were strung on a wire. Evergreens were used as a background and the potted plants from the study hall were used to decorate the stage. "Redfire, placed in iron kettles at either side of the stage, was used for the tableaux and the fumes soon set the performers, as well as the audience, to coughing."

The audience sat in wooden chairs arranged in rows, the desks having been moved for the occasion. Though the stage and the settings were somewhat amateurish, the vocal and instrumental music was of a high order. The performances were looked forward to by the Monroe residents.

The gowns and costumes were especially beautiful. "One teacher, a brunette, appeared in yellow satin trimmed with quantities of black lace over white lace; another wore pink satin with square neck and elbow sleeves; a pianist, a real blond, wore blue net with many, many ruffles, a bustle and tight waist."

At the end of the performance, bouquets were thrown. The one receiving the most was considered the most popular.

At the commencement, the young ladies wore white tarlton, net or grenadine with many ruffles, trains, and long white, buttoned kid gloves.

On the evening of February 21, 1854, Libbie took part in a "Musical Review," playing *Polanasie* Oesten on the piano. Seminary program of 1854 is in the files of the Monroe County Historical Museum library.

[14]Libbie's Diary.

[15]A perhaps typical evidence of the social feeling of the time was the expression of Mrs. C. W. Hockett in *Some Monroe Memories* (Burton Historical Collection Leaflet, Detroit, May, 1939): "We did not associate with the Custers. They were quite ordinary people, no intellectual interests, very little schooling."

"He (George Armstrong Custer) was of good character but the (Bacon) family just couldn't see him.... Margaret Custer, his only sister, was a fine girl. She became quite a cultured lady. She attended Noble's school here in Detroit."

Mrs. Hockett nee Minnie Redfield lived in Monroe at the time of the Custer Battle, being 17 at the time. Her father served as Monroe's mayor from 1871 to 1876.

[16]Malaria is caused by a parasite in the red blood corpuscles contracted by the bite of an infected anopheles mosquito.

[17]Libbie's Diary, May 18, 1852.

[18]*Ibid,* June 16, 1852.

[19]*Ibid.*

[20]*Ibid,* February 27, 1853.

[21]Bulkley, Vol. I, pp. 421-22.

[22]Reverend Seth Reed: "Pastor's Report — 1853-1855," St. Paul Methodist Episcopal Church, Monroe, Michigan.

[23]Libbie's Diary, August 27, 1854.

[24]Monroe *Commercial,* August 17, 1854. Eleanor Sophia Bacon died on August 12, 1854 at the age of 40.

[25]Merington, p. 24.

Those quotations used in this chapter without reference to source are taken from Libbie's Diary.

CHAPTER 3
POOR MOTHERLESS GIRL

Libbie had developed a love for Howlett Hill. Like the swallows at Capistrano she felt the call to the Hill. No more had school ended that spring than she headed for the East. There her aunts and cousins made much over her. These attentions were shamelessly received since she was aware they were more than usually solicitous as to her wishes because she had no mother. And encourage this attention she did for she was not reluctant to trade on it by offering excuses for not doing anything she did not want to do, knowing full well they would give in to her. She overheard them speak of "poor motherless Libbie," then remind their listeners that "Libbie Bacon has no mother!"[1]. All of it had the happy effect of aiding her to pass smoothly through the time interval necessary to adapt to a life deprived of a mother's companionship and counsel.

It soon came time to return to Monroe. It had been a summer of fun with no time to make entries in her diary until that September. Her first entry casually noted that the fall term of the Seminary began in late September. She allowed more prominence to her first shopping trip and a disappointing visit to a photographer's studio. The day had been rainy and dark so the daguerreotype wasn't taken. With teenage logic—she was 12—she had purchased both candy and a toothbrush, then returned home.

At Christmas time many of the Monroe boys home from Ann Arbor College visited the Seminary—Ed Thurber, George Landon, Hobi Miller, Lester O'Brien, Fred Skelter, Mr. Comstalk and George Babitt. The girls dressed in white. Libbie wore her hair down her back tied with two black silk ribbons which caused Mr. Zeus to say she looked like a Swiss girl.

On New Year's Day, 1856, callers were received at the Seminary. Several of the married men attempted to kiss Libbie which caused her to observe that "they thought they could because they were married men; no indeed, none did but my friend Dr. Smith. I did not mean he should but he did. I believe I slapped him but he did not care. I did not wish him to kiss me any way."

Libbie was an uncommonly attractive young lady. Though a bit plump for her five feet she displayed a pretty oval face, set with light blue-gray eyes and crowned with chestnut brown hair. Her fair complexion and alabaster skin were accentuated by full red lips. When she smiled her eyes would almost close in a fashion that magnetically caused others to smile with her.

By the time she reached 18 she would be considered by many to be the prettiest in a town that boasted of a hundred pretty girls. By that time her full height was five feet, four inches, though passports in later years reveal her as being several inches taller at times. This variance might have been due to a difference of heel height.

Things had gone well for Mr. Boyd and his girls seminary. Now well into its sixth year, the school had received wide notice and had established an excellent reputation. Stebbins' Academy had not been so fortunate. Whether it was poor management or an insufficient number of boys is unknown but it was unable to survive. It was forced to close its doors after only two years of existence. Several of its instructors joined the Seminary staff, Mr. Zeus, the art instructor being one of them.

Since there was no school for young men the enterprising Mr. Boyd offered morning classes in Greek, Latin and mathematics in one of the cottages on the Seminary property. A rumor, probably originated by the wishful thinking of female students, soon circulated that there would be boys on one side of the hall of the main building and girls on the other.

With the turn of the New Year, it was natural enough to think of resolutions. Turning to her diary, Libbie began what would be the last month of her entries for two years. Her very first resolution was one to write in her diary every day. The next was to "never speak ill of any one." She recalled what her mother often told her, "If you cannot speak good of anyone, say nothing at all."

She had seen the effect of big words on others, perhaps in listening to legal jargon her father used in the course of his daily work. Several such attempts by her caused her parents to admonish her that she was trying to impress unnecessarily, and that she should be her natural self. She resolved to try not to use big words.

To please her father she decided to keep an account book and enter into it all of her purchases.

JUDGE DANIEL S. BACON AND DAUGHTER LIBBIE. Ca. 1862. Author's collection.

GENERAL CUSTER'S FATHER, Emanuel H. Custer. Ca. 1870. Col. Brice Custer collection.

In memory of her mother's wish she concluded that she would read a chapter in the Bible each day beginning with Second Samuel.

On January 4th she mentioned that every letter she received from her Aunt Mary advised her to see her father twice a week. Meanwhile Libbie had taken a strong dislike to French though her father wanted her to take it and Mr. Boyd reminded her that her father wanted her to study it. She wrote, "I have never in all the time I have been here have felt so heartily sick of the Sem, Monroe, and most of the people as I am now. I do get so homesick for Howlett Hill and I am sure I shall be ready next spring to go as soon as the Sem closes to do as father wishes and spend the summer there." Then she continued ruefully, "I guess I got out of the wrong side of the bed this morning for I am cross and lonesome."

Her class on mythology was more to her liking. Miss Merrick's method of teaching from their new book "Grecian and Roman Mythology" maintained the interest of everyone. It was the one book in Libbie's small library in which she carefully recorded the names of the class, so great was her interest in it. On the back fly under the headline "Mythology Class of 1858" she listed them in pencil: Eleanor Allbright, Kate Cunningham, Julie Clark, Fannie Bagley, Maria Hickock, Sarah Stewart, Laura W. Noble, Aggie L. Shoulder, Emilie Clement, Ada A. Chipman, Annie L. Darrah, Sallie M. Webster, Libbie A. Lown and Kate C. Smith.

On January 7th she alluded to the loss of Laura Noble's affection. Laura, it seemed, had been quite taken up with two other girls and had been spending less time with Libbie. Laura was the only one she liked well enough to confide in. It was quite natural that she would miss her father at a time like that and wish she could see him oftener than just on Sunday.

On January 9th she recorded, "Father and I had a long talk together about keeping house, his marrying again and several other things. I told him if he found a person with whom he could be suited and I would be suited too, and so I will for even if I did feel so averse to his marriage a year ago I have undergone a great change since and I now feel if it would add to my father's happiness to be married again, I would advise it. But it would make me feel dreadfully to be deprived of keeping house for him for I think of it often. It is the first time father has ever spoken to me of his marriage."

Mr. Boyd appointed her the monitress which delighted her. Her duty was to awaken the girls each day—"knock the girls up, as the Sem expression goes."

On January 15th she wrote to her Aunt Mary at Howlett Hall. This made her think of her mother and how much she had lost in losing her. She knew she would be a better girl if around her Aunt Mary. She thought she was getting wild and felt discouraged in her efforts to do right. "God help me," she wrote, "for I know I do wrong everyday."

GENERAL CUSTER'S MOTHER, Maria Ward Kirkpatrick Custer. Ca. 1870. Col. Brice Custer collection.

It was while at Howlett Hill in August of 1858 that she reapproached her diary. By chance she read those last lines referring to her mother. This recalled to mind the promise she had made when her mother and father were anxious for her to develop the habit of making regular entries. She had been at Howlett Hill since the 8th of April, her birthday, having arrived there on that day with her father. The Judge had stayed only a day or two then went on to New York, stopping off in Washington before seeing some of the State of Virginia.

Before leaving he had made arrangements for Libbie to attend the fall term of a fashionable girls school in Auburn, New York.[2]

Selection of the Auburn Young Ladies Institute was wise. Now nearly seventeen years old, Libbie needed the sobering experience of living apart from the immediate influence of her family. Though it was less than a day's ride from Howlett Hill and her protective kinsfolk, there were no telephones to provide a hot line to salve her loneliness. She had to turn to strangers whenever she needed advice.

Though she spent Christmas at Howlett Hill with Aunt Mary and uncle John Case, it was a holiday without her beloved father. Aunt Eliza and Uncle Denison Sabin and her cousins were there, and though she loved them all, it wasn't Christmas without her father.

Almost 70 years[3] later she would write to her Howlett Hill relatives about the time she was "a motherless and lonely little girl" going to visit them during vacation time. She recalled the stage station near Denison Sabin's home and the stage coach with its large springs, its sway from side to side and its folding steps that gave it a touch reminiscent of royalty. It was the steep Camillus Hill that wiped away the feeling of grandeur for the fear of it caused her to hold her breath as she buried herself in Aunt Mary's seven breadths of petticoats, only to be saved from suffication when Aunt Mary called for her to come out with "Your life is saved again!"

A pleasant memory was the patience of Uncle John in allowing them to milk an old cow whose permissiveness extended to permitting an approach from either side. Her young cousin Bronson Case extended this liberty, she recalled, by crawling between old Bessie's hind legs and dodging her swishing tail as he sought to fill his small pail.

Her father had sent a pony all the way from Michigan on which all of them learned to ride. She wrote, "Cousin Bronson as a little lad gained his first equestrian success—and also mastered the seat in the saddle which can hardly be acquired too young. And I owe much to that little pony so intelligent, so tolerant . . . for I was taught to keep my seat in the saddle when so young at Howlett Hill. Afterwards on the frontier marching beside my husband on army horses . . . I was able to keep my seat in the saddle for hours on the march . . . ."

And there was no dread of going to the little cemetery in back of the Presbyterian Church on Howlett Hill. The children carried flowers to the various graves. She concluded, "I had litle assurance of a heaven awaiting me before I joined my kin on Howlett Hill. Not that I had attained to any perfection of character but to those who were working for it I was told the door was always open."

Libbie boarded with Mr. and Mrs. Mortimer Browne while attending the Auburn Institute. Their residence was called Chestnut Home. On her return after Christmas—by date it was January 8, 1859[4]—she wrote to her father that she had returned from Howlett Hill last Monday and was happy to find his letter and the "very acceptable" Christmas gift it contained. Obviously, it was money.

She told him of the merry time they had had at the Hill and of the great number of gifts received from her aunts and cousins. A plaintive note crept in when she expressed her regrets that he was not there.

She promised to improve as much as possible for him, and as a grateful daughter would commence her studies and duties with new diligence. Of the many new resolutions she had made, one of the least was "not to cry for anything, however tried I might be."

Mr. and Mrs. Browne, thinking to place more responsibility upon her, had changed her room and her roommates. She had shared a room with a teacher upon whom she depended. Now saddled with two little girls, she must set a good example. She indicated that she had accepted this move with some reservations. So she wrote, "I think you will be pleased with the idea, Father, as you wish me to become *womanly* do you not? I don't want to though—I like being a *little* girl. I dread being a young lady *so* much. I like acting *free* and *girl like.* Not being so *prim* and *particular* about what I say and do! I have to be on my guard in this room as to my actions. My roommates are not as pleasant as the other ones. They generally groan out, 'Oh I wish I were h-o-m-e.' It seems as if I should sometimes break my resolution 'not to speak cross' and 'not to cry' but I *will* not for I want to be a *good* woman and try and have you *proud* of me, not to be *ashamed* of me. Which I sometimes fear you are ashamed of me .... Oh, how *stiff* I have to be. Why father, when I get on H. Hill how I do *act* . . . But I know it is best and I must be content."

She hoped he could spare the money for the next term as she thought she would improve more that winter than ever before. She felt that the strict discipline, though exceedingly trying, was good for her.

Apparently money was a little tight at this time. With her father's impending marriage less than a month away she had thoughts of "dropping drawing and everything else which will add in the least to the expense," then adds that she *"would not go here on any* consideration if I thought it would incommode you, so don't, in wishing to please me, hesitate to tell me if it will disarrange your money matters."

To all this she complained of being unhappy because "the young ladies are *so different* from *Monroe girls."* While in this mournful state she voiced a regret because Mrs. Pitts, the Judge's intended wife doesn't answer her letter. "I am afraid she won't think much of me after she is married if she doesn't enough now to write to me."

Meanwhile Judge Bacon had been busying himself in preparation for his approaching marriage. His residence had been rented out since Sophia had died. Libbie had been rooming alternately at the Seminary and with his relatives at Howlett Hill, and for the past few months at Auburn. He had made the rebuilt Exchange Hotel his abode. It required some time before he could obtain possession of his house. He had to obtain a place for him and his wife to room and board until he could paint and repair his house, a period of time that would extend well into summer.

Rhoda Wells Pitts had been born in New Bedford, Massachusetts, June 29, 1809. She and her former husband, the Reverend Samuel Pitts, who was six years her junior, came to Tecumseh, Michigan, to lead its Congregational Church. In ill health when

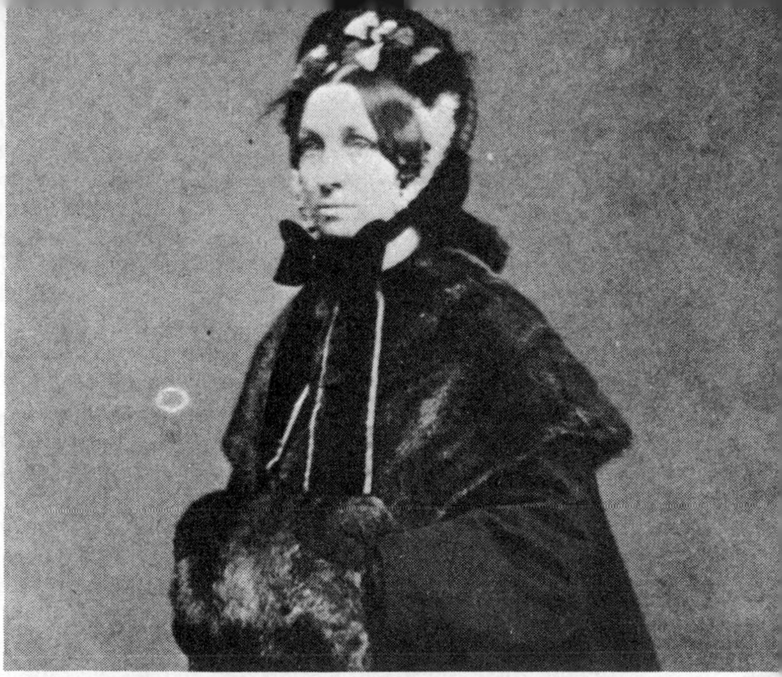

GENERAL CUSTER'S HALF-SISTER, Mrs. Lydia Ann Kirkpatrick Reed, mother of Autie Reed who was killed with his Uncle Autie Custer at the Little Big Horn, June 25, 1876. Col. Brice Custer collection.

he arrived, he succumbed to consumption early in 1855.

Several years later Judge Bacon made a business trip to see his old friend Judge Stillman Blanchard in Tecumseh. Judge Blanchard introduced the subject of matrimony, counseling him to remarry. Daniel voiced his reluctance to accept any thought of doing so and stated that others had offered the same advice. He believed any such move would be disloyal to the memory of the mother of his children. Blanchard thought otherwise and said he knew the very woman for him.

All of Blanchard's well-developed promotive instincts came to the fore. This woman, he explained, was attractive, intelligent, sensible, well off, an excellent housekeeper—and available.

Purposely he escorted the now curious Daniel down the village street past an attractive house. In the yard tending her flowers was a well-formed woman in her late forties dressed in starched calico, sun bonnet and gloves. Judge Blanchard tipped his hat and Daniel did likewise. Daniel's next trip to Tecumseh was more purposeful than this one.[5]

Libbie's letter of January 15th[6] indicated that she had found her room and roommates pleasanter than the previous week, an indication that she was accepting and adapting to conditions.

She patiently awaited a letter from Mrs. Pitts, adding that, "I can't help feeling she don't like me much." Apparently she had forgotten her concern for her father's financial situation of a week earlier because she warned him of two large bills he would be receiving since, so she states, "I have to dress more here than I do at Monroe."

The Judge's reply received on January 24th caused her to cry, *"for nothing at all."* She answered it the very next day,[7] by assuring him she would like to remain at the Young Ladies Institute "but if it is going to make you so much trouble to raise the means or if you feel you cannot afford it, be *assured* I will *willingly* go to Howlett Hill for I know full well your expenses at this time are great . . . . I shall be delighted to remain here if it will be *convenient* to you but shall not be happy if I think it troubles you."

She re-emphasized her willingness to economize, again offering to give up drawing lessons, which seemed to her to be the greatest sacrifice one could make. She continued deploringly, "I wish I only knew enough to earn something and in that way help you. But Father, are you really so *poor?* I shall not tell the girls my father is *too poor* to send me here! I expect I have too much pride."

Reiterating her feeling that Mrs. Pitt didn't like her because she hadn't answered her letter, Libbie gave her father some advice: "If she wants to put off the marriage, don't *you,* will you father for I am so anxious to get to living with you again? We shall all be so happy. Oh! won't we? . . . Will you tell me the exact day you will come? I have counted the days."

Three days later, on January 28th,[8] she wrote that she had received his letter informing her he would not be in Auburn until the middle or last of February. Petulantly she responded, "I was very much disappointed indeed and I think I can safely promise you that I will never 'count the days' again or anticipate too much." She concluded by asking for a supply of stamps.

The correspondence between them in the ensuing months was meager. Knowing that Libbie was in good hands, the Judge poured all his energies into his nuptial preparations.[9] Following his marriage to Rhoda he entered a rapidly changing world, and a welcome change at that.

Though 61 years of age, he adapted to the new life readily enough. It wasn't a case of trying to teach an old dog new tricks. He was truly an old dog, but the tricks were not new.

The new Mrs. Bacon insisted on using some of her own furnishings; her bed, for one thing. Her former husband seemed to have had no difficulty in using it but Daniel ran into a problem. Being somewhat taller than his predecessor he had to occupy it on the diagonal, a situation he referred to with some humor.[10]

By the middle of May Libbie was back at Howlett Hill. She missed Mr. Browne's counsel and fine example as a Christian and knew of no other she could turn to as a friend for guidance. Mrs. Browne merited considerable praise too for Libbie wrote with deep feeling and gratitude when referring to her as a mother to her. In her summation of them in her diary she said, "I went there as a stranger. They took me into their hearts as if I were their child and ever, *ever* will I thank them for it. I had remained at the Seminary at Monroe so long that I was not what I should be, but even although there is *much* to do to make me what I should be, yet I cannot but feel that I have improved much. I went there a *child*—but came away a *woman.* God be praised!"

DAVID REED, with whom George A. Custer lived in 1849 when first attending school in Monroe. Col. Brice Custer collection.

In early June Libbie's father advised her that the cost of repairing their house exceeded his expectation. He was happy with the outcome though and was looking forward to the comfort and domestic happiness that he expected they all would enjoy. He assured her that, in spite of her newly acquired reluctance to leave Howlett Hill, all of the Monroe ladies who had become acquainted with Rhoda felt that she and Libbie would get along like sisters.[11]

Soon afterward Libbie returned to Monroe. The Bacon home was not ready for occupancy which made it necessary to share lodging with her father and new mother at the Lawrence residence. Near the end of summer they moved into the Bacon house, Libbie returning to her studies at the Seminary nearby. This was a new and pleasant experience for Libbie. She and Rhoda got along very well and the Judge was a contented man again. Libbie expressed her feelings to her cousin and confidant, Rebecca Richmond, by writing, "Mother and I laugh and grow fat."[12]

The winter months were marred by Libbie's illness. There was doubt in the doctor's mind. Consumption? He could not be certain. Rest and the ministrations of her new mother pulled her through. An added benefit was the bond that developed between the two, a result that added to the Judge's contentment.

Though a sober-minded man by nature, the Judge enjoyed the sound of laughter in his home. To hear

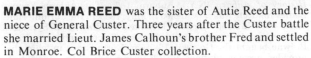

MARIE EMMA REED was the sister of Autie Reed and the niece of General Custer. Three years after the Custer battle she married Lieut. James Calhoun's brother Fred and settled in Monroe. Col Brice Custer collection.

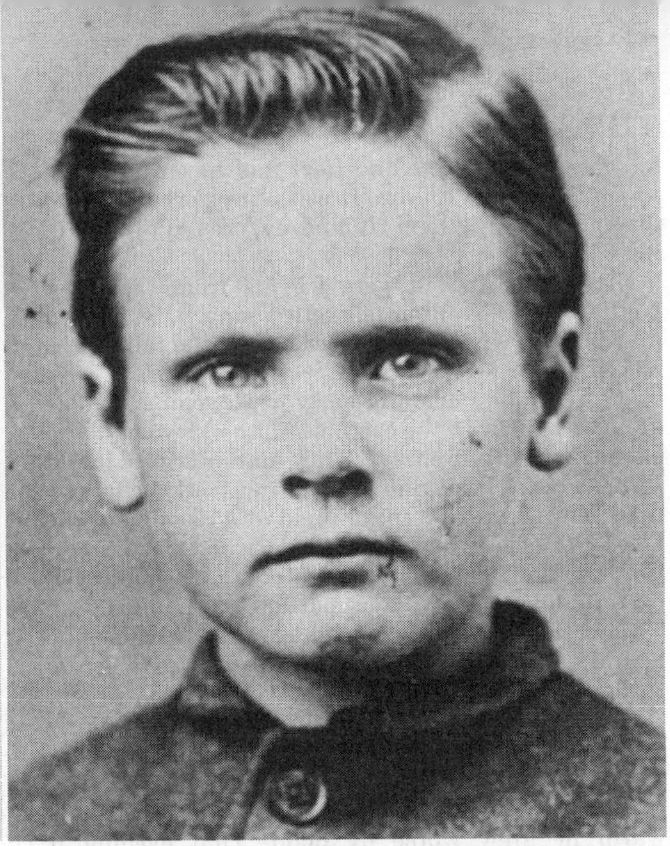

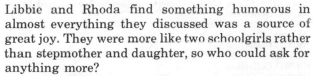

AUTIE REED, christened Harry Armstrong Reed, was 18 years old when killed by Indians with his Uncle Autie Custer in the Battle of the Little Big Horn, June 25, 1876. Col. Brice Custer collection.

Libbie and Rhoda find something humorous in almost everything they discussed was a source of great joy. They were more like two schoolgirls rather than stepmother and daughter, so who could ask for anything more?

He had obtained spiritual peace of mind in joining the Presbyterian Church four years before.[13] Of a religious nature and upbringing he had made that final step in the knowledge that it was the right thing to do. His first wife had been a member of the church since transferring by letter from her Congregational Church in Rutland, Vermont, two years after their marriage.[14] Perhaps he affiliated after her death in the knowledge it would bring them closer together. The month following his joining the church he assumed the responsibility of teaching a boys Sunday school class.[15] A most unusual occurrence, and indicative of his high moral character and community acceptance, was his election to the Board of Elders in the Presbyterian Church just four months after he had formally joined it.[16]

He had attended Sunday services regularly for years with his first wife and had continued to do so after she had passed away. Frequently he was seen to arise sobbing during the service, then hurry down the aisle to the outside, fists clenched all of the way. No one laughed at this disclosure of his deep emotion. He was respected rather than censured for it.[17]

His second wife had religious convictions that ran as deep. One of her first acts on assuming the role as his wife was to seek membership in the Monroe Presbyterian Church. This she did on July 3, 1859 by a letter of transfer from the Tecumseh Presbyterian Church.[18]

The following September (1860) Libbie resumed her studies at the Boyd Seminary. Though there were thoughts of graduating, she did not, for she had missed most of the school year because of her protracted illness. She loved school so this proved to be no deterrent.

General Levi Humphrey and his daughter Nettie were house guests of the Bacons for the last three weeks of September. They were awaiting the final construction stages of the new Humphrey House hotel Levi was to manage and were to move into it while it was being completed.

Levi had just disclosed that he had been married for two or three years, his wife and two boys residing at Buffalo in the interim, while Nettie, his small son and their cousin were staying at Montpelier, Vermont. This had been an astonishing bit of news for the townsfolk to absorb. Judge Bacon too had found it rather surprising for, as closely associated as they had been over the years, Levi had never disclosed any of his secret to him. It was a mystery to all and no one, including Levi Humphrey, offered to explain it.

Nettie and Libbie were friends from the start. Nettie was a lovely, intelligent young lady, refined and dutiful, who Libbie described as the tallest girl she had ever seen.

On a Monday evening early in November, Libbie arrayed herself in the costume of an old woman and called on the Humphreys. They all had a good laugh at her appearance. She and Nettie spent the following evening with Fannie Fifield at a meeting of the Literary Society. Eve Frost read an historical essay; Fannie read Poe's "The Raven" quite dramatically, then followed it with a portion of Longfellow's "Hiawatha." The girls thought Fannie brilliant, the training she had from Mrs. McCrady years before being quite evident.

General Humphrey became quite ill that evening, so much so that Judge Bacon went after Dr. Landon. In spite of contrary advice Levi got up and went to the hotel the next day. Though his room there was warm he grew worse by noon. That evening it appeared he would not live through the night. Libbie stayed with Nettie, keeping her company that night while Mr. Dunning sat up with the General. In a few days he fully recovered.

The following morning a telegram arrived announcing that Mrs. Humphrey would leave Rochester that day. She arrived in Monroe Friday noon. Libbie described her as a short woman with black hair and black eyes, between the ages of 30 and 40, "and is much more than I expected." She had two children, Frankie age three and a baby age five months. Frankie was handsome but sickly.

Though few people knew it, Mrs. Humphrey had once been the General's servant. He would refer to her as "his pet wife Katie." And Nettie seemed to like her too.

Several evenings later Libbie attended a lecture on philology. She was escorted home from the Seminary by Joseph Dansard, an event that her mother laughed over considerably and caused Libbie to note that it was the first time he had offered and would probably be the last.

Between Christmas and New Year's, on the Thursday evening, Libbie and her father and mother attended a grand New England Supper at the Humphrey House. There was a meeting of the Literary Society at the City Hall several doors away. After the reading of several papers, there was dancing for the young people. Libbie wrote in her journal "and *of course* we went home."

The following week of vacation provided time to attend a series of events: The Episcopal Festival on Saturday, the Bell Ringers Concert on Monday evening, the Presbyterian Festival on Tuesday, tea at the Jos. Clarkes with Laura amd Mary on Wednesday, an overnight stay at Nettie's on Thursday and a party on Friday evening at which one of the boys was tight "though he denied it."

Libbie received quite a few holiday gifts: a Philapena from Mr. S.; "Welles Poens" in blue and gold, a handkerchief and a dollar bill from her father; a pin and wristlets from her mother; "Wide Awake" from Laura Noble; and a pen from Mary.

Saturday was reserved for callers. On Monday, Connie Noble invited Libbie for a sleigh ride to Newport. Sorrowfully she wrote, "Father said No for I went last year to my first ride and the company didn't get home till 5 o'clock. Mr. B. told Con, Mary could go, to my *wonder*. They went and I have stayed home. 'Tis, of course, all right and Father knows best but its hard and a great disappointment."

NOTES—CHAPTER 3

[1]Merington, p. 38.

[2]Syracuse (N.Y.) *Herald Journal,* November 29, 1859; Henry Hall; *History of Auburn* (N.Y.), Auburn, 1869. The Auburn Young Ladies Institute was established in May, 1855, in the Corning Hall block by Winthrop Tappan. Mortimer L. Browne of Syracuse became a joint principal until 1859, when Tappan retired. In 1859, Browne bought the Goodwin Place on North Street in which he provided accommodations for 25 young ladies. The institution won a superior reputation for its religious and cultural influence.

Libbie, in her letter of January 15, 1859, to her father, gave her Chestnut Home address in Auburn as 187 West Genesee Street. Col. Brice C. W. Custer Collection, hereinafter referred to as BCWC Collection.

[3]Libbie's letter of August 16, 1927. Copy in collection of John Manion, Camillus, N.Y.

[4]BCWC Collection.

[5]Merington, p. 39.

[6]BCWC Collection.

[7]*Ibid.*

[8]*Ibid.*

[9]February 23, 1859. Bacon Family Bible. The marriage was performed by the Rev. Mr. William B. Brown. There is mystery to this wedding. Why did Judge Bacon, a prominent member of the Monroe community, and Rhoda Pitts, the widow of a Tecumseh, Michigan, Presbyterian Minister, elect to wed in far away Orange, New Jersey. Rhoda's brother, Postmaster Wells lived in Paterson, New Jersey, but this doesn't explain why they did not marry in their own communities where each was well known.

The Orange Library newspaper files reveal that they were married at the residence of William B. Russell.

[10]Merington, p. 40.

[11]*Ibid.*

[12]*Ibid,* p. 41.

[13]Dorothy Robinson, Records, First Presbyterian Church of Monroe. D.S. Bacon joined March 27, 1856.

[14]*Ibid,* Eleanor E. Bacon joined January 1, 1839. Carrie L. Boyd, in her letter of February 1, 1945, to Major E. S. Luce (copy in files of Monroe County Historical Museum Library) stated that in her father's Sunday School record book under August, 1856, he, Wm. H. Boyd wrote, "Mrs. D. S. Bacon, formerly a teacher in the Sunday School, died in August this year. She was a good woman and much beloved."

[15]*Ibid,* April, 1856.

[16]Bulkley, Vol. I, p. 531.

[17]Merington, p. 21.

[18]Monroe Presbyterian Church membership records.

CHAPTER 4
SEMINARIES AREN'T SINFUL

It was war, civil war, that was the principal subject of conversation. The newspapers had been full of it and the hawks and the doves were having a field day. Libbie found it so when she visited the Nobles on New Year's Day of 1861. Fifty or more guests called on David Noble and his wife that day, Libbie and their daughter Laura acting as hostesses for them.[1] Their guests could talk of nothing else.

The old year had ended with the State of South Carolina having seceded from the Union. Some thought that the Federal government would oppose the secession, though no one knew how. Other Southern states were expected to follow. Many believed that a compromise might be worked out though neither side appeared willing to make a settlement. President-elect Lincoln was opposed to a compromise[2] and violently opposed to secession.[3] South Carolina was setting up an independent government complete with a cabinet. As a result there was considerable talk of a new Southern Confederacy. The guests expressed feelings both of apprehension and resentment. Mr. Noble, usually unemotional, was particularly distressed about the state of the nation.

Mrs. Noble discretely broke up this rather intense discussion by inviting the young men present over for ice cream that evening. Joe Dansard, John Bulkley, Harry Conant, Connie Noble and two friends of theirs by the name of Oliver and Rode were quick to accept. The early evening was occupied by playing cards, which Libbie mentioned in her journal, adding "but of course I did not join in."[4] Just after nine o'clock, all went over to Mary Landon's house to join several other boys home from college. Her journal records that they laughed, talked, sang and danced, "promenading I mean, for we could not dance."

Though she mentions there were no regrets because she could not go on the sleigh ride the night before, nothing was said of the restrictions on card playing and dancing. The Judge ruled with a kindly though iron hand. Libbie was wise enough to refrain from expressing her disappointment in her journal. She loved and respected her father so much she would not openly disagree with what he considered wise decisions in her interest.

There were no present restrictions on being walked home by a young man of respectable family, so Conway Noble did walk her home that evening, at least as far as Nettie Humphrey's, where she was to spend the night. Nettie was in bed but glad to see her. Sometime after retiring, both were awakened by a mysterious rapping at the head of their bed. Though the soft rapping was repeated whenever they blew out their oil lamp, it soon stopped, and their fright with it. The next morning they decided it must have been mice.

She dressed in the school clothes at Nettie's the day before, picked up her volume of "Moral Science," then headed for the Seminary. It was rather a lonely day, for many of the girls had not returned. The blackboards painted on all sides of the classroom give it a depressing air "as if draped in mourning." Miss Griswold, the instructor in the General History class Libbie was attending, asked Professor Kellog "if it were draped in mourning because of the fearful state of our country."

Bert Conway spent that evening at her home saying many things "he'll wish to forget when he sees Nan." He must have seen the disbelief on Libbie's face while she listened to his remarks since he mentioned that she didn't believe him at all. Libbie admitted that she didn't in some things, because she had heard he had been quite wild in Ann Arbor.

On the following day, January 3, she watched Alice and Cora Woodruff skate on the pond in back of her father's office. She would like to learn to skate but ruefully recalled "father thinks it not best." That afternoon the entire house was swept with the expectation that her father and mother would be returning that day. They arrived at four o'clock. Mother Bacon had thoroughly enjoyed herself at her brother James' home in Clinton even though he had been ill while she was there. Millie Wells had sent along a large piece of cake and a very pretty headdress made of braid for Libbie.

Nettie and Mrs. Hammond were the first to call on the Bacons and welcome them home. Nettie, in particular, wanted to issue an invitation for Libbie to attend a "hop" at her place that night.

Henry and Mattie Williams, Mary and Niv Beaver called for her that evening on their way to Nettie's. They had stopped for Nan but she told them to go on without her as she was expecting Tate Thurber to escort her as soon as he arrived. At Nettie's the conversation centered on poetry and romance, mostly criticizing the work of Tennyson, Scott, Goldsmith and Willis. The party broke up early, allowing time for Libbie to note in her journal all that had occurred that day. She concluded that she liked Niv Beaver, thought Hen Landon a jolly, splendid fellow, and believed he might be engaged to Mattie Williams.

It was Friday, January 4th, a day proclaimed by President James Buchanan to be spent nationwide in fasting and prayer. Both the Episcopal and the Presbyterian churches in Monroe observed it, Libbie along with her mother and father attending services beginning at 11 at the latter, and staying until half past one. The meeting was well attended, the church being filled to capacity. Libbie observed that Reverend Strong read the psalm "God is our refuge, a very present help in our time of trouble," which he followed with appropriate remarks. She went on to write that she thought it remarkable that the "first fast day was held for the *peace* of our country," adding, "I hope God will give ear to the many cries going up from the thousands of hearts. It is fearful to think of Civil War."

She went home with Mrs. Landon to find many of her friends there. Hen and Niv Beaver sang several college songs for her — "Vive a la! vive a la!" etc., "Cococholunk chulunk che-le-le," and many others. The backgammon board was brought out to tell fortunes and, again, Libbie was the favored one. The board prophesied she would marry Will Robinson in 11 years on the eighth of June which caused her to proclaim, "I don't feel very much elated for even it they think I do, I *do not* love Will Robinson or any other man."

Once home Libbie changed to more comfortable attire. Though not dressed for callers she was happy to receive Eve Frost. Their time was occupied with chatting, Eve telling her much about Conway Noble's scrape in Ann Arbor. Conway and Mr. Martin had been arrested for assault and battery with attempt to kill, but were cleared of the charges. It all started when some hackmen remarked that the two boys were overly familiar with the servant girls. The men wanted money to keep quiet. They got a beating instead.

Libbie seemed to think Conway was so wild because he didn't go to church but Eve assured her she had heard in Ann Arbor he attended church regularly and also took communion. This was a delightful thing for Libbie to hear. She knew he was in a group of wild boys who belonged to the two wildest college fraternities — the Delta Phis and the Sigs — and was faced with many temptations.

Reverend Strong's Sunday sermon dwelled on duties for the New Year. In retrospect Libbie's past seemed like a dream to her. Not many sorrows and much to be thankful for. There had been many hours wasted foolishly and many neglected opportunities. She had many faults to correct. This might be her last term in school. She resolved to overcome her faults, feeling that if she did not she would "never be of any use to anyone and would be but an idle consumer."

Judge Bacon did not write often to his sisters, Eliza Sabin and Miriam Case, in Howlett Hill. When he did his letters were concise. A letter addressed to the both of them at this time described Libbie as "well and fleshy and full of fun and wit."[5] Their house was quite comfortable, for it now had a furnace, and was the *"neatest house you ever saw."* He disclosed that his wife had means of her own she used to purchase things for herself and the house. He had industriously applied himself to the building of a grape arbor and planned a piazza Libbie had asked for. He was doing such chores as firing his furnace, and feeding his cows and two pigs though he had a man cut and split his wood.

The war to him was a formidable rebellion that would take "time, lives and treasure to put down," but things did look better. Pridefully he mentioned that Monroe had supplied one company of men, two lieutenant colonels and three captains.[6]

One cold day John Rauch, a promising young attorney, called to see if Libbie would ride with him in his single cutter on a business trip 12 miles west of town. On their return they stopped off to get warm at the farm home of Alfred Bates and his wife just north of the River Raisin. Libbie's good friend Nellie Bates served tea with plenty of broiled chicken. Little was said when they arrived at seven o'clock.

The middle of January saw a change in the weather. A rising temperature and rain made walking surfaces sloppy and insecure. The seminary girls were praying that a heavy snow fall would cover the slush so they could participate in a sleigh ride to Ann Arbor the next week.

Libbie, knowing she would not be permitted to take the sleigh ride to Ann Arbor, turned her thoughts to the subject of style. She had obtained the Balmoral shoes Mr. Newell had made for her. Accustomed to footgear made of cloth or kid leather she wrote, "It seems funny to wear calfskin and regular men's soles." She did like the style of the Balmoral skirts worn with the Balmoral boots and she also approved of the new skating caps and the bell-shaped crinoline and ottoman cloth dresses. Somehow the corded ottoman dress cloth blended in attractively with the heavy, laced boots and the striped Balmoral materials. She decided to get some fleece lined stockings to wear in the new boots.

One evening while Nettie Humphrey was visiting the Bacons, the judge, who was in a playful mood and teasing Rhoda considerabley, turned his attention to the two girls. Selecting a volume of poetry he requested their attention while he read "love-sick" poetry to them. To even the score they criticized his pronunciation.

Professor Kellog had certain feelings about schoolgirls attending parties during the school year. He firmly believed there was a conflict of interest and had expressed himself at length along those lines at several of his classroom sessions. Libbie listened attentively, then decided it would be better for her to stay home from the party the girls had planned. She had a composition she wanted to try her hand at and then her Moral Science studies needed some homework. She felt good about not going because she didn't really want to go.

Those who attended the party came to school the next day in good spirits. They had completed their studies after the party, determined to show Professor Kellog school and parties could survive together. All had a splendid time. Libbie learned that the party had been a stylish affair, the girls having donned their very best—Fannie in her brown silk with a cherry silk Grecian waist; Nan Darrah in her drab silk and ditto waist; Kate in her organdie and white tulle cape; Nettie in her flounced braize and opera cape; Laura in a new multicolored tarleton; Hattie Cole in a pink one; Marie M. ditto, and Helen Wing in a white tunic with black velvet.

Refreshments were served at ten and consisted of oysters, ice cream and many kinds of cake, pyramids of macaroons, kisses, candy, fresh pineapple and many other fruits. There was no dancing as a matter of course. The party broke up at twelve.

Libbie, after hearing all this, said she was glad she didn't go, writing "I should have felt badly to be the only one in a thick dress. And then I do, in reality, feel that schoolgirls cannot go to parties and improve." This last sentence must have sounded rather weak after she had reread it for she added, "We can't make dresses to go then we feel so mean the next day."

An invitation to a party at Nettie Humphrey's did much to eradicate any feeling of disappointment she may have entertained. There were 70 or 80 people there when she arrived. With the three parlors and Mrs. Humphrey's room used as one large dining room, a supper was served to the guests. Following it some professional musicians played dance music. One of the gentlemen urged Libbie to dance one set, which she did. Immediately afterward she went upstairs to sit with the womenfolk, thinking afterward, "I wanted to dance so badly that I almost cried several times but I knew father wouldn't like it so I did not."

Later that evening after a lunch, she and Nettie went to their room where they decided to put on a private theatrical performance for their own amusement. Arrayed in their nightdresses they went through a series of recitations, burlesque roles and dramatics that were definitely too loud for the thin walls of the hotel. From the rooms of Mrs. Humphrey, Mr. Rauch and Mr. Sackett came evidence that their performances were not quite appreciated. "We got poundings on our ceiling and wall to pay for it all," she recorded.

After several weeks of February had passed she turned over to a fresh page in her journal and began with, "I am sorry to acknowledge my negligence but this book shows fully my 'bump of perseverance' needs enlargement. I had much to do before and after our jaunt to Ann Arbor so neglected my Journal." She made note of a trip to Nell Bates the day before to learn how to skate. She had learned to stand and to move over the ice ever so little so was greatly encouraged. From Nell she learned that her brother Elliot was going to West Point.[7] She thought Elliot a fine fellow.

April 8, 1861, was a day to reckon with, for Libbie was 19. Preoccupied with the reading of David Copperfield she found it difficult to leave just to write in her Journal. That Reverend Strong visited that afternoon at tea time was important enough to enter. He had received a call from Galena and had not reached a decision whether to accept it. The Bacons used every argument they could think of in an attempt to persuade him to remain in Monroe. Before he left Mr. and Mrs. Noble arrived. Mr. Noble had been reading the news in the latest paper and was concerned about the political affairs of the nation. Conditions at Fort Sumter were serious.

The conversation changed to local happenings. There had been a lot of talk about a new hotel to be built out on the La Plaisance Road at the site of the mineral springs. Did Mr. Noble know anything it? Indeed he did. He thought Shawnee Springs—that would be the name of the combination hotel and "Watering Place"— would be a certainty. Why Ned Clarke had nearly $3,000 subscribed. But this would have no effect upon General Humphrey who was going to finish off the third story of his hotel.

On April 13th, Fort Sumter surrendered to the Confederates.[8] The matter was of great concern to the military[9] as well as to the civilians. It was war and Michigan was destined to fill an important role. Monroe boys were volunteering; its streets were full of Michigan's gray uniforms. Henry Landon had become a second lieutenant in the 7th Michigan Volunteer Infantry and had been appointed Col. Ira Grosvenor's adjutant.

Libbie noted, "Hen is a splendid fellow and Mattie a lucky girl," this after Hen walked over to the Seminary to watch them make paintings of strawberries and cherries. The girls were concentrating on still life in their art class, special emphasis being placed on fruit arrangements.

Nettie Humphrey was leaving for several months in the East. All of her girl friends walked down to the railway junction with her and there was much kidding on the way. One girl brought along a bottle of camphor to pour on Nettie's bouquet to preserve it. Much fun was made of it.

A feeling of dejection come over Libbie after Nettie had departed. She knew Nett would return in September, but that was three months away. What would she do all of that summer without her? There was Howlett Hill and there were young men but so many of the nicer ones were enlisting. Then in a spirit of bravado she wrote, "I do feel so supremely indifferent towards all the young men here and as to what they think of me that I just take comfort in having as much *fun* as possible. I don't see the use in stewing as some girls do for fear the fellows won't like them and they won't ever be married. If no one ever comes that I love then I shall be a 'spinster' but to be one from necessity or one from pleasure are different things. I am sure of never ranking among the first named!"

An organdie dress occupied her mind and time. The finishing touch was three flowers sewed around the bottom. From that she began sewing a "side-awake cape" for it. She was extracted from this occupation by the arrival of Mr. and Mrs. Johnson and their daughter Delie inviting her to take a carriage ride with them along the lake. Nearing Brest they began their return, for the hour was late. As the sun began to set it lit up the sky in gorgeous colors, bathing the woods they passed in a dramatic red. Once home, her first reaction to the lovely ride was to sit down at her piano and play, then to her room she went to read Pickwick Papers.

Wednesday evening Bible class didn't hold her attention as much as usual. Once Rev. Strong asked her a question which she was able to answer partly right. Her attention was diverted by the face of Miss Aunt Stevens who "looked so interesting I had to immortalize on paper." The evening wasn't a total loss, for John Conant asked to walk her home. "I didn't refuse . . . for it was a splendid evening." Mother Bacon, after John had left for home, made fun of his nervous habit of wiggling. In spite of her mother's kidding Libbie thought him to be "absolutely pleasant and I am very agreeably disappointed in him."

Libbie was displaying considerable interest in her painting at this point. Mr. Highwood was the class instructor. He had taken a rather special interest in her, offering to take her out to paint from nature. She noted, "He is rather an impulsive man. He appears to like me and is rather too affectionate for my taste. He put his arm around my waist and I had a pin there so he picked himself and took it away whereupon I told him I should put the pin there after that and I guess he understood."

She referred to another occasion on which she was painting strawberries "Mr. Highwood was as loving as usual. I drew myself back and sideways and twisted generally to get away from him. I believe him to be *licentious beaucoup.* And if I made the slightest advance he would take me in his arms and kiss me to suffocation! But he is a fine teacher and 'tis a pity we can't have everything good combined." She was glad she knew a thing or two and didn't fall in love with him.

Highwood kept trying. After a Saturday morning of painting, he asked her to come to his studio that afternoon so he could paint her hair down. She told him that the picture might be called "Mary Queen of Scots before her execution!" He confided to her that he wished to go with the 4th Michigan Volunteer Infantry as an artist to sketch battle scenes. If he couldn't, he would go up through the lakes, Mary (Libbie failed to mention her last name) accompanying him on a sketching tour. Libbie's response: "I think I see myself alone with that licentious man."

On the Monday after the June Commencement, Libbie met her Uncle James Wells at the Clinton Inn. He drove her out to his farm where she had a delightful stay. It was harvest time and a novel experience for her. Mr. Conklin took Sarah Wells, Miss Hampton Mill and Libbie on a boat ride one day, then showed them the process of making meal-flour at the Globe Mills. Another day was spent in a ride to Tecumseh and the next in a trip to Jackson to view the Jackson State Prison, though Uncle Jim was having a great deal of difficulty in breathing because of his asthma and severe coughing attacks. Late that afternoon they stopped to have tea at Miss Nimock's hotel in Clinton.

That fall, Daniel wrote to his sister Miriam that it had been 39 years since he had left home and that he had written on that same day each year. He wanted her to know that Rhoda was nearly well though she had been an invalid since April. Libbie was well and he was never better.[10]

Six days later Libbie wrote to her cousin Rebecca Richmond that she had received her long awaited letter at her uncle's farm near Clinton. "Minnie Wells, as I told you, spent the winter here attending school a year ago so I knew her. She has a number of brothers—country boys and rather verdant—but with unbounded hospitality and quite gallant withall." She had been there four weeks and had been introduced to the Clinton society whose charming girls were by no means rustic.

She told her that on her return to Monroe, the 7th Infantry under Col. Grosvenor was "under guard on our Fair Grounds. It was fun to visit the camp ground and witness either Battalion Drill or Dress Parade.

"The Adjutant is from Monroe—Henry Landon—he has been my playmate from infancy to girlhood almost. He makes a splendid officer and I regret he has left Monroe." She told of being invited to the

Officer's Grand Military Dress Parade to which her father would not permit her to go. Fannie Fifield went though. Libbie had just received word that her Aunt Mary (Miriam) with whom she had lived at Howlett Hill, and who had been a second mother to her, had died that day from consumption.

The 7th Infantry had already left for Washington. They had been given a collation before they departed—cake, pie, etc. The town seemed desolate and forlorn to the girls after they left. "Stupid and subdued described it," according to Libbie. Then she wrote that Monroe was "a right pretty place in the summer . . . but there is nothing going on here, no concerts, lectures, parties or anything and I must confess it is *stupid.* People seemed happy to visit though . . . to see a young gentleman is a rarity.

"This is such a pleasant month. This and next month, for Monroe has many trees to display autumn beauties. . . . I beg you to come. . . . I am not going to school this fall and do not wish to graduate at all, but probably shall next year. I shall not resume my painting lessons until next year."[11]

Libbie was thinking of other things. Young men of her acquaintance were disappearing from the streets of Monroe. Those who were not attending college had enlisted. She had reached an age when the company of women, when constant, was blunting her sensibilities. She recognized the need for male companionship, and appreciated it. She was quick to analyze each male she met, ofttimes reaching conclusions which surely must have brought a smile when she read them in her journal in the more mature periods of her later life.

On the Friday before Christmas, Mr. Perry and Mr. Ball escorted a half dozen students over to Toledo to the High School to see an exhibition of gymnastics. On a large stage at the end of the hall, the girls performed with Indian clubs and the boys with dumbells. Afterwards their party went shopping, had their supper at the Island House, then returned home on the cars. Libbie was aware of Mr. Ball's considerable attention to her, noting in her journal that "Mr. B's blue eyes followed me about somewhat closely. I believe him to be licentious for he wouldn't look so out of his eyes if he wasn't. Foolish for me to write all this but how could I but be flattered by his marked attentions preferring me to the rest."[12]

New Year's Day of 1862 was a matter of an open house. Libbie noted that they had 54 callers, several of whom received her particular attention. Will Oliver had the contents of a cake basket spilled all over his new suit, much to Libbie's embarrassment. Charlie Miller may have been the cause, though she didn't say. He impressed her to the extent that she said of him, "O he's so homely but the keenest man I ever saw. He can turn and twist everything I say to suit him . . . O! He is so cute. He has the strongest hands with long slim fingers which are always where they shouldn't be and which without *seeming* to do anything will take your fingers in spite of you."

At the Seminary Mr. Boyd presented some of the writings of Shakespeare in his class of English literature. King Lear was assigned but Libbie spent an evening reading other plays he had written, then concluded that he was "awfully vile for girls to read but one of the girls told me and so I thought I should." She was enjoying her senior year and had decided that "if I don't get the valedictory I am amply repaid for going in by the pleasure I feel in studying and feeling how much interest Mr. Boyd takes in our class."

John Bulkley called on her for the first time in the new year. He returned her locket and chain he had borrowed several days before, and in which he had placed his photograph. He invited her to attend a masquerade party in Ann Arbor. She was in one of her gay moods that day and her actions seemed to have upset the staid young attorney. Libbie apparently enjoyed his discomfiture for she commented, "John is much disappointed in me and thought before I was the demure kind. Ha! Ha! Who's had more fun than Bill in her day? I would have fun in a prison."

She was beginning to get a touch of the euphoria that is induced through popularity. Evidences of the stimuli appear in the journal from this point on. She followed her reaction to John Bulkley with, "Mr. Vrormian has been telling around the state that he could have Fannie Fifield or Laura Noble or me. Laura was the richest but I the prettiest. On the whole he didn't know but he believed he liked me best?"

The Bacons were having a house guest for the balance of the winter: nine year-old Sammie Russell, a nephew of Rhoda, who had traveled the 900 miles from Newark, New Jersey, alone, arriving in Monroe at 4:30 in the morning. He immediately became a member of the family and showed a strong attachment for Libbie. When John Bulkley, who was to be seen at the Bacon residence with greater frequency, learned that young Sammie was getting into the habit of crawling into bed with Libbie—now nearly 21 years of age—he wrote to her imperiously, "Let Sammie sleep alone," then added discerningly, "boys of 9 often know as much as boys of 19." John tempered his straightforwardness by inviting Libbie on a sleighride to Newport with a party of young folks. On discovering that she couldn't go he was "elegant enough" to take her out riding the next evening alone, which she thoroughly enjoyed.

Near the end of January a young man by the name of Dutton alternated with Mr. Taylor while Rev. Strong was away as chaplain of the 7th Michigan Infantry. Libbie liked him but couldn't follow him too well since he wandered in his sermons. He dropped in on a social call and had tea with the Bacons one Sunday afternoon, saying to Mr. Bacon,

"I don't know as you want to see me but I am tired of seeing myself." Libbie enjoyed his company because he was so agreeable and smart. She had heard he was engaged to Kate Wing, and wondered if there was any truth to the rumor.

At a party on the following evening, Mr. Dutton came over to her to state that he had been informed by Kate Wing she had been making sketches of his colleague Mr. Taylor while he preached. Libbie had a feeling of sinking through the floor, then recovered and turned all colors. Seeing her discomfiture he kidded her and got her to laugh. A while later he came over and asked, "Do you prefer charcoal or crayon for drawing?" She mumbled something in reply and he said he was just paying her off. She vowed then and there to concoct something to tease him with. Her escort, Mr. Brown, took her home, staying until one o'clock.

On the next day Mr. Brown read Shakespeare for one hour in class. After lunch that noon at the Bacons he stayed on until four, then went to Fannie Fifield's for tea. He was back at the Bacons early that evening, staying until 11:30. Libbie enjoyed his company. He read to her a great deal and had her read to him. In her journal she commented, "In the evening Father monopolized him and I sat by mending his gloves. He has such a little hand for a man." It was pouring rain that evening and poor Brown had to walk in it, having missed the conveyance to the coach.

The girls at the Seminary were quick to note Libbie's newest conquest. They plagued her with, "the next wedding bells would be hers," then advised her solemnly to wait until she graduated.

On the last day of the month—January—she arrived home to find Mr. Dutton there taking tea. She told him she was glad to see him, but he said he thought she wouldn't be after last Monday night; then he asked her to forget. She replied, "I'll forgive, but could I forget?" In the way of reconciliation he offered her an invitation to attend the lecture with him. She had been invited to Nan's for a reception being given the newly married Hen Landon and Mattie Williams so couldn't go to the lecture. He offered to walk her to Nan's and as they neared their destination she said, "If you come in I don't believe they'll turn you out." In he walked and stayed until all were ready to leave. He enjoyed himself thoroughly, playing such pranks on Libbie as pinning her lunch box to a chair, to which she responded by stealing his oysters. John Bulkley took exception to Libbie's escort and almost bit Mr. Dutton in two, according to Libbie. She recorded, "Mr. D. is too cute for life," and, "Mr. D. is quite likely to turn my head with his brightness."

In the following two weeks Mr. Dutton and John Bulkley were alternate entries in her journal. She enjoyed Dutton's sermons and Bulkley's escort service home. She particularly enjoyed Mr. Dutton but wished her father wouldn't monopolize him so completely. To her way of thinking, "Mr. Dutton is just the kind of man to please me. His eloquence in the pulpit astonishes me, holds me enraptured. His musical powers are past my knowledge. He converses eloquently and is too cute for anything—*there!*"

Dutton had other talents. One day he came over to tune the piano. Libbie was at her saucy best that day. He would make some sharp remark and she would respond in a similar manner. "He does just make *anyone* laugh," she thought. "I guess he thinks I am the most harum scarum girl ever living. He is just nice anyway."

The Judge had become quite ill. "Liver complaint, we think." But that didn't stop the callers, for tea was a ritual in the Bacon household. The Thurbers and the Wrights dropped in to inquire as to the Judge's health, and Mr. Brown and Fan Fifield brought along Mr. Bissell to meet Libbie. "I was so delighted with Mr. Bissell," she observed, "splendid black eyes, a black mustache and ditto hair. Yes, I like him and we became acquainted quickly. He gives compliments under such a garb of beautiful language it makes me swallow them with pleasure."

Mr. Brown, who had stayed on after they had left, chatted with her until car time. "He is very pleasant and *looks books full* out of his eyes. But I guess I am not very deeply in love with him." While jotting down these thoughts, an envelope directed to Elliot Slocum kept falling out as if to warn her not to fall in love, for Elliot, so she thought, "is *better, truer, loves me more.*"

On the evening of Washington's Birthday, after attending a prayer meeting, Libbie spent the night at Mary Hines'. Joe Dansard was there, staying on till midnight. Libbie thought he was quite fond of Mary. She had told Mary she didn't care much for him perhaps because he was sort of soured on Monroe. Mary said Joe thought Libbie was "sort of proud and felt above people." To this Libbie exclaimed, "*Me* above all persons feeling above people." She admitted she did not like Joe's "course of life" and could not like him as she did John Bulkley. "But if he's reformed, I want to encourage him."

She did not go to church or Sunday School because of a bad cold. She wished all day Mr. Dutton would visit for tea, and sure enough, he did. She enjoyed him so—his brightness, his cheerfulness. He played for her and both sang though Libbie had to limit her singing because of her hoarseness. She recorded, "I am quite taken up with him. Yes, indeed I could learn easily to love him. I wish I wasn't so susceptible. I fear I shall never know who I do love! If I know a man likes me I'm almost sure to do the same. I don't know if he intends to marry or no. A wife would, in getting him, get a jewel! But yet he has the vapors sometimes. As Mother says, she could bear it or some other disagreeable trait once in a while if a person was so fascinating at other times. The last would counteract the first. She says so of Judge Wing. Mr. Dutton is as quick about gallantry as a young man." With that she concluded, "I must go and study and not think so much of males."

Girls will talk of matrimony, and those at the Seminary were not exceptions. After considerable discussion, they arrived at some conclusions as to who would be the first to get married. By unanimous vote it was to be Miss Rider. Fannie would marry in ten years, and Libbie in two. Miss Conor expressed the thought that Libbie would be an old man's darling, this thinking apparently the result of Mr. Dutton's frequent visits to the Bacon residence. Miss Conor said she intended being an old maid, and Libbie agreed that she might be.

It was now the end of February and nearing the end of the school year. Commencement Day would soon arrive and Libbie, in a moment of self-appraisal, felt herself inadequate. Modeling after her father was natural enough since she admired and loved him. His precise, deliberate ways were the distinctive characteristics of a man in his profession. His speech was clear, crisp and unhesitating. Libbie tried to imitate him. Conscious of her errors in speech, she tried all the harder. The net result was entered, "Recited as usual this morning. *As usual* means the same stammering, stuttering manner. Why can't I recite fluently?"

Her mind was relieved of this introspection by a busybody she met on the street. Libbie Wing was extremely interested in the Dutton visits to the Bacon home. She slyly plied Libbie with questions and got in answer the information that Mr. Dutton made his calls on the Judge.

On the way home she met Jimmie Little who handed her a letter from Elliot Slocum. After reading it she thought awhile, then concluded, "He wrote a dear, good letter. I'd give my old shoes to know if I love the boy. I am so susceptible I can't tell. If there wasn't any other fellows around I might be certain but I am not. *Time will tell. Patience.*"

That Sunday afternoon, March 2nd, Libbie found she had the entire house to herself; but not for long. Mr. Dutton had hardly entered the front door when Mary and Mattie Landon arrived closely followed by four Seminary girls. Mother Bacon soon arrived and served tea with some of her excellent sausages and mince pie. After the crowd had thinned out Mr. Dutton chatted with Libbie about her laughing in church, advising her she should laugh about things other than people. She didn't record her reactions to this unrequested advice.

This seemed to have no cooling effect upon their relationship for on March 30th, in perusing the last few pages of her journal, she noted the frequency of the letter D. Over the past two weeks she had seen Mr. Dutton nearly every day and "'tis no use of talking about his coming to see pater and mater familias; I know he don't. I am certain now that he loves me and nobody else and it makes me feel terrible for the prediction above (I shall cease to like him or do more) has come to pass. I was mighty near loving him but I am just as far away now from it. I never can. There are feelings in the bottom of my heart that have never been stirred. . . . I do not, cannot love him."

On her birthday, April 8th, she said an everlasting farewell to her teens. She didn't feel as old as she did at 17 but decided she would soon reach her second childhood—"say at 30." She had changed her views about aging, having decided, "I used to think that 20 was immensely old but now I think 26 is."

A week later Mr. Dutton asked for a place in her heart, then kissed her for the first time. Somehow that kiss didn't start any fire. "I knew *then* he loved me . . . but no love was in my bosom for him, simply admiration for his intellect." All of a sudden she had grown up. That afternoon she wrote him a note telling him she esteemed him only as a friend. As she did so his words, "Lizzie Bacon, you are charming!" kept ringing in her ears. Dutton took the rejection in stride, though he didn't visit the Bacons that evening. And Libbie missed his visit.

The Monroe *Commercial*[13] contained an announcement that was of particular interest to the Bacons. Their pastor, the Reverend A. K. Strong, had resigned as chaplain of the 7th Michigan Volunteer Infantry and had returned home to his congregation on May 31st. The last information they had received of him had appeared in the *Commercial* in a letter to the editor from Fort Benton, in which he stated, "I regret to say that the Seventh Michigan Regiment has had much sickness and have lost a number of men by death since it came into this state. The measles have made havoc with the soldiers, leaving them, in many instances, with severe colds and affections of the lungs; while typhoid has laid low on a bed of sickness many others, and in a few instances, some of these in the grave."[14] His return meant Mr. Dutton would be leaving Monroe.

Isaac P. Christiancy, who already had made a name for himself as an Associate Justice of the Michigan Supreme Court,[15] had brought additional honor to the city by his recent appointment as one of the Visitors to the United States Military Academy.[16] This bit of news was announced along with that of Daniel Bacon being made the Moderator of the Board of Trustees of the Union School. The Union School, well into its fourth year, was the community's first public school.[17]

FIRST CUSTER FAMILY RESIDENCE IN MONROE, MICH. On the west side of the South Dixie Highway, one mile south of Monroe, it was rented by Emanuel Custer in 1842 for about six months, after which he returned to New Rumley, Ohio. He left Monroe because his horses had been stolen. His daughter Lydia Ann left a good impression, for David Reed of Monroe married her four years later. Author's collection.

Monroe was displaying its progressive tendencies. The Common Council, acceding to the request of petitioners, passed an ordinance prohibiting cattle from running at large at night in the city streets. To this was added an amendment to include horses and ponies," said animals to be shut up from 8 P.M. to 5 A.M. each day."[18]

June 25th was Commencement and the close of the twelfth year of the Seminary. It was a banner day for Libbie. Her cousins Mary and Rebecca Richmond, and her Uncle Abel Page from Grand Rapids, had arrived on Monday evening just to see her graduate. She read an original composition as her part in the ceremony prior to the presentation of the diplomas. Entitled "Crumbs," its simplicity and originality rated it as the best by the Detroit *Free Press*. The local press said, "'Crumbs' by Miss Libbie Bacon of Monroe, was well arranged, exhibited good humor and good sense, and appropriately called to the minds of the graduates many scenes and incidents connected with their school days, to be pleasingly remembered in after life, when more trying realities are encountered."[19]

NOTES—CHAPTER 4

[1]Libbie Bacon's Journal, No. 2, (1861-1864) BCWC collection.
[2]E. B. Long: *The Civil War Day by Day,* Garden City, 1971, p. 19.
[3]*Ibid,* p. 20.
[4]Libbie's Journal.
[5]Merington, p. 42.
[6]*Ibid.*
[7]William H. Powell: *Records of Living Officers of the United States Army,* Philadelphia, 1890. Alfred Elliot Bates, born in Monroe, Michigan, July 15, 1840, was appointed to the U.S. Military Academy June, 1861, and graduated July 1, 1865.
[8]Long: *Day by Day,* p. 57.
[9]*Ibid,* p. 59. Maj. Robert Anderson was to say, "Our Southern brethren have done grievously wrong, they have rebelled and attacked their father's house and their loyal brothers."
[10]Sept. 5, 1861. To Howlett Hill. Author's collection.
[11]Sept. 11, 1861. To Grand Rapids, Author's collection.
[12]Libbie's Journal. Throughout her journal Libbie consistently employs the first letter of a person's name. At times absolute identification is impossible.
[13]June 5, 1862.
[14]Monroe *Commercial,* Dec. 12, 1861.
[15]Monroe *Monitor,* May 28, 1862.
[16]*Ibid,* June 4, 1862.
[17]Wing, p. 524. Cornerstone was laid June 24, 1858. Classes began April, 1859.
[18]Monroe *Monitor,* June 11, 1862. It was also ordained that sound white oak plank sidewalks, four feet in width, be built on certain residential streets. The business section had sidewalks of large flagstone.
[19]*Ibid,* June 25, 1862.

CHAPTER 5
AUTIE CUSTER WAS HIS NAME

Rhoda and Daniel Bacon were at the peak of their happiness. Both loved Libbie and gloried in her graduation. As valedictorian of her class, Libbie had been most impressive. Her simplicity, her sweetness, affected everyone, but her father the most. He was an emotional person in spite of his outward calm, for he was a person of deep feeling. The poise of this girl who so resembled her mother was just too much. Mustering his entire reserve he writhed within so he could appear as emotionless as possible while she made her presentation. His was a performance that outperformed the best in the tradition that "the show must go on." Not for one moment would he allow himself the luxury of wilting.

The Richmond girls were having the time of their lives. As Rebecca had written to her parents in Grand Rapids, "Though Uncle Bacon will not allow dancing in the house we have a delightful time, singing, playing games and promenading on the long piazza."[1] Rebecca spoke highly of Rhoda as a wife, mother and housekeeper and of the wonderful relationship that was maintained between her and Libbie. She was lavish in her praise of Libbie's "splendid disposition and lovely temperament." She never saw Libbie's parents restrain her since they seem to "encourage her mimicries, drolleries and schoolgirl gaieties."[2]

Judge Bacon enjoyed their visitation so much he had to express his delight to their parents. With judicious caution he advised them he had told the girls they could laugh and play and walk in good weather to their hearts' content "but must not ride after fast horses, and no boat rides, and have as little to do with fast young men as is consistent."[3]

The Richmond girls stayed on for three weeks. They urged Libbie to go home with them but she refused to go until fall. She had developed a deep feeling of admiration for Rebecca, who was three years her senior. Mary was a fine girl though quite a flirt, and "hardly the equal of her sister."[4]

Early in September the Judge addressed a letter to his sister Eliza at Howlett Hill in which he recalled that he had left there 40 years ago that day. He lamented the fact he never saw his mother after that. Knowing Eliza wished news of Libbie, he told her she "is well and lives by eating, as the old saying is, for but few persons like better food or more of it. Since she has been out of school she has enjoyed herself well." He closed by saying they would soon be visiting Grand Rapids.

On the 17th of September Mary Landon married Joe Dansard, Libbie acting as the first bridesmaid and John Bulkley as the groomsman. When asked to assume this role Libbie was quite surprised since Nan had been more of an intimate to Mary. In response to her question Mary said her family liked Libbie the best and Mary did too. Mr. Boyd performed the ceremony in the absence of Rev. Strong.

Libbie traveled with them as far as Trenton, Michigan, where she met Elliot and Alice Slocum. After having tea they visited a charming island at the mouth of the Detroit River. On the day following she went on to Romeo to visit Helen Sill and Louise and Belle Slocum. They took her over to Pontiac where she remained overnight with Mallie Gustine. On board the train to Grand Rapids were Alice and Elliot Slocum as she had expected. She had been decidedly interested in Elliot until she discovered he had not a spark of sentiment. Even so she enjoyed the trip with them. They were getting off just east of Grand Rapids to visit their uncle. Libbie couldn't very well refuse their invitation to go with them so she stayed at their uncle's from Tuesday till Saturday. But her interest in Elliot had cooled. "Uncle's charming place, the beautiful evenings and all aroused not a spark of sentiment in Elliot Slocum."

The stay at the Richmonds was to be an interesting experience. Boarding next door was a young Yale graduate by the name of Coyt. He offered to take the girls on a ride the next day, an offer they accepted. Unfortunately Rebecca fell down in the process of entering his carriage and knocked out her four front teeth.

Encamped just two blocks back of the Richmonds were two regiments of volunteers. Libbie soon became acquainted with the young officers, particularly Capt. Drew, Lieut. Littlefield, Lieut. Burge, Lieut. Bolza, Lieut. Hall and Capt. Weber. She was particularly impressed with Capt. Drew because he was practical, businesslike, devoted to duty; no flattery from him, and he sported a big mustache under a big nose. She decided, "he is something — my style of man."

Mary had started an affair with Con Noble back in Monroe and carried it to a point that enraged Libbie. Mary became cool toward him almost to the point of rudeness, yet had to be polite to him when he visited her in her home. She, of course, had to tell someone of her conquest and Libbie was nearby. "Mary poured her confidence in my ear. She is a sad flirt; has already had seven proposals and lots of less intricate flirtations. Rebecca was as noble, self-sacrificing and dignified as ever.... She is one of the loveliest girls I ever knew."

Libbie returned to Monroe in time to be invited to a Thanksgiving party at the Seminary. There were many young men invited to it from Toledo, Detroit and Adrian, but Libbie was most interested in Mr. Utley. She had been informed that he had liked her composition and her humbleness on Commencement Day for he had been the one to give her such a fine press notice in the Detroit *Free Press*. Libbie had noticed how his eyes had followed her around the room. She found he was extremely bashful and liked this characteristic. It was refreshing to meet a modest man for most she met had been so conceited. Rev. Strong came up at this time to talk to him so Libbie excused herself and while walking across the room was introduced to Capt. George A. Custer of Gen. McClellan's staff. This meeting, which was to change her entire life, is barely mentioned in her journal though one wonders what was written on a small portion of about six lines that was torn out of the book just under her simple statement that she had met him.

George Armstrong Custer was destined to be a warrior. He was born in New Rumley, Ohio — an overnight stage stop half way between New Philadelphia and Steubenville[5] — December 5, 1839. The ring of steel was early in the youngster's ears for his father Emanuel was the village blacksmith.

Emanuel, though a founding member of the New Rumley Methodist Church that year,[6] had militant forebears. He responded to the call for recruits in the New Rumley Invincibles, a local militia preparing for what might be a war with Mexico. Autie, as George was nicknamed by his family, attended drills with his father when about age four. He soon learned to go through the old Scott manual of arms with his toy musket. One day his father heard him lisp through a line one of his elder half-brothers was committing for school, "My voice is for war."[7]

Emanuel, dissatisfied with the income derived from his blacksmith shop and the post he had held as justice of peace for 12 years, moved his family to Monroe, Michigan, in May, 1842. There he remained six months, just long enough to make good the losses he acquired through the theft of his horses, then returned to New Rumley to engage in farming.[8]

Emanuel's first wife had died six years after their marriage, leaving him with three small children. Three years later he married Maria, the widow of Israel Kirkpatrick who had been left with three children. The marriage was a happy one. From it were born in or near New Rumley, Ohio:

1. George Armstrong Custer, December 5, 1839.
2. Nevin Johnson Custer, July 29, 1842.
3. Thomas Ward Custer, March 15, 1845.
4. Boston Custer, October 31, 1848.
5. Margaret Emma Custer, January 5, 1852.[9]

Lydia Ann Kirkpatrick was 14 when George Armstrong was born. It was natural enough for her to assume the caring for him through his early years for theirs was a household of divided responsibilities. She loved the flaxen-haired boy from the start for he was gentle though full of life, and never quarrelsome or quick tempered.

When he became 12 while staying with his sister Ann in Monroe he returned to New Rumley to help his father on a farm purchased two miles out toward New Market.[10] Here he mowed, plowed and handled an axe, ofttimes helping his father in his blacksmith shop. This gave him the opportunity to handle and ride the horses brought there for shoeing for he loved horses. In school he was naturally bright but hated to study, doing most of it in school by skimming over his lessons. He managed to receive respectable marks.[11]

At the age of 14 he returned to Monroe to live with the Reeds. While there he attended the Stebbins' Academy, the name popularly applied to the Boys' and Young Men's Academy. His schoolwork was acceptable though not outstanding. He would smuggle novels with military backgrounds into the class and read them behind his large geography textbook.

Schoolmaster Stebbins was an individualist with sore feet. He was not above wearing carpet slippers in the classroom to provide the comfort necessary for a "standing" teacher who ofttimes found it necessary to move rapidly and quietly around the rear of the room. Custer's geography covered the smaller volumes of Lever's *Charles O'Malley, Irish Dragoons* or *Tom Burke of Ours*. He read in stealth. More than once was he caught by the watchful teacher.

The Stebbins Academy remained opened for two years, 1853 to 1855, during which time Custer attended, then returned to New Rumley to attend the McNeely Normal School at Hopedale, Ohio.[12]

His father Emanuel had expected him to become a clergyman and wanted him to go to college at Meadville where he had owned a scholarship.[13] But Autie took his future in his own two hands. He had thoughts of attending the United States Military Academy.

Ronsheim mentioned that Autie taught in two Harrison County schools, starting about 1854, attending McNeely Normal School between periods.[14] I have three of Autie's "School Examiners Certificates" indicating that he could teach school, but only from 1856 on. The earliest is dated March 28, 1856, at Smithfield, Ohio. It is issued by the "Jefferson County Examiners of Teachers of Public Schools" and shows that he was qualified to teach Orthography, Reading, Writing, Arithmetic, Geography and English Grammar. The other two were issued by the Harrison County Board of School Examiners on April 5, 1856, and June 7, 1856, at Cadiz, Ohio, the latter for a period of 12 months. These certificates indicate he returned to Ohio later than 1854. And Custer did attend the Stebbins Academy through the spring of 1855. This permitted him to return to New Rumley in time to participate in the fall and winter terms at McNeely Normal School.

That summer he taught at the Locust Grove School at a monthly salary of $26. Though he, like any boy of 16, had dreams of many things money would buy, the first month's pay was taken home and poured onto his mother's lap.[15] He knew his parents had deprived themselves and the other children to give him an education. An appreciative son, he did the right thing.

An opportunity to earn several dollars a month additional caused him to teach at the Beech Point School near New Athens during the fall and winter terms.[16]

During this period he entertained a strong desire to enter the United States Military Academy. The Custer family was a close knit clan. With such deep feeling for each other it was natural for all to discuss the future plans of any member. Autie was no exception. Mother Custer was the chief opponent to any schooling at West Point whereas Father Custer and David Reed were very much in favor of any such move. Autie had convinced his father that a military career was the only path to happiness.

While attending the normal school at Hopedale, Autie wrote a letter to Representative John A. Bingham on May 27, 1856.[17] In it he requested information about the qualifications for admission to West Point and added that his parents had given their consent to his wish to attend the Military Academy.

Bingham promptly replied that a young man from Jefferson County had been appointed for that year. Following the adjournment of Congress that summer, Bingham returned to Harrison County. Autie, to the consternation of his strongly Democratic father, participated in a Republican parade so he might have the opportunity of shaking Bingham's hand. Later he arranged to talk with him, the frankness and modest determination of the young man so impressing the congressman that he promised to nominate him for the next year's vacancy.

Autie was jubilant. His ambition had been keyed to attending the Military Academy. "Had I been thwarted in this," he wrote, "my intention was to work my way through one of the great Eastern colleges, and qualify myself as a teacher, educator."[18] He was determined to have an education and was willing to throw all his energies into the task of acquiring one. So strongly did he feel that way that he wrote in a letter, "Should accident cast me adrift and I be thrown upon my own resources I have not a fear but that energy and a willingness to put my shoulder to the wheel would carry me through triumphantly and with reasonable success. In this country, no man, particularly if moderately educated, need fail in life if determined to succeed — so many and varied are the avenues to honorable employment which open on all hands before him."[19]

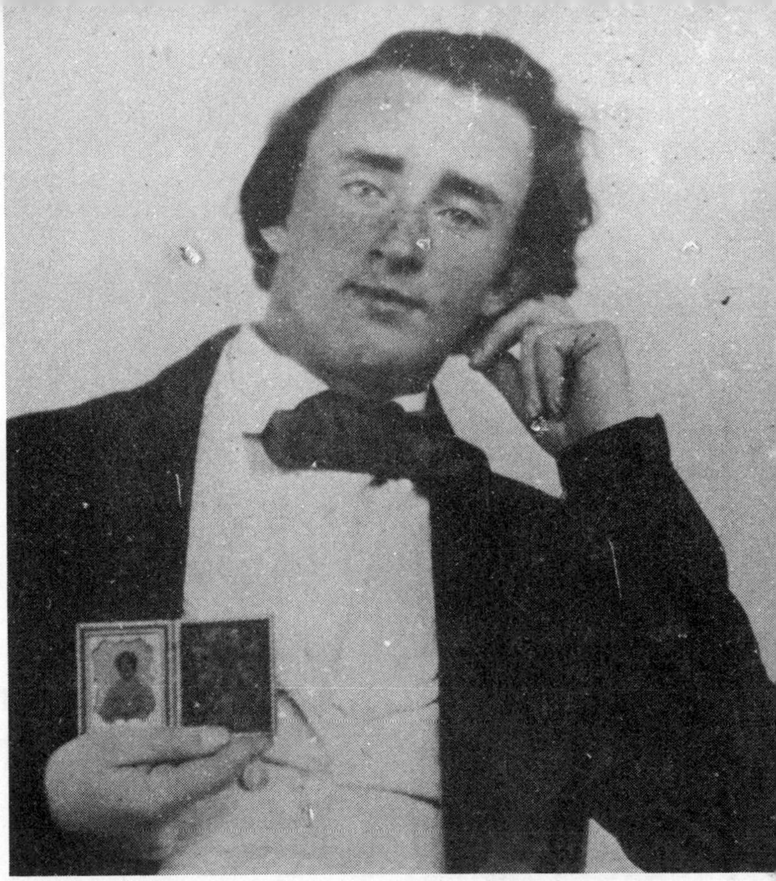

GEORGE ARMSTRONG CUSTER—his family called him Autie—as he appeared about 1856 when 17 years of age. The photo he displays is that of a passing fancy. Courtesy of Mrs. Milton Ronsheim, Cadiz, Ohio.

He had a year before him to prepare for the entrance examinations which he knew to be rigid. A special effort was made to master mathematics, a subject he applied himself to diligently. In consequence he was able to pass the entrance exam with little difficulty.

He was a popular teacher with his students for he had a sunny disposition and a well-developed sense of humor like his father, characteristics that are a common trait in the Custer family today. His love for practical jokes, which, in later years, often served to carry him through situations that other men would have found extremely annoying, was a Custer family characteristic.

Music always fascinated and entertained him though the only instrument he could play was the accordion.[20]

CADET CUSTER AND HIS FIRST GUN. Ca. 1859. The far away look may have been a daydream of battle. Author's collection.

The year soon passed and Custer was on his way to West Point. Soon after he left, Congressman John Bingham gave a talk at the Cadiz Methodist Church. In his remarks he spoke of the young man who had just left the community and that he "had impressed him as one of the most honorable and truthful men he had ever met."[21]

In June of 1857 he landed at the wharf at West Point. This was to be a new way of life for him. His previously independent life now became one of restriction and orderliness. Unused to rules and regulations governing his every move, he soon began accumulating demerits for indiscretions and irregularities in behavior. He loved the Academy but his high spirits involved him in a series of minor difficulties. He was indifferent in his attitude toward many of the subjects, yet on June 30, 1858, he wrote home, "I could not leave this place for any amount of money because I would rather have a good education and no money than a fortune and be ignorant."[22]

There is some dispute as to Custer's actual height. In later years his wife referred to him as being "not quite six feet" tall, and weighing about 170 pounds.[23] In his letter of nomination to Secretary of War Jefferson Davis, November 18, 1856, John Bingham indicated Custer was five feet nine and three-quarter inches (5′9¾″) tall, this less than three weeks before his 17th birthday.[24] On admission to the Military Academy his height was given as five feet eight and one-eighth inches (5′8⅛″).[25] A strange difference persists. Yet a classmate, Morris Schaff, wrote of a schoolmate over six feet tall who threatened him. He related how Custer and "deacon" Elbert of Iowa who "were about the size of the Southerner," had said to him, "if he lays a hand on you, Morris, we'll maul the earth with him."[26] Here we have a classmate who saw him daily for four years refer to Custer as being over six feet tall. Could Custer's admission measurements have been made or entered in error? There is the possibility, that Custer, hardly 17, had not reached his full growth when he entered the Academy.

Custer's passage through four years at the Military Academy was not unattended with problems. His interest in his studies was intermittent; his interest in fun and frolic was constant. There was no restraint to his exuberance, consequently his demerits piled up almost to an amount demanding his dismissal. Many of his classmates were dismissed but he, with studied dexterity, managed to escape each time he neared the posted limit.

On August 7, 1859, he wrote to a girlfriend that he had become accustomed to the strict discipline and had escaped with few demerit marks, this at a time when 150 demerits would have meant dismissal. By the following January it would require only 100 marks in a year to result in a dismissal. He was now liking West Point as well as if not better than at first, and had reached a point of thinking it the most romantic spot he had ever seen.[27]

He proceeded to tell her of the nocturnal pilgrimages bolder cadets made "to a small village two or three miles down the river for the purpose of gettings things which are not allowed, such as ice cream, candies, fruit and (I am sorry to say) some even go for wine and liquors."

Autie was not reluctant to visit Benny Havens, the off-limit purveyor of contrabands to cadets. Benny Havens was the favorite resort of cadets after taps, his cottage being established at the base of a high cliff near Highland Falls.[28] To be caught there might mean dismissal, yet it was not the liquor that lured the boys but anecdotes of the military famous that Havens could supply in a continuous flow. The relief from irksome discipline added zest to the occasion.

Though he was extremely popular with his classmates, Custer's disregard for regulations kept the unsympathetic eyes of his superiors constantly glancing in his direction. As Brig. Gen. Evan Andruss recalled in a letter to Mrs. Elizabeth B. Custer, "His boyish pranks—but harmless—frolics kept him in constant hot water. . . . He was beyond a doubt the most popular man in his class. . . . "[29]

The fact that he was the strongest man in his class, or that he displayed unusual athletic abilities such as being able to spring to a standing position while lying flat on his back, or to excel in riding and jumping a horse to a point of attaining the highest on record next to that of Cadet Ulysses S. Grant, had little to do with his popularity though it must have commanded respect. Perhaps Brig. Gen. Peter Michie gives an inkling when he wrote, "He (Custer) had more fun, gave his friends more anxiety, walked more tours of extra guard and came nearer being dismissed more often than any other cadet."[30]

His friends called him Fanny. His fair complexion, blond hair and temperate habits earned him that. The yellow hair that was to become the symbol of his later fame was allowed to grow *a la Cody,* a length not permitted on the post. After he was reported several times for long hair, he instructed the barber to give his head a clean shave. Relentlessly he was pursued and reported at all inspections and "on sight" for "Hair out of uniform." To prevent his dismissal he was forced to wear a tan wig until his head evidenced enough growth to permit the wig to be abandoned.[31]

When plebe Jasper Myers of Indiana first arrived at the Academy he displayed a great beard. Custer was the first to meet him and, on doing so, told him he should go home and send his son since it was the boy that was wanted and not the old man.[32]

In Spanish class he asked the instructor to translate "Class is dismissed" into Spanish. When the request was complied with, the entire class arose and left the room.[33]

The practice march on horseback was an exercise all hated. It was a walk all of the way, never once breaking into a trot or a gallop. As the squad passed the Cozzens Hotel it was not unusual for a member to drop out "to water his horse at the trough in front of the bar of the hotel." Never once was he caught, the squad member being Custer.[34]

Though none of the demerits he had accumulated were obtained through any serious transgressions — playing cards, talking in the ranks, throwing snowballs at passing columns and hiding cooking utensils in his fireplace chimney were the principal charges — he managed to acquire 98 demerits in his first half and 94 demerits in his second half of his second year.[35] He needed but 100 marks, at that point, to be dismissed. In his first half-year he had accumulated 129 which somehow was reduced to 69.[36]

There was a constant flow of letters to his family and to several girl friends in the New Rumley area. His sister Ann was his favorite correspondent though he wrote to his parents with great frequency. Most of his writing was done at night by candlelight after hours, a habit he maintained throughout his life.

He complained to Ann about his father's refusal to sign a permit so that he could use tobacco. He didn't want the tobacco for himself but for his roommate who smoked, and who would get things for him in exchange for the favor. He bemoaned the fact that Tom and Bos could smoke and chew because they were at home where they could be controlled but he, because he was away from home, could not have a permit. He concluded by saying that nothing could induce him to either smoke or chew as he considered it a filthy and unhealthy habit.[37]

Apparently his parents were not doing too well on their farm outside of New Rumley. The area was growing slowly in comparison to the region around the west end of Lake Erie. Autie had been trying to induce them to move to Monroe County and buy a farm there, so he wrote Ann. The country wasn't as pretty as it was in the rolling farmlands of Harrison County, for Monroe could offer no hills. It could offer soil that was highly productive, and it was near the Reeds. Just 40 miles to the south, near Tontogony, Ohio, his half-brother David Kirkpatrick had a farm. Members of the family did try to keep close together.[38] He expressed some anxiety because they were unsettled, then added, "I would feel much more contented and could attend to my studies much better because I am thinking of them and always have an anxiety and fear that they will not be able to buy a farm where they can get along comfortably."[39]

Emanuel elected to move to Wood County, Ohio, for the records show that he purchased 80 acres in Washington Township on the Tontogony Creek Road for $2,000 on March 1, 1861. His son Nevin lived just north of him on the George Fulmer Farm.[40] This didn't lessen Autie's determination to move him into Monroe County but it took more than two years to convince hardheaded Father Custer he could do better in Michigan. Then it took an offer to send sister Margaret to the Boyd Seminary.[41] Margaret was 11 years old.

Autie continued to enjoy his cadet life. He lived in the tower room of the 8th Division. Lieutenant Douglas had a flock of chickens and a buff-colored rooster in a garden just under Autie's window. The rooster was a tempting morsel and Autie had cooking utensils hidden in his chimney. The cadet assigned to dispose of the feathers failed to wrap them securely. A trail of yellow feathers could be seen leading from Autie's tower room.[42]

Autie was impressed with the sectional lines established by the cadets. This was evident when political problems were discussed, each cadet expounding and defending the feelings of the Congressional District he represented. The subject of abolition was one that developed considerable heat. The advocates for and against slavery were equally vociferous in their arguments, those from the South being the most talkative.

The Presidential campaign was hotly contested. Those with Republican leanings supported Lincoln and Hamlin while the adherents to the extreme Southern Democrats followed Breckenridge and Lane. Lane's son was a member of Autie's class. The more moderate Democrats declared themselves for Douglas and Johnson.

Feelings ran high. Breckenridge followers announced, as did their senior in Congress and at home, that if Lincoln was elected the South would secede. One night an effigy of Lincoln was hung to the limb of a shade tree in front of the cadet barracks. It was removed early in the morning so that few ever knew of it.[43]

During the winter preceding the opening of hostilities between the North and the South Autie and his classmate P.M.B. Young were discussing national events. Young, as Autie recollected, said to him in a half jocular, half earnest fashion, "Custer, my boy, we're going to have war. It's no use talking; I see it coming. All the Crittenden compromises that can be patched up won't avert it. Now let me prophesy what will happen to you and me. You will go home, and your abolition Governor will probably make you colonel of a cavalry regiment. I will go to Georgia, and ask Governor Brown to give me a cavalry regiment. And who knows but we may move against each other during the war. You will probably get the advantage of us in the first few engagements, as your side will be rich and powerful, while we will be poor and weak. Your regiment will be armed with the best of weapons, the sharpest of sabres; mine will have only shotguns and scythe blades; but for all that we'll get the best of the fight in the end, because we will fight for a principle, a cause, while you will fight only to perpetuate the abuse of power."[44]

This prediction was fulfilled to a remarkable degree. Custer did lead an abolition governor's cavalry, but not of his native state but that of-Michigan. Young led a Georgia cavalry regiment. Both met on the field of battle and both rose to high command.

One by one the Southern cadets resigned to enroll in the ranks of their seceding states. In a matter of a few weeks there was scarcely a Southern cadet remaining. The separation was a painful act for the bond that tied these young men together was strong, yet each respected the other's viewpoint.

The attack on Fort Sumter had united the North like nothing else could. Political opponents became friends; all differences vanished in the unity provided by a common cause. On April 14, 1861, when the defeated garrison marched out of Fort Sumter, the entire South rejoiced. Commandant Robert Anderson responded by saying, "Our Southern brethren have done grievously wrong, they have rebelled and attacked their father's house and their loyal brothers. They must be punished and brought back, but this necessity breaks my heart."[45]

The depletion of officer candidates through cadet resignations was a matter of concern. Competent officers to train troops were in great demand. In order to fill this great need it was decided to reduce the five years of instruction to four years. This would permit two classes to graduate in the spring of 1861, Autie's being the four year class.

This was a time for recapitulation and self-objurgation. Always honest even though it hurt to be so, Autie wrote some months before his death, "My career as a cadet had but little to commend it to the study of those who came after me, unless as an example to be carefully avoided. . . . My offenses against law and order were not great in enormity, but what they lacked in magnitude they made up in number. The forbidden locality of Benny Havens possessed stronger attractions than the study and demonstration of a problem in Euclid, or the prosy discussion of some abstract proposition of moral science. My class numbered upon entering the Academy about one hundred and twenty-five. Of this number only thirty-four graduated, and of these thirty-three graduated above me. The resignation and departure of the Southern cadets took away from the Academy a few individuals who, had they remained, would probably have contested with me the debatable honor of bringing up the rear of the class."[46]

When June arrived he was assigned to a tour of duty as officer of the guard, a novel situation for him since he had been compelled to act as a private on numerous extra tours of guard duty for violating regulations. At dusk one day he heard a commotion near the guard tents. Hurrying to the area, he discovered two cadets about to engage in fisticuffs. Several of their friends were attempting to separate them when he, instead of placing the two combatants in arrest for violating Academy regulations, pushed back those who would interfere and called out, "Stand back, boys; let's have a fair fight."[47]

In referring to his part he wrote, "The instincts of the boy prevailed over the obligation of the officer of the guard." For the remainder of his life these instincts prevailed. This event might well have been a portent of things to come. This quickness to act won many battles, made many friends, created many enemies, led to a tragic end.

Autie was to regret his thoughtless act. Hardly had he uttered the words than the crowd begin to disperse. Approaching him were two army officers, Lietuenants William B. Hazen and William E. Merrill. The officer in charge, Hazen, asked him why he had not suppressed the riot that had occurred a few moments ago. Stunned by the thought that two boys fighting could be considered a riot, he could not answer. He was ordered to report to the commandant, Lieutenant Colonel John F. Reynolds, the following morning. Unable to provide a satisfactory explanation of his conduct, he was ordered to his tent in arrest to await a court-martial.[48]

To add to his discomfiture news came to him several hours later that his class had been relieved from duty at West Point and had been directed to report to the Adjutant General in Washington for further orders. His name was not on the list.

Lieutenant Stephen Vincent Benét presided as judge advocate. And Autie pleaded guilty. He produced the two combatants as witnesses, principally to prove neither was injured in the fray. In a matter of minutes it was over and he was returned to quarters to await his sentence. Meanwhile classmates with important connections busied themselves in his behalf while they were in Washington. Several days later the superintendent of the Academy received a telegraphic order directing him to release Autie at once and order him to report to the Adjutant General of the Army for duty. Autie never learned the decison of the Court.

According to Special Orders No. 187 of the Adjutant General's Office, dated July 15, 1861, the Court sentenced Custer "to be reprimanded in orders. . . . The Court is thus lenient to the peculiar situation of Cadet Custer represented in his defense, and in consideration of his general good conduct as testified by Lieutenant Hazen, his immediate commander."[49]

On the 18th of July he hastened to Washington, stopping off at Horstmann's in New York just long enough to purchase his lieutenant's outfit of sabre, revolver, sash, spurs, etc. Early on the morning of the 20th he arrived at the Ebbit House in Washington where he hoped he would find some of his classmates. There he found his roommate James P. Parker of Missouri. Parker told him he had received an order dismissing him from the rolls of the Army for having tendered his resignation in the face of the enemy. Two other classmates have been included in the order. All had sympathized with the South but had remained at the Academy long enough to graduate. The other two had obtained commissions in the Egyptian army.

Bidding Parker farewell, Custer proceeded to the Adjutant General's office where he presented his credentials. Accepting an opportunity to meet General Winfield S. Scott, he was asked by Gen. Scott, after being presented, just what type of duty he preferred. He managed to stammer that he earnestly wished to see active service with the Second Cavalry he had been assigned to.

"A very commendable resolution, young man," Gen. Scott replied, then turning to the Adjutant General, he continued, "Make out Lieutenant Custer's orders directing him to proceed to his company at once." Turning back to Custer, he said, "What I desire to say to you is, go and provide yourself with a horse if possible, and call here at seven o'clock this evening. I desire to send some dispatches to General McDowell, and you can be the bearer of them. You are not afraid of a night ride, are you?" As well ask an angel if he feared the devil.

It was near three o'clock in the morning when he neared the army at Centerville. Picking his way through sleeping and breakfasting men, he reached McDowell's headquarters and delivered the dispatches. While eating breakfast he learned that the army was to move against General Beauregard that day. Just three days out of West Point and he was about to witness the first grand battle between the Union and the Confederacy.[50]

A short time later he had remounted his horse and made his way to the head of the column, taking his place with Company G of the Second Cavalry. He soon learned that the two contending armies were nearly equal in size with a slight advantage on the part of the Union troops and that the cavalry was to be used only as a support for the batteries of artillery.

By mid afternoon when the force under Irvin McDowell had the situation well in hand, several thousand fresh enemy troops flanked the victorious Union force, causing them to panic and run. Autie, who with a classmate observed this from a vantage point on a high ridge, concluded, "A moderate force of good cavalry at that moment could have secured to the Confederates nearly every man and gun that crossed Bull Run in the early morning. Fortunately, the Confederate army was so badly demoralized by its earlier reverses, that it was in no mood or condition to make pursuit, and reap the full fruits of victory."[51]

This first battle of Bull Run or Manassas, though a military disaster, roused the people of the North. Like the attack on Pearl Harbor it unleashed the spirit of patriotism at a time when most Northerners were indifferent to the dangers. In seeking a cause for the defeat the press spread the story that General McDowell, after having won a substantial victory, had lost the battle because of his drunkenness. Autie, in his *War Memoirs,* investigated these charges and arrived at the conclusion that McDowell had "always practiced the rule of total abstinence from the use of all wines and spiritous liquors, refusing even the luxury of a cup of tea or coffee." He allowed that the defeat was entirely due to a timely flank attack by enemy reinforcements when the Union forces were driving their opponents in a disorderly retreat.[52]

The natural result was the removal of McDowell. The unjust criticisms showered on him brought a demand for replacement and General George B. McClellan was the one selected to take command. In the reorganization that followed, General Philip Kearny assumed command of a brigade of New Jersey volunteers to which Autie's company was attached. Autie was first made his aide-de-camp, then later his assistant adjutant general.

Kearny was a strict disciplinarian. Some regarded him as a martinet though the unfortunate victims of his displeasure were usually the high brass. He was a man of violent passions and haughty demeanor, extremely brave, distrustful of those who differed with him, and was bored with inactivity. Autie found him "ever engaged in some scheme either looking to the improvement of his command or the discomfiture of his enemy."[53] Autie remained his aide until an order came through forbidding regular Army officers from serving on the staffs of officers holding volunteer commissions.

In the early fall of 1861 the regular and volunteer cavalry, under the command of Brigadier General Philip St. George Cooke, assembled near Washington to form into one organization. Cooke, who had authored a book on cavalry tactics, was bypassed at this point by the appointment of Brigadier General George Stoneman as chief of cavalry on General George McClellan's staff. As Autie later wrote of Stoneman. "He failed, however, in every respect to realize the expectations of those to whom he owed his selection as chief of cavalry. He proved himself deficient in almost every necessary requisite to the success of a cavalry leader. Active and somewhat enterprising when in pursuit, but not in the presence of the enemy, he seemed to be forsaken by both these qualities when actual conflict and offensive movements were necessary. The record of the cavalry while operating under Stoneman contains nothing to its credit as a separate organization. . . ."[54]

WEST POINT GRADUATE. Though encountering some difficulty before graduating in 1861 he had the good fortune to be present at the battle of Bull Run. Courtesy of the United States Military Academy Archives.

NOTES—CHAPTER 5

1 Merington, p. 43
2 *Ibid.*
3 *Ibid.*
4 *Ibid,* p. 44.
5 A. D. Cole and Jacqueline Hencken: *New Rumley,* Strasburg, Ohio, n.d., p. 4.
6 *Ibid,* p. 8. Emanuel Custer was on the first board of trustees of the New Rumley Methodist Church. His uncle Jacob Custer, who platted New Rumley in 1813,is buried in the Lutheran cemetery.
7 Milton Ronsheim: *The Life of General Custer,* Cadiz, O., 1929, p. 1.
8 Wing, p. 318.
9 Lawrence A. Frost: *The Custer Album,* Seattle, 1964, p. 18.
10 Lawrence A. Frost: "Let's Have a Fair Fight!", *Chicago Westerners Brand Book,* Vol. XIV, No. 4 (June 1957), p. 1.
11 Ronsheim, *op. cit.,* p. 3.
12 *Ibid.*
13 Wing, p. 318.
14 Ronsheim, p. 3.
15 *Ibid,* p. 5.
16 *Ibid,* p. 3,5; letter in Custer Battlefield National Monument files, G. A. Custer to Mrs. David Reed, Dec. 12, 1856.
17 Frederick Whittaker: *A Complete Life of Gen. George A. Custer,* N.Y., 1876, p. 13.
18 Merington, p. 7.
19 Yale University Library, manuscript collection.
20 Ronsheim, p. 4.
21 *Ibid,* p. 5.
22 Elizabeth B. Custer collection, Custer Battlefield National Monument. Hereinafter called EBC-CBNM.
23 Elizabeth B. Custer: *Tenting On The Plains,* N.Y., 1887, p. 23.
24 National Archives, Record Group No. 94.
25 *Proceedings of Medical Board,* 1857-1865, U.S. Military Academy Archives.
26 Morris Schaff: *The Spirit of Old West Point,* N.Y., 1907, p. 84.
27 G. A. Custer to Minnie St. John. Author's collection.
28 Joseph R. Farley: *West Point In The Early Sixties,* Troy, N.Y., 1902, p. 195. Benny Havens, years before, had sold buckwheat cakes, ale and liquor inside the lines in violation of Academy regulations. When discovered he was expelled from the post.
29 Brooklyn, September 27, 1905. Custer Battlefield National Monument.
30 A. Noel Blakeman: *Personal Recollection of The Rebellion,* N.Y. 1897, p. 194.
31 Farley, p. 78.
32 Schaff, p. 66.
33 Merrington, p. 8.
34 Farley, p. 75.
35 Frost: *The Custer Album,* p. 22.
36 G. A. Custer: *My Life on The Plains,* Chicago, 1952 (Quaife ed.), p. XXV.
37 Merington, p. 9; Monaghan, p. 34.
38 Monaghan, p. 34.
39 Letter of February 18, 1860 to Mr. and Mrs. David Reed. Author's collection.
40 Bowling Green (Ohio) *Daily Sentinel Tribune,* July 26, 1949.
41 Margaret Custer's letter of August 27, 1863 to Autie. Author's collection.
42 *Custer Album,* p. 22.
43 G.A. Custer: "War Memoirs," in *Galaxy,* Vol. 21, No. 4 (April 1876), p. 449.
44 *Ibid,* p. 451.
45 Long, p. 59.
46 G.A. Custer: "War Memoirs," in *Galaxy,* April, 1876, p. 454.
47 *Ibid,* p. 455.
48 Frost: "Let's Have a Fair Fight," p. 27.
49 West Point Library files.
50 G.A. Custer: "War Memoirs," in *Galaxy,* April, 1876, pp. 458-460.
51 G.A. Custer: "War Memoirs," in *Galaxy,* Vol. XXI, No. 5 (May 1876), p. 628.
52 G.A. Custer: "War Memoirs," in *Galaxy,* Vol. XXI, No. 6 (June 1876), p. 809.
53 *Ibid,* p. 815
54 *Ibid,* p. 817.

CHAPTER 6
BY CHANCE THEY MET

It was a typical Michigan October — cool, crisp mornings and a sun that warmed the farmer in the field. Autie was to find it so when he arrived in Monroe on a sick leave. His sister Ann and his brother-in-law David Reed made him more than welcome for they regarded him as a son. Emma, his niece, was now a young lady of 13, and his little nephew Autie was three.

Autie was to find his homecoming pleasant in many ways. The River Raisin abounded with small mouth bass and the lake-shore marshes teemed with a variety of ducks and the Canada geese that stopped off on their trek south each fall.

The table at the Reeds groaned with the results of a bountiful harvest for David had a large garden and shared in the produce from a number of farms he owned. Autie found convalescence a pleasant experience though he never succumbed to the luxury of becoming neurotic over illness.

His blue clad figure adorned with brass buttons commanded considerable attention as his measured gait carried him through the business area. Monroe's only officer in the regular army and the first to be under fire in the war, he was the subject of conversation everywhere, though it was of a hushed nature among the young ladies.

He, like many other lads, had acquired some of the bad habits prevalent in the service. Proficiency in swearing was one; drinking, another. Meeting a few of his old school chums in one of Monroe's saloons, he celebrated the occasion by having a drink with them. One drink led to another. When it became time to go home it was evident he could not walk the mile to the Reed residence without assistance. One of the boys helped him. The first block had a flagstone walk; the rest of the way was a footpath. As the story is recalled by members of his family the two boys occupied the whole of the stone walk, but no account is given of their problems on the narrow path.

As they passed the Bacon home, which was on the opposite side of the street, Libbie chanced to be at the window. Years later she referred to it as "that awful day."

Arriving home, Autie was left on the porch to maneuver for himself. The Good Samaritan who had accompanied him had been willing to face the public gaze in getting him there but could not face Ann Reed at the moment of crisis.

When sister Ann saw Autie she took him into her bedroom where she kept her Bible, then closed the door. What transpired there has never been fully known. We do know that he gave a solemn pledge of total abstinence which he kept until his dying day.[1]

In February, 1862, he returned to Washington.[2] One of the first people he met was his classmate Deacon Elbert whose news of the moment was his announcement that he was about to get married. This was something to celebrate. A band was a necessary accessory so one was obtained at the regimental headquarters. After serenading Elbert's sweetheart they proceeded to the homes of friends to entertain them. Everyone offered them wine and liquors. Autie, true to his pledge to Ann, refused to touch a drop.[3]

There was an air of expectancy around camp. The President wanted General George B. McClellan, the newly appointed commander of the Army of the Potomac, to move against the Confederate forces at Bull Run and fight a second battle there. The Confederate encampment appeared as a constant threat to Washington and Lincoln was under continual pressure to do something about it. McClellan was of the opinion that his army should be transferred by water to the Peninsula and move from there against Richmond. He believed this movement would force the enemy to abandon its fortified positions at Bull Run and thereby free Washington from any menace of attack. His opinion finally prevailed. As soon as the transfer was ordered, the enemy evacuated its fortified position in front of Washington and withdrew to Richmond.

On March 10th the cavalry moved forward, Custer now taking turns with other company commanders in assuming the point of the advancing column. Temporarily his company was without its captain and first lieutenant. His regiment was no longer called the Second Cavalry, having been redesignated the Fifth Cavalry under a program of enlarging the cavalry corps.

On this advance toward Bull Run he experienced his first charge upon enemy cavalry pickets. General Stoneman ordered that the pickets be driven back across Cedar Run. Custer requested permission of his regimental commander, Major Charles J. Whiting, to lead his company in such an attack. He received permission and led a gallant charge that drove the pickets across the bridge at Cedar Run. In the exchange of fire one of his men was wounded in the head though not seriously.[4]

Members of the press accompanying the column made much of the affair, for skirmishes and battles were relatively uncommon. The wounded man received considerable attention, his being the first wound received in the Army of the Potomac.

There was evidence that the Army of the Potomac was showing signs of life. It had appeared to be a loser up to this point. The first battle of Bull Run had a demoralizing effect upon the men but now, with McClellan in charge, things were beginning to shape up. Not only did he appear to be doing something but he seemed to know what he was doing. The move toward Richmond away from those fortifications about Washington was the sort of thing that meant action. McClellan had stirred the imagination of the men. He had breathed life into a comatose army. Custer felt the stimulous and expressed his feeling in a letter to Mother and Father Custer on March 17, 1862: "I have more confidence in General McClellan than in any man living. I would forsake everything and follow him to the ends of the earth. I would lay down my life for him. He is here now. Every officer and private worships him. I would fight anyone who would say a word against him."[5]

By the end of the month the cavalry embarked on steamers to be transported in an atmosphere of absolute secrecy. No one knew where they were bound but all expected they would end up at Richmond. They discovered their destination when the boats docked at Fortress Monroe. The troops moved from this point forward to face the enemy's earthworks at Yorktown and at Lee's Mills. A Union reconnaissance in force against the Confederate entrenchments at this time ended in failure. Finding it impracticable to assault this impregnable position, the Union forces settled down to a siege.

There was a demand for young officers to serve under the engineering officers engaged in planning and erecting defense works. Since West Pointers were assumed to have a practical knowledge of such matters, Custer was assigned to Lieutenant Nicholas Bowen, chief engineer for Gen. William F. (Baldy) Smith.[6]

Smith's position was on the left of the line opposite Lee's and Wynn's Mills. In constructing earthworks Custer was assigned the task of preparing a simple rifle pit in close proximity to the enemy's artillery and sharpshooters. This he accomplished overnight with a work force of 100 men. Daylight found the rifle pit occupied by two companies of Berdan's sharpshooters who ended the annoyance of an enemy fire upon men constructing the large earthworks.[7]

Professor T.S.C. Lowe, a professional balloonist, was receiving considerable attention and ridicule because of his captive balloon reconnaissances. General Smith had employed Professor Lowe and his assistants to make ascensions to observe the enemy and report any changes in its position or numbers. An element of doubt had entered into the reports since there was no means by which they could be varified or denied. It was thought that the reports might be padded with exaggerations in order to augment their importance and thereby insure continued employment of Lowe's staff.

General Smith decided that an officer would be best qualified to make and report these observations. Apparently reasoning that a young, single officer would be the most expendable, he ordered Custer to the detail. Not exactly air-minded, Custer had expressed a preference for horse transportation — the first ascension was encountered with considerable trepidation.

His first attempt had been preceded with the news that General Fitz John Porter had made such an attempt alone. The rope, weakened by the acid used in manufacturing the inflating gas, had broken. The free flight that ensued was partially controlled by Porter's presence of mind in opening the escape valve which permitted the gas to escape and the balloon to drift downward. The descent was both rapid and dangerous. Fortunately the balloon was snared by the branches of a tree and the General escaped unhurt.

Custer took with him his field glasses, compass, notebook and pencil. Accompanied by one of the balloonists, he was elevated to a height of 1,000 feet, much to his discomfort. The enemy's camps, much like his own, were located in the woods where it was coolest during the summer. He soon discerned outlines of earthworks and gun emplacements and an occasional tent. Making sketches in his notebook[8] and making mental notes of important details, he signaled to be lowered. General Smith was pleased with his report and continued him at the detail on a daily basis.

Custer suggested that a night ascension would provide a view of the enemy campfires and provide a more accurate means of determining the enemy strength and any change in position. Discovering there were few evening fires because of the summer heat, he resolved to ascend just before daylight to observe the mess fires that were necessary for the morning breakfast. The fires were easily seen and proper conclusions were drawn from their positions and numbers. At 2 A.M. on the morning of May 4th large fires were seen near Yorktown as if houses were being burned. With the approach of daylight the fires usually observed along the enemy line were found wanting. Repeating his observation at dawn, he concluded that the enemy's works were deserted.

Following a rapid descent he reported to General Smith. Smith had just received similar information from several contrabands. The word was the enemy was retreating toward Williamsburg. Since Custer's report confirmed the contrabands' report, Smith wired General McClellan. McClellan ordered Smith to advance and obtain verification. Smith complied and found that the enemy had moved out. Stoneman's cavalry was sent in pursuit, the infantry following to support it. That afternoon Stoneman's force was defeated. Custer, who would have been with Stoneman but for his peculiar assignment, had been given permission to accompany General Winfield S. Hancock as he moved his infantry up to support Stoneman. Hancock acquitted himself honorably by routing a Confederate force that outnumbered him ten to one.

Hancock, in his report, mentions a spectacular charge of the enemy's works led by Custer,[9] which resulted in Custer's second citation that day.[10] Custer said nothing of his own exploits in his letters home though he did describe the scenes before him. On the few occasions he did describe some act of his own, the letter was intended only for the eyes of his immediate family. On this occasion his letter said little. In it he enclosed a penciled scrap of paper that told more of the story of that fierce charge than could have been told by an eyewitness. It read: "Notice — To those concerned — $50.00 bounty & one quart whiskey to the Yankees that charge this Battery. May 2nd, 1862. A Conscript Sasafrass Tea Drinking Rebel." There was a nail hole in each corner.[11] One wonders if the Tea Drinking Rebel paid off and, if so, what coffee-drinking Autie did with the whiskey.

McClellan's army moved forward slowly, cautiously for the next two weeks. On May 22nd he established his headquarters near the Chickahominy River, seven or eight miles north of Richmond. Brigadier General John G. Barnard, McClellan's chief engineer, was out reconnoitering along the Chickahominy that day. Seeing Custer sauntering around off duty, he beckoned to him to follow. Reaching a swampy portion of the stream across which were enemy pickets, he ordered Custer to "jump in." Custer immediately obeyed, then forded the stream and ascended the opposite bank, expecting any moment to be fired upon. His feet sank into several inches of muddy bottom and the water rose to his armpits but he held his revolver above his head as he crossed. On the opposite side he could see the enemy's picket fires and several pickets obviously unconscious of his presence.

Barnard tried to signal him back but he was busy exploring the enemy positions in an attempt to locate the main picket post, which he succeeded in doing. In his mind he planned a way it could be cut off. Once satisfied, he returned to the other side and reported to Barnard that the river was fordable. Barnard told him to follow him back to McClellan.

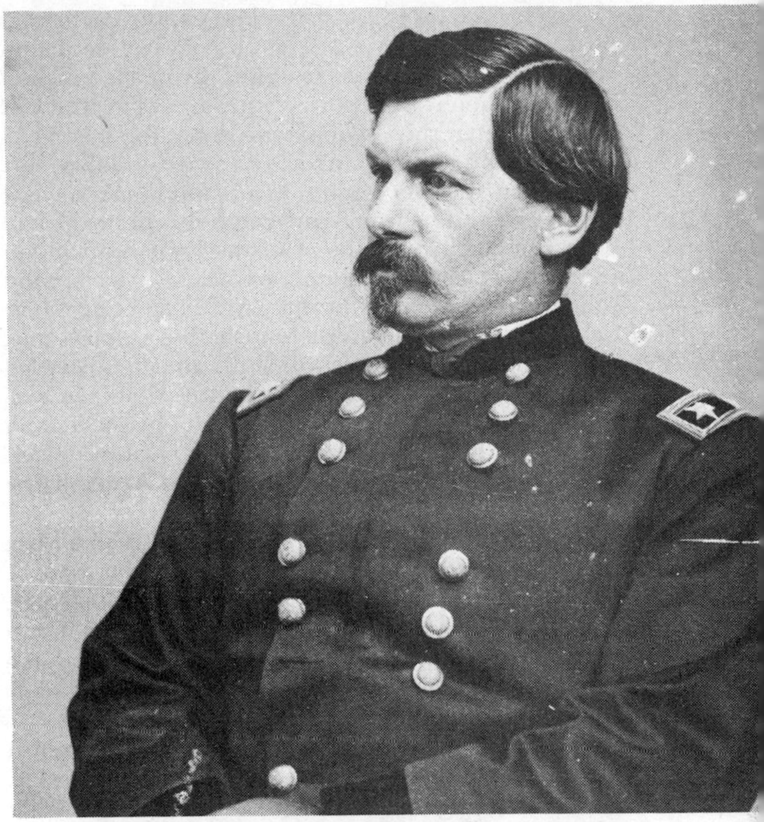

MAJ. GEN. GEORGE B. McCLELLAN gave Custer his first recognition. Custer responded by offering complete devotion. Ca. 1863. Library of Congress.

When Barnard approached McClellan, Custer dropped back out of sight. The contrast of his mud-covered, shabby uniform to that of the glittering staff attendant to General McClellan was overwhelming. In receiving the report, McClellan observed that Barnard had not made the river bottom survey; he was too immaculate and dry for that. In questioning him he learned that it was a young officer who had rendered the service. McClellan wanted to meet him so the word was passed down the ranks that "General McClellan wanted to see the officer who had been down to the river with General Barnard."

Custer stepped forward shamefaced at his careless attire but McClellan put him at ease and asked him many questions about the other side of the river. Forgetting himself, Custer told about the enemy pickets and the ease with which they might be overrun. McClellan said, "Do you know, you're just the young man I've been looking for, Mr. Custer. How would you like to come on my staff?" Would he accept? As he said later, "I felt I could have died for him."[12] Soon after, he received a notice that the President had appointed him an "additional aide-de-camp" on the staff of Major General McClellan with the rank of captian as of the 5th of June, 1862.

Custer had asked for a detail to capture the picket post on the other side of the river. McClellan consented and he was assigned two companies of cavalry and one of infantry with orders to attack at dawn. Custer then waded the river for a mile to explore it and be prepared for any eventuality.

When he met his column before daybreak, several voices asked if he was Armstrong. By chance he had been assigned Company A of the Fourth Michigan Infantry, most of whom were old friends and schoolmates from Monroe. After shaking their hands he called out, "All Monroe boys, follow me; stick to me, and I'll stick to you! Come!" Custer led and they followed. He and his 4th Michigan surprised the pickets, taking a number of prisoners and one color. The latter was taken by Custer himself and was the first to be taken by the Army of the Potomac.

Custer and Lieutenant Bowen had become close friends; sharing danger had cemented the process. The two had fought in this engagement together, almost side by side. During the Seven Days' Campaign that began on June 25th, they seemed to have been inseparable. The Campaign came to an end at Malvern Hill on July 1.

McClellan's slowly retreating army had taken a strong defensive position against General Robert E. Lee's advancing forces. The position was one readily adaptable for both his artillery and his infantry. McClellan was being forced to withdraw from the proximity of Richmond despite his superior numbers. It was Lee's hope that he could destroy the Union forces at this point.

Here at Malvern Hill, Custer and Bowen were well in the advance as usual. With their orderlies they decided to explore an area in plain view of the enemy line. Six or seven Confederate cavalrymen suddenly charged them to which they responded by flying back toward their own lines. Seeing their pursuers strung out behind them, they called to their orderlies to charge their pursuers. Acting in unison the four captured each man separately and compelled them to give up their arms since they were too close to the enemy lines to bring the men in. The two returned to camp in full sight of both sides, loaded down with revolvers, sabers, carbines and belts,[13] to the delight of the Union observers.

Lee's attack was unsuccessful. Though his forces now were superior in number his losses exceeded those of McClellan.[14] McClellan had been unsuccessful in taking Richmond. Lee had been unsuccessful in taking McClellan. This was just the beginning of a long war.

A long period of rest followed, for both sides were exhausted. Early August saw Custer in the saddle again. He had been, intermittently, several weeks before, but this time it would be continuous. By this time he had acquired a few possessions as a result of his forays, a dog he called Rose, the first of what would be a long string of dogs; a Confederate saber; a blooded horse; a double-barreled shotgun which he sent to his brother Boston, and a Negro servant boy to tend his horses and keep his boots polished. The last was a must now that he was a captain and aide.

That September, Custer wrote to his sister Ann from Sharpsburg, Maryland. He hadn't written to her for some time and apologized for not having done so. He said he had no excuse — he had been busy but not that busy. He told her that on reaching Williamsburg he had inquired about his wounded and captured classmate Gimlet Lea. He found him staying in the house of a "secesh" friend, his wound almost healed. After several pleasant hours of conversation he returned to camp after promising he would be back to spend the night with Lea.

Receiving permission from the General for the visit, he returned. Lea introduced him to two beautiful young ladies, one of them as his fiancee. The wedding was to take place the following week. Lea was anxious for Custer to be present but this was out of the question as Custer was of the opinion he would be moving on. A consultation was held and it was decided that the wedding would take place the following evening so Custer could be present. The other young lady, who proved to be the bride's cousin from Richmond, was to be the bridesmaid. Custer was to act as groomsman.

Custer returned to camp the next day to put on his full blue uniform, returning well before the appointed time. Lea was in the new grey uniform trimmed with gold lace. The two girls were dressed in white with a simple wreath of flowers upon their heads.

A strange wedding, this. Both had been warm friends at West Point. Now thrown together by an unusual twist of fate, they faced each other in the uniforms of opposing forces. Lea had never met the young lady until after the battle in which he had been wounded. She and her mother had visited the wounded to care for them and had decided to take him home where he could receive more attention. He fell in love with her and courted her, then decided to bring the romance to fruition by marrying her.

After the Episcopal service was concluded the bridesmaid sat down and cried. Lea concluded she was doing so because she wasn't being married. He said to her, "Here is the minister and here is Captain Custer, who I know would be glad to carry off such a pretty bride from the Southern Confederacy." She replied, "Captain Lea, you are just as mean as you can be." Autie said he told her he could not see how so strong a secessionist as she could consent to take the arm of a Union officer. She replied, "You ought to be in our army."[15]

Following the battle of Antietam, in which the enemy was permitted to safely escape, General McClellan was removed from command, Major General Ambrose E. Burnside replacing him. McClellan had been overcautious to the point of procrastination. But he had developed an excellent *esprit de corp* in the Army of the Potomac, having organized it to a high degree. The army was excited and the officers were furious. They idolized this man for they believed him a military genius.

McClellan was on "waiting orders," which meant that his staff was about to be dissolved. Since Custer's appointment as captain was not a commission but only for the period designated as at "the pleasure of the President," he would revert to his regular army rank of First Lieutenant. McClellan advised him to go home to Monroe and remain there until his appointment as a captain was revoked.

It was November, 1862, when he arrived in that sleepy little town on the shores of Lake Erie. It was a pleasant homecoming for he had acquired status since leaving there. He had left as a Cadet and was now a Captain, and a member of General McClellan's staff. There were some members of the older generation who were reluctant to forget his humble beginning, that his father was a blacksmith-farmer, untutored and of ordinary means. The younger generation accepted him at face value for he was a hirsute young Hussar who had proven that long hair and a mustache did not interfere with success. And there were many senior citizens who agreed that nothing succeeds like success. As Custer's biographer Whittaker stated, "Monroe was beginning to forgive Captain Custer for not being born with a silver spoon in his mouth."[16]

The next few months passed pleasurably enough. Living with the Reeds as he did meant that he would have food quite different than the army fare. He had written Ann that he did not intend to eat hard tack, salt pork or to drink coffee without milk when he got there. His doting sister saw to it that his wishes were complied with.

Reverend and Mrs. Erasmus J. Boyd gave a Thanksgiving party that fall at the Seminary. Graduates were invited as a matter of course, Libbie Bacon among them. To add luster and an additional male to a predominantly female party, the local war hero was invited. With all of Monroe's beauties to be at the party, Autie had no intention of refusing the invitation. There was no thought of meeting anyone in particular. Each knew of the other but had never been introduced. Their families were unacquainted for social life tended to follow church affiliations. The Bacons attended the Presbyterian Church, while the Reeds attended the Methodist Church across the street from the Bacon residence.

This chance meeting occurred when Conway Noble, in an effort to appease Libbie for having annoyed her with some small matter, offered to introduce her to Captain Custer. She consented merely to be left alone. Once introduced, the conversation between them was rather stiff. Politely but coolly she made some mention of his rapid promotion. His response was to say that he had been most fortunate. There was little more to say.

NOTES—CHAPTER 6

[1]Frost: "Let's Have a Fair Fight!" p. 30; Merington, p. 26, 48, gives a variation; Whittaker, pp. 89-91; Monaghan, p. 61.
[2]Whittaker, p. 93; Monaghan, p. 61.
[3]Merington, p. 26.
[4]G. A. Custer, "War Memoirs," in *The Galaxy,* Vol. XXII, No. 3 (September 1876), p. 299.
[5]Merington, pp. 27-28.
[6]G. A. Custer: "War Memoirs," in *The Galaxy,* Vol. XXII, No. 4 (October 1876), pp. 454-55.
[7]G. A. Custer: "War Memoirs," in *The Galaxy,* Vol. XXII, No. 5 (November 1876), pp. 684-685.
[8]Notebook in author's collection.
[9]Whittaker, p. 105; Merington, p. 30.
[10]Monaghan, p. 75. His first citation that day was given for capturing a rebel flag.
[11]In author's collection.
[12]Whittaker, pp. 108-114.
[13]*Ibid,* p. 121.
[14]Long, p. 235: The Federals lost, in killed, wounded and missing, 8,036 out of some 83,000 engaged; the Confederates lost 9,477 out of a total of about 86,500 engaged.
[15]Whittaker, pp. 126-128, letter to Ann Reed dated September 21, 1862.
[16]*Ibid,* p. 136.

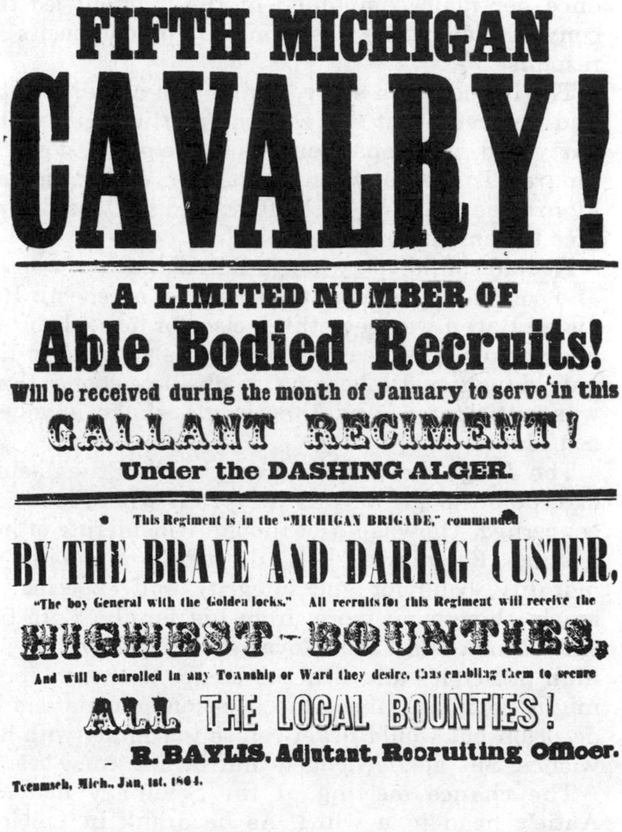

FIFTH MICHIGAN
CAVALRY!
A LIMITED NUMBER OF
Able Bodied Recruits!
Will be received during the month of January to serve in this
GALLANT REGIMENT!
Under the DASHING ALGER.
This Regiment is in the "MICHIGAN BRIGADE," commanded
BY THE BRAVE AND DARING CUSTER,
"The boy General with the Golden locks." All recruits for this Regiment will receive the
HIGHEST BOUNTIES,
And will be enrolled in any Township or Ward they desire, thus enabling them to secure
ALL THE LOCAL BOUNTIES!
R. BAYLIS, Adjutant, Recruiting Officer.
Tecumseh, Mich., Jan, 1st, 1864.

RECRUITING WITH CUSTER. Tecumseh, Michigan, just north of Monroe, used this broadside to attract embryonic cavalrymen. The Custer name was magic. Col. Brice Custer collection.

CHAPTER 7
FATHER KNOWS BEST

"Tonight is the anniversary of our first meeting," so Libbie wrote to Autie on Thanksgiving Day of 1863. "I suppose it was *willed* that we should meet . . . and what we said I am dying to know for I remember nary a word."[1] In this statement Libbie was sincere for she had been disturbed over something Conway Noble had said to her, and in the unexpected introduction to Autie she had been taken completely off guard. A mutual friend had tried to bring them together previously but on such occasions either Libbie was engaged or Autie was not in Monroe. The very suddenness of the introduction had given her no time to prepare some opening pleasantries. For once her male companion of the moment led the conversation while she fumbled for comments in response.

The introduction served to blow on a spark. Autie had observed that she was the prettiest girl at the party and, by comparison, easily the prettiest girl in Monroe. To see her was to pursue her. With kinfolk in Monroe he would be back often. And she would be so nice to come home to.

He had confidence when in the company of women and confidence when in the pursuit of an enemy. But Judge Bacon was something else, for he could be an obstacle once he learned of Autie's interest in his only daughter. He became an obstacle sooner than was anticipated, and that would shake anyone's confidence.

The Judge exercised a strong hand in the raising of Libbie though he was no tyrant where she was concerned. He was strict though considerate of her feelings. For himself he had set high standards of morality, behavior and integrity and expected as much, though no more, from his family. Both his wife Rhoda and Libbie loved and respected him for high principles and firm adherence to them. Libbie might complain about his decisions on matters of decorum but would never refuse to comply with his wishes. She acknowledged that father knew best.

The chance meeting at the Seminary had set Autie's head in a whirl. As he drank in Libbie's beauty and observed her every move he said to himself she reigned supreme in all of the youth and beauty around her. From that meeting he went home to dream, and to plan, for all good officers survey the field, then lay out a plan of attack.

The day after the party Libbie, with a coat over her arm, approached the residence of her seamstress Miss Milligan. After ringing the bell she turned to look down the street. Facing her was Autie Custer, a smile on his face. She had not been aware of his proximity but the meeting pleased her. He recognized her interest, the smile on her face making it evident. The rest was up to him.

It was not a question of love at first sight for Libbie, though what young lady in Monroe would refuse the attentions of an attractive young officer? She found him an interesting, delightful companion, and always, always available. He seemed to be at the gate each time she prepared to leave the house, and always he saw her back to it. His was a constant vigil.

When she wrote to Cousin Rebecca Richmond about her social activities she mentioned "the escort of one of General McClellan's staff whenever I put my nose out of doors . . . a Captain Custer."[2]

In discussing Autie in a letter to her good friend Laura Noble who was visiting in New York, she summed up her feelings by saying, *"I don't care for* him except as an escort."[3]

In the middle of December the Bacons received a visit from Libbie's uncle, Abel Page of Grand Rapids. Uncle Abel had taken an interest in Helen Clarke and he gave Libbie no rest until she went with him on an evening visit to her home. It seems he thought that by taking Libbie with him his visit would appear casual rather than serious. As Libbie noted in her Journal, "Uncle evidently is smitten with Helen. I don't think it will do any good."

On the biting cold morning of December 17th she got out of bed rather reluctantly, complaining, as she addressed her Journal, neither ideas nor ink flowed readily. She noted that Autie had called Thursday morning while she was sweeping but she had declined to see him. "Sunday he was there and in spite of rain and sleet went soldierlike without an umbrella, for which I admire him."

Sunday evening he met her at the door of her church and asked to escort her home to which she responded affirmatively. On the way he invited her to attend the Seminary concert with him. She tried to laugh off the invitation with, "I couldn't because the girls would plague me," but he refused to accept the excuse. Squirming a bit she said, "Well, I must go with Mother because Father wouldn't." He quickly responded, "I would be happy with Mrs. Bacon's company too." She said that wouldn't do, and when asked why, Libbie fell back on what she termed "an old woman's reason — 'Because'." He had heard that before, and wouldn't accept it. Finally, she decided to go with him. Autie's quickness of thought and speech drew the conclusion from her that "he was so bright I couldn't but like him."

The next morning, after soberly considering that her mother and father would disapprove of her going with him, she wrote Autie a note saying she could not attend the affair with him. She justified her action by recalling that "the servants even talk about your going with Captain Custer." She had heard her name linked with his and also had heard it said that he was in love with her. This could make a problem if the rumors reached her father. She wrote, "But I do like him and admire his courage and bravery. The note said 'twas no ill will I bore Captain Custer that caused me to decline, but Father had signified his desire to go and it was so wonderful I could not but accept."

That afternoon Jacob Greene, who later in the war would become Autie's assistant adjutant general, called on Libbie to invite her to go to the concert with him. Of course she declined the invitation, though he urged her. She was glad she was able to refuse for, had she gone with him, it might have offended Captain Custer.

As it turned out she went with her father. Just back of them sat Mr. Greene and Captain Custer without escorts. As she left the performance she had difficulty opening the gate. Someone stepped up and gallantly opened it for her. It was Captain Custer. She could only stammer, "Thank you sir."

On the following evening, about 9 o'clock, the Judge came home after an evening at the Humphrey House. He told Libbie he had just left Captain Custer who had informed him he was leaving for the Chickahominy at midnight. Libbie had a sinking feeling. She hadn't thought of it all ending like this. In a reminiscent mood she took out her Journal for she hadn't made an entry in nine days. Briefly covering that period she then wrote, "I felt so sorry for him. I think I had something to do with his going. I believe he liked me and felt my refusals to go with him. I wish him success and hope he'll come back a 'Gigodeer Brindle.' 'Tis best as it is for I never should encourage such attentions when I know that I cannot return them with the right spirit. Good Bye to him then! I shall miss his daily walk up and down the street for he walks and rides superbly. He was in too much haste tho' I admire his *perseverance.*"[4]

Judge Bacon had known Captain Custer for only a short time. He had asked his friend and partner Levi Humphrey to introduce him when he overheard the young officer being questioned one evening by a group that surrounded him. The Judge was impressed with the manner in which he answered their questions.

This chance meeting at the Humphrey House gave the Judge an opportunity to obtain firsthand information about military matters. He plied Autie with questions at every opportunity in an effort to satisfy his hunger for knowledge of activities in the field. The relationship was pleasant though casual for the two had nothing else in common.

The Judge was aware that Libbie knew Autie for he had seen him address her occasionally when he attended the Presbyterian Church services. For that reason he had informed Libbie of Autie's leaving for the Chickahominy. He was not aware of Autie's beginning siege for the attention of Libbie.

Father Bacon frowned on excessive fraternization with soldiers. He was extremely patriotic and had an avid interest in military affairs as they pertained to the war. But for his daughter to marry a soldier was unthinkable! She might be left a widow, or worse, with a maimed husband. Libbie had been cautioned about such things.

Libbie was not one to refuse the attentions of an eligible male, be he soldier or civilian. She knew her limitations and abided by them for her father had defined the word eligible. The legalistic training of Judge Bacon made such a definition mandatory. An obvious limitation was the set she traveled with. Generally they were the "haves," the "have nots" being unacceptable. And a higher education was a factor, too.

There was no effort to arrange marriages as in Europe but there was a suggestion of supervisory control and parental approval. By present day standards the Bacons would be considered snobs. Libbie was brought up to be a dutiful daughter and to believe that "father knows best." He hadn't said anything to indicate that he considered Captain Custer an ineligible escort mainly because he was not aware that his daughter had been encouraging the Captain's attention.

Libbie had been aware that Autie had returned to Monroe just before Thanksgiving. He had been passing her house forty times a day, according to her observation, "and is gentleman enough not to gaze into my ladies' chamber every time he passes." At the Sunday evening choir practice Mrs. Cole called her over to where she was sitting with Captain Custer. She went back to sit with Mary Cole, picking up some Christmas candies on the way which she wrapped in colored paper, then tossed them to Autie in typical schoolgirl style. He responded by sending her a note of thanks. Libbie was quite aware that her moment of fun would encourage Autie to renew his siege. And so he did.

As the days passed Libbie was beginning to feel some twinges of conscience. Autie was laying a heavy siege to her heart. He went everywhere with her, filling the role of a devoted escort. One evening early in January, during a rainy spell, he carred her across a muddy crosswalk. It was an act that left a deep impression.

They talked of many things; a long discussion covered the subject of drinking. He told her of his promise to his sister a year ago never to touch drink again. He said he knew himself well enough to be certain he never would break that promise. Libbie wrote, "I hope he never, never will."

Several times Autie had tried to tell her of his devotion to her. She managed each time to change the subject without hurting his feelings. Near the end of January he told her that he loved her. She suddenly realized that her flirtation had gone further than she had expected it to. Autie was serious, very serious. This happened one evening on their way home from choir practice. She told him she could not listen to him because it was wrong to. He wanted to know why. She could not entertain such feelings from him without reciprocating and that she could not do, was her response. He asked for some hope but she told him it would be wrong to build a hope on so uncertain a foundation as the future. She had to tell him that a gulf stood between them that could not be crossed and that gulf was love. It hurt her to say it but she had to tell him she was not in love with him.

Remorsefully, afterwards, she addressed her Journal in an attempt to purge her mind from the thoughts that tortured her. "I cannot tell anyone how badly I feel. No one can ever know but I will write some of the deep and tender feelings I cannot suppress. I am wholly free from blame. Captain C says so. But I cannot but mourn to think I have saddened a life. . . . Oh it is sweet to be loved but it is *sad* to see a man suffer, to feel that he is giving to you what he can never offer to anyone else — just love — to see him in agony and not be able to hold out any hope.

"He is noble, brave and generous and he loves, I believe, with an intensity that few know of or as few ever can love. . . . He tells me he would sacrifice every earthly hope to gain my love and I tell him if I could I would give it to him. I told him to forget me and he said he *never could* forget me and I told him I never should forget *him* and I wished to be his true friend through life but it is no use to offer myself as a friend for he will never think of me otherwise than his wife. . . . Oh, *Love, love,* how many are made miserable as well as happy by the all powerful influence."

Autie Custer was not one to give up easily. He had a Teutonic quality some called stubbornness; others might call it determination. In seeking a solution to his problem he resolved to arouse a base emotion in his lady fair. Libbie had never evidenced any sign of jealousy, quite probably because she had received the attentions of all of the eligible young men in Monroe. Autie was aware of this but he had noticed her Achilles Heel — none other than her schoolmate Fannie Fifield.

Fannie was a natural flirt and undoubtedly the most predatory of the young set. She was pretty and talented, one who took top honors with her dramatic recitations. For her to see an attractive young man was to pursue him, and all young men to her were attractive.

Autie had noticed that Fannie was not above flirting with the escorts of her girlfriends. This irritated all of the girls, Libbie among them. Autie thought it would be just the right time to show Fannie some interest for she had just returned from a visit in the East and was looking for a male companion to amuse her. The opportunity arose several days after Libbie and Autie had their heart-to-heart discussion about the state of their affairs. The place was a house party at the Netters. John Rauch was Libbie's escort. They arrived to find most of their friends there: Helen and Kate Wing, Maggie Goodman, Jacob Greene, Jennie and Fannie Fifield, the Pauldings and the Johnsons. The evening was spent playing Blind Man's Buff, and Jacob and Ruth. Fannie and Autie were observed flirting and holding hands by both Nettie and Libbie.

Libbie revealed in her Journal that this bit of flirting she observed for the several nights that followed. It read as though she was whistling in the dark, "It is the richest joke to see them flirt," then continuing, "John Bulkley told Nan that Custer knew Fan as well as any of the boys do!"

In an apparent effort to arouse some additional feeling of jealousy in Libbie, Autie flirted with Fannie upstairs, then when he came downstairs to the parlor he sat down beside Libbie. Afterwards the girls told Libbie they thought it a good joke on Fannie after the flirting upstairs to see Autie sit with Libbie and chat with her. What none of them knew was the subject he chatted about for he asked Libbie repeatedly to make him happy by thinking as he did. Nor did they learn she gave him her ring that had the letters L A engraved in it which by a strange coincidence were the initials for Libbie and Armstrong. His mother was to ask about it since he never wore a ring she had given him.

Sunday he walked her home from church. He attended church regularly, obviously to see and meet her. Connie Noble had told her he had seen him peering through his fingers at her during the prayers. When Libbie accused him of this blasphemy he told her he just happened to do so on Sunday and Con was looking at him when he did — when they looked at each other they both laughed.

Judge Bacon was beginning to hear rumors that linked Captain Custer with his daughter. Never once had Autie mentioned her name in their conversations at the Humphrey House. As the rumor grew, fear struck the heart of the Judge. Sensing a potential love affair that could end in marriage and tragedy, he took steps to terminate it. He concluded that the wisest thing he could do would be to get Libbie out of town for awhile. Recalling Annie Colten's repeated invitations asking Libbie to visit her in Toledo, he suggested to Libbie that she invite Annie to their home now that it was mid-January and the holidays were past. Libbie complied with his wishes and Annie made the 20 mile trip to Monroe.

The inevitable happened. Annie invited Libbie to return with her to her home in Toledo, and Libbie accepted. Before she left, Father Bacon had a long discussion with her about the rumors he had been hearing and the gossip that had been circulating around town. He preferred that she break up the affair. It had reached a point that disturbed him very much and it was his opinion that no good could become of it should it continue any further. Libbie listened respectfully but gave no sign of complying with or rejecting his suggestion.

Prior to leaving for Toledo she told Autie he must never meet her again, that it was her wish and her father's wish. Though he tried to talk her out of it, she insisted that he could not walk down the street with her nor could he call at the house except to say goodbye. She did permit him to accompany her and Annie Colten to the railway station the day they left. Unhappily the Judge went along. When he saw the attention Autie showered on the girls he had an attack of paternal jealousy. Several weeks later, when the matter was discussed with him, Libbie insisted that Autie assisted her no more than he assisted Annie. The Judge was unconvinced. He had gone through an emotional crisis at the station to a degree that he was barely able to speak to Libbie, all because he was fearful that Autie would go to Toledo with them. He might have gone into shock had he learned that Autie had asked her if he could go along. Wisely, Libbie told Autie he could not.

Libbie found Toledo a lively place. The Coltens were more than cordial. Lectures, concerts and teas followed, and a solicitous beau made her stay most enjoyable. A grand party at the Oliver House was planned and all insisted that Libbie send home for a party dress. Father Bacon send her bandbox of apparel by way of the conductor, Mr. Colten picking it up at the station. With it came a letter from her father expressing some doubts about her attendance at the party. It tended to dampen her spirits to the point she wrote him a letter chiding him for sending her clothes if he did not wish her to go, then needling him with, "I think Mother, who wants me to enjoy myself supremely, was instrumental in having them so kindly sent."

After telling him of the concert and lecture she had attended, she advised that she had relayed his wishes to Captain Custer. It was a situation that had made her feel badly since she liked Captain Custer very much and had found him to be a pleasant escort. She had told him never to meet her but nothing had been said about never seeing him again. She did not blame Captain Custer for he had many fine traits.

Irritably she concluded, "You have never been a girl, Father, and you cannot tell how hard a trial this was for me. . . . And Monroe people will please mind their own business, and let me alone. . . . I wish the gossipers sunk in the sea. It would give me great pleasure to know that you place entire confidence in me."[5]

The party was a gala affair, lasting until three in the morning. Libbie realized she was most attractive in her simple dress. General Hunt had asked her to lead the promenade with him and then asked her to open the ball by dancing the first set with him. Gentlemen, young and old, came from all parts of the ballroom to be presented to her, she receiving more dancing invitations and attention than she could cope with. It was very flattering to her and did much for her ego. But several days later she was back in Monroe.

Visiting Nettie, she found Autie there as she suspected he might be. She managed to get him alone and ask him if it was true he was leaving town that night with Major Fifield without seeing her. He said, yes. She told him it would be cruel and heartless to do so and if duty didn't take him, why didn't he stay? After further urging he promised he wouldn't go.

Libbie had begun to realize that Autie meant much more to her than she was willing to admit. When she had learned that he was leaving town with Major Fifield she had become frightened over the thought. She had implored him to stay, knowing that she would not be able to see him very much. She realized she was getting into the bad habit of requiring his attention and when she did not receive it she did not enjoy herself.

She had come to realize that whatever Autie did he threw his whole soul into. She knew how much he loved her for, as she said, "He acts it, speaks it from his eyes, and tells me every way *I love you.*" Knowing this she was undisturbed with his act of publicly flirting with Fannie, knowing he did it to take the onus of gossip from her.

Though he took Fannie to an oyster dinner, it was Libbie he took aside in the hallway to talk to. And it was there in front of a large wall mirror, as if imitating a picture in a frame, she thoughtlessly placed her head on his shoulder. He responded by putting his arms around her and asked to kiss her. She refused him with burning cheeks, saying she was not Fannie Fifield. He apologized and begged for a kiss, but she refused and was glad she did.

She recorded, "I am *so* ashamed tho' to think I endeavor to behave myself and not let even an edge of my affectionate loving nature show itself in the presence of the gentleman I like, but I cannot always battle against temptation successfully. I yielded and I hope it won't happen again. I wrote him an answer to his little note and said I was ashamed and did not wish the program repeated positively one night only."

Following this was a short account of a surprise party for Reverend Strong on February 26th. The young lady was beginning to have some second thoughts about her clandestine meetings with Autie. Remorsefully she wrote, "No one but God knows how badly I feel. O how can I stand such a trial as I have to bear? How can I do what duty points me to? I know that after I had once told him I could not go with him anymore it should have been so. Oh, we should not have even seen each other after those painful meetings when he told me he loved me and me alone. But I thought if I could not give him all I would give him what I could and so I continued to meet him. He has written notes and I have answered them and tho' I've not been with him but little still I've seen him when I've been out and we've passed much time at the parties together. But Monday and Tuesday I was so depressed I could not account for it. Tuesday evening I went to Nettie's. I knew he would be there for I told him the night before *I* was going. Fortunately he didn't come."

At home she found a letter from her cousin Albert Bacon. Albert had recently been a house guest of the Bacons so knew quite a bit about the Custer courtship. The letter was one of advice, outlining her duty to her family and to herself in the matter of Captain Custer. Reading it brought tears and a measure of relief. With her pent-up emotions relieved, she felt happy yet with a degree of sadness.

She saw Nettie the next morning and told her that her duty was plain. Nettie said she had come over to tell her she was doing wrong in giving Autie a little hope knowing that eventually she would have to dash every hope. Libbie excused herself by saying, "I only did it from kindness of heart. He knows what I meant. But oh! how can I do my duty? How can I battle with so great a sorrow? I grieve for him all the time. I feel so very, *very* sad."

Nettie told her of talking to him in a similar fashion just the night before and that he was much affected by her comments. She felt as if she was removing the last plank from a drowning man. This caused Libbie to say, "O how *can* I do what grieves him so? How can I?"

Thoughts of Autie continued to plague her. She had the feeling she had been tried by God and had not been found entirely wanting, so she wrote in her Journal. "I was not in love — yes I was, perhaps, but I am sure that the deep feelings which I know have not been stirred by anyone — the chords of my heart strings were not swept by him. Yes, I like him so much now — no one knows how much — but I feel that it is proof that I do not really love for how could I silence so soon feelings that are always so deep. I think often will anyone ever *touch* those feelings hidden so far as to make me doubt almost that I have them."

It was nearly a month before she saw Autie again and then it was to meet him face to face and discover he would neither look at her nor speak to her. She recalled that he had said he would do just that and, though she had begged him not to, he had. On reaching Nettie's, for she was walking toward the Humphrey House to see her, she sat down and wrote him a note imploring him not to hurt her so for it would bring down upon them again the tongues of the gossips.

Nettie delivered the note with an ambrotype of Libbie. There was no answer for a few days and then she received his reply. So upset was she that Nettie had to tell Autie the answer could not be given in writing but must be given in person. For over two hours they discussed their differences at Nettie's, both having ten thousand things to say but not covering a quarter of them. He drew their discussion to a close by stating he would do what she wanted him to and that he would abide by her judgment.

In final judgment she said they could "never go together again *never* but he must recognize me and we would meet as acquaintances."

It had not been as hard to part with him that day as it had been that Friday night four weeks before. When she first saw him tears rushed to her eyes but did not fall. And he showed his actions as deeply as any man could. She said she would send his notes back to him if he would send hers back to her. This he refused to do, nor would he ever part with her picture.

When Autie left Libbie on this occasion Nettie, who came into the room prior to his leaving, saw the old happy look on his face she had missed lately.

Later Libbie took particular pride in noting he had been talking about kissing at the time and that she had refused him for the 4,000th time. She recalled, "I long so to put my arms about his neck and kiss him and how often I lay my head on his breast — in imagination — and feel how sweet it would be to make him entirely happy. But he don't know it. Dear,

dear man, I never can tell him how deeply I have felt for him, yes and toward him. It is *hard* to crush out the affection I feel for him but if we had been together as we were for some time — every day — till now, it would have ripened into love."

After writing, "A JOURNAL IS A SAFETY VALVE," she continued, "Would it not be a blissful delight to anyone to have a man like he is willing to sacrifice everything but honor to the girl he loved as he is to me. When every word I say he prizes and remembers, and every action he looks upon as right and is sure I cannot do wrong. I fear it spoils me for all other men. . . . Certainly I don't believe I shall *ever* find some qualities that C has so admirable combined in his character in anyone else. . . . I wish I could . . . kiss him a thousand times and say everything I desire or think to him and then blot that day out of my mind forever. Wishing for *impossibilities* is unsatisfactory but wishes and desires for improbabilities are not; they are harmless and I shall indulge. So then, to be reasonable, I'll wish just for the reason last stated that I could just spend a quiet evening with him alone without fear of improprieties and control myself as I know I can do. Every time I see him I think it may be the last scene in the drama that has lasted four months."

On Wednesday evening, April 1st, Libbie went over to Nettie's to stay with her all night. Nettie was leaving for Chicago the next day. After they played backgammon and chatted awhile, Jacob Greene dropped in. He being a jolly young man, the fun began. Though full of the Old Nick he never took advantage of Libbie though he had numerous opportunities to put his arm around her and kiss her. He bought a pitcher of beer and invited all to join him. Libbie didn't like beer but drank some to see how it would affect her. All laughed at her because of her silly actions and foolish laughter. She told him not to ask her to do anything for she would be foolish enough to do it if he did.

In time they quieted down. Nettie meanwhile was packing her things in preparation for her departure, occasionally hinting to Jacob that the hour was growing late. He pretended not to understand just to tease her. Libbie had become seated in a large chair and he had perched on one arm. Gradually he slid into the chair aside of her, crowding her somewhat. Suddenly the door opened. It was Autie. He said something about it being after twelve, asking why such late hours. The frustrated Libbie hurried over to the door, took him by the hand and led him into the room. She was determined not to let him leave without an explanation, for she saw he was disturbed by what he had seen. She told him of the beer and that she was not accountable for her actions. Cheerfully he accepted her explanation. He sat down to talk to Nettie and to write while the three proceeded to tease him. Nettie, in fun, took a scissors and cut a curl from his head and gave it to Libbie. Nonchalantly Libbie asked why it was given to her.

There were more hints from Nettie that it was time the men went home. Autie said he thought it not worthwhile as he had to catch the five o'clock train to Detroit. With that Greene turned the gaslight down and called for Libbie to sit on one sofa with him; Autie and Nettie were sitting on the other. Libbie refused, then sat down in a chair next to Autie. Greene got up and turned off the gas light which caused both girls to run for the door. Autie took her hand and drew her to the sofa. As she described it, "Darkness reigned. That hand, that tenant hand! He would not let go but held it and kissed *oh so passionately.*" Greene soon opened the door to have a look at the scene, so he said. He saw nothing, but Nettie's discerning eyes saw Libbie's hand locked in Autie's hidden by Libbie's dress. With a parting squeeze he released her hand, bade Nettie goodbye, then said goodbye coolly to Libbie who answered in similar fashion.

The next morning she had time to reflect. She was pleased with the knowledge that Autie was happy. That moment in the darkness had undone time's healing work completely. She knew she was not as strong as she had thought and that she longed for what she did not have. So she penned in her Journal, "I have everything I wish and have had nearly all my life and now one thing is refused me I sometimes almost rebel. But I shall conquer. In time I'll learn not to regret or reprove."

Libbie's uncle Cyrus Wells of Brighton arrived on April 3rd to spend a few days with his sister Rhoda and to meet Albert Bacon while he was visiting the Judge.

There was a surprise for Libbie when she walked into church on Sunday, April 5th. There was Autie seated so he could look at her as she moved down the aisle to her pew. She was glad to see him in church for he had not been there except once in more than a month. As they were leaving at the conclusion of the service, he managed to time his exit so he could walk at her side. It was then he told her he thought he had better stay away from church since he could not prevent his eyes from wandering when they ought not to be. Reaching the door they parted without another word.

That evening she attended prayer service with Albert. After being seated she saw Fannie come in with Autie. He sat down, brushed back his hair, looked around and on seeing Libbie looked directly at her for an instant. The glance was so brief no one could have noticed it but the two. Though Libbie kept him under constant surveillance he did not repeat that glance during the rest of the service. The recollection in her Journal stated, "It is strange how little jealousy I have. I certainly have none at all. I only wish myself where she is often and wish rather I had the privilege she has. But I think my reputation is of more account and so I am content tho' the chain frets me often."

On April 6th she wrote, "In two days I shall be twenty-one! I am first going to try and write for a month steadily in my journal. I find that what I can relieve myself of saying with my pen to these trusted pages I have no fear that I shall say to others and regret it in ashes."

On the following evening while visiting Fannie, who drops in to visit but Autie. Fannie promptly showered him with attention. He, in turn, was very quiet. Libbie managed to talk to him about Nettie. At one point she told him to write to Nettie, so he took down her address. In discussing the evening at Nettie's in which beer had been served, Autie made several implications Libbie took exception to. She responded to them rather spiritedly, then both quieted down.

Seeing the other side of his nature made her realize she had seen him only as a lover. She decided he was quite set in his ways and that he fibbed occasionally. She persisted in the belief that he had some splendid traits she had never seen so finely developed in any other man. And she just couldn't believe he was a man of transient love.

The next day was spent in analyzing suiters, past and present. There was France Chandler, Belle's brother, whom she had been thrown with at the last commencement. She had liked him last summer better than any young man she had ever met. They had corresponded ever since. He arrived in White Pigeon a week ago and had concluded on coming to Monroe to see Libbie. She was surprised to see him but after an hour with him realized she didn't care for him as she once did.

France, in her opinion, indulged in the hope that he might sometime marry her. And so had others — Elliot Bates, Mr. Dutton, Captain Custer, John Rauch and George S. She didn't love any of them or any man on earth, or so she thought.

She sort of believed she liked Frank Earle because he was gay and had the indescribable air of a wellbred city gentleman. He had lost his wife which made Libbie think he would find consolation in taking another.

Autie left Monroe on the evening of her birthday. She didn't see him go but began to miss him immediately. While she was at Mary Noble's party Jacob Greene, came over to tell her Autie had left. Once home from the party she concluded that she didn't enjoy parties and gatherings or have nearly as much fun now that Autie was gone, yet she knew it was best that he had gone. She was doing her duty and had been removed from temptation.

On April 18th she wrote, "I heard yesterday he was assisting General McClellan make out his report in New York. I wonder if I shall ever see him again and how and under what circumstances. Time will heal and *does* for I don't think about it near as much as I did. The affair seems so like a dream. I hope he will get over it too but if he has as easily as I do I should certainly think he had not felt as deeply as he said he did.

"Whatever happens I won't allow myself to think lightly of what had happened between us. I am very sorry for it all. I wonder if he has written to Nett. I wonder if he told Fan he loved her. Fan, when she told me about her proposals the other night, tried to lead me into the belief that he thought so much of her, and I am sure she would have been glad enough to have been able to say he proposed, for the sake of a triumph, but she couldn't consistently. The idea that C — knowing the low-minded girl as he does, should wish to *marry* her. He, like others, takes all she gives which I sometimes think is *everything,* but when a man has all he desires in one he rarely desires the girl for his wife. And he has as exalted ideas about what a woman should be as anyone.

"I *know* the reason he loved me because I wouldn't let him kiss me and treat me as if we were engaged. Yes indeed, for on that memorable Friday night he said, 'Libbie, you are so different from other girls. I know girls better than you. A man knows a lady better than her lady friends do.'

"He said he had been introduced to a lady one afternoon and had met her in the evening and went home with her and she asked him to set on the step which he did when she sat on his lap and he kissed her as he liked. Then from his remarks I know he knows Fan. He told me I hadn't read her wrong. She little knows he made her a convenient tool to carry out his plans.

"Fan is now crazy over the vilest looking man, a perfect rake. He stared me right in my face yesterday. He owns a leopard dog and I hear he is a dog breeder. Now Fan has caught his eye and he asks 'who that handsome gay girl is.' He is a healthy looking fellow — and maleish. But of course, dresses elegantly as all that style of men do."

One afternoon a week later someone called to see Mrs. Bacon who was in bed ill at the time. Libbie entered the parlor and found it was Major Earle. She was quite agreeably surprised and quite happy when she learned he had called primarily to see her. She noted the elegant manner in which he used his handkerchief, his genteel way of walking and talking, his exquisite hair. She pronounced him right handsome but for a horrid nose one forgot when he talked. He told her he planned to leave the army soon to enter the salt business at Saginaw. At the moment he was on Merrell's staff.

Libbie treated him quite openly in the fashion she had first treated Autie. She felt that she liked him much as she might like a girl. She believed that Frank Earle was more devoted than France. She liked a man who was so pleased with what she had to say as to listen and treasure her words. France, she thought, was either too conceited to wish to listen or wasn't interested in her remarks. She knew he liked her a lot though she disliked the way he broke in on a sentence when she was saying something. She noted, "C has quite spoiled me. Everything I said or did was remembered and treasured by him. He was more devoted than I ought to expect in any other man."

In Bible class that day Fan had told her Autie had left New York and was now in Washington. General McClellan wouldn't allow him to take his captain's commission until he had a colonelcy. Fan said he had left a "good bye" for her and since then had sent his love to her. The two had been writing to each other.

Artfully, Libbie asked her when they were to be married. Fannie responded in the negative but in a manner that was intended to leave the impression they were engaged. Libbie wasn't taken in by the pose. She reasoned that Autie had too exalted an idea of what his wife should be to marry Fannie. She said to her, "Captain Custer loves me too much to go away and never say good bye to me!"

Fannie answered, "Yes, he does like you but I guess he thinks you don't like him much."

This last statement remained in Libbie's mind until she opened her Journal that evening. In thinking of the various young men she had liked or thought she had loved she decided that she didn't care for any of them and didn't know of a man she would marry for any consideration. She was determined that she would not be married until she was past 24.

Quite naturally her thoughts returned to Autie. He had begged her to kiss him or let him kiss her. She could now write, "Thank Heaven I refused. I told him he was not my lover. I could not give him a lover's privilege. I am glad because if I had yielded once alas, how many times would he have taken what I know he would prize beyond every other girl's caress. He left with a respect for me he wouldn't have had if I had yielded."

Then after a further analysis of her several current love affairs she wrote, "Yes, now comes the tug of war. Whether I am to be Mrs. Frank Earle or Mrs. France Chandler or Mrs. Elliot Bates. I shall see the two last, perhaps the three, in the next month and I must not be too susceptible but remember that it is a question for life and not a week or a month."

Such flights of matrimonial supposition led her into thinking of Autie again. "Dear C. I love him so in one way. But I am getting over my *violent* fancy and feel that I have been fascinated. Dear, *dear* soldier boy, he didn't forget me as Nan's letter shows how dear he is. How much I think of him still. It is best that he is away, that we are separated by miles and miles of distance and unsurmountable obstacles. God knows best."

NOTES—CHAPTER 7

[1]Merington, p. 46.
[2]*Ibid*, p. 48.
[3]*Ibid*, p. 49.
[4]E.B.C. Journal, December 17, 1862.
[5]Merington, p. 50.

Details and statements in this chapter, quoted without the use of reference numbers, are taken from Libbie Bacon's Journal. It was Libbie's practice to record her thoughts in the privacy of her bedroom just prior to retiring.

CHAPTER 8
RIDE A SADDLE TO A STAR

It had been a laborious though illuminating experience for Custer. He had been ordered to General McClellan's Trenton, New Jersey home to assist him in completing the official account of his campaign. From his mentor he learned something of the art of describing a skirmish or battle. Reports always read better if you augmented your role in an engagement and diminished that of the adversary. In any case it was a matter of "gilding the lily" should the occasion demand it. Custer never received the complete course for, in one week,[1] he was ordered to join his company in Washington.[2]

Returning to Washington meant a demotion. With his appointment as an aide now terminated, he would revert to his regular army rank of First Lieutenant. In no way did this diminish his respect for McClellan since his tenure as an aide had developed a feeling for him bordering on idolatry.

Judge Bacon had been a strong supporter of McClellan. In May he wrote Custer that he thought the removal of McClellan from his command of the Army of the Potomac was a mistake. In this Custer concurred. The Judge had frowned on any correspondence between Libbie and Custer, yet he did not consider it improper or a breach of principle if he maintained one with him. How else could be obtain observations of a military nature from one so close to the scene of action?[3]

Major General Joseph Hooker was in command of the Army of the Potomac when Custer reached Washington. A boresome desk assignment was soon interrupted by an order to join Brigadier General Alfred Pleasonton at Falmouth, Virginia. Pleasonton headed a division of the newly reorganized cavalry corps under the command of Major General George Stoneman. The other two divisions were headed by Brigadier General David McMurtrie Gregg and Brigadier General William W. Averell.

Pleasonton was all but pleasant. He was a sarcastic martinet, so exacting and difficult to please his men had little love for him. The redeeming feature in his personality was his backing of any good officer to the limit. We shall see where he backed three of his officers by recommending them for high promotion. By doing so he was gambling his own future.[4]

Almost on arrival, Custer was asked to join Pleasonton's staff, a position he wrote home about in the middle of May as being quite comfortable.[5] A lover of animals of all kinds, he had adopted a two-months-old hound pup. The handsomest of his two horses he named *Harry* after his young nephew Harry Armstrong Reed. And he had adopted a black waif named Johnny. Johnny rode his extra horse on the march and in general acted as a servant for him.

Pleasonton demanded a constant supply of information as to the conditions on his front. An extremely active officer, he expected the same response from his subordinates. He wanted no excuses; he expected results.

Custer, the indefatigable, was the one who supplied him with most of the information of enemy movements and positions in the area. He took it upon himself to do much of the dangerous reconnoitering which ofttimes carried him across the enemy lines.[6]

He messed with his general and the other staff officers, enjoying a variety of fruits and vegetables not available to others. Pleasonton had a Negro woman doing his cooking, her husband waiting on the table and making himself generally useful. This Custer related to his sister Ann to allay all her fears of his being underfed. He assured her that in spite of their moving around he didn't go hungry. And there was band music to entertain them in camp each night.[7]

Near the end of May he wrote to his friend Nettie Humphrey who, by agreement, read to Libbie the letter from him. Nett was acting as a go-between and self-appointed matchmaker for the pair, a responsibility she had accepted readily enough when urged to do so both by Libbie and Autie. Judge Bacon had ruled against any correspondence between the two. They abided by his wishes but had felt free of any conflict with this request by having Autie write to Nettie and she, in turn, replying but only after she had read Autie's letter to Libbie and obtaining her reactions so she could incorporate them in her reply.

He wrote to Nettie on May 26th as to his part in the triple entente, describing an expedition of 75 cavalrymen he had led into Dixie, in which he returned with 12 prisoners, 30 horses, two large boxes of boots and shoes and two barrels of whiskey which he had destroyed. As a result of the success of this expedition General Hooker sent for and complimented him.[8]

May 25th had been spent visiting a number of friends, some of whom were in the Fourth Michigan Infantry. One of them, Lieutenant George W. Yates, he introduced to General Pleasonton with the suggestion he be added to the staff. Pleasonton acquiesed.[9]

It had been 18 months since Autie had joined Kearny's staff. The experience he had gained since then had tempered him for war. His boundless energy and enthusiasm applied to all tasks, no matter how minor, had made him stand out conspicuously on Pleasonton's staff.

Pleasonton was rapidly welding his forces into a unit to be reckoned with. No longer were they used only as guards and message carriers. It was cavalry against cavalry and, at this time, Pleasonton against Jeb Stuart.

On June 9th the Confederate Cavalry forces were discovered at Beverly Ford where they were concentrating preparatory to a move around the Union right flank in an effort toward Maryland and Pennsylvania. In the cavalry fight that day, Custer took over the command on the field of battle when his superior, Colonel Benjamin F. Davis, was shot down.

Near noon Pleasonton arrived to learn that his underrated cavalry had nearly defeated Jeb Stuart's cavalry. This would give his corps the necessary shot in the arm, by the knowledge that Stuart was not invincible. But this inspiring information was not all for he soon learned that Lee was moving north. Hooker had to be advised at once.

Autie was sent to General Hooker's headquarters with a captured flag and a list of the prisoners captured. He and his friend George Yates were cited for gallantry. Marcus Reno, a captain at the time, was wounded in the engagement.

Several weeks earlier, Autie had learned that the Seventh Michigan Cavalry was seeking a colonel. In making an application to Governor Austin Blair for the appointment he had been endorsed by Generals Pleasonton, Burnside, Copeland, Humphrey, Stahl and Stoneman, all of whom strongly recommended him. Judge Isaac P. Christancy, the United States Senator from Michigan, had also supported him in his quest for the colonelcy.

Governor Blair denied the request on the basis that such commissions were given only to those who had assisted in obtaining the enlistments that filled the ranks of that regiment. The rejection, so Custer believed, was actually based on his being a McClellan supporter. As future events proved, it was a blessing in disguise. He continued to serve in a role that permitted him to display his qualifications for higher command before a man who recognized his true worth.

Cavalry skirmishes followed in quick succession. Beginning at Aldie on June 17th and followed by Middleburg on the 19th and Upperville on the 21st, Custer was seen in the middle of each action. It was at Aldie that he gained particular recognition for the part he played in leading a cavalry charge against Stuart's men. In the melee the audacious young lieutenant found himself surrounded by rebels and cut off from his own men. Owing to a broad brimmed rebel hat he wore he was at first mistaken for one of them. Hastily he cut down a man in his way, then put spurs to his horse and escaped. The rebel hat had saved him.

Alfred Pleasonton had been placed in command of the Cavalry Corps, Army of the Potomac, on June 3, 1863. On June 22nd he was made a Major General of Volunteers.[10] This was exciting news for Custer. He would now be made a captain.

Pleasonton had organized his Cavalry Corps into three divisions. The First Division was placed under Brigadier General John Buford, the Second under Brigadier General David M. Gregg and the Third under Brigadier General Judson Kilpatrick.

Pleasonton wasn't one to permit any coffee cooling. He was a man of action and expected as much from every man in his command. With Lee's invasion well under way he had a job to do and he needed active officers who could lead the men in battle. Strategists he had in abundance, including the Washington politicians who constantly meddled in the game of war. Overly supplied with older officers who seemed to go out of their way to avoid exposure to enemy fire, he had under his surveillance some of his young officers who had shown audacity and coolness under fire.

Lincoln was deeply concerned with the advancing Confederate Army. Pressure on him had reached a new high. Hooker had advised him that Harper's Ferry should be evacuated. If it was not, he wished to be removed from command of the Army of the Potomac. Lincoln obliged by removing him and placing Major General George Meade in command on June 27th.[11]

Several evenings later, after having posted a large number of pickets, Custer entered the headquarters tent only to be greeted by various staff members with, "Hello, general." "You're looking well, general." "How are you, general?" The banter continued until he responded with, "You may laugh, boys. . . . I will be a general yet, for all your chaff."[12]

George Yates, thinking it had gone far enough, said to him, "Look on the table, old fellow. They're not chaffing."[13]

There lay a large official envelope addressed "Brigadier General George A. Custer, U.S. Vols." Custer was overcome. In an instant his old friends surrounded him, shaking his hand and congratulating him. This time there was sincerity in their actions. It was only after a time that he could regain his composure and read the orders that directed him to report to General Pleasonton for instructions.

Pleasonton had rewarded the three he deemed most worthy and whom he thought would most capably fill the urgent need in the Cavalry Corps. He had sent in the names of Wesley Merritt, Custer and Elon J. Farnsworth.[14] Pleasonton had endangered his own future by appointing these intrepid youngsters. Time would prove his judgment sound.

By advancing over the heads of overcautious officers with greater seniority, they became the objects of much jealousy. Envy, and even hatred, would result in some instances.

Custer met with Pleasonton, receiving his instructions and the news that he was to command the Michigan Cavalry Brigade composed of the 1st, 5th, 6th and 7th Michigan Cavalry Regiments together with Battery M, 2d U.S. Artillery. He proceeded to join his brigade that same evening and select his staff. He now commanded the 2d Brigade in Kilpatrick's 3d Division. All of his staff members were selected from the brigade, and many of them were old Monroe acquaintances.

As the youngest general in the Federal Army — he was but 23 years of age—he thought it prudent to assume a cold and somewhat distant air with his colonels. Because they were older he was fearful they might give way to clapping him on the back and giving him advice. That they envied him he could see. He was confident that one battle would change all that. And that opportunity would come soon enough.

One of the first things he did to add to their dislike was to tighten up the discipline. Unlike the regular cavalry the volunteer cavalry had been governed rather loosely. His first order required a commissioned officer to supervise the grooming of the horses. This meant getting up a bit earlier.

Regulations were to be adhered to and Custer was quick to find fault with any deviation from them. He wanted the baggage load lessened on his horses; he insisted on it for there was rough work ahead. He expected his men to salute as regulations required. The officers fumed and the men cursed. There were no explanations and none were asked for.

Custer sought out his bugler Joseph Fought, who had acted as his orderly while he was on Pleasonton's staff. He told him he wanted something to show his new rank. Fought searched until late that night, finally finding two stars he sewed on the corners of Custer's collar. In telling of this incident Fought noted the jealousy of the other officers and that "not one of them but would have thrown a stone in his way to make him lose prestige."[15]

Custer had talent for attracting attention. Up to this time there was no need to attract it. It had come to him naturally enough through his unremitting enterprise and audacity as a cavalryman. He had observed older officers remaining back of the lines as they sent their men into a battle and had beheld the many lost opportunities to win an engagement because of the delay in receiving information and the time lost in sending orders back to the front line. It was quite apparent that observations and decisions should be made at the front line by the commanding officer, and that timing of the charge was all-important. This increased the risk for the commanding officer; one could get killed up in front. But it also meant more battles would be won. And a general at the head of his troops, sharing their dangers, was an inspiration to them. Who wouldn't fight for an officer who said, "Come on, boys!" instead of "Go in, boys!"

Custer had led in enough engagements to know the value of being in front. His intuitive sense of timing and tactics had won the appreciation and support of Pleasonton, who was revamping the cavalry from a scattered force of messengers to a mobile, compact corps of fighting men capable of stopping Stuart.

Custer had seen what leadership could do in the heat of a battle. He had worn an old hat which, when he was carried into the ranks of the enemy, had identified him as a rebel. Having the privilege of wearing a uniform of his own design, he planned one that would identify him as the commanding officer in any part of the field. Like a personal guidon it would show his men where he was at all times while sharing their danger. This would, of course, draw the enemy fire. Knowing that a moving object was harder to hit than a still one, he kept constantly on the move in front of his troops, using a fastgaited horse in doing so. At the same time he was able to observe the positions and movements of his adversary, choosing, and instantly ordering, the moment he wished to strike.

Joe Fought did better than scrounge two general's stars. He managed to obtain the materials necessary to complete a general's uniform. It was the next day at Hanover that the brigade saw Custer for the first time. Major James H. Kidd of the 6th Michigan Cavalry heard a voice new to him giving orders in a clear, calm, resonant voice. Looking back a few feet he saw a figure that both amazed and amused him. He described him as:

"An officer superbly mounted who sat his charger as if to the manor born. Tall, lithe, active, muscular, straight as an Indian and as quick in his movements, he had the fair complexion of a school girl. He was clad in a suit of black velvet, elaborately trimmed with gold lace, which ran down the outer seams of his trousers, and almost covered the sleeves of his cavalry jacket. The wide collar of a blue navy shirt was turned down over the collar of his velvet jacket, and a necktie of brilliant crimson was tied in a graceful knot at the throat, the long ends falling carelessly in front. The double row of buttons on his breast were arranged in groups of twos, indicating the rank of brigadier general. A soft, black hat with wide brim adorned with a gilt cord, and rosette encircling a silver star, was worn turned down on one side giving him a rakish air. His golden hair fell in graceful luxuriance nearly or quite to his shoulders, and his upper lip was garnished with a blonde mustache. A sword and belt, gilt spurs and top boots completed his unique outfit."[16]

When Custer joined his brigade Kilpatrick's command was badly scattered. They had spent the early morning hours of June 30th searching the countryside for news of Stuart. Major General George G. Meade had taken over the command of the Army of the Potomac on June 28th[17] and had moved it north to meet Lee's invasion of Pennsylvania. A climax between the forces of Meade and Lee was near.

Stuart's force was reported near Hanover about noon. Kilpatrick, being nearer, reached Hanover first. The result was a clash between the two forces in which Stuart was forced to move north on a line further to the east, and further than ever from General Lee. Stuart led his column to Carlisle while General Lee was moving toward Gettysburg.

It was only after Stuart had reached Carlisle that he received the first reliable information as to the location of Lee's forces. Immediately he began the 30 mile trek toward Gettysburg, arriving there in the afternoon of July 2d. The battle of Gettysburg had gone into its second day and the outcome was still in doubt.

Lee greeted him sharply, "General Stuart, where have you been? I have not heard from you in days and you the eyes and ears of my army."

"I have brought you 125 wagons and their teams, General," he replied.[18] These had been captured from the Federals just north of Washington with some 400 prisoners. The prisoners had been paroled, the loaded wagon train he had retained. All this and the detour resulting from his skirmish with Kilpatrick's column at Hanover had delayed his juncture with Lee. The diversions had prevented him from reconnoitering for Lee. Lee had been groping in the dark without him.

Early on the morning of July 3d, Custer received an order from his commanding officer Kilpatrick to move his brigade out of Two Taverns toward Gettysburg. Farnsworth's First Birgade was in the lead. As Custer moved out he received a countermanding order from General Gregg to move his command northerly into a position on the pike between Hanover and Gettysburg.

Union scouts on Cemetery Ridge had seen Stuart moving out on the York Pike and had informed Gregg. Gregg, excellent general that he was, realized that he had no chance in leading his two small brigades against Stuart's four brigades and three batteries. With a premonition of a serious disaster he acted by intercepting Kilpatrick's largest brigade — Custer's Michigan — and turning it off to the right. It was a bold and decisive move.

Custer arrived at the designated point and positioned his command so that it faced Gettysburg. All was quiet until 10 A.M. when Stuart appeared on his right flank and opened fire with a battery of six guns.

Stuart had moved east from Gettysburg on the York Pike for two and a half miles. Seeing no enemy he turned to the southeast where he positioned his command in the Rummel woods. From this ridge he had a commanding view of the rolling farmland around him, and of Cemetery Ridge to the west. It was then he had ordered a battery to open up before he left this strong postion, presumably to determine if any Federal Cavalry were in the vicinity. Had he discovered there were none, or had there been the pitifully small command of Gregg's without the aid of Custer, Stuart undoubtedly would have attacked the rear of Meade's forces on Cemetery Ridge at the moment Pickett was occupying Meade's attention on his front. Had this occurred, the Union defense position might have been overrun by Stuart's cavalry. In that case, as some think, the North might now be talking with a Southern accent.

Custer's battery of 3-inch rifles opened fire on Stuart's and soon silenced them. Following a period of brief calm the thunderous sound of the cannonading that preceded Pickett's charge rolled upon them. It was then that Custer directed Colonel Russell A. Alger to advance and engage the enemy now in the vicinity of the Rummel barn. The 5th Michigan moved toward the Rummel woods, its flanks protected on the right by McIntosh's brigade and on the left by part of the 6th Michigan. As they moved from fence to fence the Confederate cavalry moved forward to engage them. The gray line, though superior in numbers, was unable to withstand the superior firepower of the 5th Michigan's eight-shotted Spencer carbines, and had to fall back.

Within several hundred yards of the Rummel woods the 5th Michigan found itself out of ammunition. When Stuart's men discovered this they sprang forward with renewed zeal. The blue line fell back stubbornly, the Confederates pursuing it toward Randol's battery. When near it, the 7th Michigan advanced toward the Confederate line with drawn sabers. Gregg, who was now on the field, ordered a charge. As they cleared the battery, Custer drew his saber and took a place at their front, shouting, "Come on you Wolverines!" As they charged, the dismounted Confederate line broke and fled, the 7th Michigan after them.

Following several charges and countercharges was one grand charge Gregg had ordered. It was a frontal attack personally led by Custer against a foe that outnumbered his men three to one. As Custer struck them head on, the 3d Pennsylvania hit their left flank and the 1st New Jersey and 5th Michigan struck their right flank. The Confederates were driven from the field. There was no attempt on either side to continue the engagement. That night Stuart withdrew to the York Pike and camped. On the following morning he rejoined Lee and his retreating army.[19]

Though the loss on both sides was about equal, Custer's Brigade lost 219 men as compared to the 35 lost in Gregg's Division.[20] Later Custer wrote in his official report, "I challenge the annals of warfare to produce a more brilliant or successful charge of cavalry than the one just recounted."[21] Typical of him he made no mention of himself but was lavish in his praise of others in the engagement.

The day before, Custer had led one of his companies in a skirmish, just to win the respect of his men. On this day he had led two charges, the last against heavy, almost hopeless, odds. His unique uniform identified him. His position at the head, leading the charge and sharing their danger, inspired them. After that there was no question of loyalty or *esprit de corps*. Where he led, they followed.

Lee's bold plunge into Pennsylvania had been thwarted at Gettysburg, his failure being blamed on many things. He had assumed the initiative from the beginning and had maintained it to the very end. There was no waiting when he thought he could gain an advantage, but to gain it he had to have knowledge of Hooker's movements. Without Stuart he did not know where Hooker or Meade were. Lee didn't miss the cavalry; he missed Stuart.

July 4th was a day of intense gloom for the Confederate Army. Adding to the universal discomfiture was a torrential downpour that bogged down and retarded its full retreat.

It was Kilpatrick's assignment to harrass its slogging column and destroy its wagon train. Most of this task fell on Custer. Indefatigable, he pressed the retreating foe, captured large numbers of prisoners and a wagon train.

There were times when Confederate sharpshooters or a battery were encountered whose task it was to cover the retreat of Lee's army. Units of the Michigan Brigade made short work of these, their adversaries having little desire to fight under the circumstances that prevailed.

The days that followed were employed in pursuit and harassment. Custer tempered his audacity with discretion. Mounted charges were used against equal or inferior forces; dismounted skirmishers were used in defensive actions against superior numbers.

On July 14th, at Falling Waters, through a mistake in orders, Custer was directed to advance on earthworks held by four Confederate brigades. These were the remnants of Lee's retreating army, the rest having crossed the Potomac into Virginia.

Obeying the command to take them, Custer's brigade captured 1,500 prisoners,[22] losing 33 killed and 56 wounded in the action. Three battleflags were captured along with several Napoleon guns. Up to this point in the Gettysburg campaign, Custer had seven horses shot under him.[23]

According to Whittaker[24] the battle of Falling Waters illustrated the power of discretion in Custer in contrast to the "headlong rashness of Kilpatrick." He indicates that "Custer came up alone, saw his enemy wavering, and with the use of only four companies *put in at the right moment,* captured a whole Confederate brigade. Then he stopped — he knew when audacity had been pushed far enough. A moment later up comes Kilpatrick. Not satisfied with a single brigade, he must needs attempt to take *four,* with an inadequate force, and ordered the charge of the Sixth Michigan *continued.* . . . The surrendered brigade, thinking no quarter was to be shown, resumed the struggle, and the victory gained by Custer's tact, was nearly lost by Kilpatrick's foolhardy assault."

Kilpatrick had ordered Captain Peter A. Weber — who had rendered outstanding service at Gettysburg on July 3d—to mount his 6th Michigan and charge the Confederate works. With less than a hundred men, and outnumbered ten to one, he obeyed, losing his life and most of his command in doing so. When given the order by Kilpatrick, he was in the act of obeying Custer's order to advance a line of dismounted skirmishers toward the hill to determine what would be encountered on their front.[25]

So ended the Gettysburg Campaign. At this point Kilpatrick left on sick leave, Pleasonton giving Custer command of the division in Kilpatrick's absence.

In August, Kilpatrick, concluding his report to Pleasonton, wrote, "To General Custer and his brigade, Lieutenant Pennington and his battery, and one squadron of the Eighth New York Cavalry, of General Buford's command, all praise is due."[26]

Pleasonton was unhappy with Meade. Meade seemed content to rest on the laurels gained at Gettysburg. Earlier — on July 6th — Custer had met enemy pickets below Williamsport he was able to push back with ease. Convinced they were only an advance guard sent by Lee to secure the river crossing, he resolved to hold the crossing and prevent Lee's escape into Virginia. His brigade was too small to hold off the entire Confederate force. With Kilpatrick's and Buford's divisions the enemy could be delayed until Meade's infantry arrived, so Custer reasoned as he began the fight. Soon after,

Kilpatrick ordered him to withdraw. It was Pleasonton who revealed later that Meade was afraid to fight Lee, for it was Meade who had given the order to Kilpatrick to withdraw.[27] Another Union general fearful of Lee's shadow.

On July 23d, Custer and his 1,200 men neared Culpeper Court House. From information he had obtained he learned that Confederate General A. P. Hill was approaching it. He concluded that if he could get between Hill and General James Longstreet, Meade could move forward and defeat them separately. It was only a matter of divide and conquer.

Finding Culpeper unoccupied, he pushed forward toward Orange Court House. Hill, in a surprise move, cut off Pennington's battery and the 5th and 6th Michigan. In an act of desperation they broke through and rejoined their brigade. Custer, realizing his position was precarious, requested reinforcements from Meade through Pleasonton. The request was denied, the procrastinator Meade refusing for a second time to fight Lee. Pleasonton was more than annoyed, he was disgusted. Irately he reported his feelings to his superiors in Washington.

On August 4th, Kilpatrick resumed his command. He, in turn, was curbed. Meade wanted no confrontation with the enemy at this time. He had an insufficient number of troops, so he said. With the expiration of enlistments, many men would be going home. It would take time to fill their places with draftees. Meade, like McClellan before him, would make no move until he had a numerical superiority.

There was little for the cavalry to do during August. Ranks thinned by the vigorous action in the Gettysburg Campaign were filled with new recruits and veterans who had recovered from their wounds. Horses were rested and equipment repaired or replaced. There was to be more action ahead once the cavalry corps was made ready. Pleasonton would see to that.

Meanwhile Custer used the lull to catch up on his correspondence. On August 13th he wrote "Friend Nettie" from his headquarters at Hartwood Church, Virginia, that they were living in magnificent style. From the rebel farmwomen they were obtaining ample supplies of butter, eggs, milk and vegetables in exchange for coffee, sugar and salt.[28]

Knowing it would be of particular interest to Nettie, he indicated that her sweetheart, Captain Jacob Greene,[29] was developing into an Adjutant General beyond his expectations. "I tried him the other day, took him where bullets flew thick and fast. I watched him closely. He never faltered, was as calm and collected as if sitting at dinner."

Autie was satisfied with the capabilities and efficiency of his staff officers. All, in his opinion, were refined, sociable gentlemen.

What seemed to concern him was the opinion Judge Bacon might have of his promotion. Had he indicated whether he thought it deserved or not? Had he said anything at all? Though he didn't he might as well have asked Nettie if the Judge thought better of generals than he did of captains where his daughter was concerned.

Nettie soon answered. Her letter of August 24th[30] declared that Libbie was away with her mother, while Judge Bacon was boarding at the Humphrey House each night until they returned. "He has never said anything *to me* about your promotion, in fact your name is seldom if ever mentioned between us. In some respects he is a very prejudicious man I think, and does not interfere with the friendships of his neighbor's children, however much he may attempt to control his own in that respect. He is truly a good man and a fond, devoted Father who would feel ingratitude or deceit on the part of his child, most keenly. An act of disobedience from Libbie, in a matter of importance would almost kill him I think. This is one reason why I so often say 'it is not best.' He is a man of strong prejudices — you and I think some of them unfounded — but — what necessity for me to go over the reasoning I have used so often before! If the time ever comes when I find myself able to assist in removing any of those prejudices, you know I will enter the work most heartily."

Nettie's letter was not mailed until August 27th, there being additional news she thought Autie would be interested in. Judge Bacon had received a letter from Albert Bacon saying that Libbie and her mother had arrived safely at Traverse City. This, Autie would want to know. She had some other thoughts for him.

"Do you think I avoid mentioning her (Libbie) in my letters of late? Well, maybe I have done so, because sometimes I think it is not quite right to talk constantly upon themes which suggest forbidden hopes, though my principal motive in commencing this correspondence was that I might be able to afford you the gratification of occasionally hearing of her welfare, at the same time I gratified myself in not losing sight of a friend whom I esteemed, amid the fortunes of war.

"Perhaps too, I thought it might not be displeasing to another person to hear now and then, of one whom 'destiny' had so strangely brought into the story of her life. I am not sure however, that the whole thing is not wrong. Why should we sip from the cup we are not permitted to drink? And yet I am convinced that so far, it has done us no harm.

"In this way she is not likely to be banished from your mind as she might be, in a measure, did you never have your remembrances of her reminded by these letters, and it may increase the pang should the time ever come when you *must* give her up utterly and forever. You have taken this responsibility upon yourself so I have no right to worry about it. . . . As long as you hear from me you shall hear from her if possible. Love to Capt. Greene."

Custer's response was immediate. He saw that Nettie was concerned about him so he thought he should put her anxiety to rest. He wrote, "That time may come, perhaps soon. When it does come, I hope it will find me the same soldier I now try to be, as capable of meeting the reverses of life as I am those of war. . . . You, fearing that disappointment might render me unhappy, are doubtful as to whether it is best for me to cherish the remembrance of one who is now to me, all that she will ever be. . . . Do not fear for me. . . . What you have hinted as being probable in reference to Libbie *may* occur. . . . Rest assured, that whatever fortune may have in store for me will be borne cheerfully. Now that you know this, you need not hesitate in future to tell me *all*."[31]

Custer was displaying the art of positive thinking. He thought, as he thought all through his short life, that to win one had to think positive. The thought of defeat he never entertained. It might enter his mind but it was never permitted to dwell there. His philosophy, in the event of a reversal, was to accept it and move on to the next objective. There was no room or time for lamentation. He had written Nettie in May that he followed a rule "never to regret anything after it is done."[32]

Near mid-September Meade began to move down the Rappahannock River. Hampered by ignorance of Lee's exact position, he had his cavalry cross the river on September 13th and advance toward Culpeper.[33] As they neared Brandy Station along the line of the Orange & Alexandria Railroad the enemy began resisting their advance.[34] The fighting grew fiercer as they passed through Brandy Station and on toward Culpeper some six miles away.

Apparently there remained many who were curious as to how the flamboyant Custer would acquit himself. Captain Willard Glazier, a participant in the battle at Brandy Station, said, "It seemed to be the general impression that he would not have the nerve to 'Face the music' with his bandbox equipment, but he soon proved himself equal to the occasion. . . . No soldier who saw him on that day at Brandy Station ever questioned his right to wear a star, or all the gold lace he felt inclined to wear. He at once became the favorite in the Army of the Potomac."[35]

Gregg and Buford followed the railroad while Kilpatrick was on the left with Custer covering his left flank. In a form of a crescent they approached Culpeper where the Confederate artillery had opened up on them.

Stuart was getting ready to leave and a locomotive and load of cars had a head of steam preparatory to pulling out. Custer had his artillery turned on the locomotive but was unable to stop it. Suddenly he led a charge against three cannon positioned within the town, capturing all three guns and their caissons. A shell fragment tore through his boot and leg, killing his horse under him.[36] The wound was painful though not serious.

Colonel Lyman, who had watched Custer's charge on the three cannon, wrote, "This was a really handsome charge and was led by General Custer, who had his horse shot under him. . . . he has a very merry blue eye, and a devil-may-care style. His first greeting to General Pleasonton, as he rode up, was: 'How are you, fifteen-days'-leave-of-absence? They have spoiled my boots but they didn't gain much there, for I stole 'em from a Reb.' And certainly, there was one boot torn by a piece of shell and the leg hurt also. . . ."[37]

Pleasonton was happy with what his cavalry corps had accomplished and the part Custer had played. Fifteen days had been asked for by this lad. Why not add five days travel time so he could visit this Fannie Fifield whose picture he had seen?

Custer received the 20 days with a whoop. That would be ample time to heal his leg wound and just might be enough time to settle a problem that had been troubling his mind for some time. Hurrying on to Washington, he was able to procure rail transportation west for the day after his arrival there. It was all aboard for Monroe!

NOTES—CHAPTER 8

1There is some discrepancy between biographers as to Custer's time with McClellan. Whittaker (p. 139) indicates he was summoned by letter "in the middle of January (1863)."

Monaghan (p. 113) mentioned that with the news of the Battle of Fredericksburg (December 13, 1862) "came an order for Custer to report to McClellan in Trenton," where he assisted him in preparing the official account of his campaign.

Libbie's Journal entry of December 17, 1862, states that on Sunday, December 14th, Autie met her after the evening church service and escorted her home. She recorded that on the evening of December 16th her father told her he had just left Autie who was starting for the Chickahominy at midnight. Later, she notes that Autie had returned on Christmas Day. She refers to him continuously up to the time he left for McClellan's home in New Jersey on her birthday, April 8, 1863.

2Special Order, April 16, 1863, C.B.N.M.

3Merington, p. 52.

4Frost: *"Let's Have a Fair Fight,"* p. 30.

5Whittaker, p. 148.

6Frost: *The Custer Album*, p. 34.

7Monaghan, p. 117.

8Whittaker, pp. 149-51.

9*War of the Rebellion* hereinafter referred to as the O.R. (Official Records), Vol. XXVII, I, Part III, pp. 97-98, Gen. Orders No. 19, June 13, 1863, assignments as aides-de-camp to General Pleasonton included First Lieutenant G. W. Yates and Captain E. J. Farnsworth.

10George W. Cullum: *Biographical Register of the Officers and Graduates of the U.S. Military Academy*, New York, 1891, Vol. II, No. 1212.

Army Register for 1864, pp. 18, 68.

11Long, p. 372.

12Whittaker, pp. 162-63.

13Francis B. Heitman: *Historical Register, United States Army*, Washington, 1903, Vol. I, p. 1065. George W. Yates began his service on June 21, 1861, as quartermaster Sergeant in the 4th Michigan Infantry. He served as a captain in the 7th U.S. Cavalry, dying with Custer on the Little Big Horn, June 25, 1876.

14*Army Register of 1864*, p. 70. Merritt, Custer and Farnsworth were commissioned June 29, 1863. Farnsworth was not listed in the 1864 Register having been killed in action July 3, 1863, just four days after receiving his commission; O.R., Vol. XXVII, I, Part III, p. 373, Special Orders, No. 175, June 28, 1863, Brigadier General George A. Custer was assigned to duty with the Cavalry Corps and ordered to report to Major General Pleasonton. On p. 376, Special Orders No. 98, June 28, 1863, signed by Pleasonton, assigned Custer to duty under the Third Division commander, Brigadier General Kilpatrick. On June 29, 1863, Special Order No. 2, signed by Kilpatrick placed Custer in command of the Michigan Cavalry Brigade (2d Brigade, 3d Division of the Cavalry Corps), E.B.C. files. On June 29, 1863, Custer acknowledged and accepted his appointment by the President (file RG #94, National Archives).

[15]Merington, p. 60.

[16]James H. Kidd: *Personal Recollections of a Cavalryman,* Ionia, 1908, p. 129.

[17]Long, p. 372.

[18]Burke Davis, *Jeb Stuart,* New York, 1957, p. 334.

[19]Kidd, p. 136-155.
William Brook Rawle: *Gregg's Cavalry Fight at Gettysburg,* Philadelphia, 1884, pp. 9-28.

[20]Kidd, p. 155.

[21]Whittaker, p. 178; O.R., I, XXVII, part 1, p. 998.

[22]Kidd, p. 189; Monaghan, p. 155; Whittaker, p. 189, states there were 1,200 prisoners captured; Willard Glazier: *Battles For the Union,* Hartford, 1878, pp. 305-306.

[23]Kidd, p. 171.

[24]Whittaker, pp. 191-192.

[25]Kidd, pp. 185-86.

[26]Glazier: *Battles For The Union,* pp. 305-306.

[27]Alfred Pleasonton; "the Campaign of Gettysburg." in the *Annals Of War,* Philadelphia, 1879, p. 455.

[28]Merington, p. 63.

[29]George A. Turner: *Record of Service of Sixth Michigan Cavalry in the Civil War,* Kalamazoo, 1905, p. 62. Jacob L. Greene had served in the Seventh Michigan Infantry, resigning as a First Lieutenant, January 20, 1862. He was commissioned a captain in the Sixth Michigan Cavalry, July 14, 1863, being appointed Assistant Adjutant General as of September 4, 1863. The *Official Army Register of 1864,* p. 73, and Jno. Robertson: *Michigan in the War,* Lansing, 1880, p. 94, both indicate he was made an A.A.G. as of September 4, 1863. It appears that Custer had appointed him as Acting Assistant Adjutant General until the appointment was officially confirmed.
On May 20, 1863, the Monroe *Monitor* printed the following business card: "Jacob L. Greene, Attorney, Counselor and Solicitor, Office in Washington Block, Washington St."
William Cahn: *A Matter of Life and Death,* N.Y., 1970, p. 81, described Jacob Greene, who was born in Waterford, Maine, in 1837 as "not physically big, but his erect posture made him look taller than he was. His eyes were gray and his manner reserved." He "was an unusual mixture of conservatism and a reckless willingness to act."

[30]Letter in author's collection.

[31]Whittaker, p. 206; Merington, p. 63.

[32]Whittaker, p. 151.

[33]Long, p. 408.

[34]Whittaker, p. 194: "Each brigade had an average of four regiments, with a regimental average of 300 men. Thus the whole force (the three divisions consisting of nine brigades) was near 12,000 strong. In front of each brigade was a full regiment, deployed as skirmishers, each man riding some 20 feet from his fellows, carbine in hand. Behind the right and left of this open line of men, at a distance of some 200 yards, were two regiments with drawn sabers, in line of battle, but moving at a walk. In rear of the center, and retired some 200 or 300 yards further, was the last regiment, in column of march. Before this was the brigade commander, and in front of him was his battery. Each brigade occupied more than half a mile, and the whole line was between five and six miles in length."

[35]Willard Glazier: *Ocean to Ocean On Horseback,* Philadelphia, 1898, p. 276.

[36]Monaghan, p. 162; Whittaker, p. 196, 205.

[37]Theodore Lyman: *Meade's Headquarters,* Boston, 1922, p. 17.

TWO STAR GENERAL. Custer was made a major general on April 15, 1865. Matthew Brady made this photo soon afterward. Courtesy of Ansco Corp.

AUDACITY, ALWAYS AUDACITY. Custer was one of a daring new element in the Federal Cavalry Service. His audacity and excellent sense of timing made him appear invincible. 1865. Brady photo. Library of Congress.

CHAPTER 9
NETTIE HUMPHREY - MATCHMAKER

Libbie was battling bugs while Custer battled rebels. The buzzing flies had been annoying her ailing mother so she spent part of the afternoon disposing of them. Then there were those multilegged creatures "with the long legs and ferocious gait" she was so terribly afraid of. The June beetles that besieged their house had been particularly annoying but less to be feared. Even while she wrote in her Journal one of them hovered close enough to be dispatched. Her technique merited a description for others to follow so she wrote, "I take my slipper and murder them."

But as she wrote that June 15th, "I didn't take my pen to write of bugs, but perhaps of big bugs viz.: men." Her immediate thoughts turned to her mother's illness and the observation that there was improvement under the ministration of Mill Wells who had been visiting for the past week. With that thought recorded she returned to the subject next to her heart, men.

Mr. Moore had reappeared on the scene. He had taken her to church that evening and then afterward had sat on the steps with her for awhile. His invitation to go on a buggy ride the following evening was alluring and she would go if Mother was well enough. So she noted, "After a fast horse but not with a fast man for I believe him to be good. O dear, I hope I shan't get into any scrape and have him telling me he loves me and I have to endure the agony I have. I cannot be different from what I am. I am so lively and unreserved and talkative, and I can't be cold and dignified and treat them as if they were wood and marble. I must be natural."

Recent letters from Frank Earle and France Chandler made her recall their manly characteristics, and then there was Elliot Bates—and Captain Custer. They all loved her and she loved them. What to do? So she penned, "I wish everything wouldn't crowd upon me so. I live years in months. I wonder if every *affaire du coeur* is coming now and the future will be barren of everything?" The frustrations and pressure of indecision were becoming difficult to meet without consultation with a trusted friend. It was time to talk to Nettie.

Belle and France Chandler were expected in two days, France arriving in time to escort Libbie to the commencement exercises and party at the Seminary. There was some concern as to an escort for Belle. And as much concern as to the proper response to France. No need to plan. Just meet each problem as it came.

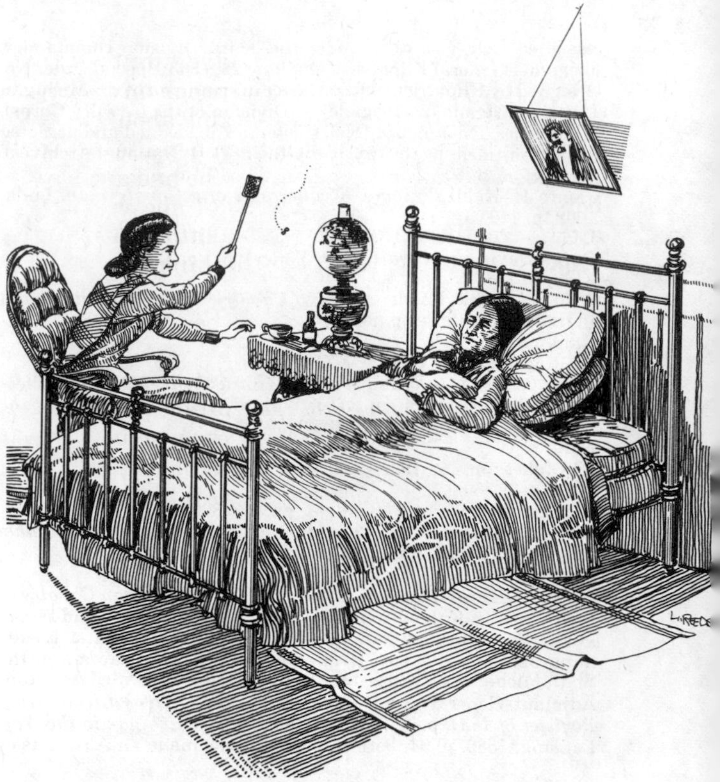

On June 22d, Libbie was fairly bubbling with thoughts that had to be expressed. Better to write them down than tell them. Secrets were no longer such when told to another. And some of the thoughts that raced through her brain were better left unsaid.

In recording some of these thoughts she reverted to the use of French phrases. She wrote of an unnamed suitor who she did not like because he lacked animation and was no Christian. That night, after she had retired, she presumed he would make her happy and she could learn to love him. "Untroubled night gives counsel best," she recalled, which made her think that she should listen more to the thoughts her mind offered during the quiet hours.

It became apparent that the subject was France Chandler. France had tried on her a system that other suitors had not tried. He had been extremely attentive to Nettie in Libbie's presence, then talked constantly of her to Libbie when she was absent. He got to Libbie and provoked in her a feeling tinging on jealousy, though she was not aware of it. It was an obvious response to Libbie's frequent chatter about her fondness for Jacob Greene and Mr. Utley.

Chandler was reserved, a bit stand-offish. She had tried to analyze him but with little success. He was hard to get acquainted with, yet he had displayed affection for her in the way he took her hand or by the frequent looks that he sent her way. He had observed that she gave an impression of indifference to him. She had done so because she knew he would love her if she displayed any interest in him.

She had resolved not to have him think she was ripe and ready to drop like a peach on a garden wall. To be sure she had been thinking about him that day and wondered if he had given her a second thought. At least he would never know he had a good many of hers. "I do love him a little," she wrote, "for his attention to Annette awoke a little spark of jealousy I am a stranger to. If I didn't think and almost know that he almost loved me I would banish my thoughts of him." With that she closed her Journal and turned out the light.

Just a week later, Elliot Bates visited the Bacon home. Her previous letters to him had been paving the way toward a negative response in the event he might think of proposing marriage. She hadn't told him in so many words she was interested in another. Wisely, he suggested that she would get to know him much better before the summer was over. He added that unless Libbie Bacon would be his wife, no one else ever could be. He had loved her since he was a boy, he reminded her, feeling it within him as something God had put there. At the very least, he would be her staunch, true friend forever.

Fannie Fifield was the harbinger of news that delighted Libbie. Seeing Libbie downtown on July 5th, she rushed over and told her that Captain Custer had been made a Brigadier General for his recent bravery. Libbie accepted the news with no show of emotion, her gray eyes barely blinking as she thought how Autie had rebounded to Fan and had become so devoted to her she believed he wished to marry her. Giving the matter a second thought, she was undecided as to whether he was flirting with Fan desperately knowing it would be quite a conquest to jilt such a renowned flirt or whether he was in earnest.

Anyhow, she was indignant at him. Fan had talked to her of ambrotypes and, in doing so, said, "Lib, that one Captain Custer has of you is the best I've ever seen." Libbie's face was a mask as Fannie continued, "You look so careless like, to the plaid Garibaldi, the little bow on your head and the curl."

Once back home in her room, Libbie stormed. "He promised me he never would show it, only to his sister. His word I *trusted.*"

The next day she told Nettie. Neither would believe he would break his promise until they had more proof, though Nettie was as enraged as Libbie over the possibility he could have. Libbie angered at the thought that he had been writing passionate messages to and about her at the same time he had been writing love letters to Fannie. She decided he was nothing to her and never would be, yet she liked him very much. Now that he has been promoted Fan would probably marry him.

Meditating over the Journal that evening she wrote, "After all the trouble I can't help but feel so delighted that I sent him away instead of his leaving me. He should marry and I want him to do so but I want his wife to be other than that unprincipled flirt, Fan Fifield. She is *dead in love* with C, especially his new appointment! Bah! If I loved a man I should love him just as much at the foot of the ladder as at the top. C I loved for a time but I never thought of marrying him. My parents wishes have too much weight with me to let me."

Nettie had agreed to write Autie and determine if he was not keeping his promise. If he wasn't Libbie would send him word through her that he had forfeited his claim and right to her picture by breaking his promise. She really didn't expect it back for he had told her, "Libbie, *whatever* happens, I will never give this up."

She firmly believed he had been too deeply in love with her to get over it so soon. Fan's dash, fine looks and stylishness may have captivated him but that was all. In any event, his response to Nettie's letter would help them decide if he was true or false. The two of them fairly exploded over the idea of Libbie being Fran's bridesmaid and *more especially* should Autie be the bridegroom.

On the following evening Libbie visited Laura Noble. Laura read aloud a letter she had received from Emma Bougher who was living in Frederick, Maryland. She told of Captain Custer calling on her as the Union army passed through. Though he was wearing his hair longer than ever he was a favorite in the army.

Emma had told him of Libbie and Major Earle going together while he was in Monroe. Autie asked her three or four times if she thought there was any truth to it being a serious affair. Then they discussed Monroe folks in general, especially the girls. Autie thought Nan Darrah had the prettiest face in Monroe, and so on. When he took an ambrotype out of his pocket, Emma asked, "It's Fan?"

"No, her's is down at the hotel." She was quite surprised to see that it was Libbie. Then he asked her if she corresponded with Libbie.

The letter brought new pleasure to Libbie. He had been true to his promise. She had been warmed by the thought he carried her picture on his person, while Fan's was left with his baggage.

Nettie was surprised to learn of this development. She had prepared a letter to Autie reproving him for his alleged actions and demanded an explanation of his showing Libbie's picture to Fannie. She told him Fannie had given Libbie every reason to believe there had been a greater intimacy between them than Libbie had supposed, yet this didn't credit him in showing what he had so solemnly promised not to show.

The letter, as she read it to Libbie, had been written in a sisterly fashion that ended with the thought they both hated to believe he had changed so soon. Both were willing, and Libbie desired, that he marry, but thought that if he was engaged to Fan he had no right to write to Fan about Libbie as he did.

This was no letter to send to Autie, thought Libbie, now that Emma Bougher's letter had proven to her satisfaction that Autie was not engaged to Fannie. Nettie agreed.

Strand by strand a web was being woven around Fannie. All she had been representing was not as it seemed. Several days before, she had pulled out an old letter from Autie to wave in front of Libbie, as if she had just received it. When told of this Nettie recalled meeting Fannie on that same day and discussing with her the void in correspondence from Autie. Fannie admitted not having heard from him since the last of June. As later proved, Autie had corresponded with no one until the Gettysburg Campaign had concluded. There was no time for it with his new responsibilities suddenly thrust upon him. So, by displaying an old letter, Fannie had used an old trick to arouse jealousy. Libbie now felt that Autie was as true as steel.

That morning the door bell rang. Libbie answered it and, to her consternation, who faced her but Mr. David Reed. As he stood there, a huge envelope in his hand, he said, "You know me, I suppose?"

With a sinking feeling she responded, "Mr. Reed, I think. Captain Custer's brother-in-law. I have seen you on the street and know you through him. Will you walk in?"

"Yes," he replied.

Both sank into chairs facing each other, he the color of a beet and she with the expression of a spanked baby. She thought at the moment that Autie, as pink skinned as he was, never looked so red during one of his most embarrassing moments. Both were obviously embarrassed.

Opening the envelope, Mr. Reed withdrew a picture and handed it to her with a shaking hand. It was a drawing of Autie by the famous Civil War combat artist Al Waud. How peculiar his uniform appeared; his beardless, wind-burned face and long locks topped by an old slouch reb hat, a brigand jacket and shirt with a scarf over one shoulder, and a pair of old fallow pants thrust into some cavalry boots that had seen better days.

Libbie said he looked like a pirate or a brigand to which Mr. Reed agreed. Then he handed her a letter that came with the picture. Blushingly she read it. Autie had written a description of a battle he had been in and the manner in which he had been saved by the reb hat he wore as shown in the drawing. He asked his brother-in-law to show the letter to Fannie, Colonel Winans and his other friends. Mr. Reed brought it for her to see since she was a friend of his.

All Libbie could do was to express her gratitude, then add that she was not surprised that Autie had been made a general, only it was so soon.

"Yes," he said, "we had not anticipated as sudden a promotion."

Then speaking of Fannie, Libbie said, "She has led me to suppose she was engaged and I didn't know but what Autie would be home this fall to be married to her."

"*Do* you think so?" he replied. "If you don't know his feelings, he doesn't know." By his manner, she was aware he knew Autie loved her. She was uncertain as to whether he thought she returned the love and her father objected, or whether she was indifferent to Autie's feelings for her.

A variety of thoughts raced through her mind as she sat there facing him. "I am trying hard to tear Autie's image from my heart. No, I am not! I will too! I love him still. I know it is love from fancy with no foundation, but I love him still and theory vanishes when practice comes in to play. There is no similarity of tastes between us and I will never think of it, but *I love him*. His career is much to me."

Mr. Reed broke into her thoughts by saying he didn't know when Autie would be back in Monroe but he was certain it would not be until after the conclusion of the summer campaign. Libbie asked to be remembered when next he wrote to Autie.

After he had left Libbie's emotions reached a point that required an outlet. Running upstairs to her room, she threw herself on her bed and wept. In time the tension was relieved. Time had not wrought its healing power as she had hoped. The first appearance of Mr. Reed had been embarrassing yet somewhat amusing. After he had talked awhile she came to realize how kind it was of him to attempt to do what would have been an extremely delicate matter for anyone. It was then the seriousness of it all had struck her.

Drying her tears, then powdering her nose, she went into her mother's room. Mother Bacon had been slowly recovering from her illness. There had been some backward movements in her recovery but for the past month there had been progress. That day she was feeling much better, so much so that Libbie told her of the Reed visitation. She asked her not to tell Father Bacon and, though there was no answer forthcoming, Libbie knew she wouldn't.

Nettie had to be told. She was dumbfounded when first she heard Libbie's story, then she laughed, and Libbie laughed with her. Both concluded that the entire meeting and every word Libbie had uttered would be carefully chronicled in the next letter the Reeds would send to Autie. "And to think that I was to be her bridesmaid!" said Libbie. With that they fairly exploded with laughter.

"Dear, dear Autie. I wish this moment I might see him face to face," she penned in her Journal that evening.

The evening of August 3d was rather dull, perhaps because it was Monday. It was warm and somewhat humid, better adapted to reading than a walk down town. The Journal could stand being brought up to date, thought Libbie. Why not work on it?

As she opened the volume and stared at a blank page she thought of Elliot, dear Elliot, and wondered why she hadn't filled it with everything he had said to her. She enjoyed every word he uttered but it all seemed a matter of course and never surprised her.

She thought a great deal of him but wondered if she truly loved him, enough to marry him. It would be two years before he graduated from the Military Academy. A lot could happen in that time. She might see many men and meet one who would make her forget all others.

So she wrote in her very legible hand, "But it would almost kill dear Elliot to have me finally refuse him. I tell him over and over again *I do not* love him now enough to be forever. . . . Perhaps I may be able to judge my feelings after a year when my violent fancy for C shall have passed away. But I am under the influence of it *now*. It seems as if devoted love for me influenced me even at this distance. If it were possible I should say his spirit influenced and partly controlled mine tho' miles separated us. He is coming next month and I'm afraid I shan't see him."

Libbie thought she wouldn't be seeing Custer when he would return to Monroe on leave because she would be visiting Albert Bacon in Traverse City with her mother. Custer arrived in Monroe on September 16th, just the day prior to her return. Her mother had gone on to Clinton to visit her relatives there while she and her father boarded at the Humphrey House for the remainder of the month.

In a letter to her cousin Rebecca Richmond she said she saw Autie the moment she arrived "because I could not avoid him. I tried to, but I did not succeed."[1] One can be certain she expended very little effort and no thought in attempting to avoid him. A wounded war hero is not the sort of person a friend would avoid.

Rebecca Richmond traveled in a Grand Rapids social set equivalent to that of Libbie's. Custer, had he lived in Grand Rapids early in his career, would have received the same disapproval from the Richmond family he received from Judge Bacon. An awarenes of this caused Libbie to color her relations with Autie whenever she wrote to Rebecca.

In one letter that fall she told Rebecca Autie had proposed to her repeatedly last winter and she refused him because of her father's unconquerable prejudices. She added that she had never *"even thought of marrying him."*[2] It was not until he left Monroe in the spring that she discovered she loved him.

That Custer was lionized by all of Monroe, one can be certain. The Eastern press had made numerous references to the "Boy General." The notoriety he had received for his exploits and gallantry had made no change in him. He talked freely enough of the battles he had seen but was always modest in respect to his own endeavors. Though it is not recorded, it would be in keeping with his propensity as a showman to use a cane while his minor leg wound repaired.

On the day of his arrival the Monroe *Monitor*[3] told of his being wounded "while gallantly charging a battery of the enemy in which four guns were captured."

On the following day the Monroe *Commercial*[4] mentioned that "Gen. Custer was slightly wounded by a shot that killed his horse." Neither of the articles could be considered any more than a brief notice of an event they wanted to let their readers know they were aware of. But this was equally true of their accounts of most of the Civil War engagements that had taken place up to that time.

The Monroe *Commercial* managed a somewhat better coverage on a fancy dress and masquerade party given at the Humphrey House on the Monday evening of September 28th by the young men of Monroe for General Custer. There were some 10 or 12 gentlemen in costume and about double that number of ladies.

Custer was dressed as Louis XVI and Libbie as a gypsy with a tambourine. Dancing began at 9 o'clock and continued until a supper was served at midnight after which the dancing was resumed. "A large number of spectators filled the hall who enjoyed the fun fully as much as the spectators."[5] Custer, to be sure, had disposed of his cane if he was using one at all. Painful or no, he would not have missed the opportunity of leading Libbie around the dance floor.

The time passed rapidly enough for the two lovers. Autie had talked to the Judge frequently for the latter's professed interest in the war brought them together on that subject. Though Libbie insisted that her father should be informed of their present feelings for each other, Autie, who had never hesitated to charge a rebel battery, veered away from any such confrontation as he would from peering into the mouth of a loaded mortar. The Judge appeared to be the only man he feared on earth.

Libbie had set the ground rules and Autie had agreed to them. There had been, and would continue to be, no exchange of letters. Nettie could convey messages from each but only in her handwriting. Libbie's ambrotype was never to be shown to Fannie Fifield. Though the two had arrived at an understanding, there would be no engagement or marriage until Father Bacon consented. To all this Autie agreed. He had developed into a master tactician on the battlefield. Instant decisions had won him many engagements but the approach to the Judge could not be hasty. Autie was checkmated.

The time for departure had arrived and still the Judge had not been confronted. On the afternoon of October 5th Libbie and Autie met for the last time before he returned to his troops. It was a painful parting for they could not be together as they wished. A large group of friends had accompanied him to the depot, the Judge, Nettie and Libbie being among them. Judge Bacon took him to one side of the station platform where he drew an encouraging picture of Autie's prospects in the service, then ended by telling him he would be quite disappointed if he did not receive excellent reports of his activities. Autie listened politely enough until he was through, then told him he "had desired to speak to him, but being prevented from doing so, (he) would write to him." The Judge replied, "Very well."[6]

It was a sad evening for Libbie, one in which many things burdened her mind. She could not become reconciled to the plight she found herself in. The time had arrived in which she must have a heart-to-heart talk with her father. She had observed her father's kindly feeling for Autie at the depot. He rarely displayed such a personal interest in young men and never went out of his way to give advice to them when it was not asked for. With Autie he had made an exception. She wondered if this interest was even deeper than he knew. It would be better to write out some of her thoughts before they were spoken. The Journal was the place for that. Taking it out of the drawer she began to jot them down.

"I little thought that these few pages would be devoted to a name which has figured so largely thro' this book. The last few leaves will bear a name I love—Dear C—try as I did to suppress the 'fancy' for six months it did no good. The *fancy* I know was more, it was *love.* I do love him and have all the time. He is *dear, dear.* I *tried* so hard to think it was an idle, passing fancy. But I love him. I believe I shall marry him sometime. This afternoon I parted from him and it was such a hard trial for us both. I cannot go on tho' until I talk to Father. I am going to do so tonight if I can. It is very hard for me to do so but I *must* and, if Father says *no* I shall abide by his decision. O how I have felt. 'Tis sad at his going, so full of dread for the future and a dread to say a word to Father. For two weeks I've been at Nett's and have seen him three times a day. It has been perfectly open tho', no clandestine meeting. Nothing could be more open than the parlor of a hotel.

"Oh how dear he is. I love him so. His words linger in my ears, his kisses on my lips. I forget everything sometimes when I think of him. Then a thousand doubts come into my mind like tormenting devils and I doubt if I love him. I do tho' and I shall sometime be his 'little wife.' "

On board the steamer *Morning Star* a few hours out of Toledo, Autie sat down to pen a few lines to Nettie, to drive his cares away. A day of separation from Libbie had made him lonely and sick at heart. The rhythmic movement of the boat as it plowed its way through foam-capped waves reminded him of the sea of life and the storms encountered as he charted his course over it. He was grateful to the divine power that had guided him safely thus far. Then he ended the letter, "How I wish I could be with my little girl tonight, and yet I cannot complain."[7]

On the following afternoon at Baltimore, an hour before his train left, he again wrote to Nettie. Monroe had been constantly in his thoughts and the Judge in particular. What to say in that letter he had promised to write to him. "My mind has been alternating between hope and fear, hope that my letter will be well received. . . . And yet I cannot rid myself of the fear that I may suffer from some unfounded prejudice. Oh, I wish some guardian angel would tell me what course to pursue."[8]

On that evening of October 7th he occupied a box in a Washington theatre. Appreciative of showmanship, having a personal use for it at times, he delighted in observing the professional at work. It was unfortunate that his mind was beclouded with thoughts of home for as he left the theatre at the conclusion of the performance he purchased a small bouquet from a flower girl. Inadvertently he forgot to put his purse containing 70 dollars back in his pocket.

The following day he wangled transportation back to Culpeper and enough credit from a Washington photographer (probably Brady who had photographed him previously) to sit for a $30 portrait he ordered for Libbie.[9]

By evening he was back in camp near the Rapidan River. The warm welcome he received made him feel at home. Though there was much to attend to he could not help meditating about the vast responsibilities thrust upon him, the many, many lives committed to his care. He realized that he was just entering manhood and because of that and his rank, he must assume the reponsibilities of both. There was no fear attendant with this thought, only determination. He would continue to follow the simple motto that had brought him success to this point, "First, be sure you're right, then go ahead."

On the evening of the 9th, following an extremely busy day, he borrowed time to correspond with Nettie. Disturbed in mind about not having written to Judge Bacon, he told her, "I would have written *that* letter to her father today, but that I knew I should be interrupted, which I did not wish to be, when writing so important a document. How much depends upon the results it obtains. All my future *destiny* hangs on the answer my letter shall bring. I will not despond, nor will I take trouble before it is upon me, but I cannot be anxious."[10]

There would be no opportunity to write that letter for some days to come. Lee's army was on the move. Custer had learned that Jeb Stuart's men were less than 20 miles away. Lee was moving northward once more in an attempt to turn Meade's right flank and push through to Washington.

On the 12th he found time to bring Nettie up to date on the activities of the preceding days. His troops had moved forward to probe into Lee's advance and determine the meaning of it. On Saturday, the 10th, he faced Stuart's entire cavalry command at James City and, though successful, was ordered to cover the retreat of Meade's infantry the next morning to the north side of the Rappahannock.

At one point on the 11th, his brigade was entirely surrounded by a superior force of cavalry. Placing a regiment on each of the four sides of Pennington's battery as they advanced, he ordered his men to draw their sabers, then told them all they had to do was to open a way with their sabers. The men gave three cheers as the band played the inspiring tune, "Yankee Doodle." In a series of charges they reached and crossed the river.

He told Nettie that the color bearer carrying his new guidon had his horse shot and he had two horses killed under him within 15 minutes. During the entire action he carried Captain Greene's saber. He concluded by asking her to "give my love to Libbie, and tell her I thought of her so often during the battle yesterday."[11]

Lee's army was gaining momentum in its drive northward, so much so that President Lincoln asked Meade on October 12th, "What news this morning?"[12] From all reports, Lee had moved around Meade's right flank toward Washington. Each side was trying to ascertain the intentions and strength of the other and it was the cavalry's obligation to probe and find this out.

From the 11th to the 15th of October, the Michigan Brigade was delegated to the task of picketing and guarding the flank and rear of the Army of the Potomac. On the 15th, the Army of the Potomac and the Army of Northern Virginia faced each other along Bull Run. Custer's scouts in a reconnaissance ascertained that the enemy strength near Gainsville was considerable.

Custer had informed Nettie he was camping on the Bull Run battlefield as he wrote, where as a second lieutenant he had heard his first shot in battle. He described the battle scarred area and the graves washed open by heavy rains revealing their contents of skulls and skeletons. He wondered if Judge Bacon had received his letter.

Three days earlier—on October 16th—he had approached the task of composing the letter that meant so much to him. It contained the same elements of frankness and honesty that had so impressed Congressman Bingham when Custer had asked for an appointment to West Point.

Humbly he told of his former intemperance, an error of judgment as it was, which led to "the solemn pledge I made my sister with God to witness." This pledge he had kept for two years.

If he appeared trifling in his attentions to other Monroe girls after he discontinued calling on Libbie, it was only to divert the gossipers. Libbie, he was certain, could explain his conduct satisfactorily.

Gently he reminded the Judge he had not corresponded with his daughter. He had hoped for a personal interview to seek this permission and to ask for her hand. As if in a summary and requesting an acquittal of charges placed against him, he ended, "I left home when but sixteen, and have been surrounded with temptation, but have always had a purpose in life."[13]

It was a dark October 18th for Libbie. She had awakened with thoughts of Autie on her mind and a few lines that kept running through her mind all that day:

"O that were possible after long grief and pain
To find the arms of my true love round me once again."

They were lines Autie had marked in her copy of Tennyson.

She took his picture from under her pillow and lay there for some time gazing at it as she talked to him. "Certainly, dear old fellow, our prospects are dark. Father but consents to listen because he feels much harm has often been done by parents utterly refusing—but after all Father is, to my surprise, on my side. Mother cannot, and will not see him in my light but that she herself has seen. And Albert is *so* bitter. Everything sometimes seems against me and I sometimes think is it not best to give it up? I shall not marry anybody else if I continue to love him. If I don't marry him I will be single forever."

There was no escape. He remained in her mind all of that day. When evening came she sought solace in her Journal. After recording her thoughts of the morning she had more to add. "My last thought at night and my first in the morning, my dreams too, have somebody like him as their hero. When I read I make applications to us. When others talk of my subject I connect it with the dearest one on earth to me.

"Albert in his cruel letter says 'Do you see with Libbie B's eyes, etc.? Wait two years before you take any steps.' I never expect to marry him for years. In two years Mother and Father and Bert will see 'if the character he is developing now will hold out.'

"How delighted I was to hear Colonel Winans talk of him this afternoon. He spoke of him so splendidly. It made me love him to hear him justly extol my lover as he did. O but he is witty. Colonel Winans answered Mrs. Thurber's questions so spiritedly. She, doubting like, asked, 'Was it not good fortune that gave him his promotion? Was he wanted, etc. like some home people I knew?' Indeed, I so often hear him or know him to be looked upon in an insignificant light that to hear right downhearted praise *delights me* intensely. And Net and Nan were never so enthusiastic over anyone.

"I wonder if he has thought of what I said to him two weeks ago tonight—that *happy* Sunday night. I have been with him in spirit the two Sundays he had been gone. . . . I can't ever tell him how his ambrotype has delighted me. It is so large it seems like the Boy General himself—and Mother thought it was such a fine picture, but of course she had to give me a little 'dab' by saying I was taken with the stars on his matchless shoulders!

"I felt so badly over Albert's letter I cried myself almost sick. It was hard for him to talk so to me but I know he did it in the kindest of spirits. Of *if* only he could look at him as Colonel Winans and all his good friends do. He was considerate enough to call him Mr. C. and in the other letter it was only C."

Forgetting for the moment that time passes rapidly with lovers when they are together, she added, "And he had not been home a week hardly before he was again in the midst of a fight. Victorious too. Colonel Winans says, 'In *all* he has ever undertaken he *succeeds.*' Two horses shot under him and he escaped. I thank the One who holds us all in the hollow of his hand. When I thought of what he has passed through and the dangers on all sides I can only look about feeling that God alone dictates it. . . . But God alone has kept him and I can only pray that he may be ready always to acknowledge the power of his protecting God.

"General Pleasonton says he is the most remarkable cavalry officer living. Well his 'little girl' cannot give testimony (to) his heroism on the battlefield but she can whisper in his ear *he is a dear. . . .* "

On the following evening she attended a meeting of the Aid Society. After an election in which she was elected treasurer, Mrs. Paulding told her that Fannie Fifield had called on her a few days ago. Before she left she discussed Autie disparagingly, then cried and called him names. For the Journal Libbie wrote, "What a vile girl to say such things. I think tho' if I had been jilted I should be pretty mad but I would not have talked of it to anyone I am sure.

"I expect and yet fear every day Father will get a letter from C. It is such a delicate and important matter. I love him though—'not withstanding all.' "

Custer had been operating with a reduced staff, several of them having returned to Monroe to recuperate from the effects of their campaigning. Jacob Greene, who was responding to the tender, loving care of Nettie Humphrey, wrote to him on October 19th that he was doing well, being able to sit up all day, walk and ride. He expected to be back in the saddle the following week. George Yates would leave for camp that morning.

Jacob saw Libbie quite often since he spent most of his time at the Humphrey House, and he had had a talk with Judge Bacon the other day. As for the Judge, he added, "I think the leaven is at work and may leaven the old lump after awhile if it is not interfered with. . . . Keep cool and steady. Your chances are coming about pretty good I should think. You ought to be satisfied with the present accomplishment.

"Miss F (Fifield) is having some tantrums. I shall be compelled to have a short, sharp conflict with her before I leave. It is necessary for her good and possibly for yours. You will not speak of it to anyone, but she has been circulating some reports that I know to be false, but which are prejudicial to you if anybody believes them, which they do not. I propose to stop that kind of a game and in the meantime give her a little good advice. She is making a ridiculous exhibition of herself.

"Jim (Christiancy) is improving fast. The doctor says he will be able to work soon."[14]

On the following day Custer wrote Nettie from Gainsville, Virginia, that yesterday the 19th, he had met a superior force under General Stuart and Fitz Lee. In requesting but not getting support from Kilpatrick although the other brigade was inactive and only four miles away, he managed to drive them from a strong position. Kilpatrick soon came up and complimented him, then went on ahead. Custer had advised him of heavy infantry columns moving up on his flanks but Kilpatrick ignored the intelligence. Custer was ordered to bring up the rear of the marching column. Once the First Brigade had passed, the enemy fiercely attacked both his flanks, forcing him to retreat.

Unknown to Custer, Kilpatrick had ordered a battalion of the 5th Michigan under Major John E. Clark to skirmish in a woods. All were taken by the enemy.

To add to Custer's discomfiture his headquarters wagons which he had ordered to the rear had been ordered by one of Kilpatrick's staff officers to follow the other brigade. The wagons of Kilpatrick and the First Brigade were captured. Custer lost his official reports of Gettysburg and other engagements and Captain Greene's desk with his reports. He concluded the recitation of this unhappy affair with, "I presume my letter to Judge Bacon has been received."[15]

The Judge's reply was slow in coming, so it seemed to Custer. For three days following the last engagement the command had been in camp repairing its losses, outfitting the men and resting the horses. To add to his quandary was a move on the part of friends to have him transferred to the Southwest to take over the command of an entire division of cavalry, all from Michigan. There was the realization that his present situation was one in which he had established a reputation. In the event of a blunder it would be overlooked. In the West he would have to produce a series of unmarred successes to establish himself.

General Pleasonton had been like a father to him. Solicitously he would greet Custer after each battle with, "Well boy, I am glad to see you back. I was *anxious about you.*" Custer wrote Nettie, "He often tells me that if I risk my life so much he will place me in such a command that I shall never have the opportunity."[16]

Continuing his correspondence, he reminded her he was not surprised at Fannie's telling everyone she carried his likeness in her locket. He would not be surprised at anything she did and just hoped she would not annoy Libbie.

He asked Nettie to tell Libbie that no Sabbath passed without her words coming back to him. At eleven-thirty in the morning he could see her at the end of their corner pew in the church.

A note of apprehension crept in. "I grow more anxious each day to learn how my letter to Judge Bacon has been received." He was not fearful of Mrs. Bacon but could not understand why Albert Bacon was using his influence against Autie since he knew nothing of him in any respect. Perhaps it was because of his strong attachment to Libbie.

Then the long awaited letter arrived! Dated October 22d, it began by reminding Custer that the subject was one of vast moment "requiring weeks or even months before I can feel to give you a definite answer." The Judge recalled a deathbed scene in which Libbie's mother had simply expressed to him, "I want you to be a mother as well as a father to Elizabeth." He said he had felt the responsibility beyond anything in his life before or since and felt thankful to a kind Providence that had spared his life and permitted him to consummate the wishes and desires of her mother.

He was grateful for the adopted mother who had shared his interest in Libbie's welfare. "You will not therefore be surprised that we have had a watchful care over her and have guarded her reputation with intense parental solicitude," he continued.

In conclusion he alluded to his feeling for Autie. "Your ability, energy and force of character I have always admired and no one can feel more gratified than myself at your well-earned reputation and your high and honorable position. The evening you left here I had a full and free interview with Libby (sic) and shall talk with her more upon this important subject which she is at full liberty to communicate to you."[17]

NOTES—CHAPTER 9

All material is this chapter is based upon Libbie's Journal unless there are other source indications.

1Merington, p. 64.
2*Ibid.*
3September 16, 1863.
4September 17, 1863.
5October 1, 1863.
6Whittaker, pp. 210-11; Merington, pp. 64-65.
7Whittaker, p. 210, October 6, 1863.
8*Ibid*, p. 211, October 7, 1863; Merintgon, p. 65.
9G.A.C. to Ann Reed, October 25, 1863. EBC-CBNM.
10Whittaker, pp. 212-13, October 9, 1863.
11Merington, pp. 65-67.
12Long, p. 421.
13Merington, p. 67; Whittaker, pp. 214-15.
14Letter in BCWC collection.
15Whittaker, p. 214; Merington, pp. 68-69.
16Merington, pp. 69-70.
17Original letter in author's collection.

BRIG. GEN. JUDSON KILPATRICK led a celebrated but unseccessful raid on Richmond in 1864. Author's collection.

CHAPTER 10
OTHER MEN SEEM ORDINARY

Custer was in a quandary. He had asked for a whole loaf of bread and had received what appeared to be but a slice. The slice could not, in his opinion, be interpreted as meaning he could communicate with Libbie beyond that of discussing the subject of matrimony.

After first writing to Nettie, giving her the Judge's reply in some detail and asking her for an interpretation of the thoughts it contained, he decided to ask the Judge for permission to correspond with Libbie. Already it was the 27th of October. Why not send it along with that one to Nettie? To think was to act. The brief letter was soon ready and on its way.

Two evenings earlier—it was Sunday the 25th—Libbie sat down to write in her "dear old safety valve." She began: "Love him! I have loved him all the time and I need no clearer index of past feelings than this old book. I have written once of his taking my hand and kissing it and how he looked and how I felt. O tho' he kissed me when he was here last, my lips used to thrill with them after I had left him and was in bed. Affectionate, I never saw a man more so.

"When I told him he might be released from his promise I never saw him more happy. I used to call him my anaconda because he used to 'squoose' me so. How I laughed at the impress of the American eagle being stamped on me. He went to sleep on my bosom one night, he was so tired, and so those two weeks at Net's were so full of such perfect happiness.

"I never was kissed so much before. I thought he would eat me. My forehead and my eyelids and cheeks and lips bear testimony—and his star scratched my face. I have so much to write.

"I said just three weeks ago tonight in Marie's organ nest to my lover that I would be with him in spirit on Sundays. Spirits commune I think and the poetry he sent me shows he thinks so too.

"Two weeks ago today he was in a fierce fight when he cut the way for Beaufont[1] and Kilpatrick. Perhaps he may have been today.

"My prospects are so bright now. Father is more than reconciled and Mother getting to look more favorably. They both joke me about the dear man. And I am happy. I felt that time, these past three weeks, have increased the love I feel for him. I *know* now I do truly love him. I doubted it or doubted its lasting at first. Yes, I love him devotedly. Every other man seems so ordinary beside my own bright particular *star*.

"O if I could only see him tonight and feel his strong arms around me and his dear lips to mine.

There *is* nothing half so sweet in life as love's young dream. The doubts I have felt seem to be vanishing like the morning dew. How I wish I might see him tonight.

"His letter to Father was well received. Mother and he read and reread it and Father wrote an answer the next day. I saw it and it was good tho' not so well written as his impromptu efforts. Father's was, of course, not decided in the affirmative but he far from discouraged his suit. Dear man, if he were here and listened to our talk and even *jokes* over the matter his spirits would rise as they never have done before I fancy.

"He wrote Net he felt more anxiety over his answer expected from Father than about the battle imminent. I hope he will be preserved. Indeed I never have a fear except a passing one. I seem to feel that 'he'll come back to me.'

"F. F. talks as usual. She tells such terrible stories about him it fairly startles me. It annoys me to hear them. I can't bear his name to be so common.

"Father asserted positively he thought I'd be married the coming February. I certainly won't be for two years yet. Albert is cool as a cucumber over his wedding coming off this week. I should fly into atoms if it were *me*. I *think* of it. I wish I had the wings of a dove just this moment. O just to be able to see him from now till midnight as I did three weeks ago." With that, Libbie placed her Journal in the dresser drawer and prepared to retire.[2]

By this time the Confederate cavalry had retired across the Rappahannock, the campaign around Manassas having ended. There had been little change in territory and the losses had been low. Lincoln, not satisfied with the situation, instructed General Halleck that the Army of the Potomac must get ready to attack Lee immediately. Meade made an effort to follow the order but stopped at Brandy Station. There his men were detailed to sawing boards for tent floors and winter huts. Custer stewed over the probability of an inactive winter in camp.

On Sunday evening, October 25th, in camp at Bristoe Station, Virginia, a sentry's challenge rang out, "Who goes there?"

"Friends."

"Advance and give the countersign!"

"Haven't got it. I want to see General Custer!"

"That's Captin Greene's voice and Jim Christiancy's laugh," exclaimed Captain Judson. All the staff jumped up from around the fire to welcome them back. After plying them with questions about Monroe they settled down to singing songs accompanied by a violin and a guitar. As they sang "Then You'll Remember Me" it reminded Custer that Libbie promised to sing it to him the next time he visited Monroe.

He and Captain Greene spread out their coats on the ground beside the fire and talked about many things. How was his mother and father, Ann and all the others? How was Libbie? Had the leaven reached the Judge? Was Fannie Fifield upsetting Libbie? The stimulus of Greene's presence fresh from home was enough to make him forget time until they saw the servants preparing breakfast, at 5 A.M.[3]

Several days later he received a letter from his sister Ann. Ann mentioned Mother Custer's wish to be back on their old farm in Tontogony, Ohio, where she wouldn't feel so shut up. The Reed house, though having a large yard, seemed too confining to her. Father Custer and Maggie were happy where they were.

Ann announced that Maggie had not commenced attending school. "We all think she should go to the Union School. Armstrong, you don't think what it takes to send a girl to the Seminary. It takes a little fortune to send her there until she graduates." This last was in response to Autie's desire to see his sister Margaret attend the Boyd Seminary.[4] He knew one fine example of what the Seminary could produce and saw the potential for his little sister if a similar background could be provided for her. With a display of that affection and loyalty characteristic of all the Custers he insisted that Maggie attend the Seminary, he providing the funds that she might do so.

On the 27th, Ann mailed another letter to Autie that evidenced her concern about Maggie's schooling. "I wish you would give your consent for Maggie to go to the Union school. Thare (sic) is just good children go thare (sic) as at the Seminary. I would like to have Riley (Maria Reed) and Maggie go to school together. Now please say yes. You are under no obligation to Mr. Boyd to send Maggie. I think it would be much better to take the tuition and by (sic) her a piano but if you should not do so it is better to go to Union school."[5]

Father Custer, apparently yielding to the counseling of his wife, "guessed he would move back to Wood County (Ohio)," but Ann was of the opinion her mother would be better satisfied after she had lived in Monroe a few years.

Father Custer had not written Autie because he was awaiting the arrival of a horse Autie was sending to him which should arrive on the following day. Meanwhile he was using Roanoke to haul the winter wood.

Monroe folks were permitted a brief glimpse of their boys on the Virginia front when a letter from Orderly Fred A. Nims of the 5th Michigan Cavalry was published in the *Monitor*. He told his mother of the pleasure they all experienced at seeing Custer rejoin his command that past week. The day before he had written had been a gloomy one, for Kilpatrick's Division had been routed by Stuart at Buckland Mills. The 5th Michigan had lost 60 men and five officers and the other regiments had lost in proportion. He concluded by saying that the 4th Michigan Infantry had camped nearby for the night and he intended to see the boys after supper.[6]

On the evening of November 1st, Sunday, Libbie sat down to a labor of love—her Journal. In utter frankness as always, she wrote, "It seems Sundays I am having a nice little chat with my absent lover when I take up this good old friend. I wish I could write in a language no one but myself could understand. I wish I might see *mon cher* my hero tonight. Ah, wouldn't I devour him with kisses. But like a silly little girl that I am I say to myself, 'I love my love and my love loves me.' How dear, how nice it is to have a love.

"How many hours I spend thinking of him. I sew him into my work. I read him in all my books. When I take in the book heroes there comes dashing in with them my live hero, my dear boy General. I know he wishes tonight he might be where he was four weeks ago tonight—in Marie's little organ nest.

"Net brought a splendid letter from him last night. He writes finely. I wonder if *mon pere et ma mere* will object to my writing myself soon. How I want to, I have such hosts of things to tell him. I hope he has gotten—yes, I think he has—the last Sunday's letter when I made Net write—his dear, his dear—so many times. I love you Armstrong Custer. I love *you*. I love my love and my love loves me — and I am happy."

About a week after Libbie had made this last entry in her Journal, Custer received a letter from Judge Bacon that cleared the air and the way for him. Concisely phrased and unconsciously touched with legal parlance, it granted Custer permission to write to his daughter. Though the Judge had not said it in so many words, Custer assumed that this permission to correspond carried with it a consent to their marriage. And he was right.

Finding time on the evening of November 10th, he prepared a letter to Nettie. After relating some details of the capture and killing of some of his orderlies by Mosby he informed her that General Kilpatrick was to be made a major general and ordered to the West. This he was pleased with since Kilpatrick was his senior. He reasoned that had the promotion come to him rather than his commanding officer the latter's friends would have attempted to defeat his nomination. In any respect, if Kilpatrick did not go West, Custer was sure to go.

"However much I wish to add a star to the one I wear," he observed, "yet would one word of disapproval from Libbie check my aspiration." In this he was quite certain that Libbie would not interrupt his plans or ambitions.

It was while writing this letter to Nettie that he received Judge Bacon's letter referred to before. Already having stated that he was anxiously awaiting an answer as to whether he could correspond with Libbie, he now concluded his letter to Nettie with:

"What makes you think I am going to take a young lady on my staff and who do you think is the young lady? I must close. I have another letter to write. . . . to a Young Lady in Monroe."[7]

Meanwhile Libbie had made her Sunday evening entries in her Journal. She had attended services at the Episcopal Church that day presumably because Autie had told Nettie he liked its form of worship.

After noting that five weeks ago this evening *"we* were together in Marie's organ loft," she mentioned that Autie had written her father for permission to correspond with her and that "Father answered yes and he'll get the letter tomorrow and I shall get my letter from him by Saturday I hope."[8]

She continued, "I suppose I shall soon be busy writing to my dear boy, my anaconda. . . . I wish I could see my boy tonight. I believe I would kiss him. I *know* I would kiss him.

"Only five weeks since he left, and I never saw time pass so slowly in that time. So many important things have transpired in that time. Especially regarding my affair with Armstrong. How dark it has looked sometimes but I am happy enough now to make up for it."

In mid November, while the Union guns were thundering against Fort Sumter, Custer thundered against the Quartermaster's Department. In a letter of complaint formally drafted so that General Pleasonton could add his endorsement and have it forwarded to the authorities in Washington, Custer called attention to the unserviceable condition of the men and horses being sent to him from Dismounted Camp. It seems that of a detachment of 80 men just returned to him, 17 were unable to reach his command because their horses could not carry them that far.

He went on to say that he had numerous complaints from his regimental commanders about the inferior quality of the horses sent to them with men from Dismounted Camp.

LIEUT. GEN. PHILIP H. SHERIDAN, like Custer's previous commanders, was quick to recognize his unusual talents. Ca. 1869. Denver Public Library photo.

In a final charge he asserted, "So far as my experience and observation extend, my command suffers about as much from the influences and effect of the Dismounted Camp as it does from the weapons of the enemy. It is an actual fact that there are men in my command who have been captured by the enemy, carried to Richmond, and rejoined my command in less time than it frequently requires for men to proceed to the Dismounted Camp and return mounted."

General Pleasonton, in his endorsement, fully concurred and requested an immediate change in a system "so radically wrong."[9]

A reply from the Office of the Cavalry Bureau, dated November 23rd, stated there were few if any of Custer's men in the Dismounted Camp, and that the writer "understood that Custer's brigade are horse-killers, and it is very likely that the 17 horses were used up as stated, though they were serviceable when they left the depot."

During the first two years of the war there had never been more than 60,000 cavalrymen in combat areas at any one time. During this same period they were provided with 284,000 horses.

It was an accepted fact that it took two years to train a cavalryman as compared to the much shorter period to turn out a competent infantry or artillery soldier. Northern recruits had little or no experience with horses and had to be trained for this endeavor from the ground up. The high casualty rate amongst horses could be due to anything from poor horsemanship, hardship, improper care, to gross inefficiency on the part of the officers and men involved.[10]

Another week had rolled around, but it had been a rewarding one for Autie's letter had arrived on Saturday, as Libbie had predicted. Taking her pen in hand she began: "My more than friend, at last, am I a little glad to write you some of the thoughts I cannot control. . . . I was surprised to hear how readily Father had consented to our correspondence. . . . Didn't Father and I sit down beside the fireplace last Sunday night and talk until the fire died out about one General Custer. . . . Few know what a splendid old gentleman he really is."

Responding to his inquiry as to her objections to an early wedding, she teased him with, "Ah, dear man, if I am worth having am I not worth waiting for? . . . If you tease me I will go into a convent for a year. . . . I implore you not even to mention it for at least a year."

On Sunday evening, November 15th, she made what would be the last entry in her Journal. "Tonight Father began talking to me about General C. Well, he thought the letter C wrote last implied in this remark 'he would wait patiently for his decision,' that should he get Father's consent he might play the hypocrite, and if he did, what would I do?

"I said what I feel now. If General C dies it will be a terrible blow to me, it would almost kill me but if he should play the hypocrite my pride would support me and all my love would vanish. Father was satisfied. I guess if he had read all Nett's letters, which are the same as mine, he wouldn't worry.

"Love me, I never doubt that. Then when I say anything that would seem an impediment to my marrying Armstrong, Father is the one to explain it all away instead of me. 'His family, daughter, are as good as ours or your mother's. About his going with those little girls, daughter, why he was a boy then, never had been in society, etc.' I love him and wish I could see him."

Libbie's letter of the 15th was answered on Sunday evening of the 22nd from Stevensburg, Va. Custer opened it with the observation that they were quietly preparing for a forward movement and a general engagement but hadn't moved that morning because of a heavy rain that rendered the river on their front impassable. "Perhaps as this reaches you, by the telegraph wires will come the news that the Army of the Potomac is moving or that a great battle is being fought. . . . It is the plan at present, to throw four pontoon bridges across the river, upon which to cross the infantry and artillery. The cavalry will probably, with their usual independence, cross by fording."

Nettie Humphrey's nursing had done wonders for Captain Greene. His continual improvement drew the comment from Autie that he had never seen a person improve in health as he had in the past three weeks. "He is actually becoming corpulent and will, if he continues to improve (?), resemble Dr. Landon or Mr. Dunning in appearance, only imagine it. Yesterday I heard him complain about his clothing fitting him too tightly. His cheeks almost rival yours in their rosy complexion." All of this was written so that it could be relayed to Nettie.

James Christiancy, the son of Judge Isaac P. Christiancy, had been the cause of considerable parental concern. His liking for liquor and the circumstances he placed himself in while under its influence had caused his father to petition Custer to make a man of him while he served on his staff.

Autie wrote to Libbie that Jim had done remarkably well since his return with Greene. "He has not in a single instance acted contrary to my wishes, has committed no excesses, and instead of foolishly squandering his money and calling upon his father for more as heretofore. I induced him to send home more than half of his last month's pay to be deposited to his credit at Wing & Johnson's. He has the elements of a noble man. He only needs proper restraint. He is young and fond of excitement and pleasure. As he grows older his habits will improve and become more settled." These sage comments seem to come from a mature man of sixty rather than from a lad who would reach his twenty-fourth birthday in two weeks.

Continuing his letter, he turned "to something more interesting. . . . When first I opportuned you to *'promise some day to be my darling wife'* you *did* reply *'if father consents and I love you.'* I deemed it discouraging enough to get rid of one 'if,' let alone two. I was not content to let the subject rest and trust to time to remove all hindrances. I continued my appeals from day to day until a few days prior to my leaving (The night of the masquerade while seated upon the sofa in Mrs. Hammond's room). You promised me that 'if father will give his consent, *Yes.' N'est ce pas* Gypsie? Since the above was written your *dear* letter written the 17th was handed to me. I read it *twice,* something unusual for me, and I propose reading it again before I go to sleep.

"Like you, the pleasure of the present moment repays me for the trouble and vexation of the past. How truly glad I am that in no instance did we ever act in opposition to the expressed will of your father. . . . Speaking of your father in such high and eloquent terms of praise as you do only confirms my early impressions of his character. This is why throughout the darkest period of our acquaintanceship I have never cherished or felt one unfriendly sentiment toward him but on the contrary have always entertained the highest respect and esteem for him because I know he acted from a sense of duty and in a manner which he deemed best calculated to secure your happiness and welfare. I only regretted that he should differ so much from me. Happily that difficulty is removed. . . .

"I am sorry that I cannot accede to almost the first *written* request my little Gypsie has made, but such unfortunately is the case. You bid me maintain strict silence upon a certain subject until next winter and then we are to discuss the subject of your becoming Mrs. - - - and arrive at a conclusion the following winter. This like all other bargains requires two to complete it. Now had you presented a single, good reason why the course you make out should be adopted, I might have yielded assent, but you have not done . . . I shall not *urge* you to act against your own wishes.

"One of your objections to becoming Mrs. - - - is that you want to remain 'Libbie Bacon for an age,' but that need not be an objection. Can you not be Libbie Bacon Custer? There is one objection removed!

"Again, you say 'girls have so much fun.' I do not doubt it but I am unable to see how getting married will curtail your pleasures as a girl. I will become responsible that your pleasures are not diminished.

"Then you say I know what your idea of marriage, or rather matrimony, is. Yes, I do, but your idea is incorrect and has no foundation in fact. You have no reason for entertaining such an incorrect idea. Good bye objection No. 3.

"You ask me if I do not 'take into consideration that women are as changeable as the sea.' If I thought you were changeable that would be an argument in favor of an early marriage.

"You say, and truly too, that if you are worth having, you are worth waiting for, all of which I admit. You do not doubt my willingness to wait indefinitely long if there is any necessity for doing so but, my dear, what motive can there be for delaying our marriage after it has once been decided upon?

"Now dear one, I have another request to make. While your letter contained that which implied that some day you would be, instead of my 'little girl' my darling little wife, yet you did not say as much. Now won't you on your next letter *say* that you will, without interposing one of those hateful 'ifs?' Please do. I will be so glad if you will, then I will know that we are 'solemnly engaged' and will be ever so good.

"Next Thursday is Thanksgiving. One year from that date we were introduced to each other. I was speaking to Captain Greene about it today and told him if we were not on the march I would celebrate the anniversary by a great dinner, etc. but I fear we will otherwise be engaged. However I will celebrate it in memory if in nothing more. I wish I could be in Monroe the 5th of next month which is my birthday. Your is the 8th of April is it not?

"I will now tell you something and then something else. You probably would be surprised at the great majority of officers who delight to play cards and attend racing of horses. Scarcely a pleasant day passes that the officers of this Division do not assemble to witness and stake money on races between favorite horses. Even General Pleasonton sometimes lends his presence and General Kilpatrick invariably does. Between the latter and myself frequent wagers have been laid.

"Again, if the vast number of officers who, to kill time, play cards, there is not one in 20 but will, 'to make the game *interesting,'* play for some stake, generally for cigars or for champagne but most frequently for money, the stakes however being merely as they say large enough 'to make the game interesting.' I have heard many persons remark that they would 'never think of doing such a thing at home.'

"Now no person enjoys witnessing a race or a game of cards more than I do and I frequently attend the former and participate in the latter but since my return from Monroe I made a resolution to myself intending to delay putting it into execution until I receive a letter from you. I recd your letter today. I will now tell you what I have resolved.

"Never to engage in any game of chance with the intention of staking money or to participate in any game played for stakes of any kind. I have never participated in either of these amusements with any other purpose but to kill time, and while I condemn both as hurtful to most persons, and apt to be engaged in to excess, yet I never feared their consequences to myself.

"I have made the resolution to abstain in future from both simply because I knew, first, that they were wrong in principle, second, and more particularly, I was convinced that you would not like to have me engage in them.

"Am I not right darling to tell you of my faults and tell you I have discarded them forever? You know I will keep my promise don't you? You know how solemnly I have observed the promise to my sister.

"I have bad adieu to every vice except one. You are already aware of the existence of that one. I will admit that I still cling to the habit of profanity. . . . Do not understand me to say that I am now free from faults.

"I have a strange belief in regard to profanity. I am not ignorant of its magnitude as a sin nor of its inelegance as a habit but I have always believed, without reason perhaps, that the sin did not appear so great in me as others. I seldom indulge in it except when I am angry and then it seems to afford me so much satisfaction. I always try to justify myself by saying that I do not mean what I say. . . . it is a satisfaction I am loth to deprive myself of.

"Whatever mistakes you detect in my correspondence must be overlooked as I never read what I have once written. I will write to you twice a week as you have chosen to do."[11]

It was Thanksigiving Day that George Gordon Meade had his Army of the Potomac cross the Rapidan in an attempt to turn Lee's right flank. Responding to the oft-repeated urging from Washington, he led 85,000 troops aginst Lee's 48,500 in an effort to force him back toward Richmond.

Custer had moved to within a mile of the Rapidan near Morton's Ford the night before, where he had his men build bivouac fires up and down the river for miles to give the impression that a large force was readying to cross there at dawn. Emphasis was added by having the band play at various points during the night.[12]

Custer was instructed to make a feint as if to cross from Morton's Ford upward the moment he heard cannonading from below where Meade was to cross. He complied when the artillery sounded and managed to draw the fire of 30 enemy guns who were accompanied by a large infantry force. The maneuver was highly successful.

Once Lee had discovered the intentions of the Federal Army he withdrew his artillery and infantry and developed strong defensive positions along Mine Run. By the end of the month it was evident that Lee had halted Meade's offensive, preventing him from reaching his objective. The campaign had ended in failure.[13]

There was peace of mind in letter writing, and there was always time when the letter was to be addressed to a loved one. Thanksgiving Day had been a hectic one for Custer, and he had had no sleep the night before. Virile, energetic and youthful, with an enormous capacity for work, he had the ability to lie down on the ground, even in a driving rain, sleep soundly for 20 minutes, then arise completely refreshed. With a competent staff responding to the duties he had assigned them, he found time to write a letter to Libbie. Unknown to him, she had written to him that same day.

Nettie too had written to Autie on Thanksgiving Day. She began by briefly describing the wedding of Henry Noble and Addie Martin in the Presbyterian Church that evening. She had attended the affair and the reception afterwards with Libbie, the two conducting themselves "like respectable spinsters." The letter she was writing in Libbie's room in response to his *"order"* not to discontinue her letters to him. As she wrote, she reminisced:

"Oh, Armstrong Custer, who could have thought last Thanksgiving evening when we so coolly received our mutual instruction that in one short year I would be writing *this* letter. When we first used to meet at Mrs. Paulding's, when you followed me to Mr. Bacon's, where that oyster supper and surprise party were carried out, who would have thought that Elizabeth would have sat at my feet, as she does now, writing to *you,* almost betrothed!

"I am looking back over a year, and tracing our intimacy step by step. How strange it seems, far more so that you and I should be such friends, than that you and *she* should be lovers. I believe you are a noble, true man and I thank you for strengthening my faith in any fellow creatures.

"You ask what I think about hurrying my adoption into this family—Elizabeth protests—but I believe it *is possible.* I think Judge Bacon and his wife are prepared for anything from the audacious soldier who has won the affections of their idol. I think they consider her a 'gone case.' (pardon slang and don't tell Jacob I used it) Use your influence with her, selfishly or unselfishly as it may be. I am rather inclined to your side, still I am not the proper person to insist upon the matter.

"Libbie declares she will do nothing of the kind for a long time but she may be induced to bow to *'destiny.'* I hope you will be able to come home this winter. If you do, perhaps you will be able to carry her back with you.

"I am glad you saved some of your 'golden locks.' You know you promised me one (or at least I *asked* for it) and did not give it to me. I could weep (tears of vexation) at the downfall of your hair and Jacob's beard, *'Ichabod!'* Love to Jacob."[14]

The exchange of letters continued. Autie tried to convince Libbie an early marriage was desirable and that early winter would be ideal. Realizing the intimate friendship that existed between Libbie and Nettie could be useful, he tried to secure the latter's assistance to convert Libbie to his way of thinking. Better yet if she could be convinced she should join him in Virginia after the wedding. The insistence, the repetition of the request, soon wore away the resistance, first of Nettie, then of Libbie. Autie was able to write to Nettie:

"I am glad you incline to my way of thinking in regard to my little girl coming to the army this winter. Why shouldn't she? I have been earnestly pleading with her in my last letters to tell me when I can come for her. I can come whenever she bids me do so. . . . You know if I don't come this winter, it is not probable that I shall be granted a leave before next winter. Cannot you *threaten* her, or use your influence to induce her to do as she *ought?* If I was there, how I would talk to her! She would be glad to say yes to get rid of me. . . ."[15]

Early in December Custer advised the Judge that he was mailing a large colored photograph to him to be placed in Libbie's room as a surprise just prior to Christmas. This, Judge Bacon advised Custer, he was more than happy to do as he could anticipate the strength of her hugs when first she saw it.

"You cannot at your age in life realize the feelings of a parent," he divulged, "when called upon to give up and give away an only offspring. I feel I have kept you in suspense quite too long, and yet when you consider my affection and desire for her happiness you will pardon me for this unreasonable delay. I feel too that I have no right to impositions on my daughter requiring her to remain single to marry and settle near me that I may enjoy the pleasure of her company the little time left me, or to make choice for her. I have too much regard for her present and future happiness for which I have lived.

"Your explanatory and excellent letter, a full, free and personal interview with our reliable and mutual friend Col. Winans, to say nothing of incidental interviews with Judge Christiancy, Col. Grosvenor and others, as well as letters from the Potomac independent of interviews will, as well as the wishes of my daughter, perfectly reconcile me to yield my hearty spirit to the contemplated occasion.

"I may add further that as present advised you are the object of my choice. I would feel perhaps more gratified if you were a possessor of the Christian religion, but it would ill become me to require such at your hands, when I consider at your age my morals and my future were far short of what you are now.

"As a Michigan man I cannot but feel gratified at your wellearned reputation which is now fully established, and your last act in keeping so large an army in check for so long a period may be looked upon as your greatest military achievement.

"It will not be impossible for me to say at this time that I am not a wealthy man. My property is mostly real estate, its sale and price depending on unseen contingencies.

"I secured to Elizabeth's mother in her lifetime my homestead. This by the laws of descent is hers subject to my occupancy during my lifetime. I also secured to her a few hundred dollars that she might not be dependent on me and this I treat as any other indebtedness which will be mainly absorbed in her outfit as the wife of a General. Beyond this she may never be the recipient of another dollar but circumstances occurring ever so favorable, she would not have a patrimony at my death exceeding $10,000."[16]

Several days later Autie received a letter from his sister Ann. She told of having her picture taken at Wing's studio on Front Street and meeting Annie Darrah, John Bulkley and Libbie Bacon there. Hearing that Custer had had two taken there, she wondered who the other one was for.

She, having a bit of the reformer in her makeup, could not miss the opportunity to advise him, "If you give it to a stranger there will be hard feelings among some of the folks." Knowing he would read her letter to the very end, she continued:

"I am willing to give you up to another. I do hope and pray that you will be a better and happier man. I am not acquainted with Libbie but believe she is a good girl and will make you a good wife. . . . I do hope your best days are coming, and let me caution you to be saving and try to lay something aside for yourself. Monroe folks will have something to talk about, but there is some good folks in Monroe."[17]

Ann had some additional thoughts about the photographs after she had posted the letter. She wasn't one to waste a lot of paper with fancy prose. Using a half sheet she began as if adding a footnote to the letter she had mailed the previous day: "I am afraid if you give it to Judge Christiancy, Col. Winan's folks will think hard of it and you know they are warm friends of yours. You have a good many warm friends in Monroe and I fear if you give the Judge such a nice picture the rest will feel slighted. Maggie starts school Monday."[18]

Libbie could be a tease at times. General Pleasonton, according to Autie, had been suggesting he had to contend with many rivals. Libbie insisted that the General had underestimated the number of men courting her. There was a prominent Chicago attorney—with a long, dyed beard—who invited her to a concert. There was Francis Chandler who liked her, and the likeable Elliot Bates, and John Rauch, of course, who would bring her nuts and candy. "Ah, if only gentlemen know how ladies can be won!"

Then, as if realizing she had been flippant, she wrote, "Do not think me immodest. Had these gentlemen put into words what it may be they desire I should not treat the matter so lightly.

But then a very important letter arrived at Autie's headquarters. After reading it he sat down and addressed a letter to Libbie:

"Your letter, the dearest of all, dated the 14th awaited me on my return this evening from General Pleasonton's where I had been spending the day. How can I find language expressive of my joy and thankfulness upon reading your consent to yield to my entreaties and becoming my darling wife? I am so supremely happy that I can scarcely write, my thoughts go wandering from one subject to another so rapidly that it is with difficulty that I return one long enough to transfer it to paper. Am I not dreaming? Surely such unalloyed pleasure never before was enjoyed by mortal man.

"Words seem weak, powerless, when I attempt to describe my heartfelt joy. I will wait until I see you, for then I can make up in action what language fails to make clear. In one full loving embrace I can testify more clearly than in words the ecstasy I feel at this moment. Everything seems propitious.

"I returned to my headquarters this evening intending to write to you tonight informing you that circumstances here would prevent me from spending Chirstmas with you but that I should see you before New Years. I had been talking with Gen. Pleasonton about *our* affairs.

"Your last letter had led me to believe that we would be married *before* next winter, the precise time was not mentioned. I presume that I would be expected to pass the holidays with you, then return to the Army and in a short time, again visit Monroe, this time claim my darling gypsie bride. The difficulty with which Gen. Pleasonton and I labored was how to obtain the *second* leave of absence from Gen. Meade. We deemed it very uncertain, at any rate I could only have received 15 days each time but you dear girl come to my rescue by sending me the sweet and gratifying intelligence that I might soon come and claim my beloved and further, that you would accompany me back to my Army home. Thank you darling. You do indeed deserve a kiss and how gladly I will give it when I see you.

"Now then, to be practical I can bring Jacob (Greene) home with me and expect to bring all the members of my staff. I am confident that I can obtain a leave of 30 days 'owing to the peculiar circumstances of the case.'

"You did not tell me what day in February your father's wedding occurred nor did you say positively that that would be *the* day. I hope it was early in the month. Supposing that I receive a leave of 30 days. How many days do you wish me to be in Monroe before our marriage? Remember, I would like to visit my friends, also spend a very short time in Ohio. I think it would be *short* as possible. But it is necessary that I should know the *exact* day as soon as possible in order to arrange it in reference to my leave and the leave for Jacob and the others. There will be quite a number of officers present. Where is Conway Noble now or at least what is his address?

"We must not forget our wedding cards. I wish you could be with me in Washington to select the style and I think it advisable to obtain them there rather than at Detroit. Perhaps I can obtain specimens and send them to you for your selection.

"Libbie, upon which finger did you wear the ring you gave me?

"I am real glad that you mentioned Conway as he first introduced us to each other. Of course we couldn't get along without Jacob. I agree perfectly with you as to the bridesmaids. They are the very persons I would have desired. How pleasant you have arranged it.

"I wrote to my sister this evening informing her of our intended marriage and telling her to mention it to none except my parents. You mustn't fail to call on my sister and parents also. If you call on Mrs. Reed first she would be glad to accompany you to my mother's and it would be less embarrassing for you. I wish I could be there to accompany you.

"Won't the good people of Monroe 'gossip' when it becomes known that Libbie Bacon is no longer Libbie Bacon by somebody else? I wonder what Miss FF will say? Probably that she knew of it long ago.

"I received such an excellent long letter from your father this evening. How kindly he wrote to me and how encouraging his words. What do you think he told me darling? Nothing more nor less than that I was *'the object of his choice!'* Would you believe it? I will let you see the letter sometime. I will write you tomorrow if possible. Pardon the brevity of this letter, it is unavoidable. Good night *my little wife*. I will soon come to you. Armstrong."[19]

The next week dragged for Custer. No word to indicate what the family reaction had been. It took at least two days for a letter to travel each way but the impatient lover couldn't wait it out. On the 22nd he wrote to his sister Ann to see how his family and more particularly how his mother reacted to the news. Unable to pass up an opportunity of joshing anyone, he told her to "tell Pap I forgot to get his consent."[20]

On the 23rd Libbie wrote to her "Beloved Star" expressing her happiness over finding his new photograph in her room. It had reminded her that Autie was to be shorn for their wedding. She asked him to save his golden curls from the barber, adding teasingly "when I'm old I'll have a wig made from them."[21]

The afternoons were being passed in hopeful waiting by Libbie. It had been a lonely Christmas without him but he had helped her immensely with his letters. It had become a ritual with him to end each day with a long letter to her, a ritual he maintained afterward whenever they were separated.

Her father habitually stopped at the post office after closing his office for the day, the mail carrying train from Toledo having arrived shortly before that. On December 27th (?) she wrote: "My dearest Armstrong, I believe you would love me a little if you knew how I say, afternoons, 'Half-past four—Letter *please* arrive!'"[22]

On the 27th, Libbie was able to tell Autie Christmas was nice though not merry. Before church Fannie, in elegant new furs, had called on her for the apparent purpose of seeing what Autie had given her as a Christmas gift. Libbie made no move to tell her.

She had asked Nettie afterward, "Is Libbie's diamond larger than mine?"

Nettie replied, "Did Libbie say it was a ring?"

Then Fannie continued, "Is General Custer engaged to be married?"

Several of the boys, John Bulkley being one of them, stopped over at Nettie's on Christmas day, tight. Nettie voiced her disapproval and Libbie hers when she wrote, "Oh, it is shocking. Both old enough to know better and to have fixed principles. My dearest, if you are not already repaid for your abstinence, my pride in you would repay you."

Someone had told Judge Bacon that General Kilpatrick used an oath in every sentence and that General Custer was nearly as bad. Libbie thought this a stain on Autie's character and was not hesitant in telling him so. She said, "I know this is exaggerated. But . . . God cure you of it."

She admitted, "Religion is a part of my life. It is hard to give up my place in church. But thankful I am that I am marrying a man who, though not professing religion, is not an unbeliever."[23]

On the 29th, Judge Christiancy wrote Custer that he was happy to see he would marry "one of the best girls in the city." But there was more on his mind than the wedding. His son Jim, now on Custer's staff, had become the greatest trial of his life. In an act of friendship Custer had agreed to help Jim stay away from liquor. Periodically he had given Judge Christiancy a progress report. In response the Judge remarked: "I am glad to hear you speak encouragingly of him. I love the boy as well as I do any of my children. But until he makes up his mind not to taste a drop of intoxicating liquor (except as medicine) I do not want to see him.

"He has done too much to disgrace himself and his family and he comes here without fully resolving to abstain from liquor and keep out of drinking saloons. . . . I shall feel that he is received and shall treat him as an abandoned reprobate and no son of mine. But if he behaves himself like a gentleman as he is capable of doing there is no person I could like to see better.

"He must know by this time that liquor is to be his name unless he at once abandons it. And I hope you will not permit him to come home with you till he has given his solemn pledge not to drink or frequent bawdy houses. I am under great obligation to you for the care you have taken of him and the influence you have exerted over him in this respect. I fear he will not appreciate your kindness as he ought."[24]

Unfortunately this was not the end of the Judge's troubles with his son Jim, though it was the end of another year. For Libbie it was a time of joy and anticipation. Together on New Year's Eve as had been their custom for some years, Libbie and Nettie sat on the floor of Libbie's room writing notes to each other after having opened at midnight those they had written the previous December 31st. On the envelope of the new note, each wrote, "Break not this seal at your peril until December 31, 1864."

After reaffirming her great admiration and friendship, and expressing her happiness over Libbie's love for Autie, Nettie wrote, "Shall we ever spend such another New Year's Eve together?"[25]

NOTES—CHAPTER 10

[1]Libbie must mean Captain Eugene B. Beaumont, 4th U.S. Cavalry, and Aide-de-Camp.
[2]The aforegoing was from the EBC Journal.
[3]Merington, pp. 71-72.
[4]Letter of October 26, 1863, in BCWC collection.
[5]Letter of October 27, 1863, in BCWC collection.
[6]Monroe *Monitor,* October 28, 1863. Letter dated October 20, 1863 at Gainsville, Va.
[7]Merington, pp. 71-72.
[8]Merington, p. 71, in obvious error, dated a letter Custer wrote to Nettie as November 1, 1863, in which he tells of his first direct letter to Libbie. Whittaker, p. 215, indicated erroneously that Custer had no consent until late in November. Libbie, in her Journal entry of November 8, 1863, proclaims that her father's affirmative reply should be in Custer's hands on November 9th. The Merington letter referred to should be dated November 10.
[9]November 12, 1863, O.R. Vol. XXIX, Pt. II, Series I, p. 448.
[10]Charles D. Rhodes: *History of the Cavalry of the Army of the Potomac, Kansas City, Mo., 1900, pp. 74-75.*
[11]Letter of November 22, 1863, in BCWC collection.
[12]Monaghan, p. 172, O.R. Vol. XXIX, Pt. I, p. 811, November 26, 1863.
[13]Rhodes, pp. 93-94; Monroe *Commercial,* December 3, 1863; Monaghan, pp. 172-173.
[14]Letter of November 26, 1863, in BCWC collection.
[15]Whittaker, p. 216.
[16]Letter of December 12, 1863, in BCWC collection.
[17]Letter of December 14, 1863, in BCWC collection.
[18]Letter of December 15, 1863, in BCWC collection.
[19]Letter of December 17, 1863, in BCWC collection.
[20]Letter of December 22, 1863, in EBC files, Custer Battlefield.
[21]Merrington, pp. 74-75. This letter of December 27th must be wrong. Libbie writes as if the wedding date was to be a year away, and in the hope he would be home for the holidays. Obviously it was written prior to Christmas and Autie's letter of December 17th.
[22]Merington, pp. 76-77. This letter was written on a Sunday so probably was written on December 27 rather than 26.
[23]Letter of December 29, 1863, in BCWC collection.
[24]Note in author's file written by Nettie to Libbie, December 31, 1863.
[25]*Ibid.*

CHAPTER 11
ARMY WIFE

Jacob M. Howard[1] of Michigan served on the U. S. Senate's Committee on Military Affairs. The committee, in its considerations, had before it a number of officers recommended for advancement and confirmation by the Senate. Custer was among them. He had been appointed a brigadier general by Secretary of War Stanton as of June 29, 1863. The appointment would not be confirmed by the United States Senate until its Committee on Military Affairs presented it with its recommendation.

A Washington friend had written to advise Custer that both Howard and Michigan Senator Zachariah Chandler opposed his confirmation on the grounds that he was not a Michigan resident. Should they vote for him it would deprive a Michigan man of the appiontment.[2]

This may have been argument in the committee meetings but more than likely it was known that his father was an active Democrat and he was a strong "McClellan man."

Custer knew that Secretary of War Stanton, though from Cadiz, Ohio, was a Democrat. He might help but such help could be harmful. Judge Christiancy, on the other hand, was a Republican well up in Michigan politics. The senators from Michigan would listen to him with respect.

On January 4, 1864, Custer wrote to Senator Howard reminding him they had met in Detroit in the fall of 1863 and that the senator had offered his aid at any time. He understood that he was being objected to on the basis of his extreme youth and because it was thought that older men desired and should have the position. He asked him to contact Major General Pleasonton "asking him to give his opinion as to my merit and ability, also to mention my services." He then requested that the senator use his influence in his behalf.[3]

Several days later he wrote to Judge Christiancy informing him of the situation and that Pleasonton had advised him to obtain all of the political influence available. Time was growing short. Custer wanted to meet his wedding date with the assurance he would remain a brigadier general of volunteers. How else could he be certain that he could maintain Libbie in the manner to which she was accustomed? Certainly not on a captain's pay.[4]

An encouraging letter from Judge Christiancy soon arrived. And on January 19th he responded to Senator Howard's letter of the 16th which afforded him the opportunity of giving a brief expression of his "views regarding the war policy of the Administration." Howard had made it evident that Custer's feelings for McClellan politically were of more concern to the committee than his own abilities or contributions as a soldier.

Custer, as in one of his charges, went right to the focal point:

"Having, at an early age, adopted the profession of arms, I have never deemed it proper or advisable to assume an active part in politics. I have endeavored to be a soldier and not a politician. So far has this sentiment controlled me that, at the last presidential election, of the three candidates who were nominated for the presidency I never expressed nor entertained a preference for either.

"The President of the United States as Commander in Chief of the Army and as my superior officer cannot issue any decree or order which will not receive my unqualified *support.* This much would, to me, *as a soldier,* be my duty, but I do not stop there. I do not merely tender my support of the war measures of the President, but all his acts, proclamations and decisions embraced in his war policy have received not only my support but my most hearty, earnest and cordial *approval.* And furthermore I am convinced upon every principal of reason and by the light of experience, that it is only by the adoption and execution of the present policy of the President that we can help to establish and secure an *honorable* and *lasting* peace.

"I seldom discuss political questions but my friends who have heard me can testify that I have insisted that so long as a single slave was held in bondage, I for one, was opposed to peace on any terms, and to show that my acts agree with my words I can boast of having liberated more slaves from their masters than any other general in this Army. This is a fact which can be verified by referring to Maj. Gen. Pleasonton and a host of other officers.

"As to 'compromise,' I know of no compromise with rebels by which we could retain our dignity and self respect as a nation of freemen. If I could decide the question, I would offer no compromise except that which is offered at the point of a bayoonet.

". . . with regard to the coming presidential election I say frankly that I am not committed to any one man, but that of all that I have been prominently spoken of for the position I know of none who would in my estimation conduct the affairs of government as ably and successfully as Mr. Lincoln for the past three years.

"I regret Mr. Howard that it has become necessary to defend myself from such slanderous charges. . . .

"I will now explain how and why the rumors arose which have reached you, to the effect, that I was an appointment of the Administration. I was promoted and appointed on the staff of Gen. McClellan for an act of gallantry, and at a time when I was almost a total stranger with McClellan he having seen me but *twice* before and never had spoken twenty words to me. During the time McClellan was in command I, *as any soldier would,* supported him, but I have never allowed my personal obligation to him for his kindness and favor toward me, interfere with my duty. . . .

"The real reason why this charge has been brought against me is simply for the lack of some other. There are those who desire to see me defeated and no effort has been spared to bring influences to bear with you and Hon. Z. Chandler to prejudice my case. My conduct in the field has afforded these enemies no opportunity to defame or injure me and as a last hope they have chosen the one more lacking in truth and correctness than any other which they could bring."[5]

Libbie, with all of the unreasonableness that can spring from a woman certain of her conquest, continued to dally in setting her wedding date. Custer's convenience or problems seemed not to matter. She had appeared to capitulate when she gave up plans for the following winter and settled on February 23rd. This was a huge concession in her way of thinking. In Autie's it meant a very short honeymoon since he had to be back well ahead of a campaign planned for the first of April. Admonishingly he wrote, "My own loved little one, do dispense with some of your superfluous preparation."[6]

"Father," she replied, "says I ought not to keep Armstrong waiting. . . . My preparations are not elaborate, only for the bridal tour and the summer in Washington, but they will tax Mother to the utmost."

Mother Bacon had said to Libbie, "It's just what we might have expected. February. But I'm afraid you'll have to yield to him, though I don't see how it's possible."

"But Mother," she protested, "if I yield now to such teasing I shall always have to do so."

"No, no," she advised, "for I consented to hasten my own wedding because my former husband Mr. Pitts insisted on it. . . . And I always had my own way afterwards in Everything!"

On Sunday, January 10th, Autie wrote Libbie two letters, the last being the third in 24 hours. Displaying his anxiety because of the anticipated move of the army early in April, he noted that this letter was "one more final desperate and reasonable attempt to induce my darling to name an early date for our marriage. . . ."[7]

Libbie had advised her cousin Rebecca Richmond in Grand Rapids of the impending wedding. She told her of her wedding plans for the next winter, then the change to February because "Armstrong pleaded so urgently."

In describing his character she wrote, "I do not say Armstrong is without faults. But he never tastes liquor, nor frequents the gaming table, and though not a professing Christian yet respects religion."[8]

It became apparent that Libbie weakened a bit. Rebecca made a notation in her diary on January 14th that she had received a letter from Libbie the day before advising her that the wedding day had been changed from the 23rd to the 10th of February. "She is very urgent for me to be present and wishes me to be one of the bridesmaids, four in all: viz., Laura Noble, Nettie Humphrey, Annah Darrah and 'Bess' (Rebecca Richmond). 'Bess' replied this morning, declining the proposed honor of bridesmaid, but accepting the invitation to be present."[9]

Libbie had other ideas, too. Sending to New York for her silks, she went to Detroit to have her dresses made and her "underclothes made on a machine," quite a novelty at that time.

She had changed her mind about not wanting ostentation. She let it be known she wanted an evening wedding, and in church. Autie was to wear his full-dress uniform for he had indicated his entire staff would be present. And dear Mr. Boyd should perform the ceremony—"You are willing, are you not?"—having been Libbie's friend so long.

Almost defying tradition, she planned a pea green silk wedding dress to the top of her gaiters, looped with yellow military braid. The veil would be of green silk, and her corsage of red roses would be tied with a yellow cord. So she described her dress to Autie. But perhaps she was teasing him for at the wedding she wore the traditional white.[10]

Late in January Senators Chandler and Howard and Congressman William Kellogg had taken Custer's side in the issue regarding his confirmation hearings. Having no fear of his promotion being defeated now, he could travel to Monroe with but one thought in mind. He admitted to Judge Bacon the matter had caused him no little anxiety and that he had not written to him about it for fear of upsetting Libbie.

He had been surprised at the persistence of the men attempting to defame him but he had trusted to time for vindication. It had been learned that he had been charged with being a "copperhead", but this had been disproved to his satisfaction.

Near the end of January, Custer and his staff set off for Monroe. Judge Bacon had wanted the wedding to be on his own wedding anniversary, February 23rd. Realistically he had withdrawn his request and the date had been moved up to the 9th.

It was a three-day trip from the brigade camp to Monroe. Relief from the routine of winter camp and the anticipation of the festivities ahead had everyone keyed up. There was little sleep on the way but that was not unusual for cavalrymen. They had learned to get it in the form of cat naps. In this they emulated the master of the technique for Custer employed it regularly.

On the way to Monroe Tom Custer joined the party. It had been four and a half years since the brothers had seen each other. Autie had been home on his vacation from West Point in the summer of 1859 at which time Tom was a stripling of 14.

Tom, now tall, brown-haired, broad shouldered and blue-eyed, was a Custer through and through. His uniform sleeves displayed the stripes of a corporal and his kepi the insignia of the 21st Ohio Infantry, an outfit he had joined at the age of 16. He exhibited the same Custer restlessness and energy.

Autie hardly recognized him. Learning that Tom had not been home since he enlisted, a plan was immediately formulated to pass him off at home as Major Drew.

Once home, Tom was introduced as Major Drew to everyone including his father. No one recognized him. Mother Custer thoroughly enjoyed the deception, having been informed who he was immediately upon their arrival. She particularly enjoyed the mystification of his older brother Nevin.[11]

Nevin Custer was the only one of the three older brothers who remained at home and farmed during the war. He had responded to the call for volunteers but he had been rejected at the Cleveland recruiting office because of his chronic rheumatism.[12]

Monroe was in a hubbub. It was winter and there was snow on the ground, a good time for cutters and bobsleds. The village hadn't had as much excitement since the River Raisin massacre 50 years earlier. The news of the unusual wedding visitors had passed around quickly enough so there was a sizeable crowd at the railway depot to greet them.

THE BRIDE WAS LIBBIE BACON. The ceremony took place in Monroe's Presbyterian Church, February 9, 1864, at 6 p.m. Rev. Boyd, assisted by the Rev. D. C. Mattoon, officiated. Col. Charles Custer collection.

Members of the staff accompanying Custer included such Monroe boys as George Yates, Jim Christiancy and Jacob Greene.[13] Greene had little interest in the crowd; Nettie Humphrey was there and that was enough for him.

All of the party were driven to the Custer house where they greeted Autie's family.[14] The well-built house literally shook from the activities of the merrymakers.

Autie, having seen his family and having indulged in the usual civilities of introducing his staff to the numerous neighbors and friends who dropped in to greet him in an almost continuous stream, impatiently steered his party toward the door and the cutters outside for he had been waiting a long time to see Libbie.

Around the corner they drove down Monroe Street to the Bacon home. The Judge was at the door when they arrived. One can well imagine the scene when Autie, lean and tan, threw his arms around Libbie who stood beside her father, her cheeks redder than usual, her eyes filled with stars. This was the first of many such moments for there was to be a lifetime of partings and meetings.

Emanuel Custer had taken the events in stride. In December he had broken down and wept when he learned that Autie was about to marry. He felt he could hardly give Autie up he was so dependent upon him.[15]

Emanuel was property poor. He owned a farm of 80 acres on the Tontogony Creek Road about a mile north of Tontogony in Wood County, Ohio,[16] from whence he had moved to Monroe to live with the Reeds. It was not until August, 1865, that he sold it, realizing $3,000 on his original investment of $2,000[17] — a profit of $1,000.

Nevin farmed just a mile north of Emanuel's property during the same period of time, moving his family to Monroe just after the war. David Kirkpatrick, a son by his mother's first marriage, remained a resident of Wood County much longer.[18]

Ann Reed thought her father in such dire straits financially that she appealed to Autie to give hin $20 for an overcoat. He needed it badly, and moreso if Autie expected him to go to church for the wedding. She indicated in her letter that the Custer family was more opposed to his getting married than she was. She gave no reason for this opposition. One might obtain a slight lead into their thinking from the concluding lines of her letter: "I think they all love Libbie and all things will be right. Your paw says you are the only child he could depend on for help."[19]

Pressed as he was financially, Autie sent Ann the $20 for "Paw" Custer shortly before Christmas. On February 2nd she wrote Autie: "Grandpa was very much pleased when I gave him the money and told him you sent it to get him an overcoat. He says he needs a dress coat very much . . . . Our folks seem to feel much better about your getting married than they did at first. I told them I thought they would like Libbie.

"Nevin said he had a letter from you and was perfectly surprised to hear of the matter. None of the family seemed to think you was going to get married for a number of years."[20]

Though Libbie had a head start, Monroe folks were not long in preparing for the wedding. There were receptions, teas and visitations, and the usual gossip. Not to be outdone, the military members of the community took a hand. A committee consisting of Colonels Luce and Clark, Captain Greene and General Humphrey organized a complimentary party for the evening of Friday, February 5th, to be held at the Humphrey house. Tickets were issued to limit the attendance.[21]

All went well at the wedding. The Presbyterian Church that Tuesday evening of February 9th was filled to overflowing, standing room in the aisles and vestibule being fully occupied.

Soon after 6 P.M. the bridal party reached the church, the bride leaning on the arm of her father passing down the east aisle of the church while the groom with the bride's mother passed down the west aisle. Each was preceded by a bridesmaid and groomsman. It was with some difficulty that they made their way down the crowded aisles to reach the altar.

The Reverend Erasmus J. Boyd, Principal of the Young Ladies Seminary, assisted by the Reverend D. C. Mattoon, performed the short though traditional ceremony. The bride was given away by her father.

The bridesmaids, Nettie Humphrey, Anna Darrah and Marie Miller, with the groomsmen, Captain Jacob Greene, Conway Noble and John Bulkley, escorted them to the Bacon residence where there was a reception from 7 until 10 P.M.[22]

The Bacon residence was pressed for space, some 300 people making an appearance at the reception. Of particular interest to the women was the large display of wedding gifts, the principal one being a six-piece silver tea service consisting of a teapot, coffeepot, water urn, sugarbowl, creamer and a slop bowl; a pitcher, waiter, two goblets, castor, cake basket, pair of salt dishes and a berry spoon, all presented by the officers of 1st Vermont Cavalry. All of a Grecian pattern, they were engraved with the word "Custer." A companion present, an eight-piece solid silver tea set, was presented by the officers of the 7th Michigan Cavalry.

At midnight the four couples of the bridal party took the train to Cleveland, arriving there at nine in the morning where they stopped off at the Waddell House. That afternoon Charles Noble gave them a reception and then a party at his home. It was not until the following morning that the newlyweds left for Buffalo.

Several days after the wedding, Judge Bacon wrote to his sister Charity that he was satisfied with the way everything had gone, including his own behavior. He had feared he might act the role of a baby when parting with Libbie but had schooled himself so that he hadn't.

An added fear was that of burglary. The Bacons and their house guests, Rebecca Richmond and Mrs. Bacon's niece Mrs. Baggs of Detroit, were kept awake the rest of the wedding night because of false burglar alarms. The following morning the Judge carried all of the silver to the bank for safe keeping. That evening the tired family was in bed by seven o'clock.

Rebecca Richmond hadn't met Autie until her sojurn to Monroe for the wedding. In writing to her sister Mary a lengthy feminine version of it, in contrast to the short and unimaginative one the Judge wrote to his sister, she told her that none of them had been favorably impressed with Autie prior to being introduced to him. Somewhere they had obtained the impression he was foppish and conceited and put on airs. After meeting him she was "most agreeably disappointed," finding him simple, frank and manly. Everyone had been immediately taken with his personality.

She described Libbie as wearing "a rich white rep silk with deep points and extensive trail, bertha of point lace; veil floated back from a bunch of orange blossoms fixed above the brow." The trousseau consisted of a large variety of dresses and included "a waterproof with armholes, buttoned from head to foot," and an opera cloak white merino, silk lined, that included a silk hood.[23]

High-minded Judge Bacon, in keeping with his principles, had given Libbie a copy of the Holy Scriptures to take with them as a token of his affection in the hope that it would be her companion in camp or in the field. An additional gift was a watch as a further testimonial of love and affection. To Autie they gave their dearest possession, Libbie.[24]

From Buffalo the newlyweds went on to Onondaga, stopping off in Rochester just long enough to enjoy a play. The production was *Uncle Tom's Cabin* based on Harriet Beecher Stowe's book by the same name.

Libbie's Aunt Charity and Uncle Oren Smith welcomed them to their home at Onondaga where they visited during several days of inclement weather. On Monday they made their way toward Howlett Hill and Camillus and the scenes of Libbie's childhood visits to the Bacon lineal descendants.

It was as they were packing Libbie's wardrobe prior to leaving Onondaga, and following a display to her relatives and friends, that Autie became enmeshed in a hoop skirt. Libbie had called for assistance in packing and Autie, anxious to please her but unskilled in handling the gadgets on women's clothing, became so tangled he had to cry out for help. One of the assisting women cried out "Surrender?" while the others laughed hysterically. He had no other recourse but to comply.

Soon they left, everyone waving handkerchiefs. Libbie responded by waving Autie's hat until the hatband fell off, to add to the merriment.

At Camillus they were met by Libbie's Aunt Eliza and Uncle Denison Sabin. Once in the Sabin home at Howlett Hill they were greeted by her many relatives, among them the cousins she had spent such pleasurable hours with her in her childhood.

NEWLYWEDS. The bridal party took the train for Cleveland at midnight to attend another reception the following evening. Courtesy of Monroe County Historical Museum.

Cousin George played his fiddle in the big kitchen of the farmhouse while everyone danced. Uncle Den and Aunt Eliza had started the dancing in the old-fashioned manner they had known from youth. Their bounding up and down so amused Libbie she had to sit down and laugh before she fell down from doing so.

On their way to New York City the newlyweds made a stop at West Point. The river was frozen solid when they got off the train so the ferry was not running. A husky man pulled Libbie across the Hudson River on a sled while Autie pushed from behind.

At the Military Academy he was greeted as a distinguished alumnus. Everyone was most cordial, even the dogs, for they seemed to remember him. When Autie was engaged in conversation with some of the instructors and left Libbie for a time, the cadets showered Libbie with attention, showing her the many points of interest which included Lovers' Walk. One old professor claimed, quite openly, the privilege of kissing the bride.

Later, on the train to New York, Autie vehemently made evident his disapproval of the attentions she received from the male element at the Academy. After his display of jealousy and her fearful protest, she managed to reproach him by saying, "Well, you left me with them, Autie!" And so he had.[25]

Their address in New York was the Metropolitan Hotel, a fine old hotel "where the cadets came after graduation to have their formal banquet before separating." It was here that Autie stayed while assisting McClellan with his reports in the spring of 1863.[26]

The Judge, who was a believer in phrenology, had asked Autie to visit the phrenologists Fowler and Wells in New York City. Libbie said that the professor who made the examination had not the slightest idea of the identity of his client. She supposed that they both provided every evident sign of newlyweds—"newness of clothes, consciousness of the event, exuberance of manner—the General's face an open book." Once the examination had been completed Professor Fowler addressed Autie as follows:

"You should always avoid overdoing. It is as natural for you to overdo as it is for birds to spread their wings when they feel in a hurry, and it makes little difference what your business is, you would contrive somehow to overdo at it. You make work of pleasure. If you were an overworked citizen and went to the country to rusticate for a month in the summer, you would get up all sorts of enterprises, and excursions to mountain tops, romantic ravines, fishing grounds and what not; and you would blister your hands with rowing and your feet with tramping, and your face with unaccustomed exposure to sunshine, and you would be a sort of captain-general of all such things. If you were an army officer and in active service, you would get as much work out of a horse as General Custer or Phil Sheridan would, that is to say, as much as the horse could render. If you were running a machine, that machine would have to go a few turns faster than machines of that sort are generally run."[27]

Their stay in New York was short. From the moment of their arrival telegrams were handed to Custer asking when he could return to his brigade. They became increasingly urgent. Finally, in Washington, came the order to join the Army of the Potomac by a certain date.

"Washington was bewildering and delightful to me," Libbie noted. "The city was made gay from having so many troops. The corridors of the hotels were full of officers on leave in shining new uniforms for few wore civilian clothes.

"There were camps all around the city and the bugle calls were mixed in with the other sounds of town life. I do not believe my husband was loth to leave for there was danger being classified with those who by every kind of subterfuge and personal influence strove to escape returning to their regiments or commands.

"Senator Chandler (of Michigan) said that some one attempted to throw a stone across Pennsylvania Avenue and it hit five brigadiers, and I remember years later that the habit of officers loitering around Washington seeking some 'featherbed duty,' as it was termed, was brought home to one of them at a dinner where a French woman was taunting a colonel whose regiment was in the field and finally silenced him completely by saying, 'Ah, Gen-e-*ral,* it is up and down Pennsylvania Avenue that you would chase the *Eendeen* (Indian).' "[28]

Though Libbie was quite impressed with the distinguished Congressmen and Senators she met at several dinners they were invited to, she remembered more distinctly her chagrin when overturning a wine glass on one of them.

Libbie had never been permitted to see a play as a girl. The newlyweds had stopped in Buffalo on their way East purposely so that she could see one for the first time. Her second had been seen at Rochester. It was natural enough for the two, while in Washington, to take in the melodrama *East Lynn.* She had discovered that her husband "laughed at the fun and cried at the pathos in the theatres with all the abandon of a boy unconscious of surroundings."

As a result of her involvement in the first act of the melodrama her lace handkerchief with its tiny cambric center became a sodden rag. Turning to Autie to beg for his handkerchief, she found him red-faced from weeping. He handed his damp handkerchief to her and said, "Don't keep it long, Libbie. I need it."[29]

The Michigan Cavalry Brigade was camped near Stevensburg, a small town about five miles south of Brandy Station, Virginia. Custer took Libbie with him but under his protest. He believed she would be safer and more comfortable in Washington. She believed not. She had known only a sheltered home where she had been spared all anxieties and cares. Stevensburg was at the extreme wing of the Army of the Potomac, almost on the firing line. There might be long periods of time Autie would not be near her but she would be content if only to see him for the time in between. Willingly he acceded. He had found it was futile to argue and unwise to command.[30]

The three upstairs rooms of a farmhouse serving as their living quarters were meagerly furnished with a few camp articles and some furniture loaned by the Virginia family who occupied a portion of the ground floor.[31] The house was used as a headquarters, the staff living in tents in the garden and the brigade some distance away.

It was here Libbie met the members of her household staff, the waif by the name of Johnny Cisco Autie had adopted to care for his horses, and a Negress cook named Eliza.

Eliza had joined "The Ginnel" as she called him at Amosville, Rappahannock County, Virginia, in August, 1863. Custer, then a fledgling general with a staff of his own, prepared to adopt Pleasanton's habit of hiring a Negress cook to handle his mess. There was an abundance of such contraband to select from, many having left their plantations to seek the new freedom endowed them by Lincoln and his army.

In search of a woman well-qualified to handle food often scrounged as well as rationed, General Custer and Captain Farnham Lyon walked up to Eliza. Custer asked, "What's your name?"

"Eliza," she replied.

"Well, Eliza, would you like to come and live with me?"

She looked him over a full minute then replied, "I reckon I would."

She was lonesome at first and afraid of everything connected with the war, often wishing she was back on the plantation with her mother. It was a happy day when "Miss Libbie" arrived for there were weeks on end in which she didn't see a single female.

Eliza was cognizant of a color distinction in her own race, having no part of those suitors—of which she had many—who were dark of skin. Of one such suitor she said, "Why, Miss Libbie, he needn't think to shine up to me; he's nothing but a black African."

Once, in 1865, Eliza stood in front of a bronze medallion of the General, then said, "Why, Ginnel, they have made you jest my color," this to his great amusement.

In age she possibly was in her mid-thirties though Libbie, when they first met, thought her older. In reminiscing later, Libbie believed she thought her so because Eliza mothered and comforted her in her loneliness.

Many Negroes had accepted emancipation and moved into the Northern cities. Eliza elected to see the war to the end. As she commented, "I didn't set down to have 'em all free me. I helped to free myself." There is no doubt she did, and when the war ended she had commanded the respect of all the men and officers she had come in contact with.

FAITHFUL ELIZA. Liberated as a slave in Virginia, Eliza attached herself to Autie as his cook before he married Libbie, then continued to be their maid afterward. She traveled with them to Texas, Michigan and Kansas, before marrying a black attorney and retiring to Ohio. Custer Battlefield National Monument.

Though she admitted to fear, she was exceedingly courageous. Once captured by the enemy, she escaped and made her way back to camp after nightfall. Shellfire didn't disturb her while she was cooking a meal though it did force her, at times, to move her outdoor cookfire whenever a shell dropped close by. This she did begrudgingly because she considered it an inconvenience rather than a danger.[32]

Eliza began to "mammy" Libbie as soon as they arrived and she criticized Autie whenever the chance arose for she could hardly believe that at his age he could make a model husband of himself without her guidance. Eliza became such an important member of the family that the Custers believed they were blessed with her presence.

From the day Libbie arrived Eliza managed the Custers in a masterful manner and, though the General did not permit her to manage his Brigade, she had supreme control elsewhere.

Libbie, in wedding notes written years later, said of her:

"She accomplished everything by wheedling, some scolding that was not dangerous, and by as delicate diplomacy as many a subtle, deep-thinking person could have exercised. It was not necessary for me to learn to be a housekeeper as she was far more competent than I could ever be and beside my husband did not wish me to have care. My life was such a hard one for the years of privation and dangers that ensued that he considered that all my strength should be given to the taxing life of any woman who follows troops in the field.

"So Eliza had sole control of the kitchen and was most ingenious in getting something to eat when everyone else failed for there was no market and the plantations had been stripped by the foragers of both armies. She was so frugal in saving something if she thought we were going to camp where there would be no chance to get supplies when we were on the march, but she was frugal in nothing else.

"Her pocket was rarely without some money and when she got her handkerchief out a bill was very apt to tumble to the floor. She had no sense of the value of money but took it with some appreciative word if the officers gave it to her when she mended for them or took care of their uniforms.

"She could have made off with quite a little fortune after an expedition had started if she chanced to be left behind for everyone came and deposited their valuables with her. She had sleeve buttons, studs, watches, chains, rolls of bills, for officers rarely carry purses, and their valises and papers, and yet she covetted nothing apparently.

"My bridal finery was a delight to her and I have to thank her for confining her fancy to some of the plainer things for she had a way of admiring a garment right off one's back. She preferred clothes and finery that someone she liked had worn and I remember what an amount of stretching one of my gowns was subject to and how much Eliza expected from the buttons of the dress given her, for her plump proportions really needed more room than they were allowed.

"She had a very attractive face. Her voice was so soft and she had a way of putting so much affection and tenderness in it that it was a real rock-a-bye-baby sort of tone and you felt just as she wanted you to feel—as if you were a little child and had a nurse.

"Although this faithful creature directed and managed her new master and scolded when he was late to dinner or did not get up on wash days when she told him, and tho' he was very much superintended and advised how to care for me, corrected if she thought his shirt fronts were too mussed or the dogs allowed too much liberty lying on the bed—the white counterpane being her especial pride—she exacted from other servants and Johnnie all the deference for her 'Ginnel' that might be expected for a Czar of the Russias.

"The first meals in our Virginia house found Eliza opening the door to the room we used for dining to admit her small minion who carried on a tray as big as himself the dishes she had so carefully cooked for us over a very poor fire and in an improvised kitchen with only a camp outfit. Apparently she closed the door again but it was shut, as the darkies pull doors, with a crack left large enough to follow Johnnie with her watchful eye as he handed the food.

"When her embryo butler went to the kitchen, she took him to task for passing everything to my husband first—something I had not noticed—and said, 'Don't you know, Johnnie, that ladies has always to be helped first?"

"In apologizing for him afterward she said, 'And what do you think, Miss Libbie, that little, puny mite up and told me that he knew he was right for didn't the Ginnel have the most rank? Now, Miss Libbie, we don't know whar he cum from and he may belong to quality, but one thing sho', he don't have their manners.'"[33]

In defiance of convention Libbie had joined the troops at the front. At that time there was a feeling prevalent that a military camp was no place for ladies. Her arrival was the subject of a great deal of comment.

Prior to her arrival the presence of respectable women was almost unknown. There were a few noble, dedicated women like the sister of Senator Harris of New York, who took charge of front line hospitals as an errand of mercy.[34] More frequent were the camp followers who plied their trade openly or in the guise of laundresses. Annie Jones was another matter.

Annie Elinor Jones was not an ordinary camp follower. This intriguing young lady from Cambridge, Massachusetts, came to Washington with the 135th New York Infantry as a "daughter of the regiment." The War Department records now in the National Archives indicate that she was an orphan, "very well educated and intelligent," and one who "easily interests and engages the attention of officers."

Little orphan Annie, in a sworn statement, admitted that she had been the friend and companion of many general and lesser officers over a period of two and one half years. She maintained that her original intention was to offer her services as a hospital nurse but had been refused because of her youth. She remained with the army "out of mere curiosity."

Having access to rations, horses, a tent and passes to come and go as she pleased, she crossed the lines into rebel territory a number of times and finally was arrested by Federal authorities on the charge of being a spy.

Her lengthy statement alleged that "General Kirkpatrick (sic) became very jealous of General Custer's attention to me, and went to General Meade's headquarters, and charged me with being a rebel spy. I was then arrested. . . ."

The War Department, through General Pleasonton, sent a copy of her statement to General Custer and General Kilpatrick for their comments. There is no evidence in the file that Kilpatrick complied. Custer in his reply admitted that Annie had been around his headquarters for eight days, but contended that conditions were not quite what Annie represented them to be.

He added that she arrived with passes from the War Department giving her permission to visit the Army. "She expressed a desire to attach herself to one of the hospitals connected with the 3d Division. I gave her permission to remain at my Headquarters until she could ascertain whether her services were required at any of the hospitals in the command. She remained at my Headquarters about one week and desired to remain longer but I denied her permission to do so. After I had informed her that I could not consent to her remaining longer with my command, a general order was issued from the Headquarters, Army of the Potomac, prohibiting all females from accompanying the Army. This order hastened her departure. Upon leaving I informed her that she must never visit my command again. A few weeks later, she came to my Headquarters near Hartwood Church. She came in an ambulance and under an escort furnished by Maj. Gen. Warren. At first I refused to see her and told Adjutant General Captain Greene to order her to return to General Warren or at least to leave my command; it being nearly dark and she representing herself very much fatigued from having ridden nearly 30 miles, I gave her permission to delay her departure until morning. . . . Since then I have never seen her. . . . Her whole object and purpose in being with the Army seemed to be to distinguish herself by some deed of daring, in this respect alone she seemed to be insane. . . . So far as her statement in relation to General Kilpatrick and myself goes, it is simply untrue. I do not believe she is or ever was a spy. This part of her reputation has been gained by her imprudence."

Following her several arrests and confinement at the Old Capitol Prison in Washington and finally in Boston, on charges of either spying or breaking her parole, she obtained the interest of a New York congressman, Fernando Wood, to the point of getting him to seek her release through a request for intercession by President Lincoln.

On January 24, 1864, Lincoln sent a note to Secretary of War Stanton ordering the U.S. Marshal at Boston, on July 9, 1864, to release Annie from the House of Correction there.

According to a letter of March 6, 1865, from the judge advocate general of Massachusetts, William S. Burt, to Secretary of War Stanton, Annie had been detained since March, 1864, under a restraining order issued by Stanton.

On March 19, 1865, Annie wrote a letter to Stanton from New York requesting permission to go to New Orleans to seek employment. Her parole restricted her to the country north of the Susquehanna River during the war.

"Give me passage to New Orleans and I will never trouble you further."[35]

The transition from a small town to the proximity of an army of many thousands with all its hustle, bustle and strange noises was a bit disquieting. Indulged and shielded from the seamy side of life, Libbie found the new way intensely interesting though filled with adjustments.

She was amazed to find mature officers reporting for duty, standing at attention in front of her youthful husband, their gray heads uncovered. She could hardly wait until they left to ask, "Do *they* obey *you?* I wouldn't if I were them."

"Yes," he replied laughingly, "and I shall reduce you to subjection sometime." All the sides of his character she had seen were merry, boyish and absolutely unconscious of a rank unusual for one so young. It took her a long time to adjust to the fact that these officers under him had observed on the battlefield a side of him she had never seen.

She remarked that it was fortunate such manners were not expected from his family. He laughed and replied that she could be punished for insubordination and that there were rules for camp followers. Later he admitted he could command his Division of thousands but not his wife.[36]

Adaption was made easier because of the happy military family they were surrounded by. Soon after his appointment to a brigadier and assumption of command of the Michigan Brigade, Autie began appointing many of his old Monroe schoolmates to his staff. Libbie knew all of them and thoroughly enjoyed their company.

"Hazing a plebe or freshman at college was nothing to what I endured for it required so much more study and finesse to torment a verdant girl who could not be subjected to the rough treatment of a college boy," she recalled. If not perpetrating a joke of their own they would join her husband in some such endeavor.

If she said she did not mind smoking that was the signal for all of them to drop in one by one, apparently without premeditation, and casually close the least crack in the windows, and then light every kind of pipe, cigarette and vile cigar. When her eyes filled with tears from the smoke and her coughing became constant, it occurred to her she was being smoked out. In a short time she learned to disregard the effects of the tobacco. Though she was teased unmercifully by these fun loving men, all were too tenderhearted to carry their jokes to a point of hurting her.[37]

Autie had obtained a pony for his bride, having it ready for her when they arrived at their new home at Stevensburg. She had been taught to guide her horse by the bit. Cavalrymen sway their animals to the right or left by the pressure of the bridal rein on the opposite side of the horse's neck. Scarcely a spoken word is used other than a caressing word to the animal. If they wish to ride faster they touched the spurs or tightened the reins.

The gait of her pony was slow compared to the usual gallop of the cavalry. Despairing at the slow pace of her mount, she would forget herself and give a low but emphatic "cluck." The enlisted men, having learned that she could be teased, would call out, "Stop that, now. That's the way the infantry ride."[38]

She had been used to a curved saddle in Monroe. The pony had a flat English saddle that gave her the feeling she was sliding back toward the animal's rump. The one thing that provided her with an element of pride was the animal's ability to perform tricks. It could waltz a little and could rear up and take a few steps on its hind legs. It knelt for Libbie to mount and had a number of other tricks in its repertory which she would gladly have exchanged for a little speed. He had about the same speed as that of a child walking home from school.

She felt rather humiliated seeing the staff officers strike off into a long-strided lope while she attempted to keep up with them at a choppy little canter. The officers held in out of politeness but had great difficulty holding back their snorting, impatient beasts.

When the cavalry column with its thousands of snorting, careening, hard breathing horses moved out with the caissons, batteries and lumbering supply wagons following in the rear, she would recall how gratifying it was that she had learned to take all of this as a matter of course.

She feared that the staff and whatever generals were with them would think her husband had married a noodle because she couldn't talk and couldn't ride. Inwardly she feared she was a failure, a fear that made her resolve to try harder. Glancing at her husband from time to time as the column rode along, she observed "only the utmost patience and heard constant commendation if I got the pony into his clumpety little canter. The officers said and did everything they could to put heart into me and if tears of fright ran into my eyes they made believe not to see them. The bravest are the tenderest."

She went on, "I was frequently the only woman in the whole Division of 3,000 men and once was the only woman in the whole Army of the Potomac. Naturally the men were curious at sight of a woman riding near them and tho' they might not turn their heads their eyes showed the whites on the side furtherest from me."[39]

Finally the day arrived on which the cavalry would leave on its special mission, the mission for which Custer had been ordered to cut short his honeymoon. General Kilpatrick was seeking a little glory.

Eager to obtain distinction at any cost, Kilpatrick had promoted a plan in Washington that had received official approval. He was to lead a cavalry force of 3,500 men with the intent of penetrating a rather weakly defended Richmond and to release the 15,000 Federal prisoners there. As a diversion, Custer was to make a raid into Albemarle County, Virginia, by passing around Lee's left flank, tear up a railroad, then destroy the Confederate supplies at Charlottesville.[40]

Of course, this was a "secret" raid. Like most of the Union secrets, most of the Confederacy knew about it. Certainly more than Libbie knew.

Some years later Libbie learned from a friend that Autie had told him that "he went out to that raid with little hope of return." In this raid he was asked to lead strange troops and not his Michigan Brigade, all for the purpose of a feint toward Richmond which would bring the whole of General Lee's army in pursuit so Kilpatrick would reach his objective.

Some officer had said to Kilpatrick, "Well, that feint promises to be the death of Custer for he is not likely, with the comparatively small force assigned him, to escape the whole Confederate Army coming down on him." Kilpatrick replied with great nonchalance, "Somebody had to be sacrificed and why not Custer?"[41] General Farnsworth had been sacrificed at Gettysburg by the imprudent Kilpatrick. Custer was to be next.[42]

On the evening of February 28th the cavalry force rode out. It was the first of a dozen such goodbyes, none less painful for the pair. Though Libbie was unaware of the circumstances and was quite upset at his leaving, Autie, who knew his assignment was extremely hazardous with many odds against him, maintained his composure and managed to keep her in ignorance of the peril he was to face. He said it was only a raid. Libbie, not then knowing what a raid was, supposed it was nothing compared to a battle. It was only after he had returned that she learned of the risks involved.

When the troops had pulled out Libbie had a sensation of bewilderment and terror over the strange position in which she found herself. It was one almost of having been abandoned in a desolate place. The Southern family downstairs could have no feeling but that of hostility toward her, she reasoned. She was one of the invading "yankees."[43]

Since it was well-known that this raid expected to encounter superior numbers, the need for men was so urgent even the escort had gone along. It was

General Pleasonton who came to her rescue almost at once, with all his staff to ask if he could do anything for her. Assuming an air of bravado she replied, "Nothing, oh *nothing.*" She longed to ask all of them to remain in the tents vacated by Autie's staff until the return of the expedition, but she did not. It was Eliza who tried to dry the tears.[44]

GENERAL AND MRS. CUSTER IN GRAND RAPIDS.
Both wear the badge of the Michigan Cavalry Brigade, 1865. Courtesy of Frank Mercatante, Grand Rapids, Mich.

NOTES—CHAPTER 11

[1]Charles Lawman: *Biographical Annals of Civil Government of the U.S.,* Washington, 1876, p. 211. Howard had an impressive background in law and politics. He had drawn the platform of the first convention held by the Republican party in 1854. F. A. Barnard: *Representative Men of Michigan,* Cincinnati, 1878, p. 80.
[2]Monaghan. p. 176.
[3]Hamilton G. Howard: *Civil War Echoes,* Washington, 1907, p. 304.
[4]Letter of January 7, 1864, to Christiancy. Custer Battlefield National Monument.
[5]Howard, pp. 306-13.
[6]Letter to Libbie, January 10, 1864. In BCWC collection.
[7]*Ibid.*
[8]Merington, p. 79.
[9]Rebecca Richmond diary in Grand Rapids Public Library.
[10]Merington, p. 80.
[11]Wing, p. 318.
[12]*Ibid;* The Custer family informed me Nevin, who farmed at the westerly edge of Monroe on the North Custer Road, was afflicted with rheumatism until the end of his days. See p. 180, Frost: *The Custer Album.*
[13]After the war, George Yates died with Custer at the Little Big Horn in 1876, James Christiancy became a practicing attorney, and Jacob Greene became president of the Connecticut Mutual Life Insurance Company.
[14]The house still stands on the southeast corner of Cass and Third streets across from the former Boyd Seminary property. According to Monroe County Court House records Emanual Custer bought it for $800 on September 1, 1863. On August 22, 1871, he sold it for $1,500. David Reed deposited several hundred dollars on the original purchase to hold it until Autie could come up with the sum needed.
[15]Letter of Ann Reed to Autie, December 22, 1863 in BCWC collection.
[16]Wayne Coller article in the *Daily Sentinel Tribune,* (Bowling Green, Ohio), July 26, 1949. Wood County records show it to be the east half of the southeast quarter of section 31, Washington Township.
[17]*Ibid.*
[18]*Ibid.*
[19]Ann Reed's letter of December 22, 1863. BCWC collection.
[20]Letter of February 2, 1864 in BCWC collection.
[21]Monroe County Historical Museum.
[22]Monroe *Commercial,* February 11, 1864; Monroe *Monitor,* February 10, 1864; Merington, pp. 81-82; Detroit *Free Press,* February 10, 1864.
[23]Merington, p. 83.
[24]Libbie's penciled noted in author's collection. Hereinafter called Libbie's notes.
[25]Merington, p. 85.
[26]Libbie's wedding notes. Author's collection.
[27]*Ibid;* also *Phrenological Journal,* September, 1876.
[28]Libbie's wedding notes.
[29]*Ibid.*
[30]"February 24, 1864—Pass Mrs. Gen. Custer to Army of the Potomac and return. By order of Sec. of War." Author's collection.
[31]Frost: *The Custer Album,* p. 58.
[32]E. B. Custer: *Tenting On The Plains,* N.Y., 1887, pp. 39-47; E. B. Custer: *Boots And Saddles,* N.Y., 1885, p. 10.
[33]Many of Libbie's notes in the author's collection made reference to various materials and subjects she could refer to in her future writing.
[34]Whittaker, p. 218.
[35]Annie E. Jones in Provost Marshal's File, RG 109, National Archives.
[36]Libbie's notes.
[37]*Ibid.*
[38]*Ibid.*
[39]*Ibid.*
[40]Long, p. 469.
[41]Libbie's notes.
[42]Monaghan, p. 181.
[43]Libbie's notes.
[44]EBC files at Custer Battlefield.

CHAPTER 12
ALL IS NOT QUIET ON THE POTOMAC

An empty cavalry camp was no place for Libbie. Once buzzing with activity and now literally deserted, it was no place for a lonesome, almost homesick girl. Eliza was a source of consolation but the absence of Autie and the growing fear of hostile neighbors caused her to take heed of Autie's request to go on to Washington and await news of his return. There were friends there she could stay with until he sent for her.

Nineteen days after their wedding she was in Washington; Autie was on his way to Charlottesville and Jeb Stuart's winter quarters.[1]

The two cavalry columns under Kilpatrick and Custer had moved out at 7 P.M. on February 28th, taking advantage of the darkness to penetrate deep into enemy territory before being discovered. Kilpatrick's 3,600 men headed southeast with Colonel Ulric Dahlgren, son of Admiral John A. Dahlgren, and a force of 460 men in the lead. Dahlgren crossed at Ely's Ford, capturing the enemy's pickets. He then pushed on with his small force through Spottsylvania Court House to Frederick's Hall where he captured a Confederate court-martial consisting of 13 officers.

In a mixup on directions thought to be due to the treachery of a guide, Dahlgren was led away from Richmond rather than toward it. He managed to reach the outer limits of Richmond on March 3d but was ambushed near there by Fitzhugh Lee's men. Dahlgren and many of his men were killed, the remainder of the 150 being captured.[2] It was said later that papers were found on Dahlgren indicating there was a plot to assassinate President Jefferson Davis.[3]

Kilpatrick had taken a course to the southeast until he had struck the outer perimeter of Richmond's defenses. Reaching the main barricade without serious opposition, he prepared for an assault while waiting for Dahlgren, who was to attack the other side simultaneously. When Dahlgren's fate became known, Kilpatrick elected to withdraw his column.

Meanwhile Custer, who led the diversionary force of 1,500 cavalrymen, had struck out to the southwest for Madison Court House. Following a bivouac there that night the column moved along a road leading from Wolftown south, paralleling the Blue Ridge Mountains, until it struck the Rapidan River. On the 29th Custer's troops pushed through Stannardsville toward their objective, Charlottesville. One regiment was sent ahead to scout the area while he rested his brigade. An artillery outpost near Charlottesville was surprised by the regiment, resulting in its taking 50 prisoners.

The prisoners falsely reported that Fitzhugh Lee held Charlottesville some two miles away. That evening, after burning a Confederate mill and a bridge on the Rivanna River to prevent pursuit, Custer started north in a cold, spring drizzle. The rain soon froze to cover everything with a sheet of ice.

All that night they stumbled and skidded along a course led by one of the prisoners who claimed to know a shorter route north. Custer was suspicious from the start, his suspicion being confirmed when the early morning sun revealed the sun's rays on the sparkling snow capping the Blue Ridge ahead, an indication they had been traveling west rather than north.

Now concerned about being led into a trap, for there were scouts' reports that Confederate cavalry were seen all around them, Custer decided to deceive the guide. Sending along a squadron to follow the guide, Custer dropped back with the major portion of his column and took them to another ford. At the very last moment the lead squadron, at a given signal, raced to join him and thus escaped a trap they discovered at that point. It was a running fight for some distance but all of Custer's men escaped though a few were wounded.[4]

On March 1st Libbie received a message from General Pleasonton: "I have just heard from the General. He has returned safe to Madison Court House with his command. I congratulate you!"[5]

Libbie's joy knew no bounds. Autie would soon be home safe from all harm. She had learned that horses and men on a raid returned fatigued and worn. It would be weeks before they would be in condition to return to the field, many of the men having to go to the remount camp for fresh horses. This meant that Autie's duties would be minimal, his staff well able to assume the routine required to recondition the brigade. The disrupted honeymoon could be resumed.

Custer's raid had been substantially successful. Kilpatrick's had not. Kilpatrick's daring plan to capture the city of Richmond and liberate the 15,000 Union prisoners had failed pitifully. Eager to obtain glory, he had lost the opportunity of taking the city by becoming irresolute when at its very door. His strategy had been bold in concept. Where he had failed had been in the faulty execution of his tactics. He had unwisely divided his command and had then failed to attack the city immediately upon his arrival. And he had not aided the moral of the seasoned veterans under him when he issued a last minute order to his commanding officers that they were to make their own arrangements for their wounded, there being no ambulances available.

Kilpatrick reported afterward: "The expedition failed in its great object, but through no fault of the officers and men accompanying it. . . . If Colonel Dahlgren had not failed in crossing the river. . . . I should have entered the rebel capital and released our prisoners."[6]

Confederate cavalryman General Wade Hampton wrote to General Jeb Stuart on March 6th: "My observations convinced me that the enemy could have taken Richmond, and in all probability would have done so but for the fact that Colonel Johnson intercepted a dispatch from Dahlgren to Kilpatrick, asking what hour the latter had fixed for an attack on the city, so that both attacks might be simultaneous."[7]

From this it can be seen that Richmond had received information as to the strategy being applied to Kilpatrick's audacious enterprise. It already had previous knowledge of the "secret" raid. Everyone at Washington's Willard Hotel knew about it. Kilpatrick had been summoned by the President which was interpreted to mean that a raid was forthcoming since a cavalryman was involved in a high-level consultation. The information soon filtered southward.

When Custer and his cavalry headed south through Culpeper on the Sunday of February 28th, well on the Union right, followed by Kilpatrick on the extreme left, there was little doubt at Richmond, when this intelligence was received, that their city was the destination. The concerned inhabitants rallied to its defense by mustering the home guard, factory and office workers, and the wounded.

When Colonel Dahlgren approached from the west to within two miles of the city and learned that Kilpatrick had failed to penetrate the inner defenses, he withdrew. And so the raid ended. Dahlgren, as the sacrificial lamb, lost his life.

Washington abounded with rumors. No rumor was the news that Congress had created the rank of lieutenant general. It was reported that General Ulysses S. Grant would be given that rank when he assumed command of all Northern armies. On

SHERIDAN'S DEPENDABLES. Left to right: Major General Wesley Merritt, Major General Phil Sheridan, Major General George Crook, Brigadier General James Forsyth, Major General George A. Custer. 1864. Brady collection, Library of Congress.

March 1st President Lincoln nominated him for the new rank. The Senate confirmed the nomination the very next day.

Autie arrived in Washington several days later to claim his prize. Ebullient and inexhaustively he transported her around the city to see the sights. He displayed no evidence of the exhausting campaign he had just completed. His enthusiasm and his boundless energy kept them moving constantly; to the theatre, on visitations to some of the friends they were unable to see when their honeymoon had been cut short, and to various restaurants they had been advised not to miss. Those several days passed all too rapidly. Once more they were on their way back to Stevensburg.

Life at the capital had been exhilarating but camp life proved to be more exciting for Libbie. This was her husband's life, the life she had elected to lead. Though it would soon become commonplace, it was interesting to watch the veteran troopers train the recruits sent up to fill the ranks depleted by Kilpatrick's raid.

The Michigan boys took a lot of pride in their brigade. They saw to it that each new man was well-equipped and well-trained to handle the horse and weapons issued to him. The horse was the cavalryman's insurance to reach a destination and return from it. It was his obligation to see to his mount's health and welfare before his own. And he was reminded again and again that the badge of Custer's brigade—the red necktie—was a badge not to be dishonored. It was a badge of courage.

Autie had provided Libbie with a touch of elegance. Springless army ambulances were usually

SECRETARY OF WAR STANTON AND LIBBIE receive captured Confederate flags from Sheridan's cavalrymen. October 23, 1865. J. E. Taylor drawing, Western Reserve Historical Society.

furnished as transportation for officers' wives. Having "liberated" a fine carriage with its silver-trimmed harnesses the summer before, he purchased two fine horses to draw her about. Because of the nearness to the front line he had four or six troopers ride as an escort wherever she went.

"Such styles as we go in!" she proudly wrote to her parents. "Such styles as these army dinners. General Pleasonton has six courses. It would delight your hearts to see Armstrong refuse wine when offered him by his best friends. They honor him for it."

She made note of a picturesque ride to the signal station from which could be seen the vast tent city of the Army of the Potomac stretching out as far as the eye could see. There was concern for the cavalry because its quarters were not as nicely finished as those of the infantry who, during the winter months, had little to do and no horses to care for.

The newspaperman's old story that "All is quiet along the Potomac" was a bit of rubbish to her way of thinking. "Something is happening all the time," she continued. "One day this week six rebs escaped from the Davis dominions across this river. Four got within out lines before daybreak."

There were orderlies from different army posts interrupting their sleep at all hours of the night. On one such occasion, to her great concern, Autie was ordered out at dawn with 300 men to scout the rebels at Ely's Ford. The seemingly impromptu and emergency orders that prevailed in the life of the cavalryman caused an infantry general's wife to tell Libbie she wouldn't want her husband to be in the cavalry for the world. As Libbie expressed, "Their work, like a woman's, is never done."

Accounts were filtering through that a large portion of Confederate General Rosser's command in West Virginia was on furlough and that General Early's command was inactive.[8] Since this information reached Washington with little difficulty it could have been information released to lessen the vigilance of the Federals. In consequence 100 of Custer's men were sent out on a scout toward Blair Mountain in Madison County, Virginia, to determine what the enemy might have in mind. They returned with 20 captured guerrillas, their horses and 10 slaves.[9]

On March 8th the 42-year-old Grant registered at the Willard Hotel in Washington, his only companion being his 14-year-old son Fred. That evening the President held a reception in his honor in the East Room of the White House. On the following day at the Executive Mansion Lincoln presented him with his commission.[10]

Grant immediately proceeded into the field to confer with Generals Meade and Sherman. At Nashville, Tennessee, while with General Sherman he announced that his headquarters would be in the field with the Army of the Potomac. On his way to Washington he stopped long enough with the Army of the Potomac for Autie and Libbie to board the special train back to Washington. Autie had been thrown out of his carriage and injured[11] enough to obtain 20 days sick leave.

The train trip was one of great interest to Libbie and was reported in detail to her parents.[12] It was her first meeting of the hero of Vicksburg. She saw a short, very unassuming, ordinary person with sandy hair and beard, and eyes of a greenish blue. No mention of his habit of stroking his beard with his left hand or of raising and lowering his partially clenched right hand from his knee to the table while he talked.[13]

That she mentions he talked a great deal and was humorous is interesting. Grant was known for being quiet and very reserved in the presence of strangers. It was only in the presence of his close friends that he opened up in this manner. Libbie, with her sweetness and interest in others, obviously put him at ease.

She enjoyed his remark that "small army men invariably ride horses 17 hands high," and appreciated his considerateness when he retired to the back platform of the car to smoke his cigar so that he would not make her uncomfortable. She counted five cigars he disposed of on the way back after she and Autie insisted that he remain inside to enjoy his tobacco. The scant two hours it took to travel the 57 miles to Washington was all too short a time for her.

Washington seemed like home to Libbie. Her previous trips had resulted in many friends so it wouldn't be quite as bad separated from her husband. They spent as many evenings at the theatre as they could for they both enjoyed a good laugh and even a good cry together.

The Sanitary Commission Fair was closing when they arrived there. They were not too late to learn that the President, while attending it, had stated, "If all that has been said by orators and poets since the creation of the world in praise of woman applied to the women of America, it would not do them justice for their conduct during this war."[14] Lincoln, at least, was recognizing the valued services of womankind during the war. In another area of interest that continuously occupied his mind he wrote, "I never knew a man who wished to be himself a slave."[15]

The two were delighted when *Harpers Weekly*[16] appeared on the newsstands that Saturday; its entire front cover pictured Al Waud's drawing of Autie leading a cavalry charge on the Charlottesville raid. The issue of the following week contained a double centerpage spread covered with Al Waud's drawing of the raid.[17]

Libbie was astonished at the attention Custer received wherever they went. Senators and Congressmen flocked around him to be introduced, and he was presented to President Lincoln.

On March 25th General Pleasonton was relieved of his command of the Cavalry Corps of the Army of the Potomac and ordered to the Department of the Missouri.[18] His command in Virginia was temporarily assumed by Brigadier General David McM. Gregg. A rumor was circulated that Pleasonton was removed because of excess drinking. In a letter to her father Libbie denounced it as false. Teetolar Autie, having messed with him over a long period of time, had told her that Pleasonton did drink wine with his dinner, but never excessively.

It was Libbie's observation that Pleasonton's clear eye and general demeanor was in contradiction to such a charge. She considered Washington a Sodom and Gomorrah where everyone drank. Indeed she could recall one night when Senator Chandler was sober.

Grant, shortly after taking Fort Donelson, had similar charges made against him. One of his staff members, Colonel James H. Wilson, reported that a group of citizens descended upon President Lincoln to counsel him on Grant's alleged drunkenness while on duty. The President told them: "I can't say whether Grant is a drinking man or not, but if he is, I should like to know where he buys his liquor as I wish to present each one of my army commanders with a barrel of the same brand."[19]

Grant survived the charges, then became the general-in-chief of the Union armies. Pleasonton too had been a winner but apparently had been demoted on a much weaker charge. But time breeds rumor. The next one held that Pleasonton was removed because of an ill-feeling that had developed between him and General Meade. Then was heard what appeared to be the real reason—his two unmarried sisters living in Washington had talked so disparagingly about the President and the Secretary of War it was supposed they were repeating his views.

By April 11th[20] Custer was back with his troops. Though his long hair was shorn and he sported some side whiskers, he was the Custer of old. His old friend and mentor Pleasonton was gone and Gregg, who had directed him into the action at Gettysburg, had been temporarily in command of the Cavalry Corps but had been relieved by a new man from the West. This man, Major General Philip H. Sheridan, once had been colonel of the Second Michigan Cavalry.[21]

Grant had been looking for a cavalry commander who was aggressive. In his *Memoirs* he wrote: "In one of my early interviews with the President I expressed my dissatisfaction with the little that had been accomplished by the cavalry so far in the war, and the belief that it was capable of accomplishing much more than it had done if under a thorough leader. I said I wanted the very best man in the army for that command. Halleck was present and spoke up, saying, 'How would Sheridan do?' I replied, 'The very man I want.'"[22] Sheridan took over his cavalry command in the Army of the Potomac on April 5th.

Sheridan immediately set about correcting certain deficiencies in the cavalry corps. He maintained that cavalry should be used to fight cavalry and not wasted on picket duty, escort duty or in carrying messages. Pleasonton had started a changeover by using his men in combat but only in the face of resistance from older commanders.

Meade tended to follow the traditional views of the military. Who would protect the front and flanks of his marching infantry? Who would escort his wagon trains? If the cavalry was concentrated they would not be able to provide that protection.

Sheridan had found his new command well equipped but the cavalry horses painfully thin and worn from unnecessary picket duty. Much of the rundown condition of the horses he discovered to be due to picketing a line sixty miles in length with hardly a Confederate facing it.[23]

He expressed the opinion that the superiority of the Confederate cavalry had been due to its employment in a body. With an army of 10,000 cavalrymen he intended to defeat the Confederate cavalry in a general engagement which would result in instilling confidence in his men to such a degree he would be able to attack them at any point.

Meade agreed to diminish much of the picket duty but insisted that Sheridan should remain at headquarters and operate his corps through him. It was evident that the two, with such divergent views, would soon clash.[24]

In early April Custer's appointment as a brigadier general was confirmed by the Senate. It was a happy day, for his sick leave was drawing to a close and he was expected back with his troops by April 4th. His leave was extended to April 11 to insure a full recovery.

Soon after he arrived at the cavalry camp at Stevensburg he reported to General Sheridan's headquarters. It was their first meeting. He had heard of his new commander's success in the West but was not quite prepared for what he saw. The closely cropped man before him sat foreward in his chair so his short legs would reach the floor. The large head moved spiritedly as he spoke. Each sentence was spiced with an oath that never seemed to be repeated. His manner was cordial but his speech was brusque.

He asked Custer to remain at his headquarters overnight so they could become better acquainted. Custer stayed until 4 o'clock the following afternoon. He learned that the cavalry corps had been shuffled, and that he and the Michigan Brigade had been transferred to the 1st Brigade of the 1st Division—"the post of honor in the cavalry corps."

Brigadier General David McM. Gregg, whose prescience placed Custer where he could stop Stuart at Gettysburg, retained command of the 2d Division, and Brigadier General James H. Wilson led the 3d Division. Wilson had been an engineering officer on Grant's staff and had never commanded a company of men. According to Custer, Wilson made himself look ridiculous by displaying his ignorance of cavalry. The two had been aides for McClellan at Antietam. Wilson had learned how to polish the apple.

An old friend of Custer, Brigadier General Alfred T. A. Torbert, was placed in command of his 1st Division. Torbert he considered an able officer.[25]

After his conference with Sheridan Custer presented himself at Kilpatrick's headquarters where the latter was throwing a farewell party. Kilpatrick was being transferred to the West, Wilson taking his place. Though Kilpatrick had displayed a certain ruthlessness in risking the lives of his men, he was a magnificent cavalry leader. There was considerable doubt as to Wilson's ability to fill such large shoes; later events proved the reasonableness of such doubts.

When Custer had arrived at camp he had been informed that some of Grant's favorites had attempted to have him relieved of his command of the Michigan Brigade and assigned to another. Since it was the largest—and considered by him the best—cavalry brigade in the army, these were fighting words. He repaired to General Meade's headquarters and told him that "if such an order was issued I should apply at once to be relieved from duty with this army and sent elsewhere. General Meade at once assured me, as did General Sheridan, that I should retain my Brigade."[26]

Custer was supported by quite a few of his officers, including the commanding officer of the 1st Vermont Cavalry, all of whom were determined to resign if he was removed.

Sheridan told Custer that he was entitled to the command of a division. Meade had told Kilpatrick that there was no reason why Custer should not have succeeded Kilpatrick in the command of the 3d Division. But there was a reason. Grant was moving in and taking his friends with him. Custer knew that the removal of his mentor Pleasonton to an obscure command had removed his own chance of commanding a division at that moment. What he couldn't know was that he would soon become Sheridan's favorite. For the time he had been mollified by the knowledge he would continue leading his faithful Wolverines.

Though lonesome for her Autie, Libbie was finding Washington extremely interesting. She had easily become acquainted with a large number of the most prominent men there in military and political life.

Autie had assured her father that he regretted that Mrs. Bacon could not see some of them: "Even her refined taste would be more than satisfied."[27]

Libbie's Sixth Street boarding house was pleasantly situated close to a fine church. She visited the Capitol quite frequently so that she would be familiar with the faces of those members she read about so much in the papers. To her most of them appeared very ordinary. She realized that she, with her rosy cheeks, looked like a Dutch milkmaid compared to the pallid city girls.

In a moment of loneliness she wrote a letter to her parents asking them to send her palette and box of water colors, and to write. A morning Presidential reception was described which she attended in the company with Representative and Mrs. Kellogg. Once through the throng that crowded the doorway to the White House and into the Blue Room, she was presented to President Lincoln. The President shook hands with her as he did everyone in the long line, then, hearing her name, he halted the line and shook her hand again quite cordially and said, "So you are the wife of the general who goes into battle with a whoop and a yell? Well, I'm told he won't do so anymore."

She replied that she hoped he would. Then he quipped, "Oh, then you want to be a widow, I see." With that they both laughed. The impatient line in pushing on made her wish she weighed 180 instead of 118 so that she might hear more of Mr. Lincoln's knowledge of Autie.

She noted Mrs. Lincoln standing near the President, a rather plain, squatty figure, dressed in white moire antique with black lace bertha and white ribbon quillings.[28]

In the East Room Mr. Kellogg introduced her to the Speaker of the House, Schuyler Colfax, who thrilled her with the remark, "I have been wishing to be presented to this lady, but I am disappointed she is a Mrs.!" On meeting one of Lincoln's Secretaries she asked him to tell the President he would have gained her vote if soldiers' wives were permitted one.

On the following day Congressman Bingham called on Libbie. She found him to be quite charming and affable. Though now a Judge Advocate he continued to regard Autie as his protégé. He still retained Autie's letter referring to his appointment to West Point, a copy of which he gave Libbie.[29]

Washington had its glitter but it also had its seamy side. Libbie observed that it "was crowded with strangers and as the summer advanced, they increased. All seemed to be working to get something from the Government. There were gamblers, thieves, lawless people, from all over the country." She viewed it as a Gomorrah belonging to no one. The streets were unsafe at night and the parks were unsafe even in the daylight.[30]

Letters from home did help while away the time. Cousin Rebecca brought her up to date on family matters. Mother Richmond had been suffering with the ague for five weeks but was showing some improvement. They had gotten a chuckle out of Autie's reference to Libbie as the "Light Cavalry Brigade."

It took little time to devour the few pages of the Monroe *Monitor* thoughtfully forwarded by her father. Monroe, once expected to outdistance nearby Detroit in growth, was having problems because of growing pains hardly attributable to a population explosion. The *Monitor* in its April 13th issue recommended: "1. rigid economy; 2. a good sewer to suitably drain the business portions of Front, Washington and Monroe streets, but by assessment rather than a general tax; 3. open up Monroe Street to its full width as originally planned to provide more rooms for teams. The four corners by the bridge are rapidly becoming the center of the city and business; 4. an Artesian well on the public square; 5. one or more reservoirs to supply fire engines with water. Taxes are enormous already."

Mention of the meetings of some of the women's aid societies recalled to mind her schoolgirl efforts to knit hose and make havelocks to send to the locally recruited troops. She had since learned that the havelocks had become quite handy in cleaning their guns. At least they had found a certain usefulness, but what about the fate of those rough, cumbersome socks they had knitted that contained so many dropped stitches they were bound to provide excessive ventilation for the wearer in those wintry winds of Virginia? The girls would slip a piece of doggerel into the toes of their contribution, hoping for a reply. A few received responses.

Libbie was maturing quite rapidly. In looking back she saw herself as irresponsible and immature, coddled by aunts and relatives, excused from everything arduous while attending an Eastern boarding school, pampered by E. J. Boyd at the Seminary where she began as a boarder at age nine.

Having lost his only son and an adored wife, Judge Bacon was an overindulgent father to her. Even his friends extended this feeling in excusing her from any responsibility by explaining, "She has no mother, you know." Her stepmother, fearing to be judged severe, permitted her to dance and sing through childhood.

Knowing her father's feelings about a soldier son-in-law, she did not tell him of the impetuousness of a young captain who conducted his matrimonial affairs quite on the plan of a cavalry charge by proposing the second time he saw her. He had explained his ardor by saying that he had made his choice of a wife when a little girl of seven, though not knowing him, had audaciously called as he passed her house, "Hello, you Custer boy!"[31] To tease her on occasion in the years that followed, he would recall this highlight of his early years in Monroe.

She had declined the honor at once and mentally vowed that if she ever did marry—for she had determined to remain single and study art—it would *never* be to a man with light hair or who wore what looked like a theatrical cloak lined with yellow. She didn't know it was a regulation cavalry coat.

Her father, objecting at first, had reasoned that there was something in that young Custer after all, "that no man could be made a general at 23 without influence unless there was something in him as a man and soldier." Libbie was in complete agreement for, well before that time, hadn't she fallen completely and absolutely in love with him?[32]

On April 23d, Sheridan held his first review on the open ground near Culpepper. The magnificent spectacle of the 10,000 mounted cavalrymen breaking into columns as they passed the generals assembled was a sight that none there ever forgot. If only Pleasonton could have been there, and with them from then on in, to share in the coming glory. He had done so much to make the cavalry an effective arm. He had acquitted himself creditably in the battles of Chancellorsville, Middleburg and Brandy Station and had shown himself to be a match for Stuart. His reward was an ignoble assignment with Rosecrans in Missouri.

His successor, Sheridan, was equally as quick to reward his subordinates. The review brought special mention from him to Colonel George Gray and his 6th Michigan as the best marching regiment in the entire command. The entire Michigan Brigade was commended as the best.

Several days later Generals Sheridan and Torbert sent Autie to Washington for 48 hours on a special assignment. His arrival was a complete surprise to Libbie. The haste with which he climbed the stairs and burst open her door made some think the house was on fire.

She knew there was something different in the way he kissed her. Those were kisses without his mustache for he had shaved it off and mailed it so that she had received it just the day before. He looked quite funny and so very young without it she thought but dared not say. And his smooth skin gave her the sensation of kissing a girl.

Libbie kept her parents informed of all that transpired in the Capitol. Her long letters ofttimes evidenced the homesickness she experienced. She would tell of her pleasure and joy in attending church, and of her studied plainness of dress and her use of somber colors to avoid appearing like *persons of a certain class.*

There was ample evidence and numerous rumors that everyone was readying for a great battle. Long wagon trains rumbled over the pavement and regiments tramped by with greater frequency. No one knew what Grant was going to do. For once the newspapers were silent.

For a certainty the Army of the Potomac was going to strike in Virginia. When or where were the questions uppermost in Lee's mind. He was ready though he knew his men were not fighting with the vigor and obstinacy they had in 1863. Their equipment was inferior and their ranks were thinning. The infantry fought hard but the cavalry was beginning to lose some of its dash.

Grant began his big push early on the morning of May 4th, crossing the Rapidan in a move to pass around the left of Lee's entrenchments south of the river. The country before him was covered with a forest and almost impenetrable undergrowth through which even small bodies of men found it very difficult to move. Large bodies of troops would be exceedingly difficult to maneuver and artillery would be of little use. It was the sort of terrain in which the enemy could assume the defensive quite effectively, and so it did.[33]

Torbert's Division was assigned the task of bringing up the rear of the 4,000 wagons that composed the slow-moving train. This was not to Custer's liking for the action would be at the front. Sheridan too chafed at this escort duty. "Why cannot the infantry be sent to guard the trains and let me take the offensive?" was the question he put to Meade.[34]

The advance soon entered the dense jungle and was met by a withering fire from the Confederate forces. It was evident that Lee was going to make the most of ground he was thoroughly acquainted with. So began the Battle of the Wilderness. It wasn't the sort of fighting either side enjoyed though the Southerners had the advantage. The slaughter was dreadful. Both sides took fearful punishment. There was no retreat for the North.

Grant operated on the premise that the North had unlimited manpower and industrial strength. His solution was a war of attrition. Hammering the enemy he called it. Heavy losses would not deter him. He could replace men; the South could not. He had to destroy Lee's force to win. That meant moving forward. To remain inactive could deplete his fighting force to nearly as great an extent through the ravages of disease.[35]

As the battle progressed, Sheridan had some problems as a result of Meade's modification of orders previously given to the cavalry. In Sheridan's opinion one of them resulted in an unnecessary battle at Spottsylvania. Meade's redirection of some of the cavalry had caused the cavalry and the infantry to intermix in the dark in hopeless confusion.

This was enough to fire up the fighting Irishman. Arriving at Meade's headquarters during the dinner hour on May 8th, Sheridan went directly to the point. In sharp tones Meade told him he had ordered him to keep his cavalry off the road so that it would be clear for the infantry. Sheridan said he had received no such order. Meade apologized but Sheridan was not through. In vehement language well spiced with his fluent profanity he said he thought the behavior of Meade's infantry disgraceful and implied that he thought as much of Meade's by his interference and countermanding of the cavalry corps orders, that it endangered and rendered the cavalry useless.

MAJOR GENERAL PHIL SHERIDAN was no armchair general. 1864. Brady photo, courtesy Chicago Historical Society.

GENERAL ULYSSES S. GRANT, a man Libble had little use for in her later years. 1865. Gutekunst photo, Philadelphia. Courtesy Chicago Historical Society.

Meade was not altogether speechless. One word led to another, then Sheridan astounded Meade with the statement he could whip Stuart if he was permitted to but, as he wrote later, "since he insisted on giving the cavalry directions without consulting or even notifying me, he could henceforth command the Cavalry Corps himself, that I would not give it another order."[36]

Meade immediately reported the conversation to Grant who calmly replied: "Did he say that? Then let him go and do it." By 1 P.M. Meade had made out the orders for Sheridan that would mean the end of Stuart.

Before the campaign into the Wilderness had begun, Custer wrote to Libbie every day. There was a constant stream of couriers to Washington and he took advantage of every opportunity to convey his thoughts to Libbie.

On May 1st, from *Camp Libbie,* he praised her religious earnestness, then admitted he was a non-professing Christian though not an unbeliever.[37] He confessed that on the eve of battle he always offered a devout, inward prayer in which he commended himself to God's care, then asking forgiveness of past sins and requesting care for those dear to him in the event he fell. He had a deep conviction that his destiny was governed by the Almighty, a belief that dispelled all of his fears in battle.[38]

Several days later—May 4th—he wrote his last letter to her from *Camp Libbie* to let her know that the army was moving out that night and that there would be no communication with Washington for a time, the knowledge of which should not worry her.

Sheridan had long maintained that cavalry should fight cavalry. On receipt of Meade's order he had three days' rations issued to his men after which he advised Gregg, Merritt and Wilson they were going out after Stuart in what would be a cavalry duel behind Lee's lines.[39]

Starting early on the morning of May 9th, the 13 mile-long column marched around the flank of the enemy unsuspectedly, Custer's Brigade leading the way. It was Stuart who discovered its advance, responding by having Fitz Lee attack the rear of the column. Meanwhile Custer's brigade had recaptured about 400 Union prisoners near Beaver Dam Station who were being taken to Richmond. He proceeded to destroy the station, two locomotives, three trains of cars, about ten miles of railroad and telegraph lines, 90 wagons, a million and a half rations and nearly all of Lee's medical supplies.[40]

Stuart's men continued to attack the Federal cavalry column but were repelled repeatedly. Finally realizing that Sheridan was heading for Richmond, Stuart drew his troops off the rear of the Federal column and hurried them forward to attempt to interpose his force between Sheridan's and Richmond. By forced marches he managed to reach Yellow Tavern on May 11th, ahead of Sheridan.

In the battle that followed the Michigan Brigade played a dominant role, Custer leading it in a daring charge. Sheridan, who witnessed it, ordered Merritt to send an officer to Custer and express his compliments. Later he breveted him a lieutenant colonel for gallant and meritorious services.

While the battle was in process, Jeb Stuart had ridden up to the firing line to observe his 1st Virginia defend itself against a mounted charge. While there a dismounted Union cavalryman, Private John A. Huff, Company E of the 5th Michigan Cavalry, fired across a fence with his pistol, mortally wounding Stuart in the side. He was taken to Richmond where he died on the following day.[41]

Having accomplished what he had set out to do—defeat Stuart—Sheridan, following a series of lesser engagements, reported to General Meade at Chesterfield Station on May 24th. He had broken up Lee's railroad communications, destroyed huge quantities of his supplies and drawn off Stuart's cavalry. Most important was the defeat of Stuart. His defeat had a disheartening effect on the Confederate cause and when the news reached Lee he said: "I can scarcely think of him without weeping."[42]

Then began a series of cavalry actions between Sheridan and Wade Hampton, the new commander of the Confederate cavalry. Many of Sheridan's command were sorry for the change; they considered Hampton a superior officer.

On May 27th, during the heavy cavalry action at Hawe's Shop, one of Custer's aides, Lieutenant James Christiancy, had the end of a thumb shot away and was seriously wounded in the thigh and hip. His horse was shot under him as was that of another aide from Monroe, Lieutenant Frederick Nims.[43] On the following day, a third member of Custer's staff from Monroe, his adjutant Captain Greene, was struck on the head by a spent ball but was not injured. Another horse was shot from under Custer. Two weeks later, while on the Trevilian Raid, Greene was captured and placed in Libby Prison.[44]

There was some discontent in the Union ranks. The slaughter in the Wilderness made some of the infantrymen feel that if such butchery lasted all summer on this line there would be only a few left of the original Army of the Potomac. "Grant, the Butcher," was a common phrase. As one wrote: "What would be the cry against our old commander, Little Mac, if he lost so many men in such a short time? The cry would be long before this, perhaps, to hang him for incapacity to handle so many men .... surely, we cannot see much generalship in our campaign so far, and the soldiers are getting sick of such butchery in such a way."[45]

Both Grant and Lee had their eyes on Cold Harbor because the road to Richmond led past it. Sheridan arrived there on May 31st, attacking and taking an entrenched position, then pushing on to Bottom's Bridge three-fourths of a mile beyond. A heavy counterattack forced him back to Cold Harbor which he reoccupied on Meade's order. At dawn of June 1st his small force held its position against two fierce onslaughts.

On June 7th Sheridan moved north with 6,000 men to destroy the Virginia Central Railroad, then move west to draw the Confederate cavalry after him to relieve Grant's wagon trains while they crossed the James River.

Sheridan's move was a partial success. He returned to White House on June 20th with 500 prisoners, having drawn off Hampton and Fitz Lee and after destroying some of the railroad at Trevilian Station. There Custer and his men were caught between Hampton and Fitz Lee. Custer had been ordered to Trevilian Station to join two other brigades and turn the enemy's flank. Arriving on time—the others arrived three hours later—he was surrounded and attacked from all sides.

Up to that point he had captured more than 1,500 saddled horses, 250 wagons, six caissons of ammunition and several hundred prisoners. To hold it all was impossible. He was overwhelmed and was fortunate to escape though he lost all he had captured including his headquarters wagon containing his bedding and clothing. He had lost everything except his toothbrush.

Eliza, who was with him, was captured along with Johnny Cisco and three extra horses, including the one he had named Clift after Libbie's family. The subject of much kidding, Jacob Greene's flute, along with its owner, was captured.

The greatest regret, Autie wrote Libbie, was the loss of all her letters to him. He just did not relish the thought of others obtaining amusement reading them. With that in mind he cautioned Libbie about the use of certain expressions in the future.

Though the occasion had been a disastrous one, "Custer's Luck" had been evident. When his color bearer, Sergeant Mashon, had been mortally wounded at the head of a charge he had given the flag to Custer who, to save it, tore it from its staff and stored it under his shirt. A short time later Custer was struck on the shoulder and the arm by spent balls but suffered no ill effects other than bruises.

Libbie must have shuddered when she read his letter relating how he had rushed forward to drag back a 5th Michigan man who had been shot through the heart by a sharpshooter. Autie could not bear the thought of the man being struck again as he lay there in a death struggle. When Custer picked him up and turned, the sharpshooter fired, the ball creasing and stunning him for a few minutes but doing no perceptible harm. He managed to bring the body back to a safe position.

He expressed one regret at the end of the letter. Her beautiful ambrotype she had given him before their wedding was in the desk captured by Hampton.[46]

In previous letters he had told Libbie that he had sworn less in battles than he had before, all because of her influence. By mid-August he would write her that he had gone through an entire engagement, and a severe one, without uttering a single oath. He admitted that this was the first time he had not been remarkably profane during the heat of battle, an event that his staff spoke of afterwards. Certainly not an easy accomplishment with the stimulus of Sheridan's fluent profanity ever present.

It was on June 9th the Monroe *Commercial* carried the story of Custer's exploits at Cold Harbor,[47] "Custer with his demoralizing seven shooters." It also announced that Lieutenant James J. Christiancy was severely wounded the following day, and that a letter to Judge Christiancy indicated that the ball had passed through the upper part of his hip, making it a bad wound. The Judge left immediately for Washington.

Jim had been moved to Miss Hyatt's boarding house where Libbie was staying. Libbie would not permit him to stay in any of the over-crowded and undermanned Washington hospitals, preferring to care for him herself. At this point she indicated that Washington was not a disagreeable place though it was rather sad. The hospitals were overcrowded with both sick and wounded, and there were so many crippled, bandaged and limbless men on the streets—and so many funerals. She had made it a point to visit the wounded at the hospitals, enabling her to decide what was best for Jim.[48]

Having been modestly successful in remolding Autie's personal habits, she confidently approached the invalided and defenseless Jim with the same ulterior motive. She "talked to him of leading a useful life, of reformation, of a wife who would save him from wrong and of a God who came to save sinners, not righteous men."[49]

Jim did well enough under Libbie's gentle care. As fragments of clothing came out of his wound his recovery progressed. She enjoyed his companionship and the thought that he did not have to stay in one of those horribly odorous hospitals.

She wrote to Autie telling him that she could never give up Jim's friendship. It was her sincere belief that he had been "without the influence of good Christian women." Her missionary instincts were rallying to the challenge of converting the young man. But there was pity welling up into her heart for she confessed to Autie: "I hope, my dear, that you do not think I did wrong because when he came he had such a fever and was very sick and I in my sympathy kissed the poor boy as I should have done had I been unmarried."[50]

Reassuringly Autie responded: "You know what ample cause I have to be suspicious or doubtful in regard to the conduct of women. . . . But I would as soon harbor a doubt of my Creator as of my darling little wife."[51]

There is no doubt that Jim responded to her ministrations; what man could resist the sympathetic understanding of a beautiful woman? At least he did while directly under her influence, but six months later he was up to his old tricks.

While in Monroe on leave, he got half drunk one evening at the Humphrey House. While there several women called for a doctor to assist a woman in confinement. Jim passed himself off as an army surgeon and went with them to the house. The woman had completed her delivery of two children by the time he arrived. One had been born dead. Jim examined her, then prescribed hot applications of whiskey, a hot whiskey sling and hot bricks to her feet. His patient lived in spite of his treatment.

As Judge Christiancy wrote to Custer: "Jim may look upon this as a fine joke, but to me such recklessness appears shockingly frightful besides being a black disgrace. I am now entirely discouraged at the prospect of making anything of him. . . . I implore you to cure him of his drinking propensities if possible. . . . I hope I shall never see him again till he is thoroughly reformed."[52]

NOTES—CHAPTER 12

1. Charles F. Bates: *Custer's Indian Battles,* Bronxville, N.Y., 1936, p. 7.
2. Rhodes, p. 100.
3. Long, p. 471.
4. Monaghan, p. 184.
5. Original in author's collection.
6. Rhodes, p. 101.
7. *Ibid,* p. 102.
8. Washington *Daily Globe,* March 21, 1864.
9. *Ibid,* March 17, 1864.
10. Lawrence A. Frost: *U.S. Grant Album,* Seattle, 1966, pp. 86-87, 92.
11. Washington *Daily Globe,* March 18, 1864, reported that he had been thrown from his horse and injured.
    The Monroe *Monitor,* March 30, 1864, states: "Gen. Custer is recovering from injuries received by being thrown from a carriage."
12. Merington, pp. 87-89.
13. Horace Porter: *Campaigning With Grant,* New York, 1897, p. 15. Porter, who was on Grant's staff and traveling with him at this time, was Custer's West Point schoolmate, having graduated one year ahead of him.
14. Long, p. 476, March 18, 1864.
15. *Ibid,* p. 477.
16. March 19, 1864.
17. *Harper's Weekly,* March 26, 1864.
18. Long, p. 478.
19. James H. Wilson: *The Life of John A. Rawling,* N.Y., 1916, p. 78.
20. On April 10, 1864, Judge Bacon wrote to his sister in New York that Custer had been thrown out of his carriage and injured his head. "He obtained a furlough of 20 days which expires tomorrow for recruiting his health. He has not fully recovered but will be able to take the field again." He expressed his major worry by telling her: "What awaits Custer no one can say. Libbie may be a widow or have a maimed husband." Letter in author's collection.
21. Robertson: *Michigan In The War,* p. 191.
    Sheridan became the colonel of the Second Michigan Cavalry, May 25, 1862, remaining in command until the fall of 1862. He then commanded infantry as he had prior to taking command of the Second Michigan. See Lawrence A. Frost: *The Phil Sheridan Album,* Seattle, 1968, pp. 30, 34, 49.

[22]Ulysses S. Grant: *Personal Memoirs,* 2 Vols., N.Y., 1895, Vol. 1, p. 60.
[23]Rhodes, p. 103.
[24]Frost: *The Phil Sheridan Album,* p. 70.
[25]Rhodes, pp. 103, 186-87; EBC—CBNM, G. A. Custer to Judge Bacon, April 23, 1864.
[26]*Ibid.*
[27]*Ibid.*
[28]Libbie's notes in author's file; Merington, p. 91; Bates: *Custer's Indian Battles,* p. 7.
[29]Libbie's notes in author's collection. Letter of December 12, 1856 from Cadiz, Ohio stating that he is teaching about four miles from Cadiz on the Athens road for $30 a month. He expected to go to West Point in June though, "Mother is much opposed to my going but father is in favor of it."
[30]EBC—CBNM, micro film roll #5.
[31]Libbie's notes in author's collection.
[32]*Ibid.*
[33]Andrew A. Humphreys: *The Virginia Campaign Of '64 And '65,* N.Y., 1883, pp. 10-11.
[34]Rhodes, p. 105.
[35]Frost: *Grant Album,* p. 88.
[36]P. H. Sheridan: *Personal Memoirs of P. H. Sheridan,* N.Y., 1888, 2 Vols., Vol. 1, pp. 368-69; Agassiz, pp. 105-106; Frost: *The Phil Sheridan Album,* pp. 70-71; Monaghan, pp. 191-92.
[37]A search of the St. Paul Methodist Episcopal Church records of Monroe reveals that all of the Monroe Custers and the David Reed family were its members, George Armstrong Custer being the exception.
[38]Lieutenant Frederick A. Nims of Monroe, according to his daughter Katherine, said that Custer always entered his tent before a battle and got down on his knees to offer a prayer. Nims observed this while serving as an aide on Custer's staff. Merington, p.95.
[39]Sheridan: Memoirs, Vol. 1, pp. 370-71.
[40]*Ibid,* pp. 374-75; *Michigan In The War,* p. 422; George Price: *Across The Continent With The Fifth Cavalry,* N.Y., 1883, p. 396.
[41]Kidd, p. 306; Burke Davis: *Jeb Stuart—The Last Cavalier,* N.Y. 1957, pp. 405-406; *Michigan In The War,* p. 423. Custer, in his report, gave Private John Huff credit for bringing Stuart down. "Huff had won first prize for shooting while serving in Berdan's Sharp Shooters. . . . He was from Macomb County, Michigan, and died June 23d, 1864, of wounds received in action at Hawe's Shop."
[42]Sheridan: *Memoirs,* pp. 386-87.
[43]*Michigan In The War,* p. 425.
[44]William Cahn: *A Matter of Life and Death,* N.Y., 1970, p. 83. Greene was imprisoned at Libby, Macon and Charleston prisons over a period of 11 months. He was exchanged on April 7, 1865, two days before Lee surrendered. He then served as Custer's Chief of Staff in Texas.
[45]D. G. Crotty: *Four Years Campaigning in The Army of The Potomac,* Grand Rapids, 1874, p. 134.
[46]G. A. Custer to Libbie, June 21, 1864.
[47]Cold Harbor was frequently called Coal Harbor.
[48]Libbie's letter to Aunt Eliza, from 471 Sixth Street, Washington, July 3, 1864. EBC files—CBNM.
[49]Libbie to Autie, June, 1864, Merington, p. 100.
[50]Merington, p. 101.
[51]*Ibid,* pp. 101-102.
[52]I. P. Christiancy to G. A. Custer, February 8, 1865. Original letter in author's collection.

CAPTAIN THOMAS WARD CUSTER, General Custer's younger brother, was twice a Medal of Honor winner. From a tintype in the Col. Brice Custer collection.

THE INSEPARABLES. Autie and Libbie Custer with brother Tom Custer standing. 1865. Brady photo. National Archives.

CHAPTER 13
LITTLE ARMY CROW

Now that Sheridan's corps had reached the James River it was time for rest and recuperation. With spirits buoyed in anticipation of some leisure the men crossed and camped ten miles below City Point on June 28th, there to begin the procedure of obtaining clothing and equipment as they rested their wornout horses. The process of rejuvenation began.[1]

It was a relieved Libbie who wrote to Custer each day. Wisely she told him of various advances made by some of the gentlemen with whom she came in contact. Some she excused because they were tipsy.

In several of her letters there is mention of the period following the war when they could raise a little boy and girl in a time of peace, a time she could hardly wait for. A sketch of her dreamchild was enclosed in one.[2]

Libbie was changing her opinion of Washington hospitals. On learning that many of Autie's men, wounded in the Trevilian engagement, were in Mt. Pleasant Hospital, she went with Dr. Bliss to visit them. The men were surprised and pleased with her visit when they learned her identity. She experienced a great sense of satisfaction in having given them some pleasure on that extremely warm June day.[3]

Her experience caused her to advise her parents that any patient was better off in a Washington hospital than at home because of the better medical attendance, nursing, dict and medications. The wards were light and airy, the beds were clean and neat and the female volunteer nurses were efficient.

The maimed and the bandaged soldiers on the streets, the numerous embalming establishments, the flag-wrapped coffins in the many hearses escorted by cavalry, and the story that 60 to 100 die in the hospitals each day, gave her the impression this was the saddest of cities.

All was not sadness. She had to laugh every time she thought of Autie and his toothbrush. He had lost everything at Trevilian except it and that had been saved because, like his saber, it was always with him. Too good a story to keep, she revealed it to her parents and then added that he had a habit of using it *after every meal.* To her it was as humorous as his habit of frequently washing his hands.

One of the senators had obtained the use of the Presidential yacht *River Queen* for an excursion to City Point. When Libbie learned that Congressman Kellogg was to be a member of the party she turned on all of her charm in an effort to obtain an invitation for herself. It was obtained without unusual difficulty. According to an account of the meeting with Kellogg which she wrote to Autie, he was "very cordial. Too much so, for I avoided his attempt to kiss me by moving aside and offering him a chair. Any lady can get that man to do anything. But all I want is that he shall take me on that trip to you."

The trip down the silvery Potomac was a pleasant one. The evening they docked at City Point General Sheridan brought his band aboard to play for a dance. Libbie enjoyed watching him enjoy himself. He entered into it wholeheartedly, having learned to dance that summer. It was comical to watch his short figure bob up and down, she told her old Monroe schoolmate Laura Noble. The booming of the siege guns at Petersburg seemed not to detract from the gaiety of the occasion, the officers intent on enjoying the fun at hand.

On the following day, Saturday, July 9th, the *River Queen* docked at Washington. Their time together had been short. In a matter of 24 hours Autie had to return to camp.

But Libbie was due for a surprise. On Wednesday, the 13th, while reading in her room she heard someone bounding up the steps two at a time. It was Autie. This time his stay was longer.[4] Apparently he had obtained leave to return because of his fear for Libbie's safety.

Confederate soldiers under General Jubal Early had reached the Washington perimeter. There had been skirmishing at Frederick, Maryland, and at Fort Stevens in Early's attempt to determine the strength of the capital's defenses. When Early observed Federal troops moving into the city's fortifications he relinquished his plans for an assault. It was considered more expedient to skirmish along the northern boundary of Washington.[5]

Libbie was concerned for her husband's health when he left. The arduous campaign had left him gaunt and tired, yet he would not rest like others. His concern for her happiness made him shield any evidence of fatigue he could, but she saw through his act. His ability to slide into a comfortable position and instantly fall into a sleep for 15 to 30 minutes and awake refreshed didn't fool her. It was obvious he needed a good rest away from the strenuous life.

Phil Sheridan must have thought so too for hardly a day had passed before Autie was back for Libbie with a 20-day furlough. On July 18th they arrived in Monroe to discover that the Judge and his wife were in Traverse City settling the affairs of the late Albert Bacon. The next day they were on their way there to visit them.[6]

On July 30th a mine was set off under Lee's Petersburg defenses. The result was a crater 30 feet deep, 170 feet long and 60 to 80 feet wide. About 278 Confederates were killed in the blast, yet the Federal forces failed to take advantage of the surprise. Grant was blamed for the failure and more particularly, Lincoln was. With a fall election in the offing, this could seriously hurt his chances.

On the same day, Early's men entered Chambersburg and burned it to the ground when the townspeople failed to accede to the demand for $500,000.

The daring moves of the Confederate cavalry were causing much concern in Washington. Using the Shenandoah Valley as a base of operations, the Confederate forces were again threatening the capital. There was a hue and cry to defend it. Lincoln, in an unusual display of courage, and disregarding what would have been politically expedient, wired Grant on August 3rd: "I have seen your dispatch in which you say: 'I want Sheridan put in command of all the troops in the field, with instructions to put himself south of the enemy and follow him to the death; wherever he goes, let our troops go also.' This, I think, is exactly right as to how our new forces should move. . . ."[7]

On August 7th Sheridan was assigned the command of the newly created Middle Military Division, the army of which was known as the Army of the Shenandoah. Grant wired him: "What we want is prompt and active movements after the enemy, in accordance with the instructions."[8]

Grant had noticed that Lee's men had used the rich valley of the Shenandoah to make his raids into the North. He had briefed Sheridan on the political and military situation in Washington on the 6th, then had given him explicit instructions to push up the Shenandoah for the express purpose of stripping it of all forage, stock and provisions needed by his command and destroying whatever he could not consume. No buildings were to be destroyed, however, and the residents were to be informed that this would continue as long as they provided subsistence for an enemy army.[9]

The Shenandoah Valley was 150 miles long, varying from 10 to 20 miles in width. The gently undulating bottom was carpeted with fertile fields that had supplied the Confederate armies with ample food and forage. No terrain could be found more ideal for cavalry combat.

Sheridan had 8,000 men on horse in his army of 30,000 men. His adversary, Early, had almost as many.

Early was no man to run but it was near harvest time and the ripening fields were a matter of concern to him. He would wait for the harvest, and wait he did. It was near mid-September before the action began.

Nor was Sheridan to be hurried at this time. He was turning over another page in what was becoming a brilliant career. Exaggerated accounts of Early's strength had come to him—40,000 men. It was no time to take an unnecessary risk until he had adequate transportation and supplies and had thoroughly studied the topography.

He had headquartered at Harper's Ferry and it was out of there he conducted a series of inconclusive engagements against Early. He left, then returned to Harper's Ferry so frequently the numerous military critics referred to his army as the "Harper's Weekly." This criticism was of little concern to him. He was biding his time for he knew the right opportunity would come.[10]

In one of the engagements Custer had a bullet graze the right side of his head and cut off several locks of his hair.[11] Libbie's heart sank when she heard of it. There was no use to complain or worry. She knew his life would be one of risks. The less she said about it the easier it would be for the both of them to bear.

Early in the spring Autie had appointed her family treasurer. From time to time he sent her any monies he had no immediate use for. He had suggested that she be as economical as possible but not deny herself any necessary items.

The word economy was an unknown in her vocabulary. Born in a fairly affluent family, she had never suffered for the want of anything even when the Judge hinted at an austerity program while she attended the Auburn Institute shortly after her mother had died.

In early September Autie had placed $500 in her account. After having paid her board bill, $300 had been spent for an entire summer outfit—an expedniture she did not consider extravagant when compared to the $600 Mrs. T. had spent. She did want a black silk dress that would cost $60, a small expenditure to her way of thinking.

When writing to her father, some idea of their finances was recounted. There was $100 for Autie; $190 for Libbie. Autie's commissary bill for the large part of the summer was $70; she had spent $600 in over four months. She was determined to be economical, of course, for the pay of a general would only be temporary. Autie had never complained about her forage on their treasury. And now she was just beginning to understand why her father had tried so patiently to teach her how to keep accounts.[12]

She noted that the price of gold had dropped as a result of the military victories. In July the Federal dollar had dropped in worth to 39 cents, its lowest price during the war.[13]

The coming presidential election was creating considerable excitement. Soldiers when passing a Lincoln flag or a McClellan banner, would either groan or cheer, depending upon their sentiments. Senator Chandler made a series of caustic speeches against the Copperheads. As the election approached, the radicals on one side and the peace proponents on the other hammered the Lincoln Administration.

Libbie confessed to her father she didn't know how Autie felt about the candidates. To Autie she had written that the general feeling in Washington that fall was favorable toward Lincoln. She added that she did not express any observations for fear people would think she was repeating his views, views which she did not know. It was her personal feeling that McClellan would be elected "and that would mean peace—perhaps dishonorable." Then in a twinge of conscience she admitted that it was treasonable and unwomanly to think that way. Deep within her was the desire for peace on any terms—she loved her country, but she loved him more. This she had to tell him.[14]

In his response he expressed the belief that if the North and the South could get together it would result in a better union that formerly. As to politics, it had always been his doctrine that soldiers should not meddle in them.[15]

In sharing Libbie's love of good poetry, Autie had purchased for her a copy of Alfred Tennyson's *ENOCH ARDEN,* at Philp & Solomons Book Store in Washington. There were other Tennyson poems in the small volume but it was in Enoch Arden that each marked favorite passages so that the other would take note. On the flyleaf was inscribed in brown ink: "Philapena from Autie, August 5, 1864." Autie had noticed earlier that Libbie had written "Philapena" rather than her own name in her copy of *THE POEMS OF NATHANIEL PARKER WILLIS.*[16]

There seemed to be a stalemate in the Shenandoah and this was disturbing to both Lincoln and Grant. Grant, occupied with the siege at Petersburg, had expected Sheridan to break Early's back. The cavalry skirmishes between the two forces during August and early September had gained no advantage for either side.

On the 15th of September Grant headed north from Petersburg to interview Sheridan. On the following day at Charles Town, West Virginia, Sheridan showed him a plan to sever Early's lines of supply and retreat. Grant approved it without showing him his own.[17]

Sheridan had been on the offensive in accordance with his orders. He had employed his cavalry in harassing the enemy infantry almost daily, with the end result that his cavalry were becoming quite proficient in attacking infantry positions.[18]

"My dear little Army Crow," was the way Autie opened his letter of September 11th. You may be certain it was addressed to Libbie. He had just returned to his camp at Berryville after visiting her at a boarding house at Sandy Hook a mile from Harper's Ferry where he believed she could safely reside. It was 16 miles from camp, a short distance when traveling toward her. The ride back, even though in the company of two of his officers, was much longer and made more so by his unsocial introspection. Leaving Libbie had left a lot on his mind.

Like all of his letters, there were anecdotes and observations of interest. One of his officers had been

BRIGADIER GENERAL CUSTER AND WIFE. Brady photo. 1864. Courtesy of Frank Mercatante, Grand Rapids, Mich.

captured by the guerrilla raider Mosby. He had discovered that one of his guards was a fellow Mason. Between them it was arranged that he might escape during the night. To cover the intrigue the guard fired several shots toward him as he made his escape but was careful to aim wide. Though pursued over miles of mountains, he escaped successfully.[19]

Sister Ann did not enjoy writing. Composition was a chore and her spelling at times was disastrous. Conscientiously she wrote to Autie to inform him about the family and to keep him writing to her. Though but 14 years his senior she had been more than a sister, her sickly mother having assigned to her the task of raising him. Truly she had served as a second mother.

Ann was a gentle soul whose life was spent in the service of others. Her deep religious convictions governed the Reed family and had an effect on all others she came in contact with. Her charities were many but unknown to all but the recipients.

Autie had been a special concern to her. He had not been a bad boy when he lived with her in Monroe or while they lived at New Rumley. His overabundance of energy—a Custer trait—and his propensity for playing harmless jokes, — another Custer characteristic—had been rather taxing at times. He might have replaced the table sugar with salt or switched the setting hen's eggs with those of a duck but there was no evidence of meanness or maliciousness in any prank of his.

His inventiveness in such escapades was not limited to his home or school. An evidence of it was related by the Methodist pastor, Reverend Seth Reed:

"While his (George Custer's) deportment in church or Sunday school would be nearly so respectful that it could not well be reproved, yet it was so sly and concealed that he would plan fun for a half dozen other boys older and larger than he to execute, while he would look sober as a deacon. Sometimes in prayer meeting we could hear, but could not see, small bird shot snapped from the thumb nails of the boys and rebounding over the carpeted floor, while not a smile would appear on the face of any of them. We knew who was the promoter of such schemes, for George was easily their leader."[20]

Ann had little difficulty getting him to attend Sunday school. It was only a half mile from the Reed home, on the edge of the business district, and a short distance from the River Raisin. But she could never quite convince him that he should join the church. Perhaps it was the influence of David Reed. David supported the Methodist church though he did not become a member until some years after Autie's death.[21]

Ann persistently applied her evangelistic tendencies. She had converted Autie to a life of abstinence and she knew of Libbie's success in stemming his flow of profanity in the very presence of Phil Sheridan, the master of malediction. It was her mission to convince him that church membership was the only means by which he could reach heaven.

While Autie was at Harper's Ferry he received a letter from Ann telling him that Mother Custer and Maggie were at Tontogony where they had been visiting the past three weeks and that his horse had arrived in Detroit but Paw had been unable to go for it. In conclusion she wrote: "O my dear brother I think of you every day. I do wish you a good Christian. I have often thought that was the only thing you needed to make you a perfect man. I want to meet you in heaven."[22]

She enclosed a clipping from the Monroe *Monitor* that arrived just before she posted her letter. Headed "GEN. CUSTER AND HIS CAMPAIGN," it began by telling of the fresh laurels he had gained in Sheridan's campaigning in the Shenandoah Valley around Front Royal and Winchester, then quoted a New York *Tribune* correspondent's tribute to him as follows:

"Future writers of fiction will find in Brig. Gen. Custer most of the qualities which go to make up a first-class hero, and stories of his daring will be told around many a hearthstone after the old flag again kisses the breeze from Maine to the Gulf. With a small, little figure, blue eyes and golden hair which will persist in curling around his head, dressed in a navy blue shirt and dark blue pants, and wearing a slouched black hat ventilated by holes cut in the sides, Gen. Custer is as gallant a cavlier as one would wish to see. No officer in the ranks of the Union army entertains for the rebel enemy more contempt than Gen. Custer, and probably no cavalry officer in our army is better known or more feared than he. Always circumspect, never rash, and viewing the circumstances under which he is placed as coolly as a chess player observes his game, Gen. Custer always sees 'the advantage of the ground' at a glance, and like the eagle watching his prey from some mountain crag, sweeps down upon his adversary and seldom fails in achieving a signal success. Frank and independent in his demeanor, Gen. Custer unites the qualities of a true gentleman with that of the accomplished and fearless soldier."[23]

Sheridan had learned that Early had sent troops down to Petersburg, thus weakening his own force. With Grant's approval of Sheridan's proposal to cut Early's retreat and supply lines south of Winchester as soon as Early's reinforcements were far enough south so they were unable to get back in time of need, it would be only a matter of timing.

Early had a force of about 12,000 men remaining as opposed to Sheridan's total force of more than 40,000. Learning that Early's four divisions were precariously spread out, Sheridan decided to strike.

Sheridan's force moved out on the 19th of September, beginning the action near Opequon Creek, about ten miles from Winchester. The action in the early part of the day was predominantly one of infantry.

Custer's Brigade moved out that day soon after 2 A.M., taking an across country route to Opequon Creek in advance of the Division. At daylight he received orders to move up stream to a ford and attempt a crossing. Though fierce resistance was encountered the ford was taken.[24]

From this point on Sheridan's veterans drove Early's force before them along the pike to Winchester. At the edge of town the enemy rallied. It was then that Sheridan's cavalry, driving Lomax and Rosser—the "Savior of the Valley"—before him, arrived on the scene. Until that time the engagement between the infantry forces had been even.

The following excerpts from his official report will give some idea of Custer's part in this engagement though it should not be thought that his was the only cavalry used even though cavalry became the deciding factor in the battle of Winchester:

"One continuous and heavy line of skirmishers covered the advance, using only the carbine, while the line of brigades, as they advanced across the country, the bands playing the national airs, presented in the sunlight one moving mass of glistening sabres. This, combined with the various and bright-colored banners and battleflags, intermingled here and there with the plain blue uniforms of the troops, furnished one of the most inspiring as well as imposing scenes of martial grandeur I ever witnessed upon a battlefield.

"No encouragement was required to inspire either men or horses. On the contrary it was necessary to check the ardor of both until the time for action should arrive. . . . The enemy relied wholly upon the carbine and pistol; my men preferred the sabre. A short but closely contested struggle ensued, which resulted in the repulse of the enemy."[25]

The Confederates rallied later and again were driven back. A final attempt to make a stand was unsuccessful when Custer led his men in a saber charge that forced them into a full retreat up the valley. As Custer stated in his report: "My command, which entered the last charge about 500 strong, including but 36 officers, captured over 700 prisoners, including 52 officers; also seven battleflags, two caissons, and a large number of small arms. . . . Night put an end to the pursuit."[26]

Losses on both sides were heavy. Of the 12,000 men under Early, almost 4,000 had been lost including a general officer. Sheridan had lost nearly 4,500 of his 40,000 men, General D. A. Russell being among those killed.[27] Though the losses were about the same for each contestant the losses of the South could be considered to be serious. There just were not enough replacements to fill their depleted ranks. As a Federal officer remarked following an August engagement in which the Confederates won but had lost an equal number of men: "The Rebels licked us, but a dozen more such lickings and there will be nothing left of the Rebel army!"[28]

When the news of Sheridan's capture of Winchester reached Washington there was exultation. The good news was announced to all by the booming of a hundred cannons. Lincoln's immediate reaction—with an election in the offing—was to send a dispatch to Sheridan: "Have just heard of your victory. God bless you all, officers and men. Strongly inclined to come up and see you." In addition to this he promoted him to the grade of brigadier general in the regular army and gave him permanent command of the Middle Military Department. The congratulations of Stanton, Grant, Sherman and Meade followed.[29]

Libbie had reason to be joyful. Autie had figured prominently in the news. He had taken a principal part in the battle and had been breveted a colonel in the regular army for gallant and meritorious service at Winchester. With only 500 men he had captured 700 prisoners and seven battleflags. Not bad.

The Federal force continued moving south following the main highways of the valley. Retreating Confederate forces entrenched on Fisher's Hill, four miles south of Strasburg, planning to stay the Federal advance. With every hope of destroying Early once and for all, Sheridan ordered a surprise infantry attack for the marooning of the 22nd. It was overwhelmingly successful at the outset but was hindered later by Rosser and his cavalry who checked the Union cavalry long enough to permit Early to retreat. Custer followed closely on his heels for 20 miles but was unable to capture anything worthwhile.

Sheridan was thoroughly disgusted with Brevet Major General William W. Averell's failure to pursue the retreating foe when he had the advantage. Relieving him from command of the 2d Division, he replaced him on the 26th with Custer. Four days later—the 30th—before Custer had assumed full command, Sheridan gave him command of the 3d Division, Wilson having been sent on to join Sherman.[30]

Averill had failed to press the enemy while they retreated and Sheridan's chief of cavalry, Torbert, had failed to arrive when most needed.[31] Sheridan believed he could have destroyed Early at Fisher's Hill if they had obeyed orders. He wanted men in command who obeyed orders with promptness and courage. He offered no quarter to the Confederates and none to incompetent or apathetic subordinates. He expected his cavalry commanders to lead with celerity and courage. He had no room for others.

To command the 3d Division again was the very thing Custer wanted. He had won his star with this Division and it was while leading the Michigan Brigade in this very Division that they had won acclaim at Gettysburg. This outfit had a service record under Kilpatrick of having done more fighting, marched further and killed more horses than any other in the service. Veterans they were.

Under the cautious Wilson it had avoided rather than sought action. The heart of the Division had been removed—the Michigan Cavalry Brigade. The Division had a respectable reputation but it wasn't what it once had been. To rebuild it was a challenge Custer accepted readily.

Merritt commanded the rival division, a division that contained Custer's favorite fighting men, the Michigan Brigade.

Libbie must learn of the change—but she probably knew for she had contacts that would inform her of any change that affected her life. So he wrote to her at the end of the month: "Had she learned that her Boy General had been assigned to the permanent command of a division?" He had to leave his old brigade and staff but his bugler Fought and Eliza he was able to retain. Sheridan had promised him the Michigan Brigade would be transferred to his command as soon as practicable. With it back in the fold he couldn't ask for anything more.[32]

Libbie immediately advised her father of the new honor and that Congressman Kellogg, who had been visiting the front, wanted to go to Monroe to speak on the fighting qualities of General Custer.

Her mother responded with some advice as to the sacrifices a wife should make in the matter of clothing. Clothes should be plain and, quite properly, never over $12. Armstrong will be happy to learn she is making her own coat for "all husbands like to have their wives ingenious as well as industrious."[33]

Libbie didn't have to be told that all husbands like to hear they are loved. Intuitively she did so at every opportunity. Perhaps she was influenced by the knowledge her husband's occupation was hazardous. Then again her mother and father had showered her with affection and she was intelligent enough to realize that this was a trait to be appreciated and emulated.

So to Autie she wrote that she loved him and wished to look up to his judgment and experience and be guided by it though she could hardly be a submissive wife. Their love was such that their lives blended without the loss of individuality.

On the evening of October 3d, Lieutenant John R. Miegs, Sheridan's engineering officer, was returning to camp with two of his assistants. Meeting three men dressed in Federal uniforms, he rode with them a ways. Suddenly they ordered him to surrender, then fired at and killed him. One of his topographers escaped and reported the murder to Sheridan. He immediately ordered Custer to burn all the houses in a five mile area, reasoning that the assassins had been harbored by some of the local people. Once a few houses were fired Custer was ordered to discontinue the house burning and arrest all able-bodied men.[34]

Sheridan had decided to contract his lines of communication and supply. With winter coming on he began moving down the valley on the 6th of October toward Strasburg. The infantry led the march northward, the cavalry taking up the rear and spreading across the valley as it systematically destroyed everything of military value though respecting all dwellings and civilians. The smoke from burning barns darkened the sky as they moved on. For a week afterward a heavy haze clung to the bottom land, refusing to allow the sunlight to pierce through.

At first the Confederate cavalry followed at a respectful distance. It was led by Custer's old classmate Tom Rosser who had joined Early on the 5th with an additional brigade. On the third day his men began to annoy Sheridan's rear guard. That evening, aggravated by Rosser's display of confidence and still irritated with Torbert because of his dillydallying at Fisher's Hill, Sheridan ordered Torbert to give Rosser a whipping the next day or get whipped himself.[35]

Merritt was instructed to move down the Valley Pike and strike Rosser at Tom's Brook in concert with Custer who was to take the back road along the Blue Ridge paralleling Merritt's route though three miles away. At 7 o'clock in the morning of the 9th, Custer confronted Rosser.

Rosser and his 3,500 men occupied a position on the south bank of Tom's Run behind some low hills, his dismounted men taking a position behind stone fences at the base. Custer, across from this position, could not help but view the level valley bottom as a splendid site for a cavalry engagement. There were no trees or rail fences, for the latter had long since been used for soldiers' fires. There was ample room for maneuvering for not an obstruction could be seen.

He deployed his 2,500 men in full view of Rosser for there was no way their movements could be shielded. The skirmishers had moved forward to develop Rosser's position and shown it to have the advantage for he had posted his six guns on the summit of a hill in a strongly defended position.

Once this was determined, Custer rode out alone far in advance of his front line. Bringing his mount to a halt, he removed his broad rimmed hat and swept it to his side as he bowed in Rosser's direction. Like a knight in the jousts of King Arthur's day he had indicated to his adversary—an old friend—this was to be a fair fight to the finish and there was no ill feeling.[36]

Returning his hat to his head, Custer gave the signal for his 3d Division to open with a trot. Leading the way, he soon set the pace at a gallop as his men waved their sabers and came on. The Confederate cavalrymen fired repeatedly but did little damage as the blue clad boys raced toward them and their batteries. The suddenness of it all, though occurring in plain sight, permitted the three Federal brigades to curl around Rosser's force and almost envelop it. The Confederates became demoralized and took to their heels, being driven for two miles before making a stand.

Again they were charged by Custer's men and thrown into confusion. Now completely demoralized, and with their six guns gone, they began their flight to Mount Jackson 26 miles away. In the pursuit Custer's men took 300 prisoners, 6 cannon and their wagontrain and ambulances.

This Donnybrook, officially referred to as the "cavalry fight at Tom's Brook," and unofficially and facetiously as the "Woodstock Races," so demoralized Early's cavalry he asked Lee that it be dismounted.

With time to do so Autie wrote to Libbie to allay her fears. He spoke with pride of his new command and then of the headquarters wagons captured in the recent engagement. Surprisingly he had recovered Libbie's ambrotype lost at Trevilian Station. Cheerfully, always cheerfully, he wrote. Never did he describe the death and desolation wrought by battle.

He knew that Libbie would take great interest in his victory over his old friend Rosser for he had told her of their escapades together at West Point. The affection and deep respect for him was evident in every line. He delighted in telling her he was wearing a new Confederate uniform coat he had found in Rosser's baggage. To take the edge off his old friend's embarrassment, he had written him a playful letter that evening, thanking him for presenting him with so many new things. He concluded the note by asking Rosser to "direct his tailor to make the coat tails of his next uniform a little shorter." Rosser was the taller of the two.[37]

In a letter some days later he told of finding the private correspondence of General Mumford in the captured papers. He had been the one who had captured Libbie's letters at Trevilian Station. Autie had tied Mumford's wife's letters into a bundle without reading them or permitting others to do so. He thought that to be an invasion of privacy that even a war should not violate.

There was quiet for the Federal cavalry during the next ten days. On the 13th of October, Secretary of War Stanton asked Sheridan to come to Washington and discuss several points.[38] A demonstration on the part of Early delayed him until the 17th at which time he departed for Washington in answer to General Halleck's request.[39] Returning to Winchester late on the 18th, he retired about 10 o'clock.

Early in the morning of the 19th—near six o'clock—he was advised of irregular artillery fire from the direction of Cedar Creek. Because of the irregular fire he considered it a probe and was not alarmed by it. But uneasy in mind he arose, dressed and ate his breakfast. Near 9 A.M. he mounted his horse *Rienzi* and rode toward the Valley Pike. Past Mill Creek he was met with the shocking spectacle of a panic-stricken army.[40]

MAJOR GENERAL THOMAS L. ROSSER, CSA., left Custer's West Point class two weeks before graduation to join the Confederate service. Courtesy of the Confederate Museum, Richmond.

Almost unnerved by the sight, he stopped some of the men and ascertained that the army was in full retreat. Quickly he sent word to a brigade in Winchester to spread out across the valley and stop all fugitives but allow all wheeled traffic through.

Soon receiving full intelligence from the front that his troops had been scattered, he took two aides and 20 men, then started for the front. As the retreating men along the road saw him they shouted, shouldered their muskets and followed him. As they threw their hats in the air Sheridan took his off and waved it in acknowledgement, galloping forward as he did so. The word passed quickly to all the stragglers well off the road and they too turned their faces toward the front. When he arrived there he found Getty's Division and the cavalry attempting to resist the enemy.

Once he had received an account of the day's events he rearranged his line just in time to repulse an attack. Then began his counter-attack along the entire line, driving everything before it. Merritt uniting with Custer fell on the flanks of the retreating foe. All of the lost artillery, transportation and equipment was recaptured along with 24 cannon, 1,200 prisoners and five battle flags.

HON. ISAAC P. CHRISTIANCY. A founding member of the Republican party in Jackson, Michigan, a justice in the Michigan Supreme Court, United States Senator and finally, a minister to Peru. He was a staunch friend of General Custer. Library of Congress.

Early's supreme effort to crush Sheridan had failed. Early had been a three-time loser and this had been his last chance. The Governor of Virginia had asked for his removal, and there was much dissatisfaction in the Confederate Army as well as in the government. Lee evidenced his confidence by advising him, "One victory will put all things right." The chance for victory had slipped out of his grasp. His prestige was gone.[41]

Sheridan's victory was hailed throughout the North. As Grant wrote to Stanton, Sheridan had turned "what had bid fair to be a disaster into a glorious victory." Meade referred to it as "one of the most brilliant feats of the war." Gratefully President Lincoln wrote to Sheridan: "With great pleasure I tender you and your brave army the thanks of the nation. . . ." Sheridan had illustrated what the unexpected could do in a battle.[42]

Little Phil, as he was popularly called following his famous ride, directed his men to mop up the valley. There was continued resistance so it was not until December that the devastation of the Shenandoah was complete. It was said that a crow would have to carry a lunch to travel through it.

Libbie was enjoying her stay with the William D. Russells in Newark, New Jersey. It was a much slower pace than that of Washington. What she missed were the products of the Washington rumor factories. There were few letters from Autie for he was active in the Shenandoah and had no time to write. It had not been easy for her to wait for the infrequent letters so she had decided to avail herself of the invitation of her old friends and relatives in Newark and meet another old family friend, Mrs. John S. Bagg of Detroit, who would be visiting there at the same time.

A letter was sent to Autie so that he would know of her safe arrival. Travel had been a bit more difficult than usual. At Philadelphia she had to change trains, the one she had taken from Washington not stopping at Newark. In the change it was necessary to travel through Philadelphia on a horse-drawn streetcar for five miles to reach the other depot. There she boarded a sleeping car—a new and somewhat frightening experience for her.

Autie had to be filled in on her shopping trip to New York with Mrs. Bagg and her ultimate purchase of some purple poplin worsted and silk for a mere $35 that a fashionable Broadway dressmaker would make into a dress. The silks were so outrageously high she intended waiting until spring when the prices would come down, so she said. Then to soften the blow she concluded with: "I don't care if 50 rebels read this letter. I miss your kisses."[43] Did he know that John Rauch had married Reverend Mattoon's daughter Frances on October 5th?[44]

On October 16th Libbie received a letter from Congressman F. W. Kellogg in Washington addressed to her in care of her host Mr. Russell.[45] He had written a letter to the Detroit *Advertiser And Tribune* as to what he thought of General Custer. He enclosed a copy and hoped it suited her. Eagerly she read its contents:

"Of General Custer . . . I pronounce him one of the best if not the very best cavalry officer anywhere in the service. Under his command the Michigan Brigade has achieved a reputation, and secured for itself frequent and honorable mention in the history of the way. Their devotion to their lion-hearted leader is almost idolatrous and they never once failed to follow him when they heard his ringing voice give the word of command.

"Said a general officer to me the other day, 'The finest sight you ever saw is Custer when leading his old Brigade in a charge.' He seems to be a stranger to fear, and his old veterans, who have followed him to victory on a hundred fields, affirm that he wears a charmed life, and is not destined to fall by a rebel bullet. He is indeed the Murat of the American Army, and resembles that famous chief of the cavalry of the great Napoleon in his dashing, daring manner, and in his reckless bravery and audacity on the field of battle, but, with all this, he is cool and thoughtful, and quick to take advantage of the errors of an enemy. In his habits he is strictly temperate, never using intoxicating liquors, for which he cannot be too highly commended."[46]

It was Sunday morning, the 23d, while Libbie was eating breakfast that Mr. Russell brought in a copy of the New York *Times* and began to read to her. Thinking that he was making up a story when he read that General Custer had arrived in Washington with flags captured at the battle of Cedar Creek, she jumped up and began reading over his shoulder. When she saw that all he had read was true she began to cry. The more she realized she had missed Autie by not staying in Washington the harder she cried. Seeking solitude, she ran upstairs to her bedroom to continue her tears.

In a short time several members of the family came to her room to console her. Hardly had they entered her room when they heard the children below scream: "He's come! He's come!" And so Autie had come. Gently he dried her tears and told her he was taking her back to Washington. The Secretary of War had been ill and would not be able to see them till the morrow.[47]

Custer was the pride and joy of the Russell family. Mrs. Wells, a sister of Libbie's stepmother, made it quite evident that she approved of the Boy General, a reaction that delighted Libbie.

The staff of the Newark *Advertiser* soon learned of the presence of the distinguished visitor and had a reporter knocking at the door. There was little difficulty in interviewing Autie for he enjoyed presenting his observations to an appreciative audience. Though not a polished speaker his animation and vivacity, his colorful description as an eyewitness, held the attention of the listener.

He gave a description of the affair at Cedar Creek, venturing that "the victory was the most complete and decisive which had yet been achieved in the Shenandoah."

General Ramseur, who was killed in the engagement, was a classmate of Custer at West Point. Before his death he sent for Custer. "The two, thus strangely brought together, reviewed in the presence of death the reminiscences of their cadet life."[48]

Monday Custer and his wife returned to Washington on a fast train which, according to a Washington press release, ran 40 miles an hour. On arrival they took an omnibus to Libbie's boarding house on Pennsylvania Avenue, a Confederate battle flag flying from each of its windows. This display brought tremendous cheers wherever they went.

On the morning of October 25th at 10 o'clock Autie and his ten men walked to the War Department bearing the captured rebel flags.[49] Once there each man, in reply to Secretary Stanton's query, gave a brief account of the trophy he was presenting. Following this Stanton told the men that each of them would receive a medal from the Government and, that in answer to General Custer's request, each would receive his pay as if on duty, while in Washington awaiting their medals, and that they would have their fares paid for a trip home, then back to their command.

In conclusion he announced: "To show you how good generals and good men work together I have appointed your commander, Custer, Major General." Then turning to Custer and shaking his hand he added, "General, a gallant officer always makes gallant soldiers." As the crowd finished cheering this statement one lad who had presented a flag said: "The 3d Division wouldn't be worth a cent if it wasn't for him." Everyone laughed and Custer bowed his head in embarrassment.[50]

As the crowd dispersed Secretary Stanton asked Custer if he was related to Emanuel Custer of New Rumley, Ohio. Custer said Emanuel was his father. The Secretary then told him that he was once his client but hadn't associated the two because he had learned that the General was from Michigan. Then Stanton asked: "Why have you never been to see me?" The General answered: "Because I never had any business to bring me to your office, sir." Father Custer had told his son to "go see Stanton. He'd be glad to see you." Custer never did. He did not want the Secretary to get the impression he was seeking a favor.

THREE VIEWS OF LIBBIE IN 1865. Author's collection.

NOTES—CHAPTER 13

[1]O. R. Vol. XL, Series 1, pt. 1, p. 201.
[2]Merington, p. 102.
[3]Libbie's letter to Aunt Eliza, July 3, 1864, EBC—CBNM.
[4]Monaghan, p. 210; Merington, pp. 113-14.
[5]Long, p. 537.
[6]Monroe *Monitor,* July 20, 1864; D. S. Bacon to his sister, September 5, 1864, author's collection.
[7]Frost: *Phil Sheridan Album,* p. 74.
[8]Adam Badeau: *Military History of Ulysses S. Grant,* 3 Vols., N.Y., 1881, vol. 2. p. 502,
[9]Frost: *Phil Sheridan Album,* pp. 74-75.
[10]*Ibid,* p. 76; George E. Pond: *The Shenandoah Valley,* N.Y., 1882, p. 137.
[11]EBC—CBNM. G. A. Custer letter to his sister Ann, August 24, 1864—"On August 16 a bullet grazed the right side of my head and cut off several locks of my hair. Eliza is still with me.... I thought of sending Eliza's daughter to you by David (Reed);" Kidd, p. 377.
[12]Merington, pp. 92, 112, 116-18.
[13]Long, p. 537.
[14]Merington, p. 118.
[15]*Ibid,* p. 119.
[16]Both volumes are in the author's collection. The *Random House Dictionary of the English Language,* N.Y., 1966 states under *Philopena:* 1. a custom in which two persons share the kernels of a nut and determine that one shall receive a forfeit from the other at a later time upon the saying of a certain word or the performance of a certain thing. 2. the thing shared. 3. the forfeit paid.
[17]John W. DeForest: *A Volunteer's Adventures,* New Haven, 1946, p. 172; Long, p. 569; Jubal A. Early: *A Memoir Of The Last Year Of The War For Independence,* Lynchburg, 1867, pp. 91-92.
[18]Rhodes, p. 130; DeForest, p. 166.
[19]Merington, p. 119; George A. Custer's letter to sister Ann, September 17, 1864, EBC—CBNM.
[20]Reverend Seth Reed: *Pastor's Report—1853-1855,* St. Paul Methodist Church, Monroe.
[21]David Reed joined the Monroe Methodist Church on December 30, 1883, according to Mrs. Polly Sprague, Methodist Church historian.
[22]Ann Reed to George Custer, August 30, 1864, BCWC collection.
[23]Monroe *Monitor,* August 31, 1864.
[24]O. R. I, Vol. XLIII, pt. 1, pp. 454-59; *Michigan In The War,* pp. 430-33; Long, p. 571; Kidd, pp. 385-89; Whittaker, pp. 234-46.
[25]*Michigan In The War,* pp. 431-32.
[26]*Ibid,* p. 433.
[27]Sheridan: *Memoirs,* Vol. 2, p. 29; Long, p. 571.
[28]Agassiz, p. 226.
[29]Sheridan: *Memoirs,* Vol. 2, pp. 29-31.
[30]*Ibid,* pp. 45-52.
[31]Early, p. 94, stated: "If Sheridan had not had subordinates of more ability and energy than himself (at Winchester), I should probably have had to write a different history of my Valley campaign."
[32]Merington, p. 119-20.
[33]*Ibid,* p. 121.
[34]Sheridan: *Memoirs,* Vol. 2, pp. 51-52; Early, pp. 98-99.
[35]Sheridan: *Memoirs,* Vol. 2, p. 56; Whittaker, pp. 255-56; Kidd, p. 401; O.R., I, XLIII, pt. 2, p. 327.
[36]Whittaker, p. 258; O.R., I, XLIII, pt. 1, p. 32.
[37]Elizabeth B. Custer: *Boots And Saddles,* N.Y., 1885, pp. 91-92.
[38]Sheridan, Vol. 2, p. 60.
[39]*Ibid,* pp. 65-66.
[40]*Ibid,* pp. 67-76.
[41]Kidd, pp. 424-25; Early, pp. 111-12.
An excellent and understandable account of the Battle of Cedar Creek may be found in Willis C. Humphrey: *The Great Contest,* Detroit, 1886, pp. 435-445, as prepared by General James H. Kidd; O.R., I, XLIII, pt. 1, pp. 527-28.
[42]George Pond: *The Shenandoah Valley In 1864,* N.Y., 1883, pp. 240-41; Frank Moore: *The Rebellion Record,* N.Y., 1868, Vol. XI, pp. 740-41; O.R., I, XLIII, pt. 1, pp. 527-28.
[43]Merrington, p. 124.
[44]October 12, 1864, Monroe *Monitor.* Reverend Mattoon officiated at Libbie's wedding. Libbie didn't quite approve of "Frankie" marrying John Rauch the reason for which is not known. Later Libbie engaged John as her attorney to handle her father's estate (1866).
[45]BCWC collection. Letter dated October 14, 1864.
[46]Detroit *Advertiser and Tribune,* October 11, 1864.
[47]O.R. I, XLIII, pt. 2, p. 437; Merington, p. 126.
[48]*Michigan In The War,* pp. 434-35.
[49]Monroe *Monitor,* October 26, 1864; Monroe *Commercial,* October 27, 1864.
[50]Washington *Star,* October 25, 1864.

WEST POINT CLASSMATES—Lieut. James B. Washington, while a Union prisoner, discusses the past with classmate Capt. George A. Custer, May, 1862. Brady collection, Library of Congress.

CHAPTER 14
LET THE THING BE PRESSED

The camp near Martinsburg was a dull place without Libbie. There was one way it could be brightened and that was to send for her. On the 28th Custer did and, in doing so, advised her there would be fewer comforts since the life she would be leading would be that of a soldier. A riding habit and a small trunk would suffice for there was no place to wear nice dresses. And it would be well to retain her room in Washington. Plans could be changed suddenly, for this was the army.

Libbie broke all records packing a small trunk. Her reply to Autie indicated she would gladly give up luxury, dress, comfort—she loved them all—just to be with him.[1] A week earlier she had written her friend John Sherman Bagg in Detroit: "But it was never intended by the Creator that husband and wife should be separated and so I am sometimes quite ready to rebel against this living alone like a little old maid."[2] Life could be beautiful.

Several days before leaving to join Autie she addressed his letter: "My own dear love—Gen. Torbert called for about five minutes today. He seemed thoroughly tired out. Nobody seemed to make the slightest fuss over his arrival and I couldn't but draw contrasts upon his and somebody else's arrival. . . . I scarce ever saw a gentleman with so little animation and spirit as he has. I think I can never endure again anybody but one who has life and animation.

"Oh Aut, give me men for action who have the enthusiasm, energy and ardent temperament of my warrior brave. . . . I cannot help but compare other men with my hero and how far, far they come from being like him!

"The longer I am your wife the more heartily I admire thorough earnestness and ardency and animation because these traits are all so prominent in my Boy General.

"While attending an Episcopal Church service I prayed that I might be given a child that I might try and make it a cornerstone in the great church of God—and Autie, if God gives me children I shall say to them: 'Emulate your Father! I can give you no higher earthly example.' But *then* I can say to them: 'Emulate him in his Christian as well as his moral character,' can I not?"[3]

When the train pulled in at Martinsburg, Autie was there to meet her. He hardly evidenced his new brevet rank of major general. Bundled up in a Confederate overcoat, old rebel hat and gauntlets—Virginia was cold in early November—he presented the appearance of a rebel leader rather than a member of the Federal forces.

The evening was spent in Martinsburg at the home of a Union sympathizer. Leaving the following morning at seven, and escorted by 150 cavalrymen, they traveled the 40 miles to camp in a light spring wagon. The thrill of their meeting was augmented by the knowledge they were passing through a countryside ravaged by Mosby and his guerrillas.[4]

The camp was pleasantly situated. Custer had established a pattern he would use during the balance of his military career by joining two wall tents so that one served as a bedroom and the other as a living room. The latter flaunted floors of liberated barn doors. Eliza's tent nearby often served as a dining room.[5]

Autie had much to show her, much to tell her. Did she know that since Jim Christiancy left her care and went to Monroe with his father he had several pieces of bone removed from his hip? Judge Christiancy had written that the four inch incision was healing and Jim was moving about on crutches.[6]

The best news of all he had held back until last. Brother Tom would be joining his staff any time now. Tom, who was a corporal in the 21st Ohio Volunteer Infantry when she had met him at their wedding, had obtained a discharge from that outfit to accept a commission of Second Lieutenant with the Sixth Michigan. Once Tom was in the Cavalry Corps it was a simple matter for Autie to ask Sheridan's permission to add Tom as an aide. Autie's old friend and Colonel of the Sixth Michigan Cavalry, James H. Kidd, had made room for Tom so that a commission was available.[7] It was then that Secretary Stanton ordered the discharge of Tom from the 21st Ohio with the express understanding Tom must accept the commission or remain with the 21st, or he would be considered a deserter.[8]

Tom was quick to join Autie for there was nothing he wanted more than to be with his older brother. He had joined the 21st Ohio when only 16 years old. Now a mature stripling of 19 years with three years of military service behind him, he was ready to try his wings. When barely 20 years of age he would be awarded his first Medal of Honor, his second one less than a month later, for his role in the Appomattox campaign.[9]

About the time he arrived the cavalry had been ordered to fall back. Sheridan had been searching for winter quarters near Winchester. Autie was able to obtain the use of a large Virginia mansion owned by a Mr. and Mrs. Glass. The owners, grateful for the protection they offered against marauders, made their stay very pleasant.[10]

Libbie had found this new life quite exciting. She had ridden at the head of the troops in her Virginia carriage and had graduated from the pony riding class to a saddle horse if she cared to ride it. Arising before daylight and eating breakfast by candlelight, then waiting by the campfire while her tent was being packed, fascinated her. Sleeping in a tent was a novel experience that seemed a bit strange and had a certain appeal, yet she welcomed the hominess of the roomy mansion they now occupied near Winchester.

Her older brother had died just a few days after her sixth birthday. Having had no extensive exposure to a brother during her childhood, "brother" Tom's presence in the camp was a pleasurable sensation. She had written in her notes:

"We could not help spoiling him owing to his charm and our deep affection. When Tom came in to report he was the most formal of them all standing at attention and using a tone of voice that betrayed no signs of anything but the strictly disciplined soldier.

"The two called each other 'Sir' and until I had become accustomed to this I used to think that Tom had surely been offended by some dereliction and I prepared to take his side and plead his cause whatever might be the right or wrong of the case. As soon as the report was made and the commander had said, 'I have no more orders, sir, for the present,' Tom flung his cap off, unbuckled his saber and the two were calling each other by their first names and with some teasing words in the midst of a scuffle as vigorous and rollicking as when they were boys on the Ohio farm of their childhood.

"It was a long time before I became accustomed to the instantaneous transformations from the overflowing exhuberance of the boy to the grave, dignified manner of the commanding general when he was suddenly arrested in a frolic by the appearance of an officer who came to make an official report.

"Sometimes I took the first position of a soldier and then saluted this head of our household when he forgot and spoke in the quick, authoritative tone of official life and I soon caught up the expression—'Is that a military order or a request?' This brought him to a realizing sense that in his absentmindedness he made me jump with momentary fright at the abrupt and austere tone of voice he had unconsciously assumed.

"And I remember that peals of laughter that followed at my affronted air and the apology that immediately ensued and when the sky had cleared somewhat a tantalizing query made behind a barricade of chairs for safety, 'It didn't want to be a solder did it?'"[11]

It was during this period she thought how difficult it must have been to learn to compose military reports. Enthusiasm was natural after winning an engagement. The desire to describe in detail how officers and men had carried out orders or displayed heroism had to be condensed and personal feelings suffocated. She delighted in some verbal order given by a great soldier, e.g. "go in and give them hell," but the brevity and suppression of reports distressed her.[12]

Custer was now beefing up his Division. It was the strongest of the three at Winchester but that did not satisfy him for he had plans to make it even stronger in readiness for the spring campaign. Believing in the principle Secretary Stanton had offered the previous month that "a gallant officer makes gallant soldiers," he was procuring the most competent and experienced field officers he could find to add to his staff. Raiding the staffs of Generals Sheridan, Stoneman and Torbert was the first step. Another member was obtained from the teaching staff at West Point.

A respected associate who had served him admirably at Gettysburg, Colonel A.C.M. Pennington, was given command of a brigade. Captain L. W. Barnhart, Captain F. Lyon and of course brother Tom were made members. Tom began rapidly developing into a competent aide.

When Libbie and Autie received an invitation to attend the wedding of her cousin William P. Bacon at New Haven, Connecticut,[13] it was her natural inclination to attend. They had hoped for a 30 day leave which Autie reminded her would quite probably be reduced to 20. Her parents had been strongly urged by her to visit them but neither felt inclined to leave the comforts of home. Rhoda had been unwell most of the year and the Judge had been unwell off and on.

It also was noted that the wedding day was November 9th, the day after the Nation's day of decision between Republican Abraham Lincoln and Democrat George B. McClellan. Anything could happen at that time either in the field or at Washington. There was no question where Autie would be needed, so they both stayed home.

The once popular general received 1,835,985 votes to Lincoln's 2,330,552 votes. Thus Lincoln received a plurality of 494,567. Of the total vote he had received 55 per cent.

General Sheridan was suffering interference with the distaff residents of his Winchester encampment. The wives of many of the officers, failing to recognize that they were permitted to join their husbands only because of the graciousness of the commanding general, were a source of constant irritation to him. Family squabbles that left the officer in a perturbed state of mind when he joined his command, and attempts to counter regulations and orders, were but a few of the problems Sheridan encountered.

Sheridan was a bachelor and a soldier through and through. He enjoyed the company of attractive females but there was never any question in his mind that duty came first. He was not interested in winning a popularity contest. His main purpose was to win battles, and win them he could not with line officers either hesitant or upset because of disruptive influences at home. Aroused to a point of action, he finally ordered the wives of all line officers out of camp. There was one exception—Libbie. She had thoroughly won him over. Through keen eyes he saw her as an inspiration rather than as a deterrent to her husband's fighting abilities. Her influence on the behavior of the officers had been noted and seemed to have been the basis for Sheridan's permissiveness in allowing other wives to join their husbands in the field. Not wishing to understand that permission to join their husbands was a privilege rather than a right—under army regulations they had no status—many of them abused it.

As Libbie viewed her situation in December, all of the line officers' wives had been ordered out and she was the only lady permitted to remain.[14] In one of her lectures in later years she said: "To General Sheridan I owed so much for, after testing General Custer to see if he still charged the enemy with the same impetuosity after as before marriage he never refused to let me come to camp. It had been necessary for him to make very strict rules as women who joined their husbands often interfered with official duties. But, I took no credit to myself. It was my husband's devotion to his profession that enabled him to resist any plea on my part."[15]

The month of December was not one of rest. Though the Federals had considered Early to have been emasculated he continued to worry Sheridan. His raids into the valley were a source of irritation requiring some response. Merritt and Crook were sent out to check these activities. They were not successful. Merritt then sent Custer toward Taunton to make a demonstration that would draw enemy troops to him while Torbert moved toward Charlottesville. Torbert was checked by General Lomax and his Confederate cavalry while Custer was the recipient of a surprise attack from Rosser that forced him to withdraw his troopers rather hurriedly, losing horses and men in doing so.[16]

The weather had been extremely unpleasant, men and animals having been exposed to rain, sleet and finally snow. The temperature frequently dropped below zero with the result that many of Custer's men arrived at Winchester severely frost bitten. That concluded all campaigning for the rest of the winter.

Christmas Day was one of rest for most of the 3d Division. The Custers had expected to get the long awaited furlough and be in Monroe on this day. As it turned out Autie was ordered to preside at several courts-martial. There was nothing he could do but comply.

Libbie had continued imploring her parents to visit them but had received no encouraging replies. The last letter received from her father had amused her because he had implied that they could get as long a leave as they wished and whenever they desired it. After all, wasn't his son-in-law the general that put Early on the run?

Libbie's Christmas Day reply reminded her father that everything in the army was so uncertain. At that very moment Autie was out on a raid. He had been keeping in touch with her by sending back notes sewed to the hem of the pants of those scouts carrying dispatches to General Sheridan.[17]

On the following day Judge Bacon wrote to his sister Eliza Sabin in Onondaga that "Libbie and Armstrong are expected over the holidays and may arrive any time now. The cavalry are on a raid which may defer his visit a week or two." He told Eliza that Libbie had been wanting them to visit her. "We do not want to go but Rupels, our friends in New York, said that my wife governs me and that Libbie governs both."[18]

Rebecca Richmond accepted Libbie's invitation to visit them that winter. The two girls always had enjoyed each other's company and this visit to the 3d Division headquarters would supply an opportunity to see each other, the first time since Libbie's wedding.

In accordance with their established custom, Nettie Humphrey sat at her desk on New Year's Eve to write Libbie a letter after opening the one Libbie had written the year before. She wanted her to know that Captain Dodge[19] no longer was anything to her, that for the second time she had changed her mind about Jacob Greene who was now home.

There had been some differences between Nettie and Jacob Greene. Dodge, who seems to have been in Monroe during one of them, had captured Nettie's interest to a point that she had asked Autie's confidential opinion of him that summer. Greene had just been released from a rebel prison camp and was now home to pursue his courtship.

Nettie's letter was missent and returned to Nettie who on January 10th readdressed it and added that she hoped it would reach them so that their minds would be prepared for the announcement of her approaching marriage.[20] In the confusion of the preparations she must have forgotten she had written to Libbie just two days earlier that she was to marry Jacob Greene in a very quiet wedding on January 12th, and that she would tell her all when she came home.[21]

Libbie and Autie were unable to leave Winchester until the middle of January. On the 15th, the day before they left, General Sheridan and his staff gave them a surprise party. After spending a day each in Washington and New York they arrived in Monroe on January 20th accompanied by the General's staff.[22]

Autie must have chuckled when he picked up the January 19th issue of the Monroe *Commercial* and read *"Who Pays Income Tax In Monroe."*

"Names	*Taxable Income*	*Income Tax*
James Armitage . . .	$2,000	$100.00
Wm. H. Boyd	5,111	205.55
B. H. Campbell	5,000	250.00
George A. Custer . . .	2,000	100.00
Benjamin Dansard . .	2,254	112.70
J.L.C. Godfroy	2,000	100.00"

A roar of laughter surely greeted the February 2nd issue of the *Commercial* when the Custer family read a front page sketch headed *"Brevet Maj. Gen. George A. Custer."* Reprinting a copy of the Michigan *Western Rural* published several weeks earlier it went on to state: "The name of his parents was Fitzhugh, but his father having died in infancy, his mother married a gentleman named Custer, and the son has took and has since born the name of Custer, which he had rendered historical." The balance of the article was highly laudatory, having been taken from the Philadelphia *Press*. The editor of the *Commercial* drew attention to the error of parentage, obvious to everyone in Monroe.

Custer's entourage stayed in Monroe, then went on to Grand Rapids, the home of many of the men serving under him. Time passed so rapidly he found it necessary to request a five day extension which was granted. The Judge wrote to his sister Eliza: "There was a good deal of ceremony & display at the Rapids and on the way, too much for a man of my cloth, so I left and came home alone. All left here on Monday morning the 6th (of February), my wife and Rebecca Richmond of the number. . . . I leave on Monday the 27th, shall first visit Washington intending to be there at the inauguration and then to the army where I shall probably remain until the opening of the campaign.

"The spring and summer will open bloody, and no one can tell whose son or brother will die on the battlefield, It is a miracle how Custer has escaped, yet he may be the next victim. He is not so much exposed since commanding a division."[23]

Colonel Kidd had wired to his father in Ionia asking him to visit Grand Rapids while Custer was there and intercede for him and the Sixth Michigan as it was their desire to again be a part of Custer's Division. Mr. Kidd was unable to see Custer since the latter was staying at the William A. Richmond residence with his father-in-law Judge Bacon. Mr. Kidd did, however, extract a promise from Colonel Gray that he would do everything in his power since it was his design to see the Michigan Brigade all together.[24]

It may have been the unconscious coalition formed by Libbie and Ann Reed that caused Autie to take the final step in his acceptance of Christianity. Both women had expended considerable time and thought to the endeavor. Each saw Autie as a lost soul unless he professed a kinship. And each used every opportunity to encourage his affirmative decision.

That Autie finally yielded to their desires is to their credit. Unquestionably they influenced him for they were the two great influences in his short life. He loved them above all others and any wish of theirs was almost a command. Though pleasing them played some part in his final decision, unquestionably he also was influenced by the daily scenes of death and destruction. His daily observations were constant reminders that life was uncertain.

The Monroe Presbyterian Church was offering a Week of Prayer. It was while attending one of these sessions with Libbie on Sunday evening, February 5th, that he reached a decision. Two weeks later, while at his headquarters in Virginia, he wrote to Rev. D. C. Mattoon:

"It was about this very hour two weeks ago tonight that I knelt with you and your family circle in Monroe. . . . In your presence I accepted Christ as my Saviour. . . . Years of reflection and study had convinced me that I was not fulfilling the end of my Creator if I lived for this world alone. . . . I felt as if I saw the hand of Providence in the fact of being at home during a period of such religious interest.

"I feel somewhat like the pilot of a vessel who has been steering his ship upon familiar and safe waters but has been called upon to make a voyage fraught with danger. Having in safety and with success completed one voyage, he is imbued with confidence and renewed courage, and the second voyage is robbed of half its terror. So it is with me."[25]

Lee was worrying about the potential disintegration of the Confederacy. Though General W. T. Sherman's corps were bogged down by rain in the Carolinas it would just be a matter of time before he confronted the weakened force of General Joseph E. Johnston. Sheridan's forces were coming to life in the Shenandoah Valley and he would soon have to be reckoned with.

Mistrusting Torbert's ability to conduct the expedition because of his disappointing conduct at Fisher's Hill and more recently at Gordonsville, Sheridan appointed General Merritt as the Chief of Cavalry with Custer's and Devin's divisions assigned to his command.

Sheridan had received orders from Grant to destroy the James River Canal and the Virginia Central Railroad, then take Lynchburg and either join Sherman or head back to Winchester. On February 27th his force of 10,000 cavalrymen moved south, Early's depleted forces offering little resistance."[26]

At Waynesborough—on March 2d—Custer led his division against two Confederate infantry brigades and some supporting cavalry and defeated them. Early barely escaped while Custer captured well over a thousand men, 200 wagons, 17 battle flags and 11 guns.[27]

The next day he was met just outside of Charlottesville by a delegation of citizens led by the mayor who turned over the keys to the public buildings and the University of Virginia. At their request he moved his headquarters into the university and, by placing a guard, saved it from destruction.[28]

Judge Bacon had gone East just as much to see the inauguration as to see his family. He had never witnessed one such affair in his 66 years and he didn't intend missing this one. No sooner had Autie led his troops out of camp than the Judge packed his bag. But he had three women to reckon with—Rhoda, Libbie and Rebecca—perhaps four, though we have no record to indicate whether Eliza traveled with them. We can only presume so for Libbie was going back to her room in Washington.

The Judge was rather inept at travel arrangements. Had it not been for the kind attention of a colonel traveling in the same car Libbie was certain they would have been lost. They were loaded down with so much baggage in addition to a bird cage and plants, two ambulances were necessary to convey it all.

Senator Chandler took Libbie and Judge Bacon to the War Department where he presented them to Secretary Stanton. Stanton spoke highly of Father Custer and of their long friendship, then said of Autie: "I am glad he has been as judicious in love as he is wise in war."

From the gallery of the Senate Chamber Libbie, Rebecca Richmond and Judge Bacon were able to see and hear all of the inauguration ceremony. The shock of seeing Vice President Andrew Johnson, obviously drunk,[29] take the oath of office, then ramble through a disjointed address, awakened the large audience. Surprisingly, Libbie barely mentioned the incident in a letter to Autie. Perhaps the life around camp had inured her to the sight of overindulgence.[30]

The thought of Johnson's conduct soon passed out of mind when President Lincoln began his second inaugural address. Briefly, eloquently, he presented his thoughts, his hopes and aspirations, concluding: "With malice toward none; with charity for all; with firmness in the right, as God gives us to see the right, let us strive on to finish the work we are in; to bind up the nation's wounds; to care for him who shall have borne the battle, and for his widow, and his orphan—to do all which may achieve and cherish a just, and a lasting peace, among ourselves, and with all nations."

Now that Early was disposed of, Merritt directed Devin to march along the James River and destroy the canal while Custer moved on toward the Virginia Central Railroad to break it up. The streams were swollen, the roads were muddy and the weather miserable but on they went. Sheridan now completely controlled the country north of the James River. On March 9th the main column moved eastward, destroying locks, dams and boats on their way. At Columbia they met Devin's column where they bivouaced for a day until the supply trains could catch up. It had continued raining and the mud had reached a point in which Sheridan considered abandoning his wagons. Fortunately some 2,000 Negroes who had been following the column literally put their backs to the wheels and virtually lifted the wagons out of the mud, thereby rendering an invaluable service.[31]

Once the column reached the Pamunkey River opposite White House, Custer wrote to Libbie assuring her of his and Tom's safety. They were drawing forage and rations that day, March 11th, from supply boats and would cross the river the next day. They had taken 3,000 prisoners and 16 battleflags with neither General Sheridan nor General Merritt within 10 miles when the captures were made.

No others could claim the laurels for no others had been near. There had been instances in the past when Custer's men had charged a battery or a position and taken men and guns, then dashed on to additional situations while their captures were left in the hands of a few, that other troops came up and took over the booty, laying all claim to it.

The enemy had withdrawn to Richmond, unable to deter Sheridan's column. In spite of heavy rains, bottomless roads and swollen streams the enemy's means of subsistence had been destroyed beyond comprehension or computation. The railroad and canal had been destroyed and the raid in the Shenandoah had ended as a signal success.

March 19th Sheridan's command reached White House Landing where five days were consumed in rest for a very weary corps. On the way there was an engagement at Ashland during which Custer escaped a tragedy. His new horse *Jack Rucker* slipped into a hole, causing him to take a complete somersault, rolling over onto Custer's prostrate form. Had he struggled as his full weight rested on Custer's back, Custer would have been crushed or crippled. The intelligent animal remained motionless until he was rolled off his rider. Custer's injuries were minor and did not hinder him from continuing to direct the fight.[32]

From White House Landing the march across the Peninsula was extremely difficult. Half the horses were unfit for service, their riders having to walk. After using a pontoon bridge to cross the James River they continued on, joining Grant's army near Petersburg on the 26th.

Custer had time in which to read the letters Libbie had waiting for him. She had been delighted to read of his success in the raid, the New York *Herald* giving quite an account of his defeat of Early. Of equal interest to her was the knowledge that he read a chapter in the Bible each night, and that he had not uttered a single oath since last seeing her. The chessmen obtained from Early's captured headquarters wagon that he had forwarded, Rebecca and Major Farnish had found quite useful entertainment. And she had been looking for a new boarding house.

Previously, he had written her: "I long for the return of peace. I look forward to our future with earnest hope. . . . We may not have the means for enjoyment we now possess but . . . above all, we shall have each other."[33]

In response she wrote: "Don't expose yourself so much in battle. Just do your duty, and don't rush out so daringly. Oh, Autie, we must die together. Better the humblest life together than the loftiest, divided."

In the torrential downpour the Northern Army of the Potomac and the Army of the James moved out toward Richmond and Petersburg. It was March 29th they left, numbering together about 125,000.

Sheridan had joined Grant after the last raid because he had been unable to get through to Sherman. Grant had now directed him to pass the left flank while moving southward, cut loose and join Sherman. Sheridan vehemently protested for he knew the days of the Confederacy were numbered and he wished to be in at the kill. He offered that it would be a bad policy to be sent to the Carolinas to crush Johnston's army and then return to wipe out Lee. It would give the impression that Grant could not crush Lee unaided, and arouse Northern public opinion. "In fact," Sheridan said, "my cavalry belongs to the Army of the Potomac, which army is able unaided to destroy Lee." Grant replied that the written order was a blind to cover up the army's movements. With a sigh of relief Sheridan returned to his command, secure in the belief he was not to join Sherman.[34]

It was still pouring down rain on the 30th, the countryside being a sea of mud around Dinwiddie Court House. This important crossroads could boast of a half-dozen shabby houses, a tumble-down tavern and a timeworn courthouse. Sheridan had bivouaced there for a day, waiting for the rain to cease and Custer to bring up the mired-in wagon train five miles back. While there he received orders from Grant to discontinue his raid toward Sherman and instead, seize Five Forks.[35]

Merritt and Crook were ordered to Five Forks in an attempt to dislodge Lee's entrenched troops. Lee saw an opportunity. Making what was to be his last lustrous move in the war, he struck Devin at Five Forks and rolled him back toward Sheridan at Dinwiddie to the south. It was his plan then to crush Sheridan before Grant could intervene. He had a corps of 11,000 men under Pickett facing Devin's force of about 4,000. Devin's dismounted cavalrymen fought a delaying but futile battle. Devin was reinforced late in the day by two of Custer's brigades, a division of the latter being left to bring up the train. The victorious enemy was restrained just north of Dinwiddie.

This change of events found Sheridan separated from Grant, a circumstance Lee could not pass without taking advantage of. In doing so he had detached Pickett and his infantry to engage and destroy Sheridan. Pickett's move in following Sheridan in Dinwiddie isolated him, providing Sheridan with what he called "a rare opportunity."[36] Sheridan made plans to attack Pickett's rear but the latter foiled him by quietly falling back to Five Forks early the next morning.

Libbie and Rebecca Richmond were in Washington at this time. The news that came to the Capital was good but Libbie waited anxiously. Autie may lead a charmed life but she was realistic. Anything could happen.

Rebecca was good company—always happy, always singing. And then there were callers like Chaplain Theodore J. Holmes of Autie's command. He was on his way home to his congregation from whom he had received urgent calls to return. Holmes, when leaving the 3d Division, had told Autie of his gratitude to the Almighty for having made him a General and an unusual man. He was delighted with Custer's decision to lead a religious and moral life since it was having a great effect upon his staff, his command and the entire army. To Libbie he confided that Autie was almost alone in his decision to lead a Christian life.[37]

Libbie hadn't been spending all of her time socially. She had promised her husband she would make him a new personal flag and had spent every moment she could to complete it in time to be carried in the Appomattox campaign.

Fashioning the swallow-tailed guidon from a double layer of silk—a red bar over a blue bar—she bound the outer edge with a heavy silk cord, then stitched white crossed sabers in the center of the field on each side. In size it was three feet wide and six and one half feet in length. Certainly it was a labor of love and pronounced by all who saw it "the handsomest flag in the army."[38]

Lieutenant Peter Boehm had been sent to Washington with letters to the War Department by the General. When he was through with his assignment he carried an additional letter to Libbie. She completed her colorful flag by embroidering her name on one of its points, then entrusted it to Lieutenant Boehm who wrapped the flag around his body under his clothes for fear he might be captured and have to surrender it. In this manner it was delivered to General Custer on the evening of the 30th in the midst of a raging battle. It was immediately attached to a staff, and a breeze unfolded it as if to greet its new owners as an omen of good fortune.

Late the next day during the engagement at Five Forks, Libbie's name was shot off the guidon and Private Huff who carried it was mortally wounded. An inspiration to Autie, the guidon was with him until the end came at Appomattox ten days later.

Lee had told Pickett to "Hold Five Forks at all hazards," but it was an assignment impossible to achieve. His army was cut to pieces, separated as it was from Lee, and he barely escaped. Devin's cavalry had borne the brunt of the cavalry fighting for they had taken the center with Custer taking the left and receiving almost as much punishment.

Sheridan thought it apparent that Lee would retreat toward Amelia Court House. The big question was how to prevent his reaching it. His decision was to head him off, then attack him.[39] In the pursuit of Lee's forces the Federal cavalry was in the advance with Custer well in the lead. On April 3d, Custer's men struck the rear of the retreating column, finding that its resistance was feeble. The gray force had been abandoning equipment along the way. The road was strewn with broken-down ambulances, caissons, wagons and debris of all kinds. Artillery ammunition had been thrown into the woods and along both sides of the main road leading from Namozine Church, the woods and fences then having been set on fire. Some 1,200 prisoners had been taken and reliable information had been obtained that not more than one in five of the rebels had arms in their hands.[40]

Just the day before, while in a skirmish at Namozine Church, Second Lieutenant Tom Custer had captured a battle flag and 14 prisoners, three of whom were officers. For this Sheridan bestowed upon him the brevet of captain and recommended that he be awarded a Medal of Honor.[41]

Lee was now traveling light. He had maneuvered to escape toward Burkesville. Sheridan moved across country paralleling Lee's line of march, ever watchful for a weak point he could take advantage of. Now in open country, Devin and Custer charged the enemy train at intervals, reaping considerable destruction. The policy now was to strike and harrass the rebels on the march, to delay them until they could be intercepted.[42]

The opportunity for a major attack occurred at Saylor's Creek on April 6th. The Sixth Corps under General Horatio G. Wright had arrived. Sheridan had thought Lee's army could be destroyed at this point and Lee's men, obviously thinking the same, fought with desperation. Sheridan's men, eager to end it all, fought determinedly. It ended that evening with the capture of General Richard Ewell, six of his generals and almost 10,000 of his troops.[43]

Sheridan had written to Grant at this time, "if the thing is pressed, I think Lee will surrender." President Lincoln telegraphed Grant, "Let the thing be pressed." And it was.[44]

Custer's role in the battle of Saylor's Creek was nothing short of phenomenal. Early that morning while his command was watering the horses he received orders from General Merritt to move his command at once to an attack upon the rebel wagon train. His column moved out, he leading it toward the point designated. When it was reached he saw a more desirable point to attack. As he moved toward it he saw a nine-gun Confederate battery being positioned. His seeing it was to charge it, taking all nine guns and 800 prisoners.[45]

Continuing his charge another mile he struck the enemy wagon train, capturing and destroying 1,000 wagons. Reforming his command in a small valley, he prepared for the day's work. Over the hill General Joseph B. Kershaw and his rebels had thrown up some earthworks. All that day Custer charged this fortification, reforming each time in the valley, then returning to attack. He knew the Sixth Corps was having a successful engagement on the other side and would soon be turning the flank.

As the sun began to settle beyond the western horizon Custer and his staff were picking their way across the debris littered battlefield. They passed groups of enthusiastic blue clad men herding large groups of rebel prisoners. Among those captured were six Confederate generals: Ewell, Kershaw, Barton, Corse, De Barre and Custis Lee, son of Robert E. Lee.[46]

When Custer arrived at the spot he had previously designated as his headquarters, it was twilight. Awaiting him was the newly surrendered Confederate General Joseph B. Kershaw who described the meeting in an account to Mrs. Custer years later:

"A spare, lithe and sinewy figure, about medium height, bright, dark blue eyes, ever restless—a florid complexion, brown wavy curls, high cheek bones, an acquiline nose, firm-set teeth, a jaunty close-fitting cavalry jacket, large top boots, handsomely ornamented Spanish spurs, golden aiguillettes, a serviceable sabre, a quick, nervous, energetic movement, and an air of hauteur, telling of the habit of command, announced the redoubtable Custer whose name had become as familiar to his foes as to his friends.

"After being introduced by an aide, 'Why General,' said Custer, taking my hand with a kindly smile somewhat tinged with humor, 'I am glad to see you here. I feel as if I ought to know about you.'

"'Yes,' said I, 'General, we have met very often but not under circumstances favorable to cultivating an acquaintance.'

"This little passage of pleasantry made us quite at home immediately, and very soon the conversation became free, general and kindly around the camp fire. With a soldier's hospitality, we were made to feel welcome by our host, and notwithstanding our misfortunes, enjoyed not a little the camp luxuries of coffee, sugar, condensed milk, hard-tack, broiled ham, etc., spread before us upon the tent fly converted into a table cloth around which we all sat upon the ground. Custer and his Rebel guests.

"After supper we smoked and talked over many subjects of interest to all of us dwelling however, almost wholly upon the past. The future to us, was not inviting, and our host with true delicacy of feeling, avoided the subject. We slept beneath the stars, Custer sharing his blankets with me. . . . as I lay watching the cold insensate stars, I buried all my dreams of Southern independence.

"When I awoke the sun shone brightly and all was brisk and activity. Our host was already up and gave me a cheery greeting as I arose and joined him standing near the fire. He wore an air of thought upon his face, betokening the work of the day that lay before him, and received and sent many rapid communications. While at breakfast, one after another some 30 troopers rode up within a few rods, each dismounting and aligning himself, holding his horse by the bridle. Each also carried a *Confederate battleflag,* except my captor of the previous day whom I recognized in the ranks, and he bore two of our flags. He also, as he caught my eye and bowed, pointed to my own sabre worn at his belt with an air of pride and pleasure. (Corporal Lanham of the 25th Ohio Cavalry had promised Gen. Kershaw he would conduct his party directly to General Custer without insult or molestation. He was intercepted by a lieutenant of the 8th Illinois Cavalry who relieved Kershaw of his saber. Kershaw had reported the incident to Custer who, without comment to him, had righted the wrong. Kershaw had requested that Lanhan should have it.)

"My curiosity was greatly excited by this group and I asked General Custer what it meant. 'That,' said he, 'is my escort for the day. It is my custom after a battle to select for my escort a sort of *garde de honeur* those men of each regiment who most distinguish themselves in action, bearing for the time, the trophies which they have taken from the enemy. These men are selected as the captors of the flags which they bear.'

"I counted them. There were 31 captured banners representing 31 of our regiments killed, captured or dispersed the day before. It was not comforting to think of.

"Finally, the General turned to me and said, 'You will remain here for a few moments when horses will be brought for you and your companions and you will be conducted to Burkesville where you will find General Grant. Goodbye.'

"He shook my hand, mounted a magnificent charger and rode proudly away followed at a gallop by his splendid escort bearing the fallen flags. As he neared his conquering legions cheer after cheer greeted his approach, bugles sounded and sabres flashed as they saluted. The proud cavalcade filed through the open ranks and . . . I saw Custer no more."[47]

His West Point schoolmate Morris Schaff wrote: "He was always a boy, and absolutely free from harboring a spirit of malice, hatred or revenge. Whenever fortune made any of his West Point friends prisoners, he hunted them up, grasped their hands, with his happy smile, and, before parting, tendered generous proffers of aid."[48]

Custer had revealed a technique he had been using in rewarding valor and in developing an *esprit de corps*. Kershaw was aware of another capability Custer had evidenced in battle—his unusual tactical judgment.

Most officers commanding any body of men from a company to an army were in the habit of taking a battle position in the center rear of the troops. From there they could see most of the men on the front line which would enable them to send reserves to any weak point. McClellan liked to take a position on high ground well back and observe the movements through his field glasses.

In both instances if the country was open and the enemy easily seen, the position of the commanding officer would be ideal. In situations like Five Forks or the Wilderness nothing much could be observed from the center rear because of the heavy woods obstructing the view of the enemy. He would have to depend upon the sound of firing and upon constant reports from the front line. By the time he would get a report and send back an order the situation could have changed radically.

Custer's method differed from that just described. He believed that the commander should be in front of the skirmish line, keeping constantly in motion on a fast-gaited horse. The position gave him the advantage of seeing the ground over which his men must travel, seeing as much as they could for he was nearest the enemy, and on observing an enemy weakness he would take instant advantage of it by giving an order to his men which they obeyed in a flash. There was no loss of time by sending an order through an aide.

The very presence of the commanding officer on the skirmish line indicated a willingness to share their danger. That he would do so by exposing himself to sniper fire by wearing a red necktie and a bizarre uniform so that his men could observe his presence, was sufficient to inspire the most timorous.

Custer could get shot up there and his horses did use up rapidly. Who knew that better than he? He had lost many fine horses by enemy fire and he knew the rebels hadn't been shooting at them. The secret of his success was not luck. It was to be in front where the action was and to keep his horse moving, always moving, back and forth, keeping his eyes on the enemy and not on his troops.[49]

Sheridan, Pleasonton, Phil Kearny, Kilpatrick and Custer were firmly of the opinion that a cavalry fight could best be won by being in front of the line in motion with their eyes on the adversary. Each had won often enough to attest to the technique.

NOTES — CHAPTER 14

[1] Merington, p. 129.
[2] Letter of October 20, 1864 from Newark. Burton Historical collection, Detroit.
[3] Libbie to G. A. Custer. Letter of October 30, 1864. Original in author's collection.
[4] Merington, p. 131.
[5] Frost: *Custer Album,* pp. 79-80.
[6] Judge I. T. Christiancy to G. A. Custer. Letter of October 15, 1864. Author's collection.
[7] Letter of October 3, 1864, G. A. Custer to J. H. Kidd, Michigan Historical Collection, Ann Arbor.
[8] Special Orders No. 340, War Department, October 10, 1864, EBC-CBNM.
[9] *Michigan in The War,* p. 61; *Record of Service of Michigan Volunteers in the Civil War,* Sixth Michigan Cavalry, Vol. 36, pp. 42-43.
[10] Frost: *Custer Album,* p. 58.
[11] In the author's collection.
[12] EBC - CBNM.
[13] Invitation to the marriage of Wm. P. Bacon and Emma Whittemore at New Haven, Connecticut, November 9, 1864. Author's collection.
[14] Merington, pp. 134-35.
[15] EBC - CBNM.
[16] Sheridan: *Memoirs,* Vol. II, p. 102; Sheridan gives no indication Custer repulsed Rosser. The Washington *Daily Globe,* Dec. 28, 1864, states: "The Third Division of General Custer returned on Thursday (December 22) from a reconnaissance up the valley.... Before daybreak on Thursday morning, Rosser's rebel cavalry attempted to surprise their camp, but were repulsed with a loss to them of 15 killed and many wounded. Our loss was two killed and 25 or 30 wounded." O.R., I, Vol. XLIII, pt. 2, p. 821, December 22, 1864—Sheridan in a communication to Grant stated that Custer had captured two flags and 33 prisoners in an encounter with Rosser, p. 825, December 24, 1864—Sheridan notified J. A. Rawlins, Grant's chief of staff, that Custer had 230 men frost-bitten on the expedition.
[17] Merington, p. 135; Sheridan: *Memoirs,* Vol. 2, p. 104.
[18] December 26, 1864, D. S. Bacon to Eliza Sabin. Letter in author's collection.
[19] It is assumed this was Captain Horace W. Dodge who was mustered into the 5th Michigan Cavalry in Detroit and was discharged for disability on October 21, 1864, for wounds received at Trevilian Station. Later he became a major by brevet.
[20] Original in author's collection.
[21] *Ibid;* Cahn, p. 83, notes that Greene, after eleven months in Confederate prisons, was exchanged on April 7, 1865. The Monroe *Monitor,* January 18, 1865, states: *"Married*—on the 12th ult. at Monroe by Rev. Safford, Capt. J. L. Greene of Gen. Custer's Staff to Annette M. Humphrey of Monroe." It is very unlikely the Confederate captors would have given Greene a leave of absence from prison to visit Nettie.
[22] The Monroe *Monitor,* January 25, 1865, stated that Custer and his staff arrived in town Saturday (Jan. 21st). The Monroe *Commercial,* January 26, 1865 stated that General Custer and staff arrived in Monroe on Friday morning (Jan. 20).
[23] Monroe, February 17, 1865; original in author's collection.
[24] J. H. Kidd papers, January 30, 1865. Michigan Historical Collection.
[25] *The Evangelist,* March 16, 1865 (Union Theological Seminary). Letter of G. A. Custer to Rev. D. C. Mattoon dated February 19, 1865. Rev. Mattoon had assisted at the Custer-Bacon wedding ceremony one year earlier.
The Monroe County Historical Museum display a photo album containing *Cartes-de-visite* of about 40 prominent Monroe men given by George A. Custer to his former Presbyterian Church Sunday School teacher S. M. Sacket in 1862.
[26] Sheridan: *Memoirs,* Vol. II, pp. 112-13.
[27] *Ibid,* pp. 114-16.
[28] *Ibid,* p. 118; Monaghan, p. 228; Brown, John R. and Anne Freudenberg—"General Custer At Piedmont," *Magazine of Albemarle County History, Charlottesville, Va.,* 1964, wrote: "Custer moved his headquarters into the University of Virginia and by the intervention and requests of the people and a committee of the more important men of Charlottesville, the University of Virginia was saved from being burned."
[29] Poor Johnson, unused to whiskey in any amount, had been induced to take some as a medicine for an indisposition. An amount that the average drinking man could handle was more than his teetotaling body could handle.
[30] Merington, p. 136.
[31] Sheridan: *Memoirs,* Vol. II, p. 121; *Rebellion Record,* Vol. XI, p. 636; Rhodes, p. 157.
[32] Merington, p. 141; Rhodes, p. 158.
[33] Letter of March 20, 1865.
[34] Sheridan: *Memoirs,* Vol. II, pp. 127-28.
[35] *Ibid,* p. 145; Whittaker, pp. 286-87.
[36] Sheridan: *Memoirs,* Vol. II, p. 154.
[37] Merington, p. 147.
[38] *Ibid;* Frost. *Custer Album,* p. 61 (illustration); H. Michael Madaus, "The Personal And Designating Flags of General George A. Custer, 1863-1865," *Military Collector And Historian,* pp. 1-14.
[39] Newhall, F. C.: *With Sheridan In Lee's Last Campaign,* Philadelphia, 1866, p. 132; Sheridan: *Memoirs,* Vol. II, p. 174.
[40] O.R., I, Vol. XLVI, pt. III, p. 531, Sheridan's report to Grant, April 3, 1865.
[41] *Medals Of Honor,* War Department Circular, Washington, 1897, p. 37. The award was for "Capture of a flag, April 2, 1865, at Namozine Church, Va." Date of issue, April 24, 1865. Stillman, Sue: *Medal Of Honor Men,* Michigan Military Records, Lansing, 1920.
[42] Tremain, Henry E.: *Last Hours Of Sheridan's Cavalry,* N.Y., 1904, p. 141; Rhodes, p. 164.
[43] Sheridan: *Memoirs,* Vol. II, pp. 180-184; Humphreys, Andrew A: *The Virginia Campaign Of '64 And '65,* N.Y., 1883, pp. 380-81.
[44] Rhodes, pp. 105-106; Newhall, pp. 179-80; Sheridan: *Memoirs,* Vol II, p. 187.
[45] Tremain, pp. 154-56.
[46] *Ibid,* p. 161.
[47] Account of Major General Joseph B. Kershaw, C.S.A. Original manuscript in author's collection.
[48] Morris Schaff: *The Sunset Of The Confederacy,* Boston, 1912, p. 114.
[49] Whittaker, pp. 283-84.

WAR OF 1812 VETERANS—On June 15, 1871, resident survivors of the Battle of the River Raisin met on Guyor's Island near Monroe. Gen. Custer (center standing) was a speaker. His father Emanuel is directly in front of him, first row. Courtesy Monroe County Historical Museum.

CHAPTER 15
SURRENDER

Tom Custer had done it again. Leading a valiant charge on horseback, the youthful lieutenant was the first to leap his horse over a breastworks at Saylor's Creek, seize the rebel colors and demand their surrender. As he seized the flag the color bearer shot him at such close range the powder burned his face, the bullet entering his right cheek and passing out the back of his neck. He responded by retaining the flag, then drawing his revolver and killing the rebel.

Autie arrived just as Tom, the front of his shirt covered with blood, had handed his trophy to one of his men, had taken another and was preparing to go on. Autie firmly ordered him to a surgeon in the rear, an order which he obeyed only after Autie placed him under arrest. He was proud of this young brother who had taken three stands of colors in four days and had two horses shot under him in the process. He had been concerned about his brother's conduct when first he transferred to the cavalry but it was with a feeling of pride he could note that Tom was moderate in his drinking, had discontinued the use of tobacco and was respected and admired by all who knew him. To crown it all he had displayed unusal judgment in observing enemy activity and in deciding when to press them. He had become a superb tactician.[1]

As a result of this act of bravery Sheridan made him a major by brevet and recommended him for his second Medal of Honor. Later he was breveted a lieutenant colonel.

For Lee the situation was critical. Grant had written him on the 7th of the hopelessness of further resistance on the part of the Army of Northern Virginia and suggesting its surrender to prevent further loss of blood. Lee's reply on the following day was in the nature of a request for the terms offered with such a surrender.

He was looking for a way out. He had learned that evening just before dusk that Custer had charged in to Appomattox Station and captured four trains with their locomotives loaded with sorely needed supplies.[2] This was a low blow; his men had been marching without food for nearly two days. This discouraging intelligence along with the knowledge his front was blocked by a formidable cavalry force was a matter to discuss that evening at what was to be his final council of war. It might be possible to break through the cavalry but were there Federal infantry beyond? If so it would be impossible to break through.

The day dawned on a Palm Sunday as the Confederates attempted to force a way through the Federal line. Gordon's infantry and Fitz Lee's cavalry met with some success but soon encountered more infantry than either could cope with. There was no hope, no escape. Lee could do nothing but surrender.

It was near noon of the 9th that Grant received Lee's request for an interview to discuss a surrender.[3] Meanwhile a flag of truce had been sent by General Gordon just in time to stop a charge Custer was preparing to lodge.[4] In an exchange of notes Grant and Lee agreed to meet at the village of Appomattox Court House.

They met in the stately Wilmer McLean house to complete the details of capitulation. By three o'clock the terms of surrender had been written out and accepted. Grant and Lee shook hands, Lee departing on his gray mount into history.

The moment he had turned away there was a rush up the steps, the waiting officers eager to purchase the objects in that historic room. Phil Sheridan managed to give Wilmer McLean a twenty-dollar gold piece for the small pine oval-topped, spool-legged table on which the terms of surrender were written. Calling Custer, he presented the table to him with a note he had penned to Libbie that read:

"Appomattox Court House
April 10th, 1865

My Dear Madam,

I respectfully present to you the small writing table on which the conditions for the surrender of the Confederate Army of Northern Virginia were written by Lt. General Grant — and permit me to say, Madam, that there is scarcely an individual in

our service who has contributed more to bring about this desirable result than your very gallant husband.
Mrs. Genl. Custer
Washington, D.C.

Very Respectfully,
Phil H. Sheridan
Maj. General."[5]

Custer, his golden hair falling to his shoulders, carried the table down the stairs on his shoulders as he hurried to his tent pitched to the right of the McLean house. It was there that evening he would entertain a number of his old West Point classmates and friends. Seven of them, all Confederate officers, slept with him that night under his blankets in the same tent with the table.[6]

Many years later Libbie wrote that the surrender table "may have been a reward of merit to me for not interfering with the services of one of his generals whom he generously acknowledged had done so much to lead to his success. General Sheridan never hesitated during his command of the cavalry to express to his officers and to others what he owed

SURRENDER TABLE AND ACCOMPANYING LETTER FROM GEN. SHERIDAN. May be seen in the McLean House at Appomattox Courthouse, Va. Photo in author's collection.

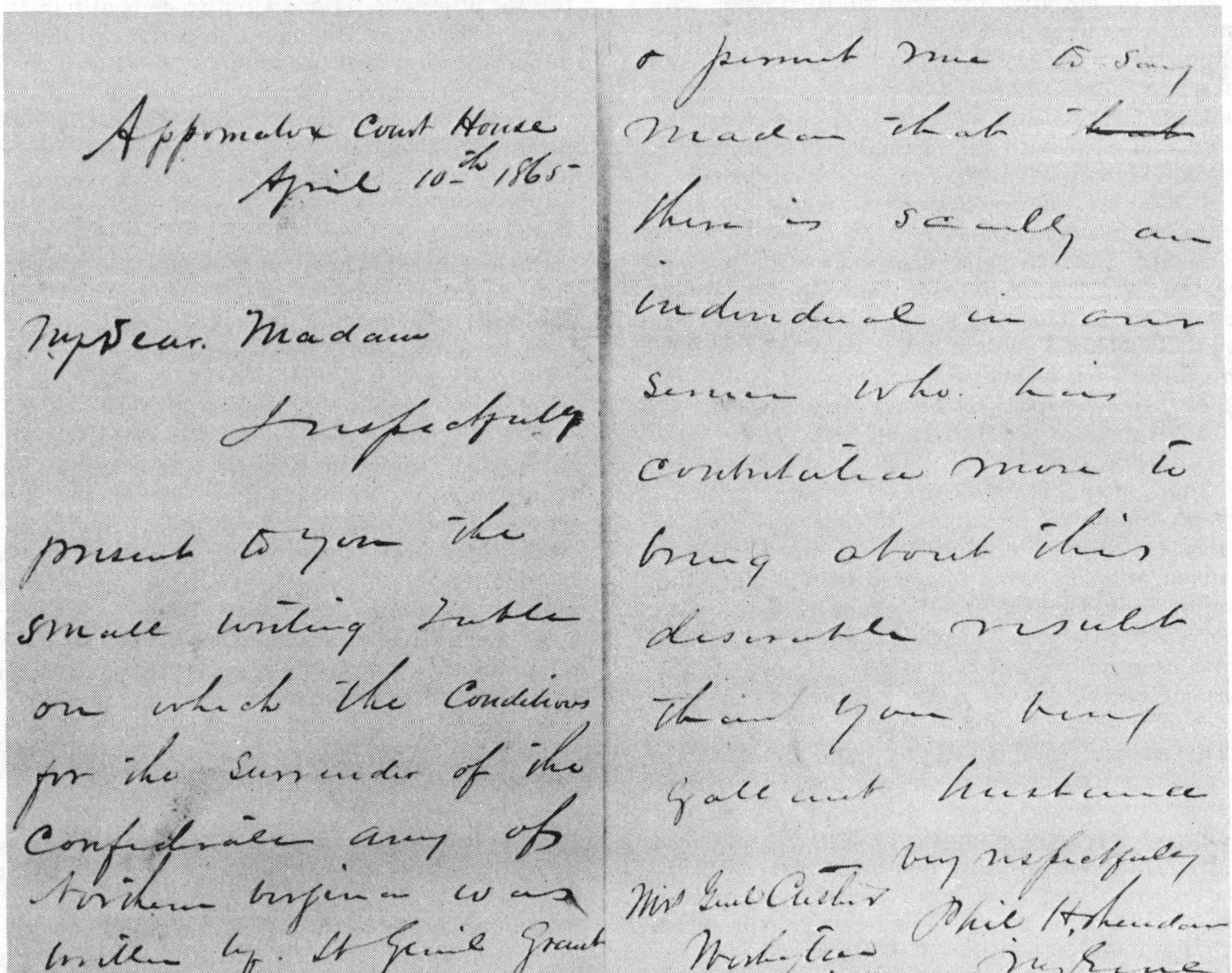

Appomattox Court House
April 10th 1865

My Dear Madam

I respectfully present to you the small writing table on which the Conditions for the Surrender of the Confederate army of Northern Virginia was written by Lt Genl Grant & permit me to say Madam that ~~that~~ there is scarcely an individual in our service who has contributed more to bring about this desirable result than your very gallant husband

Very respectfully
Phil H. Sheridan
Maj Genl

Mrs Genl Custer
Washington
DC

them. But he groaned when they became engaged and was utterly discouraged when they married.

"However, to my husband he said in time: 'Custer, you are the only man whom matrimony has not spoiled for a charge.' This was a royal accolade to me but I feared that it was undeserved for, though I never attempted to 'spoil' General Sheridan's cavalryman I do not remember a time when, if I could, I would not have prevented one of those desperately perilous charges for which he was noted. Patriotism and renunciation do not appear to be ruling spirit either in ancient or modern history with girls who are in love."[7]

Libbie beat Autie into Richmond. With the news of the surrender at 5 A.M. on the 10th, she could stay in Washington no longer. Boarding the train at 2 P.M., she arrived at Fortress Monroe four hours later in time to board the President's gunboat *Baltimore*. She disembarked in Richmond that evening to observe that it looked "like a dead city." Though her thoughts were occupied with the anticipated meeting with Autie, she was impressed with one of the other passengers—Admiral Porter—who she thought "assumed more style than Farragut but is very much a gentleman."[8]

Before Libbie had her trip to Richmond with Senator Chandler and the members of the Joint Committee on the Conduct of the War her husband had some thoughts he had to express to his gallant Division. Grant's military operations had virtually drawn to a close with the surrender at Appomattox. The men were to begin their march to Petersburg on April 10th and expected to be mustered out upon their arrival there.

Knowing that the end was near and that circumstances might not afford the opportunity of showing his deep feelings for his men and the service they had rendered, he immediately prepared a statement and had it issued to his men:

"Headquarters Third Cavalry Divison
Appomattox Court House, Va.
April 9, 1865.

Soldiers of the Third Cavalry Division:

"With profound gratitude toward the God of battles, by whose blessings our enemies have been humbled and our arms rendered triumphant, your Commanding General avails himself of this first opportunity to express to you his admiration of the heroic manner in which you passed through the series of battles which today resulted in the surrender of the enemy's entire Army.

"The record established by your indomitable courage is unparalleled in the annals of war. Your prowess has won for you even the respect and admiration of your enemies. During the past six months, although in most instances confronted by superior numbers, you have captured from the enemy, in open battles, 111 pieces of artillery, 65 battle flags and upwards of 10,000 prisoners of war, including seven general officers. Within the past ten days, and included in the above, you have captured 46 pieces of field artillery and 37 battle flags. You have never lost a gun, never lost a color and have never been defeated; and notwithstanding the numerous engagements in which you have borne a prominent part, including those memorable battles of Shenandoah, you have captured every piece of artillery which the enemy has dared to open upon you."

Following a few additional remarks he concluded:

"And now, speaking for myself alone, when the war is ended and the task of the historian begins; when those deeds of daring, which have rendered the name and fame of the Third Cavalry Division imperishable, are inscribed upon the bright pages of our country's history, I only ask that my name be written as that of the Commander of the Third Cavalry Division."[9]

On the following morning, the 10th, the cavalry began its march to Petersburg.[10] By the evening of the 11th it had reached Prospect Station on the Petersburg Railroad. Once routine matters had been disposed of, Custer sat down to write his first letter to Libbie since the surrender. Beginning: "My Darling—Only time to write a word. My head is too full for utterance. Thank God peace is at hand and thank God the 3d Division has performed the most important duty of this campaign and has achieved almost all the glory that has been won."

Proudly he told of the 40 Confederate battleflags at his headquarters obtained because the 3d Division had won every battle and had always been in the advance. The cavalry was now moving back to Brandy Station.

Physically exhausted but mentally exhilarated, he exclaimed: "Hurrah for peace and my little durl!" And then to advise her that he could soon be back on the pay of his regular army rank, he ended his note: "Can you consent to come down and be a Captain's wife?"[11]

With the termination of the war and the natural cutback of the armed forces there would be a reduction in the number of general officers. Those who held such rank in the volunteer army or those who held a brevet rank would be reduced to their regular army standing, which in Custer's case would be that of captain.

No sooner had the note been dispatched than a telegram arrived from Admiral Porter advising him that Mrs. Custer had arrived in Richmond. The next morning Autie, as he walked into her room in the Confederate White House, found her asleep in Mrs. Jefferson Davis' bed. She had slept in Jeff's the night before.

Once awake she perceived that he was tired, very tired; his face was thin and drawn, the high cheekbones more prominent than ever. The tan of his sun-reddened face was accentuated by the pillow he was napping on while she dressed. Awakening him, she conducted him on a tour of the famous house under the ever watchful eye of the housekeeper who had been left behind by the Davis family when they fled from Richmond. Much of the furniture had been left—a grand piano in the parlor, mirrors, drapes, a sewing machine, the Sevres china and a tiny black-and-tan dog remained.[12]

The two had little time to spend in Richmond for Autie must return immediately to his command. There is no evidence he was on furlough. With him he had the surrender towel he had received at Appomattox Court House. He gave it to her for safe keeping.[13]

Rejoining his command, they moved with it toward Petersburg. At Nottoway Court House they heard the dreadful news of Lincoln's assassination the evening after it occurred. The first story indicated that the President had been shot at Willard's Hotel that morning — April 15th — a story General Sheridan believed to be false because he could see no reason for Lincoln visiting that hotel. The following morning an official telegram verified the story of the assassination though giving no details.[14]

As the cavalry column moved along Libbie rode at its head in a spring wagon most of the time with the wife of brigade commander Col. A.C.M. Pennington, finding it more comfortable than the jolting ride of the springless ambulance that had been assigned.

It was fatiguing but such a novelty she thoroughly enjoyed the ride. Eliza brought up the rear in her battered carriage.

Autie reminded Libbie of another novelty she had experienced—she was the first woman to ride over the South Side Railroad following the evacuation of Richmond.[15]

At Petersburg Autie gave her a horse called *Custis Lee* he had captured from a staff officer of that general at Five Forks. He was a blooded bay pacer, very spirited though very kind.[16]

On the 24th the cavalry column moved out toward Danville, Sheridan having received orders to march it and the Sixth Corps to Greensborough, North Carolina, to aid Sherman in an effort to quell General Joseph E. Johnston. Libbie returned to Washington, taking the surrender table with her to ship home to Monroe. She cautioned her father to take good care of it and not give away one splinter. She was fond of the table but the letter that Sheridan had sent with it was her pride and joy.[17]

Libbie had wanted to go home with Tom who had become quite a hero in his own right but preferred not being so far from her husband. Senator Chandler, she had learned, had just said to Secretary Stanton, "Don't you think Custer had done enough to have a full commission?" Stanton replied, "My God, what hasn't he done?"

When the cavalry arrived at South Boston on the 28th, Sheridan received a notice from Halleck that Johnston had capitulated and that he should return to Washington immediately.[18] He set out at once for Washington, the cavalry corps returning leisurely to Petersburg for some days of rest.

On the move toward North Carolina, Sherian had ordered that horses were to be taken from the country through which they were passing, to be pressed into public service. One of the horses was claimed and purchased by Custer from the Provost Marshal for $125. The 12-year-old bay stallion described as being 15 and a quarter hands high had been purchased by him after it and several hundred others had been appraised by a board of officers.[19] He determined later that this animal he called *Don Juan* was valued at $10,000 and had a remarkable track record.[20]

At Petersburg Custer received a letter from his friend Judge Christiancy expressing fear that his son Jim had not done as well as he ought to though he was glad he had taken a pledge of abstinence. "If he keeps it fairly," he wrote, "he may be a man yet. If he don't I hope never to see him again. His conduct has nearly worried the life out of me and my kindness to him has always rendered him worse."[21]

Judge Christiancy indicated that he had given the Detroit *Advertiser* a portion of Custer's letter of April 21st, which it intended publishing soon. The letter appeared in the issue of May 1. Since it clearly expresses Custer's views at this time and the views of Christiancy, who was a ranking Republican in Michigan, it is reproduced herewith:

"I confidently believe that the policy which President Johnson will pursue toward the rebellion and its leaders, will not only be the wisest, but in fact is the only one which can be adopted to secure safety for the future. I may be mistaken. . . . I agree fully with the sentiment expressed in his speech (a recent one to an Illinois delegation) that the sooner the people learn that treason is the blackest of crimes and that traitors must be punished, the sooner shall we be prepared to treat properly the leaders of this unprovoked and unholy rebellion.

"For myself, I can express my opinion in a few words, and in doing so, I believe I express the universal opinion of the army. Extermination is the only true policy we can adopt toward the political leaders of the rebellion, and at the same time do justice to our posterity. No other course is safer or politic toward such of them as dare to remain in the country. Let all of those who have occupied prominent positions in the rebel State Governments or the so-called Confederate Government—all the editors and others who, by their traitorous harangues or speeches, have stirred up the people to revolt, be condemned as traitors and punished with unrelenting vigor, until every living traitor has been swept from our land, and our free government and free institutions shall be purged from every disloyal traitor. Then, and not till then, may the avenging angel sheathe his sword, and our country emerge from this struggle regenerated, and with renewed confidence in the ability of a free people to govern themselves."[22]

Meanwhile Judge Bacon had arrived home, having left Rhoda at Canandaguia, New York, on their return from Washington. He informed Custer they had received the news while at Canandigua of the battle of Waynesborough and of the presentation of the captured flags in Washington.

The kindly judge wanted him to know that he took a great pride in Tom's heroism and had gone to his mother and sister to dispel their fears, then added:

"I feel that a kind Providence has watched over and protected you and that God should be praised. I feel a thankfulness and gratitude that no language can express in the thought that there is to be no more fighting, that we are to have a country without dismemberment, and a government to be feared and respected, and one without civil war during the lifetime of our children's children."[23]

A week later he wrote to Libbie in Washington that he was taking her mother to Traverse City for three months in the hope that the erysepilas about her face would improve in that climate.[24] But the Judge didn't leave immediately for on May 5th he wrote to Autie, "You have been truly and emphatically among the most fortunate of men not only in this but in all previous ages. You have been providentially spared on the battlefield and I am not aware that you have ever made a mistake." He continued:

"Tom, the young hero, has gone to the (Grand) Rapids to see Rebecca. I wanted him to go with me to Detroit on Monday but he declined. He is the lion of the day for one of his age and rank. Many inquiries are made about him personally and by letter. He was made for the army and I hope he may be continued in service with a command and promotion."[25]

The Judge noted that, "The *table* is feasting the eyes of many. Even the unlettered French look upon it in the light of an antiquarian." It appears that Tom had carried the surrender table home with him from Washington.

On May 14th the Judge wrote Libbie that they were leaving for Traverse City in the morning, an act that he regretted as his fruit trees looked beautiful in blossom, and there was unfinished business that should be cared for. Tom would leave the first part of the next week. "Like all other soldiers he is restless and uneasy and wants to be with his command." Then he assured Libbie that the colored man—Henry—they had sent home to take care of *Phil Sheridan* was very faithful and competent.[26]

With the rest at Petersburg concluded, the cavalry corps under command of General George Crook commenced its homeward journey. Proudly it passed through the curious crowds in Richmond, through Trevilian Station and Brandy Station, then finally camped on the battlefield of Bull Run where Autie had had his first taste of action. There were several days of rest, then a move across the Potomac River to a new camp ground.

The Grand Review of the Army of the Potomoc was scheduled for May 23 and 24. Phil Sheridan, who had led the army to Appomattox Court House, could not be there. He had been relieved of his command and sent to the southwest to restore Texas and the enemy held portion of Louisiana to the Union in the shortest possible time. General Kirby Smith was the culprit holdout rebel and he was to be treated as an outlaw if he did not surrender. He was to be accorded the same terms as those offered Lee and Johnston, said Grant. If he refused. . . .[27]

Sheridan attempted to get an extension from Grant so that he could participate in the Review. It would be the last chance to see the men he so highly regarded. Grant was adamant. There was no time to lose for there was more than met the eye or than in the written orders.

Emperor Maximilian and Empress Carlotta of Mexico had been holding conferences with Confederate officials at Brownsville, Texas. Maximilian's invasion of Mexico had been encouraged by the Confederacy and, because of it, had been considered a part of the rebellion. As a result, many hundreds of Southerners had crossed into Mexico retaining their feeling of hostility toward the Union. Grant wanted the north side of the Rio Grande controlled by Federal troops and would not be content until the French and Austrian invaders of the Mexican soil were forced to leave.[28]

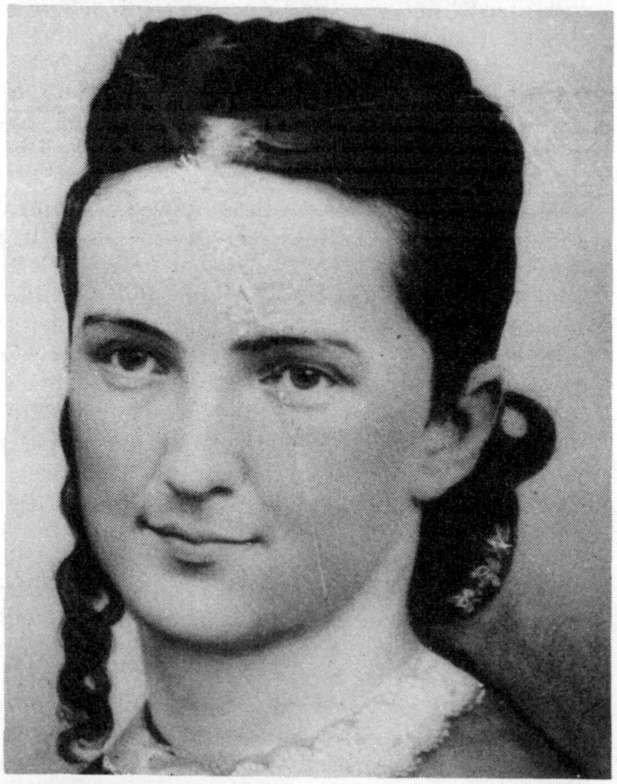

LIBBIE IN NEW ORLEANS, July, 1865. From a miniature on a vase painted in New Orleans by O. Lux. Photo in author's collection.

Sunday morning was dull and overcast. It had been raining the night before and large pools of water stood in Pennsylvania Avenue. The cavalry corps had been ordered to a more accessible camp ground for the Tuesday Review. Word had been received that Sheridan would leave them without leading them in the parade. As the squadrons of cavalry splashed their way down Pennsylvania Avenue they purposely passed Willard's Hotel where Sheridan was quartered. Sheridan and some members of his staff appeared on the hotel balcony to view for the last time this remarkable army. The following day he was on his way to St. Louis where he embarked on a steamboat for New Orleans. Before he reached his destination he was informed that Kirby Smith had surrendered.

Merritt, who had taken over Sheridan's command, had placed Custer and the Third Cavalry Division first in the order of march in the coming review.[29]

On the following day both Custer and Merritt were ordered to take their staffs and report to General Sheridan in New Orleans.[30]

It was appreciation time for the Army of the Potomac. The Grand Army of the Republic was passing in a last review before the crowd-lined streets and the bunting-draped Presidential reviewing stand. A cannon blast at 9 A.M. had started the parade down the hill past the newly finished Capitol. As it moved along in the bright sunshine the crowds cheered and children sang patriotic songs and waved flags. The flag before the White House was at full mast for the first time since that terrible day in April.

Custer rode proudly in front of his 3d Division. His dress was subdued, for he wore the full dress uniform of a major general. He sat *Don Juan* his dark bay stallion with the white saddle marks, as if they were one. The temperamental animal, sensing the unusual, champed at the bit as he eyed the throngs of people carpeting the buildings and sidewalks on each side. The bands were blaring and the crowds shouting as they moved down the avenue toward the reviewing stand.

Some 200 yards from it, so the story is told in an eyewitness report, a group of 300 girls began singing "Hail to the Chief," and throwing bouquets and wreaths at Custer as he passed. As Custer slacked his reins to catch a bouquet, the fractious animal took off toward the reviewing stand before Custer could gather up his reins.

Down the avenue they raced, Custer's yellow hair and red flannnel necktie floating in the air. In rocketing past the reviewing stand Custer thought to draw and present his saber in full salute to President Johnson and General Grant. In doing so his saber caught his wide hat, causing it and the saber to fall to the ground. With both hands now free he easily brought the terror-stricken animal under control. Retrieving his saber and hat from an orderly, he returned to the head of his command.[31] There had been a charisma about this flamboyant young warrior that endeared him to many. This last incident had augmented his admirers.

After having bid his devoted men a painful farewell that afternoon, they packed and boarded a train that evening heading southward. His eyes remained moist with the thought of those fine men he was leaving, of the feeling in their cheers and the final cry of one of them, "A tiger for old Curley!" Truly he believed that there was no friendship like that cemented by mutual danger on a battlefield.[32]

Custer's move south was not unexpected. Soon after reaching Arlington to go into camp in preparation for the Grand Review, Sheridan had queried him as to his interest in taking command of a cavalry division on the Red River in Louisiana, then marching into Texas and possibly on into Mexico. Though Custer advised Libbie he had accepted Sheridan's offer he did not tell her it might end in a campaign to drive the French out of Mexico. Libbie had said: "He preferred transportation by steamer rather than to be floated southward by floods of feminine tears."[33]

Their train trip to Louisville was a merry one for it was crowded with discharged officers and soldiers anxious and happy to be returning home to friends and family. The war was over. There was no time for serious thought; a carnival spirit was prevalent everywhere.

At each station stop the returning heroes were welcomed by bands, friends and loving arms. There was none, and would be none, of this for Custer and the members of his staff. For them the war was not yet over. As they witnessed these receptions and welcomings they must have felt a bit of envy, of loneliness, and thought a little of the folks back home. Libbie sensed this feeling carried deep within them though no look or word betrayed their innermost thoughts. It became more apparent to her when they reached the deep South for the Southern women, evidencing a false sense of patriotism, would haughtily spurn the slightest advance from even the handsomest of the command.

There was no parlor car on the train but it did boast of a ladies' car in which no man could enter unless accompanying a woman. Since most of the staff were unmarried this broke up a happy family until one of the more inventive members came up with a plan to circumvent the carrier's regulations. Borrowing Libbie's bag, and waiting until Autie and Libbie were seated, he strode up to the conductor and requested permission to deliver it to his lady friend on board. It worked. The others, soon equipped with Libbie's umbrella, cloak, books and lunchbasket, made similar requests quite successfully.

It was customary for Eliza to eat with them while traveling since no table was provided for servants. At a dinner stop the proprietor refused to serve

Libbie's maid, stating there was no table for servants. Custer insisted that she sit down between them which she did reluctantly. The proprietor demanded that she leave, insisting black people were not permitted to sit at the table. Poor Eliza, her appetite gone, said she was willing to go back to her car but Autie, quietly but very firmly, insisted she would stay and she would be fed. Suddenly his entire staff arose and civilians about them did likewise. One of the latter spoke for all: "General, stand your ground; we'll back you; the woman shall have food." The proprietor served poor Eliza her food though she was unable to eat it.[34]

The trip down the beautiful Ohio River from Louisville on a river boat was a new experience for Libbie. Accustomed as she was to lake boats setting deep in the water, she was a bit concerned with these shallow-draft vessels with their upper decks loaded with cargo. The thought of those sudden squalls that frequently arose on Lake Erie during the summer was uppermost in her mind. Surely these top-heavy boats would capsize in a high wind.

There was a certain restfulness to sitting in the deck chairs as the steamer glided smoothly past an ever changing landscape. The movement at night was even more restful and quite a contrast to the noisy, jerky railroad cars they had just left. The river sounds intermingled with the rythmic thump of the engine in the hold and the continuous swish of the water rushing over the stern wheel had a tranquilizing effect on the two. Autie used the first few days to advantage by relaxing in the novel atmosphere and getting a thorough rest.

It was not long before his restlessness returned. The *Ruth* was a larger steamer—one of the largest on the Mississippi—that provided him with many areas to explore. He had his two horses, *Jack Rucker* and Libbie's *Custis Lee,* below deck. Frequent trips down to visit them and then up to the pilot house over the texas helped dissipate his excessive and pent-up energy.

The trip down the Mississippi was a totally pleasurable experience. It had been restful at a time Autie needed rest; the food had been excellent; everyone aboard had been sociable and agreeable. When they arrived at New Orleans it was with regret they disembarked.[35]

It was play-day in New Orleans for the Custers. Detained by orders for a short time, they took advantage of the opportunity by strolling through the French quarters, visiting the fine French restaurants and brousing in the many fascinating shops. Canal Street was an object of daily visits. The flower stands perfumed the air with their fragrance and the colorful clothes of the Creoles promenading leisurely created an atmosphere wholly foreign to them.

When it was learned that General Scott was staying at their hotel—the St. Charles—they called on him. Scott had been a legendary figure in Libbie's earliest recollections. Her father had hanging in his home a picture of General Scott, his huge figure seated on a prancing steed surrounded by the smoke of battle during the Mexican War. Here before her was this same man, a tall, decrepit figure of a once glorious image. Disillusioned, she said: "I was almost sorry to have seen him at all, except for the praise that he bestowed upon my husband, which, coming from so old a soldier, I deeply appreciated."[36]

General Sheridan had occupied an elegant mansion for his headquarters one block from the St. Charles Hotel, for he was now commandant of the Department of the Mississippi. Sheridan was in a gay mood when he entertained them at dinner. He could not help but contrast the daintily prepared French cooking of his Negro cook Mary to that prepared over a campfire in Virginia. After dinner the two men moved out onto the veranda where they could discuss, out of Libbie's hearing, a possible campaign into Mexico.

Custer, in anticipation of just such a move, had been studying his Spanish. On the Monday evening before the Grand Review in Washington, he had been called upon to give a speech to a serenading crowd but refused by saying he was so busy studying the Mexican language he had no time to make a speech in English.[37]

German born Rudolph Lux had been making quite a name for himself at his Camp Street studio. During the Union occupation of New Orleans he had been painting miniatures of porcelain jars, pitchers and vases for many of the soldiers in a style that evidenced great skill and feeling. Prior to the occupation he had become well known for rendering likenesses in oil of children in many prominent New Orleans and St. Louis families. The Custers, having heard of his laudable ability, had requested that he prepare a miniature in oil, of each of them on a separate porcelain vase. In early July the two vases were shipped to the Custer family in Monroe.[38]

Rebecca and Libbie kept in constant touch with each other. In a letter at this time Rebecca referred to Tom's recent visit to Grand Rapids and the pleasure she experienced in becoming acquainted with him. She reasoned, "He is going to be so much like Armstrong. Under his air of abandon and carelessness he has great thoughtfulness and ambition. . . . He feels his lack of schooling and would make a devoted student could he once overcome the natural reluctance to entering school at his age."[39]

Tom evidenced his air of abandon at frequent intervals. One occurred during the last week of June when the steamer chartered to take the horses, freight and troops up the Red River was preparing to leave. Captain Greathouse, master of the vessel and a dyed-in-the-wood Hoosier, offered to take the officers and men as his guests until they could pay him the traveling expenses allotted them but not yet received.

Tom, who had but 26 cents to his name, jingled it against a knife in his empty pocket and put on an air of affluence as the captain approached to offer his invitation. Before the offer could be made Tom majestically asked as to the cost of the trip because, he explained, it was his rule to pay in advance. This was too much for Autie. Hurriedly he left so his laughter would not be viewed by the hospitable captain.

The trip up the Mississippi, and then the Red River to Alexandria, did not take long. Sand bars, tree stumps and red clay banks lined their way. Autie and Tom amused themselves by shooting at alligators sunning themselves along the banks. Each morning and evening they would have a shooting match, Autie using a new rifle a Washington friend had presented him. It received his approbation after he managed to place a shot through a vulnerable point just behind the eye of one of the reptiles.[40]

Libbie was quite disgusted about the appointment of one of the officers to her husband's staff. She fully approved of all the others, she told Rebecca—Lieutenant Fred Nims, Tom, Lieutenant James Christiancy, Major L. W. Barnhart, Major Jacob Greene, Captain Farnham Lyon and Major George Lee—but Captain Edward Earle was something else. All of the staff were Michigan men though Earle didn't act like the rest.[41]

Accordingly, Libbie revealed to Rebecca: "I don't like him; he's a bore and I dread his anticipated arrival. He gives the whole staff reason to think he is engaged to Mary (Rebecca's sister). That she gave him the locket with her picture in it he wears, construes her very coolness into a feeling of love she tries to hide, and otherwide tries my patience to such a degree that I have thought of asking Mary not to *notice* a man who can neither take a hint nor tell the truth but must needs misconstrue the simplest act of friendship into some supposed feeling of affection for him. Try and induce Mary not to write to him. None of the staff can endure him. And those that *men* hate must indeed be insufferable."[42]

At Alexandria the Custers were destined to live in a house the six weeks they spent there. It had been occupied by General Nathanial P. Banks during the war. While they were disembarking, a tall Southerner stepped forward with extended hand, an unusual act considering Southern hostility in those times. Libble did not recognize him as having been a visitor to Monroe ten years back until he introduced himself. Then she recalled the flowery and imaginative descriptions he inscribed in her arithmetic of his ancestral mansion in the South. The ancestral mansion turned out to be a very ordinary white cottage. This discovery did not interfere with a pleasant visit and no allusion was made to his once fanciful descriptions of home.

Judge Bacon was a bit concerned. His dutiful daughter had corresponded quite regularly up until her arrival at Alexandria. The last letter had taken 20 days to reach Traverse City where he was settling Albert Bacon's estate. He suggested that she should take into consideration the time it took for him to receive her letters. Paternally he advised her in many things—obtain a letter press; watch out for the damp mornings, the sun and her diet; obtain a blank book and keep a daily journal, then "record all important incidents. Such a book will be valuable and interesting to you in after life, as well as to those who survive you and those to *come after you.*"[43] The Judge had a feeling for history.

Though the summer heat was overpowering and the humidity suffocating, the drinking water brackish and the mosquitoes huge and inexhaustible, Autie and Libbie took the greatest pleasure in riding their horses along country roads hedged on one side by Osage orange and on the other by double white roses growing 15 feet high. The fragrant air, the deep, rich colors of the sunset and the warmth of their love for each other made her regret leaving Alexandria, the pleasures of their stay having outnumbered the drawbacks.

On one such ride they crossed the river and visited an empty school still called the Sherman Institute. Before the war General Sherman had conducted a military school there. Subsequently it became a hospital, but now was unoccupied.

Custer's major task was that of organizing and unifying a division of fighting men out of the troops being sent there from all points in the West. They were a restless and insubordinate lot who, not having served out their enlistment time, had seen those more fortunate go home to their friends and families. Many had seen no combat.

Each order was met with growls and grumbling and finally with outright insubordination. One of the colonels told Custer his men did not like a certain order. He wanted the General to visit his regiment and give them the reason for it.

Rumors of a proposed attempt on Custer's life was circulated. When Libbie heard of the plan she wept and begged him to protect himself. To soothe her he put a pistol under his pillow. It was not until that winter that she learned he had no cartridges in the house.

The men became so bold and rebellious they were almost beyond control. When this was reported to General Sheridan, he replied to Custer: "Use such summary measures as you deem proper to overcome the mutinous disposition of the individuals in your command."[44]

One military observer noted that Custer's command was made up of Western regiments who, at most, had been involved in guerrilla warfare as small independent squads. There was little discipline and no regimental pride. Facing one good battle as a unit would have developed a regimental pride they lacked.

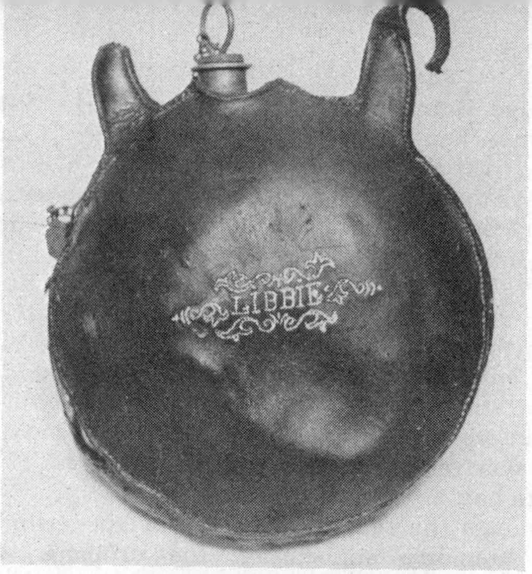

IF LIBBIE'S CANTEEN COULD TALK. The canteen she carried with her through Texas. Photo in author's collection.

Disgruntled to the point of becoming reckless, they began raiding the countryside, robbing and pillaging without regard for the rights of the residents. Custer was under orders to respect the rights of all civilians. He expected his command to follow those orders to their fullest extent.

One officer aroused the ire of his men to the point they signed a petition demanding that he resign. Fearful of his life, he went to Custer asking for protection. All who signed the petition were placed in arrest, and all but one apologized and were released. The holdout—a sergeant—was sentenced to death as a result of a court-martial on the charge of mutiny.

Those men who had been released were quite upset and asked for the man's pardon. And the officer they had attempted to have dismissed circulated a petition that requested mercy for the sergeant. A week passed with no evidence of response to their request other than a promise of consideration. By the time the day of execution arrived the men were in a vengeful mood. Custer was aware there would be an attempt on his life and Libbie was aware of it too. Though she had been protected by those around her from hearing alarming rumors, they advised her of the circumstances so she could use her influence to get Autie to take some precautions. He refused to wear sidearms or permit the members of the staff to do so.

When the execution time arrived, he had his 5,000 men form a hollow square while he and his staff slowly rode around the entire square almost, it appeared, as if in a display of defiance. A wagon bearing the sergeant and a deserter sitting on their coffins followed, the guard and the firing squad bringing up the rear. On arriving in the center at two open graves, the coffins were placed on the ground as the two men stood nearby.

One carbine was loaded with a blank and the other seven with live ammunition as the eyes of the victims were bandaged. The red-faced firing squad and the breathless onlookers made a sight to behold. Except for the reading of the warrant, not a sound could be heard. As the provost marshal prepared to give the fatal command one soldier quietly took the sergeant by the arm and moved him to one side. With the crash of the carbines the deserter dropped dead and the sergeant fell back in a faint. When the sergeant regained consciousness he was told that General Custer had decided to pardon him long ago, believing he had been unduly influenced.[45]

Custer's role was somewhat like that of a military governor. The task of maintaining military discipline was an unenviable assignment, yet it had been accomplished. Piled on it was the difficulty he was having with the freedmen, the Negroes who refused to work in the expectation of Government support the rest of their lives. And there was occasional trouble with former Confederate soldiers who made boastful comments for the benefit of Federal soldiers listening which frequently resulted in a minor riot. For a young man of 25 it was quite a responsibility to command 5,000 men and govern a once rebellious people, acting as judge and conciliator for all. He did so without any hesitancy, governing his actions by the orders issued by General Sheridan.

It was nearing time to start west for Texas. The disciplinary measures were beginning to pay off. The men grumbled but accepted the inevitable. It was pretty hard on them to see other soldiers go home, Custer told Libbie, and not be able to go home too.

Autie did his best to keep all official matters from her. It was a policy he maintained all of his military career. She amazed him at times by speaking of something he had thought to be a confidential matter, unknown to her, as if someone on his staff had confided in her.

When asked how she knew they were ordered to Texas, she explained that it was easy enough "when he had been sending for the quartermaster and the commissary, and looking at his maps for ever so long before. It was not much of a mystery to solve when the quartermaster meant transportation, the commissary food and the maps a new route."[46]

While they were awaiting stores, a spring wagon was prepared for Libbie to travel in. Fitted up as a dressing room with adjustable seats, a roof of rubber sheeting covered with canvas and canvas side curtains, it was drawn by four matched grey horses. However it was intended that Libbie ride on horseback some of the way.

The 200 mile march to Houston, Texas, was made in the cool of the morning and evening. A pontoon train was taken along though it was expected that Libbie could ford most rivers on horseback, having had previous experience in doing so. Autie proposed that the march would take 13 days in spite of a late start. They had planned to leave in July but left in August instead.[47]

NOTES—CHAPTER 15

[1]Whittaker, p. 303; Merington, p. 151; Monaghan, p. 238; Silliman, pp. 179-182; War Department Circular "Medals of Honor," p. 37; April 16, 1865 letter of Tom Custer in National Archives.

[2]O.R. I. XLVI, pt. III, p. 653, Sheridan to Grant, April 8, 1865, 9:20 P.M. In addition, Custer captured 25 pieces of artillery and a number of prisoners and wagons. Sheridan added, "I do not think Lee means to surrender until compelled to do so"; Tremain, p. 359, at 9:40 P.M.; Sheridan advised Grant that Custer now held 35 pieces of artillery, 1,000 prisoners including a general officer and nearly 200 wagons; Rhodes, p. 167; Sheridan, Vol. II, p. 200.

[3]Tremain, p. 368-69.

[4]*Ibid,* p. 371; Humphreys, p. 398; Sheridan, Vol. II, p. 194.

[5]Frost: *Custer Album,* pp. 61, 67.

[6]EBC-CBNM; John Gibbon: *Personal Recollection Of The Civil War,* N.Y., 1928, pp.317, 331-34, Gibbon refers to seeing Custer carry a *marble-topped* table and of obtaining an old *pine* table on which, he claims, the surrender was signed. Colonel Charles Marshall, who was Lee's only staff officer present, told how Grant made the first draft of the terms on a small, varnished pine table found in the corner of the room by Colonel Horace Porter. After Lee had approved of the terms, Colonel Ely S. Parker took the pine table back to the corner and made a copy in ink on it. Colonel Marshall then used the table to draft Lee's reply to Grant. Colonel Parker then placed the table at Grant's side with the ink copy of it, which he signed. Colonel Marshall laid Lee's copy on the square marble-topped table and he signed it.

Somehow, Gibbon had the impression he had placed a pine table of his own in that room and it was the one used. In his account he tells of seeing Custer with a table just before being told that Grant and Lee were in the McLean house in a conference. Fourteen pages later he states: "Mindful of the prize I had seen Custer carrying off and having no surplus $20 gold pieces to pay out, it occurred to me to secure a cheaper table! I therefore directed the old pine camp table which I had used all through the war to be placed in the room. This was covered with a blanket and when at 8:30 P.M. the members assembled to sign the final agreement, they signed on this table."

It appears Gibbon became quite confused in this portion of his "Recollections." A footnote in Grant's *Memoirs,* Vol. II, p. 345 (N.Y., 1885), states: "There is a popular error to the effect that Generals Grant and Lee each signed the articles of surrender. The document in the form of a letter was signed only by General Grant, in the parlor of McLean's house, while General Lee was sitting in the room; and General Lee immediately wrote a letter accepting the terms, and handing it to General Grant (F.D.G.)." See Frost: *U.S. Grant Album,* pp. 131-33.

Grant, soon after Lee's departure, telegraphed Secretary Stanton of Lee's surrender that afternoon. It was sent at 4:30 P.M. Grant's *Memoirs,* Vol. II, p. 347. Sheridan, in his *Memoirs,* Vol. II, p. 202 stated that about 3 P.M. the terms of surrender were written out and accepted, General Lee leaving immediately afterward.

The oval pine table Sheridan gave to Libbie was sent to Judge Bacon for safe keeping. Monroe *Monitor,* May 3, 1865.

In the May 18, 1865 issue of the Monroe *Commercial* it was announced that a "Curiosity Shop at the City Hall" displayed a collection of rebel flags, swords, pistols, etc. "In one corner of the room a couple of ladies were in charge of the table on which Gen. Lee signed his capitulation, and for the modest sum of ten cents visitors could write their names in a blank book on the said table—the book to be presented to Mrs. Custer."

[7]EBC-CBNM.

[8]Libbie to Rebecca Richmond, April 11, 1865; EBC-CBNM.

[9]Copy amongst Libbie's notes, author's collection.

[10]Sheridan, Vol. II, p. 205.

[11]G. A. Custer to Libbie, April 11, 1865, Yale University Library.

[12]Merington, pp. 163-64.

[13]Frost: *Custer Album,* pp. 56-57.

[14]Sheridan, Vol. II, p. 165.

[15]Merington, p. 165.

[16]Libbie to Rebecca Richmond, November 17, 1865, EBC-CBNM.

[17]Merington, p. 165.

[18]Sheridan, Vol. II, p. 206. Sheridan wrote Stanton on April 19 requesting that Custer be promoted to a Major General of volunteers, O.R. I, Vol. XLVI, pt. I, p. 1112.

[19]CBNM files, July 1, 1865 and July 9, 1865.

[20]G. A. Custer to D. S. Bacon, July, 1865, Yale University Library.

[21]I. T. Christiancy to G. A. Custer, April 28, 1865, BCWC collection.

METAMORPHOSIS OF A TRUNK. This bow-topped leather trunk first was Libbie's while single, as evidenced by "Elizabeth C. Bacon, Monroe, Mich, 1862," painted on the end. When she married General Custer it was covered with canvas and stencilled on top, "Col. G. A. Custer, 7th Cav., U.S.A." When widowed in 1876, "Mrs." was lettered in front of her hero's name, and "Monroe, Mich." added below. It was sent to Monroe as it was addressed. Photo in author's collection.

[22]New York *Times,* May 7, 1865 reprinted Custer's letter in the Detroit *Advertiser* of May 1.

[23]Judge Bacon to G. A. Custer, from Monroe, April 13, 1865, BCWC collection.

[24]Judge Bacon to Libbie, April 22, 1865, BCWC collection.

[25]Judge Bacon to G. A. Custer, May 5, 1865, BCWC collection.

[26]Judge Bacon to Libbie, from Monroe, May 14, 1865, BCWC collection.

[27]Sheridan, Vol. II, pp. 208-209.

[28]*Ibid,* p. 210.

[29]O.R.I., XLVI, pt. III, p. 1190, May 21, 1865.

[30]*Ibid,* p. 1195, May 22, 1865.

[31]Whittaker, pp. 312-14; Tremain: *Last Hours,* p. 319; O. L. Hein: *Memories Of Long Ago,* N.Y., 1925, pp. 36-38.

[32]Eliz. B. Custer: *Tenting On The Plains,* N.Y., 1887, pp. 28-29.

[33]Though Libbie makes no mention of traveling to Louisville via Monroe, it has since been learned that General Custer and his staff, according to the Monroe *Monitor,* May 24, 1865, were expected in Monroe on Saturday, the 27th, and would leave from there "for Texas or the country west of the Mississippi."

The May 31st issue reports that, "Gen. Custer and staff leave Monroe this morning for Texas."

The July 5th issue states: "Gen. Custer's arrival at New Orleans is announced. He takes command of the cavalry and marches overland to Houston, Texas, to which point letters can be addressed to him and other Monroe men."

Eliz. B. Custer: *Tenting,* p. 31. But for Libbie Custer's *Tenting On The Plains,* there would be no primary source for their life in Texas.

[34]*Ibid,* pp. 36-37.

[35]*Ibid,* p. 61.

[36]*Ibid,* p. 66; Libbie to Rebecca Richmond, June 29, 1865, EBC-CBNM.

[37]Monroe *Monitor,* May 31, 1865.

[38]Frost: *Custer Album,* p. 72 for reproductions. *"250 Years In New Orleans"* exhibit at the Presbytere.

[39]Rebecca Richmond to Libbie, May 30, 1865, EBC-CBNM.

[40]Libbie to Rebecca Richmond from Alexandria, La., June 29, 1865, EBC-CBNM.

[41]*Ibid; Army Register* for 1865.

[42]Libbie to Rebecca Richmond, June 29, 1865, EBC-CBNM.

[43]D. S. Bacon to Libbie, from Traverse City, Mich., July 10, 1865.

[44]Eliz. B. Custer: *Tenting,* p. 98.

[45]*Ibid,* pp. 100-105.

[46]*Ibid,* p. 112.

[47]Merington, p. 168.

CHAPTER 16
BREAKBONE FEVER

Texas had been untouched during the entire war. With Federal troops moving onto the soil, the very worst was expected. But to the amazement of the Texans no acts of lawlessness were perpetrated by Custer's marching column. The quartermaster purchased all food and forage, none being taken from the country they traversed as in time of war.

There is little doubt the men in the ranks nurtured a healthy hate for the Boy General but that, as Libbie thought, was the penalty a commanding general pays for the questionable privilege of rank and power. Basically they were good men who had knuckled down to soldiering, which was Custer's major concern.

Libbie and Eliza were the only two women with the entire command. Unused to hardship, Libbie had been exposed to heat and humidity, unpalatable water, mosquitoes, alligators, anxiety and mutiny, without complaint. She laid no claim to being a hero nor did she aspire to being one. Letters from her parents had strongly urged the General to send her to Texas by way of New Orleans and the Gulf of Mexico. The officers had added their bit by advising her husband that they would never think of exposing their wives to that wilderness. Libbie was determined not to be separated from her husband. To have endured uncomplainingly in the past was to bolster her argument that she could meet any situation they might encounter in the future. Once she had neutralized his arguments of opposition, the rest was easy.[1]

The cavalry march was limited to about 15 miles each day for the going was a bit rough. Libbie had begged off sleeping in the tent. Most insects and underbrush seemed poisonous so why not sleep in the wagon above all that was noxious in nature? Aside from an occasional horned toad, a Texas Swift or the eye-smarting smudge to ward off insects, the wagon seemed the most desirable place in which to sleep. Autie willingly performed the task of lifting her small figure in and out of the high bedroom each morning and evening.

Libbie's adaptability was nothing less than remarkable. The endless hairpins, buttons, hook-and-eyes and petticoats could have been the basis for a nervous breakdown to a conscientious woman like Libbie. The knowledge that an army on the march moved and operated in clocklike precision was a constant source of frustration and terror. Ever mindful that she could keep thousands of men waiting by being late she systemized her bathing and dressing to such a fine point that she was able to do so completely in seven minutes. Unbeknownst to her, Autie timed her one morning and established it as a fact.[2]

Father Bacon's paramount objection to her marriage to an army officer was based on his observation of the deprivations endured by officers' wives during his early days in Michigan. He reasoned that she might have to travel "in a covered wagon like an emigrant." Autie, who had heard the story and had quite a laugh over it, would lift her out of her penthouse apartment and frequently quip, "I wonder what your father would say now?"[3]

Custer's pride in Libbie was evidenced by the way in which he would introduce her to some close friend of his. He usually opened with, "Oh, I want you to know my wife; she slept four months in a wagon."[4]

As the column moved along, potable water became more difficult to obtain. The intense heat forced them to conclude each day's march before the sun neared its zenith. Years later Libbie would write, "I do not remember one good drink of water on that march. When it was not muddy or stagnant, it tasted of the roots of trees."

Each day brought an encounter with scorpions, centipedes and tarantulas. Seed tick and chiggers were a continual source of discomfort. The latter would bury their heads under the victim's skin to fester painfully until removed surgically.

Breakbone fever—sometimes called Dandy fever, Sun fever or Dengue fever—seemed to be a nemesis for having traveled into Texas. An infectious, eruptive, tropical disease transmitted by mosquitoes, it would manifest its presence by a high fever, sore throat and severe pains in all the muscles and joints. Rest and heavy doses of quinine was the treatment. Both Tom and Jacob Greene had attacks of breakbone fever, Tom suffering from inflammatory rheumatism attributed to it for more than a year afterward.

Libbie too became one of its many victims. The surgeon compelled her to lie down on the march, a painful experience at best, the wagon jerking con-

BENHAM, TEXAS, October, 1865. General Custer near his cavalry camp. His companion is unidentified. West Point Museum collections.

tinuously as it traversed a topsoil filled with roots. Each turn of the wheels caused a joggle painful in the extreme, and exaggerated by an unevenness of the ground not evident while riding horseback.

When the wood was cut for the campfires, the men on that detail would build a pine branch shelter over Libbie's wagon to shade it from the fiery afternoon sun. Soon afterward they were out of the pine forest and on the prairie. Farmhouses began to appear which meant that eggs and butter could sometimes be purchased. In a short time they reached their permanent camp at Hempstead.

General Sheridan and his staff paid a call soon afterward, bringing with him General Custer's father. Sheridan was quite pleased with the condition of the men and the horses and the fact that there had been no insubordination on the march. After commending Custer, he placed him in command of all cavalry in Texas.[5] Hempstead was to be the headquarters for the Federal "Army of Observation."[6]

With the mail that arrived from Houston were letters to Libbie from her father. Writing from Traverse City late in July, he advised her he would be leaving there in two weeks, having been delayed because of illness. He had noted Autie's interest in real estate in Louisiana and advised against such speculation. "Forty years experience ought to make me a judge and good adviser. If you have a surplus, invest in bonds and not engage in real estate speculation." He noted that he had been a real estate man all of his life, yet considering what he had lost and had paid to others and how much he had made, he was against it. Then he advised Libbie to remain free from encumberances so she could be on the wing. He wanted her to realize the power of interest on money—that she would be surprised what $1,000 will produce in 25 years.[7]

His next letter indicated he remained "in this out-of-the-way and unsocial place"—Traverse City. Again he reminded her to keep a journal. When he reached Monroe he intended to thoroughly repair the house. "I want the passerby to feel that the father-in-law of General Custer lives in *good style.* It will be a treat for a stranger to see the house that General Custer was married in." In conclusion he advised her he was in easy financial circumstances though "not perhaps quite income enough to support me but as I have no children dependent on me for bread, I hope to get along."[8]

In the last of the three letters awaiting Libbie he advised her they had reached Monroe four days earlier and were glad to be there. He seemed concerned about any investment they might make in real estate and indicated his feelings again: "With all my high estimate of Texas and the great chances to engage in purchase and sales of real estate, still my advice to you is to invest in bonds and then when you leave there is nothing to leave behind."[9]

The cavalry camp was set up on the banks of Clear Creek where Camp Groce once stood. Camp Groce had served the armies of the Confederacy. Ironically, perhaps humorously, Clear Creek was the color of ashes.[10]

Nearby was the plantation of Liendo, owned by Leonard Wharton Groce and his wife whose four sons had fought under General Lee. When Mrs. Groce learned that Libbie was living in a tent, she

AUSTIN, TEXAS HEADQUARTERS. The Custers and the members of his staff and their wives were quartered here during the latter part of 1865. Some of them are shown on the steps. Mrs. E. B. Custer collection. Custer Battlefield National Monument.

offered her the use of Liendo. The offer was refused but not so the mutton roasts, milk and jellies sent over from time to time.

Though Libbie never forgot the snakes, scorpions, chiggers, horned toads and the extremes of Texan temperature, those memories were more than offset by the hospitality, friendliness and tall tales of the Texans.

Leonard Groce and the other friendly plantation owners taught the General the etiquette of deer hunting with a pack of hounds and the technique of controlling the pack through the calls of a hunting horn.[11]

Custer's first experience hunting with one of the planters and his pack of 37 dogs, all of whom responded to the horn, simply delighted him. Presented with five hounds after having procured a horn, he nearly split his cheeks attempting to sound the notes he expected to emanate from the horn.

Not long after they had reached Hempstead, Libbie's dearest girlhood friend Nettie Humphrey, now Mrs. Jacob Greene, arrived with Mrs. Farnham Lyon. Late in the day, when the heat had subsided, all of them would go on a long ride in the country. Father Custer, who was an excellent rider, was frequently the butt of some prank his two sons perpetrated. The boys might come up on each side of his horse, one asking him some political question while the other, seeing his father's attention diverted, would give the horse a rap across the back. The horse would lower its head and raise its heels in an attempt to throw Emanuel. The old gentleman sat his seat as if glued there.

Sundays were a void for there was no hunting and no church service. Libbie used the day in letter writing, the one to her parents having all priority. In doing so her eyes would grow moist with the thought of her family attending church services and of the pleasant home she had left there for a life in a tent. One luxury stood out in her memory as an almost impossible item to obtain. Apples did not grow in this area, one man telling her he hadn't seen one in five years. She knew there was a large plate of rosy, red apples on the dining room table in Monroe that very moment, a mouth-watering thought.

Knowing of her parents' interest, she told them there were no churches in the area, that such structures were the last to be thought of for cotton was king. She wanted them to know she had turned down $500 in Alexandria for *Custis Lee* even though he had been having trouble with corns.

With mosquitoes as plentiful as they were, it was no surprise that malaria struck the members of the staff. Father Custer was one of the first to succumb, others following. Finally Autie yielded to the enervating ailment. Quinine there was aplenty, the surgeon seeming to have it by the barrel.

Libbie too had her siege of illness. One of Custer's young troopers who had known the Groces before the war asked them for the loan of a rocking chair for

RECONSTRUCTION STAFF at Austin, Texas, 1865. 1. Emanuel Custer, 2. Col. Jacob Greene, 3. Libbie Custer, 4. Eliza, 5. Lieut. Tom Custer, 6. Gen. Custer. Mrs. E. B. Custer collection. Custer Battlefield National Monument.

Libbie so she could be made more comfortable. When the Groces learned she was quite ill they removed her to their house and nursed her back to good health.[12]

Her father should have seen her about this time for he had been bragging to his sister Eliza in Onondaga how Autie had said "few living women can ride a horse equal to her and but few better." Though the Judge had been suffering with dysentery and the ague since coming back to Monroe, he was not that sick but what he could appreciate Libbie's qualities and that she had married well.[13]

Realizing that he was advancing in years—probably enhanced by his recent bout with dysentery—he made out a will. Eight lots in the Bacon Plat of Monroe were bequeathed to George A. Custer. His daughter Elizabeth was to receive his homestead on Monroe Street, all household furniture used by her mother, and several lots west of the homestead known as the Chair Factory and Kilbaum lots. The American Bible Society would receive one-tenth of the sale of his property near Traverse City and his wife Rhoda would receive all family articles purchased since their marriage in addition to the interest on $5,000 invested in government bonds and other securities during her lifetime, Libbie to be the final heir of the $5,000. He added that he desired his wife Rhoda to be amply provided for in the way of maintenance and support. And he did request that his brother George of Indiana receive $100 a year for his support if he needed it.[14]

In November, the command moved toward Austin. The anticipated orders to move had been lost en route and duplicate orders had not been received until October 21st. Custer was bubbling with anticipation. Always the optimist, he expected nothing but improvement with any such move.[15]

It was no longer necessary to arise before dawn as they had in August. The unbearable heat had left so that the days were moderate though the nights were chilly. Libbie's attempts to sleep in each morning were aborted by her husband's comment that "the officers will surely think you a 'feather bed' soldier." Only her unwillingness to be an object of soldierly scorn prevented her from continuing her objection to being an early riser.[16]

In a letter to her parents, Libbie expressed considerable interest in the renovation of the "Bacon Mansion." She indicated her concern that father's income was not larger, especially since he had been so charitable to others all of his life. Autie had been telling her that had all of the Judge's land been converted into money and invested in Texas he would be wealthy in a short time. Cotton and land seemed to be the way to make money speedily.

Many opportunities of becoming wealthy were before Autie each day—horses, cotton, land and Government claims—but it was his conviction he should not invest as long as he was an employee of the Government.

The two had been able to save considerable money. They were living on less than $150 a month and would reduce that amount so they could be accustomed to the smaller salary he would get when he no longer received a major general's pay.

As a major general Autie's annual pay and subsistence amounted to $5,772. When the army would

LIBBIE IN 1867. Author's collection.

be reduced to a peacetime level he would revert to his regular army rank of captain and receive $1,645.

This part of the country had been great for them. Prominent and active rebels had treated them with great kindness and consideration. It was Libbie's conviction that "no country in the world can equal the South for hospitality."[17]

Her husband was in complete accord with her feeling for their Southern friends around Hempstead. He had found happiness there in the amiable atmosphere. His troops were acting like soldiers and Libbie was never in better health. She had become an expert horsewoman. Riding was their principal source of pleasure and she had become so proficient she could outride any of the staff officers' wives and many of the staff.

Father Custer was enjoying himself too. He hunted when he wasn't at work for the army, and was enjoying the best of health.

In response to a query from Judge Bacon, Autie wrote: "I regard the solution of the Negro problem as involving difficulty and requiring greater statesmanship than any political matter that has arisen for years. . . . I am in favor of elevating the Negro to the extent of his capacity and intelligence, and of our doing everything in our power to advance the race morally and mentally as well as physically, also socially. But I am opposed to making this advance by correspondingly debasing any portion of the white race."[18]

Near Austin several of its townspeople offered Autie the use of their homes which he refused. Instead he accepted the vacant Blind Asylum the new Union Governor invited him to use. It had ample room for the entire staff in addition to a dining room and a long saloon-parlor large enough for their winter dances.

Libbie accepted her new home with some regrets. She missed her wind-swept wagon that had rocked her to sleep so many times. There had been some hardships on the trip but all had been erased by the pleasures. True, she wouldn't have to jump out of a warm bed each morning at the first notes of reveille.

Her new home was a modern structure, the main building being square with two long one-story wings attached. From their room upstairs over their parlor there was a grand view of Austin and the hills beyond. Nettie Humphrey Greene lived in a room just back of theirs and the Lyons occupied one across the hall. A fourth room was occupied by a Mrs. Coffee who was living there when they had arrived. The fireplace in each room was quite a luxury after having lived in the open air for four months. Libbie found it impossible to sleep there the first night for she had become so accustomed to sleeping in her bed in the wagon.[19]

Just across the Colorado River was the Deaf and Dumb Asylum. The General appeared to be fascinated with the children there and took every opportunity to ride over to it for a visit. The students were from 10 to 16 years of age.

Custer was fascinated with the graceful manner in which they used their hands and the speed with which they sent their silent messages. Loving children as he did, it was natural enough for him to learn the sign language so he could become adept in communicating with them. They welcomed his visits and would bring him their compositions and maps for his gestures of commendation. Little did he know that the technique of communication he was learning here would enable him to be understood at the Indian council fires on the Kansas plains two years later.[20]

There are some who have the opinion that Custer had been ordered to Texas for the purpose of keeping an eye on the Emperor Maximilian, seated as he was on a shaky Mexican throne. In actuality there was so much lawlessness throughout Texas it became necessary for the President to send in troops to establish law and order. The very presence of General Custer's 13 regiments of infantry and an equal number of cavalry scattered throughout the state had the very desirable effect of diminishing lawlessness.[21]

Texas had been a state of turmoil. Bandits, bushwackers and jayhawkers had terrorized the citizens since the disbanding of the Confederate forces. It did not take long for the civil authorities, once there were troops present, to bring matters under control. It was accomplished before the winter was over.

All was not work. There was a great deal of horse racing for the Texans loved their horses and enjoyed nothing more than a worthy opponent. Autie had three race horses and a racing pony at this time. A tiny mulatto boy was his jockey, Libbie having made the lad a flannel jacket of Autie's favorite color—red. Libbie and her friends attended the races. There was little betting, Auto and Tom betting not at all.[22]

The two Custer boys badgered their father at every opportunity. Father Custer might be reading a paper when one of them would tie firecrackers to his chair leg and light them. Then again they would throw the firecrackers or a handful of blank cartridges into the fireplace while the old gentleman was leaning peacefully against the mantel smoking. Little did any of these pranks bother him. Biding his time, he evened the score.

It soon came time to move out. Autie's Adjutant General, Captain Jacob Greene, had been detailed to act as an undercover agent in the distant parts of the state to determine the sentiment of the people so that it could be decided if it would be wise to withdraw the occupation forces.

Greene's report indicated that a large minority intended to pay back the North, and that they would handle the Negroes in their own way. These dissidents were submissive only because they were forced to be. The freed man had obtained his natural rights but had been prevented from obtaining his legal rights because of existing state laws. As a result the freedman needed the protection of the Federal Government. It was Greene's opinion that it would be a catastrophe if the troops were removed. The result could end in a war between races.[23]

The troops moved on to Hempstead and Galveston where they embarked on a steamer for New Orleans. While crossing the Gulf of Mexico the small vessel was struck by a hurricane one night. Libbie was terrified, only the soothing, crooning ministrations of her faithful Eliza preventing her from becoming hysterical.

Autie, responding to the calls of the women begging to know if the ship was going down, struggled to reach the pilot house to talk to the captain. There the brave captain informed him the machinery had been disabled and that all was uncertainty.

Autie returned to the women with a half-truth to calm their terror, then crept into his berth completely subdued with *mal de mer*. The rolling vessel had taken him down to a point where he could barely utter a few words and cared little whether the ship stayed up or went down. The sea had accomplished what no adversary had been able to do.

With the approach of daylight the storm began to subside. Autie's voice grew stronger and to a point where he began to cheer Libbie and jibe at Nettie Greene in the adjoining cabin for permitting herself to succumb to seasickness. Soon Father Custer made his appearance and brought shouts of laughter when he remarked to Autie, "Next time I follow you to Texas it will be when this pond is bridged over."[24]

They arrived in New Orleans on February 20th,[25] there to enjoy the gastronomic delicacies they had talked about in Texas. Having regained their land legs they took a river boat to Cairo, Illinois, where a part of the staff would leave them. The tranquil trip up the Mississippi was a contrast to their experience across the Gulf. Every moment of their slow passage was enjoyable, the dinner hour an event in itself. Father Custer read the menu aloud to himself in the same fashion he did the newspapers.

His boys would engage him in a political argument—easily started by criticizing the Democrats or praising the Republicans—while Tom would slip his father's plate away, eat the food, then return the plate empty and unnoticed until Autie would say, "Well, come, come, come, father, why don't you eat your dinner?" The blank expression on the old gentleman's face was worth the price of the warm dinner they had brought to him later.[26]

The boys' tendency to tantalize their father had developed naturally enough. In their early childhood he had played a variety of tricks upon them and they were trying to get even. Play tricks on him they did but it was an unusual occasion when they got ahead.

They had made several attempts to obtain his money but he had been too cautious for them. One evening on board the boat he retired to his cabin with Tom. Tom climbed into the upper berth and was soon asleep. Emanuel, having sewn some bills in his vest, placed it and his purse under his pillow. While pulling off his boots he thought he saw something go over the transom. Looking under the pillow, he saw both his vest and purse were gone. Surmising what had happened, he ran down to Autie's cabin and pounded on the door. While people opened their doors to see the cause of all the commotion a glass of water was thrown through the transom onto his head. Emanuel decided it would be better to wait until morning. At breakfast both boys innocently asked what the cause was for all of the racket. They thought it shameful that he would pound on a young lady's door like that and she have to defend her honor by pouring a pitcher of water on him. They thought he should apologize to the young lady since she was Libbie's friend, and that he should do so at once before they all would be compromised by the scandal that would result.[27]

To get even he went to Autie's stateroom one morning and found Autie's pocketbook under his pillow. Confiscating it, he kept away from them for a few days until they cornered him, Tom seizing him from behind while Autie emptied his pockets. While he was penniless they had the purser ask for his ticket. His excuse that it had been stolen was not acceptable so he had to ask Autie to pay his bills until he got to Monroe. Once there the boys had a good laugh telling mother Custer the tricks they had played on him.

The Custers arrived in Monroe on March 3rd. Their homecoming was overwhelming. Families and friends kept them busy every minute until the time came for Autie to report to Washington. He took leave on the seventh.[28] With an annual income of nearly $6,000 now reduced to $1,600, it was imperative that he travel alone.

Money had never meant much to him except what it might do for Libbie and his own family. Many opportunities were being presented to him that promised great wealth. At a time when his name was a household word businessmen tempted him so they could use his name as a corporation officer. Others sought to entice him into politics. Congressman? Governor? Soldiers and civilians alike talked openly of his potential.

Just a few days before he arrived the Monroe *Commercial* — March 1, 1866 — had published "LETTER FROM GEN. CUSTER," stating:

"The *World's* Washington Special says a letter has been received from Maj. Gen. Custer, dated Austin, Texas, in which he denies the statement published in December that he has been making secession speeches. He says: 'I have made no speeches since coming to Texas, but if I had, my voice would not have been raised in support of any in sympathy with statements and doctrines of ex-rebels whose hostility and opposition to the Government is now as strongly manifested as at any time during the rebellion. I hope my course during the war will be accepted as bearing me out in this statement'."[29]

Custer arrived in Washington on Friday, March 9th. On the following day he was sworn in before the Joint Committee on Reconstruction. In answer to a lengthy series of questions he delivered the opinion that the majority of the people of Texas were unfriendly to the Government, that the lenient policy of the Government had permitted the people of the South to forget the enormity of the crime they had committed by engaging in rebellion, that the majority of the Texans would secede if they could without war, and that the Negroes generally did well at their work and were loyal and friendly to the Union.

To a final question he replied: "I do not regard the people in that portion of the Southern country in which I have been as in a proper condition, or as manifesting a proper state of feeling, to be restored to their former rights and privileges under the general government. And I do not think they have been taught the enormity of the crime they have committed by rebelling against the Government. I think the Government ought to maintain control of those states that were in rebellion until it is thoroughly satisfied that a loyal sentiment prevails in at least a majority of the inhabitants—that certainly does not exist now. . . ."[30]

The ordeal of testifying now disposed of, Autie addressed a letter to "Dear Old Sweetness." A note of loneliness crept in. He had decided to isolate himself in his hotel room. Seeing many friends that day who had inquired about Libbie only augmented his dejection. First he met Senator and Mrs. Chandler, then Major and Mrs. Fred Grant. All regretted that Libbie was not there. Others followed suit.

When Autie paid Secretary Stanton a call he was very cordially received. The Secretary after having inquired about Libbie, said he had read the account charging Custer with disloyalty but thought it absurd. He advised Autie that he had honored his request by appointing Tom a second lieutenant in the 1st U.S. Infantry as of February 23rd,[31] then added that there was nothing in his power to grant that he would not do if Autie asked.

Several days later Autie wrote to Libbie that Eliza, who had accompanied him as far as Washington, had gone on to visit her former owner "ole Missus," to show where she had hidden and buried the family treasures for her before the plantation was overrun by Federal troops. She would return directly to Monroe when through. Colonel Greene and Nettie also had accompanied him and had gone on to the Greene home in Pittsfield, Massachusetts. Greene had applied for a commission in the regular army but on observing the turmoil and clamor in Washington had decided he had better take the offer of a job from a New England insurance company.

He had written to Autie later asking why there had been no letter from him. Nettie had heard from Libbie that Tom had his appointment, which he was glad to hear. "Of course I have none or you would have written before this. I am still waiting for my muster out to go into business. My place is open and waiting. I am tired of suspense."[32]

Autie was unable to obtain a commission for Greene even though the latter had a fine military record, had been wounded in action and had been a prisoner of war. In the case of George W. Yates he was more successful. Yates had been breveted a lieutenant colonel. On March 26, 1866, he was commissioned a second lieutenant in the 2d U.S. Cavalry.[33]

Autie had confided that Washington artists and photographers had been besieging him. Brady wanted more photographs. Noted sculpturess Vinnie Ream wanted to make a medallion of him. Another sculpturer wanted to make a cast of his head for a bust.[34]

Though he was spending much of his time seeking appointments in the regular army for friends of his, he was seriously thinking of leaving the military service. An opportunity of being appointed Foreign Minister with a salary in gold of seven to ten thousand dollars a year held considerable appeal to him though it would be for just a few years.

Thinking, as he usually did, of the welfare of his family, he told Libbie he was expressing a box of military books so that Tom could study tactics of the cavalry and infantry, a subject Tom would have to be conversant with in the coming examination.

Several days later his communication to his "darling little durl" indicated that, expense or no expense, she would accompany him next time. Aside from missing her, he was suffering from a severe sore throat and, like most males, would have liked to have her near so that she could sympathize with him.

He had gone to a dinner party at the home of Chief Justice Salmon P. Chase at which most of the Supreme Court judges attended. Chase called to the attention of his guests that Custer was the youngest brigadier general and major general in the Army at the time of his appointment. Later he told Custer he expected to see him the lieutenant general of the U.S. Army some day. A pretty heady statement for a 26-year-old boy to hear.[35]

On March 28th he wrote to Libbie from the Fifth Avenue Hotel in New York that he was having a wonderful time seeing all of the New York plays. He visited Ole Balling's studio on Eighth Street to see the artist's large painting "Heroes of the Republic." All the generals were on horseback and 11 wore hats except Grant and Custer. Custer was the only figure with a sword in his hand, carrying it as if to deliver a blow in a charge. He thought that while the likeness "is extremely good (it) would have been more natural but probably less artistic and picturesque if my hair was not of such a perfect golden hue."[36]

Several days later, after having had breakfast with General Pleasonton, he called at the office of *Wilkes' Spirit of the Times* to obtain *Don Juan's* pedigree and racing record from the Turf Register. Custer knew he owned a fine bit of horseflesh in *Don Juan* but was amazed at the information they had shown him. It seems the horse had run some of the best races in the country up to that time. His quickest time had been a mile in 1:46 (one minute and 46 seconds). The fastest time ever made was 1:44, making *Don Juan's* time almost unsurpassed. The Wilkes office told Custer that only six horses had ever beaten *Don Juan's* time. And his pedigree was superb. As the Assistant Editor said, "General, you have one of the finest horses in America; there is none better." General Pleasonton was anxious to obtain one of *Don's* colts.[37]

Though he was not having too much success obtaining the kind of employment he wished, Autie was enjoying himself. He was received with deference and admiration wherever he went. Dinner affairs were arranged in his honor and he was lionized by important business and professional people.

COUSINS. Left to right: Rebecca Richmond (Grand Rapids, Mich.), Mrs. Mary Richmond Kendall and her husband Charles Kendall (Topeka, Kansas), General Custer with Libbie seated to his left. Mrs. E. B. Custer collection. Custer Battlefield National Monument.

Colonel Howe introduced him to many prominent capitalists on Wall Street who invited him to attend a session of the Broker's Board where a member unknown to him introduced him, then led the Board in six cheers and a tiger. Asked to speak, Autie acknowledged their recognition, said he was no speaker, then sat down. To this a voice from the floor responded, "You are a fighter!"[38]

At a breakfast in his honor he met William Cullen Bryant the poet, historian George Bancroft and many other well-known people.

He attended a rehearsal of "A Child of Fortune" at Nibol's with Maggie Mitchell, then walked with her to her playhouse at the Winter Garden.

Though he was enjoying the matinees and evening performances of the musicals and plays, he was not too successful in obtaining employment. It is quite likely he was seeking it with a prayer on his lips that none would be available. His heart was in the military service.

Just at the time that employment possibilities appeared the bleakest, he received a letter from General Phil Sheridan from New Orleans. Enclosed with it was a copy of a letter he had written to Secretary of War Stanton making application for Custer's appointment to the rank of colonel under the reorganization of the Army. It concluded, "The record of this officer is so conspicuous as to render its recital by me unnecessary. I ask this appointment as

CUSTER'S HEADQUARTERS ON BIG CREEK. Kansas in the spring of 1867. Left to right: Lt. Tom Custer, Mrs. G. A. Custer, Gen. Custer, Dr. Dunbar, Mrs. Capt. Smith, Mrs. Donald McIntosh standing. Mrs. E. B. Custer collection. Courtesy Custer Battlefield National Monument.

a reward to one of the most gallant officers that ever served under me."[39]

What better news could one receive? Perhaps it would be better to go back to Monroe and see what developed as a result of Sheridan's request. Stanton had indicated his interest in Custer's career. Surely he would do all in his power to honor Sheridan's petition.

New York was intriguing but the Army was more so. After the theatre one evening Custer, in company with several West Point officers, visited several shooting galleries and then some saloons operated by pretty girl barmaids. Feeling their oats, they bantered with several streetwalkers he referred to as "Nymphes du Pave" in his letter to Libbie describing their sport, then ended it: "At no time did I forget you."

It was a common practice for Custer to write of Libbie or of himself in the third person, e.g., "he will do so and so," or "I hope she will do thus and so."

One evening after returning to his hotel with General Pleasonton from a reception, Pleasonton, with an almost fatherly interest, advised him to write his letter to Libbie, then get some sleep. Custer had not been averaging more than five hours each night. At the Barlows' reception he had met General Gordon Granger and Paul Murphy, the world's greatest chess player. The event caused him to remark to Libbie: "What would sedate Monroe say to Sunday night receptions!"[40]

On the following evening he wrote: "I ask our Heavenly Father each day to give me the wisdom and enable me to choose that which will most likely secure our happiness and prosperity." With no word from Washington, the search for employment continued.[41]

Several evenings later he was invited to dinner at the L.P. Mortons where he met many prominent Wall Street capitalists and many notables including Mrs. General Fremont. The men were dressed in formal attire and many of the elegant ladies in low neck dresses. The latter caused him to relate to Libbie his experience with a baroness whom he does not name in his letter. "The Baroness wore a very handsome satin, and oh so low. I sat beside her on a sofa and 'I have not seen such sights since I was weaned' and yet it did not make my angry passions rise, nor *nuthin* else. But what I saw went far to convince me that a Baroness is formed very much like all other persons of the *same sex*."

He reassured her with: "It is for you dear one that I am so anxious to make such a change in my business—a profession as will render me more able to shower you with the comforts and luxuries of life. For you and you alone I long to become wealthy, not for wealth alone but for the power it brings. I am willing to make any honorable sacrifice. Once acquired we will enjoy it together with no more separations. My cup of happiness will then be full."[42]

On Saturday, April 21st, he advised Libbie he expected to conclude his business on Monday, then leave for Monroe on the following day. His loneliness was indicated with, "I wish her was here with her horse to ride with him in the park.... You know I am a gread advocate of exercise as a promoter of good health. I *firmly* believe that I require a ride every morning before breakfast."[43]

The nearer the time to leave for home the lonelier he became. Sunday was a particularly quiet day as all New York Sundays tend to be. Taking his pen in hand, he began, 'Dearest and best of Sweethearts—Would I were with thee every day and every hour. This evening I feel as if it would be particularly pleasant to be seated beside my little durl knowing that her heart is all my own with none to challenge my claims. I miss you oh so much. People think, and correctly too, that I am having a magnificent time, but how much more my enjoyment would be increased if my other and better self was with me. I think of you in all my pleasures, in all my plans of business for the future and in private meditation but I miss you most darling mine when the day with its mingled cares and pleasures is ended and retire to my room to sleep and gather rest for the labors of the coming day, then I miss my sunbeam, my peerless little one and long to hasten to her side where I know a warm welcome awaits me. Never will I cease to thank that kind Being who so arranged it that you should be mine. My jewel, my crown, daily I am in the society of the fairest of our land, but in none of them nor in all combined do I see the loveliness, that purity of mind and character which I find centered in the person and mind of my own lovely bride.

"I suppose you will have a great many nice *things* for me when I return. I will be in good condition to appreciate them. *Tell Tom to study*. I intend to examine him when I return and on what progress he had made on tactics."[44]

On the following evening, April 23rd, he wrote Libbie his final letter before leaving New York. He had attended a dinner given that evening for him at the residence of John Jacob Astor, having been seated on the right of Mrs. Astor. General Pleasonton also attended.

All of the attentions he had received and all of the attractive women he had met during his stay in New York had augmented his love and admiration for Libbie. Her superior qualities, her purity and virtue in comparison with all other women he had seen made him conclude that he had "cause to congratulate himself upon the possession of so rare and priceless a gem." He was eager to be back in Monroe alone with her, his family and his writing.[45]

NOTES — CHAPTER 16

1Eliz. B. Custer: *Tenting*, pp. 114-15.
2*Ibid*,p. 129.
3*Ibid*, p. 127.
4*Ibid*, p. 129.
5 On August 7, 1865, just before the command left Alexandria, General Custer issued his General Orders No. 15. (See EBC files-CBNM). He drew attention to the necessity for exercising "the most scrupulous regard for the rights and property of those with whom they may be brought in contact."

The rules were to be strictly observed. Columns of fours were to march in close formation with no intervals between companies. The Provost Guard were to march in the immediate rear of each brigade and arrest any enlisted man who left the ranks with his horse and unattended by an officer. An enlisted man might leave the ranks for water or attend to the wants of nature if he left his horse to be held in the ranks. Any act of lawlessness by an enlisted man would mean he would be punished as well as be deprived of his horse and forced to march on foot. And no foraging parties were permitted since all supplies could be obtained from the Supply Train.

6Denison, p. 192.
7D. S. Bacon to Eliz. B. Custer, July 25, 1865, BCWC collection.
8D. S. Bacon to Eliz. B. Custer, July 31, 1865, BCWC collection.
9D. S. Bacon to Eliz. B. Custer, August 21, 1865, BCWC collection.
10Vernon Loggins: *Two Romantics*, N.Y., 1946, pp. 198, 209.
11*Ibid*, p. 210.
12Houston *Chronicle*, September 21, 1930.
13D. S. Bacon to Eliza Sabin, October 10, 1865.
14Last Will and Testament of Daniel S. Bacon, October 23, 1865, Probate Court, Monroe County, Michigan.
15Merington, p. 169.
16Whittaker, p. 201.
17Merington, pp. 170-71.
18G. A. Custer to D. S. Bacon, October 5, 1865.
19Eliz. B. Custer to Rebecca Richmond, November 17, 1865, from Austin, EBC - CBNM; Frost: *Custer Album*, pp. 74-76, photos of Blind Asylum.
20Eliz. B. Custer: *Tenting*, p. 222; Ralph W. Yarborough: "General Custer Learned Sign Language at Texas State College," *Texas Good Roads Association Newsletter*, December, 1970.
21Eliz. B. Custer: *Tenting*, pp. 177, 260-62; O.R.,I, XLVI, pt. 2, pp. 1035-36.
22Eliz. B. Custer to Rebecca Richmond, November 17, 1865; Eliz. B. Custer: *Tenting*, p. 243.
23Merington, p. 176; Greene was mustered out on April 20, 1866, Cahn, p. 84.
24Eliz. B. Custer: *Tenting*, pp. 276-82.
25Monaghan, p. 264; General Orders No. 168, War Dept., December 28, 1865, mustered out of the Volunteer Service as of February 1, 1866, Major General Geo. A. Custer, with an additional leave of 30 days. Author's collection. See National Archives file—RG #94-1239-ACP, 1871, Wm. W. Belknap.
26Eliz. B. Custer: *Tenting*, pp. 286-87.
27*Ibid*, pp. 292-94.
28Monroe *Commercial*, March 8, 1866.
29Monroe *Commercial*, January 18, 1866, stated: "A report was published some days ago that an officer in Texas had been charged with uttering treasonable sentiments, and that Gen. Custer was the officer referred to. It is now stated that Gen. Merritt is the officer referred to, and not Gen. Custer."
30"Report, Joint Committee on Reconstruction," 1st Session, 39th Congress, 1866, pt. IV, pp. 72-78; Monroe *Commercial*, March 22, 1866.
31*Official Army Register* for 1866, p. 34.
32Jacob Greene to G. A. Custer, March 20, 1866. BCWC collection.
33*Official Army Register for 1866, p. 34; Merington, p. 179.*
34Merington, p. 178.
35G. A. Custer to Eliz. B. Custer, March 23, 1866, BCWC collection.
36G. A. Custer to Eliz. B. Custer, March 29, 1866, BCWC collection. The painting is now owned by the National Portrait Gallery in Washington.
37G. A. Custer to Libbie, March 30, 1866, BCWC collection.
38Merington, p. 182.
39April 6, 1866, EBC-CBNM.
40Geo. A. Custer to Libbie, April 15, 1866, BCWC collection.
41Geo. A. Custer to Libbie, Monday, April 16, 1866, BCWC collection.
42Geo. A. Custer to Libbie, April 20, 1866, BCWC collection.
43Geo. A. Custer to Libbie, April 21, 1866, BCWC collection.
44Geo. A. Custer to Libbie, April 22, 1866, BCWC collection.
45Geo. A. Custer to Libbie, April 23, 1866, BCWC collection.

CHAPTER 17
SOLDIER OF FORTUNE

Trouble was brewing in Mexico. President Benito Juarez had an ample supply of men to resist the advances of the Imperialist army under Emperor Maximilian but had no arms, equipment or money to maintain his Liberal Government army.

The French and Austrian soldiers who had invaded and occupied northern Mexico observed a military demonstration of strength and firmness at Matamoras on the part of General Sheridan and quickly withdrew to the south.

Secretary of State William Seward protested Sheridan's act as contrary to his own feeling that strict neutrality should prevail along the Rio Grande. Sheridan saw the Imperialist invasion of Mexico as an aggressive act that threatened the security of Americans along the border. He had kept General Grant advised of all movements of the Imperialist forces and of the impoverished conditon of the opposing Mexican forces under Juarez and his general, Jose' Caravajal. Grant was in accord with Sheridan's conclusions about checking Maximilian's troops but was in the unenviable position of having to subscribe to the policies of President Johnson and his Secretary of State.'

Custer had learned from Sheridan that the Mexican Liberal Government was in dire need of cavalry leadership such as he could provide. The thought of action intrigued him for he was champing at the bit. A sedentary serfdom as a civilian might appeal to many after four years of combat but to this wild young stallion it was appalling. He seemed to obtain nutriment from the excitement of a conflict.

Back in Monroe he pursued the matter further. While in New York he had been in touch with Don Matias Romero, Minister of the Mexican Legation in Washington. Romero had been seeking a qualified officer to become the Adjutant General of the Mexican Liberal army and on inquiry had received a letter from General Grant endorsing Custer. This letter of Grant is in great contrast to his opinion of Custer some ten years later when his views and observations were that of a politician rather than of an unbiased soldier:

"Headquarters Armies of the United States,
Washington, D.C., May 16, 1866.

Dear Sir:

This will introduce to your acquaintance General Custer, who rendered such distinguished service as a cavalry officer during the war. There was no officer in that branch of the service who had the confidence of General Sheridan to a greater degree than General Custer, and there is no officer in whose judgment I have greater faith than in Sheridan's. Please understand then that I mean by this to endorse General Custer in a high degree.

General Custer proposes to apply for a leave of absence for one year, with permission to leave the country, and to take service while abroad. I purpose to endorse his application favorably, and believe that he will get it.

Yours truly,
U.S. Grant"

To Sr. M. Romero, Minister

Judge Bacon had been unwell for some time. Libbie and Rhoda were doing everything possible to ease his suffering but it was to no avail. He realized his time was limited for the diagnosis of his ailment was cholera[2] and with that there was little hope. Calling Libbie to his bedside, he begged her to forget herself and endeavor not to interfere with her husband's career. As if in prophecy he said: "Armstrong was born a soldier and it is better even if you sorrow your life long that he die as he would wish, a soldier."[3]

On Friday, March 18th, 1866, Judge Bacon passed away. He was 68 years of age. Libbie was happy in the thought that her father, knowing that his end was near, was contented with her marriage to Autie. He had said of her: "Elizabeth has married entirely to her own satisfaction and to mine. No man could wish for a son-in-law more highly thought of."

Libbie wrote to her Aunt Eliza Sabin that Mrs. Jefferson Thurber had helped nurse her brother, and that Father Custer stayed with them while Autie was in New York on business. Walter Bacon had taken over the family affairs as the Administrator of the Judge's will. Libbie learned from the will that

$5,000 was to be set aside and the interest from it to be given to Rhoda for her support. This with her own money would permit Rhoda to live quite comfortable. At the moment she was visiting her relatives in Clinton. Her health was quite bad and it appeared she would never be strong enough to keep house again.

Walter Bacon was endeavoring to sell some of the Bacon land holdings at a time when real estate was moving poorly. But it was a necessity for there was insufficient cash from which to draw interest to provide Rhoda with the money stipulated by the terms of the will.

Libbie took the death of her father rather hard. Though there had been more than the usual age difference between parent and offspring—he was 68 and she 24—there had been an affinity and mutual admiration seldom seen in that period.

Autie, knowing the deep hurt that Libbie suffered, did everything possible to divert her attention from her loss. He planned activities that carried them to Toledo and Detroit where she had friends to visit. Drives into the beautiful countryside and up to Tecumseh to determine how *Don Juan* was doing in the hands of Elliot Gray got her out of the Bacon house with its constant reminders of her pleasant childhood there. And Autie insisted that she refrain from wearing clothing that indicated deep mourning. There was no percentage in a constant remembrance of the past.

The local papers had eulogized the Judge. A clipping Libbie preserved stated that he "was noted for his promptness, decision, strict integrity and excellent judgment in all his business and was known to be influenced and controlled by exalted Christian principles. . . . was always a friend to the poor . . . interested in the young . . . . and for years past taught a class in Sabbath School."

Libbie wrote her own eulogy. Briefly penciling a description of his early years in Onondaga, New York, and his professional accomplishments in Monroe, she continued:

"He maintained his faith and loyalty to Monroe having seen or watched its rise and gradual decline, overshadowed as it was by larger cities on either side. He was first and foremost in every movement that would benefit the city.

"His goodness to the poor was proverbial. He was pleased at the immigration of the Germans to this city, speaking of them always as law-abiding, industrious, honest people.

"Always a moral man, he had not until after his first wife's death made a profession of religion. He was wont to ascribe his conversion to her prayers offered up for so many years in his behalf. He united with the Presbyterian Church at the age of 60 and was soon after made an elder.

"The Judge watched the career of every county man that entered the service in the Civil War, and was the first to welcome them home with congratulations. When young Custer appeared in Monroe the story of his first victory had preceded him and Judge Bacon walked up to him introducing himself and praised this golden haired boy for his daring. His first words to him were thanks that a Monroe boy should have earned such a distinction, and reflect such honor on the town. For though Custer had spent but a brief period in the place as a schoolboy the Judge claimed him as a townsman. When however the lad chose his daughter for a sweetheart and boldy laid siege to her heart the Judge felt for a time that his patriotism could hardly make him sufficiently self-sacrificing to give up his only child to one of his country's defenders. Soon perceiving, however, that it was no idle fancy on the part of either, he gave his consent."[4]

On their wedding day Libbie turned to her father and said: "Father, I have proved my admiration for your belief in selfmade men by marrying one."

With the definite knowledge now that Judge Bacon had not been overly affluent and that Libbie's chief inheritance would be in the form of real estate rather than in money, Custer felt the need more strongly than ever to obtain highly remunerative employment. The offer of the Mexican government to pay him twice his major general's salary in gold—a total of $16,000—was highly tempting.[5]

Libbie was strongly opposed to his accepting the offer. She did not want him to go into combat again, ever, but if he did she would go with him. Fresh in her mind was the admonition of her dear father to forget her own selfish desires. He had advised her to "put no obstacles in the way to the fulfillment of his destiny. He chose his profession. He is a born soldier. There he must abide."[6] High sounding advice to a young woman intelligent enough to know that glory demanded too great a sacrifice.

Autie listened to her, of course, but not as attentively as usual for he was making plans. Sheridan had responded to his many questions at some length. He was stationed on the border where he could observe the situation firsthand. It was his view that 10,000 cavalry could take the country from Maximilian in six months. He advised against bringing in the 1,000 or 2,000 American men Caravajal had stipulated Custer would have to bring. Sheridan observed that unless the Americans were well paid and well rationed they would soon get disgusted at conditions in Mexico.[7]

On July 26th Custer received a letter from Sr. Romero indicating he had received his confidential letter with a copy of General Grant's introduction, then stating: "It is very pleasant for me to inform you, General, that I have known you to be one of the good and earnest friends that Mexico has in this country," then adding that his case would receive "special attention." Two weeks earlier, on July 13th, William D. Barpin of the Financial Agency of the

Republic of Mexico had written Custer that "everything is working splendidly at Washington."[8]

All seemed to be going well, then bad news arrived. Custer's request for a year's leave of absence from the army was denied. The General-in-chief, Grant, had approved of Custer's plan. Secretary Stanton would grant any reasonable request for Custer. The big block was Secretary Seward and his desire to have the United States maintain an air of neutrality. This could hardly be, with a member of the Federal Army on leave to take the post of Adjutant General in an army opposing France's finest.

Custer could resign. Libbie had asked him to do that but not for the purpose of fighting in another country. She admitted her purpose was to have him with her all of the time. There would be no more separations, no more dreadful suspense. But Custer would not desert his first love, the army, anymore than he would have deserted his second love, Libbie.

The K. C. Barkers of Detroit wanted Autie and Libbie to visit them. Kirkland Barker was serving out his final year as Mayor of Detroit and apparently wanted a little break from postwar political problems. He and Autie had mutual interests — dogs, fishing, hunting and fine horses. His tobacco factory known as K.C. Barker & Co., the predecessor of the American Eagle Tobacco Company, had been founded by him and had afforded him a considerable measure of affluence.[9] On this occasion he wanted Custer to join him on a trip to the Lake St. Clair flats, an area noted for its muskellunge fishing. Libbie was invited to stay with Mrs. Barker at Trenton, Michigan, while the two men enjoyed the excitement and diversion of trolling for the "tiger of the Great Lakes."[10]

As enticing as this invitation was, Custer was faced with more immediate problems. His celebrated stallion, *Don Juan,* died very suddenly at Tecumseh. The loss of the $10,000 animal was quite a blow.[11] Not much over six weeks earlier Custer had visited Tecumseh and was satisfied that the horse was quite healthy, though it was not doing very well in servicing the mares brought to him.

Considerable feeling had developed amongst the returning veterans. It had become apparent that the maimed and crippled veterans were not receiving the care, consideration and support due them for the sacrifices they had made. A meeting of Monroe County soldiers and sailors was held in the Court House on August 4th to organize a Soldiers and Sailors Union. In the election held, General Custer was made president of the organization. It was resolved that they would support the Constitution of the Union of the United States and that they would show a preference to their unfortunate soldier brothers who bore the stamp of battle, in such public offices they might be competent to fill.[12]

Custer was breaking away temporarily from his general policy of avoiding politics. Now on inactive duty he took exception by aiding the cause of his fellow soldiers.

On August 9, 1866, Custer attended a mass meeting in Detroit where the National Union platform was endorsed. He was one of the four delegates appointed to attend the national convention to be held in Philadelphia on August 14th.

Setting aside his personal interests and those of many of his best friends and supporters such as John A. Bingham and Zach Chandler who were radical Republicans, he opposed their efforts to enfranchise the freed slaves, disenfranchising prominent whites.

From a practical political viewpoint the Republicans were trying to save their party with a "slave vote." Without it the Democratic Party would take over. As a matter of principle he had differed with his father's extreme Democratic views. His opposition to the views of his friends was a matter of principle. Summarily he had said:

"Under no circumstances would I vote for a man who in time of war had sympathized with the enemies of Government . . . I believe that every man who engaged in the Rebellion forfeited every right held under our Government—to live, hold property. . . . For the Government to exact full penalties simply because it is constitutionally authorized to do so, would, in my opinion, be unnecessary, impolitic, inhuman and wholly at variance with the principles of a free, civilized and Christian nation, such as we profess to be."[13]

The Radical press used fair means and foul to discredit the National Union Party and President Johnson's reconstruction plan to restore self-government to the seceded states should they abolish slavery. When Custer, with five others, signed a petition to call a grand rally of ex-soldiers in Cleveland on September 17th, he became a prime target for the Radical press.

President Johnson had a plan to bring his reconstruction policy before the people in a manner that would sway their vote to his way of healing a national wound. He believed that merciful treatment of all Southerners would be a big step in that direction.

Picturing the Union as a large circle broken at many points by war, he proposed uniting it by clemency and commonsense legislation. The time was ripe for his proposed "swing around the circle" for a series of speeches at strategic points. A cornerstone of a monument being erected to Stephen A. Douglas in Chicago would serve as a public reason for starting on the tour, then he would swing down to Springfield to visit Lincoln's tomb. By making these two stops he would be paying respect to both a Democrat and a Republican.

As a practical politician he invited members of his cabinet, Admiral Farragut, General Grant, Senor Romero and General Custer to accompany him.[14]

The Presidential party left Washington on August 28th and was joined by General Custer at Manhattanville where all boarded a steamer for West Point.[15] After watching the cadets in review the party moved westward toward Niagara Falls, stopping at points along the way to greet the assembled crowds. At Auburn, where Libbie had attended school in her teens, all were invited to attend a picnic at the Willowbrook estate just three miles to the south.[16]

On September 3d, the New York *Times* made mention of General Grant seated outside the Presidential ball at Niagara Falls sampling whiskey. Grant was ill at Buffalo when called upon for a speech, and later at Cleveland, Monroe and Detroit. Grant's samples were usually of such size neither he nor any other human could carry them.

A large crowd greeted the President in Cleveland, evidencing marked respect and cordiality as the party left the station for the hotel. Once at the hotel the President began to speak from the balcony but was shouted down by a pugnacious crowd sent there by his antagonist Senator Ben Wade. Wade's gorillas continued their tactics for the rest of the way across Ohio for Wade the Radical controlled Ohio politics.

On its way to Detroit the special train backed off the main line onto a spur leading to the Loranger Square in Monroe. There General Custer, acting as host and master of ceremonies, introduced the President, Admiral Farragut, Senor Romero[17] and other notables after which the train pulled out of Monroe and headed for Detroit.

Libbie had joined the party at Monroe. Previously she had written her cousin Rebecca[18] that Autie had accepted the invitation of the President to travel with him to Chicago and that he had left on the 28th "to join his Excellency Mr. My Policy in New York" on the 30th. She asserted:

"It is my wish to have Autie avoid politics but I can say nothing to prevent him because I know that he is so conscientious in what he is doing. He believes as I have feared and thought for a long time that there will be another war if such a congress is allowed to dictate laws to our country as did last winter. He believes men, soldiers and all should work to prevent it and so I do not oppose his present movements.

"He has positively declined running for Congress and will do so on no consideration — much to my delight.

"He declined to remain (in Washington) on account of some 'engagements with parties in the west' — which, Rebecca dear, was his wife. He is growing so much dearer and dearer every day I am at loss to know how he can get any better."

Libbie was delighted with Secretary Seward's remarks in the courthouse square when he said to the assembled Monroeites: "I find that General Custer had a differnece in the way he enter towns. When he enters an enemy town he goes in straight forward and the enemy backs out. When he brings us into his own town he backs us in."[19]

Libbie was having to take the bitter with the sweet. She was relieved to see Autie's Mexican temptation removed and delighted to see him repel the invitations to run for office. What pained her at this point was the reaction to her husband's support of Andrew Johnson and the National Union party. The Radical press in Cleveland had declaimed him in an editorial with:

WITH FRIENDS IN DUNDEE, MICH. To the left of the seated Custers is Mrs. Rose Flint, a newspaper woman who had accommodations for troupers playing at Haynes Opera House over Dr. John B. Haynes Drug Store in Dundee. The couple standing are unidentified. Ca. 1868. Courtesy of Lisle Reedstrom.

"The very dress of the man stamped him as an egotist before he (Custer) had uttered a word. What business has a lieutenant colonel — for that is the rank to which President Johnson has recently promoted Custer — to wear the uniform of a major general, a rank he has not held, even in the volunteer service for months."[20]

The Radical Monroe *Commercial,* once so friendly to Custer, gave a brief description of the Presidential visitation to Monroe on Tuesday, September 4th, but studiously avoided mentioning Custer's name. The very least the editor (who quite probably doubled as the reporter on the weekly paper) could have done was to mention Custer though he could have misspelled his name. It is hardly unlikely anyone in Monroe did not know Custer was in the Presidential party. The article asserted that:

"In short the President is disgracing his high office by turning his trip to Chicago into an electioneering tour, and lowering himself to the level of a common stump politician.

"The Bread and Butter party, anticipating a crowd, erected a platform on the Court House square. . . . The President's train arrived about 4 o'clock and backed up to the public square, when the President and party left the train, were escorted to the platform and introduced to the crowd."[21]

A week later the same paper took President Johnson to task in an editorial, then went on to say:

"True, the President's party were engineered into Monroe by our townsman, Gen. Custer, but he with other place-seekers has proved as recreant to his avowed principles as has the President himself. And it is understood that Gen. Custer carries in his pocket a commission as colonel in the regular army, as the result of his 'fawning.'"[22]

In Detroit the party was received respectfully enough. It was Zach Chandler's domain. Chandler was a party man but not a crude politician like Ben Wade of Ohio. It was peaceful there but not so in Chicago, St. Louis, Terre Haute or Louisville. There were hecklers everywhere and the President, his patience worn thin, erred by answering back.

On the trip back to Washington[23] the Custers left the party at Steubenville, Ohio, returning from there to Monroe. No sooner had they arrived than Custer hurried on to Cleveland to attend the Soldiers and Sailors Convention. The meeting was not too well attended on its opening day, September 17th.

The Convention was vehemently attacked by the Radical press. Lies and distorted interpretations were printed about the proceedings and the individuals involved. Autie was seeing politics from both the inside and out. When a letter denouncing Secretary Stanton was circulated for signatures, Custer thought it a propitious time to leave. He had had his fill of politics.[24]

Autie escorted Libbie to Monroe, then proceeded on to Washington, arriving there on the evening of September 21st. The following morning he called on Secretary Stanton who, aware that Custer had not signed the round robin letter in Cleveland denouncing him, warmly welcomed him. Stanton's first question was of Libbie's health, then he asked: "Is she as pretty as ever?" Custer replied: "She is still improving." Stanton said: "She ought to be."

The first business he transacted regarded Tom. No sooner had Custer expressed a desire to have Tom transferred to the Seventh U.S. Cavalry than Stanton sat down and wrote out directions for the order to be made out. While doing so he said: "I will not only transfer him but I will promote him to 1st lieutenant." Stanton then informed him that Andrew J. Smith would be the colonel of the Seventh, a choice that made Custer quite happy. General Alfred Gibbs was made one of the majors. General William Price of Ohio was being considered as a major which would have meant that with Custer as the lieutenant colonel there would be four West Pointers on the staff, a welcome arrangement indeed.

The regimental ranks had been fully recruited, Stanton informed him, and all were at Jefferson Barracks, the regimental headquarters. The captains and lieutenants would be appointed in five days.

Though Autie had written Libbie from Willard's Hotel informing her of all that had transpired that day, he wanted her to know he was staying at 339 Pennsylvania Avenue in the very room at the head of the stairs she had occupied while he was in the Shenandoah late in 1864. He concluded: "So that my darling, you see that thus far our usual good luck attends us."[25]

The press had pommeled Custer with the allegation he had obtained his lieutenant colonelcy by catering to Johnson's wishes. Hamilton Howard, at the request of his father, Senator Jacob Howard who was on the Military Committee, asked him some questions. In response Custer said:

"I have never been the supporter of Mr. Johnson's policy as represented. On the contrary I have always condemned his unlimited exercise of political power as well as the conferring of political power upon leading rebels. I attended the Philadelphia Convention not to support Mr. Johnson or his policy but with the hope that there would be arranged a plan upon which Congress and the President might unite. As soon as I saw the uses made of the movement by the Copperheads peace men who hoped to regain their former power I turned my back upon the movement. . . .

"It has been stated that the President gave me my appointment as lieutenant colonel in the regular army. This is in error. I am indebted to Andrew

Johnson for nothing. My appointment was decided upon by the Secretary of War and General Grant without the advice or knowledge of the President and before I had taken part in political affairs. This can be verified by the Secretary of War."[26]

The Monroe *Commercial* continued to give its readers "a little history of General Custer's recent political antics" by quoting out of context from his testimony before the Joint Committee on Reconstruction. The anti-Johnson editor charged:

"The President was marshalling his forces in opposition to the policy of reconstruction which Gen. Custer had declared to be the right one, and needed every man he could get. A set of political demagogues flattered Gen. Custer that by going into support of 'my policy,' he could either get the nomination for Congress in this district, or secure a promotion in the army. Either the bait was too strong for the General, or the General was too weak for the bait; but whichever way you put it, the General ungloriously yielded; and now we find him doing all in his power to prevent just what he declared under oath ought to be done.

"We find General Custer traveling with the President's political caravan, acting as one of its ushers, and it is said with a commission of Colonel in the regular army in his pocket."[27]

Ten days later the *Commercial* printed a letter written to Custer by a former colonel of the 5th Michigan Cavalry under Custer, Russel A. Alger. Alger's letter of October 1 reminded Custer of their campfire talks in 1863 and 1864 in which he had "denounced the men at home who withheld their support from us while in the field."[28]

Alger contended that he and many other old Michigan friends of Custer who had served with him had variable opinions as to his political sentiments and wondered if he had been misrepresented.

On October 3 Custer replied that with the resumption of his official duties he hoped he would not be called upon to discuss political questions now before the public. He continued:

"I claim allegiance to no political party and acknowledge no political creed. I sympathize in sentiment and action with those men only of all parties, who disregarding party ties and mere party dogmas, regard the preservation of the country upon the principles of free, enlightened and Republican government as outweighing every consideration even if it be at the sacrifice of the party. "In your letter you ask 'whether or not' I 'have been misrepresented.' To this query I can positively reply in the affirmative."

Recalling his denunciation in the field of the men at home who withheld support of the fighting men, he maintained that he still entertained "the opinion that I then expressed that, while I might be willing under certain circumstances to extend pardon to those who opposed us *in arms,* I never could forgive those of the North who not only failed to support us in the field, but placed obstacles in the way of our success. So long as I believe the war to have been just, and the duty of all loyal citizens to have been to support the Government, just so long will I hold in contempt the class of men who not only opposed the Government but acted in opposition to their respective states."

Custer noted that Alger's letter closed with the query: "Can you, and do you advise your old soldiers to support Mr. J. Logan Chipman for Congress? Does he not represent that element at home which all soldiers in the field well know prolonged the war? Do you favor the appointment of such men to office?"

To the first question he admitted that he would not know Chipman if he would see him and that his knowledge of his principles was all hearsay. He would advise the soldiers to vote as their consciences dictated. He had understood that Chipman, for the past few years, had "been included in that class of men who, during the war, failed to give the Government that support which is due from every loyal and patriotic citizen." He had never seen this opinion contradicted but had heard it expressed by Democrats and Republicans alike. It was his opinion that for such an important office "we should have a man *without reproach but above suspicion.*"[29]

Purging his mind of all politics, he applied his energies to the task of moving to his new post on the Great American Desert.

Since he was taking three of his horses — *Jack Rucker, Phil Sheridan* and Libbie's *Custis Lee* — with him to Kansas, he was quite anxious that arrangements be made so that they would not have to change cars in Chicago. Mayor Barker had suggested that railroad superintendent C. F. Hatch might permit the car carrying the horses to be attached to a morning passenger train to St. Louis so as to arrive there the same time the Custers did.[30]

On October 8th the Custers left for St. Louis on a special car at the invitation of a Detroit friend. The car was filled with pretty women eager to see the great Fair at St. Louis.

The horses had been sent on with the two dogs, *Byron* the Lordly greyhound given to them by a Texas planter and *Turk,* a ferocious-looking though very gentle English bulldog. Eliza went along, of course, and with her a lazy, worthless Negro lad who was supposed to tend the General's horses. Tom, newly assigned to the Seventh Cavalry, went along with them too.

Tom had been in Monroe most of the summer. Still single, he spent most of his time dating the local beauties. Near the end of his visit he became involved with an older woman whose advances were obviously those of one whose object was matrimony. Libbie was worried over the affair. The woman did not merit her approval.

Libbie had mothered the boy, had ironed out a few of his rough spots and, realizing he would always live with them, had a fear that this woman could end up as her sister-in-law. Somehow Tom threw off the fetters and was able to travel with them a free man.

The remaining member of the Monroe party was one of its prettiest, Diana. Libbie's close friend, Laura Noble, had planned to go but at the last minute withdrew. She announced she had suddenly become engaged.[31]

St. Louis was a gay place. The war was over and the Fair was the first opportunity to give expression to peacetime pursuits without a feeling of remorse. Autie had the time of his life exploring the exhibits of swine, horses and cattle and saw to it that Libbie received the fine points of their judging.

In looking over the thoroughbred horses, he expressed his wish to own a Kentucky bluegrass farm stocked with blooded horses. He had said it before and would say it again: "If I get rich, I'll tell you what I'll do. I'll buy a home for father and mother." Then would come the horse ranch where he would retire to follow his second choice of professions.[32]

One evening they attended a performance of *"Rosedale."* Lawrence Barrett, who took the role of the hero, literally charmed Autie. Feeling the urge to express his appreciation, Autie went backstage and knocked at Barrett's dressingroom door. Introducing himself to the famous tragedian, though Barrett said he instantly recognized the famous cavalry leader, he urged him to join their party. Barrett acquiesed when Custer said: "The old lady told me I must seize you, and go you must, for I don't propose to return without fulfilling her orders."[33]

Barrett had protested at first, not wishing to be presented in his rough gray traveling suit. The insistence of Custer and the concluding "orders" from the "old lady" made him decide in favor of accompanying him.[34]

Barrett soon forgot his dress when he met the happy party from Detroit. An hour went all too rapidly. Realizing that he had considerable studying to do in preparation for a role, he asked permission to retire.

His meeting Custer meant an immediate and lasting friendship between the two. They were kindred spirits, each respecting the superlative qualities of the other.

Libbie took great pleasure in their friendship. She observed the strong bond that seemed to have developed instantly between the two men and that would grow stronger in the next ten years. Since both lived roving lives and kept track of each other's movements, Autie managed to pay a visit whenever Barrett was playing a town near enough to reach. It touched Libbie to see them part for tears would stream down their faces while they held hands as if it was to be a final farewell.

NOTES — CHAPTER 17

1Sheridan: *Memoirs,* II, pp. 214-15; See also *Message of the President of the U.S. of January 29, 1867 Relating to the Present Condition of Mexico,* H.R. Exec. Doc. No. 76, 39th Congress, 2d Session; Whittaker: *Life of Custer,* pp. 340-41; Eliz. B. Custer: *Tenting,* pp. 308-10; Merington: *Custer Story,* pp. 183-84.
2EBC-CBNM, Nos. 6318, 6349.
3Libbie's notes in author's collection.
4*Ibid.*
5Eliz. B. Custer: *Tenting,* p. 308
6*Ibid,* p. 312.
7Merington, p. 184; Eliz. B. Custer: *Tenting,* p. 308.
8BCWC collection.
9Farmer, Filas: *History of Detroit,* II, Detroit, 1890, p. 1044.
10BCWC collection, letter of August 3, 1866.
11Monroe *Commercial,* August 2, 1866.
12Monroe *Commercial,* August 9, 1866.
13Merington, pp. 187-88.
14Geo. A. Custer to Libbie, August 24, 1866, telegram from Wheeling, Va. advising her he would be in Monroe the next day and would "leave in two or three days to accompany the President to Chicago." Author's collection.
15Monaghan: *Custer,* p. 272.
16Mrs. Enos T. Martin: *The Old Home, pp. 1894.*
17*Message of the President . . . Relating to the Present Condition of Mexico,* pp. 125-26.
18Libbie to Rebecca Richmond, August 29, 1866, EBC-CBNM.
19New York *Times,* September 5, 1866.
20Cleveland *Leader,* September 6, 1866.
21Monroe *Commercial,* September 6, 1866.
22Monroe *Commercial,* September 13, 1866.
23Ronsheim, p. 63; Monaghan, pp. 277-78.
When the train pulled into Scio, Ohio (then called New Market), Custer got off and shook hands with some of his friends as he was but a few miles from his birthplace. While doing so he heard uncomplimentary remarks made about the President, loud enough for the latter to hear. Furious because of the discourtesy to Johnson he resolved never to visit Scio again.
24The New York *Times,* August 22, 1866, had printed a letter Custer had written to J.W. Forney, Secretary to the U.S. Senate, castigating him for his "wilful perversion of the truth" in a publication he edited. He asked: "What have you done or accomplished to justify you in maligning and traducing those whose patriotism has undergone the test of battle? . . . As to the propriety of my course in attending the National Union Convention, I recognize in neither you nor in those you represent, the right to question my motives. If I satisfy my God, my country and my conscience, I achieve my highest aim."
25Geo. A. Custer to Libbie, September 22, 1866, BCWC collection.
26Hamilton G. Howard: *Civil War Echoes,* Washington, 1907, p. 316; The Army Register for 1865-67 gives Geo. A. Custer's date of commission as July 28, 1866, for the rank of lieutenant colonel in the Seventh Regiment of Cavalry.
27Monroe *Commercial,* September 20, 1866.
28Monroe *Commercial,* October 11, 1866.
29*Ibid.*
30Geo. A. Custer to C. F. Hatch, October 1, 1866. Letter belonging to E. H. Rankin, Marquette, Mich.
31Eliz. B. Custer: *Tenting,* p. 329.
32*Ibid,* pp. 340-41.
33*Ibid,* pp. 344-45; Whittaker: *Life of Custer,* pp. 631-32.
34Eliz. B. Custer: *Boots and Saddles,* N.Y., p. 223. The habit of referring to Libbie as "the old lady" began in 1864 when Custer met an old Dutchman in the Shenandoah Valley. The old man tried to forestall Custer's use of his house as a headquarters by saying: "Gentlemens, I have no objections to your coming in, but the old lady she kicks agin it." Any protest on Libbie's part thereafter drew reference to the fun one might have "if the old lady didn't kick agin it."

CHAPTER 18
SPARKS ON THE PRAIRIE

Fort Leavenworth was the next stop west. There the men obtained their supplies as the officers went into nearby Leavenworth City to purchase camping equipment. Those with families bought condemned ambulances that they outfitted with iron stoves and bedding.

Ten miles east of Fort Riley the railroad track came to an end. General William Tecumseh Sherman was there to greet them when they arrived. He had been invited to drive the final spike of the division just completed, acting as the commanding general of the Army's Department of the Missouri.[1]

A waiting wagon took the luggage while Libbie, Diana and Eliza were transported in an ambulance. The narrow and slippery carriage cloth covered seats with their low back rests held her attention until the military reservation came into sight.

Both Libbie and Diana had envisioned a stone fortress with turrets and a deep moat. They were astonished to see instead a post consisting of six magnesium limestone two-story barracks built around a parade ground nearly 600 feet square.[2] Situated on a high plateau at the union of the Republican and Smoky Hill rivers, it provided a beautiful view of an endless sea of prairie grasslands. The plateau was barren of all trees, the cottonwoods lacing the rivers below providing the only evidence of green foliage.

Though Libbie's first impression was not one of enthusiastic acceptance, Autie accepted his lot with his usual zeal. Always the optimist, he could see their new home only through rose-colored glasses.

The purple haze that cast a transparent veil over the surrounding land had new meaning for Autie. He had seen it in Bierstadt's paintings of the West without understanding its significance. Now he knew and was delighted with the scene before him.

Libbie had said: "I was avowedly romantic and the General was equally so, though, after the fashion of men, he did not proclaim it."[3] This was Libbie's observation but others had noted his effervescent spirit on occasions where all thoughts of military protocol had been cast aside or where Libbie's presence undeniably occupied his attention. He did not have to talk in a romantic vein to Libbie for others to know his feelings toward her. The way their eyes met or his conversation ceased when he saw her enter a room of guests was observed by all their friends. His habit of writing lengthy letters to her each night before retiring while out on a campaign was well-known. To gently chide each other was a habit of the Custers then as it is today. He took great pride in all she did and made it known in his comments to others. Their's was no ordinary love affair.

There was no hotel to house them that night. The commanding officer's quarters, that of Major Alfred Gibbs, was the only furnished habitation available. General Sherman, having arrived earlier in the day, occupied a room in the small house. Libbie was deeply concerned over the crowded condition the five of them created, but Mrs. Gibbs acted as if it was commonplace.

On the following day Custer moved their few belongings into the large empty double house that had been built for the commanding officer. He had taken command.

Gibbs had been appointed major of the Seventh Cavalry at the same time Custer was made its lieutenant colonel.[4] He had graduated from the Military Academy the same year Libbie was born—1842—and had served conspicuously in both the Mexican and Civil wars. In the latter he had become a brigadier general of volunteers and a brevet major general. He died December 26, 1868, from a lance wound received before 1860.

Gibbs had joined the regiment at Fort Riley on October 6th to take over its organization from Major John W. Davidson, 2nd U.S. Cavalry, until the arrival of Custer.[5]

Andrew J. Smith, the first colonel of the Seventh who had been appointed with both Custer and Gibbs, had graduated from the Military Academy in 1834 and had served in the Civil War as a major general of volunteers. He joined the regiment on November 26th but, from all accounts, left the matters of organizing and training entirely in the hands of his subordinate, Custer. From that time on it became known as Custer's Seventh.

There were eight captains appointed on the same date. They were William Thompson, Frederick W. Benteen, Myles W. Keogh, Edward Myers, Robert M.

West, Louis M. Hamilton, Albert Barnitz and Michael V. Sheridan. None had attended the Military Academy.[6] The six first lieutenants appointed at the time were Samuel M. Robbins, Mathew Berry, Owen Hale, Myles Moylan, F. V. Commagere and Thomas W. Custer. And none of these had attended the Academy though, like the other officers appointed on that date, all had served during the late war.

The tedious and irksome task of training began at once. So wearisome did the life appear that 80 enlisted men deserted before the year 1866 ended. By that time the regiment had a total of 963 enlisted men and 18 commissioned officers. Companies A, D and H had been assigned to Fort Riley while the others had been stationed at Forts Lyon, Hays, Harker, Dodge, Morgan and Wallace.[7]

More than half the recruits were native born, the balance being immigrants from France, Germany, England, Italy, Ireland, Scotland, Switzerland and Canada.[8]

They came from all ranks of life: a dentist, a blacksmith, a farmer, a bookkeeper, an artisan, a gentleman or a Bowery tough.[9] Many had seen service in European armies and most had served in our Civil War.

An enlisted man would draw $13 a month. Some men joined because they were tired of working 16 hours a day for 50 cents a day, and others for $2 a week. Many under the age of 21 were lured by adventure or the glamour of the uniform. Army fever—the burning desire to be a soldier—burned out long before the termination of the enlistment.

The army had its caste system. Officers seldom spoke to an enlisted man except in the line of duty. There was no fraternization. The gulf was a broad one between the commissioned and the non-commissioned personnel. It was maintained to aid the issuance of orders, to place responsibility and to draw lines of authority.

During the rigors of a campaign the caste system was less evident. While rigidly following army protocol in garrison, these same officers relaxed regulations in the field. Campaigning brought them in constant contact with their men. Exposure to the elements, sharing the same mess, wearing similar clothes, fighting side by side, permitted a relaxation of an otherwise mandatory system.[10]

Colonel Smith arrived at the Fort shortly after the Custers. As the senior officer he ranked them out of their living quarters much to Libbie's relief. Their few pieces of furniture hardly could be seen in the barracks-like structure. Moving into smaller quarters, since army regulations permit an officer to evict a junior officer, solved this problem.

Libbie quickly adapted to the garrison way of life. The air was pure and dry. The best attempts at rain were feeble drizzles, which made her write to Cousin Rebecca: "In Monroe there is rain, snow and mud. How can they live in such a vile climate?"[11]

She had a home more comfortable than that at Winchester. It wasn't exactly crowded with furniture but there was enough to be comfortable. She mentioned an oak and green carpet, and a round table covered with a green and black cloth on which rested albums and a card basket. There were lace curtains like her mother's, and a cane seated oak chair she had purchased for Autie. Meager furnishings but a palace in comparison to life in a wagon.

Since there was considerable leisure time her easel had been placed by one of the windows. On it was displayed a picture she had just finished for Autie—a handsome portrait of their bulldog smoking a pipe.

Libbie related their meeting Lawrence Barrett after seeing his performance of *"Rosedale."* She was impressed with his gentlemanliness and was interested in knowing he had once been a bell boy in Detroit's Russell House. She wanted Rebecca to know that "this is not a *fort* tho' called so. It is a garrison, for there are no walls enclosing it."

Her description of the post gave the impression it was of some size, "the appearance of a little city," and that they were living "almost in luxury."[12]

Tom had not been too well. He had been lame with rheumatism, the result of his illness while in Texas. Anna[13] Darrah was enjoying herself to the fullest for there was no competition. Both Anna and Tom lived with the Custers, Anna intending to stay for the entire winter.

Tom had just returned from his examination before the army examining board in Washington and had passed. Autie had to take the examination along with all of the appointments to the new regiments as required by Congress. Though mandatory for all, the West Point graduates thought the examination a farce. Younger inexperienced officers found it quite severe; many were found to be deficient and were dropped.[14]

Those were happy, delightful days for Libbie. Her husband was occupied with the serious business of readying his troopers for a prospective campaign. She, with no knowledge of Indian warfare, enjoyed riding around Fort Riley, blissfully content with the thought that the Indians in question were many, many miles to the west.

As busy as Autie was he accompanied Libbie on most of her rides. She had been brought up in an atmosphere of calm and quiet. Her parents rarely had exhibited any degree of emotion, and never raised their voices. The Custer clan was a different breed. Emanuel Custer never hesitated showing his emotions. He rallied his sons with an enthusiastic shout, a practice that he introduced them to in their boyhood. In preparing for a ride the noise and hubbub created by the dogs and the Custer males was akin to a midway. It was always a merry affair that had a contagious effect upon all who participated.

Libbie was tossed onto her saddle by her admiring husband. Then, swinging blithely into his saddle

FORT LINCOLN DESERTED—so the post appeared when the temperature went well below zero. Indians were no problem in the winter. 1875. David F. Barry photo. from author's collection.

while blowing his hunting horn to call his pack of dogs, he led off with a trot.

General Sherman had told Libbie that she would find the air of the Plains like champagne. And so she did. Inhaling the fragrance of it was a heady business they both enjoyed. To this was added the pleasure of watching the fetters drop off her husband's personality. At the garrison "he was bound by chains of form and ceremony—the inevitable lot of an officer, where all his acts are under surveillance, where he is obliged to know that every hour in the day he is setting an example."[15] Away from the garrison he became a light-hearted boy, free of all cares and responsibilities. He would lead them in a race at a breakneck gallop, then rest their horses as they dawdled along to look at desert blooms or observe the dogs chase some game in the distance.

One stretch of land almost table top smooth was used to race their equally matched horses. On one such occasion, while their horses were racing neck and neck, Autie reached over and with one powerful arm lifted her from her saddle. She had seen both Tom and Autie pick up their 150-pound mother and carry her around the house, and had been toted up and down stairs by them herself. The stunt promised to be but the beginning of a series of such feats.

Drunkenness was the major problem at a frontier garrison. The life there was one of monotony. The men were away from home. There was little to do when off duty. Most of the recruits were green, coming into a strange way of life. In time they seem to resolve in doing one of two things—desert or get drunk.

Drunkenness was not reserved for the enlisted man. The officers provided a goodly number of cases for they too felt the pangs of monotony. It was the drunkenness among the officers that provided Custer with his major problems. Though a total abstainer, he never attempted to interfere with those officers who drank in moderation. He had found that he was of a temperament that made him unfit to indulge in the use of alcoholic drinks. Tom, who was of a similar temperament, had taken the pledge to abstain from the use of liquors, his brother being influential in his decision. On occasion Tom would drift away from this pledge, influenced by others when away from home. Acknowledging his weakness, he would ask for a transfer so he could be near and under the influence of his brother and Libbie.

At Fort Riley Autie stood almost alone in his convictions about temperance. Never did he attempt to force his views on others though he strove patiently to influence those officers who he thought might be salvaged.

Libbie had been accustomed to seeing gentlemen "politely tight" back in Monroe. On the frontier drunkenness was commonplace among men holding positions of authority. Drunkenness among enlisted men on payday was the rule.

Whenever Custer was confronted with a brave or competent officer who was becoming addicted to the use of alcohol, he would do everything in his power in an attempt to save him from what he knew would be inevitable. Libbie observed that: "His own greatest battles were not fought in the tented field; his most glorious combats were those waged in daily, hourly fights on a more hotly contested field than was ever known in common warfare."[16]

In those instances where an officer indulged while on duty, Custer endeavored to obtain a pledge of sobriety from him or obtain a promise that he would do his drinking while off duty and out of sight. If this did not produce results he would prefer charges for a court-martial or use means to force him to request a transfer. He did what he considered to be the right, the just thing. He insisted from the first that the Seventh must be a sober regiment.

FORT ABRAHAM LINCOLN WAS A LONELY POST IN THE WINTER. Headquarters for the post was the third residence on the left, the Custer home. 1875. David F. Barry photo. Author's collection.

There was another problem—that of developing an *esprit de corps*. A lot of Custer's thought went into molding an incompatible body of men. It was his aim to shape the Seventh into the finest regiment in the service. Libbie had noted the inharmonious feeling evident but Autie reminded her that it was on the battlefield that the strong bond between soldiers was developed. Only when men faced death together did this feeling for each other and for their regiment arise.

With winter forcing them to greater confinement, Libbie found more time for letter writing. James W. Forsyth, a close friend of theirs while he was on Sheridan's staff in the Shenandoah campaign, was stationed with his former commander at New Orleans.[17] She wanted Tony—so they called him—to know they were enjoying the luxury of cream in their coffee as their discussion turned to him and they asked: "Why didn't a kind fate give your majority in the 7th?"

She told him they liked Generals Hancock and Smith and the Gibbs very much. She detested Captain William Thompson because she knew him to be Autie's worst enemy though Autie would not acknowledge it. Autie had told her that when a man of Thompson's age asks for assistance and his wife with him, he could not let personal affairs interfere with what seemed to be his duty.[18] Thompson was nearly 60.

Because she was sublimely happy, Libbie asked Tony if he still entertained "that most cruel and absurd idea of remaining single," then added the ageless admonition: "'Tis my sincere desire that you get married for will it not be terrible when you are old and all by yourself?"

Having made her point, she mentioned her lack of success in inducing Autie to write letters, then added that Tom had been confined to the house with rheumatism but was improving and had asked to be remembered in her letter.

Autie was not having enough trouble with drunks and alcoholics. A letter from his sister Maggie informed him that David Reed was taking to drink again. Nevin had told her that he drank "very hard," and that he had sold his land and had taken part of his pay in old horses, harnesses and wagons. David would have been too shrewd to accept the latter unless his judgment had been altered with excess alcohol.

Since Autie had agreed to pay for Maggie's education at the Boyd Seminary, it was quite natural for her to enclose its bill for her tuition and music lessons during the second quarter, a mere $24.83.[19]

The Governor of Kansas, Samuel J. Crawford, had been having trouble with the Indians in the summer of 1866. He claimed they had murdered, robbed and raped hundreds of Kansans and had been driving construction workers from their work on the Kansas Pacific Railroad. With the melting of the spring snows the Indians had resumed their depredation practices of the previous summer.[20] Railroad grading parties, wagon trains, stage lines and settlers were feeling the increasing pressure of the Indians.

Crawford made repeated requests for military intervention. General Sherman, having become concerned about the territory under his supervision, made his own inspection along the Platte River, then reached the conclusion: "As usual, I find the size of the Indian stampedes and stories diminish as I approach their location."[21] But by the time he had reached Fort Laramie killings had occurred along the Smoky Hill route. The net result was his recommendation to General Grant that the land between the Arkansas and Platte rivers be cleared of Indians so it could be used exclusively for overland transportation.

Before the Indians could be confined to their reservations the Sioux took command of the situation.[22] Sherman ordered Major General Winfield S. Hancock, then commanding the Department of the Missouri, to open a spring campaign against the depredating Indians and offer them "no quarter."[23]

Hancock was in a belligerent mood. Taking charge of the expedition in person, he announced that "no insolence will be tolerated from any band of Indians who we may encounter."[24] Reflecting on it later, Custer wrote: "Of the many important expeditions organized to operate in the Indian country, none, perhaps, of late years has excited more general and unfriendly comment, considering the slight loss of life inflicted upon the Indians, than the expedition organized and led by Major General Hancock in the spring of 1867."[25]

Libbie had little realization of the changes the coming campaign would bring. She had been separated from Autie before but, in each instance, the time of separation and the capacity of the enemy was known.

Her husband had convinced her "that the Indians would be so impressed with the magnitude of the expedition that . . . they would accept terms and abandon the war path."[26] Obviously, he believed what he was telling her.

There were to be about 1,400 men—eight troops of cavalry, seven companies of infantry and a battery of light artillery made up the imposing force.[27] Custer was placed in command of the cavalry.

During the days of preparation the anguished screams of sabers being sharpened on grindstones came constantly to Libbie's ears. She had thought she had heard the last of it on the road to Appomattox. By the end of March General Hancock arrived at Fort Riley to join his infantry force with the cavalry under Custer. By the 7th of April they arrived at Fort Larned, more than 150 miles distant, where arrangements were made through Indian agents to council with the Indians on the 10th.

When it became evident to Hancock that the Indians were using a recent snowfall as an excuse for postponing the council, he decided to move his troops to their camp.

Though Hancock explained that the purpose of his expedition was to promote peace, the Indians thought it could not be or he would not have brought so many soldiers with him.[28] It became obvious that they did not intend approaching the troops nor would they allow the troops to approach them.

On April 13th, Hancock marched his command the 21 miles to the Indian encampment on the Pawnee Fork. Unknown to him the women and children fled as he approached, their menfolk facing him with a line of battle. He was unaware that his approach in force caused them to distrust his motives. They could not believe he was doing so for any other purpose than to perpetrate another Sand Creek massacre.

On November 29, 1864, Colonel John M. Chivington led 900 members of the First Colorado Cavalry in a malicious attack on Chief Black Kettle's peaceful and unarmed Cheyenne camp along Sand Creek. Flying the Stars and Stripes over their camp to indicate its pacificism—as the Indians were directed to do by their agents—the men, women and children were massacred indiscriminately. When it was all over, the body count varied from 150 to 500, the latter being the most accepted figure.

Abandonment of the Indian village angered Hancock. The cavalry was ordered in pursuit. Here Custer was to receive his first lesson in fighting Indians. The Indians had anticipated pursuit. They had no intentions of fighting—certainly not as a body of men. Breaking up their encampment into as many different detachments as there were families, each took off in a different direction with an understanding they would reunite at a point to the north.

The chase began but there was little chance of success. The warriors were hampered by their families but had a 12-hour start. The soldiers were encumbered by a tradition that required they remain together as a unit. Their horses were larger and slower, weighted down with unnecessary equipment. The cavalry had not yet learned how to live on the land and to travel light. And should the soldiers be fortunate enough to overtake one of the Indian families their victory would be an empty one.

Eventually the trail grew so faint it could hardly be seen. On April 16th, the cavalry headed north toward the Smoky Hill River to warn the stations the Indians would soon be on the warpath. There at Lookout Station, about 15 miles west of Fort Hays, Custer discovered the mangled and burned bodies of its three station keepers. When Hancock was informed of this he concluded that this must be war. With that he issued a field order directing the destruction of the abandoned Indian village. This was retribution but of a kind that would start conflagration. It was the signal for an Indian uprising. Now the plains were on fire.

Hancock had indicated earlier to the agents of the Kiowas, Comanches, Cheyennes, Arapahoes and Apaches that he desired no war with the Indians but would punish any who molested travelers across the plains or committed hostilities against the whites. Then he indicated he did not expect to make war against the Indians unless they made war against the whites.[29] All evidence suggests that Hancock burned the village *after* he learned of the burnings and massacre at the stage stations on the Smoky Hill trail.[30]

There was no end of correspondence between Autie and Libbie. He, in spite of the numerous drawbacks that interfered with western correspondence, managed to get a lengthy letter to her almost daily. Little was said about military affairs for they were well covered in his official reports. His letters to her were concerned with the camp life, the hunting and his plans for their reunion.

FUN FOR TWO. The General enjoyed swinging Libbie off her saddle as they galloped across the Plains. For the moment he forgot his cares at the post. His only thought was of Libbie. Sketch by Frederick Remington from *Tenting on the Plains.*

On March 30th he wrote from Saline he would soon be at Fort Larned where he hoped to write telling her to pack and be ready to move on 24-hour notice.[31] From Larned he wrote apologizing because no mail had gone out in two days and expressing disappointment for not being able to send out a few (that would be on a sick day) lines every day. Their next stop would be Fort Dodge, just 45 miles away. He hoped their operation would be concluded by May 18th, and their western tour to follow immediately afterward.[32]

Libbie, in willing response to his advice would send a letter by every passing stage, expressing her concern over General Hancock's intention of not letting the wives of Seventh Cavalry officers join their husbands that summer. Her otherwise chatty and cheerful letters evidenced a change when she wrote him on April 26th that she was possessed with anxiety. The depressing accounts of the Indians and the excitement of a recent earthquake had her begging him for permission to meet him.[33]

While on the train to Fort Leavenworth she met General Hancock. He told her Custer was off on a 15-day scout but when he returned he would come to Riley to take her back with him to Fort Hays. He praised him highly as a husband and a soldier, then said: "I do not know what we would do without Custer; he is our reliance."[34]

Libbie's letters were a great consolation to the lonely cavalryman. They did not arrive with the same regularity with which they were sent. The stagecoach service was irregular, and military couriers could not be sent daily when official dispatches were not indicated. When letters did arrive after an interval, there often were several. Autie would retire to a quiet spot and read them hungrily. He'd thrust them into his breast pocket when finished to return to them later and reread them. That evening by the light of a candle in his tent he would reread them, then address a long letter to her. On one such occasion, while in a philosophical mood, he observed: "When I was merging upon manhood, my every thought was ambitious—not to be wealthy, not to be learned, but to be great. I desired to link my name with acts and men, and in such a manner as to be a mark of honor, not only to the present, but to future generations. My connection with the war may have gained this distinction; but my course during the last five or six years has not been directed by ambition so much as by patriotism, and I now find myself at 27 with contentment and happiness bordering my path."[35]

Custer, now assigned to command all of the troops and posts on the Smoky Hill route, had established his headquarters at Fort Hays. He had placed five infantrymen at each mail station in addition to the five well-armed employees already there.

He announced to the regiment that on Saturday, May 4th, there would be a 300 yard foot race, the company of the winner to be excused from guard and fatigue duty for one week and the winner excused from it for 20 days. This innocent amusement provided a great deal of interest and some exercise.

Also proposed was a buffalo hunt in which everyone participated. It was Custer's opinion that there was "no better drill for perfecting men in the use of firearms on horseback and thoroughly accustoming them to the saddle than buffalo hunting over a moderately rough country. . . . Nothing so nearly approaches a cavalry charge and pursuit as a buffalo chase."[36]

The buffalo hunts served their purpose in providing training and amusement for the men while they awaited supplies for an extensive summer campaign against the marauding Indians. There had been delay because the officers of the Quartermaster's Department had not forwarded the necessary supplies. When the supplies did arrive they were often insufficient or of inferior quality.

Unbroken packages of bacon and other provisions would contain huge stones placed there by dishonest contractors to add weight. The Government had paid for it by the pound. The contents were often wormy or moldy. Boxes of hard bread were received that had been baked in 1861. Such food contributed to the appearance of scurvy and other health problems and was a prominent reason for desertion.[37]

A detachment of white scouts and another of friendly Delaware Indians had been assigned to assist the Seventh Cavalry. Wild Bill Hickok was the most celebrated of the lot. He was a handsome man about six feet tall, straight as a gun barrel, his curly blond hair reaching his shoulders. Custer was quite taken with this famous scout. The story of his courage and marksmanship had preceded him. Unlike many of the plainsmen, he was neither illiterate nor coarse.[38]

Medicine Bill Comstock was a character Custer became quite attached to soon after he became one of the scouts. Born in Kalamazoo, Michigan, he moved to the plains when a lad of 15. The newspaper correspondent Theodore Davis, who was attached to the same command, said of him: "He is quiet and unassuming in manner, small in size and compact in proportion. He is one of the best riders on the plains, with which he is probably more familiar than any other man who roams over them."[39]

To take advantage of the great knowledge Comstock had of the customs and habits of the Indians, Custer invited him to mess with Moylan and himself. Comstock was thoroughly familiar with the dress and peculiarities of the various tribes and was able to converse in their tongue. Through this constant association with him Custer was able to learn much that he would find invaluable in his future dealings with the Indians.[40]

Comstock had two prime wishes—to see George Armstrong Custer and to see a railroad engine. It was Custer who took him to the Platte River where he saw his first locomotive.[41]

Comstock provided Custer with many surprises. The one that amused him most was the discovery that Comstock had named his large dog "Cuss," after Custer.[42]

On May 4th Custer informed Libbie that Colonel Smith would leave Fort Hays that day and there was a likelihood he would be going on to Fort Riley. If he did, she could come back with him. If not, she could expect her husband within seven days. He made it plain he wanted her to "commence packing."[43]

His communication to her on the following day indicated that General (Col.) Smith had given him his Sibley tent for presentation to Libbie. Custer had refused it but Smith brushed that aside with: "I don't care about you, but Mrs. Custer must have this tent." A hospital tent was added to the gift.[44]

Libbie was cautioned to bring no more than her actual needs because of the scarcity of wagons but to be sure to include 100 pounds of butter, several cans of lard, potatoes and onions. Since she was returning with General Smith, Autie advised her to leave him if there was any delay and hurry on to him. "Do not let the grass grow under your feet."[45]

Time was growing short. A campaign was in the offing though official orders had not come through. Custer knew that when they did there would be little time to spend with Libbie. He hadn't received any indication from Libbie that she was moving on to Fort Harker to meet General Smith, in fact, he hadn't heard from her for the most part of a week.

Anxiously he wrote: "I hope you are to start for Hays soon. Days count, even hours are magnified into days when passed away from you. By all means come as soon as possible. *We are not to be at Hays forever.*"

He would be expecting her by the 16th of April, "certainly not as late as the 20th." There were things she could bring that would be most welcome: a croquet set, lard, butter, vegetables and fruits. Undetailed was his statement: "I know *something* much, very much better and be sure you bring *it* along. *I am entirely out at present,* and have been for so long as to almost forget how it tastes. . . . Remember, every moment gone can never be reclaimed."[46]

General Sherman had concluded that the area between the Arkansas and the Platte rivers should be cleared of all Indians. If this could be maintained as a neutral zone, any Indians entering it would be considered hostile and treated accordingly. Once the region was freed of this menace, settlers and miners could travel westward in comparative safety. Custer and the Seventh Cavalry were assigned this task.

His command was to "thoroughly scout the country from (old) Fort Hays near the Smoky Hill River, to Fort McPherson on the Platte, thence describe a semicircle to the southward, touching the headwaters of the Republican and again reach the Platte at or near Fort Sedgwick. . . . then move directly south to Fort Wallace on the Smoky Hill, and from there march down the overland route to our starting point at Fort Hays."[47]

Libbie, Anna Darrah and Eliza had arrived a short time before the expedition was to leave. Autie had moved their tents to the highest ground he could find, well above Big Creek on which the post had been established. A hospital tent was used as a sitting room. Attached to it was a wall tent used as a bedroom. Several other tents were placed nearby, one for the kitchen and another for the soldier assigned to take care of their needs.[48]

NOTES—CHAPTER 18

[1]Eliz. B. Custer: *Tenting*, p. 366.
[2]Circular No. 4, "A Report on Barracks and Hospitals," Washington, 1870, p. 287.
Libbie, 20 years later, described the barracks as being "a story and a half high."
[3]Eliz. B. Custer: *Tenting*, p. 354.
[4]July 28, 1866. See *Army Register* for 1866.
[5]Melbourne C. Chandler: *Of Garry Owen In Glory,* Washington, 1960, pp. 2-3.
[6]*Army Register* for 1866.
[7]*Ibid:* Chandler: *Of Garry Owen,* p. 3.
[8]Don Rickey: *Forty Miles A Day on Beans and Hay,* Norman, 1963, p. 17.

[9]George A. Forsyth: *The Story Of The Soldier,* N.Y., 1900, p. 92.
[10]Rickey, p. 66.
[11]Libbie to Rebecca Richmond, December 6, 1866, EBC—CBNM.
[12]*Ibid.*
[13]In *Tenting On The Plains,* Libbie called her Diana, though in her letters she referred to her as Anna. Such reference in Libbie's book may have been for the purpose of avoiding confusion with Autie's half sister, Mrs. David (Ann or Anne) Reed.
[14]Rebecca Richmond Diary, December 8, 1866, EBC—CBNM.
[15]Eliz. B. Custer: *Tenting,* p. 382.
[16]*Ibid,* p. 395.
[17]*Army Register* for 1867. Forsyth was made a major in the 10th Cavalry, July 28, 1866.
[18]E. B. Custer to Tony Forsyth, January 25, 1867. Special Collections, University of California Library, Santa Barbara.
[19]Maggie Custer to Geo. A. Custer, January 27, 1867, author's collection.
[20]40 Cong., 2 Sess., *House Exec. Doc. 1,* p. 28.
[21]39 Cong., 2 Sess., *House Exec. Doc.* 23, pp. 5-8; Donald J. Berthrong: *The Southern Cheyennes,* Norman, 1963, p. 266.
[22]40 Cong., 2 Sess., *House Exec. Doc.* 1, pp. 36-37; Berthrong: *Cheyennes,* pp. 267-68.
[23]Robert G. Athearn: *Sherman and the Settlement of the West,* Norman, 1956, pp. 130-31.
[24]*Difficulties With Indian Tribes,* 41 Cong., 2 Sess., *House Exec. Doc.* 240, pp. 12-13.
[25]George A. Custer: *My Life On The Plains,* N.Y., 1874, p. 22.
[26]Eliz. B. Custer: *Tenting,* p. 484.
[27]G. A. Custer: *My Life,* p. 22.
[28]Geo. B. Grinnell: *The Fighting Cheyennes,* N.Y., 1915, pp. 243-44.
[29]G. A. Custer: *My Life,* p. 22.
[30]*Ibid,* p. 42; Grinnell: *Fighting Cheyennes,* p. 244; Henry M. Stanley: *My Early Travels and Adventures in America and Asia,* London, 1895, I, p. 45.
[31]Eliz. B. Custer: *Tenting,* p. 522.
[32]*Ibid,* p. 531.
[33]*Ibid,* p. 543.
[34]*Ibid,* p. 546, Libbie to Geo. A. Custer, May 7, 1867.
[35]*Ibid,* pp. 552-53.
[36]*Ibid.* p. 579; G. A. Custer: *My Life,* p. 47; Merington, p. 200.
[37]G. A. Custer: *My Life,* p. 47.
[38]*Ibid,* pp. 33-34; Joseph G. Rosa: *They Called Him Wild Bill,* Norman, 1964, pp. 78-79.
[39]Theadore Davis "A Summer on the Plains," *Harper's Monthly Magazine,* Vol XXXVI (February, 1868), p. 303.
[40]G. A. Custer: *My Life,* p. 47.
[41]Lawrence A. Frost: *The Court-Martial of General George Armstrong Custer,* Norman, 1968, p. 39.
[42]Eliz. B. Custer: *Tenting,* p. 379; Merington, p. 200.
[43]Merington, p. 201; Eliz. B. Custer: *Tenting,* p. 580.
[44]Frost: *Custer Album,* p. 80 photograph indicates that Custer adopted the tepee-shaped tent for his personal use.
It should be noted that it was the custom in the army to call a man by the highest rank he had ever borne, be it brevet or actual, except when he was on duty. Andrew J. Smith, Colonel of the Seventh Cavalry, had been a major general of volunteers.
[45]Eliz. B. Custer: *Tenting,* p. 581, G. A. Custer to Libbie May 7, 1867.
[46]G. A. Custer to Libbie, May 9, 1867, BCWC collection.
[47]G. A. Custer: *My Life,* p. 48.
[48]Eliz. B. Custer: *Tenting,* p. 631.

PICNIC AT FORT LINCOLN. This was one of the simple ways in which the commanding officer entertained his friends and guests. Left to right, *standing:* Mr. Swett of Chicago, Capt. Myles Keogh, LTC G. A. Custer, Dr. G. E. Lord, Asst. Surgeon, Lt. R. E. Thompson, 6th Infantry; *seated:* Lt. James Calhoun, Capt. Stephen Baker, 6th Infantry, Boston Custer, Lt. W. S. Edgerly, Miss Watson, Mrs. James Calhoun, Mrs. G. A. Custer, Capt. T. B. Weir, Misses Wadsworth of Monroe, Lt. Tom Custer, Lt. A. E. Smith. 1875. Author's collection.

CHAPTER 19
A DREAM COME TRUE

June 1, 1867, was moving day for the Seventh. The cavalry column of 350 men moved northward in fours, the train of 20 wagons following. The first day's march up Big Creek valley was only 15 miles, Custer intentionally keeping the ride short to gradually toughen the men for the long march ahead.

He had stayed behind to superintend the location of Libbie's tents, establishing them on a knoll that rose several feet above the highest bluff bordering Big Creek nearby. Here Libbie and Anna would remain and await the return of the Seventh rather than retreat to the more comfortable forts further east.

Shortly after midnight Custer followed the trail of his column, accompanied by a scout, four Delaware Indian trailers and two of his enlisted men. According to a note he sent to Libbie after arriving in camp that morning, he had reached there at 4:10 A.M. Reveille was sounded at 5 A.M. Lieutenant Cooke had the officers believing Autie was lost since 2 P.M., a story Autie supported to the fullest. Later the officers, seeing through the joke, concluded that he had ridden hard and fast to reach them that night.[1]

Once the horses had been groomed, breakfast was ready. When the men had finished their coffee and sowbelly the bugler sounded the "General." Down went the tents in unison, then the packing began. Soon after, "Boots and Saddles" was blown, signaling the men to saddle their horses and ready the wagons. Five minutes later "To horse" was heard. With this the men led their horses into line to await the command "Prepare to mount." With that each man placed his left foot in the stirrup then, at the command "Mount," rose on it and seated himself in the saddle. When the "Advance" was sounded, the troops moved out in columns of fours. From that point on the average daily march was about 25 miles.[2]

Day after day they traveled over the arid prairies. The nearest they came to Indians was the sight of a four-day-old trail of a band of 15 Indians one day, and the sight of 100 warriors the next. All 100 fled when they saw the cavalry. The only incident of any importance which occurred before they reached Fort McPherson was the suicide of Major Wickliffe Cooper. Cooper, in a fit of drunkenness, had turned his service revolver upon himself.[3]

Fort McPherson was half a mile south of the Platte River, just 215 miles northwest of Fort Hays. With the burial of Cooper completed, the wagons were

loaded with supplies and forage. Then the column moved west in search of the elusive Indians. Abandoned ranches and numerous graves were grim evidence of their recent visitations along the Platte.[4]

About 12 miles west of Fort McPherson Custer made camp to await the arrival of General Sherman. He had also arranged a council with the Sioux chief Pawnee Killer and several other Oglala chiefs. Custer hoped to induce them to bring their lodges into the vicinity of the fort and live there in peace. When the chiefs arrived it became obvious their main purpose was to obtain ammunition, food and information. The Indians were given quantities of sugar and coffee and gave in return their promises to live at the fort with their families, all empty promises, Custer was soon to learn.

When Sherman arrived the following day he made it quite evident he had no faith in Pawnee Killer and that he wanted him pursued and seized. The search began the next day, the Seventh moving southwesterly toward the forks of the Republican River where Pawnee Killer's village was thought to be.[5]

Upon leaving Sherman it was understood that Custer was to search the country around the forks of the Republican River, then march northwesterly to Fort Sedgwick to receive further orders from him. On June 22nd the column searched the area of the Republican forks.[6] The guides had advised him against travel north to Fort Sedgwick, the terrain being impassable for wagons loaded with supplies. As they were equidistant from Forts Sedgwick, McPherson and Wallace, Custer decided to send Major Joel A. Elliott to Fort Sedgwick with dispatches. Sherman would be able to provide him with any orders at that point. The wagon train was then sent south to Fort Wallace for supplies badly needed to continue the search.

Elliott had a dangerous mission. His trip over an unknown terrain infested with hostile Indians would be a matter of almost 200 miles. On the 23rd he left at 3 A.M. with a detail of ten men and a scout, the darkness cloaking his movements.

Captain Robert M. West with K Company and a train of wagons had left the afternoon before for Fort Wallace. Having arrived at Beaver Creek — midway to Wallace — he sent the train on under command of Lieutenant W. W. Cooke. West used his wait to scout the Beaver Creek region.[7]

Back at Fort McPherson Custer had sent a letter to Libbie at Fort Hays advising her to meet him at Fort Wallace since he fully expected to be stationed there for several weeks after the scouting expedition had terminated. He expected her to arrive there ahead of him so he sent another letter to her by Cooke asking her to return to the Republican with his escort.

In his letter of June 17th from Fort McPherson,[8] he wrote to her: "If you get a chance to come to Wallace, I will send a squadron there to meet you. . . . I am on a roving commission, going nowhere in particular, but where I please. . . . Now that General Sherman says you can come, do not let General Hancock or General Smith have any peace until they send you to Wallace."

In the letter he sent with Cooke he said: "I never was so anxious in my life. I will remain here (at the forks of the Republican River) until Mr. Cooke returns with the rations—and you, I hope. . . . You cannot imagine my anxiety regarding your whereabouts, for the reason that, if you are now at Wallace, you can join me in about six days and we can be together all summer."[9]

Autie had reason to worry as to her whereabouts. He hadn't heard from her in two weeks. His last two letters to her requesting that she proceed to Fort Wallace had produced no answer. It was his hope she would be there for word had reached him that cholera was spreading westward from Fort Leavenworth. Some blamed its spread on the movement of the Thirty-Eighth U.S. Infantry which had been ordered to Fort Union from Fort Leavenworth. It seems that cholera made an appearance wherever it stopped.[10] Unquestionably prospectors, pioneers and transcontinental travelers played an important role as carriers of this dreadful disease for many of them succumbed along the way.

Captain George Armes, 10th U.S. Cavalry, was stationed near Fort Harker at this time. It was his observation that on July 5th two in his camp were ill with cholera. Within the next ten days 23 had died from it.[11] An examination of the dates on post cemetery markers indicates a flow of cholera westward in the early summer of 1867. Custer had reason to be concerned for Libbie's well being.

Life at the cavalry camp on Big Creek was tranquil enough after Custer and his expeditionary force had pulled out. The fort itself was but a short distance from Libbie's canvas home. Between Fort Hays and her tents the Gibbs were camped. And a sentinel walked his tour of duty on a line paralleling the nearby stream.

Libbie had ample time to do many of the things there was little time for when her husband was at home. Now comfortably situated, she was able to do some reading and some sketching. Then there was time to go over the inventory of her father's estate. Walter C. Bacon, who was its administrator, had sent her a copy from his home at Fergus Falls, Otter Tail County, Minnesota.

The total appraised value of Judge Bacon's estate was $27,225 — certainly not a large inheritance by present day standards when one considers that a third of it was real estate, mostly land, and another third in notes and mortgages. Of the cash balance, $5,000 had to be invested so the interest would be available for her stepmother Rhoda during her lifetime.[12]

The officers who remained in camp visited Libbie every day to see if they could do anything for her. She had resolved to have no wants. In that fashion she would be no burden to them. If it had been at all possible she would have preferred seclusion until her husband returned from his expedition. Her intense desire to be with him and not become a burden or responsibility had drawn the conclusions from her several years earlier to never: hamper troop movements, think of hunger if the regiment could not stop to eat, admit she was too hot or cold, ask for a drink of water between meals. While living in New York many years later, she continued her habit of using water frugally.[13]

A few nights after Autie had left to join his regiment, thunder and lightning began. The roll of thunder, sounding like volleys of artillery in a great battle, was accompanied by flash after flash of lightning. The sky seemed to be constantly illuminated by it. And in a minute and a half the girls counted 25 peals of thunder.

The wind had increased in velocity to a point that their rag house fairly shook. Autie, aware of these sudden storms, had ordered the corner posts of the tents sunk deep into the ground, the entrance flies fastened with leather straps and buckles and the ridge pole secured with picket ropes.

Then the rain came, falling in sheets. The trench that surrounded the tent was unable to cope with it and soon the floor was covered with water.Colonel Smith and his adjutant Captain Thomas B. Weir made their way to the tent accompanied by Eliza. The very thing Libbie desired the least — becoming a bother to the officers of the command — had happened.

The two officers, in surveying the large hospital tent, decided that its ridge pole could fall down. Quickly they moved all of the available furniture into a hollow square within which they placed the three women. There they sat on a large board until the thunder diminished, though the wind and the rain belabored the frail shelter unremittingly. The officers returned to their tents while Eliza helped Libbie and Anna over the pools to their bedroom tent. Into their wet beds they crawled, too terror-stricken to notice how wet they were.

Scarcely had they fallen asleep when a voice outside warned that they should arise for they were being flooded. Hurriedly they dressed and moved outside, there to see by the light of a lightning flash what had been a tiny creek the night before was now a seething torrent of water more than 35 feet deep.[14]

The water was slowly crawling upward, having reached the kitchen tent near the creek bank. The soldiers hurriedly moved Libbie's boxed household goods to the high ground next to her tents. Some of the officers arrived to render assistance but the women bravely told them they could fend for themselves. The officers then continued to aid the soldiers trapped on a water-locked area of land in a bend of the creek below.

Once the household goods were safe and there had been a moment of relaxation, the air was rent with the agonized cries of drowning men. There was neither officer nor man near enough to hear or aid them. The very thought unnerved the women. Eliza could but run along the bank and cry out: "Oh, Miss Libbie! What shall we do? What shall we do?"[15] Libbie and Anna could do nothing but stare and scream at the writhing figures flailing their arms in the torrent that engulfed them.

As several of the figures were swept by, Eliza came running to Libbie who was struggling to untie a wet piece of rope. "Miss Libbie," she called out, "there's a chance for us with one man. He's caught in the branches of a tree, but I've seen his face and he's alive. He's most all of him under water and the current is a switchin' him about so he can't hold out much longer. Miss Libbie, there's my clothes line we could take, but I can't do it, I can't do it. Miss Libbie, you wouldn't have me do it, would you? For where will we get another?"[16]

Eliza, frugal through years of necessity but benevolent at heart, had reached a mental crisis which Libbie solved by rushing to the kitchen tent for the clothesline. Making a loop in one end, they used a flash of lightning to show him how to pull it over his head. After several futile attempts they managed to throw the rope end within his reach. Pulling and tugging, the inspired women managed to get the choking and chattering half-drowned man ashore. After they warmed him up and gave him one of Autie's blue shirts, for he was naked from the waist up, he got up and left without a word. A long time afterward, and on another expedition, he met the General and told him Eliza had saved his life and asked him to thank her.

There were two more men saved by the intrepid women. Both were wrapped in blankets and rubbed with red pepper at the fire side. With the dawning of day the rain ceased and the waters of the flash flood had begun to recede. Everyone and everything was drenched. Soon the camp was covered with bedding, clothes and blankets hung out to dry. Eliza magnanimously broke up her bunk for a fire and soon had a warm breakfast for everyone.

The falling water soon exposed the havoc wrought by raging waters of the night before. Caught in the debris on the opposite bank was the swollen dead body of a soldier, his one arm raised in the air as if beckoning for help. They were unable to reach him.

In reviewing the incidents of that evening, it was determined that seven men had drowned near their tents. Then it became known that the officers had planned to strap the women to the Gatling guns nearby, they being the heaviest objects to which they might be anchored. Fortunately the rising waters

WATER SUPPLY. The Missouri River was Fort Lincoln's only source of water. It had to be crossed to reach the frontier town of Bismarck. 1873. Author's collection.

BISMARCK, D.T. First called Edwinton, the name was changed to Bismarck about the time Fort Lincoln was occupied by the Seventh Cavalry in 1873. It was a "spree" town for cavalrymen on payday. Courtesy of the North Dakota Historical Society.

had abated for, strapped to these heavy pieces, they would have been unable to escape a sure but slow death.

That evening a light rain began to fall and the skies gave evidence of more bad weather. With the news that Big Creek was beginning to rise, the officers made plans to move to higher ground. An attempt to take the women across the creek in an ambulance failed. For three days more they remained in their tents until at last the sun appeared. In company with the Gibbs family they were driven across the soggy plains to the divide. Their Sibley tent was pitched and into it they dropped exhausted and unnerved.

A short time later General Hancock arrived from Fort Harker. He told Libbie that it appeared as if Autie would be in the Platte River area for several months. Libbie's heart sank, her prospect of seeing Autie having now become almost impossible.

To add to her discomfiture a military order was issued that required all women to return to Fort Riley.[17] And return to Fort Riley they did.

Major Elliott and his detachment rode into camp on June 28.[18] They had traveled the 200 miles by night, resting in ravines each of the five days. No contact had been made with hostile Indians which was evidence that they had moved to the south between the command and Fort Wallace. This intelligence created a new anxiety for Custer.

Cooke's escort to Fort Wallace was a squadron of only 48 men. Under the command of Lieutenant Sam Robbins, it would be no match for the large number of warriors it would be confronted with. Of even greater concern to Custer was the safety of his wife. As Custer recalled later: "My wife who, in answer to my letter, I believed was at Fort Wallace, would place herself under the protection of the escort of the train and attempt to rejoin me in camp. The mere thought of the danger to which she might be exposed spurred me to decisive action."[19]

Custer was no stranger to decisive action. His reputation had been made on it. Captain Edward Myers, an officer with considerable Indian experience, was sent in command of a well-armed squadron to join Captain West, then march toward Fort Wallace to meet the returning train.

Meanwhile the wagon train had reached Fort Wallace uneventfully, had loaded with supplies and had begun its return trip over the same route. On June 26th it had reached a point half way back to the camp where it had left Captain West. Suddenly Comstock, who had been scanning the horizon in all directions, detected a few Indians in the distance. These soon increased in numbers until they totaled more than 600. As they advanced they circled the double column of wagons, then opened fire. In a series of circling charges they attempted to run over the handful of cavalrymen but were met each time by the unfaltering fire of the Spencer Carbines in their hands.

The running battle continued for three hours, then suddenly the Indians withdrew, taking their dead and wounded with them. The troopers took the respite to rest and care for their few wounded.

An hour later there was new cause for alarm. In the distance could be seen a body of unidentified horsemen. Later, with the aid of field glasses, it was determined that the figures on horseback wore the blue blouses of the cavalry. It was the combined command of West and Myers.

On the morning of the 28th all were back in the main camp on the Republican River.[20] They had no additional news of Indians in the Fort Wallace area and there was no news of Libbie or replies to the letters sent to her from Fort McPherson.

Now the stories of cholera at eastern posts and the rumor that Libbie was ill began to take their toll. With no communication from her in weeks, Custer's sternly disciplined mind began to entertain thoughts as to whether it was worthwhile to remain in the service. His chronic optimism began to yield to suspense. He had learned of her exposure to the flood at Big Creek and heard false reports of her illness. These coupled with the knowledge that cholera was moving westward and that she might become exposed to it made him think seriously of resigning from the service. The only thing that would change his resolution would be news that she was safe.[21]

Major Elliott had brought dispatches from General Sherman directing Custer to march up the north fork of the Republican River to a point on the Platte west of Fort Sedgwick called Riverside Station. The march was a terrible ordeal for everyone. The 65 miles in the burning July sun without water for the animals necessarily had to be completed in one day.

In looking over his column later that day, Custer saw the blistered faces, the bloodshot eyes inflamed from the clouds of alkali dust kicked up by the horses, the exhaustion showing in the men who followed him. The suffering was great among the men but equally so with the horses. Many of the dogs died from thirst and exhaustion. Near midnight they reached the welcome shore of the Platte.

Next morning at Riverside Station Custer received a dispatch from Sedgwick advising him that a detachment of ten men and a Sioux guide — Chief Red Bead — under Lieutenant Lyman Kidder had left that point the day following Elliott's departure, with dispatches from Sherman. This was indeed a surprise for there had been no sign of Kidder. Requesting a copy of the orders Sherman had sent, Custer learned from them that he was to march his command to the Smoky Hill River, striking it at Fort Wallace.

At 5 A.M. on July 7th the column headed back on its trail. In preparing to leave it was determined that 40 enlisted men had deserted during the night. No effort was made to pursue them for supplies were low. The hardships endured, the poor and insufficient food provided by the quartermaster's department and the nearness to some recent discoveries in the gold fields were reasons enough to encourage such desertion.

At 1 P.M. the command halted for a rest, having traveled 15 miles. Thinking this was the final halt of the day, some men passed word that there would be a mass desertion that night in which one-third of the command would move out. Custer issued orders to march another 15 miles before nightfall. While preparing for it 13 men, of whom 6 were dismounted, were seen moving rapidly to the north. The very boldness of the move took everyone by surprise.

Several of the officers, led by Major Joel Elliott, succeeded in bringing the dismounted men to bay, wounding three of them when they resisted arrest. That night the camp was patrolled by the officers fully armed with the express understanding that any man seen outside his tent after taps would be fired upon after being hailed once. There were no desertions that night or any subsequent day or night on their return to Wallace.[22]

Pursuing their way along the trail in the direction of Wallace they came upon the trail of Kidder. It was obvious he and his men had been following Cooke's wagon train to Wallace thinking it was Custer's. After following Kidder's trail some miles they came upon the mangled bodies of him and his men, hacked and disfigured beyond recognition. Quietly burying them the column moved on, arriving at Fort Wallace on the evening of July 13.[23]

Fort Wallace was besieged. The post had seen travel along the Smoky Hill route cease some weeks before. The large numbers of Indians along the route and their efforts to disrupt stage travel had resulted in the stage stations being abandoned. Neither mail nor dispatches had been received for some time.

The reserve supply of food at the post was near exhaustion and there was no knowledge of fresh supplies on the way. What food was available was inedible. To this could be added a matter of great concern—the appearance of cholera. Exhausted and half-starved from the enervating expedition, the men would be easy victims of the dreaded disease.[24] With no orders there to guide Custer, something had to be done.

Never one to shy away from responsibility or a decision, he decided to make a run for it. Fort Harker was 200 miles to the east, no short jaunt for horses generally unfit for service. In a calculated risk he selected 100 of his best mounted men and prepared for the march to Fort Harker to obtain the much needed supplies.

The detachment left at sunset of July 15th. Pushing on in the dark, they frequently halted to rest the jaded mounts and weary men. At 3 A.M. of the 18th they reached Fort Hays, a distance of 150 miles in 55 hours. With Lieutenant Louis Hamilton left in charge to bring the men on at a leisurely pace, Custer with his brother Tom and Lieutenant Cooke took fresh mounts and pushed on to Fort Harker. There he awakened Colonel Smith at 2 A.M. to report the details of the previous weeks and to arrange for a train of supplies to be in readiness when Lieutenant Hamilton arrived.[25]

Smith was quite willing to permit Custer to take the morning train to Fort Riley. There he could visit Libbie until the supplies were ready for the return trip.

Having barely arrived at Fort Riley, he received a telegram from Colonel Smith ordering him to return at once to his command. Through no fault of his own Custer was unable to return to Fort Harker. The erratic schedule of the railroad made an immediate return impossible.

On July 21st he arrived at Fort Harker where he reported to Colonel Smith. Smith placed him in arrest at the insistence of General Hancock. He was to remain there and await his court-martial on a charge of leaving his command at Fort Wallace without authority.

The Hancock campaign had served to stir up the Indians rather than subdue them. Public pressure had Congress upset. Congress passed the blame on

FIRST CUSTER HOME AT FORT LINCOLN. Built late in 1873, it burned to the ground that winter because of a defective chimney. Mrs. E. B. Custer collection. Custer Battlefield National Monument.

the military and ultimately it settled on Hancock's shoulders. In his search for a scapegoat Hancock was fortunate enough to find Custer doing the wrong thing at the right time.

Custer had followed his orders to the letter until he arrived at Fort Wallace and there found none awaiting his arrival. With communication cut off from Wallace, he had been unwilling to remain there while his men were running out of supplies. Rather than entrust the command of the relief party to another he personally led it to Fort Harker, there to be placed in arrest for leaving Fort Wallace without permission in a quest to obtain permission to leave Fort Wallace.

Colonel Smith had always been very friendly to the Custers. Knowing Libbie had been waiting for Custer's return, he ordered him to await the court-martial at Fort Riley.

Back in Michigan, the Fourth-of-July issue of the Monroe *Commercial* headed a page two article with "Painful Rumor." In a telegraphic dispatch from the West it went on to say that: "A report was current at Fort Harker last week that Gen. Custer with a small body of men had been overpowered by a large body of Indians and the General killed. The report is not well authenticated but gains some credence on account of having heard so little of Custer's command for some time."

On July 11th the *Commercial* advised that "the report we published last week concerning Gen. Custer turns out to be untrue." This was good news in Monroe. The Custer and the Reed families, like Libbie, had no letters from Autie because of the interruption of communication. The July 4th "rumor" had been extremely disturbing and was the topic of conversation everywhere. The correction of the rumor was welcomed by everyone.

Libbie's open arms made everything worthwhile. Though Custer did not confide in her on military matters, she provided a haven on all other matters. In the early part of September they had been transferred to Fort Leavenworth, considered by many to be the third finest post in the country. To Libbie's jubilation over the move there was the knowledge that General Sheridan and his staff would soon arrive at the post.

These were days of relaxation and companionship. One would hardly think that Autie faced a court-martial. The two lovers would walk down Sheridan Avenue, hand in hand, as if nothing else in their world mattered but each other. In those times a court-martial was not considered a disgrace. Such trials were commonplace. In a year in which the army number 24,000 men, 13,500 men were tried by court-martial.[26] One officer published a lengthy volume of his own manifold courts-martial.[27]

Col. Smith had charged Custer with absenting himself from his command at Fort Wallace without authority, then proceeding to Fort Harker. An additional charge was that of using army ambulances and mules as a conveyance from Fort Hays to Fort Harker. No great problem for Custer. It was not unusual for a commanding officer at a post to leave it in the charge of his subordinate for a short time without requesting permission from his district commander. He took the risk of being caught at it and being court-martialed. At most he would be reprimanded which, in effect, was a slap on the wrist. As for the use of the ambulances in the course of private business, though against regulations, it was customary with all officers and their families.

Then came the surprise! Captain Robert M. West had provided some additional charges of a very serious nature. West had previous run-ins with Custer for drinking while on duty. A capable officer and an experienced Indian fighter he, like many other officers on the plains, could not control his drinking. He had been assigned duty as officer of the day on their arrival at Fort Wallace. Though knowing that the post was beseiged by Indians, he promptly got drunk and displayed himself in that condition while on duty. Custer placed him in arrest and ordered his court-martial. As a form of retribution he provided additional charges against Custer.[28]

West reached back into a very sensitive subject — the confrontation with the deserters near the Platte River. He charged Custer with ordering their pursuit and "to shoot the supposed deserters down dead, and to bring none back alive," thus causing "three men to be severely wounded," and then "persistently refuse to allow the said soldiers to receive treatment," one of whom subsequently died.[29]

What had originated as a simple whitewash for Hancock had now become a serious situation for Custer. West's alcohol saturated mind could think of nothing but revenge. Apparently in remorse, he continued his drinking up to the time of the court-martial. During it he was afflicted with delirium tremens with the result the prosecution did not put him on the witness stand.[30]

Letters offering assistance and suggestions were coming to the Custers from everywhere. Captain Tom Weir, Colonel Smith's adjutant, wrote in a note to Custer: "Will any little favor I may be able to give be kindly received? I am anxious in the affair to go on your side."[31]

Lieutenant Charles Brewster indicated to Custer: "Lieutenant Wallingford has expressed to me that if subpoenaed he should give everything the best coloring for you that he could. That is also my resolution. There is not another officer here (Fort Wallace) whom you could count on."[32]

About this same time Custer's former Adjutant, Levant W. Barnhart, wrote him from Washington: "With the exception of a few old fogies it seem to be the general belief that the whole proceedings against you is but an outbreak of the smoldering enmity and envy which has existed on the part of some fossils whose names appear upon the Army Register, toward you."[33]

The best break of all was the news that General Sheridan would arrive to testify he had ordered Custer to shoot deserters without trial. Sheridan had called this to Custer's attention and had urged him to introduct it as evidence. He had assured Custer that Washington authorities considered the trial an effort on Hancock's part to divert attention from his disastrous Indian campaign.[34] It had every evidence of that.

Legal counsel was necessary but that was not a difficult decision to make. Charles Parsons, a captain in the Fourth U.S. Artillery, had graduated from the Point with Custer. A fine military lawyer and a Christian gentleman, he was just the man to handle the defense.

The court convened at Fort Leavenworth on September 15th with a jury of nine men. Its last day of meeting was October 11, 1867.[35] There were technical difficulties from the very beginning the details of which we will avoid. It is a matter of record that Custer was found guilty and sentenced "to be suspended from rank and pay for one year, and forfeit his pay for the same time."[36]

Libbie had worked hard during the trial. In a letter to Rebecca Richmond a day after the trial had concluded she indicated that she had copied 50 pages for Captain Parsons which, of course, was a labor of love even though she believed the trial to be nothing but a plan to persecute her husband.[37]

She was grateful that her husband had not been a victim of the cholera or of the Indians and that now she had him all to herself. Her days of anxiety and her nights of hideous dreams were over — for at least that coming year. How could she forget that day he had returned from the plains? To her, "There was in that summer of 1867 one long perfect day," she recalled 20 years later. "It was mine, and — blessed by our memory, which preserves to us the joys as well as the sadness of life — it is still mine, for time and for eternity."[38]

MORE ROOM WAS NEEDED. The Custer residence was the center of the officers' social functions, a piano and a billiard table helping to while away winter boredom. It was apparent more room was needed. The wing was added about a year after the house was completed. 1875. Mrs. E. B. Custer collection. Custer Battlefield National Monument.

NOTES—CHAPTER 19

1 G. A. Custer to Libbie, June 2, 1867. He noted that he was 16 miles from "Home." Original in author's collection.
2 G. A. Custer: *My Life,* pp. 51-52.
3 Merington, pp. 204-205; Henry B. Carrington: *Ab-Sa-Ra-Ka,* Philadelphia, 1879, p. 280; Theodore R. Davis: "With Generals In Their Homes," *Chicago Westerners Brand Book,* 1945-46. pp. 119-120.
4 Theodore R. Davis: "A Summer on the Plains," *Harper's Monthly Magazine,* Vol. XXXVI, February, 1868, p. 301.
5 G. A. Custer: *My Life,* p. 54.
6 Lt. Henry Jackson: *Itinerary of the March of the Seventh U.S. Cavalry,* 1867, p. 25.
7 *Ibid;* G. A. Custer: *My Life,* p. 56.
8 E. B. Custer: *Tenting,* pp. 581-82.
9 *Ibid,* pp. 582-83.
10 William A. Bell: *New Tracks In North America,* I, London, 1869, pp. 77-78.
11 George A. Armes: *Ups And Downs of an Army Officer,* Washington, 1900, pp. 233-35; E. B. Custer: *Tenting,* pp. 668-669, 671, 696.
12 Monroe County, Michigan, Probate Court records. Libbie inherited the Bacon homestead appraised at $4,000. Autie was left eight lots in the Bacon plat in Monroe, a valuation of $800.
13 Dorothy M. Johnson: *Some Went West,* N.Y., 1965, p. 120.
14 E. B. Custer: *Tenting,* pp. 632-49; G. A. Custer: *My Life,* pp. 48-50. Both sources provide the details of the incident.
15 E. B. Custer: *Tenting,* p. 640.
16 *Ibid,* p. 641.
17 *Ibid,* pp. 656, 667.
18 Jackson: *Itinerary of the Seventh,* p. 28.
19 G. A. Custer: *My Life,* p. 62.
20 Jackson: *Itinerary of the Seventh,* p. 28.
21 E. B. Custer: *Tenting,* p. 671-72.
22 G. A. Custer: *My Life,* pp. 72-73; see Frost: *Custer Court-Martial* for complete details.
23 G. A. Custer: *My Life,* pp. 77-79.
24 *Ibid,* pp. 79-80.
25 *Ibid,* p. 82.
26 Jack D. Foner: *The United States Between Two Wars,* N.Y., 1970, p. 34.
27 Armes: *Ups And Downs.*
28 Frost: *Court-Martial,* pp. 86, 89.
29 *Ibid,* pp. 100-102.
30 Merington, pp. 211-212.
31 T. B. Weir to G. A. Custer, August 14, 1867, author's collection.
32 Charles Brewster's letter to G. A. Custer, September 7, 1867, author's collection.
33 Levant W. Barnhart to G. A. Custer, September 9, 1867, author's collection.
34 Merington, p. 211; William E. Connelley: *Wild Bill and His Era,* N.Y., 1933, p. 103: "The complete failure of the Hancock campaign made it necessary that some victims be found. The blame was to be shifted. . . . General Custer, who had been left to his own resources and had made dangerous marches, the only officer who had shown intelligence, was now seized, charged with grave offenses, and court-martialed."
35 Frost: *Court-Martial of Custer,* pp. 96-246, provides the verbatim account of the entire court-martial.
36 *Ibid,* p. 246.
37 Merington, pp. 213-14.
38 E. B. Custer: *Tenting,* p. 702.

CHAPTER 20 POLICING THE PLAINS

As if sensing that Custer was no longer an adversary, the Indians renewed their depredations. In a raid along the Union Pacific Railroad they severed the telegraph line and prepared an ambush for the repair party they knew would come.

The repair men left the Plum Creek Station on a handcar. As they approached the break in the line they found their way blocked by a barricade of railroad ties piled upon the track. When they stopped, Indians, who had been concealed in deep grass, rushed them from every direction.

One mounted warrior singled out William Thompson, firing at him from ten feet, wounding him in the arm. Thompson turned and ran. As he did so the Indian clubbed him down with his rifle, then stabbed him in the neck. Thinking that his victim was dead—for Thompson feigned death—he twisted Thompson's hair around his left hand, then hacked and sawed at the scalp with a dull knife.

Thompson was sick and dizzy from the agonizing pain. When the last bit of scalp over the temples failed to yield to the busy scalping knife, the Indian gave a mighty jerk. With the detached and dripping scalp in his hand, the Indian mounted his pony and rode off. As he did so he dropped the scalp unknowingly several feet from Thompson. The latter gathered it in, then managed to find a hiding place in the brush and grass nearby.

Several hours later a train struck the barricade. The fireman and engineer were dragged from the derailed engine, then shot and scalped. Once the boxcars were plundered, they were set afire. Everything that appealed to the Indians was confiscated—tobacco, flour, hats, boots, shoes, saddles, ribbons and bales of calico. To their horses they attached the colorful calico and ribbons, wildly galloping around so they would trail behind them in the breeze.

The discovery of a barrel of bourbon soon added to their ferocity. Adding the emptied boxes to the burning boxcars, they had a scalp dance during which they threw the bodies of the engineer and fireman into the flames.

Thompson, taking his precious scalp with him, managed to crawl away and reach the Willow Island Station. There a rescue party took him to Omaha. The scalp went with him in a pail of water. A physician sutured the four-by-nine inch scalp in place but it failed to take. Thompson lived many years after to tell interested audiences of his unique experience.[1]

The Custers certainly didn't mind the sentence. The loss of $95 a month pay would inhibit them but they would continue to receive his emoluments which amounted to more than his pay. They could live on that.

The New York *Times*[2] mentioned that "it gives him a respite that he had desired for a long time, not perhaps in this precise way, but he seems to take his blessings as they come. He proposes to remain in Leavenworth during the winter and visit Europe during the spring."

General Sheridan had given the Custers permission to stay at his residence at Fort Leavenworth that winter. Sheridan had been relieved of his command in the Fifth Military District at New Orleans by General Hancock. He was to assume Hancock's command of the Department of the Missouri embracing Kansas, Missouri, Indian Territory and New Mexico.

Leaving New Orleans on September 5, 1867, he stopped off at St. Louis, then to comply with a technicality, traveled on to Fort Leavenworth, returning to his home at Somerset, Ohio, immediately, to remain there until March, 1868. There he recuperated his health from the ill-effects of three summers in a Louisiana climate rampant with cholera, yellow fever and malaria.[3]

Sheridan had offered to intervene in Custer's behalf in an effort to obtain a remission of part of the sentence. To this Custer strongly objected, saying he would not accept it.[4]

The Custers had an agreeable winter at Fort Leavenworth. As Western posts went it was a lively one. This was to Libbie's liking. She and her husband had been after her cousin Rebecca to join them and participate in the winter activities, and she arrived near the end of the year. The first entry in Rebecca's diary—January 1, 1868—indicated that the Custers held an open house that afternoon in the Sheridan residence the Custers were occupying. Her sister Mary and husband Charles Kendall had traveled with her from Grand Rapids. With the assistance of Anna Darrah they all received about 40 callers. Some had served on the court that had tried Custer and others had testified in it, but this was a small, close-knit community and bygones were bygones. Custer never was known to carry a grudge. Captain Weir and Lieutenants Bell, Hale, Jackson and Cooke stayed on for an evening of music.[5]

Two days later Custer and Captain Cooke were arrested by civil authorities on a charge of murder. Captain West who signed the complaint obviously was in his cups again.[6]

Justice Adams began his examination of the two men on January 8th and concluded it on January 18th by finding the charge not sustained by the evidence.[7] It was a complete vindication.

Libbie and Rebecca would take long walks on the Arsenal grounds down by the river. Though perfectly safe to do so, it brought to her mind what Captain Cooke had told her the first time they met after the three hour running fight he and his 48 men had while defending the wagontrain on its return from Fort Wallace to rejoin Custer's command on the Republican:

"The moment I found the Indians were on us, and we were in for a fight, I thought of you and said to myself, 'If she were in the ambulance, before giving an order I would ride up and shoot her.'"

"Would you have given me no chance for life?" I replied.

"Not one," he said. "I should have been unnerved by the thought of the fate that awaited you, and I have promised the General not to take any chances, but to kill you before anything worse could happen."[8]

This shocking information drove home the feeling the officers had about the atrocities committed by Indians on the women they captured. They had knowledge of numerous incidents in which white women were raped to death by those who captured them. Those who survived the ignominy were kept by some chief until he tired of them, then passed to another. The officers, knowing of this, had a pact to do what they considered to be the only honorable way. Libbie had been completely unaware of this until Cooke had informed her of their promise and determination to abide by it.

Custer had some plans to visit Europe in the spring. He had been writing his memoirs for Harper and Brothers who intended to publish his experiences from West Point to Appomattox.[9] It was a lengthy and time-consuming project. He had a lot of time to consume and hoped to use part of it on a trip abroad.

SECOND CUSTER HOUSE AT FORT LINCOLN. This was completed in the spring of 1874 and occupied by the Custers as a home and headquarters. It was built on the site of their first house. Mrs. E. B. Custer collection. Custer Battlefield National Monument.

In the latter part of February he addressed a letter to John Jacob Astor apparently asking if he could represent him in one of his foreign endeavors. Astor replied that he would be glad to serve him except that business had languished for the past six months because of the political situation in the country.[10]

With their only chance of seeing Europe unavailable, the Custers continued their stay at Fort Leavenworth. The arrival of spring provided an opportunity to do more hunting with his dogs though at one point they had become such a nuisance around the post that orders were issued: "On and after the 20th instant all dogs found running loose in the garrison will be shot by the guard."[11]

But dogs didn't receive all of the attention. On June 16th, the garrison held a mule race one mile in length, the winner to received a purse of $50. The humorous poster announcing it noted: "The money accruing from this race is to be devoted to the support of the widows and orphans made so thereby."[12]

Soon after this race the Custers left for Monroe. Cavalry detachments were being sent out each day on escort duty, in pursuit of deserters or in a vain search of hostile Indians. Observing all of this preparation and activity was too much for the action-loving cavalryman. Thinking that "out-of-sight, out-of-mind" could be a reality, the two headed for home. There in the Monroe marshes he could shoot ducks that fall, whiling away the time until then by fishing for bass in the River Raisin. Libbie would have ample time to visit with her family and friends.

Now that Sheridan had taken over the Department of the Missouri, conditions there were supposed to be peaceful. Not because Sheridan was in command but because of the agreement reached with the Cheyennes, Arapahoes, Kiowas and Comanches at Medicine Lodge.

The treaty at Medicine Lodge provided that the country between the Platte and Arkansas rivers would be released for settlement by the whites, that the railroads would be permitted to continue their construction through the region unmolested, and that the tribes signing the agreement would move on to their new reservation in the Indian Territory.[13]

Sheridan soon discovered that many of the young men of the tribes were in complete disagreement with the provisions. His efforts to avert a confrontation were useless in the face of these firebrands. By early August they began their raids.

Lieutenant Colonel Alfred Sully, who had much experience in Indian affairs, was directed by Sheridan to take immediate action. Sully met with little success that summer. By fall the Indians had run his cavalry ragged.

Back in Michigan Custer devoured an article in the Monrore *Commercial:*

"THE INDIAN OUTRAGES IN KANSAS—Dispatches from Gen. Sheridan confirm the press dispatches about the Indian outrages. Gen. Sheridan says the outrages are too horrible to detail. Gen. Sherman orders Gen. Sheridan to continue the pursuit and drive the savages from that section of the country, and when captured to give them summary punishment."[14]

The Custers' old friend Tony Forsyth had waived his rank in an effort to get some of the action. Placed in command of 51 frontiersmen, he moved out of Fort Hays on August 29th in search of depredating Indians. At what is now called Beecher's Island they were surrounded by Cheyennes outnumbering them 10 to 1. For over a week they were pinned down, with half their men killed or wounded by the Indians.[15]

By the close of the summer campaign, the Indians had suffered some losses but they had hardly been damaged enough to be peaceful.

Sheridan was quite disappointed with the results. He concluded that the only way to bring the hostiles to their knees was to conduct a campaign against them in the winter when their horses were weakened from inadequate forage and could be easily overtaken by the well-fed cavalry horses.

The veteran frontiersman Jim Bridger had made a special trip from St. Louis to advise him against it: "You can't hunt Indians on the plains in the winter for blizzards don't respect man or beast." Many others had advised him not to undertake what was considered to be the impossible but Sheridan had Sherman's blessing. That was backing enough for he knew Grant backed Sherman.[16]

Custer had found his "base of operations" in Monroe pleasant enough for there was an abundance of friends, a lot of time to spend with them, and then there was Libbie. Even so, he longed to be with his regiment in the field. The day that he could join them seemed a long way off for it would not be until the following winter. Then one evening, while he was seated at the dining table of a friend, a telegram was delivered to him which he opened and read:

"HEADQUARTERS DEPARTMENT OF THE MISSOURI,
IN THE FIELD, FORT HAYS, KANSAS,
September 24, 1868

To General G. A. Custer, Monroe, Michigan

Generals Sherman, Sully and myself, and nearly all the officers of your regiment, have asked for you, and I hope the application will be successful. Can you come at once? Eleven companies of your regiment will move about the 1st of October against the hostile Indians. . . .

P. H. Sheridan
Major General Commanding"[17]

Knowing that Sheridan and Sherman would obtain a remission of the balance of his sentence from the authorities, he wired Sheridan that he was on his way. As he wrote later:

"The following day found me on a railroad train hastening to the plains as fast as the iron horse could carry me. The expected order from Washington overtook me that day in the shape of an official telegram from the Adjutant General of the Army, directing me to proceed at once and report for duty to General Sheridan."[18]

Custer arrived at Fort Hays on September 30th, reporting to Sheridan there. Receiving instructions from him, he set out to join his regiment near Fort Dodge. Just as he rejoined his regiment it was attacked by Indians, a fitting introduction to the task before him. Once the Indians were repulsed Custer learned this had been a daily occurrence and that the camp was virtually in a state of siege.

The Seventh Cavalry was to serve as a complete regiment for the first time. Now having them all together Custer began a "coloring of the horses" whereby each company was provided with horses of one color. Then all horses were reshod. Daily target practice was ordered for everyone. It was announced that the 40 best marksmen of the 800 would become a corps of sharpshooters and would be exempt from all guard duty. He was readying for the Washita campaign.

There are a number of accounts of the Battle of the Washita the reader might wish to pursue.[19] An examination of the Custer correspondence covering this period would seem most appropriate in this account.

On October 2nd Autie wrote to Libbie from Fort Leavenworth that he was "equally if not more gratified" at his reception when he compared it to the delightful manner of their departure from there last spring. He cautioned: "Don't tell Mother but I was overjoyed to get back to the post again and the big house never seemed so welcome. I experienced a home feeling here in the garrison that I cannot find in civil life."[20]

Two days later he was at Fort Hays breakfasting with Phil Sheridan and his staff. He informed Libbie:

"All expressed their pleasure at my return. Gen. Sheridan expects me to command the expedition and has said to me twice already, 'Custer, I rely everything upon you and shall send you on this expedition without giving you any orders, leaving you to act entirely upon your own judgement.'... I start for Fort Dodge tomorrow at 6 A.M."[21]

On October 7th he was at Fort Dodge, having arrived there the night before. The 90 mile ride had been made in two days. One of Sheridan's staff officers had told him that all of the officers of the Seventh were thankful for his return and wanted him to assume the command. Pridefully, and certainly with a feeling of gratification, he told Libbie: "I would not repeat this even to you only I want you to see that even my enemies ask to have me return."[22]

Custer was now in his element. He had made California Joe Milner his chief of scouts. This loquacious, bearded character was the life of the expedition. His humorous remarks kept everyone in good spirits but did not detract from sharing his vast knowledge of Indians. Custer noted that scouts were paid $75 a month, and $100 would go to the scout locating an Indian village.

He took a particular delight in telling Libbie:

"Cooke says Tom expects that I will bring some good clothes out he can borrow. He evidently needs them this time as his dog BRANDY caught a polecat and Tom, in rushing in to pull him off, got enough perfume to last him several months. This is not exactly the country to allow a man parting with his clothes as he can't very well go back several hundred miles to replace them.

"Tom partially turned the joke so hard on him on some of the other officers in the camp. As the mishap occurred to him about dusk, he with Capt. Hamilton concluded that they would call on the other officers in camp while Tom was so highly if not fashionably perfumed. So they started on their visiting expedition. They would enter a tent where probably half a dozen other officers were already crowded. Room would be made for them when a universal remark arose, 'Some dog has been killing a skunk. I wonder where the damn brute is?' A third would reply, 'It's evidently close about here you can bet!' So the conversation would run until Tom and Hamilton, nearly busting with laughter, would betray the secret. Then they would leave and enter another officer's tent where the same scene would be enacted."[23]

As they moved toward Medicine Lodge Creek, they made camp in the vicinity of the Antelope Hills. The

GENERAL CUSTER'S STUDY AT FORT LINCOLN.
The General spent his winters here studying and writing his *Memoirs.* Libbie read nearby while he worked, for he wanted her near him at all times. 1875. Mrs. E. B. Custer collection. Custer Battlefield National Monument.

trees were literally black with wild turkeys. A former member of Sheridan's staff who was present on this expedition told the late Major Edward S. Luce that "in the vicinity of Antelope Hills . . . they killed 63 with rifles. . . . Custer cut the head off from a turkey with a Spencer repeating rifle at 200 yards."[24]

Custer's regiment at this point was composed of a large number of raw recruits, many of whom filled in the vacancies created by the past season's desertions. He had progressed rather well in their training and felt confident they would stand up in an engagement. He told Libbie: "Some of the officers think this may be a campaign on paper but I know General Sheridan too well to think he will follow any such example."[25]

He had two complaints he presented to Libbie. He wished Eliza was with him to bake some rolls "instead of the solid shot our cook gives us." And his brother Tom was pestering him for one of his stag hounds because she had told Tom he could have one, so Tom said. "I tell him they are my dogs not yours, and that if you bring any out, you are at liberty to dispose of them as you see fit; yet I might as well talk to a mule. You have had some experience in determining how persistent a Custer is when seeking anything he really desires."[26]

On October 24th from his camp 12 miles out of Fort Dodge a letter addressed to "My Darling" opened with the comment that he had just received two letters from "the sweetest girl on earth," both having been mailed from Grosse Ile, Michigan. He enclosed a letter from General Sheridan to him outlining plans for their future movements, then added:

"The Genl. has finally decided upon a winter campaign but I know this decision is conditioned. If we cannot find the Indians and inflict considerable damage upon them, we will be on the

BACK TO CIVILIZATION. Music was a solace to the soldier and a major form of relaxation. General Custer turns the music for his talented sister Maggie Calhoun. Libbie, in a pensive mood, is in the center resting her head on her hand, while brother Tom seems quite interested in the young lady in front of him. 1875. Author's collection.

wing all winter. If, however, we are fortunate to strike a decisive and telling blow against any one of the hostile tribes we will then obtain a respite and I have no doubt but that one complete victory over either hostile tribe would practically end the Indian war.

"The Indians have the belief no white troops dare follow them into this country where no whites have been before. All the tribes committing depredations the past season are in the vicinity of the Wichita Mts. He expects, once they learn of his entry into their country, that they will combine against them. This is exactly what I desire. I only ask for one good opportunity to fight them, or better still to strike a village."[27]

Captain West, who had preferred the devastating additional charges for Custer's court-martial, had been talking to Weir about Custer. He had expected Custer "to make it as unpleasant for him as I could, and when ordered to report to me, expected my first interview would to him at least, be an unpleasant one. . . . He told Weir that the easy and apparently pleasant manner in which I received him almost unsettled him. He was taken by surprise and scarcely knew how to act, that my conduct toward him since had been courteous and strictly impartial, contrary to his expectations. . . . In reference to what happened he could and would say nothing. He . . . . knew what he had done, but *henceforth he intended to support Genl. Custer to the extent of his power in anything he did.* If I had been seeking a triumph I would be satisfied. Far better is the present condition of affairs than if I demeaned myself by using my position for the gratification of private malice and spleen. . . . I hardly expect that my little durl will wholly approve of my conduct, but it is the right one."[28]

While Custer was writing the letter that morning all companies were out for target practice which to him "sounds almost like a battle." He looked about his tent as he wrote, noting that he was well prepared for the cold weather they would encounter. Many of the items before him had been provided by her—the blue shirt she had made a year ago, his dressing case and everything he looked at "is evidence of my little durl's love, and I am constantly reminded of her thoughtfulness and care from the moment I arise in the morning to the moment I fall asleep at night."

Then resorting to the military style used in reporting operations in the third person he continued:

"In his eyes his darling is perfect; he desires no change in her; he is too proud and gratified in being the possessor of her hand and heart. And he does not fear to compare her with the world knowing that she is his peerless bride. One who in all his experience with women and with the world is without equal in the traits and attributes which to render the character of women lovely and to be admired."[29]

His letter of Sunday, October 25th, was written at 8 P.M. No letter from Libbie that day but there was one bright note — they had a new cook for his mess. His breakfast consisted of: "boiled ducks, good hash, crisped potatoes, warm corn bread, light bread, butter and a good cup of coffee."

As for dinner: "splendid roast beef, tomatoes, nicely cooked corn, mashed potatoes, *apple pie,* bread, butter & coffee, with strawberries for dessert—a clean, white tablecloth with handsome *crimson napkins.* The pie was a present from Ft. Dodge. Dinner began with vermicelli soup."[30]

This was small compensation for Libbie's absence. Console himself as he might by being rid of a bad cook, Libbie's absence gnawed at him. The daily routine kept his active mind well occupied. The evenings were hard to face. He told her:

"I would gladly live on hardtack if by doing so I could have my darling with me. . . . There is nothing in this world that can at all compensate me for the loss of you. I might have all the women of the world before me (as I did once) to select from, yet I would be none the better contented unless I had you. You are everything to me, both food and raiment, yes and sleep, for even yet I am restless at night and often wake to find myself feeling for you."[31]

Custer had sent for Captain West to discuss regimental business. After it had been completed West asked him if Weir had said anything to him of their conversation. Custer recalled the conversation with Weir but not all of the remarks, so he replied. West repeated in substance what Weir had told Custer, adding: "General, I feel very kindly toward you, and in the future I intend never to do or say anything prejudicial to you."

Custer tried to steer the conversation into a different channel but was ineffective. West continued: "Well, General, I am sincere in what I say and to prove it to you I give you my hand upon it." With that he extended his hand. Custer quietly but firmly ignored it. West continued to hold out his hand then repeated his request. Custer said,: "Colonel West, I do not intend that the past shall influence my official conduct towards you. I intend to deal justly by you but to do so I do not think it necessary to take your hand. I will not take it." The interview was closed.[32]

West went directly to Weir's tent and told him what had transpired. Weir afterward, in telling Custer about it, said: "Well, it couldn't be better. You have not compromised yourself and West has knuckled down." In telling Libbie about it, Custer wrote:

"I feel I am doing right. I am not acting to gain any triumph over any person, but my conscience approves my course. It is far better to descend to a level with the man who sought to injure me. Five years ago I would have acted differently, yet not so well."[33]

His letter to her on the following day spoke of Fort Dodge as "a terrible place." He had reason to believe that most of the officers had laundresses for mistresses, the latter being young and attractive. One of them had "sworn a child" upon one of the lieutenants. It was the opinion of the officers that the year-old child was the exact image of another officer. And just the day before, one of the laundresses complained to him that an officer had attempted to break into her room several evenings prior. This matter he intended to investigate even though he had been approached in an effort to hush it up. He concluded: "Dodge is the lowest post I ever knew anything of."[34]

"You would be horrified," he wrote, "did you know the vast quantity of liquor drunk by the officers. Even some of the temperate (?) ones dispose of one canteen full each day and whiskey costs $3.75 per canteen."[35]

But enough of this, he thought, and turned his mind back to the different stages of his acquaintance and courtship of Libbie. Returning to his habit of writing of himself in the third person, he continued:

"Was there ever a lover so determined to win from the commencement as was your boy? He knew that Libbie Bacon, of all the world, was his fate and his fortune, rather his destiny as he used to term it, and feeling thus he acknowledged no obstacle and accepted nothing short of her hand and heart. A thousand times over he has been repaid for his anxiety and trouble.

"She has been to him more than his fondest hopes ever pictured a wife could be. She has disappointed him in nothing material to our mutual happiness and today he is a better, truer man for having had her society and love. And he owes her a life of devotion, of pure unbounded and undivided affection for the pure love she bears him, for his unselfish devotion to him and to his interests, and for the perfect type of a true, pure and loving wife she is and ever has been to him."[36]

On October 28th he reported to her that while he was examining the mouth of Major Elliott's horse to determine its age, the animal reared and struck at him with both fore feet, one of them striking him on the face and cutting his eyebrow to the bone. Dr. Lippincott closed the cut with sticking plaster. Custer said he did not suffer much but did miss Libbie fussing over him.[37]

And on this same day he received a letter from the Spencer Arms Company saying it was shipping by express a Spencer rifle to both General Sheridan and Colonel Schuyler Crosby at Custer's request, saying that in doing so he was the first officer to test the merits of the weapon and the company was gratified because he had. Sheridan had admired Autie's Spencer carbine very much so Autie had written in the General's behalf and also for Sheridan's aide, Colonel Crosby.[38]

Autie had just learned that one of the officers Libbie knew had become a drunkard because he was convinced of his wife's infidelity. "He scarcely notices her now and from the excellent officer that he once was he has descended to one of the most inefficient. Poor man, I am deeply sorry for him and cannot censure him. I would do no better if as well were I in his place. . . . How blessed am I that I am united to a pure, virtuous and devoted wife and I feel immeasurably thankful for it."[39]

Autie and Libbie had often discussed the possibility of having children. As much as both wanted them, it was a dream that never came true. Whether sterility was a problem with either is unknown. More than likely would be a sterility imposed upon him by the trauma of hard riding, a not uncommon occupational hazard in the cavalry.

He had been weighing carefully a matter that he believed was now the time to place before Libbie. Frankly and openly he began:

"Now I want to ask you a question and before you answer it weigh it fully in your own mind and answer me just as you feel. If you answer in favor of it, well and good; if you from any cause or reason are not inclined to the idea, be frank enough to tell me, and you disapproving of the proposition shall not in the slightest way ruffle my feelings or cause me to think one jot less of you. Your wishes shall be law and I hope you will tell me your views with your usual candor.

"What do you think of the idea of our adopting Autie Kirk (Kirkpatrick—his nephew)? He has reached that age that places him beyond the most

LIVING ROOM IN THE CUSTER HOUSE. Libbie made every effort to offer Autie some frontier luxury while home. Mrs. E. B. Custer collection. Custer Battlefield National Monument.

troublesome part of a child's life. I have proposed the idea not as a gratification to myself so much as to discharge a duty. My mind however is far from being decided either way. It all depends upon your advice, wishes and suggestions. Say and do that which you think in the end will most certainly conduce to our mutual happiness. Whatever suggestions may occur to you state them, and I may be benefited, if possible, by them. Write fully and freely and your wishes will be my guide. I will do nothing which in the future might interfere with or mar our happiness."[40]

What Libbie's objections were, if any, have not been preserved. Did she want the boy but fear that a child of her own, if she was blessed with one, could complicate their lives? Or did she realize that Autie suggested the adoption only to appease his conscience and satisfy his family? In any event, they did not adopt Autie Kirkpatrick, who was about ten years of age.

The following day, October 29th, saw Autie write three letters to his "Darling Sunbeam." He indicated that there was a question in his mind as to whether Uncle Sam would be willing to pay him for doing nothing but write letters to his "rosebud," though the thought hadn't deterred him.

In a moment of enthusiastic reverie he wrote:

"I always tell you how I miss you after each separation. I do not exaggerate darling when I assure you that never have I missed you as now. Never have you seemed so good, so pure, so lovable and so loving as now. Nor have I ever felt so desperate in regard to our separation as during this time. What is to become of us if it continues this way? I sometimes fear that I may even be induced to neglect my duty for you. You know I have never done so."[41]

As he wrote this letter Lieutenants Bell and Moylan were playing cribbage nearby. Tom Custer and his close friend Cooke came in to chat awhile, both indicating in their conversation they intended to visit Cooke's home in Hamilton, Ontario, on their next leave. Outside the tent the officers were undergoing signal practice using books sent them from Washington. Autie informed her that: "Most officers can now converse with each other quite readily as far as they can see signals. It may prove quite useful to us on the coming campaign as this is just the country to signal in, nature having formed admirable signal stations all over the country."[42]

Two days later Custer received a letter from Sheridan giving the details of an action taken under General Carr and Tony Forsyth near Sumner's Crossing on Beaver Creek. In it they had killed 10 Indians and captured 80 ponies. In relaying the story to Libbie, Custer said: "Next to the 7th I would rather hear of the success of the 5th Cav than of any other regiment, it being my old regiment and many of the present officers being my warm personal friends."[43]

In concluding this letter he told Libbie:

"I know you are in earnest when you say you mean never again to give me an uneasy moment. I have the sublimest confidence that you never will. . . . Then too I am delighted and overjoyed that my little darling bride is having an opportunity of really seeing and determining how troublesome and embarrassing babies would be to us. (Libbie was visiting the K. C. Barkers at Grosse Ile near Detroit at the time.) Our pleasure would be continually marred and circumscribed. You will not find in all our travels a married couple possessing and enjoying so many means of pleasure and mutual happiness as you and your boy. Our married life to me has been one unbroken sea of pleasure."

A week later Custer received word from K. C. Barker that Libbie had left their place for Monroe. She would leave for Fort Leavenworth on Thursday, November 5th. Barker was glad Custer was pleased with the dog he had sent to him and would send on a new litter of staghounds if he wished them.[44]

On November 4th Custer complained to Libbie because he had received no letters since her No. 7, all because of the difficulty in sending the mails through. To him "that is the greatest hardship the Indian war inflicts on me."[45]

The 5th was spent in discussing preparations and plans with his staff. Captain Henry Inman helped decide on the number of wagons that would be needed. General Sully wanted "to talk over the plans of the campaign and things in general." Lieutenant Robbins would be in charge of the escort, Custer informed Libbie, and Lieutenant Myles Moylan would be going along.[46]

WINTER PASTIME. Amateur theatricals were a means of relieving the boredeom of a confining winter. Both officers and men derived great pleasure through this means of expression. This is a Fort Lincoln *tablieux* in which General Custer and his sister Maggie Calhoun take the role of Quaker Peace Commissioners while Miss Agnes Bates of Monroe sits below them representing a Sioux chief's daughter. 1874. Mrs. E. B. Custer collection. Custer Battlefield National Monument.

The next day, soon after reveille, Custer inspected the stables. He made it a point to speak to most of the officers, noting that every company had its officers with it. Regulations had been relaxed somewhat during the summer campaigning, no attendance having been required of officers at the stables. He had ordered all to be present each morning.[47]

The next few weeks were spent in other preparatory endeavors, all focusing on anticipated situations. General Sheridan and his staff arrived on the 22d with several volunteer troops of Kansas cavalry. He issued orders for 11 companies of the Seventh to take 30 days rations and move out under Custer toward the Wichita mountains. A new lot of horses had been brought with him and from them Custer had selected a beautiful brown animal he named *Dandy*.[48]

On the morning of November 29th Sheridan received word that Custer and his cavalry had charged Black Kettle's camp on the Washita River and demolished it.[49] It was Sheridan's plan to follow this blow by moving his men south. This was delayed by the late arrival of the Kansas volunteer cavalry under Governor Crawford. When that force did arrive the expedition headed for the Wichita Mountains and Fort Cobb, following an Indian trail until it reached a Kiowa village.[50] The rain, snow and mud had retarded the cavalry's rate of travel to such an extend that on some days it made only eight miles.

Custer arrested the Kiowa leaders Satanta and Lone Wolf with several Apache chiefs and, on Sheridan's orders, threatened to hang them if their villages failed to come in to Fort Cobb peacefully. After several displays of bad faith the tribes moved into Cobb.[51]

Receiving letters from home soon after the Washita raid, one of which was from K. C. Barker asking him to resume his hunting tales in *Turf, Field & Farm Magazine* because "they would add greatly to the interest of the paper."[52] Custer wrote to Libbie, now at Leavenworth, that Sheridan had said: "The battle of the Washita is the most complete and successful of all our Indian battles and was fought in such unfavorable weather and circumstances as to reflect the highest credit on yourself and regiment."[53]

He went on to tell her:

"The sad side of the story is the killed and wounded. Hamilton . . . killed by a rifle bullet through the heart. . . . Major Elliott with but six men charged away from the command in pursuit of two Indians . . . not one escaped. . . . Col. Barnitz was wounded by a rifle bullet through the bowels. . . . Tom receiving a flesh wound in his hand from a bullet.

"Tomorrow we set out again upon the warpath. This time not alone. My command will be doubled. The Kansas Volunteers and all of Sandy's (Forsyth) scouts and a party of Kaws. We strike for Ft. Cobb a hundred miles from here. Sheridan said to me: 'Custer, I'll ask this one more trip of you and then I'll march you to Leavenworth'."[54]

From Fort Cobb he wrote to Libbie:

"On our march here we revisited our battleground (Washita) and found the bodies of Major Elliott and 16 men. They were horribly mutilated, naked and frozen stiff. We learned from the Indians that Elliott and his party followed two or three Indians a mile and a half and were then surrounded by several hundred warriors who soon made an end of them but not until Elliott and his party had killed 15 Indians and wounded many more. We also learned from the Indians that we killed many more than I reported. They admit now 133 warriors while their wounded must have been considerable. Five miles below the battleground we found bodies of a young, beautiful white woman and her baby, both killed and mutilated by Indians.

"I open my letter to add a line to tell you that you must expect to see us abused by all papers that do not believe in punishing hostile Indians, but never mind, you know how little such trifles affect me."[55]

NOTES — CHAPTER 20

[1]Stanley: Early Travels, I, pp. 155-58.
[2]New York *Times,* December 7, 1867.
[3]Sheridan: *Memoirs,* II, p. 283.
[4]Merington, p. 214.
[5]Rebecca Richmond Diary, EBC - CBNM, January 1, 1868.
[6]*Ibid,* January 3, 1868.
[7]*Ibid,* January 8, 1868, and January 18, 1868; Frost: *Custer Court-Martial,* pp. 26-63.
[8]E. B. Custer: *Tenting,* pp. 628-29; Fairfax Downey: *Indian Fighting Army,* N.Y., 1941, p. 98.
[9]Merington, p. 215.
[10]J. J. Astor to G. A. Custer, February 24, 1868, original in author's collection.
[11]General Orders No. 6, April 18, 1868, Yale University Library.
[12]From original poster in author's collection.
[13]Sheridan: *Memoirs,* II, pp. 283-84.
[14]Monroe *Commercial,* August 27, 1868.
[15]George A. Forsyth: *The Story of The Soldier,* N.Y., 1900, pp. 229-30.
[16]Sheridan: *Memoirs,* II, p. 307; Frost: *Sheridan Album,* p. 126.
[17]G. A. Custer: *My Life,* p. 125.
[18]*Ibid.*
[19]G. A. Custer: *My Life,* pp. 145-183; Monaghan, pp. 309-321; Frost: *Custer Album,* pp. 89-98; Whittaker: *Custer,* pp. 425-52; Carl C. Rister: *Border Command,* Norman, 1944, pp. 101-20; Sheridan: *Memoirs,* II, pp. 312-22; Chandler: *Of Garry Owen,* pp. 8-25.
[20]G. A. Custer to Libbie, October 2, 1868, EBC - CBNM.
[21]G. A. Custer to Libbie, October 4, 1868, EBC - CBNM.
[22]G. A. Custer to Libbie, October 7, 1868, EBC - CBNM.
[23]G. A. Custer to Libbie, October 10, 1868, EBC- CBNM.
[24]G. A. Custer to Libbie, October 18, 1868, with Major E. S. Luce's footnotes, EBC - CBNM.
[25]G. A. Custer to Libbie, October 22, 1868, EBC - CBNM.
[26]*Ibid.*
[27]G. A. Custer to Libbie, October 24, 1868, original in author's collection.
[28]*Ibid.*
[29]*Ibid.*
[30]G. A. Custer to Libbie, October 25, 1868, original in author's collection.
[31]*Ibid.*
[32]*Ibid.*
[33]*Ibid.*
[34]G. A. Custer to Libbie, October 26, 1868, original in author's collection.
[35]*Ibid.*
[36]*Ibid.*
[37]G. A. Custer to Libbie, October 28, 1868, original in author's collection.
[38]*Ibid.*
[39]*Ibid.*
[40]*Ibid.*
[41]G. A. Custer to Libbie, October 29, 1868, original in author's collection.
[42]*Ibid.*
[43]G. A. Custer to Libbie, October 31, 1868, original in author's collection; Rister: *Border Command,* pp. 89-90.
[44]K. C. Barker to G. A. Custer, November 3, 1868, BCWC collection.
[45]EBC - CBNM.
[46]G. A. Custer to Libbie, November 5, 1868, BCWC collection.
[47]G. A. Custer to Libbie, November 6, 1868, BCWC collection.
[48]G. A. Custer to Libbie, November 22, 1868, EBC - CBNM.
[49]40th Congress, 3d Sess., Senate Exec. Doc. 18, pp. 27-29; 39-41, "Indian Battle on the Washita."
[50]Sheridan: *Memoirs,* II, pp. 321-33.
[51]*Ibid,* p. 335; G. A. Custer to Libbie, December 19, 1868, EBC - CBNM.
[52]K. C. Barker to G. A. Custer, November 27, 1868, BCWC collection.
[53]G. A. Custer to Libbie, December 6, 1868, EBC - CBNM.
[54]*Ibid;* E. B. Custer: *Following the Guidon,* N.Y., 1890, pp. 45-46.
[55]G. A. Custer to Libbie, December 19, 1868, EBC - CBNM; Sheridan: *Memoirs,* II, pp. 328-29.

Some writers have made much of Elliott being left behind by Custer without having made a search for him. Terming it an "abandonment of Elliott and his men" they claim it created dissention and a divisiveness in the command that lasted and had an influence on the Battle of the Little Big Horn. This is hardly borne out by facts.

If anything, the animosity of one officer, that developed into a pathological hatred, was the seed for any such feeling existent in later years. The host and initiator of this hatred was none other than the senior captain Frederick Benteen. The origin of his intense dislike for Custer seemed to stem from their very first meeting and is best described by an extract from a letter Benteen wrote to Theodore Goldin, February 12, 1896 (W. A. Graham: *THE BENTEEN-GOLDIN LETTERS):*

"I had never seen Custer before joining at Fort Riley in '66. At my first formal call at his private quarters, he paraded his orders and books of the old Cav. Div. in the Cav. Corps, as if endeavoring to impress me with the magnitude and eminent success of his operations in it.

"I remember his orders shown me said, 'No gun has ever been pointed at that Division but what they captured it,' etc.

"Well, the impression made on me at that interview was not a favorable one. I have been on intimate personal relations with many great generals, and had heard of no such bragging as was stuffed into me that night."

A series of events followed, according to the letter cited above, that Benteen took exception to, all of which fanned his first dislike into a flaming hatred.

At the very end of the Washita battle, Lieutenant Edward S. Godfrey and his men followed some Indians eastward. As he mounted a hill in pursuit he saw hundreds of mounted warriors before him ready for battle. With difficulty he covered his retreat to the village. Custer soon had ample visual evidence of the overhwelming force Godfrey had met. In a short time the surrounding hills were occupied by additional warriors. It was then Custer learned that Black Kettle's village was only one of a number of them along the Washita.

He was in a difficult situation, obviously outnumbered. Resorting to trickery he mustered his troops and started them down river toward the other villages. Though he had no intention of attacking them the watching warriors thought otherwise and began to flee. Following two hours of such marching he reversed his direction and retraced his steps. Marching all night, with a brief rest at 2 A.M., they were joined by their wagon train. It was not until 2 P.M. that they stopped for a much-earned rest and food, a feeling of security prevailing at last. (Carl C. Rister: *Border Command,* Norman, 1944, pp. 109-11.)

Dr. B. Randolph Keim *(Sheridan's Troopers On The Borders,* Philadelphia, 1891, pp. 149-50), acting as a newspaper correspondent with Custer's expedition to the Washita had this to say:

"Although the fate of Elliott's party would appear as a gross abandonment by Custer, particularly for not even recovering the bodies, or making some effort to learn what had become of them, when found missing after the fight, the circumstances of the event were of such a character that while no attempt was made with that view, the conduct of Custer in ordering a withdrawal was justifiable according to the laws of war. He struck the upper flank of a long range of villages numbering several thousand warriors. His own force was small and without supplies. . . . The wagon train containing the subsistence stores and tents of the entire column, which had been left miles away, had not come up yet. The guard consisted of but 80 men. Custer, after the fight commenced, seeing such an extraordinary display of force, felt a natural anxiety to look after his wagons for their destruction would involve the loss of his entire command and probably defeat the entire campaign. He therefore set out for the train, and was hastened by experiencing greater opposition than was anticipated."

It was determined that Elliott and the 16 men were missing only after the battle was over and an accounting was made of the killed, wounded and missing. There was no way of determining in which direction they had gone for no one had seen them in the heat of battle. The glare of the snow-covered countryside inhibited any attempt to see for any distance.

Keim learned later that three fugitive warriors had escaped to the villages below the one Custer struck. Elliott saw them break through and pursued them. His detachment killed two of the three but the third reached a neighboring village and gave the alarm. When Elliott was several miles from his column the Indians struck him. He had no alternative but to dismount and stand them off in the hope of being rescued. He and his 16 men were finally overwhelmed.

Though Elliott was a capable and highly respected officer and his loss was felt by all who knew him, Custer's major concern was the safety of the entire command rather than that of a very small portion of it.

CHAPTER 21
FOLLOWING THE FLAG

By the time Custer and the Seventh had returned to Fort Cobb Sheridan had developed plans to strike a second winter blow. The blow just struck at the Washita had been a hard one, and on one of the tribes most guilty of depredations on Western settlements. The Kiowas had promised to come into their reservation but had not kept their word. It was time to impress them and their allies, the Cheyennes, Arapahoes and Comanches.

Sheridan was getting a backwash from the do-gooders in the East, a situation somewhat paralleling the "doves" and "peace-at-any-price advocates" during our war with North Vietnam. Sheridan chose to ignore the cries of the ignorant. He had seen too many evidences of Indian murders of women and children, massacres of settlers, rape and the destruction of property. He answered the charges against him by ordering Custer to put an end to the delays of the Indians. He wanted them on their reservations where there would be no confrontation with the whites.

Custer entered into a series of conferences, parleys and maneuvers with his Indian adversaries which finally culminated in the release of several captive white girls and the return of the tribes to their respective reservations.[1]

Historian Milo Quaife was of the opinion that "Custer's last campaign on the Southern Plains . . . was a remarkable performance which deserves far greater renown than has ever been accorded it. In its conduct he displayed a complete mastery of Indian psychology and of the art of frontier warfare."[2]

Just prior to the termination of the winter campaign Custer had written to Libbie that the Indian war was over. On this particular day he had told Captain William Thompson that he:

"Came to this command this fall determined to do exactly what I believed to be my duty, regardless of friends or foes. That I always have known that my course when on duty was not calculated to make me popular with my subordinates, that I never expected to be a popular commander in times of peace. That while I was on duty and exercising command, I intended to carry out my own views according to my best judgment, even if I knew I would be opposed by the entire command.

"I intend to let every officer in this regiment know, if they do not already, that while I prefer, if practicable, to have the approval and good will of all men, yet in my official conduct I propose and intend to follow what I think the best course whether I make friends or enemies."[3]

At this point Captain Benteen had displayed his intense dislike for Custer and had begun the process of unconsciously dividing the officers into two factions.[4] The ones closely associated with Custer were facetiously called the Custer Clan. An excellent soldier and a brave one too, Benteen had little difficulty in cultivating a following of sycophants and friends, most of whom had some reason for disliking Custer.

Custer was impatiently waiting for the campaign to end so he could get back to Libbie. He had sent one of his couriers, Stillwell, to Camp Supply with the mail. Ten days later Stillwell arrived at night, nearly naked and half-frozen, and mounted on a mule. It took a stiff drink of whiskey to bring his voice back so he could tell them the heavy rains had Medicine Bluff Creek overflowing so that it was impassable. His party and their pack mules bearing the mail were on the opposite bank a mile above the camp. The current was thought to be so rapid he decided the loaded mules couldn't cross. He partially undressed, then had his horse risk the icy water to let the General know of their whereabouts.

Knowing there were letters from Libbie on the other side of the torrent, Custer called for an unsaddled horse and some men with lariats. Galloping downstream to the point opposite the mail bearers, he had a long log rolled out into the water and from it had a rope thrown across to them, which they secured. Some of his men removed their boots and pants and made their way around to secure the rope. A volunteer stripped and made his way across by holding onto the rope. On the other side he fastened the mailbag to his neck and was pulled back by willing hands, through the raging torrent and in total darkness. Seven times he braved the current until he had all of the mail. Custer ordered whiskey from the doctor and had it given to the man, saying: "Drink my man, I don't care if you are drunk a week," then sent him to his tent to be wrapped in blankets.[5]

It was just a few nights before this that Mo-nah-se-tah, daughter of Little Rock, a chief who was killed in the Washita battle, gave birth to a baby.[6] Historical writers, more inclined to accept gossip rather than facts, have tried to link the child to Custer. One respected writer—Mari Sandoz—accepted the gossip without question. Describing the baby as light skinned and light haired, a genetic rarity under the circumstances, she repeatedly calls it Custer's child in her book *Cheyenne Autumn.* Libbie, who saw the baby that spring, described it as dark skinned and dark eyed.[7]

Writing letters at night was becoming increasing difficult for Custer. Near the end of February he was using the only piece of candle left in camp, the supplies they were waiting for not having arrived. Sheridan had left for Camp Supply in an effort to start the supply train toward them for the coming march. Autie thought Libbie would get a chuckle out of the name the Indians had given him—Mon-to-e-te, meaning Strong Arm. They did not know that his given name was Armstrong.[8]

By the first of March the Seventh Cavalry was living on quarter rations of bread. The Quartermaster and Commissary Departments had failed to provide the necessities Sheridan had ordered long before. Several days later the column moved in the direction of the Washita battlefield, arriving there on the 24th. After a few days of rest the command moved toward Camp Supply and Fort Hays, and from there to a permanent summer camp several miles out on Big Creek.

Libbie was there to join him and an additional treat was the presence of General Nelson A. Miles who was in command at Fort Hays. Though an infantry colonel he was a cavalryman at heart, Libbie observed. And it was he with his band in full uniform playing *"Garry Owen"* that greeted the Seventh when it rode into the post. Custer and Miles became firm friends from the start.

The 60 Cheyenne prisoners Custer had brought with him were placed in a large stockade at Hays. Libbie had heard so many tales of the wildness and the strangeness of Indians, her first trip to see them was attended with intense fear. She was an object of great interest to the Indians assembled there, particularly the squaws. Once she had been introduced to them they asked if she was the General's only wife. When told that she was, they evidenced sympathy for her in the belief that she had to do all the heavy work alone.

The squaws moved in to touch her and to rub their cheeks against hers in a form of caress. In Libbie's mind were the stories she had heard of the cunning and craftiness of the squaws and the readiness with which they would plunge a knife into an enemy. Though she made repeated trips to the stockade the thought never left her mind.

Libbie had been anxious to see Mo-nah-se-tah and her baby born during captivity. At her request Autie took her to see the two, something he never would have done to Libbie had the child been his own. And Benteen, hating Custer as he did, flatly stated in his letters to Goldin that the child was a full blood Indian. The time element alone crumples the story.[9] Mo-nah-se-tah's baby had been born prior to mid-January. Custer had never seen Mo-nah-se-tah before the Washita fight November 27th.

Tom, now 24 years of age, was having the time of his life. Like the rest of the Custer family he took things in stride. Not burdened with too much responsibility, and still single, he enjoyed a good time with the boys. Occasionally things would get out of hand. One such time Autie, strict disciplinarian that he was, placed him and his friend Captain George Yates in arrest. Tom laughed it off but Yates resented it for a short time. Where duty was concerned Autie had no favorites.

Basically Tom, like his brother, was quite religious. Father Custer believed that his sons, like himself, should have deep religious convictions. He also believed they should have deep political convictions provided they were of a Democratic nature. If they had any such political convictions they were only temporary; they supported a principle rather than a party.

Tom carried with him a small 4″ x 6″ volume containing THE WORDS OF JESUS.[10] Many of the passages were underlined and many of the marginal notes are in Tom's handwriting. Prophetically he had written in it: "For strangers into life we come, and dying is but going *home. Going home.* Home, Lord, tarry not, but come."

Inside the front cover one can read: "For Col. T. W. Custer, 7th Cavalry, U.S.A." And on the flyleaf: "Lulie G. Burgess, 405 Grove St., Jersey City, June 20/68."

The Seventh had arrived at its camp at Big Creek on April 8th. The men remained there for about a month, then were broken up into detachments and assigned to protect the frontier at various points.[11] Once settled down Tom would have it no other way than issue an invitation to Libbie to see his Indian trophies.

Her first visit to his tent, she recalled, never became a dim memory. There were scalplocks everywhere, even a warrior's jacket trimmed with them. Indian buffalo hide shields, bearclaw necklaces, warbonnets and weapons were his proudest possessions. Next to them he valued a collection of seven rattlesnakes he kept in hardtack boxes in his tent.

He insisted that she see them and when she demurred he said: "Well, old lady, I have some beauties to show you this time, captured them on purpose for you." She shivered as he stretched each one out to show its length and permit it to shake its rattlers. Opening one box, Tom discovered that one of his snakes was missing. It had not escaped; the larger reptile had eaten its smaller companion.[12]

Libbie tried to convince him that all of the snakes should be placed in one box since animals craved companionship. Tom was not deceived by this suggestion. In response he said: "If you think, old lady, that after all the trouble I have been to, to catch these snakes to show you, I am going to make it easy for them to eat each other up, you are mightily mistaken."[13]

On March 2d Sheridan had received a dispatch at Camp Supply from President-elect Grant to report to Washington immediately. Before leaving the following day Sheridan wrote to Custer advising of the rations and forage he was sending on to him and that he considered the campaign at an end. He wanted Custer to know he would push for his promotion as soon as he got to Washington.[14]

On March 4th, Inauguration Day, President Grant appointed Sheridan Lieutenant General of the Army to succeed Sherman who had been General of the Army. Sheridan was given command of the Division of the Missouri.

Though Sheridan continued his punishment-follows-crime policy and though he thought the campaign had ended now that they were back on their reservation, the warm weather had invited a change of attitude in the "repentant" Indians. They began slipping off the reservations until an estimated 600 hostile warriors were in the vicinity of the Republican and Solomon Rivers, north of the Arkansas.[15]

But Custer had begun a new campaign, one that would provide him with the time he wanted at home with Libbie. He had heard there was to be a vacancy at the Military Academy—that of Commandant of Cadets. Through the hands of his good friend and mentor Phil Sheridan he had sent an official application to General Sherman requesting the appointment. On June 29th he wrote to Sherman about his application. He hoped it would be received favorably, he told him, for now that Colonel Sturgis had rejoined the regiment he, Custer, would not be needed with the Seventh.[16] His companies, except for a few kept near Fort Hays, had been scattered over northern Kansas and as far west as Denver, scouting for Indians off their reservations.

Most western military posts saw towns develop nearby. Beside offering the protection of the military, these posts offered an opportunity to trade with the troops or provide them with entertainment. There was a similarity to these towns for in all of them could be found liquor, gambling and prostitutes. The elemental desires of men could be tranquilized by any one of them. There was, however, a respectable element: men who followed the ordinary pursuits of life. There were few women and children, and no elderly men.

The adventurer, the gambler, the gunfighter, took over the town. Each had to respect the lives of others; if he did not he had to resort to his gun to enforce his demands. Generally, this was a life for the young man.

Natural deaths generally were unknown, death by violence having been accepted as the way of life. Boot Hill became the popular burial ground for all those who died with their boots on. That small piece of earth was free for all who used it.[17]

Libbie left one of the few descriptions of Hays City as it appeared in 1869:

"There was hardly a building worthy of the name except the station house. A considerable part of the place was built of crude frames covered with canvas; the shanties were made of slabs, bits of driftwood and logs, and sometimes the roofs were covered with tin that had once been fruit or vegetable cans, now flattened out.

"Pistol shots were heard so often it seemed a perpetual Fourth of July. . . . It was at Hays City that the graveyard was begun with interments of men who had died violent deaths, and there were 36 of their graves before we left. . . . In our hunts and our pleasure rides I asked to shun the railroad track for I never felt sure that we might not come upon a ghastly body swinging from the beams that supported the bridge."[18]

No description of Hays City would be complete without mentioning Wild Bill Hickok, for there he was the most noted of the white scouts. Libbie said of him:

"Physically, he was a delight to look upon. Tall, lithe and free in every motion, he rode and walked as if every muscle was perfection. . . . I do not recall anything finer in the way of physical perfection than Wild Bill when he swung himself lightly from his saddle, and with graceful, swaying step, squarely set shoulders and well poised head, approached our tent for orders. . . . I do not at all remember his features. . . ."[19]

Autie remembered his features very well for they had become fast friends. He described him as being "about six feet one in height, straight as the straightest of the warriors whose implacable foe he was; broad shoulders, well-formed chest and limbs, and a face strikingly handsome; a sharp, clear, blue eye which stared you straight in the face when in conversation; a finely-shaped nose inclined to be aquiline; a well-turned mouth with lips only partially concealed by a handsome mustache. His hair and complexion were that of a perfect blond. The former was worn in uncut ringlets falling carelessly over his powerfully formed shoulders."[20]

Wild Bill had been one of Hancock's scouts during the campaign in the spring of 1867 and it was at that time Custer first met him.

While acting as a deputy U.S. Marshal Wild Bill was appointed town marshal of Hays City by a Vigilance Committee. On August 23, 1869, that county (Ellis County) elected him sheriff. (Rev. Blaine E. Burkey: Wild Bill Hickok; *The Law in Hays City,* Hays, 1973)

Known for his fast draw and his ability to defend himself at all times he, like General Custer and Buffalo Bill, became one of the noted characters of the West.

Noted Hickok biographer Joseph Rosa said of him:

> "Like George Armstrong Custer he came of a reckless breed; excitement and wanderlust were in his blood. An ancient General Custer or Wild Bill Hickok would be unthinkable. Maybe Fate felt that way too."[21]

One of the wonders of the West was the ever present buffalo. They could be seen on every side of the Big Creek encampment. Once, while standing on the crest of a divide from which the horizon could be seen in every direction, one of the officers present said: "Turn about, Mrs. Custer, and notice that you are surrounded with buffaloes. You are looking now upon a hundred thousand buffaloes."

Libbie had been victimized so frequently by their tall stories she could not help asking: "Are you really in earnest? And can I tell this to the people in the East when I get home?"

"Honor bright," he replied. "I do not exaggerate."[22]

Buffaloes were the principal source of subsistence for the Indians, providing them with food, clothing, shelter and utensils. The eventual decimation of the buffaloes by professional hide hunters did more to force the Indians onto their reservations ultimately than the forceful actions of the army. The destruction of the great buffalo herds might be compared to the destruction of the crops in the Shenandoah Valley during the Civil War, an act which deprived Lee's army of its major source of supplies.

Though garrison duty eventually became dull, the nearness of the buffalo herds, and the excitement of hunting them, offered some compensation for the officers of the command. Autie had the added joy of his reunion with Libbie. A stream of visitors, learning that the Indians had been quelled and that hunting buffalo was great sport, began to arrive from the East and from Europe. Custer's fame as an Indian fighter and as a hunter attracted them to Hays.

General Miles and Custer loved hunting together. On one of these hunts they resolved to take their wives with them on the next buffalo hunt. It took a great deal of planning for this undoubtedly was the first time women had ever been permitted to attend a buffalo hunt. Since there was great danger in riding horseback—the countryside was full of prairiedog and gopher holes that could throw or break the leg of any fine horse—a carriage had been provided. Henry, Libbie's colored servant, drove.

It was one of the wildest rides she ever experienced. Henry obeyed his orders to drive slowly—for a time. He followed the hunters, going over divide after divide, then realizing he was falling behind he gave the whip to his team and was soon galloping at a breakneck speed over buffalo wallows, prairie dog villages, cactus beds and gullies as if on a paved road. Implored by Libbie to slow down, he responded with: "There ain't no kind of danger, Miss Libbie; I'll take keer of you; you jest wait till I get to see 'em from the top of that next divide, and I'll stop."

It was several such divides before he saw them and he managed to bring the carriages up to the hunters who had dismounted and had begun to cut up their game. When Henry arrived "a shout of laughter went up from the hunters at the very idea of chasing buffaloes in a carriage."[23]

The summer saw so many strangers coming to Custer with letters of introduction, all expecting to be taken on a buffalo hunt, that it had become a bore. Whenever a dispatch arrived it was opened fearfully. Between June 1st and October 16th they had more than 200 such visitors.[24]

Though there may have been other pleasurable exceptions, the entertaining of Lords Waterpark and Berkley Paget, both presenting letter of introductions to General Custer from the Secretary of War, was an event the Custers enjoyed. Libbie had been ill with malaria the first week of their arrival but saw enough of them to say the Custers liked "their highnesses very much—they had no airs." And on one of the hunts "Autie had to remain here as it is 'pay day' soon and the men need especial charge during the spreeing time of pay day."[25]

Several days later she wrote to her Monroe friend Laura Noble that Autie was planning a grand buffalo hunt for Lord Paget and Lord Waterpark. They would establish a temporary camp about ten miles from their post since the buffaloes were not much nearer than 20 miles. The party of perhaps 20 officers, 50 soldiers on horseback, 4 ambulances and 2 or 3 wagons would start out in the morning. The wagons would be used to haul back choice cuts of meat to add to the troopers' daily rations.

Once the grazing buffalo herd was sighted, the hunters tightened their cinches, tied down their hats, loaded their pistols and carbines, then divided up the company so one portion headed off and the other drove in the rear of the herd. The ambulances, wagons and the carriage followed the chase with all haste.[26]

They—Lords Paget and Waterpark—killed 13 buffaloes in the three days of hunting the previous week, the entire party disposing of 126 buffaloes. "Autie killed seven in one day without leaving the saddle," she added. Then she went on to explain that Autie permitted the ladies to go along but "ladies had been debarred from the sport. I don't ride after the beasts because Autie thinks it too much risk as the prairie is so covered with prairie dog holes, wolf and gopher holes and buffalo wallows."[27]

A photographer accompanied the hunt, recording a buffalo at bay.[28] Other pictures were taken of the hunting party, thus enabling the two noblemen to show their friends and relatives in England some hunting scenes of the American West. So grateful was Lord Paget that he presented General Custer with a cased Galand & Somerville revolver firing a .44 Webley cartridge. Captain Tom Custer was also presented with a similar pistol.[29]

Eliza Brown had served the Custers long and faithfully. Ever since she had accepted the General's offer to take over his kitchen in Virginia, she had been loyal and reliable. She anticipated his every need, watching over him and scolding him like a mother hen. She had accepted the uncertainties and insecurity of army life. There were times when her patience reached an end. Dust blew into everything for the wind was a constant annoyance. While it rained the wind might blow a tent fly open or force smoke out of the damper on the stove in the tent. When any of these things occurred the striker, who did the chores for her, learned it was wiser to be elsewhere.

There were occasions, following a particularly trying day, when she would sit in the twilight alone. Libbie, observing this evidence of loneliness, would sit by her in an effort to console her. Eliza would respond to Libbie's questions with the unanswerable: "Miss Libbie, you's always got the ginnel, but I hain't got nobody, and there ain't no picnics nor church sociables nor no buryings out here."[30]

Eliza had many suitors for she was vivacious and entertaining. And she was generous with her cooking which had a way of getting to a man's heart. Henry was her big romance on Big Creek that summer. Henry had been sent to Monroe from Virginia by the General during the latter part of the Civil War to care for his horses. When Libbie moved out to Leavenworth to join the General, he and Eliza went along.

The romance of Henry and Eliza, like Big Creek, had its ups and downs. But when Eliza got on a spree and became insolent the Custers let her go. They had been dependent on her for so long they thought no one could replace her. To their surprise the new cook proved to be both excellent and economical. The new cook had few visitors and in consequence was able to supply the table at a considerable savings.[31]

Eliza had moved on to Leavenworth and later married a lawyer in southern Ohio. Henry married and settled in Topeka where he became a janitor in one of the public schools.

The Seventh left its camp on Big Creek in the middle of October. Marching to save expenses instead of traveling by rail, it reached Fort

A GAME OF CHARADES provided a great deal of entertainment at Fort Lincoln on those long winter evenings. Left to right: Maggie Calhoun, Tom Custer, Libbie Custer, and Agnes Bates. Author's collection.

Leavenworth soon after the first of November.[32] Foreseeing boredom in the fall duties at the post, Custer resumed his writing for *Turf, Field and Farm.* Libbie encouraged her husband to share his hunting experiences and to continue in a bent she believed he was well suited for. Signing all his articles NOMAD—he may as well have used his own name for all readers were aware of his pseudonym—he became widely read and quoted.

Late in November he visited Sheridan who was quite ill in Chicago. Sheridan, ill as he was, insisted on talking over the coming reunion of the Army of the Potomac in Philadelphia on April 9th. As its president he insisted that Custer should accompany him to it. Custer told him he would probably be on duty on the plains at that time. Sheridan told him that unless he was involved in active warfare it would be arranged so that he went with him to Philadelphia even if he had to be ordered to report to him.[33]

Custer enjoyed every moment he was in Chicago. He was treated royally by everyone. There was a profusion of invitations and not enough time to accept any more than a few of them. One night at a performance given by Joseph Jefferson he laughed until his sides ached. On another evening in company with Tony Forsyth and the rest of Sheridan's staff he attended the Opera House to see Lydia Thompson in *Blondes*. The *Times* served notice to

PORTRAITS OF LIBBIE IN 1874. Author's collection.

its readers that Custer was chasing blondes instead of Indian girls. He told Libbie that Sandy would send her a clipping that would tell all.[34]

Several days later he informed Libbie that, having just passed his birthday—December 5th—he had decided to profit from his new maturity and adopt a new resolution: "From the 1st of January, and forever, I cease, so long as I am a married man, to play cards or any other game of chance for money or its equivalent."[35]

Sheridan had requested him to travel to Washington on official business, allowing him enough time to take care of some business in Monroe. On December 11th he wrote to Libbie of his change in plans. Since it was so close to Christmas and he had been with his folks very little, he wished to spend Christmas with them and New Years with her. Cooke wanted him to go along to Hamilton, Ontario, with him. He thought he would accept Cooke's invitation since he could obtain railroad passes.[36]

General Custer arrived in Monroe on December 13th accompanied by his brother and Lieutenant Cooke. It seems that Cooke could hardly wait until he saw Diana Darrah. They had no more than arrived than Autie showed him the way to her house and told him to stay as long as he liked. Cooke took him at his word and stayed until 3 A.M.

The three visitors, after an early breakfast, went down town to play billiards, then went visiting. Their last stop was at the Darrahs where Cooke stayed for dinner.

Autie proceeded to tell Libbie:

"Tom thinks Anna (Diana) will have Cooke 'on the string' again before he leaves town. If he does become smitten I never want to see him again. But I have no idea that he will. I want Moylan to hear of Cooke staying so late last night. Cooke and Tom desire it also so I am going to write a line to Yates and he is to tell Mrs. McIntosh who will like nothing better than to tell Moylan at the first opportunity. Do not speak of it yourself until after Yates has told it as I do not want you to be connected with it and then speak only to Yates. I think Moylan ought to know it.

"I have not been so *fleshy* for a long time. I weighed 143 last summer. I now weight *164*. Everybody says I look better than for years. I feel splendidly.

"I have heard so many nice things about you. Even Tom and Cooke go into ecstacy over you. They think there never was such a woman and *strange* to say I agree with them. Gen. Sheridan desires to be most kindly remembered to you as he has done several times but I neglected to mention it. Father quit the use of tobacco last Feb. and I have never seen him look so fleshy.

"Now for a surprising piece of news. Jacob Greene *is married*. So Fannie Lewis informed me this morning. I have never written him a letter of condolence yet upon Nettie's (Humphrey) death. I think I shall write to him now.

"Cooke in a laughing manner told me some things Anna said. She told him *that her engagement with Mr. Moylan had been broken off and that she had not written to him for over a month.* Major Worrel I suppose is the one for the present but I think she would be delighted to catch Cooke but that is not on the list of probabilities. Cooke is going back to Anna's at 4:30 and at 5 goes to

Conants. If Cooke is goose enough to bite at the bait that is held out I'll tell him something that will make him think twice.

"Francis Sawyer, Anna and Major Worrell are going to the Boat Club ball in Detroit. Tom and Cooke are having a splendid time. Tell Bowers to take good care of *Maida*."[37]

Spending some time the next day with Libbie's lawyer, John Rauch, Autie was able to advise her that all of the available cash in her father's estate was needed to make up the $5,000 required by the will to be invested in securities so that her mother could live on the interest. Rauch had put the Bacon house and the lot next door on the market for $5,000. The most that had been offered for the lot was $500.[38]

Having completed his calling and Libbie's business in Monroe, Autie left for Washington. After he concluded his business there with the War Department he stopped off in Philadelphia on the way to New York long enough to get a pair of troop boots from "the only firm in the U.S. that can make them." He expected to see General and Mrs. McClellan in New York and then planned to be in Monroe for Christmas after which he would head for "11-Worth." He cautioned Libbie not to mention his delays at various points, then wished her a jolly Christmas.[39]

Libbie did have a jolly Christmas which would have been more so had Autie been there. Her cousin Anne E. (Northrop) Bingham of Howlett Hill had moved to Fort Leavenworth, arriving there on December 5th to make it her home. On Christmas Day Captain Yates escorted her and Libbie to the soldiers' quarters to see their preparations for the Christmas dinner. They were basting turkey just as they arrived.[40]

Anne observed: "My cousin seemed greatly beloved by all, and I had to notice that each officer appeared to feel that he was being specially entertained by her; such was her charm."[41]

NOTES—CHAPTER 21

[1]Sheridan: *Memoirs,* II, pp. 334-45; While Eastern do-gooders were highly vocal and critical of Sheridan and Custer for their aggressive treatment of depredating Indians, Kansans, who were the recipients of Indian terrorism, indicated their approval by a resolution passed in the Kansas House of Representatives January 10, 1869:

"Resolved by the House of Representatives, the Senate concurring, that the thanks of the people of Kansas are hereby tendered to Generals Sheridan and Custer and Colonel Forsyth, and the officers and soldiers of their commands, for the efficient manner in which they are prosecuting the War against the Indians on the plains.

"Resolved, that we have no sympathy with the Peace Commissioners and Eastern Philanthropists who seek to cast odium upon the names of the gallant commanders above mentioned by reporting that the Indians attacked in the late fight (the battle of the Washita) were friendly to the United States." (Theo. F. Rodenbaugh: *From Everglade To Canon,* N.Y., 1875, p. 553)

[2]Milo Quaife (editor): *G. A. Custer, My Life On The Plains,* Chicago, 1952, p. 596.

[3]G. A. Custer to Libbie, January 2, 1869, EBC-CBNM.

[4]W. A. Graham: *The Custer Myth,* Harrisburg, 1953, pp. 211-13.

[5]Eliz. B. Custer: *Guidon,* G. A. Custer to Libbie, January 14, 1869, pp. 47-49.

[6]*Ibid.*

[7]*Ibid,* p. 96.

[8]*Ibid,* G. A. Custer to Libbie, February 20, 1869, pp. 51-53.

[9]Eliz. B. Custer: *Guidon,* pp. 94-96.

[10]Original in author's collection.

[11]Chandler, p. 30.

[12]Eliz. B. Custer: *Guidon,* p. 114.

[13]*Ibid,* pp. 115-16.

[14]Merington, p. 228; Frost: *Sheridan Album,* p. 135.

[15]N.Y. *Times,* May 12, 1869.

[16]G. A. Custer to W. T. Sherman, June 29, 1869, *Sherman Papers,* Vol. 26, Library of Congress.

[17]James H. Beach: "Old Fort Hays," *Kansas Historical Collections,* Vol. XI (1909-1910), p. 578.

[18]Eliz. B. Custer: *Guidon,* pp. 153-54, 158.

[19]*Ibid,* p. 161.

[20]G. A. Custer: *My Life,* pp. 33-34.

[21]Joseph G. Rosa: *They Called Him Wild Bill,* Norman, 1964, p. 225.

[22]Eliz. B. Custer: *Guidon,* pp. 116-17.

General Sherman had told Libbie that from 1867 on almost nine million buffaloes had been killed. At every steamer stop along the Missouri River huge bales of skins could be seen ready for shipping. In 1874, one station on the Atchison, Topeka & Santa Fe Railroad shipped 750,000 hides. The bones were shipped East also.

An expert hunter could shoot over 100 buffaloes in one day. Using a heavy caliber rifle at long range while hiding behind a carcass he would single out and drop a buffalo. Perhaps 20 of the animals would be drawn to it by the smell of blood. While standing there he would pick them off one by one. The hunter's partners would then move in and skin the animals while he followed the herd and repeated the performance.

[23]*Ibid,* pp. 190-93.

[24]Eliz. B. Custer to Rebecca Richmond, October 16, 1869, EBC-CBNM.

[25]Eliz. B. Custer to Rebecca Richmond, September 17, 1869, EBC-CBNM.

[26]Eliz. B. Custer to Laura Noble, September 19, 1869, EBC-CBNM.

[27]*Ibid.* Frank Tallmadge, "Buffalo Hunting With Custer," *Cavalry Journal,* January, 1929, pp. 6-10, relates the story of this buffalo hunt as an eyewitness having been invited along with his father and 17-year-old sister. He was 15 at the time. He maintains that General Custer permitted his 17 year-old sister to ride sidesaddle and accompany the hunting party. On the second day of the hunt she shot and killed a big buffalo, "Her only assistance was the handing of loaded revolvers to her by special escort Captain Cooke and his orderly." She said: "Then I look around for applause. No one was in sight but my escort and his orderly, whose testimony would never do. So later in the day I killed another when everybody could see."

It is inconceivable that Custer would permit a 17-year-old stranger to participate in such a dangerous sport and would not permit Libbie to do so, expert horsewoman that she was.

[28]Frost: *Custer Album,* pp. 110-11, pictures of the buffalo hunt.

[29]John du Mont and John Parsons: *Firearms In The Custer Battle,* Harrisburg, 1953, pp. 20-22. General Custer's revolver (Galand & Somerville) is on display at the Monroe County Historical Museum.

[30]Eliz. B. Custer: *Guidon,* p. 238.

[31]Eliz. B. Custer to Laura Noble, September 19, 1869, EBC-CBNM.

[32]*Ibid.*

[33]Geo. A. Custer to Libbie, November 25, 1869, BCWC collection.

[34]G. A. Custer to Libbie, December 2, 1869, BCWC collection.

[35]G. A. Custer to Libbie, Merington, p. 231.

[36]G. A. Custer to Libbie, December 11, 1869, BCWC collection.

[37]G. A. Custer to Libbie, December 14, 1869, BCWC collection.

Annette Humphrey Greene died at the age of 28 from pneumonia following the birth of Jacob Humphrey Greene, October 28, 1868, *History of Hartford County, Conn.,* Hartford, 1928, p. 102, and *"Medical Examiner's Report,"* (Connecticut Mutual Life Insurance Co.) of Jacob Humphrey Greene, October 28, 1901.

[38]Merington, p. 231.

[39]G. A. Custer to Libbie, December 24, 1869, BCWC collection.

[40]Anne E. Bingham: "Sixteen Years On A Kansas Farm," *Kansas Historical Collections,* Vol. XV, (1919-1922), pp. 501-506.

[41]*Ibid.*

CHAPTER 22
NO TIME TO BE LONELY

Libbie maintained a great admiration for the plainswomen and their role in the settling of the West. She questioned whether the men who pushed forward so bravely in search of a new home could have done so without the encouragement and support of their wives. Looking out through the semicircle of canvas that gathered together at the front of the wagon she would give her husband a look that raised his spirits when he needed it most. Together each day they faced a hord of enemies—heat, drought, poor food, bad water, alkali dust, pommelling storms and the ever present red warrior. What woman would do this except for the man she loved?

Since Libbie had an opportunity to observe this special breed of women in most of the decade on the western plains, her observations and conclusions are of interest:

"I do not find any women in history who embody to me the very quintessence of courage like the resolute plainswomen. The Joan of Arcs, the Mollie Pitchers were examples surely of courage that poet, painter and historian have honored, but were inspired by a great courage, by a tremendous sense of the right of their cause. They were fanatics in their way. They needed the absorbing enthusiasm of their cause to make such heroines forget everything, save the work they felt they were chosen to do. Many martyrs have been supported on earth with the belief and have gone to Heaven convinced they were 'chosen' from on High to work and die for their cause.

"Our plainswomen were not so inspired. They had ofttimes no choice in their lives. Their husbands had chosen to go West and there was no alternative for them. She did not know what she was to face and she left behind her friends, her church, schools for her children, aged parents she may never see again, her family doctor, the comfort of a modern home and its fertile garden and fruit trees."[1]

Though there is no record of their opinion, the plains women probably envied army women. The latter were supplied with food and shelter, items that were scarce at times for all other women. A log cabin or a sod house, though symbols of security, were acquired under very trying conditions. Though the transition from the East to the uncivilized frontier of the West was a stunning blow to most women, it was moreso to the wives of the young graduates of West Point. Libbie took it all in stride. She had been

initiated and introduced to the hardships, to some extent, by degrees. Her first days with the army in the Shenandoah saw many of the comforts of home removed. Her first real trial, once she had become used to the army way of life, was the travel experience with Autie's troops marching across Texas.

Martha Summerhayes had observed that "throughout all our history women have accompanied their men to war, whether as the wives of common soldiers and officers, or in the capacity of nurses, laundresses or camp followers generally."[2]

Libbie was not one to allow hardship to deter her travel plans for those plans encompassed any move her husband might make that he believed would not be dangerous for her. In Libbie's mind there was no danger when Autie was near. In him she held a complete trust.

Dee Brown was of the opinion that "the most romantic husband and wife on the Indian-fighting frontier were the Custers, George and Elizabeth. Together they formed a mutual admiration society that places them in the company of the world's great lovers. . . . "[3]

Transportation on the plains was a hardship. The vehicle most commonly used for transporting army wives was the mule-drawn army ambulance. Lacking springs or shock absorbers, its oilcloth-covered seats were as hard as the terrain it traversed.[4] And the canvas covering, though intercepting the direct rays of the sun, caused the interior to reach the temperature of a sauna bath. Any cavalryman unfortunate enough to be injured or ill on the trail received the doubtful benefit of transportation in this conveyance.

During the hot summers when the army women were left alone they applied their ingenuity in creating a pleasant atmosphere in their dismal quarters. Never having enough furniture to furnish their crude dwellings, they would borrow a carpenter to fashion wood packing boxes into lounges, stools and small tables. These were covered with cretonne, calico or folded blankets. A few curtains on the windows, and four condemned gray Government blankets, darned and sewn together for carpeting, served to provide a homelike atmosphere.

A few pictures drew attention away from the bare walls. Some women, in an effort to keep the cold from penetrating their unplastered walls, would cover them with pages from the *Army and Navy Journal* and *Harper's Weekly*. Everyone took these conditions in stride and accepted them as a way of life. Like the women she was associated with Libbie concluded that "people are mistaken if they imagine for a moment that happiness arises from their accessories or surroundings."[5]

Bustles, hoopskirts and Mother Hubbards were the fashion. These billowing skirts of silk and satin offered few problems in the East. At a Western post where the high winds blew without restraint they were somewhat impractical. Even so, there was no effort made to discontinue to ignore the fashion. Libbie and her neighbors were frequently embarrassed by a sudden burst of wind that carried their skirts over their heads as they crossed the parade grounds. Autie provided the answer to their dilemma by cutting strips of lead for Libbie so she could sew them into the hem of her garments.

The happiness of the Custers was now complete. His business concluded in Washington, his visit with his family in Monroe having assured him that his aging father and his ailing mother were well taken care of, and now with his esteemed commander, Phil Sheridan, in a position of high command, he could now relax in the company of the sweetest woman in the world.

As they settled down to a peaceful winter at Fort Leavenworth they looked back upon a hectic two years. As a neophyte in Indian combat he had served an apprenticeship that had ended in court-martial. At a moment when action was imperative, he had acted. His reward was to be treated as the scapegoat for Hancock's disastrous summer campaign in Kansas.

Before his sentence had expired Generals Sheridan, Sherman and Sully and most of the officers of the Seventh had petitioned Grant for a remission of his sentence and a return to take command of a campaign against depredating Indians. The campaign had been highly unsuccessful that summer of 1868, the Indians having done whatever they wished. Custer had been tough on drunks, and had demanded a lot out of his men on the march though never more than he demanded of himself. And his pride in his regiment came first. He had studied the Indians and their way of warfare. He understood them, respected them and learned to communicate with them. In turn, they respected him.

At the end of the campaign of that past summer (1869) he had the pleasure of seeing a communication from the new commander of the Seventh, Colonel Samuel D. Sturgis, in which he said of Custer: "There is perhaps, no other officer of equal rank on this line who had worked more faithfully against the Indians, or who has acquired the same degree of knowledge of the country and of the Indian character."[6]

Captain Robert West, who had tacked on the additional charges in the Custer court-martial, left the army that year by request. Custer harbored no ill-feeling toward him and, if anything, felt sorry for he recognized in him a fine soldier whom drink had ruined.

Autie began the new year by writing his *War Memoirs*. Hardly had he started when Libbie's cousin, Rebecca Richmond from Grand Rapids, arrived. Maggie Custer, Autie's sister, was staying with them at the time. Libbie's friend Julie Thurber of Monroe was another house guest. The atmosphere was warm for this was a Michigan housewarming. And the addition of another attractive female was timely for there was to be a Grand Ball at the Arsenal Hall the following evening.[7]

Rebecca kept a running account of her stay with the Custers as she had on her two previous visits. She described the Washington Birthday Grand Ball given by the commissioned officers at Fort Leavenworth as follows:

"Dancing commenced at 9 o'clock and ending at 6 A.M. Attending were: Gen. and Mrs. Custer; Maggie Custer escorted by Mr. Nichols, and Julia by Mr. Moylan; met former acquaintances Doctor Magruder and Lippincott, Captains Yates, Noland, Moylan, Major Bell and Lieutenant Gibson; gentlemen from the City (of Leavenworth): Judge Crozier, Mr. Hoffman and Col. Rodney Smith. Music fine, floor splendid and not crowded. Hall was 140 feet x 35 feet.

"Was introduced to a Mr. Bacon (a young man) from N.Y. who immediately tried to trace a relationship through Libbie Bacon Custer.

"The ceiling was gracefully festooned over its whole surface with the American colors in bunting; walls tapestried with a background of red army blankets against which were ranged on light racks, first a row of muskets, above that a row of crossed sabres, and still above a row of cutlasses, all burnished to the last degree of brightness, and reflecting the taper lights from ten thousand angles.

"The band platform was surmounted by a canopy and enclosed by a latticework of sabres built up from a solid foundation of cannon balls. In each corner of the room stood a mountain howitzer with its accompaniment of ammunition. On the side opposite the band stand were three slightly elevated flirtation nooks ornamented with guidons. The central one bore the portrait of Gen. Sheridan hanging opposite to that of the 'Father of our country.'

"Three immense chandeliers were formed of a light framework of three tiers, from one to the other of which reach highly polished cutlasses alternating with wax tapers.

"Nice supper at about 12½. Genl. Custer, as chief of committee on decorations and, indeed general arrangements, gained much credit to himself for fine taste artistically and good judgment practically."[8]

Rebecca's next entry in her diary was one describing a Grand Masquerade the Custers gave in their home on March 9th. Rebecca, Libbie, Maggie and Julia made salad, sandwiches and taffy kisses for 60 guests, singing as they worked. Her list of guests included: Julia Thurber as *Gretchen,* Maggie Custer as *The Owl,* Libbie as *Mrs. Partington,* Mr. Nichols as *Ike Partington,* Col. Buel as *Miss Ophelia,* Mrs. Elderkin as *Night,* Col. Merrill as a burlesque *Night,* Capt. Plummer as a Harlequin, Captain Yates as Yankee schoolboy, Capt. Nolan as a Monk, Miss Couch as a Tambourine girl, Mr. Moylan as *Romeo,* Major Bell as a Turk, Genl. Custer as an English Huntsman, and Genl. Sturgis as an old vegetable huckster. They danced until 5 A.M.[9]

At intervals of less than a week there were dinner parties and dancing, and an occasional sing-along at the Custer residence. In the latter part of March Rebecca left for Topeka to visit her sister.

General Custer and Libbie planned to travel East early in April, accompanying Maggie and Julia back to Monroe, Autie going on to Philadelphia to attend the veterans' reunion just to please Sheridan. He had thought the Seventh would move out onto the Plains in early March, thereby allowing him time to accompany it and return in time to be in Philadelphia by April 9th. Orders were issued for the Seventh to move early in the summer instead. Disliking being absent from his command when it was about to move, he decided not to go to Philadelphia. Libbie stayed with him, the two girls going home without either of them.[10]

On May 3d Custer moved out with five companies of the Seventh for Fort Hays where he camped to be in a position to move in any direction in the event of any hostile demonstration by Indians.[11] The other companies were scattered to protect settlers and the wagon trains along the Saline, Solomon and Republican rivers. They usually acted independent of each other. The many miles of useless marching that summer with no apparent objective had a depressing effect upon the officers and men. Escort duty, scouting and garrison duty was a drab contrast to the exciting times they had had together under Custer the previous two years.[12]

At the regimental headquarters at Fort Hays the circumstances were different. Custer's reputation as an Indian fighter and hunter brought another avalanche of visitors. He and his charming wife had a widespread reputation as hosts. Of especial interest to the General was his good friend Mayor K. C. Barker of Detroit. Barker had repeated invitations to hunt buffalo and finally had accepted. He arrived with several other eager Detroit sportsmen; they were fed and immediately headed for the buffalo herd some 12 miles away. Unfortunately Barker and his friend Judge Beckwith were men who tipped the scales at 230 pounds. There was considerable difficulty in supplying them with horses strong enough to carry them and yet speedy enough to hunt buffalo. Nonetheless, Barker's buffalo hunt was a huge success.[13]

Mrs. George Yates had an experience in the summer of 1870 she shared with Libbie. While she was watching the General buffalo hunting one day, he rode over to her and called her attention "to a white object so far off as to look like a small pocket handkerchief hanging on a hook. I replied that it looked like a handkerchief. He said: 'No, that is the white spot on the side of an antelope and I am going to bring it down.' Dropping on one knee, he raised his rifle to his shoulder. There was a report, then a puff of dust in the distance and the 'handkerchief' dropped. We then walked out to the dead antelope which had been shot behind the shoulder. Measuring the ground carefully, we found it was 650 yards."[14]

Earlier that spring, while writing his *Memoirs* and reliving the experiences in the numerous Civil War engagements, Autie arrived at a startling conclusion—that "Custer's Luck" was not necessarily permanent. Taking his pen in hand, he wrote a last will and testament bequeathing his all to Libbie B., using as his witnesses W. W. Cooke and Jim Calhoun.[15]

Three years later his brother Tom prepared a similar instrument. His property was to be shared equally by his mother and his sweetheart, Lulie G. Burgess of Jersey City. In the event that Lulie was not alive, all of his estate would go to his mother. Following his death at the Little Big Horn his mother became the sole heir.[16]

That fall more than half the companies were stationed at posts in the field, the remaining five companies being assigned to Fort Leavenworth for the winter. General Custer was ordered to Washington where the top brass was going through the throes of a reorganization.

He had seen and had been captivated by the acting of Joseph Jefferson in Chicago the previous December. This time he stopped in New York to see him perform in *Rip Van Winkle* and was enthralled with what was Jefferson's 136th consecutive performance.[17]

While in Washington he visited the studio of Matthew Brady to have a portrait made for which he paid $30.[18] On his return west he stopped off in Detroit to see K. C. Barker, then moved on to Monroe to spend his second consecutive Christmas with his parents.

New Year's Eve saw Libbie and her husband together at Fort Leavenworth. A review of their prospects for the coming year provided them with a perspective not wholly cheerful. Autie had been informed that the Seventh was to be broken up. His request to accompany its headquarters was endorsed by Colonel Sturgis but was denied in Washington.

There was a certain monotony to the present frontier duty. Escort duty and skirmishes with a few Indians might satisfy the indolent. It did nothing for Custer. He needed the stimulus of action, the provocation of pursuit. Libbie wanted whatever her husband wanted. What made her husband happy made her happy too.

They first discussed retirement from the service but finally decided to seek a long leave and investigate employment opportunities in New York. He was granted four months of leave beginning January 11th. Leaving Libbie in Topeka with her cousin Mrs. Charles Kendall he arrived in New York in time to receive an invitation from colorful Vinnie Ream to attend the unveiling of her Lincoln statue in Washington. He declined.[19]

Vinnie Ream's invitation was one of many for within an hour after he had checked in at the Fifth Avenue Hotel he had received more than he could accept. Of particular interest, though pressing business prevented him from accepting it, was an invitation from the Northern Pacific Railroad to travel on a two-week excursion via special train and steamer to Duluth, St. Paul and return without cost to himself.

His first evening in New York was spent dining with August Belmont, John Jacob Astor, Dr. Bliss, Mr. Travers, Mr. Barker and Mr. L. P. Morton, all men deeply involved in the investment business. When Custer expressed regret to his host that the hostess could not be with them, he was shocked when the reply indicated she was ordered to remain upstairs since the men could have a better time without her. To order her to her room like a child was to him unthinkable. In contrast he thought of Libbie whose presence at his dinner table he considered highly desirable. No entertainment in his home would be complete without her. Married life in New York was not quite his idea of married life.[20]

Although he was in New York looking for employment, so his friends thought, he had an alternate purpose. Ever since the activation of the Seventh Cavalry he had been experiencing frequent desertions. Many of the men had enlisted just to obtain transportation out to Colorado so they would desert, then prospect for gold or silver. The stories of the rich strikes in that region had been the subject of conversation around the daily mess and had played a part in the desertions of some who had joined only to soldier.

Previously he had invested in several race horses, three lots in Council Grove, Kansas, and a house in Topeka, Kansas. His horses had won very few races and his house remained unrented.[21] The thought of buying into a silver or gold mine with the huge returns he had been hearing about seemed to be an attractive investment.

Hearing of several rich silver lodes in the region of Clear Creek County, Colorado, he had investigated them while in that area. One that held a particular interest was the Stevens Lode located ten miles out of Georgetown. The original lode was 1,400 feet in length, the western half of which belonged to the Crescent Silver Mining Company of Cincinnati. The eastern half was for sale though 60 feet of it had already been opened.

Pursuing financiers on Wall Street like he had pursued Libbie in Monroe eight years earlier, he convinced August Belmont to invest $15,000 and John Jacob Astor to invest $10,000 in the venture. A stock issue of 2,000 shares was being offered at $50 a share with a valuation of $100 each. Custer was listed as having an interest of $35,000. The notes he left do not indicate whether this was in cash or as a promoter's share.[22]

On April 8th, not long after he had written a letter to Libbie from the office of Frank Hames, he wrote another lengthy one from that of Osborn and Cammack. He had just returned from lunching with them at Delmonico's. Bursting with news, he told Libbie of his progress thus far.

For some weeks he had tried to interest Charles Osborn in the Stevens Lode but had made no headway. Osborn had told him from the beginning "that he would not look at a mine for investment even if he saw them taking twenty dollar gold pieces from it." When Custer had shown him and his partners that noon a note from Astor subscribing to a portion of the mine, Osborn began to show an interest. One of his partners said: "Charlie, if Astor, Belmont and these fellows are going in you had better take some too."[23]

Osborn asked a few questions, then said: "Well Custer, I want to see you further about this." Osborn's partner Mr. George said:

> "Oh General, you are bound to succeed now that you have gotten the names of those gentlemen, some of the best in New York." With that Custer wrote: "Can it be that my little Standby and I who have long wished to possess a small fortune, are about to have our hopes and wishes realized? If I succeed in this operation as now seems certain, it is to be but the stepping stone to large and more profitable undertakings. . . . I have met with many discouragements and Col. Hall felt discouraged at

OUR HOME AT FORT LINCOLN and the people who visited it. The identification underneath is in the handwriting of General Custer. 1874. David Barry photo. Author's collection.

times, and Gen. McClellan. I never have. I allowed no man's misgivings to terrify me. If I approached a capitalist and he threw cold water over my scheme, as has been often done, I looked on the bright side. . . . "[24]

It appeared that he was attempting to sell some bonds for a Mrs. Hough from which transaction he would derive $30,000 in cash as his commission. Mrs. Hough was anxiously waiting to hear about her bonds and Autie was just as anxious to be able to tell her.

James Fisk, railroad magnate and financier, offered him and General Franklin Smith the use of one of his elegant steamers to take them to Boston and back without charge or obligation. Since there would be no expense he asked of Libbie: "Do you approve?" It is very unlikely she would have disapproved had he wanted to dip into their slim savings to go by rail. He referred to it as "the usual Custer luck," then told her that he and General Sheridan were to be guests to the opera that evening.[25]

Custer had no reason to be jealous of Libbie at any time, having complete faith in her. Whether jealousy or caution entered into the advice he gave her in this letter is a matter for the reader to judge. Autie had been advised officially of the disposition of his companies in early March. One company was sent to Tennessee and the others were assigned to South Carolina and Kentucky. He was being sent to Louisville. Plans had been made to go to Louisville via Monroe, a matter known only to Libbie, so he thought. Somehow Captain Myles Keogh had learned of it and had told a friend. Autie wondered:

"How did it reach him? If I was of a suspicious disposition I would imagine you had informed him but as I am not and do not care whether you have or not I will not trouble myself about it. So far as I am concerned you write when and where you please, but for your sake the fewer notes or letters of yours, no matter how ordinary, that get into gentlemen's hands the better for your reputation for it is natural for most gentlemen to swell the number of their conquests in the eyes of others, and when a gentleman receives a note or letter from a lady and desires to create an impression, he does not tell his friends of the *contents* of the note but smugly remarks in a casual manner, 'I had a note yesterday from Miss or Mrs. So-and-So,' and leaves his friends to imagine the character of the note which nine times out of ten he does to the disadvantage of the writer. I regretted that you had written to both or either Cooke and Col. Keogh. A dozen or more persons might have heard that they had received a letter from you but not one

GATHERING ON THE STEPS of the first Custer residence at Fort Lincoln, left to right, *top row:* Agnes Bates of Monroe, Lieutenant James Calhoun, Mrs. James Calhoun; *middle row:* Libbie Custer, General Custer; *bottom row:* Fred Calhoun, Col. William Thompson. 1873. Mrs. E. B. Custer collection. Custer Battlefield National Monument.

person perhaps ever heard why or what you wrote them. Do not think I am fault finding. I am not. But did you know how often I have seen vanity prompt men to hold up an envelope between their fingers and remark, 'A note from Mrs.——' you would see why I view the matter as I do."[26]

Perhaps he was nettled because of receiving what he labeled "a characteristic letter from Col. Keogh." Keogh had asked him to send an expensive basket of flowers to one of his sweethearts and to purchase some $50 sleeve buttons for Cooke. The latter request he did honor by having them sent C.O.D.

He acknowledged receiving a letter from his sister Maggie written in answer to his. It was his observation that he usually never heard from her unless her fiance' got into trouble. Jim Calhoun, her fiance', seemingly more thoughtful, had just written him a letter of thanks from Bagdad, Kentucky, for the many kindnesses he had been proffered in his troubles. And he wanted him to know he had just received his commission as first lieutenant.[27]

A round of the theatres, supper clubs and a visit to a faro bank kept Autie occupied evenings. He remembered his resolution and made his companions understand that he did not gamble. The sheer magnificence of the casino fairly staggered him; what a contrast to the ugly gaming tables of Hays City. And what a fashionable place Johnny Chamberlain ran not far from the Fifth Avenue Hotel. Some of the most prominent men in New York frequented his casino. One could play *Rouge-et-Noir* and a new game, baccarat. Proudly he told Libbie that in the two hours he watched others gamble not once did he feel the desire to do so.

He succumbed to style and purchased a light gray top hat, for black stovepipes were seldom seen. Though not as attractive appearing in civilian clothes as he was in his uniform, his yellow hair, military bearing and measured stride made women take a second look. Dutifully, and one suspects pridefully, he told Libbie of several women he was introduced to who had made advances and of one beautiful young blonde who walked past his hotel several times trying to attract his attention. He always assured Libbie of his faithfulness, and that there never could be any other. As far as he was concerned: "He never could care for a woman who so far forgot herself as to make advances. My girl . . . to me stands all the higher by contrasts, in bright relief, true womanhood."

Late in May he received a letter from Libbie acknowledging the receipt of six letters from him in one day. In reply he reminded her:

"You shall never hereafter accuse me of indolence in correspondence—even if I do not write to other people you have ample reason to know that I am anything but indolent when you are the person I am writing to. This ought to show you what a different estimate I place upon you and upon the entire world, besides you know that except on rare *fitful* occasions you can scarcely induce me to write even duty letters to others.

"Last night the thought flashed through my brain that if I ever lost you, no other woman could or ever should reawaken it. You are irrevocably my first, my present and my last love. All the women are but as mere toys compared to you."[28]

Earlier that month he had written:

"I just received your letter written upon your return from the Mannings. Don't you think it is about time you changed the burden of your song? I refer to the explanation you have been giving me when you bring your letter to a close, viz., that you can't write any more as you are just going to pay some calls. It seems to me, judging from the calls you have reported, that the population of Monroe must have oustripped in growth that of Kansas City for I am confident there were not as many people in town when I left it as you report you have called upon. It has been nothing but 'call,' 'call,' 'call.'

"Surely you must add the Munches, the Weirs and all the other Dutch broods to your list of calling acquaintances, for I am certain that had you only been calling on the original settlers, your former friends, you would have been able to 'Swing around the circle' in less time than you have taken.

"But really, to lay all joking aside, you are extensively engaged in the calling business. Fortunately you can have no possible excuse to ask me to call when I return as you will have made the rounds."[29]

One Friday evening he attended a parade and drill of the 22d New York Guard at the Armory. He was quite impressed with the 500 men and their 40 piece band, saying of them: "I was surprised at the proficiency they displayed; their drill was excellent and their marching could not be surpassed." Many of the spectators came in full evening dress, Custer attending in uniform. The Colonel tendered him a review of the regiment which he refused. He finally compromised by inspecting them informally.[30]

Custer was a devotee of the legitimate theatre and had an equally strong leaning toward opera. He always became emotionally involved with the leading roles, running the gamut of emotions as an appreciative observer and expressing himself unashamedly in tears to laughter in response to the artist's portrayal.

He held Lawrence Barrett in highest esteem, considering him a dear friend. Similarly he deeply admired Clara Louisa Kellogg. His friendship with her was treasured and platonic. His letters to Libbie constantly referred to Miss Kellogg and, in one, he told her: I care for no one in town (he meant women) but Miss Kellogg, and I respect her and she respects me." In turn, Libbie respected the relationship and never questioned it.

One evening he went to the opera in company with the Governor Ito of Japan, the General McClellans, General Grant's brother Orville and Collector Murphy.[31]

On another evening he went to see *Rigoletto* with Charles Osborn. Miss Kellogg was playing the role of Gilda. Custer took Osborn behind the scenes between Act 1 and 2 to introduce him. She asked Custer to come back after Act 2 and tell her "how it passed off."

He replied: "Why it is no use for me to come as you will be changing your dress."

She said: "Oh yes, do come back and tell me how I got through."

As Custer related it to Libbie: "So I did, although I could only open the door a few inches and tell her, as she was dishabille. She changed her dress between each act, and in the last act she appeared in boy's clothes, the first time I ever saw her in male attire, but she was dressed so modestly and her demeanor so perfect no one could draw unfavorable inferences."

Autie described her costume and of "occasional glimpses of a beautifully turned leg encased in purple tights," then: "She told me Sunday that Edwin Booth had written her a most urgent letter making an extravagant offer asking her to play *Juliet* to his *Romeo*. Only think what a combination and what crowded audiences they would draw. He sent her the play to look over. She took the matter under advisement but finally wrote Booth saying that all things considered she had deemed it best to confine herself to her own profession."[32]

On June 3d Autie joined his wife in Monroe. The local papers indicated that he intended "rusticating in the Floral City" for several weeks.[33] Very likely he rested the first few days of his return; then his restless spirit took over and prompted him to make a round of visitations. The one person he respected most and missed talking to was Judge Bacon.

Joseph Guyor, an 88-year-old veteran of the War of 1812, was hosting nearly 100 veterans in his home at Guyor's Island. This island at the mouth of the River Raisin was once the site of a Potawatomi Indian village. Learning that General Custer was on leave and in Monroe, Joe Guyor invited him to his dinner. Following a round of speeches by Major H. F. Redford, General George Spaulding, Colonel Ira Grosvenor and Colonel Constant Luce, Custer greeted these old veterans ranging in age from 77 to 107—with an average age of 90—arousing so much enthusiasm it was decided to hold another "Veterans' Reunion." It was then decided to hold it in Noble's Grove just east of Monroe Street on July 4, 1872.[34]

In the latter part of 1865 Custer had purchased a seventh interest in the Golo Club for $28.57 from H. M. Mixer. The share in the Monroe duck hunters' club consisted of an interest in the "Clubhouse, furniture, etc." situated on the Monroe Pier.

The Golo Club had been organized in 1854 by seven prominent sportsmen from Detroit, Buffalo and New York City who wished only to hunt canvas backs, redheads, mallards, widgeon and blue bills in the famous Monroe marshes. The only resident member was J. M. Sterling. Custer retained his share until June 15, 1871, selling his share to the Hon. Harry A. Conant of Monroe.[35]

Sunday, June 11th, was a big day for Monroe's Methodists. Their new church was being dedicated. That morning the Rev. Dr. Reid announced that the total church indebtedness was $18,000. An immediate attempt to solicit additional subscriptions reduced the indebtedness to $3,000. That evening Rev. B. I. Ives announced that he had "the promise from a gentleman well known not only to Monroe but to the people of the whole country, for the last $500 needed."[36]

It was well known that General Custer was present so no great amount of guessing was necessary to determine who the liberal donor was. The $2,500 was soon raised and then his name was formally mentioned.

It was now time to return to New York. Once there he quickly obtained all the latest news and forwarded it to Libbie in a series of lengthy letters. The pet bear he had donated to the City Zoological Gardens had arrived. He hated to part with it but his change to Kentucky made it necessary. It recalled to mind a number of items he had donated to the Detroit Audubon Club two years before, sending them to his friend, K. C. Barker, who was its president. They were trophies he had obtained mostly at the Battle of the Washita and included the scalp of Cheyenne Chief Little Rock, a squaw's buckskin dress, a bow and quiver full of arrows, a buffalo hide shield and an Indian saddle.[37]

Custer considered himself quite worldly but revealed he was not entirely so when he related several instances of questionable conduct. In an instance that he admitted astounded him, a married man had taken him to call upon a married woman whose husband was away at the time. He told Custer that the woman's illness was the consequence of an abortion for which he was responsible.

A married man had told him he loved no one except his child and that as far as his relations with his wife was concerned there was "no nonsense about it." These incidents and the observation that "few wealthy people seemed to enjoy their married life" made him realize the pleasure he and Libbie derived in planning a purchase or in taking a trip together, and he told her so.[38]

While a guest at the Osborn House a few days later he told Libbie of an experience he had the night before when he, in the company of a young woman, called on a married woman:

> "We knocked at the parlor door but could get no response and were about to go away when we heard a knocking on the inside of the door. We kept knocking on the outside and during this noise the bolt was withdrawn on the inside and the door opened by a married man, not the husband of the lady. He was very much flushed and excited, while the lady was sitting in the back room endeavoring to appear calm and composed. I smelt a very large rat but said nothing. Finally, the gentleman, whom I know very well, and I were alone when he said: 'Custer, for God's sake don't you ever tell this.' I burst out laughing and teased him unmercifully. He finally admitted that at the moment I knocked at the door he was just at the height of his amusement. In other words he was performing the office between the sheets of the lady's (?) husband and he was frightened to death when we knocked at the door. He was terribly afraid the young lady would suspect something, but she did not."[39]

Osborn and his party drove Custer out to the training grounds of Joe Coburn to see the prizefighter exercise. Coburn was considered by some to be the best in America. He was preparing for a fight with the English champion Tem Mace.

There it was learned that the heavyweight championship fight would be fought in Canada not far from Buffalo and it was expected there would be 10,000 people attending it. Autie decided to go with the Osborn party if his business would permit it for Col. Hall had returned from the silver mine at Georgetown. Hall's previous report to Autie indicated that ore from the Stevens Lode assayed at $230 in silver per ton and $60 in lead per ton. The purchase of the east half had been completed for $100,000.[40]

Though Custer had long been curious "to witness one and only one prize fight," it is not known as to whether he was able to attend it. He did tell Libbie that he knew Tom and Cooke would like to see it.[41]

Custer might miss a prize fight but a horse race was something else. It was mid July and the races were running at Saratoga. It was there he met his old friend K. C. Barker. He predicted to Libbie, though he did not bet, that Mr. Harper's *Longfellow* would beat Mr. Belmont's *Kingfisher,* and he did. Such jolly time had he that he wrote Libbie: "How I wish you were here to 'double my joys and quadruple my expenses' in this enchanting place. Pardon the quotation—it seemed the place to bring it in. But you never seem any expense to me."[42]

Then, learning that the racing would conclude a day early, he asked Libbie to meet him in Detroit Saturday morning to visit with the Barkers at their Grosse Ile home.[43]

It was back to New York in August, for Custer wanted to follow up on his promotion to sell his interest in the silver mine. Late in the month General Sheridan was expected to arrive on his ship the *Russia.* It arrived a day late—September 1st—while Custer was attending the opera with Miss Kellogg. With the balance of the evening free, for Miss Kellogg retired early to rest for a performance the following day, he visited with Sheridan until 1 A.M. From him he obtained a first hand view of the Franco-Prussian war.

Indicating that he wished Custer had been with him, Sheridan went on to say: "Custer, you with that Third Division could have captured King William six times over."[44] It was good to see his old commander again and to know he retained a kindly feeling toward him.

But it was time to leave for Elizabethtown, his new headquarters. His interest in the silver mine had been sold.[45] Realizing that duty in the South involved one in politics to some extent—an arena he sought to avoid at all times—he accepted the assignment with some reservations. He had preferred assignment to the Plains but knew it would be too hard on Libbie.[46]

NOTES—CHAPTER 22

1 Eliz. B. Custer: *Women Of The Plains,* unpublished manuscript in author's collection.
2 Martha Summerhayes: *Vanished Arizona: Recollections Of My Army Life,* Chicago, 1939, p. XIV.
3 Dee Brown: *The Gentle Tamers,* N.Y., 1958, p. 67.
4 I can attest to the total lack of comfort embodied in an army ambulance of that period having ridden in one for the most part of a three-day rerun of the Butterfield Overland Dispatch over the Smoky Hill Trail during the Kansas Centennial (May, 1961). Relief came only through walking, exchanging places with passengers in the stage coach, or by making camp at the end of an uncomfortable day. Perhaps one endowed with greater posterior padding would have suffered less.
5 Eliz. B. Custer: *Guidon,* p. 256.
6 Whittaker: *Life of Custer,* p. 475.
7 Rebecca Richmond Diary, February 21, 1870, EBC-CBNM.
8 *Ibid,* February 22, 1870.
9 *Ibid,* March 9 through March 23, 1870; Rebecca Richmond to her mother, March 16, 1870. EBC-CBNM.
10 Rebecca Richmond to her parents, March 21, 1870, EBC-CBNM.
11 May 5, 1870, Monroe *Commercial.*
12 Chandler, pp. 31-35.
13 Eliz. B. Custer: *Guidon,* pp. 263-76.
14 EBC-CBNM.
15 Probate Court Records, April 5, 1870, Monroe, Mich.
16 Probate Court Records, June 19, 1873 and October 5, 1877, Monroe, Mich.
17 G. A. Custer to Libbie, December 18, 1870, Merington, pp. 230-31.
18 December 18, 1870; receipt in author's collection.
19 Vinnie Ream to Gen. and Mrs. Custer, January 25, 1871, author's collection; Gordon L. Hall; *Vinnie Ream,* N.Y. 1963, pp. 103-104; Monaghan, p. 333.
20 Merington, pp. 232-33.
21 Charles F. Kendall to G. A. Custer, Topeka, June 5, 1871. Original in author's collection.
22 Note in General Custer's file, BCWC collection. G. A. Custer to Libbie, April 7, 1871, BCWC collection.
23 G. A. Custer to Libbie, April 8, 1871, BCWC collection. This letter was written at 34 Broad Street on the stationery of "Osborn & Cammack, Bankers and Brokers."
24 *Ibid.*
25 G. A. Custer to Libbie, May, 1871, letter in author's collection.
26 *Ibid.*
27 Merington, pp. 236-37.
28 G. A. Custer to "Darling Standby" (Libbie), May, 1871, letter in author's collection.
29 G. A. Custer to Libbie, May 4, 1871, letter in author's collection.
30 G. A. Custer to Libbie, May, 1871, letter in author's collection.
31 G. A. Custer to Libbie, May, 1871, letter in author's collection.
32 G. A. Custer to Libbie, May, 1871, letter in author's collection.
33 Monroe *Commercial,* June 8, 1871.
34 Bulkley: *History of Monroe,* Vol. I, pp. 126-27.
35 *Golo Club,* Bill of Sale, June 15, 1871, EBC-CBNM. John M. Bulkley: *History of Monroe County, Michigan,* N.Y., 1913, Vol. I, p. 460; Katherine Nims: *Taped Interviews,* pp. 73-74, Monroe County Library. A Golo was a peculiarly marked duck occasionally shot in the Monroe marshes, and so named by one of the local French.
36 Monroe *Commercial,* June 15, 1871.
A former Monroe Methodist Church historian, Mrs. R. H. Sprague, advised me that at the 75th anniversary of the church a letter from General Custer was read—which has since disappeared—giving his reason for not being able to pay his pledge. I have a receipt signed by the Methodist Church Treasurer, J. M. Loose, which reads: "Rec'd from E. H. Custer, Marie Custer and Elizabeth Custer, Five Hundred Dollars to the First M. E. Church in full of Gen. G. A. Custer subscription. Feb. 27, 1877."
About 1950 a Monroe attorney thought I should know that a prominent member of the Monroe Methodist Church had told him in confidence that General Custer was invited to give the dedicatory address for the new church. Custer had arrived in Toledo, the story goes, but could get no further. Ordering a steam locomotive and a private car from the New York Central Railroad he moved on to Monroe, charging the $10,000 bill to the Methodist Church. Of course this doesn't tie in with newspaper accounts or church records, and New York Central records show no such charge or usage. It is just another incidence of the lengths and logic that some people will use to depreciate or sully a man bigger than themselves.
37 G. A. Custer to Hon. K. C. Barker, Detroit, original letter in Detroit Historical Museum.
38 Merington, p. 233.
39 G. A. Custer to Libbie, 1871, BCWC collection.
40 J. W. Hall to G. A. Custer, BCWC collection.
41 G. A. Custer to Libbie, 1871, BCWC collection.
42 Merington, p. 238; Monroe *Commercial,* July 20, 1871.
43 G. A. Custer to Libbie, July 20, 1871, letter in author's collection; Monroe *Commercial,* July 20, 1871.
44 Merington, p. 239.
45 Eliz. B. Custer to Mrs. Sabin, 1871, Merington, p. 240.
46 G. A. Custer to Libbie, 1871, Merington, p. 239.

CHAPTER 23
BETSY - TOWN

Elizabethtown was no counterpart for New York City. They varied on almost any point one might wish to discuss. Autie welcomed the change and viewed his new post optimistically. The townspeople were friendly, the air was pure and the food was good at the Hill House. Aunt Beck Hill, who managed the old-fashioned hotel he stayed at, fed him applesauce and hot biscuits at every meal, and that struck his fancy from the start.

Libbie's letter awaiting his arrival there on September 3d had asked if he had seen a physician about his cold. He answered her in the negative because: "You know my distrust of the profession." He was certain the bracing mountain air would cure him.[1]

The regimental headquarters of the Seventh Cavalry was established at Louisville with Custer commanding the post at Elizabethtown. The principal duties of its various companies scattered about the South were to assist U.S. Marshals in their arrest of illicit distillers and members of the Ku Klux Klan.[2] Custer was used principally to purchase horses for the service. Since there were few arrests during the two years they were stationed there, duty was simple compared to life on the Plains.

The first troopers arriving there consisted of A Company. They were stationed on South Main Street. The cavalry parade grounds were on Dixie Avenue while the Fourth U.S. Infantry drilled at the old Fair Grounds.[3]

After assuming command of his post, Custer returned to Monroe for Libbie. He left there on September 11th for Louisville, intending to stop off for several weeks to purchase horses for the government.[4] After a few days there he continued on to E-Town, as the natives called it, then returned to Louisville on September 21st.[5]

Libbie was not overwhelmed by the attractiveness of E-Town. She was first impressed by its dullness, quiet and antiquity. The only noise to be heard was that provided by the sheriff in the Court House calling out "Hear ye," three times for each case. The people were generally poor and uneducated. Three or four people would ride on a horse at the same time. One old fellow over 70, who boarded at the Hill House, was eager to marry a young girl. He was as unsteady on his feet as the 16-year-old dog there. Libbie observed more activity in an E-Town pig than anyone else.[6]

By the time the Custers had returned to Elizabethtown a fine house was available for rent. The owner had wanted $100 a month but finally settled for $75. It had four bedrooms and was completely furnished and carpeted, had two cisterns, a good well, stable, wood house, meat house, an outhouse and overlooked the town. They were fortunate in engaging 100-year-old Aunt Jennie to cook and wash for them at $10 a month.[7]

Custer's outgoing personality was such that he made friends easily. Lovely Libbie, whose sweet disposition and ability to be a friend made her welcome everywhere, was equally welcomed by the Kentuckians. Elizabethtown had maintained deep Southern sympathy during the rebellion but this in no way inhibited its efforts to display true Southern hospitality.

Custer hunted small game and an occasional deer with his Russian wolf hounds and English stag hounds in Kentucky, making use of his Kentucky thoroughbreds to do so.

The unmarried officers boarded at several hotels, and some of the married officers roomed at the Hill House where the Custers stayed their first days in town. Late in 1872 the Custers shared a large house with Lieutenant and Mrs. Algernon E. Smith. The house was fully furnished and the two wives alternated each week in taking charge of the housekeeping.[8]

Though Autie spent much of his time inspecting horses purchased in Louisville and Lexington he found time, while home, to play games with the children. His fondness for them was displayed many times. He played chess with his E-Town friends and squired Libbie to the dances held in Kaufman Hall.[9]

Libbie had learned the rudiments of sewing from her mother. When she evidenced a desire to save money for some new clothes by staying at home while Autie conducted some Government business in

Louisville, he bought her a sewing machine. She enjoyed making her own clothes, becoming so deeply interested in it she made Tom some underdrawers and nightgowns.

Tom appears to have been a perfectionist. He made such suggestions to her as preferring his buttonholes vertical rather than horizontal, ruffles on his nightgowns instead of lace, and a strap on his drawers to go under his feet so they wouldn't crawl on him. He concluded his suggestions to her with: "I wish you would keep your eye on that old hag that is doing my sewing and make her more careful and write oftener to your devoted brother Tom."[10]

Autie traveled without his wife most of the time. She had quickly adapted to the slow pace at Elizabethtown. Making many friends—having learned from her father that to make a friend, one had to be a friend—she found the town to be a very pleasant place in which to stay while he was gone.

Libbie observed that "everybody in Kentucky drinks." When the General was asked what he would drink for a toast before a meal he, while the others took brandy, whiskey or wine, asked for a glass of Alderney.[11]

The General was finding plenty of time to write. He had begun a series of articles for *Galaxy* Magazine entitled "My Life On The Plains," the first of which appeared in January, 1872.[12] He also spent several weeks with his good friend Lawrence Barrett while he was playing in Louisville in the latter part of 1871. Later Barrett sent Custer a beautiful cameo ring. Since he was away when it arrived Libbie opened the package. She was delighted to see how small the ring was for she envisioned it as being too tiny for Autie but large enough for her. Autie fairly smirked when he slipped it on his finger with ease.

Custer had a schoolboy love for animals of all kinds. He had owned a wide variety of animals over the years but was never known to have had a cat. Of them all he loved his horses the most though dogs took a close second place. At the time he left Kentucky it was said he owned as many as 80 dogs. And the one who cared for his dogs and horses was John Burkman.

John had joined Company A of the Seventh in the fall of 1870. He was 28 years of age; Custer was 31. John was illiterate, slow of speech and movement but thoroughly trustworthy and loyal. Libbie first saw him as a "middle-aged man" with a bad cough. When the regimental surgeon recommended light work and nourishing food for John, Libbie instructed Mary to feed him well. Long after he was pronounced fully recovered he continued to leave the cook tent after each meal with his mouth and hands full of food. It didn't take the officers long to dub him "Old Neutriment." Libble wrote:

> "My husband and I were so attached to him, and appreciated so deeply his fidelity, we could not thank the good fortune enough that gave us one so loyal to our interests."[13]

Reminiscing years later, Burkman told of the deep affection both Libbie and the General had for all of their dogs. Though most of them were quite valuable, Custer just couldn't part with one when it came down to the final sale. In one instance he turned down $500 for a puppy because of the look in its mother's eyes.[14]

The dogs were a constant source of trouble, often killing other people's pets. On one occasion they literally tore a fine bird dog to pieces. When Libbie learned of it she had Burkman take her to the owner. As Burkman said, "Arter she got through talkin' to him and sorta smilin' and lookin' up at him the purty way she had, he want mad no more."[15]

Libbie was equally attached to the dogs, giving them complete access to the house. "Most of the time they was two or three sleepin' cross the foot o' their bed," Burkman recalled. "I've knowed her to take some o' the pups to bed with her. That was arter we got up into Dakota and the leetle things, bein' thin skinned, want used to the cold and suffered considerable."[16]

Cavalrymen, generally, were sympathetic toward any helpless thing. One news correspondent told of seeing General Custer, while riding at the head of a column of hundreds of men, guide his horse around a nest of young meadowlarks directly in his line of travel, then continue on without a sign or word. All who followed him repeated his performance when they reached that spot and saw the reason for the unusual action of their commanding officer.[17]

The frigate *Svetlana,* flagship of the Russian fleet, arrived and anchored in the mouth of the Hudson River on November 19th. Aboard was the Grand Duke Alexis, third son of Alexander III, czar of Russia.[18] His arrival was headline news; his reception was larger than that given any of his royal predecessors including the Prince of Wales in 1860 and some 14 other dukes who had visited the country this year.[19]

Starting in New York, he and his party toured the principal Eastern cities of United States and Canada. In Chicago General Sheridan met him to act as his escort there.[20]

Sheridan had received a telegram from General Sherman on November 1, 1871, requesting him to provide the Grand Duke with a buffalo hunt. General George Forsyth and Doctor Morris Asch were put in charge of the mess arrangements, Brigadier General Innis Palmer was placed in charge of the hunting party, while Generals Custer and Charles Fitzhugh were invited along.[21]

Buffalo Bill scholar and authority Don Russell states that Buffalo Bill was obtained via Sheridan's order to the commanding officer of the Fifth Cavalry "not to take Cody" on its expedition to the Arizona Territory about November, presumably so he could take him on the buffalo hunt.[22] Tucker reprinted a news story dated January 10, 1872, St. Louis, indicating that Cody had called on Alexis on Monday

(January 8th) and had "proffered his services as a leader and scout for the party during the proposed buffalo hunt." Alexis had "referred him to Sheridan. . . ."[23] It appears that Cody had planted the seed for this invitation which, if true, certainly helped make the hunting party a huge success.

Custer arrived at Ft. Leavenworth where he, in company with Phil and Mike Sheridan, continued on to Omaha. There General Sheridan became the official host to the Ducal party.[24] The arrival of the royal train was greeted by several thousand cheering people.

On the morning of January 13th the special train arrived at North Platte where the royal party disembarked and loaded into ambulances for the 50 mile trip to their camp on Red Willow Creek. Two companies of infantry, two companies of cavalry and the Second Cavalry's regimental band acted as an escort in addition to Brigadier General E.O.C. Ord and Lieutenant Colonels George and James Forsyth. Buffalo Bill Cody was there too, riding around on his well-trained buffalo horse Buckskin Joe.

The camp on Red Willow Creek was appropriately named Camp Alexis. It was here that Buffalo Bill had persuaded the Sioux chief Spotted Tail and 400 members of his tribe to camp near the Ducal party and its escort.

On the morning of January 14th the hunting party guided by Buffalo Bill set out for the buffalo herd. Every effort was made to give Alexis the first shot. Though a superb and almost reckless rider, he had some difficulty in bringing down a buffalo with his revolver. Bill loaned him Buckskin Joe and his rifle, Lucretia Borgia. After a few words of advice, he then gave Buckskin Joe a crack across the rump that drove him within ten feet of a buffalo bull. Alexis brought the animal down with the first shot. With that the hunt was on.[25]

That day and the next the Grand Duke brought down eight buffaloes each day. The evenings were spent in drinking champagne, listening to the band play and watching the Indians war dance. On the last day the Indians gave a demonstration of buffalo hunting with the bow and arrow that held a great deal of interest for the Ducal party.

On the 16th the hunting party took leave of the Sioux quite early in the morning, returning to North Platte to board their train for Denver.[26] Before leaving North Platte, Custer wired Libbie who was staying at the Galt House in Louisville:

> "All returned safe and well. Hunt a splendid success. Grand Duke killed three buffalo. I killed my horse. Gen. Sheridan & Staff & myself invited by Grand Duke to accompany him to Denver and the mountains returning via Kansas Pacific. We leave tonight at ten. Will Telegraph from Denver."[27]

GRAND DUKE ALEXIS OF RUSSIA visited the western Plains in early 1872 to engage in a buffalo hunt. General Custer and General Sheridan acted as hosts. Gurney photo, 1871. Library of Congress.

True to his word he sent a wire to the Galt House on January 19th:

> "Ball tonight. To Golden City & Mountains in morning. Start in evening for Kit Carson. Stop for buffalo hunt then to Topeka. Bos meets me there. All well."[28]

Word had gone ahead that the young duke enjoyed dancing. In each of the large cities he stopped at, it became a matter of form to hold a reception and grand ball. In Denver it was decided that another buffalo hunt could be held near the town of Kit Carson. All was in readiness when they arrived. At the suggestion of Sheridan, Alexis and Custer together would start the hunt. Once Alexis had brought down a buffalo, all of the rest took part in the sport.[29]

As the train moved on toward Topeka, numerous buffalo herds were seen. The Grand Duke and General Custer used each opportunity available to fire at them with their Spencer Rifles, the train moving at about 20 miles an hour and the herds often half a mile away.[30]

Following receptions, speeches and balls at Topeka and Jefferson City, the four Pullman cars of the Ducal train arrived at St. Louis. The festivities, hunting and late hours had taken their toll. Even the young nobleman asked that all invitations be declined so that he and his party could rest.

Custer had received a wire from a Louisville delegation reminding him:

"This is a good season to visit Mammoth Cave. Am instructed . . . to cordially invite the Ducal party, through you, to accept the hospitalities of our city. A grand ball will be given at the Galt House and suitable apartments prepared. A special train and cars will be provided for the Duke's trip to the cave and everything done to make his visit to our city pleasant. . . ."[31]

On January 24th Custer replied:

"His Imperial Highness the Grand Duke Alexis and suite will arrive in Louisville at 2 o'clock AM Tuesday. The Ducal Party desires to visit Mammoth Cave on Thursday and proceed to Memphis Thursday night."[32]

The train arrived in Louisville an hour late but this did not deter the interest and enthusiasm of the huge crowd that lined the streets to see the Russians. That evening "the Citizens of Louisville" gave a ball at the Galt House in honor of the Grand Duke.[33] Alexis was at his best. Though one of his first dances was with Libbie, he pleased many by changing partners with each dance though he was careful to select a pretty woman each time. Libbie, it was noted, received a great deal of attention from the courtly Admiral Possiet.[34]

On the morning of February 1st the special train carried the Ducal party to Mammoth Cave, stopping off at Elizabethtown to pick up General Custer. He had taken Libbie there the day before, and though she had been invited along, she had elected to stay and later accept the invitation of the Grand Duke to accompany the party to New Orleans.

Custer met the train mounted on one of his horses and accompanied by his magnificent pack of hounds. Alexis was delighted to see the pack and got off long enough to inspect them but not long enough for the mayor to give a speech he had prepared.[35]

On the trip to New Orleans Libbie acted as a chaperone to Colonel Sturgis' daughter Nina and to Colonel Blanton Duncan's daughter Mate. Colonel Duncan was a local politician and former Confederate officer. Libbie found the trip to be delightfully informal. She observed that all formal uniforms and ceremony had been dispensed with and that the only ceremony continued was the custom of the Grand Duke being the first to go to the table or to leave it.

She noted that the Russian gentlemen consumed quantities of wine without becoming boresome in conversation; the same amount taken by an American gentleman would be certain to subject his female companion to a lot of idiotic verbage.

She could not help noticing Admiral Poisset's attempts to interest Alexis in the towns, rivers and general topography. Alexis had little interest in geography; his interest was in anatomy—that of pretty girls—and music. It was apparent Libbie held Admiral Poisset in highest esteem. He was a man of sunny disposition and of simplicity in contrast to the younger Alexis with his shallow interests.[36]

The party arrived in New Orleans on Sunday, February 11th, in time for the Mardi Gras. Thirty guns were fired on the arrival. The Grand Duke remained for the numerous affairs in his honor, departing on the 20th for Pensacola, Florida, where his fleet was in anchor, the Custers returning to Elizabethtown.[37]

General Custer's sister Margaret had taken a liking to Lieutenant James Calhoun from the moment she had met him on her first visit to Fort Leavenworth. The liking had blossomed into love culminating in an announcement of marriage. The General and Libbie traveled north to Monroe in time to be present at their wedding in the Methodist Church, March 7, 1872.[38] Jim was then 26; Margaret was 20.

A month later Maggie, as the family affectionately called Margaret, wrote to her half-sister Ann Reed of her reactions to E-Town. She was just recovering from "another siege of headaches with chills and fever," an ailment that plagued her the rest of her life.

To her, Elizabethtown appeared a tiny old fashioned place though there were some very fashionable people there. She and her husband were staying at the Hill House with "Aunt Beck" Hill who she considered a "queer old soul but just as kind hearted as she could be." Aunt Beck addressed them individually as "my son" or "my daughter," and when they were together she would say "my children." At the table she lent an atmosphere of dignity by addressing Maggie as "Missus Culloon."

Maggie like Libbie was impressed with the great clock in the hotel parlor that reached "from the floor to within a few inches of the ceiling."

All in all, Maggie found their rooms very pleasant but "the greatest objection we have to *this* hotel is that breakfast hour is 7 o'clock. So you can imagine our morning naps are 'nipped in the bud'."[39]

Custer had planned on attending the reunion of the veterans of the War of 1812 in Monroe on July 4th. On June 4th, while in Lexington, he visited General Leslie Combs to invite him to participate in the reunion. The 81-year-old veteran accepted.[40]

A similar invitation had been extended to General Sheridan. Sheridan expressed his regrets since he had accepted an invitation to be in Madison, Wisconsin, on that same day.[41]

Custer had extended the invitation to General Combs as the result of a meeting in Monroe with the planning committee for the reunion. He had just returned to Monroe after attending a gala day in Detroit on April 9th. It was a meeting of Civil War veterans assembled in the Detroit Opera House to organize a Soldiers and Sailors Association.

Generals Burnside, Sheridan and Custer had been introduced to the audience and each had given a short speech. After Professor Griffith had read the poem "Sheridan's Ride"—which had been loudly applauded—Custer informed the audience that the horse that had carried Sheridan was a Michigan horse. The applause was even louder.[42]

General Leslie Combs and a delegation of nearly 100 Kentucky veterans of the War of 1812 arrived in Toledo on July 4th. Custer and the Monroe Committee of Invitation were there to meet them and act as an escort. Carriages waiting at the Monroe depot transported these old warriors to the Boyd Seminary where they were housed for their stay in Monroe.[43]

The reunion was held in the beautiful wooded Noble's Grove. The crowd that came to witness the event was estimated at between 15,000 and 20,000 people, coming mostly from Kentucky, Ohio and Michigan. General Custer, acting as the master of ceremonies, read a roll of the veterans. The loudest cheer rang out for Charles Hivon for he was 102 years old. Following the ceremony the 1813 battlegrounds were visited and the battle refought.[44]

In the middle of the following month Custer received a letter from Col. J. W. Hall advising him that the Stevens mine was producing ore of the same value as of the year before "carrying 200 ounces of silver per ton and 65 per cent lead."[45] Colonel Hall also advised him that Dibbon's poor health and consequent poor management was affecting its production.[46]

In the early part of February, 1873, Libbie took a trip to Michigan. Life had slowed down perceptibly to Custer's way of thinking. He had enjoyed his stay in Kentucky at first for the Kentuckians were hospitable and friendly and the living pace, though slow, had been acceptable. But he was a man of action not accustomed to a life as a desk jockey. He had worked steadily on his Galaxy articles and, in doing so, was constantly reminded of a life which up till then had been filled with action.

With Libbie gone the house seemed empty, and so did his life. He had rambled through the house and finally settled down to the old organ, pumping away and pecking out familiar tunes with his forefingers. At intervals he would consume an apple, then return to his musical endeavors pounding out "Let Us Have Peace" and "Oh, Who Will Care For Mother Now?"

Unable to stand it any longer, he resorted to his well-formed habit of writing to Libbie. On this occasion he informed her that this would be the last leave granted by this headquarters unless she took the command with her—namely, himself. He indicated his loneliness without hesitation: "This place is called Elizabethtown, but that is a mistake. The town is here, but not Elizabeth."[47]

NOTES — CHAPTER 23

1. G. A. Custer to Libbie, September 4, 1871; Merington, p. 240.
2. Theodore J. Crackel: *Custer's Kentucky: General George Armstrong Custer and Elizabethtown,* Kentucky 1871-1873, unpublished manuscript.
3. R. G. McMurtry: "The Two-Year Residence of General George A. Custer In Kentucky," *Kentucky Progress magazine,* Summer, 1933, p. 50.
4. Monroe *Commercial,* September 14, 1871.
5. G. A. Custer to Mother Custer, September 20, 1871, original in author's collection.
6. Merington, p. 241.
7. G. A. Custer to Mother Custer, September 20, 1871.
8. Libbie to G. A. Custer, (December 15, 1872), EBC-CBNM. Date has been established on this undated letter by Theodore Crackel.
9. R. G. McMurtry: "Two Year Residence," p. 33.
10. Merington, p. 243.
11. Alderney is a breed of cattle raised on an island by that name in the English Channel. It is apparent Custer referred to Alderney milk.
12. Monroe *Commercial,* February 8, 1872.
13. E. B. Custer: *Boots And Saddles,* N.Y., 1885, pp. 67-70.
14. Glendolin D. Wagner: *Old Neutriment,* Boston, 1934, p. 58.
15. *Ibid,* pp. 60-61.
16. *Ibid,* p. 59.
17. E. B. Custer: *Guidon,* p. 188.
18. W. W. Tucker: *His Imperial Highness The Grand Duke Alexis In The United States,* Cambridge, 1872, p. 9; Don Russell: *The Lives And Legends of Buffalo Bill,* Norman, 1960, p. 174.
19. Monroe *Commerical,* November 23, 1871.
20. Tucker, Chicago, December 31, 1871, pp. 128-29.
21. Carl C. Rister: *Border Command,* Norman, 1944, p. 168.
22. Russell: *Buffalo Bill,* p. 175.
23. Tucker, p. 150.
24. G. A. Custer to Libbie, January 11, 1872, BCWC collection.
25. Bayard H. Paine: *Pioneers, Indians, And Buffaloes,* Curtis, Nebr., 1935, p. 173; Tucker, p. 162; Russell, pp. 177-78.
26. Tucker, p. 177; Russell, p. 177 quotes Cody as estimating the entire hunting party as consisting of 500 people.
27. G. A. Custer to Libbie, January 17, 1872, BCWC collection.
28. G. A. Custer to Libbie, January 19, 1872, BCWC collection.
29. Tucker, Kit Carson, Colorado, January 21, 1872, pp. 184-85.
30. *Ibid,* p. 198.
31. Louisville *Courier Journal,* January 26, 1872, quoted from Crackel manuscript.
32. *Ibid.*
33. Invitation to the Ball, January 30, 1872, in author's collection; Tucker, p. 203.
34. Louisville *Courier-Journal,* February 4, 1872; New York *Herald,* February 5, 1872.
35. Louisville *Daily Ledger,* February 2, 1872; Elizabethtown *News,* June 12, 1936, quoted from Crackel manuscript.
36. Merington, pp. 246-47.
37. New Orleans *Daily Picayune,* February 11, 13, 1872; Tucker, pp. 212-221.
38. Monroe County Court House, Marriage Records; Monroe *Commercial,* August 17, 1876.
39. Margaret Calhoun to Ann Reed, April 5, 1872, BCWC collection.
40. G. A. Custer to John M. Bulkley, June 4, 1872, Burton Historical Collections; Monroe *Commerical,* June 6, 1872.
41. Burton Historical Collection, telegram of June 10, 1872.
42. Monroe *Commercial,* April 11, 1872.
43. Wing: *Monroe History,* p. 82.
44. Bulkley: *History of Monroe,* pp. 128-133.
45. Theodore H. Lowe to G. A. Custer, August 14, 1872, EBC-CBNM.
46. EBC-CBNM.
47. G. A. Custer to Libbie, February 9, 1873; Merington, pp. 243-44.

CHAPTER 24
FIRE AT FORT LINCOLN

With a shout General Custer leaped up from his chair, grasped Libbie by the waist and swung her to a standing position on the dining room table. Then he began to dance around the table in a fashion similar to that of an Indian dancing around his bound victim, emitting howls of jubilation as he did so. Libbie laughed joyfully for this was a repetition of a scene that followed every order for her husband to move.[1]

Earlier they had received orders to proceed to the Department of Texas but the orders this day had rescinded the previous ones and had given them 24 hours in which to pack preparatory to a move to Memphis and then up to the Department of Dakota.[2]

Once the boisterous cavalryman had given vent to his feelings, the packing began. Gunnysacks, barrels and hay were brought in. Kitchen utensils and dinnerware were thrust into the barrels and packed in hay, books and pictures were crowded into foot lockers, bedding was wrapped in canvas. In no time at all the waiting wagon was loaded.

To Custer this was a delightful moment. He was being relieved from a life of idleness and returned to one of activity with his beloved regiment. To Libbie "it meant months of loneliness, anxiety and terror," for the Indians in Dakota Territory had become restless and threatening.[3]

In the summer of 1872 Colonel David S. Stanley had commanded an escort for the survey party of the Northern Pacific Railroad. Hostile Indians led by the Uncpapa Sioux chief Gall forced Stanley and the chief engineer General Tom Rosser to terminate their efforts until a larger escort could be provided by the Government.[4]

Completion of the railroad survey was essential to the development of the Northwest. It was for that reason primarily that a larger escort — namely the Seventh Cavalry — was called forth to accompany the survey party in the summer of 1873. It had responsibilities other than that of protecting the survey crew. A scientific survey was to be made of the entire region, and sites for new military posts were to be determined.[5]

While the Seventh was assembling at Memphis Custer received orders to move to Fort Randall, Dakota Territory.[6] Additional orders provided that half of the command would embark at Memphis and the other half at Louisville, all to meet at Cairo, Illinois, where all would be transported by the Illinois Central Railroad to Yankton, Dakota Territory.[7] From there they would move to Fort Rice when weather conditions permitted.

Libbie and the other officers' wives were quite concerned about not being given permission to go along. Captain George Yates, no less eager to have his wife accompany him, managed to get Colonel Sturgis to intercede in behalf of the women. General Sheridan finally told him that "railroad transportation would be furnished to officers' families free and all extra baggage could go on free to Sioux City, and there would be sleeping cars and coaches with each train."[8]

Sheridan had said he would do all in his power for the families of the officers. "They should have all the law allowed and a damn sight more" if he could manage it. It appeared that Sturgis planned to leave the families at Sioux City since it was considered the best place to take the boat to Fort Rice. The news raised Libbie's spirits to such a degree she was "as light as air."[9]

The Illinois Central Railroad soon confirmed that two sleeping cars would be provided for the officers and their families from Cairo to Sioux City.[10]

Three steamers were used to carry the 800 or 900 men with as many horses to Cairo where the trains were met. The travel from there was slow, a week or more needed to reach their destination. Long stops were made each day to water and exercise the horses. On one such stop Custer's negro cook Mary surreptitiously purchased some steaks. The General obtained some macaroons in a bakery just as stealthily. These with baked potatoes and hot coffee were served in a surprise birthday dinner for Libbie on board the train that evening — it was April 8th.[11]

A mile out of Yankton the train came to a halt. It was open prairie devoid of wood or water, yet the most desirable spot available for their temporary camp. Autie advised Libbie to go into town to the hotel with the other ladies but she preferred remaining with her new puppies and cages of canaries and mocking birds. The thought of camp life caused no apprehension. This would be an experience she had endured many summers.

While she was seated on a foot locker in her tent, the temperature dropped and the rain began to fall. Dressed as she was in muslin, the drop in temperature, accompanied by a cold wind, made her very uncomfortable. An unfinished log cabin nearby had its appeal. After arrangement were made to rent it for a few days, Libbie and Mary stretched shawls and blankets upstairs, making two rooms out of it. There was no stove so Mary walked to town and purchased a cookstove but could not get it delivered until morning. As she returned the snow began to fall.[12]

The extremes of climate the soldiers had been subjected to had made many of them ill. Indefatigable as the General was, he showed signs of complete exhaustion and finally, illness. Libbie, unbeknown to him, sent for the regimental surgeon. He prescribed a medication to be taken every hour and with it complete bed rest. Autie, too sick to argue, complied.

Earlier he had issued orders through his new adjutant, Lieutenant James Calhoun, for all of the soldiers to take their horses and obtain shelter in Yankton. It took the men little time to seek homes and stables. Soon the camp was deserted.

Libbie in *Boots And Saddles*[13] describes the ascension of the great blizzard and the terror of her isolation that first night in the Dakotas in company with a very sick husband and her two servants Mary and Ham. Without heat of any kind they, in company with eight almost frozen soldiers, managed to survive 36 hours of complete imprisonment.

Once the snow had ceased falling a group of Yankton citizens led several officers to them with food and a stove. The shelter and assistance provided by the Yankton citizenry created a warm spot in the heart of every cavalryman.

On Thursday, April 17th, the citizens, in an additional display of true western hospitality, provided a reception for the Seventh Cavalry at Stone's Hall.[14] The days following passed rapidly while the men prepared for the 500 mile march ahead. When it came time to leave Custer gave Governor Burbank and his staff a review, a gesture received by Burbank and the citizenry with grateful enthusiasm. The townspeople gave the Seventh a rousing send-off that sunny May 7th.

The first few days of marching were shortened to gradually toughen the men and the animals for the long trek ahead. Several steamers accompanied them — the *Katie P. Kountz* carried 17 sick soldiers and the *Miner* carried forage and freight — tying up at the river bank each night close to the cavalry camp.[15]

Maggie Calhoun rode with her husband and Libbie rode, as usual, beside her Boy General. The rest of the officers' wives and the laundresses traveled on a steamer. The men marched in a long column of twos followed by a long line of white, canvas-covered supply wagons and a rear guard.

A noon halt to water the horses and eat lunch provided Autie with the opportunity for a quick nap. Libbie soon acquired her husband's knack of utilizing each such opportunity and, like him, she could drop off to sleep anywhere, be it on rough ground or in bright sunlight. The 15 minutes of deep sleep was a welcome change from the long, cramped hours in the saddle.

She never tired of reaching a high bluff to view "the long line of supply wagons, with their white covers, winding around bends in the road and climbing over hills." And she loved the sight of the evening camp with its grazing horses, unloaded wagons parked diagonally, overlapping each other to form a barricade against Indian attack, and the two long rows of tents. There was time to remove her riding habit, slip into a gown, then sit beside her man and sew while he read one of his well thumbed books.

There were pleasant sounds that Libbie would never forget. The clear evening air brought the low notes of the bugler practicing his calls, the whistling or singing of a happy trooper, or the clicking of a currycomb on the back of a horse. An accordion some trooper had managed to pack, the bray of the mules or the bay of the hounds over the voices of the officers as they smoked their pipes and conversed in their tents, all played their part in the unforgetable atmosphere.

The Dakota climate was hard on everyone, the dogs included. The Custers had their large pack of hounds with them. All had marked individuality of character which noticeably increased with this change. Each encountered the traumatic experience of a cactus needle in its paw. Custer would stop and remove each offending needle. The dogs soon learned to move through the cactused areas with the skill of a veteran G.I. crossing a mine field.

The dogs seemed to have the run of the camp. They gave Libbie a look of reproach if she attempted to tie shut the tent entrance. They would be on the bed, under the bed and "so thickly scattered over the floor" she had to walk carefully to avoid stepping on tails or toes.[16]

Then came the day they arrived at Fort Rice. The log buildings there were very crude but the commandant and his wife were hospitable. It was several days before a steamer arrived with their belongings and the regimental property. To their dismay they learned that everything had been standing uncovered on the Yankton Government wharfs during the stormy weather. Most of the clothing was mildewed and damp to a point of ruin. When

Lieutenant Calhoun, gentlemanly and reserved as he was, saw his soaked uniform and Maggie's ruined silk dresses, he excused himself and went outside the tent to relieve his pent up feelings. Libbie, on seeing her mildew-spotted wedding dress, was crushed. Autie viewed the ruin of his prized books and pictures quietly, then repeated a boyhood proverb in which he stored great faith: "Never cry for spilled milk." And that was that.[17]

Early that spring the officials of the Northern Pacific Railroad had petitioned the Government for a military escort to protect their survey crew along the uncompleted portion of their road extending westward. Though the engineers and surveyors of the Northern Pacific were under the personal direction of General Thomas L. Rosser, the military escort to accompany him was under the command of Colonel David S. Stanley, a major general of volunteers during the late war. Fort Rice was selected as the rendezvous point for the troops involved. When Libbie and the other ladies learned they would be left behind, and realizing they would get letters quicker if they could remain in Dakota rather than living in the East, all descended upon the bachelors at the post in an attempt to convince them they should be permitted to occupy the empty rooms in their quarters. The officers emphatically resisted any such attempt. There had been three women at the post for some time and no two spoke to each other. The men wanted no more of that. Since no tents were available there was only one place left for Libbie to go — home to Monroe.

The expedition left Fort Rice on June 20th. There were ten troops of the Seventh Cavalry, four companies of the Eighth Infantry and six of the Ninth Infantry, five companies of the Twenty-second Infantry, four companies of the Seventeenth Infantry, 75 scouts, two Rodman rifled guns and a large wagon train. Half of the cavalry was thrown out on the sides to protect the flanks of the moving wagon train.[18]

On the second day out Colonel Stanley, obviously under the influence of liquor, ordered the sutler John Baliran to leave the camp that night or he would hang him. Back at Fort Sully, in the presence of General Custer, Stanley had given Baliran permission to accompany the command. On this occasion Custer managed to intercede so that Baliran could continue to go along.[19] This act of kindness on Custer's part led to the undoing of the sutler.

On August 4th, Baliran in company with his friend the veterinary Dr. John Honsinger, while watering their horses at the Yellowstone River, were cut off by a band of Indians and killed.[20] A sizable engagement with the Indians ensued, the Seventh Cavalry taking a paramount part.

Late in June Custer told Libbie of his meeting with General Rosser on the Yellowstone and of the delightful times they were having together discussing their various engagements during the Civil War. While he spent the evenings with Tom Rosser the officers spent most of theirs in Dr. Honsinger's tent playing poker. Autie held all of his brother Tom's surplus funds for him at his request so that he would not be tempted to play. Jim Calhoun, with no such deterrent, played and lost consistently.[21]

Calhoun's luck continued bad. He just could not hold his own with good poker players. His brother Fred, who accompanied the expedition, and Tom Custer tried to reason with him but it was of no use. He tried to borrow from his brother-in-law Tom, who responded with: "Relationships don't count in poker. Bunkey or no bunkey, keep your hand out of my haversack."[22]

Libbie was delighted with Autie's 42 page letter. She had been out in a rapidly changing world almost ten years and had returned to a Monroe that had changed little. The town had remained virtually the same size it was when she had left in early 1864. The same small talk, the same petty interests and the same store fronts remained unchanged, while nearby Toledo and Detroit had been growing by leaps and bounds, though all three towns occupied points of seemingly equal opportunity on a navigable waterway. In fact, Monroe was the only one of the three located on Lake Erie as well as on a river.

Autie's letter had sent Libbie into "the seventh heaven of bliss." Nothing in Monroe interested her like her dear one's letters. Waiting for one to arrive on the one o'clock train took precedence over any invitation she might be offered. She still enjoyed the simple pleasures of Monroe but only his letters could sent her into such ecstacy. She was biding her time until they could be together again. There was no disinclination to tell him her true feelings so she wrote: "Though we have had our trials, you have had the blessed faculty of looking on the sunny side of things. Dear Autie, you are the richest of men."[23]

She told him she was sorry for Jim Calhoun and his compulsive gambling but was more than fearful he would take to drinking. She had hinted to Maggie what had been happening in the hope that she could restrain him.

The cavalry command reached the Yellowstone River on July 15th. At the mouth of Glendive Creek it found the steamer *Key West* loaded with their supplies.[24] While resting the men and waiting for the infantry to come up, Custer provided Libbie with an account of their activities. He told her that their old Monroe friend Fred Nims[25] had been given a place with the engineers at $60 a month through the efforts of General Rosser. It was his wish that some of the Monroe boys endowed with talent and education would break their ties and go west to try their fortunes. Then, as if to reassure Libbie, he stated: "Much as I dote on my profession and am devoted to it yet, should accident cut me adrift, I have no fear that energy and willingness to put my shoulder to the wheel would carry me through to a reasonable success."[26]

He expressed a liking for Lieutenant Fred Grant, the modest and unassuming son of President Grant. Fred had graduated from the Military Academy in June of 1871 and had been assigned as a second lieutenant in the Fourth Cavalry but had been ordered to accompany Custer's cavalry on this expedition. Custer enjoyed talking over West Point experiences with him and liked him in particular because he was so respectful of his mother's wishes.[27]

About July 25th, the steamer *Josephine* was sent down the Yellowstone loaded with supplies. By this time all those who had suffered from the change to the northern climate were in robust health. Custer, who easily acquired the "snuffles" elsewhere, had to admit that his sensitive throat had suffered no discomfort.

The marching had been delayed because of Stanley's intemperance. Ten such days had been totaled unnecessarily. With a steamer charging the Government $500 a day, it was enough to disgust General Rosser.[28]

In Monroe, Libbie had been reading some of the Associated Press accounts of his Indian fights along the Yellowstone. Stirred by mixed emotions — pride, anxiety and gratitude — she wrote immediately:

"I never can so fully realize the love I bear you till suddenly some news comes of your narrow escapes. . . . Oh my dearest boy, what a life of anxiety I have before me! My heart is so full of anxiety and care for your safety and so filled with terror at the terrible danger you have been in I cannot regain my cheerfulness.

"Autie, your career is something wonderful. Swept along as I am in the current of your eventful life I can still stop to realize that your history is simply marvelous. Every event seems to fit into every other event like the blocks in a child's puzzle. Does it not seem so strange to you? Can you realize what wonders come constantly to you while other men lead such tame lives?

"Autie, does it not occur to you that we are now enjoying honors and favors that most people have to wait till they are in the sun and yellow leaf before they ever attain? And what a charm it adds to glory and honor to have the freshness of youth to enjoy it in! Thank a kind Providence we reap *now,* in the bloom of youth, many of the privileges and honors that you have worked so hard for, for 13 years. But think of it Autie, so many of our most *brilliant men* have worked 30 and 40 years before being rewarded for their labors!"[29]

Libbie had no intention of permitting Autie to rest on these honors. It was her intention to direct his unlimited energy to a planned usefulness. So let us permit her to tell it as she actually did in a letter to Autie at this time:

"Now my darling, my ambition for you in the world of letters almost takes the heart out of my body I get so excited about it. Do not hope for a moment's peace from your bunkey. I am determined now you have made such a lucky, clever hit in your Galaxy articles that the public shall not lose sight of you. It is our greatest weapon to fight the devil of temptation called Idleness in army life. Now dearie, do not fail to keep notes of everything that happened. . . .

"I do not feel worried about your hunting. I even want you to hunt on every occasion but oh I do so beg you will not grow lax. Don't ever for my sake take less than 25 men for I know you must be closely followed by Indians."[30]

Libbie was one to nurture her sense of appreciation. When away from Autie for any length of time, once the amenities associated with a return to her family and friends had been disposed of, she tended toward introspection.

At the end of August she happened to meet an old sweetheart, attorney John Rauch. It suddenly dawned on her what a humdrum life she had escaped by not marrying him. She had to admit to Autie: "I own he makes an excellent husband but oh what a life I would have led! So monotonous, so commonplace —" Then she added: "Mother Custer is in low spirits. She worries about Nevie. His poor crops, his poverty, his increasing family. . . . But I mention this mostly for one thing. It is to tell you how I am perfectly overwhelmed with gratitude when I think what a glorious disposition yours is!"[31]

On August 29, Custer's command was ordered on to Fort Abraham Lincoln. They arrived there at sundown on September 21st.[32]

Custer had acquired a new interest. Since a part of the purpose of the expedition was to make a scientific survey of the entire region, a scientific party was attached. This included the zoologist J. A. Allen of the Cambridge Museum, the geologist Dr. L. R. Nettre, the Washington photographer W. R. Powell, the Cambridge artist Edward Konipucky and C. W. Bennet, a taxidermist. Allen and Bennet taught Custer how to prepare various animals and birds he had shot, thus introducing him to the art of taxidermy.[33] Many of these specimens he had collected and prepared were given to the Audubon Club of Detroit at a time his friend K. C. Barker was president of it.

The column of 275 wagons and ambulances accompanied by close to 1,800 men and some 2,300 horses and mules[34] had accomplished its mission. The return trip was a welcome anticlimax for all were eager to see the new post and settle down to what would be a dull but welcome routine. Custer had been told by the Fort Lincoln sutler Major Dickey that the new quarters for the calvary troops were the finest in the department, and that the commanding officer's house — which would be the post headquarters — was elegant. He relayed the information to Libbie and encouraged her to interest two attractive Monroe girls to go to Fort Lincoln with her for the winter.

Captain George Dandy, the Quartermaster, had done everything in his power to make the new home of the Custers comfortable. He had bypassed the usual hooks for clothing in the bedroom by installing several wardrobes. An unusual luxury was a basement uder a portion of the house, providing thereby a place for cold storage.[35]

Sheldon and Co., the publishers of Galaxy Magazine, had been after Custer to write more articles. His previous ones had stirred considerable comment and had given an impetus to circulation. His notoriety through his writings and the newspaper accounts of his exploits had them encouraging him to write a book. As an inducement they offered to get Theodore Davis to illustrate it. In writing one of his last letters to Libbie before going East to join her, Custer said: "I wonder if the Monroe people do not think the Galaxy articles have stopped because you are not with me to write them?"[36] This he wrote in the large railroad tent General Rosser gave him to live in until the new house was completed.

Libbie responded immediately. She told him she had been glad that she had not sold the house her father had left her. It had been ready for her to come back to when he went out into the field. It would have been a lonely place to stay in had Maggie not been there to stay with her, even if Maggie did awaken her every night by grating her teeth. The thought of rejoining Autie caused her to philosophize:

> "To think that I can look forward to a long freezing winter in the very dreariest spot I ever saw," she wrote him, "with such pleasure, but proves to me over and over again that you are *everything* to me. My 'all in all' in fact. . . . I enjoy your little slips of poetry so much. I have a few lines, part of a poem I read lately I want to send to you. You know I have often said I thought I missed you far more than you did me because I immediately settle down to such a quiet and often monotonous life while you rush into excitement and danger and new scenes —
>
> 'There's something in the parting hour
> Will chill the warmest heart—
> Yet kindred, comrades, lovers, friends,
> Are fated all to part:
> But this I've seen and many a pang
> Has pressed it on my mind—
> The one who goes is happier
> Than those he leaves behind.'"[37]

Autie managed to send Libbie his summer's savings — almost $500 — to deposit in the bank. It was a fortunate move for the postwar boom and prosperity came to a sudden end on September 18th. A disastrous panic began that shook once-sound financial institutions. But Custer had other things on his mind.

He had been offered a leave but refused the major part of it. There was to be activity around Fort Lincoln and he wanted to be there and ready when it came. He had most of his regiment with him now, and the rest would arrive with the spring. Then he would be ready for anything Sheridan ordered him to do.

Sheridan was expected to attend the reunion of the Army of the Tennessee to be held at Toledo, Ohio, on October 15, 16, 17 and 18. President Grant was invited to attend, and General Sherman would be there. Sheridan expected and insisted that Custer be there. There was no reason why he couldn't for Toledo was but 20 miles from Monroe where he was heading to see his parents and obtain Libbie.

Custer sent a wire to Libbie advising her he was on his way home but would stop off in Toledo to attend the reunion. Libbie impatiently took a train to Toledo to be there in advance of his arrival. While occupying her leisure time window shopping, she was suddenly swept off her feet and lifted into the air by a pair of strong arms. It was her husband. His face, except for the bearded area, was burned a ruddy red for his fair skin had refused to tan. Where he had shaved off his summer beard the skin was a mottled pink. Those officers traveling with him had said that only a man going to meet his sweetheart would attempt shaving in a Pullman car tearing along at 40 miles an hour.[38]

On the evening of October 16th there was a Grand Reception at the Opera House which was attended by President Grant, Secretary of War Belknap, Generals Sherman, Sheridan, Custer, Noyes, Hayes and Force. President Grant stood first in line at the entrance to the staircase with General Sheridan second, General Sherman third and General Custer fourth. The last three were in their dress uniforms. It was estimated that some 2,000 ladies shook hands with all four and about 25 per cent were kissed by them.[39]

On October 18th, Libbie and her husband returned to Monroe.[40] Several weeks later, after visiting friends in Kentucky and in Detroit, they bid their family and friends in Monroe goodbye and left for Bismarck, taking Agnes Bates of Monroe with them. They arrived there in the dead of winter on the last train of the season.

Bismarck, just five miles from Fort Lincoln, was the termination of the Northern Pacific Railroad. Libbie had taken a train East from there that spring after she and the other officers' wives saw their husbands prepare to depart on the Yellowstone Expedition. The town had a frontier reputation then but had become so lawless this last train was being loaded with the undesirables being shipped out. As she stepped off the train the outlaws were being forced on.[41]

It is interesting to note the comment of one historian of the area: "After the arrival of the Seventh Cavalry the character of the town (Bismarck) changed materially for the worse. New dance halls were open on Fourth Street and demimonde congregated there in large numbers and there was no cessation in the daily and nightly routine of revelry and wickedness."[42]

The swift flowing Missouri River was partially frozen so they were able to cross that part of it on foot. Where the current was the strongest no ice had formed. Terror stricken, Libbie and Agnes Bates stepped into a small boat rowed by two soldiers. A third warded off huge cakes of ice during the hazardous crossing. Once on solid ground, Libbie vowed never to get on that river again.[43]

Tom was there to meet them and drive them to their new home. As they approached it the regimental band played "Home Sweet Home," followed by "Garry Owen." They were greeted by an additional surprise. Before the General had gone East for her he had completely settled their new house. All five fireplaces were lighted, the garrison had turned out to welcome them and Mary, the Negro cook who had taken Eliza's place and had accompanied Custer on the summer expedition, had a grand supper waiting for them.

Fort Abe Lincoln had been built with quarters for six companies, thus providing housing for half of the regiment. The barracks faced the parade ground on the side toward the river. The officers' residences were on the opposite and faced the river.

The soldiers, receiving permission from the General, used the sawmill to prepare boards from unseasoned cottonwood to construct a building in which they could hold entertainments. A rude stage was illuminated by footlights of tallow candles. The scenery was painted on condemned canvas. Seats were backless wooden benches. Officers and their ladies were offered the front row and were followed by the enlisted personnel.

Many of the enlisted men were excellent performers, some having been professionals who, on being stranded, had enlisted. The Custers never failed to accept invitations to attend their performances.

The General at this time was 35 years of age, weighed 170 pounds and was near to six feet tall. He wore his wavy blond hair short and his tawny mustache long. A daughter of Lieutenant Frank Gibson observed: "The thin, florid face, though not handome, was singularly arresting, for it glowed with an expression of combined vitality and recklessness. . . . The General was a showman it seemed, and craved an audience for his spectacle—a full-dress parade and retreat. . . . it imparted a glamor to my army life that nothing else equalled."[44]

The General loved his hounds. He had about 40, and they were a sight to see on a hunt. The foxhounds were generally used in the timber and underbrush along the Missouri in the winter. The staghounds were his favorites on the chase for large game. The foxhounds were the noisier and would attempt to strike the bugler's keynote when he was sounding his calls, to the never ending amusement of the men.

One night not long after they had settled in their new quarters, Libbie was awakened by the unmistakable sound of fire in the room above their sleeping quarters. When Autie was upstairs attempting to determine the extent of the fire, he called to Libbie for a bucket of water, thinking he could extinguish the blaze. Libbie was in the rear of the house seeking water when she heard a crash and an explosion. Thinking he had been killed, she cried out to him. He answered, ending her momentary agony. He was unhurt though surrounded by fallen bricks and covered with plaster.[45]

A defective chimney had burst, the whole side of the room blowing out at the same time. A petroleum paper used as an insulator between the plastered inner wall and the wood outer surface had emitted a gas that had exploded and ignited the roof. That too had blown off with the sound of a cannon.

Agnes Bates was unaware of her danger until plaster had fallen on her bed. She and Libbie, wrapped in blankets, hurried next door to the Calhouns. There had been no time to gather clothes. Though the air was still and very cold, the house burned quickly. There was some water but no fire engine. Because there was no wind the garrison was saved.

It was a sorry mess they had to survey the next morning. There on the parade grounds were all their remaining worldly possessions — broken, torn or marred. No silver, linen or finery. Libbie took it all in stride, accepting all her losses philosophically except that of a collection of Civil War news clippings about her husband and a wig she had made from locks cut from his head when he gave up his long hair at the end of the war.[46] It was several days later, after the shock of their loss had lessened, Autie repeated his former admonition that it never paid to 'cry over spilled milk.'[47]

The ladies of the garrison immediately outfitted Agnes. A basket of apparel was sent over to her with an unsigned note that indicated she was "the daughter of the regiment."

The commissioned officers and the wives at the post formed a group of about 40. Isolated as they were from civilization, their best source of entertainment was each other, consequently they spent almost every evening together.

Custer had made it clear from the very beginning of the married life that he would rather not have any conversation in his home that was derogatory of others. Libbie admitted it was no effort for him to curb his tongue but it was, on occasion, a great struggle for her. When she insisted that she was not above such actions, as he seemed to believe she was,

VISITORS FROM MONROE brought out the single officers. Libbie thought every officer needed the stabilizing influence of a wife and did a lot of promoting for her idea. Left to right, *top row:* Mr. Swett, Libbie Custer, Maggie Calhoun, Lieut. James Calhoun, an orderly; *middle row:* unknown civilian, Nellie Wadsworth of Monroe, Lieut. Charles Varnum; *bottom row:* Lieut. Tom Custer, Emma Wadsworth of Monroe, General Custer. 1874. Author's collection.

he asked her to use him as a sounding board when she had an urge to criticize or gossip. How could she answer him when he opened his request with: "If you wish to please me?" She realized the necessity for the commanding officer to maintain social impartiality.[48]

Official matters were never discussed. Though kept uninformed, she was close enough to gather bits of information and draw her own conclusions. On one occasion she assured an officer she could get him a leave of absence so he could straighten out some business in a nearby town. When she made the request of her husband she was quietly reminded that he was in command and that the lieutenant could make application through the usual channels.

The General had his enemies. Some resented him because he was younger and had jumped over them in rank. Some had received his reprimands with resentment. Others had real or fancied grievances. And some just disliked him for no apparent reason. Libbie instinctively knew who disliked her husband. Perhaps the aura of warmth with which she surrounded him was like a sensor when the coldness of resentment or hate made contact with it. Inwardly she recoiled when she had to welcome someone she disliked. In the long run she had to welcome everyone since eventually everyone visited them. She felt dishonest when she was obliged to speak to any person she hated. Autie appealed to her by arguing that as the commanding officer's wife she should be hospitable on principle.

A formal shake of the hand was not sufficient. Since she was inclined to do so cooly Autie would give a burlesque imitation of the manner in which she had welcomed a known enemy. She had to laugh at the exposure of her lofty mannerisms, then resolved to do better to please him.

Libbie and Autie were deeply in love. There was no room for another unless it was Tom. Tom had his two Congressional Medals of Honor; Autie had Libbie.

There was rarely a day that Tom, Autie and Libbie did not have their romps. This display of boyishness had been evident after each engagement during the Civil War and after Autie had married.[49] The exhibition was quickly transformed into a scene of official or domestic tranquility when a caller was announced.

Life at Fort Abe during the winter months was relatively quiet compared to the activity of a summer campaign. Autie rarely left the house except to hunt. If the weather was severe he would occupy his time with writing or studying. The officers congregated at the sutler's store, playing cards or billiards there. Autie rarely went to the sutler's since the latter had loaned him a billiard table he had placed in an upper

A GATHERING AT THE NEW CUSTER HOUSE at Fort Lincoln. 1875. Left to right, *top row:* Bloody Knife, Libbie Custer, Mrs. James Calhoun, unknown, Lieut. James Calhoun; *seated:* Lieut. Tom Custer, unknown, Miss Emma Wadsworth of Monroe, Mr. Swett of Chicago, Lieut. Charles Varnum, Capt. Myles Keogh, Miss Nellie Wadsworth of Monroe, Mrs. Myles Moylan, Lieut. Charles DeRudio, unknown, unknown, General Custer. Author's collection.

room where he and Libbie would play a quiet game.

The General didn't need any close friends among his officers and didn't want any. He was the commanding officer, first, last and always. His could have been a lonely position but he had Libbie and Tom with whom he could relax. A distance had to be established, a discipline maintained, with all of the officers, including Tom and his adjutant and brother-in-law Jim Calhoun. Officers like Reno and Benteen appear to have resented this barrier, though it is more likely they resented the fact that he was a younger man ranking them as their commandant.

There were a number of officers who maintained a loyalty to Custer and did many little things to display it. As previously mentioned they were referred to as members of the "Custer Clan." The phrase usually was used in a derogatory sense tinged with envy.

Lieutenant James Calhoun, his adjutant, was a well-built man, erect of carriage, standing six feet one. His flaxen hair and mustache were in contrast to his hazel eyes. He was courtly in manner and somewhat reserved with strangers.

Lieutenant William Winan Cooke was as handsome as Calhoun and fully as large. His thoroughbred features gave him the appearance of an English aristocrat. In contrast to Calhoun's blondness he was a brunette with brown eyes and long side whiskers.[50]

Mrs. Fougera describes other members of the Custer Clan of which her father Lieutenant Frank Gibson was a respected member. Her mother's sister, Mollie Garrett, was married to Lieutenant Donald McIntosh. As an "army brat" she recalled that Lieutenant Benny Hodgson was a "dapper little officer"; that her uncle, Donald McIntosh, was quiet of voice and manner, with a brilliant mind. Everyone called him Tosh. She remembered Captain Myles Moylan's sandy mustache and that his wife Charlotte was plump, with blue eyes and fair hair. The wife of Custer's Monroe friend Captain George Yates was dark and slim and impressed her as being brainy and well read. Everyone called her Annie.[51]

Of Libbie she could not forget her first impressions: "Slim, girlish looking in a light-colored, out-of-date frock, she had quiet, intelligent eyes that met one with interest rather than criticism. Her skin was soft and smooth, but her face had more than prettiness. Character was written there, and when she smiled she warmed one with her friendliness."[52]

When her mother, Katie Garrett, was proposed to by Lieutenant Gibson, Libbie counseled her. She drew a picture, in her low, sweet voice, of life in drab stockade posts, ofttimes living with uncongenial people. She pointed out many deficiencies, inequities, deprivations, dangers and periods of loneliness, then ended by advising Katie that none of it mattered if she really loved her man.[53]

NOTES — CHAPTER 24

[1]Elizabeth B. Custer: *Boots And Saddles,* N.Y., 1885, pp. 11-12.
[2]General Orders No. 2, February 8, 1873; Chandler, p. 38; EBC-CBNM.
[3]Eliz. B. Custer: *Boots,* p. 13.
[4]Mark Brown: *The Plainsmen Of The Yellowstone,* N.Y., 1961, pp. 202-3.
[5]William H. Goetzmann: *Exploration And Empire,* N.Y., 1967, p. 415; New York *Daily Tribune,* June 28, 1873.
[6]Special Orders No. 13, February 25, 1873, EBC-CBNM.
[7]*Ibid;* Special Orders No. 50, March 11, 1873; and No. 14, March 13, 1873, EBC-CBNM.
[8]Libbie to Geo. A. Custer, February, 1873, BCWC collection.
[9]*Ibid.*
[10]Illinois Central Railroad to Assistant Quartermaster James Gillis, March 15, 1873, EBC-CBNM.
[11]Eliz. B. Custer: *Boots,* pp. 13-15.
[12]According to Chandler, p. 38, the trains carrying the Seventh arrived from April 10th to 13th. Custer, who always led his troops and, in this instance, as usual, had selected the camp site. It is presumed that he was on the first train that arrived April 10th. The Dakota (Yankton) *Herald,* April 15, 1873, indicated that the blizzard began Sunday, the 12th.
[13]pp. 21-27.
[14]Yankton Dakota *Herald,* April 22, 1873; on April 22nd the officers of the Seventh Cavalry met and drafted a resolution expressing thanks "to the citizens of Yankton, Dakota," for their generous and hospitable treatment during a snowstorm that imperiled their lives. From Mrs. Nettie Bowen Smith's Scrapbook in the Brancroft Library, University of California.
[15]Yankton Dakota *Herald,* May 13, 1873 and June 17, 1873; Eliz. B. Custer: *Boots,* p. 37.
[16]Eliz. B. Custer: *Boots,* p. 57.
[17]*Ibid,* p. 88.
[18]G. A. Custer's Yellowstone Expedition Log, BCWC collection, hereinafter called "Custer's Yellowstone Log."
[19]*Ibid.*
[20]*Ibid;* Chandler, p. 40.
[21]G. A. Custer to Libbie, June 26, 1873; Merington, p. 248.
[22]Merington, p. 253.
[23]Merington, p. 251.
[24]Custer's Yellowstone Log, BCWC collection.
[25]Lieutenant Fred Nims had served as aide-de-camp on Custer's Civil War staff. He was one of a three-member commission appointed by the Governor of Michigan in 1907 to erect an equestrian statue to General Custer.
[26]Merington, p. 257.
[27]*Ibid,* p. 249.
[28]*Ibid,* p. 260.
[29]Libbie to G. A. Custer, August 26, 1873, BCWC collection.
[30]Libbie to G. A. Custer, August, 1873, BCWC collection.
[31]Libbie to G. A. Custer, August 31, 1873, BCWC collection.
[32]Chandler, p. 40; Custer's Yellowstone Log.
[33]Goetzmann, p. 415.
[34]*Ibid;* Brown: *Plainsmen,* p. 203-204; D. S. Stanley: *Personal Memoirs,* Cambridge, 1917, pp. 244-45.
[35]Merington, pp. 263-64.
[36]G. A. Custer to Libbie, September 28, 1873, Yale University Library.
[37]Libbie to G. A. Custer, BCWC collection.
[38]Eliz. B. Custer: *Boots,* p. 93.
[39]Frost: *Custer Album,* pp. 114-115; *Frank Leslie's Illustrated Newspaper,* November 8, 1873; Toledo *Commercial,* October 17, 1873.
[40]Toledo *Commercial,* October 18, 1873.
[41]Eliz. B. Custer: *Boots,* p. 96.
[42]Jessamine S. Burgum: *Zezula,* Valley City, N.D., 1937, p. 101.
[43]Eliz. B. Custer: *Boots,* p. 97.
[44]Katherine Fougera: *With Custer's Cavalry,* Caldwell, 1942, pp.77-78.
[45]Eliz. B. Custer: *Boots,* p. 115. On February 7, 1874, pursuant to Special Orders No. 25, a board of officers presided over by Lieutenant Colonel William Carlin, 17th Infantry, investigated the cause of the fire in the commanding officer's quarters on the night of February 6th. The fire had been discovered by General Custer at 3:30 A.M. of February 6th "on the floor of the attic room. . . Three feet from the chimney. . . ." In an attempt to gain control of it he threw water on it until it exploded. When the alarm was given "the Guard and men of the Garrison soon appeared and managed to save most of the effects on the lower floor." The Board observed that the chimney, which was built completely within the house was built of a single thickness of bricks through the ceiling. There was evidence of smoke escaping through the side walls. Coal-oil paper had been used as insulation. It apparently caught fire at the chimney and was conducted throughout the house acting like a fuse. The Board found Custer in no way responsible. BCWC collection.

On February 9th, Custer wrote to his mother the particulars of the fire. Everything on the lower floor was saved though scarcely a thing from the upper. They saved nearly all their furniture, dishes, carpets, chairs and books. Libbie lost all her clothing—12 dresses, four which cost between $150 and $200 each. Just a few of her every day articles were saved. Nearly all of Custer's clothes were saved; none of Agnes' clothes were saved, she escaping in her nightdress. Custer thought they were very fortunate: "to save so much as we did and have an abundance left for all their wants. It is better that we should have been burned out than that the calamity should have fallen upon others here." Original letter in author's collection.
[46]Eliz. B. Custer: *Boots,* pp. 116-17.
[47]*Ibid,* p. 119.
[48]*Ibid,* pp. 138-39.
[49]Frederick Dellenbaugh: *George Armstrong Custer,* N.Y., 1917, pp. VI.
[50]Mrs. James Calhoun: "The Personnel of Some Officers of the Seventh Cavalry," an unpublished article in the author's collection.
[51]Katherine Fougera: *With Custer's Cavalry,* pp. 69, 72, 74, 76.
[52]*Ibid,* p. 85.
[53]*Ibid,* p. 137.

CHAPTER 25
GOLD IN THE GRASS ROOTS

For some time Indian bands had been raiding settlements in the territory and had grown so bold as to run off a drove of mules belonging to a Government contractor who kept them at Fort Lincoln for drawing the army supply wagons.[1] The story of the Government's treatment of the Indians had been a sordid one. Broken treaties, the appointment of dishonest or incompetent Indian agents, dishonest judicial and ineffective law enforcement systems, played a major role in the Indians' reactive raids. The major blame for it all rested upon the apathy in Washington. In no way was the army responsible. The only part it played was that of obeying orders.

General Sheridan had recommended, in his annual report of 1873, that a large military base be established at the margin of the Black Hills "to secure a strong foothold in the heart of the Sioux Country and thereby exercise a controlling influence over these warlike people."[2] It was obvious he considered the Sioux the perpetrators of all Indian depredations in the territory.

On approval of his recommendation Sheridan ordered General Alfred Terry to prepare an expeditionary force, placing Custer in charge. Custer had displayed his capabilities while in command of a large body of men in unexplored terrain, even under the restraint of an inebriated commanding officer (Stanley). On this expedition he would be in complete charge. He had expressed a desire on many occasions to explore the Black Hills and had made known, through military channels, his impression that "it would open up a rich vein of wealth calculated to increase the commercial prosperity of this country."[3]

Custer, as usual, was meticulous in his preparations. In the latter part of April he had written to Sheridan giving him a breakdown of the costs involved, all in an effort to induce him to approve of the reconnaissance. He advised Sheridan: "It will be seen that my statement made to you last fall that the proposed reconnaissance can be made and result in an actual saving to the Government was absolutely correct."[4] It was suggested that Sandy Forsyth and Fred Grant be permitted to go along.

A month earlier, Custer had written to Terry advising him of an advertisement appearing in the Bismarck *Tribune* that called for "contributions of supplies and ammunition to a party of 50 men who proposed to start from here by the middle of next month for the alleged purpose of exploring the Black Hills for minerals." The leader of the party, according to Custer, was an irresponsible character and the keeper of a bawdy house opposite the post. It was a matter of great concern that this party of irresponsible men was inviting destruction by the Indians and would bring on future trouble.

In response Terry sent a telegram ordering Custer to notify all civilians in the area that no persons would be permitted to invade the Black Hills and, if necessary, the military would be employed to prevent it. Once this was publicized the civilians prudently abandoned their plans.[5]

Once it appeared beyond all question that the expedition would be a certainty, Custer wrote to his good friend Lawrence Barrett inviting him to accompany them. He had received definite orders from Sheridan on May 18th, he told Barrett, and would start out not later than June 15th, to be gone for two months.

"The expedition is entirely peaceful in its object" he continued, "it being the intention to explore the country known as the Black Hills and gain some knowledge as to the nature of the latter. For many years it has been believed from statements made by the Indians that the Black Hills are rich in minerals . . . . I say that our object is a peaceful one but I have no idea that our trip will be so. The Indians have long opposed all effort of white men to enter the Black Hills and I feel confident that the Sioux will combine their entire strength and endeavor to oppose us. I will have a well-equipped force however strong enough to take care of itself and of its friends who will know us by their presence."[6]

Press of obligations prevented Barrett from sharing Custer's tent.

The Seventh Cavalry had been issued new revolvers but was delayed in leaving, at the request of Terry, until the new .45 calibre Springfield carbines arrived. These were issued in time to leave on July 2d. The force of about 1,000 men consisted of ten companies of the Seventh Cavalry, one each of the Seventeenth and Twentieth Infantry, a detachment of scouts, guides, interpreters and teamsters. There were 110 wagons and ambulances. In heavy weapons there were three Gatling Guns and a 3-inch rifle.[7] There were 1,000 cavalry horses, 600 mules and 300 beeves. Unquestionably this was the best equipped expedition that had ever been outfitted for service on the plains.[8]

Accompanying them were Captain William Ludlow as chief engineer, Professor N. H. Winchell as geologist, George Bird Grinnell as naturalist with Lute North as his assistant, Dr. J. W. Williams as chief medical officer and botanist, William Illingworth as photographer, Horatio Ross and William McKay as practical miners. Major George Forsyth and Lieutenant Fred Grant arrived in time to go along.[9]

By the 15th of July the expedition was well within the boundaries of the Black Hills. The plentiful game, the abundance of wood and potable water and the excellent grazing were a wonder to all. The health of the command was remarkable, and no Indians had been encountered until two days earlier, and those were seen observing them from a distance. The scientists were making all sorts of important discoveries and observations and the soldiers were taking it as a pleasure excursion.[10] At this point they had traveled 227 miles from Fort Lincoln.

At their camping spot in Prospect Valley that day, Autie prepared a letter to Libbie informing her of much that had transpired. He told her of the beautiful country and interesting sights they had seen and of a large cave they had discovered that he had named after Ludlow. The walls were covered with numerous drawings some of which mystified him—those of ships.[11]

He was now satisfied that the commanding officer could exercise an influence for good or evil; card playing and drunkenness had been nonexistent amongst his officers from the moment they had left Fort Lincoln. Had he played cards with the officers there would have been gambling each night. As for drinking, he had seen the effect Stanley had had on his own staff the previous summer.

Practical jokester that he was, Autie could not refrain from telling Libbie about some practical joke played successfully on Tom or his other brother Bos (Boston). In this case it was on 25 year-old Bos who was on his first expedition. Good natured Bos was taking all of the jokes played on him in stride. He had been assigned a mule that had a poky gait. Autie told her:

"The land was undulating. . . . Bos rode beside me, and I invented an excuse to go in advance; I made *Vic* gallop slowly over the divide, and when out of sight on the other side I put spurs to him and dashed through the low ground. When Bos came in sight I was slowly ambling up the next divide and calling to him to come on. He spurred his mule, shouted to him, and waved his arms and legs to incite him to a faster gait. When he neared me I disappeared over another divide and, giving *Vic* the rein, only slackened when it became time for Bos to appear. Then, when I had brought my horse down to a walk I called out, 'Why on earth don't you come on?' Believing that the gait he saw me take had been unvarying, he could not understand why I lengthened the distance between us so rapidly. I kept this up until he discovered my joke and I was obliged to ride back to join him and suit *Vic's* steps to those of his exhausted mule."[12]

On one occasion Tom victimized poor Bos by giving him some stones he said were sponge stones, claiming they would soften if soaked in water for a certain period of time. Bos did this for a few nights before he realized he had been taken in by Tom.[13]

On the morning of August 2d the prospectors accompanying the expedition discovered gold.[14] That evening Custer prepared a report for General Terry. He summed up his observations of the rich soil, abundance of timber and shrubbery, pure water and excellent grazing by saying: "I know of no portion of our country where nature has done so much to prepare homes for husbandmen, and left so little for the latter to do, as here."[15]

He omitted any references to the geologists' findings, leaving that until the expedition had concluded its work, but went on to say what he thought would soon appear in public print:

"Gold had been found at several places, and it is the belief of those who are giving their attention to this subject that it will be found in paying quantities. I have upon my table 40 or 50 small particles of pure gold, in size averaging that of a small pinhead, and most of it obtained today from one panful of earth. . . . Until further examination is made regarding the richness of the gold, no opinion should be formed."[16]

Charley Reynolds, one of the guides, had the assignment of carrying the dispatch to Fort Laramie. It was a hazardous undertaking at best but none was better qualified for such dangerous work.

This young man had acquired considerable fame as a frontier guide and hunter. He was five years Custer's junior. Heavy set, about five feet eight inches tall, and quiet by nature, he was less known than other professional hunters though Custer held him in high regard. At one time he had kept both Fort Rice and Fort Stevenson supplied with meat.[17]

Libbie wrote an interesting account of him in *Boots and Saddles:*

"My husband had such genuine admiration for him that I soon learned to listen to everything pertaining to his life with marked interest. He was so shy that he hardly raised his eyes when I extended my hand at the General's introduction. He did not assume the picturesque dress, long hair, belt full of weapons that are characteristic of the scout. His manner was perfectly simple and straightforward, and he would not be induced to talk of himself. He had large, dark blue eyes, and a frank face.

"Charley Reynolds undertook to carry dispatches through to Fort Laramie, over 150 miles distant. He had only his compass to guide him, for there was not even a trail. During the day he hid his horse as well as he could in the underbrush, and lay down in the long grass. In spite of these precautions he was sometimes so exposed that he could hear the voices of Indians passing near. He often crossed Indian trails on his journey. The last nights of his march he was compelled to walk, as his horse was exhausted and he found no water for hours. . . . His lips became so parched and his throat so swollen that he could not close his mouth. In this condition he reached Fort Laramie and delivered his despatches."[18]

On his return to Fort Lincoln Reynolds was intercepted at Sioux City by reporters and asked about the rumors of gold. Like Custer he played it down but the enthusiasm of the citizens, aroused by the dispatches of the reporters attached to the expedition, could not be subdued. The bizarre and highly exaggerated reports in the newspapers had excited an interest in gold to a fever pitch.[19]

The reconnaissance of the Black Hills had occasioned great apprehension among the Sioux. To them it was a grave infraction of the treaty stipulations of 1868. They feared that this sacred ground they regarded as their home and refuge, because of the exaggerated accounts of the mineral wealth and rich soil within, would soon be overrun by the whites.[20]

During this time Custer began his return toward Fort Lincoln and, upon reaching Bear Butte, sent General Terry a dispatch bringing him up to date. It was now August 15th; he expected to reach Fort Lincoln on the 31st. He reported that the Black Hills were not impenetrable, the only obstacles encountered being near the outer base. He considered its pure water and pasturage the best in United States and, in general, an excellent area for farming and stock raising. Then referring to his former dispatch in which he mentioned gold being discovered, he concluded:

"Subsequent examinations at numerous points confirm and strengthen the fact of the existence of gold in the Black Hills. On some of the water courses almost every panful of earth produces gold in small, yet paying, quantities. . . . The miners report that they found gold among the roots of the grass and, from that point to the lowest point reached, gold was found in paying quantities. . . We have had no collision with hostile Indians."[21]

POSING WITH A FRIEND. Libbie Custer, Brigadier General Custer and a friend have a varying interest in the book before them. Author's collection.

With this dispatch to Terry went the letters of the officers and men on the "Black Hills Express," as the Indian scouts who carried the mail were dubbed. And with them went one addressed on the first letter sheet within the official looking envelope, "My Darling Sunbeam." Autie wrote with pride of the success of the explorations and almost with equal pride that he had "reached the hunter's highest round of fame. . . . I have killed my Grizzly."[22]

On August 30th, the 60th day of the expedition, the wagon train reached Fort Lincoln, having traveled 883 miles.[23] When the long train approached the post, the band that had accompanied it played the regimental marching tune, "Garry Owen." Libbie hid behind the door as the command rode into the garrison, too ashamed to be seen alternately laughing and crying in her joy at Autie's safe return. Unable to hold back any longer, she skipped down the steps and threw herself into her husband's arms oblivious to the thousand onlookers who had marched in with him. When a thousand throats burst into a cheer she became aware there were others present. This unusual reaction on the part of the soldiers caused her to momentarily lose her poise and become embarrassed. They all had loved her before; now they loved her more than ever.[24]

General Custer may have been satisfied with the discoveries made under his aegis but it brought no satisfaction to the Sioux. They had been observing his movements with uneasiness, well aware that it meant nothing but trouble ultimately. They had intercepted prospectors and hunters numerous times. As Special Indian Commissioner Chris Cox said:

"The glowing reports of General Custer (whether true or false) have aroused the frontier, and scores of organizations, more or less extended, are preparing to visit the Black Hills in the coming spring. Already small parties have ventured into the forbidden region and bloodshed has been the result. The tide of emigration cannot be restrained. The exodus will be effected. It may cost blood, but the ultimate occupation of this unceded territory by the white settlers is inevitable."[25]

Cox, as an Indian Commissioner, strangely enough, proceeded to recommend the opening of the Black Hills to settlers. Captain Ludlow, Army officer that he was, recommended in his final report:"It is probable that the best use to be made of the Black Hills for the next 50 years would be as the permanent reservation of the Sioux. . . ." He drew attention to the fact that the region was cherished by the owners as a hunting grounds and asylum which they, the Sioux, look forward to occupying as a future permanent home, the occupation of which by whites would not be tolerated.[26]

At first the Army did its best to drive out all trespassers. An instance of such an attempt was the order Terry issued to the commandant at Fort Ellis on August 18th. Terry had received a report that a party of miners was leaving Bozeman for the Black Hills. He wanted the party overtaken, their wagons burned, the men disarmed and the leaders arrested.[27]

There were repeated warnings from Secretary of War William Belknap to would-be trespassers, and repeated arrests by the military. Unfortunately those arrested were turned over to non-military courts who sympathized with the prospectors and released them.[28]

Custer had left Fort Lincoln in early July well-known as a popular writer, hunter and Indian fighter. On his return 60 days later he had additional laurels as an explorer and discoverer of gold. It was this last that created an air of ill-feeling.

The do-gooders had censured his attack on Black Kettle's camp on the Washita. These same "humanitarians" now charged him with fomenting a war by inciting a gold rush on Indian land.

As if to throw more fuel on the fire, General William B. Hazen took issue publicly with laudatory statements Custer had made in the spring of 1874[29] relative to his observations of the climate and land along the course of the Northern Pacific Railroad. Hazen condemned the land, climate and Custer's laudatory statements.[30]

Early in September the General and Libbie departed for Monroe, taking Agnes Bates back to her parents.[31] The officers all pressed Libbie to bring back another girl. It was going to be a long, lonely winter for them at Fort Abe.

After visiting family and friends they made a brief visit to Chicago where they attended the wedding of Frederick Dent Grant and Ida Marie Honore'. Ida Honore' was the sister of Mrs. Potter Palmer whose husband owned the Palmer House. The quiet, dark haired Ida was drawn to the irresistible Fred just as he was attracted to her. Their short engagement ended in a marriage in her Chicago home October 20, 1874. Many notables were present including, of course, the President and Mrs. Grant, General Sheridan and his staff in full dress uniform, the Cyrus McCormicks, the A. E. Bories, the Charles B. Farwells, the Custers and many other people of note. Fred, now 24 years old, had met Ida that spring while stationed in Chicago as a member of Sheridan's staff.[32]

Back in Monroe Libbie campaigned for the single officers in the Fort Lincoln garrison by scouting for pretty girls to bring back with them. She managed to convince the Boyds that their daughter Florence would be in safe hands while in the West.

Finding the General's parents well situated in the old Bacon house gave Libbie a feeling of satisfaction. She knew the parting would be painful to her husband, for he never knew but what it would be the last time he would see his ailing mother, but she knew he would leave happy in the thought that they had greater comforts there in town than would be available out in the country on a farm.

On November 7th they boarded the train for his winter quarters in the West. It was not an entirely sorrowful parting for he had learned shortly before leaving that his book *"Life On The Plains"* was "now in published form, making a volume of 256 pages, handsomely bound and attractively embellished."[33]

The winters at Fort Lincoln were pretty much the same. The Custer home was the center of activity for the circle of 40. Music and games helped while away the evenings.

A piano had been rented at St. Paul and added much to their enjoyment. Though many of the women could play, Maggie Calhoun had been well-trained at the Boyd Seminary in Monroe and was an accomplished pianist. Maggie was in constant demand.

They sang songs everyone knew—war songs, college songs, Negro spirituals. Hymns on Sundays were their only means of worship.

Libbie had a deep feeling of pity for the officers. After the extreme activity of the mild weather months, winter was a period of dead calm, of complete boredom. She marveled how so many of them weathered this time of year with its temptations. She felt that if she had the misfortune to be a man she could not have borne the tests to which they were subjected.[34]

The women had many simple occupations to interest them while the men had none that provided any satisfaction. There were libraries for the infantry posts but none for the cavalry. The books available were those brought back by officers on leave, and those were circulated until they became tattered.[35]

The loneliness of the men had one redeeming feature. The women at the post were placed upon a pedestal. The men were grateful to the women for the slightest kindness and, in Libbie's opinion, they overrated anything the women did or accomplished.

Libbie said she dreaded the arrival of the young officers coming directly from West Point, knowing well the temptations they would face that first drab, inactive winter. She hoped they didn't drink and had the stamina to resist evil, for Bismarck was known for its dens of iniquity.

Maggie was aware of Libbie's indelible belief that matrimony was the means of saving young officers. Maggie—a tease like the rest of the Custers—would accuse her of greeting the young officers with: "I am very glad to see you; I hope that you are engaged." Libbie wouldn't admit to saying it but did go so far as to say she thought along that line.[36]

The very close contact of the group day after day, year in and year out, through hardship, danger and deprivation, brought them together like a large family. There were times when the joking or teasing went too far but it taught self control. As Libbie expressed it:

> "Certainly it was excellent discipline, and calculated to keep one's self-confidence within bounds. It was the same sort of training that members of a large family have, and they profit by the friction, for they are rarely so selfish and exacting as only children usually are."[37]

Autie loved life. He would throw himself on the rug in front of the fireplace and reflect on his blessings. He would enumerate them in front of Libbie. First and foremost came the regiment, then the five posts in his district. His hunting, his dogs and horses, and the very room he was in was a delight to him for Libbie was there.

He thoroughly enjoyed the presence of his family, particularly Tom. In the spring of 1876 he had said of him to some friends: "To prove to you how I value and admire my brother as a soldier, I think that he should be the general and I the captain."[38] Yet no favoritism was ever shown. To the contrary, in an effort not to show partiality he would notice Tom's smallest misdemeanor.

In recollecting these delightful winters together Libbie never knew her husband to have an hour's depression. There was a reason for it, she recalled: "My husband used to tell me that he believed he was the happiest man on earth, and I cannot help thinking he was."[39]

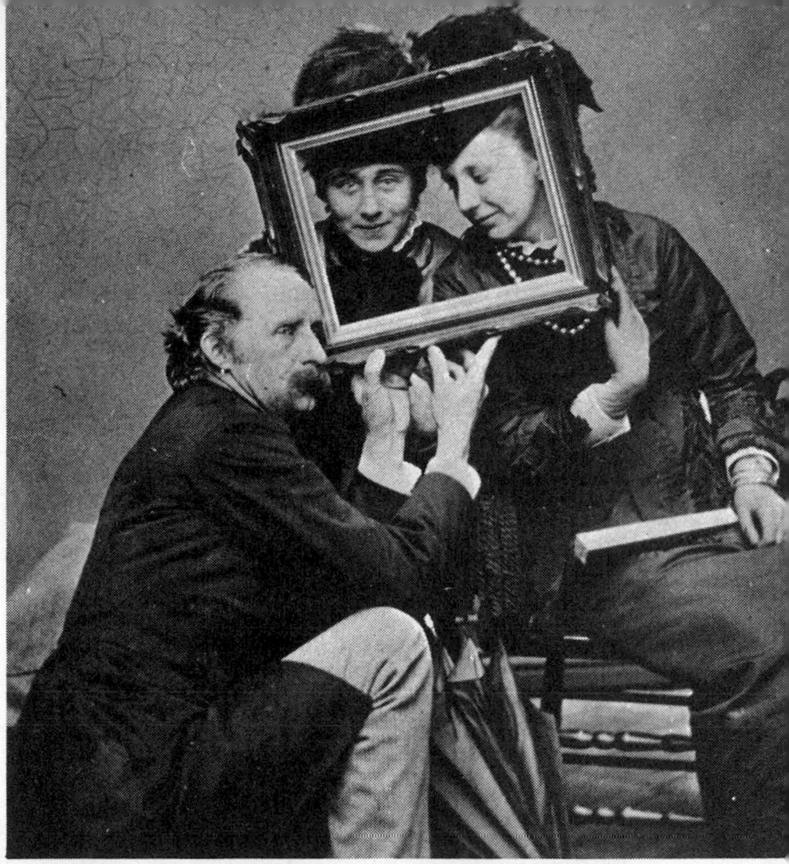

FRAMED BY A GENERAL, and the two Bates girls from Monroe enjoy it. From a tintype in the author's collection.

Custer had studied the art of communication well. He was a natural showman and, recognizing this characteristic in himself, used it purposefully. The bizarre uniform and red necktie he wore when he first led the Michigan Cavalry Brigade at Gettysburg were planned to attract the attention of his men and to communicate to them who he was, where he was and his willingness to share their dangers. He was willing to attract the enemy fire as a calculated risk in an effort to inspire his men. His long, blond hair served a similar purpose when he held lesser rank.

In 1867 as an embryo Indian fighter he studied the ways of the Indians and learned to communicate with them in their universal sign language. He found he had received preliminary training in it by accident when he had learned to communicate with the children at the deaf and dumb institute while stationed in Texas during the Reconstruction. These children and the Indians, it was observed, used hand signs remarkably similar.

The Sioux chiefs visited him at various times at Fort Lincoln to confer with him about their problems. Running Antelope and other equally eloquent Sioux would tell him how they were being cheated by dishonest Indian agents[40] out of Government food due their people. They would ask him to keep the white men out of the Black Hills as it might bring on war. They cherished the land and said they would fight to keep this land which was theirs by all rights. When they had left he said to Libbie: "The Government must keep its promises to the Indians."[41]

In later years Libbie would recall: "He recognized a true nobility in the Indian character and respected their feelings of attachment for their land. There was a time after the battle of the Little Big Horn when I would not have said this, but as the years passed I have become convinced that the Indians were deeply wronged."[42]

He was not one of those who favored taking the Black Hills ruthlessly away from the Indians. Colonel Charles Frances Bates quoted Custer in an article from the New York *Herald,* 1875, as saying:

> The success of the reservation system depends on the Government keeping its promises.... The Indians have a strong attachment for the lands containing the bones of their ancestors and dislike to leave it. Love of country is almost a religion with them. It is not the value of the land that they consider; but there is a strong local attachment that the white man does not feel, and consequently does not respect. . . . He (the Indian) keenly feels the injustice that has been done him and, being of a proud and haughty nature, he resents it."[43]

As Libbie had said: "He was a sincere friend of the reservation Indian."[44] All of his acts in attempts to aid them point to that. He was tolerant of them; he respected them as highly skilled adversaries in time of war. His intercourse with them led him to conclude:

> "If I were an Indian, I often think I would greatly prefer to cast my lot among those of my people adhered to the free open plains rather than submit to the confined limits of a reservation, there to be the recipient of the blessed benefits of civilization, with its vices thrown in without stint or measure."[45]

Spring brought welcome relief from the monotony of garrison life but only to the extent that the Seventh was used to chase bands of Indians that had gathered up stock from the settlements and run them off. Attempts to round them up generally were unsuccessful.[46]

Custer had written off his investment in the Stevens Mine in Colorado. He had heard from Colonel Hall back in August of 1874 about the Crescent Company trespassing and taking out $15,000 worth of ore from the mine. Hall was enjoining the Crescent Company on his own. It was said that Dibbon had died.[47] There had been no one left to keep an eye on the valuable property. For some time Custer heard nothing more, then in February Hall had written that he had lost all track of Custer, that Dibbon was alive, and that he, Hall, was in court trying to clear title to the mine.[48]

A month later he received another communication from Hall indicating that he "now had complete title to the Stevens Mine. I have always considered your interest in the Stevens and shall divide my interest with you under any and all circumstances."[49]

Whether this declaration on the part of Colonel Hall had anything to do with Custer remembering an unpaid debt he decided to pay the editor of the Louisville *Courier-Journal* is hard to say. Editor H. Walterson replied on April 5, 1875, that he had received the draft but could not recall any such debt, then concluded: "I make it a rule never to refuse money."[50] It is more than likely Custer had sent the draft before Hall had written him and was a bit flush through inability to spend his pay during the confining winter. The Custers were not of a disposition to save money.

Another Black Hills expedition conducted by geologist Walter P. Jenney and Henry Newton, and escorted by 400 soldiers under command of Lieutenant Colonel Richard I. Dodge, left Fort Laramie on May 25, 1875, to obtain additional geological and agricultural information. Jenney found prospectors mining on French Creek when he reached the Black Hills. Hundreds of miners accompanied him into the area.[51] His final report to the Commissioner of Indian Affairs, who had requested him to make the survey, was modest in its claims regarding gold though it substantiated Custer's report of the year before.

Prior to the appointment of the Dodge escort it had been rumored that Custer and the Seventh were to be the Jenney expedition escort.

James Bennett, enterprising publisher of the New York *Herald,* had informed Custer he had no correspondent in the West. "I therefore apply to you to keep the *Herald* ahead on all matters connected with the (proposed Black Hills) expedition. Can write over your own name of a *nom de plume.* Of course I shall be willing to pay you for whatever you send and which is printed. . . . In case you can accept please telegraph simply the word 'Alta.' If you can not accept, suggest another competent officer who would and telegraph the word "Gams" with the officer's name and rank."[52] Custer accepted.

The selection of Colonel Dodge to escort Jenney left Custer free to visit New York in a search for funds to develop the Stevens Mine. On April 27th he left, taking Florence Boyd as far as Monroe.[53] While in New York City he received word of the death of his dear friend K. C. Barker.[54] Barker and three friends drowned in the Detroit River when his yacht capsized. On his return from New York, Custer stopped off in Monroe to visit his parents. The Wadsworth girls—Emma and Nellie—accompanied him back to Fort Lincoln.

Late in September the Custers made their way East accompanied by Tom and his close friend Lieutenant Cooke. Libbie stopped off in Monroe while Autie proceeded to New York.[55] All visited the imposing new home David Reed had built on the corner of Monroe and Fourth streets just two blocks south of the Methodist Church. Of particular interest to the community was an unusual ornamental ironwork fence surrounding it that had been fashioned by the Raisin Foundry. The Monore *Commercial* had proclaimed the residence the handsomest in the community.[56]

Libbie visited the Richmonds in Grand Rapids soon after Autie left, then went on to Canandaigua, New York, to visit relatives there.[57] On her way to join her husband in New York City she stopped off a few days at Camillus to visit the Cases.[58]

Tom and Cooke had gone on to New York with Autie and were having the time of their lives. Single and uninhibited, they enjoyed everything while Autie enjoyed New York in his own way. He had gone there for purposes of investment. Having had his leave extended for two additional months, he intended making the most of it while his money held out.[59]

Lawrence Barrett was playing in *Julius Caesar.* For two nights these two friends sat side by side in Barrett's dressing room during a portion of the performance in which Barrett had a long wait. Autie was his most admiring and interested listener at each performance.[60]

Autie received many dinner invitations to men's clubs at which functions he was lauded and applauded. Though he was in civilian dress, everyone seemed to envision him in frontier buckskins. The many notables he met never tired of asking him about his views and experiences in the West. Though he preferred Libbie's company, she insisted that he accept the privilege of meeting these interesting people.[61]

After exacting promises from Libbie that she would not repeat what he had to say, since it would appear like conceit on his part, he told her what she wanted so to hear, his acceptance by these distinguished men.

Tom and Cooke had arrived back at Fort Lincoln safely enough, Tom to learn of his promotion to captain as of December 2d. Realizing Tom was outside of her direct influence, Libbie hastened to advise him:

"Don't spend more money than you can help at the Sutler's, drinking and card playing. Don't be influenced by the badness around you. Oh, Tom, if I find that the boy I have loved, and prayed over, has gone downhill. Oh, if only you had a companionable wife."[62]

Life in New York had been a continuous round of pleasure for the Custers but there had to be one bur under the saddle, one gadfly. Custer's *"Life On The Plains"* had received wide acceptance and approval. General Sherman and every member of his family had found it to be the best of any articles written about the Plains.[63] Custer had received the admiration and respect of those in the fields of literature, science and art, as well as their patrons. The Redpath Lyceum Bureau in Boston had approached him with a contract to lecture five nights a week for four or five months for which he would receive $200 a night, a tremendous supplement to his meager income that would permit him to do so much for his parents and Libbie. They wanted him to start that spring but he declined for he wanted ample time to prepare. He was a perfectionist; there was only one way to do anything—the right way.[64] Then came the gadfly.

The gadfly was General William B. Hazen. Hazen, a captain and the Officer of the Day at West Point several days before Custer's graduation, had arrested young Custer for failing to stop a fight between two cadets. Custer was court-martialed, found guilty, but never sentenced.[65] Though Custer never held this against Hazen, and there is no evidence that either disliked the other, they were born to clash.

Both men were controvesial but in different ways. Hazen was a very competent soldier but maintained a faculty for getting involved. He had appeared before the House Committee on Military Affairs in 1872 to testify as to the staff organization of the French and German armies. He had refused to answer questions about the payoffs of post traders but finally agreed to do so when he was assured it

A CUSTER AND COOKE ROMANCE. Lieut. William Cooke looks at Emma Wadsworth like Lieut. Tom Custer surveys Nellie Wadsworth. It could have been love. Owning two Medals of Honor gave Tom some advantage. Author's collection.

would be held confidential. He did not want to offend the Secretary of War. A leak to the New York *Tribune* resulted in publication of his testimony, and his transferral to remote Fort Buford.[66]

Hazen had been sent to a post consisting of seven dilapidated adobe barracks and several hundred men, completely isolated from civilization most of each year. His irascible nature already augmented into belligerency ignited to a burning point when he read the "shameless falsehoods so lavishly published in the last two years, as advertisements in the interests of that Company (the Northern Pacific Railroad)." His post had been at the mouth of the Yellowstone River for the two years prior to writing his letter to the *Tribune*.[67]

The falsehoods Hazen alluded to were statements made in the railroad advertisements that the land bordering its right-of-way through Dakota and Montana was extremely valuable agriculturally. Hazen's charge that the land was valueless stirred Custer to the point that he responded by writing a letter to the press refuting the charge. It was his opinion, contrary to Hazen's, that the land had great potential for farming.

A number of individuals took exception to Hazen's remarks, General Rosser being one of them. After General Custer's letter responding to Hazen's charges appeared in the *Tribune*[68] there were a few scattered shots from others, but none from Hazen. His withdrawal was no sign of a retreat for he was not one to do so. He needed time to get his ammunition and then his barrage began.

In the spring of 1875 he released a 53-page booklet printed in Cincinnati, entitled *"Our Barren Lands."* In it he expanded on his premise that the territory between the Missouri River and the Sierra Nevada mountains, from the Rio Grande River to the Canadian border, was not worth "a penny an acre." To this bur Custer gave no response. Perhaps he realized that he was, as historian Edgar Stewart wrote, "too much the optimist," and "Hazen was too much the pessimist, too prone to believe that what had not been done could not be done and too willing to belabor the Northern Pacific."[69] Custer had seen the country through rose-colored glasses; Hazen's were tinted grey.

The gadfly was not through. He had read Custer's *"Life On The Plains,"* published in the Galaxy of February, 1874. There were incendiary statements there. In it Custer had charged that Hazen had been deceived by the Indians at the time of the Washita campaign in 1868 and 1869, and that had he, Custer, been allowed to attack the Indians instead of being confronted by a statement from Hazen that the Indians he faced were peaceful, much future trouble could have been averted.

Hazen took exception to the remarks. He had just finished an encounter with Custer and had stirred up a hornet's nest. His wounds yet unhealed, he was readying for more of the same. This time it was in the form of an article but 18 pages long.[70] This time there was no response. Custer apparently forgave and forgot.

LIBBIE AND AGNES BATES look at a Barry portrait of General Custer. 1874. David Barry photo. Denver Public Library Western Collection.

It was February, 1876. Their money was coming to an end and so was their leave. After stopping long enough in Monroe to pick up their niece Emma Reed, they got as far as St. Paul but could go no farther. The trains would not be running again until April. The railroad officials were obliging. They had not forgotten the service the Seventh had rendered when the road was being built. Two snow plows and three large engines were pressed into service. Passenger coaches, a dining car and a paymaster's car were added. The trip was a nightmare to Libbie. Repeatedly stopped by huge drifts and snow banks, the train finally came to a halt so deeply embedded in a wall of ice the efforts of 40 miners, brought along for just such a situation, were useless.

By tapping into the telegraph wire contact was made with Fargo and Fort Lincoln. It was Tom who answered Autie's message with: "Shall I come out? You say nothing about the old lady (Libbie); is she with you?"[71]

Tom, disregarding her order not to come, hired the best stage driver in Bismarck and drove through the blizzard to the helpless train. He thoughtfully filled the sleigh with straw, blankets and mufflers for the perilous return trip.

Hardly had they thawed out at Fort Lincoln when the General received a dispatch to return to the East. Libbie hoped to return with him but Autie was adamant. From the moment he left there was no rest for her until she received a dispatch advising her that he had covered that 250 miles of hazardous terrain safely.

NOTES—CHAPTER 25

[1]Chandler, p. 41, April 23; Eliz. B. Custer: *Boots,* pp. 159-60.
[2]Chandler, p. 41.
[3]James Calhoun: *Black Hills Expedition Daily Log, 1874,* BCWC collection.
[4]G. A. Custer to General Sheridan, April 27, 1874; Calhoun: *Black Hills.*
[5]Calhoun: *Black Hills,* Custer-Terry correspondence, March 24, 28, 1874.
[6]G. A. Custer to Lawrence Barrett, May 19, 1874, Manuscript Division, Library of Congress.
[7]William Ludlow: *Report of a Reconnaissance of the Black Hills of Dakota,* Washington, 1875, p. 8.
[8]Cleophas C. O'Harra: "Custer's Black Hills Expedition of 1874," *The Black Hills Engineer,* Vol XVII, No. 4, November, 1929, p. 228.
[9]*Ibid,* p. 229; Ludlow, pp. 8-9.
[10]Calhoun: *Black Hills,* Custer-Terry correspondence, July 15, 1874.
[11]Merington, p. 273.
[12]Eliz. B. Custer: *Boots,* p. 299-300.
[13]*Ibid.*
[14]Calhoun: *Black Hills,* entry of August 2, 1874; O'Harra, p. 288.
[15]G. A. Custer to General Terry via Fort Laramie by telegram, August 8, 1874, Senate Exec. Doc. No. 32, 43d Cong., 2d Session.
[16]*Ibid.*
[17]Joseph H. Taylor: *Frontier And Indian Life And Kaleidoscopic Lives,* Valley City, 1932, p. 102; Donald Jackson: *Custer's Gold,* New Haven, 1966, pp. 20, 85-86; John and George Remsburg: *Charley Reynolds,* Kansas City, 1931, p. 24.
[18]Eliz. B. Custer: *Boots,* pp. 240-42.
[19]Jackson: *Custer's Gold,* p. 89.
[20]*Annual Report of the Commissioner of Indian Affairs for 1874,* p. 7-8.
[21]Calhoun: *Black Hills,* entry of August 14, 15, 1874; G. A. Custer to General Terry via Bismarck, August 15, 1874, Senate Exec. Doc. No. 32, 43d Cong., 2d Session.
[22]Merington, p. 275; Frost: *Custer Album,* p. 138, picture of grizzly. Though General Custer had shown a deep interest previously in Colorado Silver mines there is no evidence that he displayed any such interest in Black Hills gold mines.
[23]Ludlow: *Report,* p. 18.
[24]Eliz. B. Custer: *Boots,* p. 192.
[25]*Annual Report of Commissioner of Indian Affairs for 1874,* p. 90.
[26]Ludlow: *Report,* p. 18.
[27]Mark H. Brown: *The Plainsmen of the Yellowstone,* N.Y., 1961, p. 219.
[28]Watson Parker: *Gold In The Black Hills,* Norman, 1966, p. 127.
[29]Minneapolis *Tribune,* April 17, 1874.
[30]For comprehensive treatment of the subject read: Edgar I. Stewart: *Penny-an-Acre Empire in the West,* Norman, 1968.
[31]Boston Custer to his cousin Emma Reed, September 13, 1874, mentions that the three of them had left for Monroe. BCWC collection.
[32]Ishbell Ross: *Silhouette In Diamonds,* N.Y., 1960, pp. 34-36.
[33]Monroe *Commercial,* November 5, 1874; *Monroe City Directory,* 1874, indicated the E. H. Custer residencc as located on the northwest corner of Monroe and Second Streets (the Bacon residence).
[34]Eliz. B. Custer: *Boots,* p. 219.
[35]*Ibid,* p. 218.
[36]*Ibid,* p. 219.
[37]*Ibid,* p. 224.
[38]*Ibid,* p. 233.
[39]*Ibid,* p. 232.
[40]*Ibid,* pp. 226-27.
[41]Eliz. B. Custer: "General Custer And The Indian Chiefs," *Outlook Magazine,* July 27, 1927.
[42]*Ibid.*
[43]*Ibid,* No date is given.
[44]Eliz. B. Custer: *Boots,* p. 226.
[45]G. A. Custer: *My Life,* p. 18.
[46]Chandler, p. 43.
[47]Col. Hall to G. A. Custer, August 19, 1874. EBC—CBNM.
[48]Col Hall to G. A. Custer, February, 23, 1875. EBC—CBNM.
[49]Col Hall to G. A. Custer, April 1, 1874. EBC—CBNM.
[50]EBC—CBNM.
[51]Walter P. Jenney: "Report of Geological Survey of the Black Hills," *Annual Report of the Commissioner of Indian Affairs,* 1875, p. 181; Parker, pp. 63-65; Richard I. Dodge: *The Black Hills,* N.Y., 1876, pp. 104-107; Walter P. Jenney: *The Mineral Wealth, Climate And Rainfall, And Natrual Resources of the Black Hills of Dakota,* Washington, 1876, p. 56; Monroe *Commercial,* August 5, 1875.
[52]James Bennett to G. A. Custer, April 1, 1875. EBC—CBNM.
[53]Bismarck *Tribune,* April 28, 1875.
[54]G. A. Custer to Libbie, May 21, 1875, giving Barker's accident as occurring on May 20th. Telegram in author's collection.
[55]Boston Custer to Emma Reed, September 23, 1875, BCWC collection; Monroe *Commercial,* September 30, 1875.
[56]Monroe *Commercial,* January 7, June 10, 1875.
[57]Telegram, Libbie to G. A. Custer, October 12, 1875.
[58]Syracuse *Journal,* July 12, 1876.
[59]Bismarck *Tribune,* December 16, 1875.
[60]Eliz. B. Custer: *Boots,* p. 250.
[61]Merington, p. 276.
[62]BCWC collection.
[63]Merington, p. 244.
[64]Lawrence Barrett in Whittaker, p. 638; Barrett had promised to hear the rehearsals of his lecture after the summer campaign was over.
[65]Frost: "Let's Have a Fair Fight."
[66]Stewart: *Penny-an-Acre,* pp. 15-16.
[67]New York *Tribune,* February 27, 1874.
[68]Minneapolis *Tribune,* April 17, 1874.
[69]Stewart: *Penny-an-Acre,* p. 260.
[70]W. B. Hazen: *Some Corrections of Life On The Plains,* St. Paul, 1875.
[71]Eliz. B. Custer: *Boots,* p. 257.

CUSTER'S BLACK HILLS RECONNAISSANCE OF 1874. Rare photo in Col. Brice C. W. Custer collection. Lt. James Calhoun is at extreme right, Capt. Fed Benteen is in the center with the white kerchief around his neck and a pipe in his left hand, Gen. Custer is the upper of two figures to Benteen's right. Autie is the beardless one with the dark hat.

CHAPTER 26
I WANTED TO DIE

Why had Custer been summoned back to Washington? For what purpose was he being removed to the East at the very time he was needed at Fort Lincoln to ready his troops for a spring campaign designed to drive recalcitrant Sioux back onto their reservations?

Heister Clymer, the publicity seeking chairman of the House of Representatives' Committee on expenditures of the War Department, had a plan that would embarrass President Grant and the Republican administration.[1] His committee had uncovered evidence that Secretary of War Belknap apparently had sold a post tradership to Caleb P. Marsh. Without hesitation the committee seized the opportunity to prepare a resolution to impeach Belknap.

The agile Belknap rushed over to Grant's office with his resignation which was accepted immediately. Grant, without waiting to see the committee's evidence, accepted Belknap's explanation in good faith. Fundamentally honest, the President believed all of his associates to be of the same cloth. When anyone was charged with dishonesty, and there were many who were, he immediately came to their defense. In accepting Belknap's resignation he aided him in defeating the impeachment proceedings.[2]

Clymer and his committee continued their investigation. One of their purposes was to amass additional evidence against Belknap. Having heard that Custer had voiced his dissatisfaction with the exhorbitant charges post traders were applying to the Fort Lincoln garrison, and that it was said he knew something of the background relating to the sale of these lucrative post traderships, Clymer summoned Custer to appear before the committee. This was smart thinking on Clymer's part for Custer's popularity made him newsworthy.[3]

Sioux warriors under Sitting Bull and Crazy Horse were off their reservations and were not complying with the Secretary of the Interior Zachariah Chandler's order that "they must come onto their reservations by or before the 31st of January, 1876, or a military force would be sent to compel them." Chandler had notified Belknap of the expiration of the notice and that he was turning the matter over to him for the army to handle.[4]

Since an attempt in mid-March to force them onto their reservations had ended unsuccessfully, Sheridan had resolved on a plan of encirclement such as he had used against the Kiowas, Comanches and Cheyennes so successfully in 1874 and 1875. A simultaneous movement of three columns was to be used so that Indians, attempting to avoid one column, might be confronted by another. Since the Indians were expecting to be near the mouth of the Little Big Horn River in southeastern Montana, General Terry would command a column emanating from Montana and another from Dakota; General Crook would command the third column originating from the Platte. It was concluded that any one of the three columns could handle the hostile warriors the Indian Bureau estimated to be about 500, at the very most, 800.[5]

Custer had been at Fort Lincoln hardly a month when the summons from Washington arrived. It was obvious that Congressman Clymer was on a fishing expedition for Custer had no facts to present, only hearsay evidence. That wouldn't deter Clymer, for hearsay evidence or rumors could produce leads, and leads could produce facts.

Custer, concerned about preparing his troops for the field, and knowing his information was only hearsay, wired Terry in St. Paul asking if it was mandatory for him to go. Terry assured him that he would have to appear though he feared it would delay the cavalry column. Custer asked Clymer if he could answer the committee's questions by mail since it was expected that the Seventh would take the field early in April.[6] Clymer wanted him in front of the committee. That's where the news correspondents would be.

On March 26th Custer was in Monroe visiting his family. There was a new Secretary of War when he left there for Washington, Alphonso Taft, who received him graciously. Everywhere Custer was received with cordiality, or so it seemed on his arrival.[7]

Under the surface older politicians could sense a growing fear. The Army Ring and the Whiskey Ring had been exposed and broken up. Orville Babcock, President Grant's confidential secretary, had been charged with receiving bribes from the Whiskey Ring. Though he had been declared guiltless it had been a front page story. The Belknap resignation under the charge of fraud in the appointment of post traders was now occupying the headlines.

Grant had no great capacity for judging the character of men, nor was he an intellectual. He had no knowledge of the vast frauds perpetrated by his party members. When he was confronted with them he stubbornly protected those who had previously been loyal to him as exemplified by Babcock and Belknap.

The Republican party had been promoting Grant for a third term which the Democrats were doing everything in their power to resist. The Democrats had passed a resolution in the House of Representatives declaring a third term to be "unwise, unpatriotic and fraught with peril."[8] With a presidential election in the offing, both parties were seeking campaign ammunition. The time was ripe for political slander.

On March 29th Custer appeared before Clymer's committee and gave what he had indicated he would in a previous communication to Clymer—hearsay testimony. Some writers claim that Custer involved the President's brother Orville Grant but an examination of the testimony show this is not true. Orville appeared before the committee on March 9th, just 20 days before Custer's appearance. He involved himself. Custer had made statements damaging to Belknap, and thus arousing the ire of Belknap's friend President Grant, but had not implicated Orville Grant.

On April 4th, in answer to a question as to why he had not reported the abuses and corruption he had observed on the frontier, Custer explained that an order existed prohibiting any officer from recommending any action by members of Congress for or against military affairs. A violation of the order might cause the officer to lose his commission. The order, in Custer's opinion, was intended "to cover up the doings of the Secretary of War."[9]

Custer was retained in Washington in the expectation that he might be needed for further testimony. Though he was entertained in many quarters, he did not allow the time to go by idly. Using his contacts at the War Department to improve the Seventh, he obtained the release of four companies of the Seventh on duty in the South. They were ordered to proceed to Fort Lincoln to join the expedition. There seemed to have been needless retention in Washington at a time he was needed to prepare his troops for the field. Major Reno and Captain Tom Custer were maintaining a flow of telegrams to him requesting advice and orders relating to the coming campaign. Tom's displayed some anxiety.[10] Custer was anxious to be released in time to meet the Sioux before the various tribes had become one large, formidable force. The more Clymer's committee delayed him the greater the force became under Sitting Bull's aegis.

As was his custom a stream of letters flowed to Fort Lincoln. Libbie was kept informed as to what transpired each day. One of the letters written to her from the committee room where the Belknap exposures were made indicated he would be leaving in a few days. One reason he was anxious to leave was the continuous pressure on him to do more than he desired. He realized that any further delay might force him to give up the summer campaign. That meant he could send for Libbie—a pleasant thought. But who would enjoy a summer in the East? Many might, but not Autie.

He explained an attempt to prove he had received money from James Gordon Bennett of the New York *Herald* which was foiled by the testimony of Ralph Meeker. Meeker, as an undercover reporter for the *Herald* searching for facts on the smuggling of arms and liquor to Indians, said that the drafts were drawn for his benefit and endorsed by Custer so that they could be cashed at Fort Lincoln.[11]

When the 13th rolled around, Custer's letter to Libbie indicated the hope he would be able to start back in a few days. He had dined with his dear friend Lawrence Barrett who, a week earlier, he had no hope of seeing. Barrett had just begun his Washington run in *Julius Caesar*.

Two days later, having received a formal discharge from the Belknap Board, he was amazed to be intercepted in New York by a deputy Sergeant-at-Arms of the Senate with a summons to appear before the committee on Wednesday the 26th. He expressed the hope to Libbie that the Senate would decide, now that Belknap had resigned, the case was out of its purview. He had seen Sherman and the Secretary of War that day who were going to write to the Belknap Committee requesting Custer's release so he could return to duty.

On April 16th Custer shut himself in his room to finish an article for the *Galaxy*. The following day was spent appearing before Banning's Military Affairs Committee. He urged it to release him as he did with the Belknap Impeachment Committee on the following day when he appeared before it. He emphasized, to the latter, that nearly all of his response to their questions had been hearsay evidence. He was confident, he wrote Libbie, they would not need him further.[12] Little did he know he would be held another two weeks.

Autie expressed his appreciation for some poetry Libbie had included in her last letter. A lady he had shown it to asked: "Your sweetheart sent them. Never your wife." He told her they were one and the same. She responded: "How long have you been married?" "Twelve years." "And haven't got over that?" "No, and I never shall!"

One day, he told Libbie, General Sherman had said: "Custer, you write so well, people think your wife does it, and you don't get the credit." In response he said to Sherman: "Then I ought to get the credit for my selection of a wife."

On April 17th he had the pleasure of seeing his long-standing friend Judge Christiancy administered the oath as a U.S. senator by the Chief Justice of the Supreme Court. Christiancy was now a full-fledged senator on the very eve of the trial of William Belknap. In one of his first acts he voted for the acquittal of Belknap, saying he was unimpeachable by virtue of being a private citizen.[13]

Custer finally received his release on May 1st. Twice he had visited the White House for the purpose of paying his respects to the President and set right any misconceptions. He had heard from sources close to the President that his feelings toward him were bitter and bordering on a hatred. Custer believed he could change all this by meeting him face-to-face.

Later in the day he made a third call. On his arrival he sent in a note to the President requesting a brief hearing. Grant refused to see him. There was nothing else he could do but return to his command. He had called on General Sherman earlier and found him gone till that evening. Obtaining his train tickets, then calling on the Inspector General, R. B. Marcy, and the Adjutant General E. D. Townsend, he returned to Sherman's office. There he was informed Sherman was in New York and no knowledge of his time of return was available. Custer left for the West.[14]

Stopping briefly in Monroe the next day to see his parents,[15] he continued on the evening train to Chicago, taking his nephew and niece Autie and Emma Reed with him. On his arrival he was confronted with an astounding telegram Sherman had sent to Phil Sheridan. Referring to Custer it read: "He was not justified in leaving without seeing the President or myself. . . . order him to halt and await further orders. Meanwhile, let the Expedition from Fort Lincoln proceed without him."[16]

Custer immediately sent a dispatch to Sherman advising him of his wait at the White House from 10 A.M. until 3 P.M. with an ultimate refusal from the President to see him, of his visit to the Inspector General and the Adjutant General and receiving written and verbal authority to proceed, and of his three visits that same day to Sherman's office. Then he reminded Sherman of his frequent comment of the necessity of leaving as soon as possible for Fort Lincoln. Later he wired asking for justice in the matter of going in command of his regiment. Sherman made no reply. He was only acting as General of the Army obviously under orders of the Commander-in-Chief, President Grant.[17]

A third time that day Custer wired Sherman, this time requesting permission to serve his detention with Libbie at Fort Lincoln. This received no answer.[18]

MAGGIE CALHOUN was married to Lieut. James Calhoun in Monroe, Michigan, in March of 1872. Author's collection.

The strange part of all this is that Custer had done nothing on which a charge could be based. He had committed no crime, he had disobeyed no orders, he had followed military protocol. There was no sound, solid reason for this action on the part of Grant except to humiliate Custer for making a statement under oath about Grant's close friend and appointee Belknap. Grant's animosity was aroused toward anyone who dared question the actions of any member of his administration. Basically honest and naive when it came to judging virtues, he trusted all of his chosen associates. They could do no wrong.

New York and Washington newspapers made much of all this. It was an election year and this sort of thing, if properly headlined, would sell newspapers. When a President, already up to his neck in hot water, relieves a popular officer from his command, that's news. And it is political news when the officer is removed from command of an important expedition just after testifying against a Presidential favorite. It was a case of bad guys against good guys, and Custer was a good guy in the eyes of many partisan newspapers.

The newspapers reported that both General Sherman and Secretary Taft had protested that it would not do to remove Custer. Sherman had gone so far as to say that "Custer was not only the best man but the only man fit to lead the expedition now fitting out against the Indians."[19] Grant ignored their entreaties, saying that if they could not find a man to lead the expedition, he would.

The New York *World's* heading was "GRANTS REVENGE. The General's Reward For Testifying Against Belknap." Its editorial charged that Custer was removed "to deter other officers from telling what they knew."[20]

The May 3d issue of the New York *Sun* asked: "WILL THE PRESIDENT THINK TWICE?" It observed that this was the first time the President openly favored suppressing the truth and by doing so indicated he favored covering up frauds in his administration. They admonished that he should think twice before determining to relieve General Custer.

The St. Paul *Dispatch,* the New York *Herald* and the Paterson *News* at this time took issue with "official denials" that Sherman or the Secretary of War had protested the removal of Custer, then openly charged that the Associated Press's "contradictions and explanations and the 'official denial' are lies."[21]

At this point in time it appears the thin-skinned Grant saw in Custer an opportunity of getting at his tormentors, for he thought the antics of Clymer's committee unjustified. Sherman had been satisfied with Custer's conduct at the hearings. Knowing of Grant's wrath, he had suggested to Custer that he call on the President and explain the true condition of affairs. Grant, as stubborn and determined as he was in taking Richmond, refused to meet the slandered cavalryman, refused to listen to reason.[22]

His objective was to humiliate Custer. What could be more humiliating than to keep him in Chicago while his regiment took to the field on active duty, unless it was to permit him to reach Fort Lincoln and take command of its emptied frontier barracks? So, on May 5th, Sherman sent to Custer Grant's order that he could return to that post, there "to remain on duty, but not to accompany the expedition supposed to be on the point of starting against the hostile Indians, under General Terry."[23] Custer, in his loneliness for Libbie, had played into Grant's hands. Yet to him it was a blessing for the willing Libbie would share his burdens as she had doubled his pleasures.

Some contemporary newspapers noted this Grant tactic. One predicted Custer would be considered a victim rather than a delinquent.[24] Another, the St. Paul *Dispatch,* drew the conclusion:

> "If the President persists in his first purpose of suspending Gen. Custer, the country will accept the fact as a fresh evidence of the fixed determination of the administration to punish every witness who aids to expose wrongdoing in the public service, and it will receive this determination as an acknowledgement of guilt on the part of the President."

Custer was in Chicago when Sherman's message came through permitting him to proceed to Fort Lincoln. Taking the night train for St. Paul, he arrived there at 7 A.M. on the 6th. He left Em and Autie Reed at the Metropolitan Hotel waiting for their room while he hurried to General Terry's headquarters. Em, in spite of the two noisy canaries Custer had purchased in Chicago for Libbie, promptly fell asleep in Uncle Autie's parlor.[25]

CAPTAIN GEORGE YATES first served with the 4th Michigan Volunteer Infantry, then later on the staff of General Alfred Pleasonton during the Civil War. An able officer, he was considered one of "the Custer Clan." Author's collection.

At headquarters Custer told the kindly Terry all that had transpired. Terry, a lawyer long before he had begun his meritorious career as an officer, was accustomed to giving counsel. As a logical man he saw the great need for Custer's experience as an Indian fighter. He saw the necessity for conciliation and humbleness on Custer's part. It is said, though there is no proof, that he composed Custer's last request to the President asking for clemency. No less to his credit is the endorsement he attached to it in which he suggested that "Lieut. Col. Custer's services would be very valuable with his command."[26]

Custer's letter was all appeal. Referring to the part his regiment would take in the expedition, he continued:

> "I respectfully but most earnestly request that while not allowed to go in command of the expedition, I might be permitted to serve with my regiment in the field.
>
> "I appeal to you as a soldier to spare me the humiliation of seeing my regiment march to meet the enemy and I not to share its dangers."[27]

CUSTER AND HIS SCOUT by J. K. Ralston. 1861. Original pen sketch in author's collection.

At this point the newspapers had taken the matter into their own hands. Lead articles and editorials were beating Grant on the head with hefty cudgels. Those backing the administration were forced to fight back, and in doing so assumed a posture hostile to Custer even after his death.

The trouble had started with the malicious Heister Clymer and his political cohorts whose interests could hardly be considered altruistic. Clymer knew Custer had no important evidence to offer for Custer had told him so.

The trouble was compounded when Grant's conniving brother and the unscrupulous Belknap were implicated. Grant's stupidity as a politician and his culpability in supporting appointees found guilty of graft and malfeasance made him throw aside all reason for personal revenge.

This was an election year and Grant had visions of a third term. He might ignore the pleas and intercession of various generals in Custer's behalf but he could hardly ignore the screeches and punches from the hostile press. He relented. Custer could go with his beloved Seventh but he could not go in charge of the expedition.[28] That just suited Terry.

The first move toward the Little Big Horn originated at Fort Ellis on March 30th. Colonel John Gibbon with a detachment of 450 men—the 2d Cavalry and the 7th Infantry—arrived at the mouth of the Rosebud River on June 21.

General George Crook left Fort Fetterman on May 29th, commanding 47 officers and 1,002 men—two battalions of the 2d and 3d Cavalry and five companies of the 4th and 9th Infantry.

General Custer left Fort Lincoln on May 17th, commanding about 600 men of the 7th Cavalry.

As mentioned earlier, Sheridan's overall strategy of encirclement was to be accomplished by a three-pronged approach, the three columns to move simultaneously so that the Indians in attempting to avoid one column would be confronted by another.[29]

At the beginning of the campaign, and as late as June 21st—four days before the battle—"there was nothing official or private to justify an officer to expect that any detachment could encounter more than 500, or, at the maximum, 800 hostile warriors."[30]

Crook, in a surprise engagement on June 17th, unknown to the other two columns, was met by a large force of Sioux warriors his own scouts had failed to discover. None of his men was killed in this battle on the Rosebud River. At no time afterward were the other two columns advised of his defeat, of the size of this hostile force or of the fact that he discontinued his advance toward Terry, Custer and Gibbon, thus failing to support them.

On June 22d Custer, having received his "orders" from Terry that morning, moved his men out at noon.[31] The "orders" have always been a subject of debate, many students thinking they were but a letter of instructions giving Terry's opinions but giving Custer the right of final decision.

The Seventh moved up the Rosebud until it crossed a large Indian trail leading toward the Little Big Horn. This they followed until early morning of the 25th, arriving at a point about 15 miles from the Little Big Horn. Expecting to rest his command until the 26th, Custer was discovered by several parties of hostiles.[32] There was nothing else to do, if he hoped to prevent the Indians from escaping, but to attack at once.

Shortly after noon he divided his command into three battalions in the manner he had at the Washita. Captain Frederick Benteen with his battalion of 125 men was ordered to scout the bluffs to the left and pitch into any Indians he might find. It was hoped that he could prevent the escape of any Indians up the valley of the Little Big Horn or the valleys of any creeks running into it.

Major Marcus Reno with his battalion of 112 men continued riding with Custer toward the Little Big Horn. After traveling along Sundance Creek for a distance of nearly ten miles, they saw 40 or 50 Sioux warriors riding between them and the valley. Custer had his adjutant Lieutenant W. W. Cooke take orders to Reno: "Take as fast a gait as you deem prudent, and charge afterward, and you will be supported by the whole outfit."

Reno led his men the three miles to the river at a trot. After crossing the river he reformed his lines, then charged down the valley at a gallop. About 400 yards from the Indian village he was confronted by a body of Indians that caused him to halt and form a dismounted skirmish line across the valley bottom. The Indians, encouraged and emboldened by this halt in a charge that had pushed them before it, increased in numbers and resistance. Reno pivoted his men to the right to a woods that bordered the Little Big Horn. After fighting in the woods about half an hour, he became unnerved and ordered a retreat which he led to the river's edge. No effort was made to cover the retreat, bring the few wounded or see that all of the men were informed of the order. Some were left behind.

The river's edge was a cutbank with a sheer drop of six feet. The water was four feet deep. Horses and men piled up as the bank crumpled in their attempt to escape the blood thirsty Sioux. Once on the other side the cavalrymen had a strenuous climb up the bluffs. There the disorganized and demoralized battalion occupied a position overlooking the valley. A roll call revealed that 40 of their original 112 men were missing.

Benteen and his men reached Reno's position just afterward. He had scouted off to the left as ordered but had found no Indians. Following the trail Custer had left after splitting with Reno, he had been met by Sergeant Kanipe who carried a message to the commander of the pack train to hurry up the packs. A mile further on Custer's orderly trumpeter John Martini handed Benteen an order from Custer to: "Come on—Big Village—Be Quick—Bring Packs. P.S. Bring Pacs." It was signed by Custer's adjutant Cooke.[33]

Heavy firing was heard down stream and, though it was thought to be Custer's battalion in trouble, neither Reno nor Benteen made any effort in that direction. Captain Thomas Weir, leading his company, and without orders, struck out in that direction. He was soon followed by the other companies. All halted at a high point more than a mile distant when they sighted a large number of Indians several miles beyond. It was thought advisable to return to their former location because it could be defended more easily.

Once back on their hill top they dug in and constructed barricades from their saddles, ammunition and hardtack boxes. Soon they were surrounded by Indians. The firing continued until dark but there was no sleep. The Indians in the huge village below lit the sky with innumerable campfires. The hubbub and chants of the victorious warriors were heard until dawn, then the firing began. In the latter part of the afternoon the Indians began to withdraw.

The exhausted troopers witnessed the largest encampment ever seen on the plains depart. Moving southward up the valley of the Little Big Horn were upwards of 10,000 warriors and their families. Custer and Terry had received intelligence there would be but 800 warriors, a figure Custer later increased to 1,500. The pony herd alone was estimated to be about 20,000. And the village site was estimated to be four miles long and, at some points, one half mile wide.

But what had become of Custer? When last seen he was standing on a high promontory observing Reno ordering his skirmish line into woods below. He had waved his light hat as if, some thought, approving the move. Others believed the waving hat a sign for Reno to move on toward the village in obedience of the orders to charge it. No one knows and no one

SITTING BULL. Spiritual leader of the hostile Sioux. R. L. Kelly photo. Author's collection.

seems to know what happened to Custer immediately afterward. The best and most acceptable account is the reconstruction of his movements made by Dr. Charles Kuhlman in his exciting "Legend Into History" (Stackpole, 1951).

June 27th saw the arrival of the combined forces of Terry and Gibbon. Custer and all of his five companies of men were found dead. All were stripped and most were mutilated. The only survivor was *Comanche,* a severely wounded horse.

The next two days were used in transporting the wounded by mule litters to the mouth of the Little Big Horn where the steamer *Far West* was moored. On July 3d it began the 700 mile trip to Fort Abraham Lincoln. Captain Grant Marsh piloted the boat with its precious load, reaching its destination in a record 54 hours.

Libbie and Maggie accompanied the huge column as it left Fort Lincoln that May 17th. The officers' wives stood on their verandas as the column, some two miles in length, paraded by in its grandest style and the Seventh Cavalry band played "The Girl I Left Behind Me." There were tears, some openly, though most were hidden. It wasn't considered proper to expose such emotions before the children. The enlisted men's wives on Laundress Row openly displayed their feelings. Their tears flowed freely and they waved emotionally to their men as they passed by.

Autie rode proudly at the head of the column at the side of General Terry. He wore his fringed buckskin

RAIN-IN-THE-FACE. He boasted that he had cut out the heart of Tom Custer. Barry photo. Author's collection.

trousers and shirt. The trousers were tucked into a short pair of low-heeled boots. At his neck was the famous red necktie and on his shorn golden-red hair was a light, flat-topped sombrero. This was a big moment for him. He was again leading his beloved Seventh Cavalry.

Prior to their leaving camp a mist had covered everything. "As the sun broke through the mist," Libbie observed, "a mirage appeared which took up about half of the line of cavalry, and thenceforth for a little distance it marched, equally plain to the sight on the earth and in the sky."[34] It was as though they were marching into immortality.

At frequent intervals Autie would turn in his saddle to admire his men, then call Libbie's attention to their fine appearance. A few miles from the post a campsite was selected near a small river. In the morning the farewells were said, then Libbie and Maggie accompanied the paymaster back to the post. The paymaster had accompanied the column to this point so the men could be paid far removed from the temptations of Bismarck.

Libbie's return was far from a happy one. Her separations in the past never had been happy but this time exceeded all others in her feeling of sadness and depression. She recalled:

"With my husband's departure my last happy days in garrison were ended, as a premonition of disaster that I had never known before weighed me down. I could not shake off the baleful influence of depressing thoughts. This presentiment and suspense, such as I had never known, made me selfish, and I shut into my heart the most uncontrollable anxiety, and could lighten no one else's burden."[35]

The anguish of parting was not one sided. John Burkman, Custer's personal orderly, stood at the side of the General as they watched her ride away that morning, her head bent over as if she was crying. Custer's ruddy face turned white as he said in a low voice: "A soldier has to serve two mistresses. While he's loyal to one the other must suffer."[36]

The weeks passed slowly, drearily. An occasional steamer would drop off some very welcome mail. There were stories of hostile Indians firing at the boats from the shore. The post itself was surrounded by hostiles and its pickets were frequently called upon to defend themselves.

Each day was one of suspense, of fearful waiting and of hoping for good news. One day a dispatch arrived from Division Headquarters. The women sensed something unusual had occurred. Indian scouts were hurriedly sent to the expedition with dispatches. Once they had left the need for secrecy was unnecessary, and the women were advised that General Crook and his expeditionary force had been defeated on the Rosebud River. The Indian scouts were hastening to Custer and Terry with this information which could be interpreted to mean that the victorious Sioux were now free to join Sitting Bull against Custer. Custer never received the information.[37]

Rightly, the women concluded that the scouts could not cross the country in time to deliver the warning. Circumtances usually forced the women to be optimistic. Crook's failure produced a depressing effect. They expected their men to be overwhelmed by the large number of hostiles reported to be off their reservations and joining Sitting Bull.

It was Sunday, June 25th, that the desolate women sought solace in the Custer house. One sat at the piano playing soft chords as they joined together singing old hymns. Grief-stricken and dejected, for each expected the worst and prayed for the best, their tight throats attempted to respond in an effort to share the anguish of the others. All thought the same and felt the same for there was that common bond. While they were bravely singing their men were bravely dying.

July 5th was the day of reckoning. It was late that evening the steamer *Far West* with its precious load of wounded touched base for a few hours at Bismarck. The officers' wives had heard the whistle blast of the *Far West* as she approached Bismarck. They remained at the Custer house until midnight. Anxiously they waited and waited with heavy hearts and foreboding, then separated and returned to their homes to toss restlessly till dawn.[38]

It was Captain William S. McCaskey, 20th Infantry, who received the communication from General Terry. It was about 2 A.M. Summoning all of the officers at the post, he read them the communication. All were requested to assist in breaking the news to the widows. McCaskey selected Dr. J.V.D. Middleton, the post surgeon, and Lieutenant C. L. Gurley, 6th Infantry, to accompany him to the Custer residence.[39]

For two days the women on the post had been aware that something unusual had happened. There had been whispering and excitement among the Indian police. Rumors of a great battle had been circulated. The Indians had received information but the whites had not. The atmosphere was charged with depression.

Libbie had slipped into a dressing gown to meet the delegation. She had been lying on her bed all night partly clothed, waiting for the message she knew was coming. There was no doubt in her mind, no hope.

It was in the parlor she received them. And with her was little Emma Reed and Maggie Calhoun, large and fair like her brothers Tom and Autie.

Captain McCaskey did his painful duty. He would never forget the flood of tears, the sobs, the grief. Nor would he forget Maggie Calhoun—who had lost her brothers Autie, Tom, Boston, her nephew Autie Reed, and her husband Jim—running after him as he left and crying out: "Is there no message for me?" They left no message. They left memories, and a tradition.

Libbie, shivering in the sweltering, humid air, sent for a wrap. She had a responsibility she could not delegate to others. She must be present when the other officers' wives and those of the enlisted men were told. They needed consolation and an example in their new widowhood. It was the least she could do for them.[40] For her there was no future. Her life had ended with Autie. She could think only of one thing, she wrote later: "I wanted to die."

NOTES — CHAPTER 26

1Frost: *Custer Album*, p. 148.
2"Sale of Post Traderships," 44th Cong., 1st sess., H.R. Report No. 799, p.i.; Frost: *Grant Album*, p. 161.
3Frost: *Custer Album*, p. 148.
4*Report Of The General Of The Army, 1876*, p. 8.
5*Ibid*, p. 9.
6Whitaker: *Life of Custer;* G. A. Custer to Hon. Heister Clymer, March 16, 1876, p. 548; Robert Brekken: *Journey Back To Hawley*, Hawley, Minn., 1972, p. 150.
7Monroe *Commercial*, March 30, 1876; Merington, p. 281.
8Dee Brown: *The Year Of The Century 1876*, N.Y., 1966, p. 14.
9"Sale of Post Traderships," pp. 162-63; Cincinnati *Inquirer*, April 5, 1876; Cincinnati *Commercial*, April 5, 1876.
10Originals are in author's files.
11Clement Lounsberry: *Early History of North Dakota*, Washington, 1919, p. 314—"General Custer was instrumental in having Ralph Meeker sent out by a New York newspaper to report on this matter. He reported to General Custer. His mission was known to the writer of these pages, then editor of the Bismarck *Tribune*. . . . Custer was not backward in supplying Meeker the facts that came to his attention, and the publication of the story resulted in the impeachment of Secretary Belknap.

"General Custer was a man of action and high ideals and believed in a square deal. These rumors, backed with absolute proof, reached him. He also believed that smuggling of arms and liquor, was carried on to a great extent and that by this means also money was provided to pay the tribute exacted of the traders;" Robert C. Prickett: "The Malfeasance of William Worth Belknap, Secretary of War," *"North Dakota History*, January, 1950, p. 15; Merington, p. 289; "Sale of Post Traderships," pp. 228-235.
12Merington, p. 290.
13*Proceedings of The Senate Sitting For The Trial of William W. Belknap*, 1876, pp. 21, 238, 316-333, 1089.
14Whittaker: *Life of Custer*, pp. 552-554.
15Monroe *Commercial*, May 4, 1876.
16Whittaker, p. 554; W. T. Sherman to Phil Sheridan, May 2, 1876. EBC-CBNM.
17Whittaker, pp. 555-56.
18*Ibid*, p. 557.
19New York *Times*, May 1, 1876; New York *World*, May 1, 1876; Washington *Telegram*, May 2, 1876.
20New York *World, May 2, 1876.*
21May 6, 1876.
22Chicago *Tribune*, May 7, 1876.
23Whittaker, pp. 557-58.
24New York *Herald*, May 6, 1876.
25Autie Reed to David Reed, May 6, 1876. BCWC collection.
26Whittaker, p. 650. Custer's regular army rank was that of a lieutenant colonel. In official dispatches the regular army rank was often used. It was customary to address officers who had held higher rank previously, or had conferred upon them a brevet rank for meritorious service, by that rank. Custer was most frequently addressed as general having been a major general of volunteers, and also a brevet major general.
27*Ibid*, p. 559.
28Frost: *Grant Album*, p. 161.
29Report, General of the Army, 1876, p. 9.
30*Ibid*, p. 10, statement made by W. T. Sherman. On p. 9 he gives this as an estimate of the Indian Bureau.

General Custer's last letter to his mother "seemed full of hope and courage," and said: "they expected to meet 500 Indians," Wing: *History of Monroe County*, p. 318. This letter would have been written and mailed June 22d, three days prior to the battle.
31Alfred H. Terry: *Notebook for 1876*. Acc. 10.368, Library of Congress.
32On the morning of June 25th, Custer was informed that several Sioux Scouts were seen observing his movements. This, with the knowledge that Indians were discovered opening a hardtack box dropped by his supply train, forced him to the conclusion that further attempts at concealment were useless.
33The original order may be seen at the United States Military Academy.
34Eliz. B. Custer: *Boots*, p. 263.
35*Ibid*, p. 265.
36Wagner, *Old Neutriment*, p. 124.
37Eliz. B. Custer: *Boots*, p. 266.
38Joseph M. Hanson: *The Conquest of the Missouri*, N.Y., 1946, pp. 312-13; Fargo *Record*, March, 1897, p. 11.
39Hanson, pp. 312-13.
40*Ibid;* Merington, p. 323.

CHAPTER 27
A REASON TO LIVE

There was an immediate response to the disaster on the Little Big Horn in Washington. As expected, it was political. As early as July 7th Senator John J. Ingalls of Kansas had taken the floor of the chamber and requested a report from the President as to the purpose of a military expedition on the frontier.

He asked "whether the Sioux Indians made any hostile demonstrations prior to the invasion of their treaty reservations by the gold hunters; whether the military operations are conducted for the purpose of protecting said Indians in their rights under the treaty of 1868 or of punishing them for resisting the violation of that treaty, and whether the recent reports of an alleged disaster to our forces under General Custer in that region are true?"[1]

The Democratic press took the opportunity to attack the administration from the President on down, charging all with being responsible for the Custer disaster. Southern newspapers were particularly vitriolic in charging the Republican Party with gross misconduct, using Custer's defeat as a horrible example of the need for political reform that could be accomplished only under Democratic leadership. The mismanagement of the army, the inefficiency of the Indian Bureau and the Whiskey Ring were given as examples of an administration of incompetents.[2]

Some thought the Grant Peace Policy was one that pampered Indians with one hand while robbing them with the other, and so it appeared. Not because the policy was bad but because the policy was administered badly.

Custer's detention in Washington prior to the expedition was blamed on Grant. Bypassed was the fact that the political opportunist, Heister Clymer, had brushed aside Custer's request to be released from giving further testimony before his committee. Custer had been advised by Terry to be careful of his testimony. It appears that Custer made an effort to push or force hearsay evidence. Ever the battlefield tactician, he quickly sized up the situation. Realizing that as long as he produced evidence he would be detained from joining his command and the planned campaign, he seized every opportunity of offering hearsay evidence, thereby lessening his value to the committee. It was then that he was released.[3]

On July 15th, Congressman A. S. Williams introduced two bills for the relief of General Custer's family. The first would provide a pension of $50 a month for Libbie, and the second would provide $80 a month for the General's aged parents. In support of the latter bill he read a letter "signed by the most eminent people of Monroe" stating that the aged parents had been deprived of their only means of support. He offered the knowledge that Custer's financial affairs were in such condition the family was about penniless, and that the Custer home was "so heavily encumbered that they must lose it unless material aid is extended to them."[4]

Libbie was to be awarded $50 a month whereas the second bill was amended to provide a pension of $50 a month each to Emanuel and Maria Custer.[5] Both failed to pass. An attempt was made to grant pensions "to the heirs of the officers, non-commissioned officers, musicians and privates" who were killed in the battle, but this was rejected.[6]

Congressman Alfred M. Waddell of North Carolina, not to be outdone by the many complimentary statements made of Custer on the floor of the House, introduced a bill authorizing the erection of a monument to him. This was referred to the Library Committee and ordered printed.[7] A week later, July 25th, Congressman Williams introduced a bill "to donate bronze cannon for an equestrian statue of Bvt. Maj. Gen. Geo. A. Custer."[8]

Custer had his enemies, though none of them were Indians. He had his friends too, and where they meant the most to a bereaved family—on the frontier. In a surprise move the legislature of the State of Texas, on July 28th, approved a resolution, copies of which were forwarded to the Custer family and to the Congress. It read:

"Whereas, General G. A. Custer has endeared himself to the people of the frontier of Texas and elsewhere by his bold and dashing operations against the Indians, and

Whereas, the news of his late sudden death, while in discharge of his dangerous duties is received,

Therefore, Be it resolved by the Legislature of Texas, That we tender our sincere condolence to the family of the deceased and to the people of our suffering frontier."[9]

Other honors were heaped on the Custer name. The New York *Times,* on July 18th, announced that a new town in Will County, Illinois, had been named Custer in honor of the General. The news media printed many eulogies and letters to the editors commending Custer for his courage and contributions to national security and peace.

The New York *Herald* was the first to propose that a Custer monument be erected through private contributions from all parts of the country. It gave $1,000 and announced it would publish a list of contributors each day. Initially suggested was "a national monument erected to commemorate the heroism of General Custer and his Kinsmen who fell with him."[10]

In the day-to-day issues that followed were printed a long list of contributors, many using just initials, ranging from 5¢ up. A Custer Monument Association had been formed to receive the contributions. By July 26th it reported receipts of $3,867.[11]

Judge Henry Hilton had given $1,000; Lawrence Barrett gave $250. The *Herald* regretted that the proposal had started with so many large offers. It desired to see a host of small contributions "as an expression of the multitude of admirers."

An old army officer drew attention to Libbie's financial difficulties, and suggested that instead of a monument a fund be given to her for her support. His letter to the *Herald*[12] drew attention to the custom of presenting swords to officers when their children needed shoes. He asked: "Do you not think that if Custer himself could speak he would prefer bread for his widow to a stone for himself?"

In Bay City, Michigan, a movement was organized by Mayor McDonell to form a permanent organization to raise funds for an equestrian statue to Custer to be erected within the state. Though one person thought their association should unite with the national movement, it was decided that Michigan should have its own monument to Custer.[13]

Monroe, not to be outdone, organized a monument association. Apparently oblivious to the movement initiated by the New York *Herald,* several Monroe citizens called a meeting in the City Hall for that purpose. The meeting was held on July 17th and drew a large attendance. General Phil Sheriadan, though not present, was elected president of the newly formed National Custer Monument Association.[14]

Monroe remained in a state of shock. It had not recovered from the effects of losing six of its citizens.[15] Earlier—on July 6th—handbills had been circulated on the order of Mayor Spaulding calling for a meeting at the Court House at 4 P.M. Bells tolled as a band marched to the Court House playing a dirge. At the meeting, presided over by the mayor, various dispatches were read, speeches made and a resolution passed in behalf of the parents of the deceased. That evening a meeting was held in the Methodist Church to determine an appropriate time to hold a memorial service in the church. A portrait of Custer was displayed facing the audience, the interior of the church being draped in mourning.[16]

The July 20 issue of the Monroe *Commercial* announced that Captain Willard Glazier, who had served in the Second New York Cavalry under Custer, would lecture at the City Hall. The entire net proceeds would be contributed to the Custer Monument Fund. Glazier continued his ride on horseback across Michigan to Chicago, lecturing as he went, and sending a check to the Custer Fund after each performance.[17]

Back in New York the *Herald* continued relentlessly to hammer the Grant Administration and the Grant attitude. It had raised the big question: "Who slew Custer?" Then, before anyone could answer, it indicated that the Grant peace policy of feeding and clothing Indian families while warriors killed our troops was the thing that killed Custer—"that nest of thieves, the Indian Bureau, with its thieving agents and favorites as Indian traders . . . that is what killed Custer."[18]

On July 17th, the *Herald* challenged Grant by saying:

"Had Sheridan been killed by the Indians instead of Custer, President Grant would have published an address on the subject. But for Custer, who made Sheridan, and did more than any one man to make President Grant, the Sitting Bull of the White House has never a word to offer."

The moment David Reed learned of the tragedy he left for Fort Lincoln.[19] He knew that his daughter Emma, his sister-in-law Libbie and Maggie Calhoun would need all the help he could muster. When he arrived there on July 13th he found Libbie quite exhausted and unable to undertake the tiresome journey to Monroe. She had been receiving an avalanche of letters and telegrams from old friends.

Of 115 such letters in the author's files an even 100 contain the line "If I can be of any assistance." Many enclosed poems or biblical quotations. Old friends, and in some cases acquaintances, suggested that she should visit with them just for a change. Some observed that the Army was no longer the same; "everything has changed." Though there was solace in each, the wound was kept open.

On July 15th Jacob Greene had written from Hartford:

"Since the news of your husband's death I am continually going over the scenes of our service together. I well remember how I was perpetually

MONROE COMMERCIAL.

VOLUME 36. MONROE, MICH., THURSDAY, JULY 13, 1876. NUMBER 28.

THE COMMERCIAL.

Published every Thursday, at No. 19 Washington Street, MONROE, MICH., by

M. D. HAMILTON & SON,

[illegible] SUBSCRIPTION.—$2,00 per year, free. A [illegible]count of 50 cents for advance [illegible]

Transient advertising, one [illegible]ek, $1,00; two weeks, $1,[illegible] [illegible]r weeks, $2,50; and 25 cents for [illegible] [illegible]after.

Liberal ter[illegible] yearly advertisers.

Local business notices, 15 cents per line.

[illegible] PRINTING.—Ample facilities for all kinds [illegible] Ornamental work. Prices low and satisfaction [illegible]nteed.

CITY BREVITIES.

Hot weather the past week. See weather report.

C. G. Johnson, Esq., left for the Centennial, day before yesterday.

The Eagle Hose Co. will give a steamboat excursion to Sandusky in the latter part of August.

A good healthy summer drink is the root beer made by T. B. Case, of Lasalle, and cheap too. Mr. Case comes in town two or three times a week, to supply customers.

Last Saturday evening about 9 o'clock, a very bright meteor lighted up the sky, moving over our city in a northwesterly direction. Its track through the sky could be seen for 20 or 30 minutes.

Sackett's show window, contains the portraits of Gen. Custer, Thomas and Boston, Custer, and Armstrong Reed, draped in mourning and surrounded by a profusion of American colors.

The old friends in this city, of Miss Emma Smith, some years ago a teacher in our Union School, and who for several years past has been a resident of California, will find her marriage recorded in this paper.

David Reed Esq., left last Friday evening for Fort Abraham Lincoln, with a view to ascertain what can be done about obtaining the bodies of Gen. Custer, and the group of his relatives who died with him, and also to accompany home the sorrowing women at Fort Lincoln.

The interior of the M. E. Church has been handsomely draped in mourning, in memory of the fallen Custer and his comrads. A bas relief portrait of Gen. Custer, properly draped, occupies a conspicuous position on the organ, fronting the audience, and surrounding it, within wreaths of evergreen, appear the names of his four relatives who died by his side. Last Sabbath Rev. Mr. Casler preached a discourse appropriate to the occasion (though not a funeral discourse), from the text in Revelations, "Be thou faithful unto death, and I will give [illegible]"

Casualties.

On the 5th inst, a son of Louis Eckert ten years of age, while playing on a wagon loaded with bags of grain, fell off and was run over by the hind wheel, dislocating the left elbow joint and otherwise injuring him. He is recovering.

On the 7th inst, a son of Edward Roeder, three years of age, got his hand caught in the cog-wheel of a clothes-wringer. Result—one finger off. A rather severe initiation into the trials of this life.

On the same date, a man in the employ of Mr. Robert G. Kelly of Erie, Fred Springer by name, aged about 20 years, was thrown from a mowing machine, and falling upon the knife-bar, had his right thigh badly lacerated, with a fracture of the bone. The limb was amputated by Dr. Southworth, assisted by Drs. Gifford and Thompson of Erie. The man rallied somewhat after the operation but it is doubtless a fatal case, as at 5 P. M. full reaction had not been established.

☞ Killed in an attack made upon the Sioux Indians, in Montana, June 25th, 1876. Gen. Geo. A. Custer, Col. Thomas Custer, Lieut. Calhoun, Boston Custer, and Armstrong Reed.

At a meeting held at the Monroe M. E. Church, July 6th, the following resolutions were adopted:

Whereas, The above named have fallen gallantly fighting the foes of our common country, and,

Whereas, So many of the near relatives of the deceased are members of this church, therefore,

Resolved, That we deem it fitting that some formal action be taken, by which as a church we may recognize the high esteem in which these men were held among us, and our admiration for their valor. That as soon as possible we may fix on a suitable time, a memorial shall be held in this church. That the church be draped for thirty days in honor of the fallen heroes. That we extend our tenderest sympathies to the families of the deceased. That a copy of these resolutions be sent to each of the bereaved families, and to the press of this city for publication.

D. CASLER,
O. A. CRITCHETT, } Committee.
J. M. LOOSE,

Weather Report.

The following shows the state of the weather for the week ending yesterday.

	7 a. m.	2 p. m.	9 p. m.	Max.	Min.
Thurs., July 6	[illegible] ab.	88 ab.	82 ab.	92 ab.	67 ab.
Friday, " 7	73 ab.	90 ab.	84 ab.	96 ab.	70 ab.
Sat., " 8	79 ab.	[illegible] ab.	80 ab.	99 ab.	71 ab.
[illegible] " 9	79 ab.	90 ab.	87 ab.	101 ab.	75 ab.
10	[illegible] ab.	[illegible] ab.	77 ab.	[illegible] ab.	78 ab.
11	[illegible] ab.	[illegible] ab.	83 ab.	[illegible] ab.	[illegible] ab.
[illegible]	73 ab.	92 ab.	[illegible] ab.	[illegible] ab.	[illegible] ab.

Card.

[illegible] prepared to give lessons during the summer [illegible] nces of the scholars. [illegible] P. O. B. 227, Monroe. Respectfully,

E. HARDIX.

[illegible]ed by the same and june22w4

CUSTER FALLEN!

TRIBUTE TO HIS MEMORY!

Our City in Mourning!

PUBLIC MEETING AT THE COURT HOUSE!

BUSINESS CLOSED!

Speeches, Resolutions, &c., &c.

The news which reached this city last Thursday morning, of the death of the heroic Custer and his brave comrads is confirmed in all its fulness and terrible extent. As soon as our citizens fully realized the calamity that had befallen them—that had befallen our State and our country at large, a gloom settled upon every heart, like a pall. For Custer belonged to his country; Michigan honored him and gloried in his military career; and here at Monroe, in the home of his school days and young manhood, kindred and friends have watched his career with loving pride. They have known him as a brave, manly, heroic, chivalrous spirit, true as steel in every trial, and they have believed him worthy of higher honors than those the government has seen fit to bestow upon him. But he is now no more! All hearts are filled with sorrow; all heads are bowed in grief. We weep not alone for a friend and brother, true and good, but we weep also for a fallen brave—a friend and brother whose place in our hearts can never be filled—a fallen brave whose place among the braves of the nation no other brave can supply. Our warmest sympathies go out in hearty spontaniety to his young wife and his sister, both bereft of their companions and left alone afar off on the frontier; and most especially are our sympathies extended to his aged parents, who not only lose him, but also two other sons and a son-in-law, all brave and true; and we should not forget the parents of the younger relative, the only son of our townsman David Reed, who was in his first battle and died by the side of his heroic uncle. For the dispatches say, "the bodies of Custer his two brothers and nephew (with several other officers) were found lying in a circle of a few yards." They had made an attack, were apparently compelled to retreat, were cut off from the main body, forced into a narrow recess, where horses and men were slaughtered promiscuously [illegible] to tell the tale.

On Friday morning last by order of Mayor Spalding, bills were circulated calling a public meeting at the Court House at 4 o'clock the same afternoon, at which time business was closed—business houses had previously been draped in mourning. At four o'clock the bells were tolled, the band marched to the Court House playing a dirge, and the building was soon filled with our sympathetic and mourning populace. The Hall had been appropriately draped in mourning, and a portrait of Gen. Custer, properly draped, was arranged just back of the speakers stand.

The meeting was called to order by Mayor Spalding, who made some remarks proper to the occasion, appropriately styling Gen. Custer "the Murat of the U. S. Army."

Mayor Spalding was made chairman of the meeting, and John M. Bulkley was named as Secretary.

Rev. D. Casler offered a prayer befitting the occasion.

Mayor Spalding read a dispatch from Vice President T. W. Ferry under date of Washington, July 6th, closing as follows: "I share the grief of Gen. Custer's home in the fall of this cavalry hero. He fell as he fought—in the fore front of battle. The country will miss this brave soldier, and friends cherish his gallant memory." Also a dispatch from W. H. Walby, H. Hart and other citizens of Adrian as follows: "Adrian mourns with you on the news of the death of the gallant and chivalrous Custer and his brave comrads. We deeply condole with his amiable wife and other friends in their great bereavement."

On motion of Col. Grosvenor, a committee was appointed to draft resolutions to be presented to the meeting, said committee consisting of Col. I. R. Grosvenor, E. J. Boyd, R. E. Phinney, G. M. Landon, and E. G. Harvey.

Remarks were made by W. H. Boyd, Rev. Dr. Strong, J. D. Ronan, Frank Raleigh, J. M. Bulkley, and E. J. Boyd, each paying a fitting tribute of respect to the deceased, and of sympathy with the afflicted parents and other relatives.

R. E. Phinney, from the Committee, read the resolutions, as follows:

WHEREAS, By a Providence which only the firmest faith in the wisdom of Him who sits as the dispenser of all events, can justify, our city has been stricken with profoundest grief at the seemingly untimely death of so many of her young men, noblest in heart and life, fullest of future promise,

Resolved, That we friends and acquaintances of those who have so ruthlessly been taken from us, find most grateful comfort in the memories they have left us of their chivalric spirits and noble achievements; that in the death of Gen. Custer our city has lost one of the best beloved of all her sons, our State has lost one of the worthiest and most honored of her citizens; our nation has lost one of the bravest, most gallant and [illegible] successful of her defenders, and the world has lost a husband, brother, soldier, son and friend above reproach. That to the aged and venerable father and mother of these heroic dead, to the wife of that gallant and heretofore unconquered [illegible] Custer, to the wife of that knightly soldier, Calhoun; to the parents of the brave, pure minded boy who fell on his first field of battle, and to the whole circle of their kindred we tender our heartfelt sympathy and condolence; reminding them as we remind ourselves, that henceforth these fallen ones are no longer ours, nor theirs, but our country's and fame's, among the pure, the immortal names that are not born to die.

The resolutions were adopted, and on motion the secretary was directed to furnish a copy to the parents of the deceased.

A committee consisting of E. J. Boyd, J. M. Sterling, I. R. Grosvenor and J. M. Bulkley, was appointed to send a dispatch of condolence to Mrs. Custer and Mrs. Calhoun, at Fort Abraham Lincoln.

After another dirge by the band, the meeting was closed with prayer by Rev. D. P. Putnam. The bells were tolled during the exercises.

BIOGRAPHICAL.

Gen. George Armstrong Custer was born at New Rumley, Harrison Co., O., about 20 miles from Steubenville, on Dec. 5th, 1839. In 1852 he came to Monroe to reside with his brother-in-law, David Reed, and attended school here several years. He always after called Monroe his home. After returning to Ohio he spent a year or two in teaching, and in 1856, while Congressman John A. Bingham of that State, was canvassing his district, young Custer jocosely told him he would vote for him if he (Bingham) would send him to West Point; which Mr. Bingham promised to do if he should be elected, and he was as good as his word. Custer entered West Point in 1857. From his early youth young Custer had a great desire for military life, his ardent wish being to become a soldier. Soon after he entered West Point his parents moved to Monroe, and his vacations were always spent here. He left West Point in July 1861, went to Washington, and was immediately sent to the front with dispatches to General McDowell, and was assigned to duty just in time to participate in the first battle of Bull Run. From that time forward through the war he followed the fortunes of the Army of the Potomac, participating in nearly every battle. He rose from rank to rank, and in 1863 was brevetted Major General of Volunteers, and was afterward assigned to the command of the Third Cavalry Division. During the last six months of the war, this cavalry division, under General Custer's command, captured 111 pieces of artillery, [illegible] 10,000 prisoners. [illegible] in Texas, and then joined Hancock's expedition against the Indians since when he has been in constant service on the frontier, and by his bravery and prowess made himself a terror to the red men. In 1864 he was married in Monroe to the only daughter of the late Hon. Daniel S. Bacon, who was born and had grown to a lovely and accomplished womanhood here in this city of flowers, among the friends who now mourn with her the fall of her adored hero. After their marriage his wife was with him always at his headquarters on the frontier, and accompanied him on many of his expeditions in the field. Since the war Gen. Custer has been improving a portion of his time in the arena of literature, and with marked success. His book entitled "My Life on the Plains," which first appeared in successive articles in the Galaxy, is a very entertaining book, containing much information relating to Indian life and warfare. He spent the most of last winter in New York, revising and preparing for publication his "War Memoirs," the first two or three chapters of which have been published in the Galaxy, the remainder of the series being completed and in the hands of that journal for publication. The last number of the Galaxy contained a graphic sketch by Custer entitled "Battling with the Sioux on the Yellowstone."

Thomas Custer entered the army in 1862, as a private, and participated in Gen. Sherman's grand march to the sea. In the voluteer service he rose to the rank of Lieutenant-Colonel, by brevet. After the war he was transferred to his brother's cavalry command in the regular army, and has been with the General in most, if not all of his campaigns against the Indians. He ranked as Captain in the regular army.

Boston Custer, another brother of the General's, was in the commissary department. He has been with his brother's command several years.

Lieutenant James Calhoun, brother-in-law to the General, is the son of a widowed mother living in the State of Indiana. He was highly esteemed by all who knew him here in Monroe.

Harry Armstrong Reed, Gen. Custer's nephew, was the only son of David Reed, Esq., of this city. He was born in Monroe, was 18 years old in April last, and was known and esteemed as a very promising young man. He, with his sister Emma, left this city with the General in May last, accompanying him to Fort Abraham Lincoln. "Autie," as he was called, accompanied the expedition as a herder. His parents have a letter from him dated June 10th, and written in camp on Powder River, 20 miles from its junction with the Yellowstone, in which he speaks of Custer's command as about starting to find Indians, and said the herd had become so reduced as not to need attention, and that he had obtained permission to accompany his uncle. He speaks of writing a letter to the COMMERCIAL, and says, referring to some talk about going in another direction: "Uncle Autie says there are no Indians there: but we shall find Indians." They did find Indians—too many of them—and their friends will see them so more [illegible] the [illegible] of time.

THE REGATTA!

The Champions of the World in Monroe!

And their Names are Sho-wae-cae-mette!

The Floral City Club Captures the Four Oared Junior Prizes!

A CLEAN SWEEP FOR MONROE!

The eighth annual regatta of the [illegible]rth Western Amateur Rowing Association, held in Toledo on the 4th, 5th and 6th, was by far the finest regatta ever held by the association, and equaled, if not surpassed, any regatta ever held in the East. A large concourse of people witnessed the races each day, and the promptness with which the races came off showed that the officers were faithfully performing their duty.

The principal race of the first day was the four oared free for all, in which there were four entries, the Wah-Wah-Sums, of Saginaw: the Cincinnatis, of Cincinnati: the Puritans, of Toledo, and the Sho-wae-cae-mettes, of Monroe. The Puritans having only entered to further the success of the regatta, and with no hopes of winning the race, did not pull over the course but laid for the Sho-waes at the mile stake, coming in a half length behind. At the start the Wah-Wahs took the lead with the Cincinnatis next, until fouling an outrigger the latter fell behind. At the mile buoy the Sho-waes were some ways ahead. Here the Wah-Wahs, mistaking the buoy, lost considerable time in attempting to turn, but as soon as the Sho-waes discovered what they were at they informed them of their mistake and the race continued, the Sho-wae-cae-mettes winning in 18:25 with the Wah-Wah-Sums full twenty lengths behind. The following are the crews:

"CHAS. G. MORRIS," Sho-wae-cae-mette Boat Club, Monroe—Crew: Stroke, [illegible]phen Dusseau, 160; Joseph Nadeau, [illegible]; Moses Nadeau, 130; bow, Geo. W. [illegible]isby, 135. Total 563 lbs.; average, [illegible] lbs.

"SARAH A. BULLOCK," Wah-Wah-Sum Boat Club, Saginaw—Crew: Bow, Jas. [illegible]rome, 150; John Kellerin, 165; Henry [illegible]th, 165; stroke, P. Manning, 165. Total 645 lbs.; average 161¼ lbs.

"CINCINNATI," Cincinnati Rowing Club —[illegible] 160; F. Hecker, 160; N. G. Kenedy, 142; J. P. Numan, 135; Wm. Steinheim, 160; Henry Kalish, 140. Total 892 lbs.; average 148 2-3.

The time made in the above race was a surprise to everybody but Monroe people, as it was generally believed that no such time could be made. When the Wah-Wah-Sums passed through the city on their way to Toledo they were told that Sho-wae-cae-mettes had rowed 3 miles with a turn in 18:22, but they would not believe it and went over to Toledo confident of winning both the free for all four, and the senior four. But their hopes of remaining the champions of the North Western Amateur Rowing Association for another year were much diminished when they learned the time made in the free for all; for they frankly admitted that they never had made any such time and did not expect to.

A heavy gale on the second day prevented the races from being called at the appointed time, and the senior four did not come off till about seven in the evening. The water was rough, and it was thought by many that the Cincinnatis and Wah-Wah-Sums had the advantage on that account, but, though they may have had the advantage, it was not great enough to win them the race, as the result proved. The *Blade* says the "race for senior four oared shells was the one in which the greatest interest was manifested, for in this the Wah Wah-Sums, who sustained such a bad defeat the day before at the hands of the Sho-wae-cae-mettes, hoped to retrieve their fallen fortunes, and show the boys from Monroe, as well as boating men in general, that the old Saginaw, though once defeated, was still alive, and its crew could yet pull a boat without looking over their shoulders to see all the rest of the boats. Then the Cincinnati crew, dissatisfied with their showing on Tuesday, when, by accident to their outrigger they were thrown out, determined to make another effort to carry back a prize to the Ohio river. The Sho-wae-cae-mettes said nothing, but trusting not so much to their skill as oarsmen as to their great strength and endurance, determined that they would convince the Saginaw boys that their previous victory was not the result of an accident, but the fruit of good hard work." That the Sho-wae-cae-mettes should say nothing and the *Blade* man be so well informed, is a mystery still unexplained. The positions of the crews were Cincinnatis first, or nearest the grand stand, Wah-Wah-Sums second, and Sho-wae-cae-mettes third. At the start the Cincinnatis shot ahead, pulling a short sharp stroke, with the Saginaws second, pulling their customary long sweeping stroke. It was soon evident that the race was between Saginaw and Monroe, and at the end of the first mile the Wah-Wahs and Sho-waes were nearly even, with the Cincinnatis way in the rear. At the turn the Wah-Wahs were about a boat length ahead, and then came some of the finest pulling ever witnessed in Toledo. Though the Wah-Wahs were a boat length ahead and shoving their shell along with lightning rapidity, it soon became evident that the Sho-waes were but playing with them, as they passed them easily, gradually increasing th[e]ir stroke from 36 to 40 per minute, and winning the race by at least four boat lengths, in 18:30½. The *Blade* says the Sho-waes did not "pull well together but managed to push their boat through the water at a rapid pace." While we deny the statement that they did not pull well together, we are perfectly willing to admit that they did "*manage*" to push their boat through the water at a pace rapid enough to beat the best time on record just six and two-fifth seconds, and on the second day, when the water was very rough at the lower end of the course, they "*managed*" to beat the best time on record (made in smooth water two years ago) a little over one second. Last year Toledo papers laid their success in the junior four to "beef" and a "grindstone" stroke. This year it is their, enormous strength and endurance which they [illegible]ed in (and which enabled them to win), rather than in skill, which Toledo seems unwilling to grant them. The Sho-wae-cae-mettes handled their shell in the most dextrous and skillful manner, shooting in any direction with the velocity of an arrow; and when the boat went over the course in the race, the perfect [illegible] line which the boat took from home stake to turning stake and from turning stake to home stake was the [illegible] of all who understand boating matters. The *Blade* says they did not pull together, but there never was a more [illegible] statement than that, as each oar worked with the precision of clock work, the spoons all striking the water at the same time as though one oar. There certainly is a peculiarity in their rowing, that to the inexperienced eye, would seem perhaps as though they were not pulling together, but whether it was through ignorance on the part of the *Blade* reporter, or unwillingness to tell the truth, we are unable to determine. Certain it is that the Toledo papers have ever been willing to slight Monroe in any particular, and still more certain have they seemed unwilling to give a fair account of the races in which she has been personally interested. Why they should be so, when it is for the interest of Toledo to remain on friendly terms with the Monroe boat clubs, is more than we can imagine. However, such good time was made in the four oared and six oared races, that the association determined to challenge all amateur clubs in America to row at the next regatta to be held in Toledo next summer. [illegible] "grindstone" stroke, "strength and endurance," "beef," and the "giant" proportions of the stroke, who weighs just five pounds less than any man in the Wah-Wah-Sums crew except bow, (while the average of the Sho-waes is 20¼ lbs. lighter than theirs) have done all this. What will they not do [illegible] each them the stroke they call "skill." If the Toledo *Commercial* reporter, who is the cause of the one thousand and one mistakes that occur in that paper's report of the regatta is the one who made such a mess of it last year and then came over to Monroe and attempted to make amends by giving a miserably mixed up account of the River Raisin Navy regatta, we would advise the *Commercial* to shove a frog down his throat and tell him to go dwell with them, in some remote region where thy voice can be heard no more on earth."

The next race in which Monroe took part was the four oared junior race on the sixth. The following are the crews, giving their positions in the order named:

"FRANK H HURD," Floral City Boat Club, Monroe—Crew: Stroke, Charles Hoyt, 138; James F. Grant, 150; Geo. S. Willits, 144; bow, Walter P. Sterling, 119. Total 551 lbs.; average 137¾.

"H. B. TAYLOR," Undine Boat Club, Toledo—Crew: Stroke, C. P. Thomas, 175; L. W. Hunter, 153; A. J. Kneisser, 169; bow, J. W. Hepbourn, 143. Total 612 lbs.; average 153 lbs.

"KENILWORTH," Farragut Boat Club, Chicago—Crew: Bow, Chas. S. Downs, 185; Frank Booth, 143; Henry P. Smith, 135; stroke, A. Ogden Downs, 143. Total 560 lbs.; averave 140 lbs.

"GEO. E. HALL," Excelsior Boat Club, Detroit—Crew: Stroke, C. D. Waterman; J. E. Watson, H. E. Hass; bow, John B. Malony.

The Amateurs were entered for this race, but withdrew on account of the sickness of their stroke.

At the start the Farraguts shot ahead, but after the fifth stroke the Floral Citys were ahead and maintained the lead to the last. At the end of the first mile the Undines were close to the Florals, the Farraguts next and the Excelsiors away in the rear, when the latter gave up and returned. At the turning stake the stroke of the Undines, who were close to the Florals, broke the button off his bar, rendering it useless, and leaving the race to be contested between the Farraguts and Florals, the latter winning in 20:22.

The badges won by the Monroe clubs at Toledo this year are very beautiful as well as valuable, the twelve badges costing just $700. Those won by the Sho-wae-cae-mettes in the open to all, are by far the most valuable and we believe are considered the finest badges ever presented by the association. Each badge consists of three massive pieces. The upper piece or bar, to which the pin is attached is of Roman gold, surrounded by a raised border of polished gold with a design of vines at the bottom. In the center of this piece are engraved the words "Open to All" in plain block letters. The second piece, or badge proper, is the largest and is attached to the bar by two gold rings. This piece is also of Roman gold with a raised border, in the center of which is a representation in raised work of a four oared shell and crew. The third piece or pendant consists of a curved bar, with the word "Toledo" engraved in the center, ornamented with carved work about the sides, and hanging by a ring at each end to the piece above. They are valued at $100 each. The above description gives no idea of the beauty and richness of these badges which can only be seen to be admired.

The badges of the senior four consist of a plain bar with place for engraving the name of winner and time made in the face. Hanging from this is a design of four oars, the handles of which are fastened together at the bottom with a rope of gold, tied in a sailors knot, which describes a circle, winding about the blade of each oar, and holding them in a fan shaped position. In the center of the circle described by the rope, and lying upon the handles of the oars, is a streamer of red enamel on which in gilt letters are the words "Senior 4 Oared, Toledo, Ohio, 1876." These badges are valued at $50 each.

The badges of the junior four, though costing but half the money, are much prettier, in our estimation, than those of the senior four. The bar is plain, with a place for engraving time and name of winner. Hanging from the bar by a chain is a beautiful design of crossed oars and a twisted wreath; the blades of the oars are fastened together by a gold cord, from each end of which hangs a tassel. Upon the face of the badge, in the shape of a letter S, is a banner of blue enamel on which are inscribed in gilt the words "Junior 4 Oared, Toledo, 1876" in plain gothic letters.

The above badges can be seen in the window of L. & J. F. Grant's jewelry store.

The following is a list of the winners of each race during regatta:

Single sculls—open to all—Frank E. Yates, 140; Union Springs, N. Y. Time 14:27. Prize, gold badge, $100.

Pleasure boats—open to citizens of Toledo—"Zip"—J. G. Kaney, W. G. Alexander. Time 19:20.

Four oared shells—open to all—Sho-wae-cae-mettes—Monroe. Time 18:25. Prize gold badges, $400.

Junior double sculls—"Lotus," Farragut B. C.—Chicago—Bow, A. Ogden Downs, 143; stroke, C. S. Downs, 135. Time, 15:42 4-5. Prizes, gold badges, $50.

Senior four oared shells—Sho-wae-cae-mettes—Time, 18:30½. Prizes gold badges, $200.

Junior six oared shells—"Wm. A. Halleck," Zephyr B. C., Detroit. Crew: Stroke, E. Barrows, 138; P. W. Keating, 145; C. H. Dings, 143; David Linn, 138; Edward Sutton, 145; bow, Frank S. Bagg, 126. Total, 835 lbs.; average 139 1-6 lbs. Time, 19:15½. Prizes, gold badges, $150.

Barges—"F. G. Thompson," Phoenix B. C., Detroit. Crew: Stroke, C. Creedan: D. Creedan; P. McGrath, M. Schaffer, A. S. Martin, O. A. [illegible], [illegible] Byrne, Capt. Creedan, C. Clinton; bow, W. T. Schaffer; captain, Henry Hopkins, 135. Time, 13:12½. Prizes gold oars, $50.

Junior single sculls—"Perhaps," H. M. Butler, 120; Chicago scullers. Time, 15:56. Prize, gold badge, $35.

Senior double sculls—F. E. Yates, Grand Haven; Oscar Meday, Cincinnati. Time, 14:11. Prizes, gold badges $100.

Junior four oared shells—Floral Citys, Monroe — Time 20.22. Prizes, gold badges, $100.

Senior single sculls—"Elsie," F. W. Montgomery, Chicago scullers. Time, 16:20½. Prize, gold badge, $75.

Senior six oared shells—Wah-Wah Sums, Saginaw, Crew: Bow, James Jerome, 150; V. B. Paine, 158; B. McEigann, 158; John Kelorin, 165; Henry Smith, 165; stroke, P. Manning, 165. Total 936 lbs.; average 158 5 6. Time, 17:28. Prizes, gold badges, $300.

A Monument to Gen. Custer.

Ed. Commercial.—Believing it will meet the views of many military and civilian friends of the late Gen. Custer in Monroe and throughout the land, I would suggest that a meeting be held immediately for the purpose of taking steps to secure donations from citizens here and Gen. Custer's friends wherever they may reside, in this or other States, to erect a suitable monument in our Public Square, to him who has so greatly distinguished his own name and left so glorious an example for the young men of our common country.

I would name Col. Grosvenor, Gen. Spalding, R. E. Phinney, Harry A. Conant, John M. Bulkley and John B. Rauch, to take the matter in charge and call a meeting at such time and place as they may select,

Respectfully,
CHAS. G. JOHNSON.

Heartily concurring in the suggestions contained in a communication of our townsman, Hon. C. G. Johnson, relative to the propriety of adopting some measure by the citizens of Monroe for the erection of a suitable monument to the memory of their late distinguished fallen citizen, General G. A. Custer, unite in calling a meeting to be held on Thursday evening, July 13th, in the Court House Square, for this object.

T E Wing,	W H Boyd,
Harry A Conant,	W A Noble,
J M Bulkley,	J A Loranger,
J P Hogarth,	N Vanderheyden,
S M Sackett,	Leonard Mitchell,
C B Stoddard,	L Berthelote,
L Grant,	James L Robert,
W Stoddard,	F Soleau,
M D Hamilton,	E C Harvey
J F Grant,	L R Little,
Darius Loose,	James Little,
Fred [illegible],	Geo S Trevor,
[illegible]	J. B. Gale,
F [illegible]	A T Ward,
E [illegible]	H T Nichols,
Chas Cowan,	Geo M Landon,
Sebastian Lauer,	H M Nolte,
J L C Godfrey	J Weiss,
N. N. Kendal,	A I Sawyer,
Jas G McBride,	R E Phinney,
Thos Doyle,	H T Cole,
J H Kary,	Thos Strong.

FIRST NEWS FOR MONROE. Courtesy of the Monroe County Historical Museum.

dreading his death, and that it seemed to me I could never serve with another officer. And as he went into one danger after another & came out unharmed, and almost my first fight with him at Culpeper after which we went home together, I began to feel that the man bore a charmed life. . . .

"I never loved and admired any other man as I did your husband. What he was to you and what you were to him I well know. You were the first and only love of one of the bravest, strongest and noblest of men, whose mark in the history of this country & of his profession will never be lost, and whose death was the seal of a record, the most brilliant in deeds and without a stain of dishonor."[20]

Nearly a month later, she received a letter from General Sherman he had written after being certain she had arrived in Monroe:

"How mysterious are the ways of Providence! Custer, who for years seemed to court death when heavy columns of cavalry gave to war a glorious aspect, was doomed to fall and sleep on the far off hills of the Big Horn. Yet he was engaged in a war as necessary as any which history delights to record. A war between civilization and barbarism, a war between the peaceful agriculturist and the savage hunter. When in years soon to come, the Yellowstone becomes the highway of travel between the East and the West, when peaceful farmers and gardeners occupy the valley of the Rosebud and Big Horn, people will point to the spot where Custer and his brave companies fell that they and their children might live in peace in a land soon to be reserved from the possession of the bloody Sioux."[21]

To add to Libbie's discomfiture a letter sent by Mrs. Boyd described a sad visit to the home of General's parents where "the General's father is in tears most of the time and his mother says 'How can I bear it—all my boys gone'?"[22]

Other letters of a more cheerful content were sent by her aunts Charity and Eliza, and her Uncle Albert in Camillus, and cousins Charles and Mary Kendall in Topeka. Nellie Wadsworth's letter must have been a cheerful relief too. She wrote from Binghamton, New York, that the General had given her the happiest two months of her life.[23]

There were many decisions to make, all painful ones. Libbie knew there might be a time like this though she hoped for what she knew to be an impossible hope. Her husband was not destined to die of old age.

It would be hard to leave the white headquarters house with its green trim. It had been built expressly for Autie. There they had lived longer than anywhere—three wonderful years—and each precious minute seemed more wonderful than the previous one. It couldn't be compared in terms of comfort to the house in Monroe her father had left to her, but it held more precious memories. It would be occupied by others once she left. She would not know that no one would remember the others who would follow or what they did, though. The story of the house and of Fort Lincoln would always be a part of the Custer story.[24]

WHEN LIBBIE WAS 40. 1882. Courtesy of the Dorsch Memorial Library, Monroe, Mich.

There was not much furniture so that offered no great problem. The heavy-framed bed and dresser, the desk in his den and a few of his favorite folding camp chairs could be sent by rail with his half dozen trunks and foot lockers. The china and other fragile items could be packed in barrels of sawdust or hay. Those items remaining such as the various hanging lamps and shades were turned over to Post Trader Harmon for resale.[25]

The dogs had to be left behind. Once it was known that Libbie would present them to anyone who would provide a proper home for them, requests came in from all parts of the country. *Dandy* was another matter. Libbie wanted *Dandy* to be in the hands of Father Custer. She knew what it would mean to the old gentleman, horse lover that he was, to possess some living thing dear to his favorite son. It was decided that *Dandy* would remain behind, after he was returned to Fort Lincoln, until she sent for him.

Libbie departed from Fort Lincoln on July 30th, staying at the Bismarck residence of Colonel J. W. Raymond, formerly of Hillsdale, Michigan, overnight. With her was David Reed, Mrs. George Yates, Mrs. A. E. Smith, Mrs. Margaret Calhoun and Richard Roberts, brother of Mrs. Yates. Roberts had accompanied the expedition as a correspondent of the New York *Sun*[26] and as a herder. His pony had played out some 70 miles from the battlefield, forcing him to stay behind.

Superintendent H. A. Town of the Northern Pacific Railroad furnished them with a special car from Bismarck to St. Paul. A frontier missionary, the Reverend Mr. Wainwright, accompanied them to comfort them for the first 200 miles.

The train stopped briefly at Fargo on its way east. Sara Clarke, wife of one of the civil engineers accompanying the survey of the Northern Pacific in 1873, recalled the arrival of the train in Fargo. A large, silent crowd had gathered, not out of idle curiosity but out of deep sympathy. As the sad procession moved slowly across the platform to the hotel, which was a part of the station, a woman's sob was heard from among the onlookers. Many manly men were seen with tears streaming down their cheeks unashamed.

Libbie came first, walking slowly, a drooping, slender figure with head bent and colorless face. Maggie Calhoun followed, her eyes straight ahead into the distance as if seeing nothing near, her face like marble. The other stricken women followed.[27]

They were met by General Card of General Terry's staff at St. Paul and taken to the Metropolitan Hotel where they were the guests of the proprietor Joe Culver and his wife. That evening they boarded the Chicago and Northwestern, stopping at Harvard Junction where the proprietor of Ayer's Hotel sent a complimentary dinner to their car.[28]

Arriving in Chicago on Thursday, August 3d, they were taken to the Palmer House by Colonel Moore of Sheridan's staff. As the guest of Mr. Potter Palmer they remained until 9 P.M., then departed on the Michigan Central Railroad for Monroe,[29] arriving there on the 4th.

F. Y. Commagere, who had served in the Seventh Cavalry under Custer as a first lieutenant, covered the arrival of the sad party in Monroe for the Toledo *Journal* (August 5, 1876). Reverend Boyd was there to meet them. When Libbie, who was the first to leave the car, saw him, "her self-possession left her and she fell fainting in Mr. Boyd's arms with a cry which was almost a shriek of anguish." She was carried to the seat of a carriage and then Maggie was helped to a seat beside her. Mrs. Yates and her three small children followed. Uncharacteristic of present day reporters, Commagere, "in deference to her (Libbie's) state of mind did not interview her."[30] Mrs. Smith continued on her journey to her parents' home in Herkimer, New York.

Maggie, Libbie and Annie Yates with her three small children were taken to the Custer home, the house in which Libbie was born. For some days Libbie remained at home shut off from the world in her grief.

On Sunday, August 13, memorial services were held in the Methodist Church. Though it was a very sultry day the church was filled to capacity. On the organ facing the audience was a bas-relief portrait of General Custer surrounded with an evergreen wreath. Underneath it were two crossed sabers. Surrounding this were the names of the other five Monroeites. The entire church was draped in mourning.[31]

The service was opened with organ music after which the hymn "I Would Not Live Always" was sung. Reverend E. Casler announced Captain Tom Custer had requested that it be sung at his funeral services.

Reverend Casler prefaced his remarks with a roll call of the dead. Slowly, and enunciating carefully, he read:

"General George Armstrong Custer, aged 36, was born at New Rumley, Ohio, December 5th, 1839.

"Captain Thomas Ward Custer, aged 31, was born at New Rumley, Ohio, March 15th, 1844.

"Captain George W. Yates, aged 34, was born at Albany, New York, February 26th, 1842.

"Lieutenant James Calhoun, aged 30, was born at Cincinnati, Ohio, August 24th, 1845.

"Boston Custer, aged 25, was born at New Rumley, Ohio, October 31st, 1850.

"Harry Armstrong Reed, aged 18, was born at Monroe, Michigan, April 27th, 1858.

"These names that we come to commemorate today, no longer belong to private homes; they are the heritage of the nation."[32]

The Reverend Dr. Mattoon, in his lengthy address that followed, described an instance immediately after the battle at Waynesboro where Custer had just defeated General Early in which he had asked his chaplain, Mattoon, to pray and read a chapter of the Bible with him. It was then he had told Reverend Mattoon "he had resolved by God's help to live a Christian life and had expressed such purposes to the friends at home."

Mattoon referred to President Grant's treatment of Custer just prior to his death as a wrong done to his noble but sensitive nature. He noted: "We all felt it. The press protested against it. To the honor of General Sherman and the Secretary of War, both protested against it. But it was done. . . . We pronounce no verdict on this occasion."[33]

Reverend James Venning, who concluded the service, confined his remarks to his knowledge of Lieutenant Calhoun whom he had united in marriage to Maggie Custer in March of 1872, and of Autie Reed.

Letters of condolence continued to arrive, many of them forwarded from Fort Lincoln. There was little energy left to answer them; the women were simply prostrated. Yet there were affairs that must be taken care of for money was not plentiful.

The *Army and Navy Journal* had come out with an editorial suggesting that the New York *Herald's* "proposed creation of a Fund with which to erect a monument to those who fell with Gen. Custer" should be turned into a Widow's Fund to be collected by the *Herald.*[34] Since there was no affirmative response the *Army and Navy Journal,* in an article headed "A WOMAN'S RELIEF FUND" appealed to the members of the armed forces for contributions to alleviate the "deep distress of the helpless ones."[35]

The *Journal* indicated that it would receive and distribute all funds received and would publish a list of the contributors in each issue that followed. True to its tradition, the Old Army was taking care of its own. The response was immediate and gratifying.

Army personnel made the majority of the contributions, the amounts ranging from fifty cents up to $50. There were several larger amounts given by individuals outside the military, and there were contributions from Navy units too. By fall the fund had reached $5,000. And by November 25th, the amount totaled more than $10,000.[36]

In late August, T. F. Rodenbaugh of the *Army And Navy Journal* wrote to Libbie requesting a list of widows and orphans so that the fund could be distributed to them. He assured her there would be no publicity; it would be confidential. General Hancock and General Church were the trustees of the fund.[37]

That November, Libbie received a check of $900 as her portion of the Relief Fund. W. C. Church, editor of the *Journal,* indicated the allocations to the officers' wives as follows:

Mrs. Yates and three children—$1,050
Mrs. A. E. Smith—$510
Mrs. Donald McIntosh—$510
Mrs. James Calhoun—$510
Mrs. James E. Porter and two children—$765
Mrs. J. M. DeWolf—$510
Mrs. H. M. Harrington and two children,—$675

There were nearly 2,000 contributions, many from the Navy, he told her. $1,000 was retained to which would be added any further contributions. A final distribution was to be made at a later date.

He enclosed a leaflet giving the plan of distribution of a sum amounting to $10,270 as of November 15th. Each widow of an enlisted man received $200 and each child one-fourth of that amount ($50).[38]

Shortly before this Libbie had received a U.S. Treasury check for $197, the amount due her husband for his attendance as a witness before the Senate in the trial of Belknap. A small return for honesty of expression.[39]

The Lawrence Barretts, like so many other dear friends were concerned with Libbie's outlook on the future. Indicating to her that he would be playing in Detroit on October 23d and 24th and in Toledo on the 25th, he asked to call upon her. As Barrett explained: "My wife is in New York, and it will be a solace to her as well as myself to personally determine that you are battling with your affliction and are likely to conquer."[40] On his way to Toledo he stopped in Monroe.

Libbie always loved to hear from cousin Rebecca Richmond. Level-headed Rebecca could always say the right thing at the right time. Rebecca was in New York City when news of the disaster reached her. Now, if ever, Libbie needed her. Reaching for her pen, she began:

"If dead they are, they died as true soldiers love to die—at their posts, with their armor on and in the face of the foe. His death was like himself—rare, brilliant, startling, heroic! When I think of that my grief is swallowed up in admiration. And the plucky band that shared his fate was worthy of its idolized leader.

"The men of the Seventh prided themselves upon belonging to the Custer School. And so in death they were not divided—it was their happy privilege to fall, as they had long lived, like brothers, side by side. Hundreds upon hundreds of men would willingly pay the price to be able to share the glory which encircles the tomb of the dauntless 300.

"When I consider that probably not one of those officers would have chosen to be the one left to tell the tale; and when I think of the imposing monuments of the event which will be erected by the sculptor, by poet, by painter, and historian; when I consider this I see some reason why the selfish instincts of affection should yield, and we should try to make our hearts bear bravely the trial of a few years separation from our friends for the sake of the far more exceeding weight of glory with which they are thereby crowned.

"Libbie, how much rather would you be the early widow of such a man than the life-long wife of many another!

"Your life with Armstrong has been intense, concentrated, three or four, or a dozen ordinary lives in one, and those you can live over again quietly, thoughtfully, and I will say, pleasurably, for his is a spirit which will always be near you. You and he have had much sweet commune without the aid of language. Often he would sit for an hour at a time without speaking, but he wanted you by his side, and you loved to be there. I remember well how, after one of those long silences you would say in a slightly piqued—for I think you always rather preferred to talk with your tongue—but triumphant manner, 'I know just what you have been thinking, Autie,' and then he would laugh that peculiar little laugh of his as much as to say 'The little woman is becoming a pretty good interpreter; after awhile she shall not have to talk at all.'

"Thousands of such pleasant, significant reminiscences you have treasured away, Libbie, to cheer you in your loneliness. How thankful you should be for the happy, the honorable post of duty which was assigned you, to act as the helpmate of such a man during his term of service; and thank God too, that he enabled you ever to do that duty satisfactorily. You were a good, true, faithful wife to Armstrong, Libbie and he appreciated it with the full strength of his powerful nature. There is not a person of all my acquaintance who could have filled so beautifully, so perfectly, the position that you did.

"It is honor enough for any woman to have deserved and retained through such a varied trying career as your has been, the respect and devotion of such a man as Gen. G. A. Custer.

"Of course, at the same time you were winning the love and esteem of all observers with whom you came in contact, which made your husband the more proud of you. Yes, you made his domestic life happy which helped to make his professional life a success. . . .

"So, Libbie, your heart's desire in one respect, it seems, was accomplished. His literary reputation was made; his military record was unrivaled; and I believe there was not an officer in the Army more popular both in military and civil circles than he. He entered his public career suddenly and unexpectedly but made his influence felt immediately and wherever he has acted it has been with acknowledged ability and power.

"His exit from the stage has been even more unexpected and brilliant than the entrance; it was all in character; I believe he had finished his appointed role.

"When I read in the papers the brief line saying you were in the hospital ministering to the wants of the wounded I thought the mantle of your heroic husband had fallen upon your shoulders. Wear it, Libbie, for his sake! I know your woman's heart must ache, and your women's eyes must weep, but the latter will ease the former and then you can return cheerfully to action, for your work is not yet done. Others need your tender ministry now as he once did.

"If there is anything in the sentiment, 'It is better to have loved and lost than never to have loved at all,' it certainly means a great deal to the widow of 'Autie Custer."[41]

NOTES — CHAPTER 27

[1]Congressional Record, 44th Cong., 1st Session, 1876, No. 4435.
[2]Brian W. Dippie; "The Southern Response To Custer's Last Stand," *Montana Magazine of History,* Spring, 1971, pp. 20-21.
[3]Merington, p. 290.
[4]*Congressional Record, 44th Cong., 1st Session, Nos. 4627, 4628.*
[5]*Ibid,* Nos. 4628, 4629.
[6]*Ibid,* No. 4672.
[7]*Ibid,* No. 4671.
[8]*Ibid,* No. 4870.
[9]*Resolution Of Condolence Of The Legislature Of Texas,* August 7, 1876.
[10]New York *Herald,* July 9, 1876.
[11]New York *Herald,* July 26, 1876.
[12]July 13, 1876.
[13]Bay City *Tribune,* July 20, 1876.
[14]Monroe *Commercial,* July 20, 1876.
[15]Captain George W. Yates was considered by his contemporaries to be a Monroe resident. He served in the Fourth Michigan Infantry as a lieutenant in 1862. After his death his wife Annie returned to Monroe with her three children to live for a short time in a cottage across from David Reed's residence,
[16]Monroe *Commercial,* July 13, 1876; Minnie Redfield was 17 at the time of the disaster. When news of it became known, "A great silence came over Monroe, then all the bells began to toll—church bells, firehouse bells, every bell in town. To this day I never hear a bell that it does not bring back the memory of that dreadful day." From *SOME MONROE MEMORIES,* by Mrs. C. W. Hockett, May, 1939, p. 11, Burton Historical Collection Leaflet.
[17]John Owens: *Sword And Pen,* Philadelphia, 1882, pp. 389-93; Willard Glazier: *Ocean To Ocean On Horseback,* Philadelphia, 1898.
[18]Frost: *Grant Album,* p. 162.
[19]Monroe *Commercial,* July 13, 1876. David Reed left on Friday night, July 7th.
[20]Original in author's files.
[21]W. T. Sherman to Eliz. B. Custer, August 11, 1876, EBC-CBNM.
[22]Florence Boyd to Libbie, July 9, 1876, author's collection.
[23]Author's collection.
[24]Edna Waldo: *Dakota,* Caldwell, 1936, pp. 180-82.
[25]"Memorandum of Articles received from Mrs. General Custer for disposal," July 28, 1876, author's collection.
[26]Monroe *Commercial,* August 10, 1876; St. Louis *Globe Democrat,* August 7, 1876.
[27]Sara Clark: "The Brave Mrs. Custer," The Fargo *Record,* August, 1895.

She relates an incident that occurred in 1873 when her small daughter Nell had burst into tears because of something the child had said quite innocently that caused the adults present to laugh at her. "Custer took her in his arms, and with the gentleness and tact he always displayed with children he soon consoled her."
[28]Monroe *Commercial,* August 10, 1876,
[29]St. Louis *Globe Democrat,* August 7, 1876.
[30]Ohio *State Journal,* August 9, 1876.

Mrs. Yates, who was a native of Carlisle, Pennsylvania, was the daughter of V. Milner Roberts, chief engineer of the Northern Pacific Railroad. She had three children, aged 42 months, 22 months and 7 months. Commagere wrote that: "She has decided to establish her residence here (Monroe) so that she may be near her loved companion in suffering, and has already rented a beautiful cottage on Monroe Street, opposite the residence of David Reed. Her house is a pretty frame surrounded by a very large yard and embowered with trees."

There was little opportunity for Mrs. Yates to supplement her income in the small community. Barely able to live on a pension of $20 per month with $2 additional for each child she finally moved to Carlisle. Being very talented she made a livelihood by teaching music, dancing and languages. She had been born in Brazil and was said to speak seven languages.

Mrs. Yates never married again. As a member of the family observed: "Her children were such hellions, they made life miserable for all prospective suitors."
[31]Monroe *Commercial,* August 17, 1876.
[32]*Ibid.*
[33]*Ibid.*
[34]*Army And Navy Journal,* July 15, 1876.
[35]*Army And Navy Journal,* July 29, 1876.
[36]Edgar I. Stewart: "The Custer Battle And Widow's Weeds," *Montana Magazine of History,* Winter, 1972, pp. 54-57.
[37]Letter of T. F. Rodenbaugh to Libbie, August 25, 1876, author's collection.
[38]Letter of W. C. Church to Libbie, November 15, 1876, author's collection. Stewart (see #36 above) mentioned that Dr. DeWolf, as a civilian contract Surgeon, was omitted from the list as he was not considered an officer. It appears he was ranked as a lieutenant in the apportionment to the widows, and his widow was allocated funds accordingly.
[39]Geo. C. Gorham to Libbie, October 5, 1876, author's collection.
[40]Letter of Lawrence Barrett to Libbie, October 14, 1876, author's collection.
[41]Letter of Rebecca Richmond to Libbie, July 11, 1876, author's collection.

CHAPTER 28
SOME FREEDOM FOR WOMEN

Libbie had always been aware that it was not a woman's world though her awareness had diminished under the courtly attentions of the officers in the garrison. A shrinking bank account and the impelling desire to care for the needs of Autie's aging and ailing parents brought into focus again the distinction made between male and female in the world of employment.

Women were considered too delicate to work at any occupation other than housework, sewing or teaching. Even in teaching, males were preferred. Vermont women claimed that there were only two occupations open to them after the Civil War: 1) Teach school for five months at $3 a week or, 2) Hire out to a farmer's wife to work from dawn till 9 p.m. for $2 a week.[1]

The post-Civil War period was one of readjustment rather than reconstruction. Widows and orphans of veterans and unemployed and handicapped veterans received little assistance. Women in "men's" jobs were replaced by the returning servicemen, some women keeping their jobs only because they accepted lower wages. The employers in general were under great public pressure to hire veterans.[2]

By 1870, 14.7% of women over 15 were wage earners.[3] And from 1865 to 1890 the world of women was going through an educational revolution. Outstanding women's colleges were founded such as: Vassar, Bryn Mawr, Wellesley, Smith, Barnard and Radcliffe. And coeducation was introduced at such universities as Michigan, Cornell, Wisconsin, Kansas, California, Texas and Missouri.[4]

Women were beginning to come into their own and a foundation was being laid for the women's liberation movement that flattened all opposition in the 1960s.

Efforts were made to organize women's groups to do good for those less fortunate. There were societies developed to rescue fallen women, to support foreign missions, to establish world peace and to prohibit the sale and consumption of liquor, to name a few.

There were many women who were outspoken in their lectures around the country. Susan B. Anthony visualized the home as a detention camp commanded by a male tyrant who ruled the women in it with an iron hand. Others conducted an extensive social reform under the banner of the W.C.T.U. Though Libbie took no active role in it she had conducted a campaign of temperance among army personnel quite successfully on her own.

A more daring movement was that toward women's suffrage. It was promised that with it there would be no more crime, corruption or war. One skeptic observed that since then we've had the bloodiest wars in history, much more crime and more corruption in politics.[5]

Libbie had returned to Monroe to repair her shattered life in solitude, well away from the sympathy of an aroused nation. She had the time and quiet for introspection and objective reasoning. The newspapers had made much of the tragedy. President Grant had made an absurd statement blaming Custer for the defeat but took no official notice of the engagement. Nor did the War Department make any statement beyond its cold official report.[6]

As the stunning effects of shock lifted, Libbie became aware of the accusations made against her dead husband. Foremost was that of the President who in an interview with a reporter to the New York *Herald* had stated quite vehemently: "I regard Custer's massacre as a sacrifice of troops, brought on by Custer himself, what was wholly unnecessary—wholly unnecessary."[7] Others joined in the effort to tarnish Custer's brilliant record.

Though there were many unfounded charges, the one that irritated her most was that he allegedly disobeyed orders. Again and again she had read her husband's last letter to her in which he had enclosed a copy of General Terry's official order which began: "It is of course impossible to give you any definite instructions. . . . the Department Commander places too much confidence in your zeal, energy and ability to impose on you precise orders which might hamper your action when nearly in contact with the enemy."[8]

No other stimulus was needed. She had been the wife of this fighting man, had seen his determination and courage. He had once written to Nettie Humphrey: "First be sure you're right, then go

FIRST RESIDENCE IN BRONXVILLE, NEW YORK.
Libbie temporarily resided at the Hotel Gramatan, when first she visited Bronxville, to be near her old Monroe friends, Sarah Bates, who had married William Van Duzer Lawrence, and her sister Agnes Bates Wellington. This is the entrance to the lower level. The huge structure continues upward toward the hilltop to the rear. 1972. Photo courtesy of Gordon Corbett Jr.

ahead! I ask myself, 'Is it right?' Satisfied that it is so, I let nothing swerve me from my purpose."[9] She knew she was right.

These unfounded accusations must stop. Autie's memory must remain untarnished. She had wanted to die; now there was a reason to live. God had spared her for a reason. Now the reason was apparent.[10]

Financial conditions had improved somewhat. Libbie had received payment from an insurance policy her husband had taken out with the Life Association of America.[11] The amount is unknown though obviously welcome.

She had received a letter from the Equitable Assurance Company advising her that the June 9th premium of a $3,000 policy the General had taken out naming his parents as beneficiaries had not been paid. She informed it that her husband had told her just before starting on the expedition that "his policies were all paid up." She added:

"I remained at Fort Lincoln and had I been notified that a payment came due in June I would have promptly paid the sum. . . . We were always so prompt to keep up the payment on their policies. The General was a devoted son. He had been, since he received his first pay as a second lieutenant, their mainstay and support.

"I feel that he has left them to me as a final legacy. It is with the most intense regret that I find myself so situated financially that I cannot provide for them as I would wish. They are very old and poor and the mother is a confirmed invalid."[12]

On November 23d she received a telegram indicating that the Equitable had agreed to pay.[13]

The real boost to her morale came in the form of a check of $4,750 from the New York Life Insurance Company. Five other officers killed with Custer had taken out policies with the same company. In Custer's instance the principal sum was for $5,000 from which $250 had been deducted presumably as an extra premium for the risk the company had taken in warfare.[14]

On December 9th a telegram arrived advising her that Captain Tom Weir had passed away.[15] Weir had been a close associate of Custer. He was 38 years of age, a native of Ohio who attended school in Albion, Michigan, preparatory to entering the University of Michigan in 1857 and from which he graduated in 1861.[16]

Weir had written to Libbie in October from St. Louis to tell her:

"You know I can't tell you now but will sometime tell it to you all. . . . I have so much to tell you that I will tell you nothing now. . . . *I am coming to Monroe to see you all.* I wouldn't underline but that I mean it so earnestly."[17]

Four weeks later Libbie received another letter from him though this time from New York where he had been transferred to take charge of a cavalry rendezvous. This time he wrote:

"It is my life business to vindicate my friends of that day. . . . I know if we were all of us alone in the parlor, at night, the curtains all down and everybody else asleep, one or the other of you would make me tell you everything I know. . . . If I can get away I am going to Monroe. I know I could say something to you all that would make you feel glad for a little while at least."[18]

Libbie wrote to Dr. Orten, Weir's physician, requesting details of his death. Orten described Weir as having arrived in New York in a state of great physical and nervous exhaustion presumably due to the exposure and fatigue of that summer's campaign. He seemed to be suffering from a chronic depression that continued day after day, staying pretty much in his room and avoiding all contacts with the other officers.

Orten would call upon him under some pretext when he didn't show up for two or three days. He had not seen him professionally for 36 hours before his death and then only because he had been sent for. Weir was found excessively nervous and unable to swallow food or liquid. He was encouraged to eat lightly and get some sleep, and was then left in the care of his orderly. The morning Weir died Orten was sent for. He entered Weir's room just as he died. His death was due to meloncholia.[19]

His remains were interred at Governor's Island on December 14th, with full military honors. They were unable to locate his sister, Mrs. Samuel Brown of Greenville, Mississippi.[20]

Frederick Whittaker had begun to make waves. Immediately following Custer's death he had written his eulogy for the *Galaxy Magazine,*[21] then began a biography entitled *"A Complete Life of Gen. George A. Custer."* The latter was released on December 9th, the day Weir died. Its pro leanings portrayed Custer as a knight in shining white armor rather than a man, an unusual fighting man.

Though it was said his writing "was permeated by the influence of Mrs. Custer,"[22] she later stated that she never saw any part of his manuscript nor had she read the finished volume. Burdened as she was with family affairs and grief, it does not appear reasonable she would have either time or strength to have aided him so soon after her husband's death.

London born Whittaker came to New York to become a law clerk but turned from the study of law to writing. After serving as a lieutenant in the New York Cavalry during the Civil War, he became an assistant editor of the *Army and Navy Journal*.[23] It was while he was working in the editorial rooms of *Galaxy Magazine* shortly before Custer returned to Fort Lincoln to join the expedition that Whittaker last saw Custer.[24]

Whittaker had made the frank opening remark in his biography that "few men had more enemies than Custer, and no man deserved them less."[25] Then he concluded by demanding a court of inquiry so that witnesses under oath would not be "deterred from speaking by fear of superiors whom their evidence will impeach: . . . . The nation demands such a court, to vindicate the name of the dead hero from the pitiless malignity which first slew him and then pursued him beyond the grave."[26]

Whittaker had written Libbie he had talked to Weir shortly before his death and had obtained valuable information from him.

"Of course his death will make some little difference in the case for investigation, but not a material one. Luckily, or I should say better, under God's providence, I had a free talk with him and he told me of two officers, Edgerly and Varnum, whose testimony will corroborate his, besides which there are several others, civilians and scouts whose testimony will not be subject to intimidation. Brave old Weir!"[27]

Though Whittaker indicated that "few men had more enemies than Custer," some authors shared a belief that "many who might have been his bitterest critics withheld their fire out of consideration for Libby's (sic) feelings."[28] In retrospect, if one examines the record objectively, this does not appear to be so. President Grant, in his interview with a *Herald* reporter, was one of the first to castigate Custer. Colonel Sturgis and Captain Benteen were neither hesitant nor slow to attack the valiant dead officer. And they were followed by a host of others, some who put their ill-feeling in print, such as Brininstool, Brill, Dustin and Van de Water. Dustin called it a "conspiracy of silence." Nonsense. They were as silent as a sonic boom. There is no evidence to support the statement that there was a tacit agreement to wait until Libbie passed on before opening an attack upon the General. That was done before and during the Reno Court of Inquiry in 1879, or why else would General Nelson Miles in reference to those anti-Custer have said: "I have no patience with those who would kick a dead lion."[29]

Libbie's expressed wish to possess *Dandy* had reached the Seventh Cavalry in the field. Major Reno informed her that the surviving officers of the regiment were shipping *Dandy* by boat to her in the care of Lieutenant James M. Burns, 17th U.S. Infantry.[30]

Before the boat arrived at Fort Lincoln Libbie was well on her way back to Monroe. Lieutenant Burns wrote to her on August 19th that *Dandy* had arrived on the last steamer from the Yellowstone. He would wait to hear from her before sending *Dandy*. The beautiful animal was recovering from a wound received near Reno Hill while in the care of Burkman, and the rest, said Burns, would do him good.[31]

It was some time later, in fact about four months, that Libbie was ready for *Dandy*. On December 29th she received a notice from A. B. Bragdon, the Monroe agent of the Lake Shore & Michigan Southern Railway Co., that he had a Government Bill of Lading for one horse consigned to her.[32]

By mid-November Libbie had reached a decision. An agonizing appraisal of job opportunities in Monroe forced her to conclude there were none available. If she was to assume the obligation of supporting Autie's parents she must obtain employment soon for her funds were nearing an end. The dense population in the East with its abundant employment offered more chances for female employment. She had friends who might find a position for her in one of the many governmental departments. Frank E. Howe, for example, was an agent for the U.S. Pension Agency. He had been a friend of her husband to whom she had sent several dogs he had requested. He had offered assistance should she need it. She, in turn, asked if she could be placed in some department as a female clerk.

He hastened to advise her:

"The next day after I received your beautiful letter of November 19th I took it directly to the President in Washington, and took the responsibility of handing it to him. It touched him very much although there was a little reflection in it on him. He promptly said something must be done for you at once, and has treated the whole matter in the most tender manner. He directed me to visit the Postmaster General — Secretary of the Interior and Treasury and ascertain what could be done. I found that the highest grade of female clerk was $900 per year, and so reported to him, when he said you should have one at any moment. I then suggested that perhaps some arrangement could be made to make you Post Mistress at Monroe, when he told me to learn the situation, and to be present the next morning just before the Cabinet assembled."[33]

BROWN-SHINGLED TOWER HOUSE was the first house built by Libbie in Lawrence Park, Bronxville, N.Y., about 1892. It is at 20 Park Ave. 1972. Photo courtesy of Gordon Corbett Jr.

President Grant told Secretary of the Interior Chandler and Postmaster James Tyner that if anything could be done for Mrs. Custer he greatly desired it. The $900 a year clerk's job was available but she was to await developments on the post office appointment. Howe added that he did not have much confidence she could obtain the appointment and hoped he had not done wrong in the action he had taken.[34]

Libbie thought long and hard. Zach Chandler offered to assist her but did advise that the Congressman from her District would need to make the recommendation for the appointment of Post Mistress, that any other assistance would be only supplemental to that recommendation.[35]

Her old friend Colonel Winans got out of a sick bed to write her not to accept the Monroe Post Office.[36] Then Cousin Rebecca added her counsel. *"We sincerely hope* that when your affairs are settled you will find your income sufficient for a comfortable support *without* resort to a public office."[37]

Libbie had been quick in responding to Howe. She told him she was startled and surprised when she had learned that he had interviewed Grant in her behalf. She continued:

"It would be perfectly impossible for me to ask or accept any position from the present administration. The reasons you will readily understand.... I thought that I had asked for your aid when the administration changed or after the election of General Hayes.

"You will excuse me I know when I tell you how much I dread thinking that General Grant would be led to believe that I would ask or accept from him anything in the world.

"The appointment as Post Mistress at Monroe would be most gratefully accepted from the next administration—as for myself I told you I think I could get along very well, but with the income of the post office I could live here with my parents and assist them in many ways. I could give the General's widowed sister employment as clerk that would eke out her slender income."[38]

Ever thoughtful of others, Libbie had written an expression of sympathy to Lizzie Baliran, widow of sutler John Baliran who had been killed by Indians while with the Custer cavalry escort in 1873. Mrs. Baliran responded in kind, then added that her great comfort was her six-year-old daughter Letitia and her three-year-old son Guy Vance. She concluded: "I am sorry you are left without this blessing. My children make me very happy."[39]

About this same time Libbie received an unsigned letter from someone in Brooklyn, New York, informing her that during a seance in Brooklyn at the home of a Dr. Howard, a message was received by a Mr. Sibley with instructions to send it to Mrs. Custer at Adrian, Michigan. The message was as follows: "My darling wife, do not grieve. I am near you constantly. I am happy but wish you to be more reconciled to what has happened. It is all for the best. Custer."[40] There is no evidence that Libbie had an interest in psychic phenomena, or spiritualism in particular.

Many people, a goodly portion of them unknown to her, tried to comfort her in some fashion. The matter of *Dandy* being sent to her by the officers of the Seventh was an incident that touched her deeply, coming as it did at a time she needed moral support. Then a fine letter arrived advising her that Colonel W. H. Wood had inquired of the Indians returning to the Standing Rock Agency for relics or articles that had belonged to the husbands of Mrs. Custer, Mrs. Yates and the other widows. All of the Indians denied having any such articles even though a reward was offered for their return.[41]

Maggie Calhoun had been more fortunate than the others. Major Hughes of Terry's staff had presented her with some cartridge cases fired from Lieutenant Calhoun's revolver that had been found near his body.[42]

Senator Christiancy had occasion to meet the Governor of South Carolina, General Wade Hampton. Hampton had told him of possessing a pair of field glasses taken from one of Custer's staff and on which was printed Custer's name in gold. He offered to return them to Mrs. Custer if she would accept them, the Senator informed her. She promptly wrote to the gallant general.

Several days after Hampton received her letter, he replied, saying that he would be pleased to comply with her wish and as soon as General Custer's glasses could be brought down from the mountains he would forward them to her. "I trust," he observed, "that its value in your eyes will not diminish on account of its having served for a time *a rebel.* The war is over in which it did duty on both sides." Of

HER BROWN-SHINGLED COTTAGE IN THE CATSKILL MOUNTAINS. Libbie had this large cottage built in Onteora Park, Tannersville, on the mountainside as a retreat from the swelter of a New York City summer. Like her two houses in Bronxville, this was covered with brown shingles. 1972. Photo courtesy of Gordon Corbett Jr.

that he was certain for he had carried the glasses for a time.[43]

A week later there was more good news. Lloyd Aspinwall, president of the United States Port Military Library Association, informed her that he was placing at her disposal $500 as a part of monies received for the benefit of the Little Big Horn widows. An additional $500 was being added to that check, which was enclosed, for a total of $1,000. The latter $500 was received from the Grand Duke Alexis of Russia during a recent trip to New York City who requested that it be transmitted to her "in his name and without publicity, as a slight token of his remembrance and sympathy."[44]

In almost the same mail a letter arrived from Rebecca Richmond. She and her mother had viewed Libbie's trend toward public office with jaundiced eyes. They advised her "to dismiss that idea so long as you have so many friends willing and anxious to raise you above such necessity." They suggested that she visit some of the New York hospitals, there to spread a little sunshine on some deserving souls.[45] From this point on there is no further mention of the Post Office appointment in the correspondence between the two.

Libbie managed to probate her husband's affairs to the extent that her first account showed a cash balance of $1,447.73.[46] There being an insufficient amount of cash on hand to settle all of the claims of the estate, Libbie as executrix was forced to sell Autie's horse *Frogtown* at public auction, deriving $250 from the sale.[47] Autie's interest in the Custer farm was placed at public auction. His brother Nevin purchased it for $775 which made him sole owner of the French ribbon strip of 114 acres.[48]

A real upset for her was the claim of E. Justh for $8,500 with interest. Autie had signed a note with him while in New York not long before joining the expedition to the Little Big Horn.[49] It is presumed that Autie was straightening his accounts with Justh's investment firm as an aftermath of his silver mine ventures. In any event Libbie's attorney John Rauch proposed that the claims against the estate, now amounting to $13,291.06, be paid for at ten cents on the dollar. Cash on hand remained at $1,447.73.[50]

It was not until August 23, 1880, that a final accounting was recorded showing claims paid: "10% in claims of said estate as per order of court = $1,329.10."[51] Libbie was left with a mere $118.63 with which to pay her attorney.

There were signs of an early spring in Monroe. Adventurous robins had been seen and trees were beginning to bud in the Floral City. Cousin Rebecca had conveyed the news that Farnham Lyon, a member of Autie's staff during the Texas occupation, had visited her. Lyon was the new proprietor of a hotel in Saginaw. He was quite disturbed at Libbie seeking employment in a public position. Rebecca assured him that Libbie only wanted an occupation for her mental and spiritual needs, such as secretary to some large charitable association. Libbie had other thoughts. She needed money too.[52]

The thought of another endeavor crossed Libbie's mind, an endeavor that was not limited to males. She had been given a formal education superior to that of most people. She had been exposed to more travel, more famous people and more unique experiences than most people twice her age. Perhaps her ideas and observations could be expressed and sold. Perhaps Fred Whittaker as a professional writer could give her some advice.

Whittaker did give her advice. He encouraged her to write, and not to be afraid to write of herself. "It is through *your* memories that Custer's best traits will gradually and unconsciously expand to the world." Then he gave her some instructions and a series of tips on the art of writing:

"Use *short* sentences preferably. (Libbie loved lengthy sentences). Avoid using the *dash.* (She used it in the place of periods). Be careful of your *pronouns;* they are the cause of much confusion to all young writers. Each must have its antecedent clearly indicated, or you must change your form of expression. Don't be afraid to correct. Don't be afraid to repeat a name for the sake of clearness in a sentence concerning two persons. Talk on paper as you talk viva voce, and you conquer all mankind."[53]

The effect of spring on Libbie was far from salutary. Autie's parents were settled in her home on Monroe Street, and their health had improved somewhat. Mother Custer persisted in eating things that disagreed with her, contrary to her doctor's advice. When she did, all of the family suffered with her. The settlement of Autie's estate was progressing so that Libbie need not be present until its final accounting. She had been invited to stay with her relatives the Russells in Newark, New Jersey. Why not go? With New York City so near she would be able to pursue her quest for a job.

Before leaving Monroe she had written to Mr. I. E. Sheldon of Sheldon & Co., Autie's New York publishers, to determine if he knew of anything for her to do. His letter of May 1st addressed to her Newark address suggested that he would provide her with funds if she found hers inadequate. Referring to her husband's book he observed:

"'Life' has not done what we hoped thus far. The times have been adverse to its success but I think it has even now earned some little profit, a share of which I have always intended should go to you so feel that you have always a little something to fall back on when necessary."[54]

Rebecca Richmond was unaware of Libbie's move to Newark until she had gone. A week after Libbie had arrived there she commented:

"You really did expedite matters and were off before we had an opportunity to say goodbye. All right! We like your energy and decision! 'Be sure you are right and then go ahead' is a good motto for man or women.

"We will be in New York by the first of June (this was written on May 7th) then we can have some unrestrained talks while dining at leisure. New York is the one place in my small world where women who are rightly disposed and who know what they are about, can enjoy a great degree of the sweet freedom and independence which in other places is accorded only to men."[55]

It was here that Rebecca inoculated Libbie with the germ of an idea. Rebecca, with her level head and her feet firmly on the ground, had a great influence on Libbie. Libbie listened to her with marked respect because, not only did she dispense unusual logic, she was a friend. Such friends are rare.

Rebecca had enclosed a newspaper clipping, presumably from the New York *Times:*

"Mr. Cowdin's bill to incorporate the Society of Decorative Arts provides that Mary Penberton Sturges, Catherine Morgan Dix, Mary S. Field, Abby B. Blodgett, Annie P. Bellows, Caroline S. Choate, Sarah A. Hewitt, Candace T. Wheeler, Julia Cooper, Julia Bryant and Charlotte Bruce Arnold and their associates shall be incorporated as the Society of Art, in New York City, for the purpose of encouraging and increasing artistic industry among women, and of educating women for self-sustaining employment in the useful arts. To that end they are empowered to maintain a school of instruction and other institutions for the promotion of the general purposes named."[55]

Mr. Sheldon had thought of a better idea. Why not produce a volume of Libbie's experiences while the wife of the most talked of cavalry leader in the nation's history? He advised her to write about everything that she might think of since it would be easy to select from it that which would be best put into a book. "I would advise you," he wrote, "not to think at all of how it will read. Just write them out in the most natural way as if you were talking to a friend. . . . I think little by little you are securing the material to make an interesting book."[56]

Early in April, Colonel Mike Sheridan had written to Libbie, in reply to her inquiry, that he "had already begun to make arrangments to have the remains of the officers who fell at the Battle of the Little Big Horn brought in to Fort Lincoln with a view of the final interment of the bodies of all those who are not taken by their friends to their various homes, in the National Cemetery at Fort Leavenworth, without expense to the relatives of the deceased so far as this is practicable."[57]

He had written to General Sherman requesting full authority and had strongly recommended that the remains of General Custer be buried at West Point in accordance with Mrs. Custer's wish. He mentioned that Phil Sheridan agreed with the family conclusion that Tom, Jim Calhoun and Boston be buried at the Fort Leavenworth Cemetery, and would make arrangements accordingly.

Mike told Libbie she would be notified when the remains of her husband would arrive at Fort Lincoln though the exact time could not yet be designated owing to the peculiarity of the terrain.[58]

In early May, Mike informed her that the Secretary of War had granted permission to remove the remains of the officers. Mike would start to do this early that month but was uncertain of the date.[59]

Several weeks later he informed her:

"I have not written to any of the ladies interested (officers' wives) except yourself because there might be some difficulty about recovering all the bodies but I desired to know where they all were living so as to write them when I returned.

"It is my intention to bring the bodies down to Lincoln without caskets and have them temporarily interred at that post. . . . The General (P. H. Sheridan), if it is possible, will have the Govt. supply caskets. The Govt. will furnish the one for Genl. Custer. It is not necessary to get any other authority then that of the Sup't of the Mil. Academy to have General Custer interred at West Point.

"I expect to start next Monday the 21st and will be absent about one month I should think. Of the length of time it will take me I cannot say as the Yellowstone is very low. Captain Nowlan and if possible one Company of the Seventh, it being now on the Tongue River, will go out with me."[60]

Meanwhile Libbie was not idle. She had been investigating the possibility of becoming a hospital nurse, much to the objection of Rebecca and her mother. "Too confining and exposing from a health standpoint," they both agreed. "A secretaryship or a place on a regular visiting or distributing committee in connection with some Association is all that you ought to undertake for the first year."[61]

Libbie had progressed too far to draw back. Laura Oremieulx had made arrangements to take her on the rounds of the men's wards at Bellevue Hospital. In the envelope containing the notification of the next meeting of the Bellevue Admittance Committee Laura enclosed a circular of the Decorative Art Association. She advised Libbie that they needed an assistant for the summer—"a lady who can give information through letters or otherwise and be at the office, 67 Madison Ave., three days of the week." A small salary was provided, which she advised her to take.

Laura informed her: "The idea of the Association is to help women with more than ordinary ability to a better means of gaining their livelihood than by merely serving. It would bring you in contact with an interesting class seldom reached who are often more needy than a poorer one."[62]

Then Laura threw a fast ball. "At any rate I am asked to request you to give me an answer which I can show the ladies as a proof of your handwriting and power as a letter writer, and to say that Mrs. Lane, the President, will be at the Room, No. 67 Madison Ave. next Saturday morning at 10 o'clock unless she hears from me to the contrary."[63]

Before Libbie could regather her composure, Laura added: "I would advise you to see Mrs. Lane on Saturday at any rate and reserve your decision until after you have been to the Bellevue meeting, in case you have any doubts."

Maggie Calhoun had decided not to go to Fort Leavenworth and be present when the last rites were administered to her husband. She had been ill most of the time since returning to Monroe. Her physician, Dr. Sawyer, and all of the Custer family had advised her not to go, that it would be too much for her. Wisely, she credited her doctor's opinion as carrying the most weight.[64]

Maggie, with Mrs. Yates and her children and other members of the Custer family, joined Brother Shiers at his cottage near Petoskey in early July. The quiet, except for the noisy Yates youngsters, and the clear air soon had Maggie feeling better. Though she had occasional migraine headaches during the day, feverish spells at night and dizzy spells when she got out of bed, she decided her place was at the graveside of her dear husband. She believed she could stand it if only the rest would think so too.

From Petoskey she wrote to Libbie asking her why Colonel Sheridan did not bring Boston's remains with the others *"after promising us that it should be done* and that he should be with the others at Leavenworth."[65] Then she told Libbie of her intense desire to go to Leavenworth. She had been so much better the last ten days, her appetite was good, she felt stronger in every way. She would regret it all her life if she remained away.

When the summons arrived, she would leave Petoskey for Grand Rapids, then on to Chicago where she hoped to meet Annie Yates who went home the day before because her young son Milnor was screaming all the time.[66]

Libbie had sent a message to Major General John M. Schofield, Commandant of the Military Academy, asking his advice. Colonel Sheridan had informed her he had recovered the remains of her husband and that they were lying at Fort Lincoln awaiting her decision as to where they should be conveyed. General Custer had asked her to lay him at West Point. Could the date be fixed for his burial and would he and Mrs. Schofield "select the spot where he will be"?[67]

Major Joseph G. Tilford of the Seventh Cavalry sent Libbie a message that relieved her of present doubts and prevented considerable worry over a malicious newspaper story circulated three months later. It was from Fort Lincoln on July 28th that he announced:

"On yesterday I shipped by U.S. Express via Chicago, the remains of your heroic husband Genl. Custer to West Point, N.Y., care of the Commanding Officer of that Post. Those were my instructions from Genl. Sheridan. I presume an officer will accompany the remains from Chicago on.

"It may be some consolation for you to know that I personally superintended the transfer of the remains from the box in which they came from the battlefield to the casket which conveys them to West Point.

"I enclose you a lock of hair taken from the remains which are so precious to you. I also kept a

CUSTER GRAVESITE AT WEST POINT. General Custer's remains were removed from the Custer Battlefield in 1877 and reinterred at West Point. Libbie was buried at her husband's side. United States Military Archives.

few hairs for myself as having been worn by a man who was my beau ideal of a soldier and honorable Gentleman."[68]

The remains of General Custer, upon their arrival in New York City, were dispatched to Poughkeepsie and placed in a vault to await the final interment at West Point.

Mike Sheridan, who had been invited to be a pall bearer at Autie's services, asked to be excused. He pleaded insufficient funds to travel East and said his brother could not order him there since, unfortunately, it was outside his area of command.

He was concerned about a statement published in the New York *Herald* of the condition of the battlefield. He assured her that "*no* person connected with that paper was with me, and that any statement it may have made was manufactured in the *Herald* office and was untrue. Nowlan and myself properly identified by the stakes driven into the ground at the head of each grave the body of *every* officer I brought in without the slightest difficulty."[69]

Libbie had no doubts. The lock of hair so thoughtfully provided by Tilford was positive identification. Who else in the command had hair like her husband's?

On the afternoon of August 3d, the bodies of Captains George Yates and Tom Custer and Lieutenants A. E. Smith, Donald McIntosh and James Calhoun were reinterred in the National Cemetery at Fort Leavenworth. Captain C. S. Ilsly of the Seventh Cavalry acted as marshal of the funeral procession.[70]

Maggie rested in Monroe a few days before she wrote to Libbie the details of the ceremony at Leavenworth. It had been impressive, the guard of honor, the ceremony and the beautiful sites selected for the heroes. Fred Calhoun had arranged to be there, and Annie Yates with her small son George had met Maggie in Chicago, the three traveling together to Fort Leavenworth.[71]

Several days later Maggie was jarred back to reality. The cause of it had to be told, and who would enjoy it more than Libbie, for she was the central character in the story to be related. So, Maggie wrote to her:

"After you wrote me about your occupation and said I could make it public I took particular pains to tell *just what* you were doing, that you were a secretary, etc., and on a committee for visiting one or two wards in Bellevue Hospital, and gave full explanations.

"Result—Just before I went to Petoskey I heard that you had sole charge of two hospitals in New York City and that you were living there under an assumed name.

"I also heard you were in Europe caring for wounded soldiers. But to think Monroe people, after all my pains—knowing their propensity—should get things so twisted."[72]

Then the day of dread arrived. It was October 10, 1877. Libbie arrived at West Point in the company of Mrs. Lawrence Barrett. The General's father and his sister Maggie came from Monroe.

A cavalry detachment had received the remains on their arrival at the South Dock shortly after noon, then escorted them to the Chapel where they lay in state under an honor guard.[73]

Libbie was escorted into the chapel by General Schofield shortly before the two o'clock services began. With the flag draped coffin before her, on which had been placed her husband's sword and plumed dress helmet, she could see nothing else.

Academic duties had been suspended from 1 P.M. until Retreat so the chapel was filled to overflowing. Libbie was hardly aware anyone else was present for her thoughts were in the past.

Once the service had concluded, the pallbearers carried the casket to the caisson, then the funeral cortege moved on, a lone horse following and displaying a pair of spurred cavalry boots with toes turned to the rear.

The procession stopped a short distance from the entrance to the cemetery near the grave of General Scott who had given Custer his first assignment after graduation. The chaplain's remarks were followed by the sharp commands to fire the three traditional volleys, then it was over. Libbie had kept her promise to Autie.[74]

NOTES—CHAPTER 28

1Mary Massey: *Bonnet Brigades,* N.Y., 1966, p. 113.
2*Ibid,* p. 328.
3Anne G. Scott: *The American Woman. Who Was She?,* Englewood Cliffs, 1971, p. 13.
4Massey, p. 349.
5Lee Mortimer: *Women Confidential,* N.Y., 1960, p. 19.
6John B. Kennedy: "A Soldier's Widow," *Collier's Magazine,* January 29, 1927, p. 10.
7New York *Herald,* September 2, 1876.
8Merington, p. 307; Lawrence Frost: "Custer's Lost Orders—Found!" *Westerner Magazine,* March, 1971.
9Merington, p. 65; Whittaker, p. 212.
10Margaret Leighton: *Bride of Glory,* N.Y., 1962, p. 205.
11*Army And Navy Journal,* December 23, 1876, p. 319; letter of J. R. Rauch to Eliz. B. Custer, July 20, 1876, author's collection.
12Eliz. B. Custer to the Equitable Assurance Co., October 18, 1876, BCWC collection.
13Telegram of November 23, 1876, J. B. Kidd to Eliz. B. Custer, author's collection.
14Captain Emil Adams to Eliz. B. Custer, June 8, 1877, author's collection.
15Telegram, Lieutenant W. W. Dougherty to Eliz. C. Custer, December 9, 1876, author's collection.
16*Army and Navy Journal,* December 23, 1876, p. 308.
17T. B. Weir to Eliz. B. Custer, October 11, 1876, author's collection.
18T. B. Weir to Eliz. B. Custer, November 15, 1876, author's collection.
19Dr. S. H. Orten to Eliz. B. Custer, December 20, 1876, author's collection.
20Kenneth Hammer: *Men With Custer,* Fort Collins, 1972, p. 99.
21*Galaxy Magazine,* September, 1876.
22Robert M. Utley: *Custer And The Great Controversy,* Los Angeles, 1962, p. 52.
23Albert Johannsen: *The House of Beadle and Adams,* Norman, 1950, Vol. II, p. 301.
24Whittaker: *Life of General Custer,* p. 552.
25*Ibid,* p. 1.
26*Ibid,* p. 608.
27F. Whittaker to Libbie, December 19, 1876, author's collection.
28Utley: *Great Controversy,* p. 122.
29Nelson A. Miles: *Personal Recollections of General Nelson A. Miles,* New York, 1896, p. 100.
30Major M. A. Reno to Libbie, August 2, 1876, author's collection. Hugh L. Scott, in *Some Memories of A Soldier* (N.Y., 1928, p. 29) said: "The first subscription in the Seventh Cavalry I was asked for was in the purchase, from the government, by the officers of the Seventh, of Custer's horse *Dandy,* to be sent to Mrs. Custer."
31Lieutenant J. M. Burns to Libbie, August 19, 1876, author's collection.
32Author's collection.
33Frank E. Howe to Libbie, December 12, 1876, author's collection.
34*Ibid.*
35Z. Chandler to Libbie, December 21, 1876, author's collection.
36E. Winans to Libbie, January 22, 1877, author's collection.
37Rebecca Richmond to Libbie, January 10, 1877, author's collection. Rebecca also noted Mrs. Montague Ferry, sister-in-law of Senator Ferry had believed the newspaper report that Libbie had received the princely fortune of $85,000. "She was surprised to learn that the whole—for you and your parents—was but $15,000 minus the war risk, and that after the estate was settled and debts paid your scanty income would have to be eked out by your own exertions."
38F. E. Howe to Libbie, January 15, 1877, author's collection.
39Letter from Memphis, Tennessee, Mrs. Lizzie Baliran to Libbie, February 27, 1877, author's collection.
40Unsigned letter to Eliz. B. Custer, Adrian, Michigan, February, 1877, author's collection.
41W. D. Carlin to Libbie, January 6, 1877, author's collection.
42Monroe *Commercial,* August 10, 1876.
43General Wade Hampton to Libbie, January 2, 1877, author's collection.
44Lloyd Aspinwall to Libbie, March 10, 1877, author's collection.
45Rebecca Richmond to Libbie, March 7, 1877, author's collection.
46Monroe County Probate Court Records, G. A. Custer file, October 2, 1877.
47*Ibid,* October 1, 1877.
48*Ibid,* September 15, 1877.
49E. Justh to Libbie, September 21, 1876, author's collection.
50Monroe County Probate Court Records, G. A. Custer file, October 1, 1877.
51*Ibid,* August 23, 1880.
52Rebecca Richmond to Libbie, March 26, 1877, author's collection.
53F. Whittaker to Libbie, March 31, 1877, author's collection.
54I. E. Sheldon to Libbie, 51 Mount Pleasant Ave., Newark, N.J., May 1, 1877, author's collection.
55Rebecca L. Richmond to Libbie, May 7, 1877, author's collection.
56I. E. Sheldon to Libbie, May 16, 1877, author's collection.
57Col. Michael V. Sheridan to Libbie, April 4, 1877, author's collection.
58*Ibid.*
59*Ibid,* May 2, 1877.
60*Ibid,* May 14, 1877.
61Rebecca Richmond to Libbie, April 22, 1877, author's collection.
62Laura Oremieulx to Libbie, May 23, 1877, author's collection.
63*Ibid.*
64Maggie Calhoun to Libbie, June 14, 1877, author's collection.
65*Ibid,* July 24, 1877.
Boston Custer is buried in the Custer plot in Woodland Cemetery, Monroe, Michigan.
66*Ibid.*
67Eliz. B. Custer to Maj. Gen. J. M. Schofield, undated, EBC—CBNM.
68Major Jos. G. Tilford to Libbie, July 28, 1877, author's collection.
69M. V. Sheridan to Libbie, August 8, 1877, author's collection; General Hugh L. Scott: *Some Memoirs Of A Soldier,* N.Y., 1928, p. 48; Scott, who was with Sheridan and Nowlan, confirms this story.
70Special Orders No. 140, August 2, 1877, BCWC collection; St. Joseph (Mo.) *Daily Herald,* August 3, 1877.
71Maggie Calhoun to Libbie, August 11, 1877, author's collection.
72*Ibid,* August 15, 1877.
73General Orders No. 24, West Point, October 2, 1877, author's collection.
74New York *Times,* October 11, 1877; *Harper's Weekly,* October 27, 1877.

CHAPTER 29
TO FACE A NEW WORLD

Colonel Nelson A. Miles' disgust was evident. Outspokenly critical, he wanted action and success; the latter had to be preceded by the former. It appeared there was nothing but inaction ahead. Though the summer of 1876 had been wasted he finally got the green light to go after Sitting Bull.

Miles had indicated to General Sherman he was not receiving adequate supplies for a winter campaign, and he was not getting the support of Sheridan and Terry. Then there was Crook of whom presidential nominee Rutherford B. Hayes was inordinately fond; Crook under whom Hayes had served during the Civil War and who Hayes considered the most capable officer in the army.

Colonel Miles, a major general by brevet, commanded the Fifth U.S. Infantry. An old friend and admirer of General Custer, he and his wife had been stationed at Fort Hays with the Custers in 1869 where the two couples had "enjoyed many hunts and pleasure parties together."[1] It was with Custer he had experienced his first buffalo hunt.

The outspoken Miles was disgusted with Crook's display of a "miserable lack of cooperation," Gibbon's lack of courage in attacking Sioux villages and Terry's apathy in pursuing Indians. When he joined Terry and Gibbon at the mouth of the Rosebud River in early August, 1876, he was disturbed over what he considered useless delays. It was his opinion that Terry had lost an opportunity by retreating after the Custer battle. There had been many reports that the Indians had their fill of fighting and were rapidly retreating with their numerous dead and wounded, yet the military commanders exhibited nervous timidity. The obvious inaction at this rendezvous caused him to admire Custer all the more and to conclude that "his like will not be found very soon again."[2]

Several weeks earlier he had been at Fort Lincoln for supplies and while there had sent a note to Libbie. She asked to see him. He was appalled at the gloom around the post with its 27 widows. Libbie did not appear very strong and he doubted if she would ever regain her strength, her depression and despair were so great.[3]

He soon learned that Crook was getting ready to move against the Indians on August 1st. Crook had been getting ready for a year, constantly displaying evidence of being another McClellan. Like McClellan, Crook had a well developed habit of overrating his adversary.[4] Ever fearful of the Sioux, he moved slowly and with absolutely no evidence of that chief characteristic of the successful cavalryman, audacity.[5]

The newspapers and the public were clamoring for punishment of the Indians who killed Custer. After a delay of a month Crook went out on a scout that Miles considered senseless, useless and fruitless. Slow-moving to begin with, he followed an old trail of the fast-moving Sioux.[6] There was not the remotest chance he could catch up with the Indians, and he never did.

Miles and his men attached themselves to Sitting Bull's trail and followed it relentlessly through that winter and well into the following spring. As a result of this pursuit many of the Indians went back onto their reservations and Sitting Bull, after numerous conferences with Miles, led a small band of followers over the border into Canada.

In the middle of June, 1876, Miles had petitioned General Sherman for a good command, in the event the three columns under Terry and Crook did not succeed that summer. It was his intention to invade the Sioux country that fall and winter and "stay with them until they are worn out and subjugated." He was of the opinion that a good command of at least one-half infantry "could make their country so uncomfortable for them and give them no rest, they would be compelled to sue for peace."[7]

Libbie enjoyed the stimulus that a letter from Colonel Miles provided. He had become deeply interested in the battle of the Little Big Horn and strongly resented the misinterpretations of the press and the insinuations and charges presented by the anti-Custer faction. Showing no quarter, he had answered critics of Custer in the columns of the *Army & Navy Journal* in a fashion that made the critic think twice before continuing his tirade.[8]

In a later letter to Libbie he offered his analysis of Autie's formula for success:

> "His (Custer's) success was no more the result of luck than are the rewards of any human effort, for if there is any calling in life where the fruits are gathered in accordance with real merit it is in the profession of arms, where patient study, sleepless

vigilance, laborious toil and iron nerve are requisite in order to reap the harvest of glory. 'Custer's Luck' was the result of judgment to do the right thing at the right time, his devotion to his profession and to his great energy and persistency. Scores of battleflags, parks of artillery and thousands of prisoners taken on different fields fall not into the hand of men other than those who possess superior military capacity. . . .

"He possessed excellent judgment and studied carefully the strength of his enemy as well as the character of the country in which he was to contend, and by celerity of movements he was frequently able to strike most effectual and decisive blows where they were least expected; his natural resourcefulness enabled him to extricate his command from every menacing danger—except the last—or take advantage of successes and reap the full fruit of victory."[9]

It was not until June of 1878 that Miles had the opportunity he had been waiting for. While on a march up the Yellowstone to determine a route for a telegraph line he camped on the Custer Battlefield for several days. With him were 25 Sioux and Cheyennes who, having been in the engagement, explained it to him in detail.

The warriors told him "that *they would have fled if Reno's troops had not retreated, for the troops could not have been dislodged.*" They added that when they left Reno to attack Custer, had the seven companies under Reno and Benteen *"followed them down and fired into their backs they would have been between two fires and would have had to retreat."*[10]

Miles walked his horses over the ground from Reno's last position to the extreme right of Custer's line and it took 56 minutes by his watch. In half that time Reno could have been in action, and at a smart trot or gallop he could have been on the Indians' rear in 15 to 20 minutes, so Miles implied.[11]

In conclusion he wrote: "His (Custer's) brothers and strongest friends died with him, while his enemies lived to criticize and cast odium upon his name and fame; but it is easy to kick a dead lion."[12]

Libbie's many friends literally inundated her with their correspondence. She continued receiving letters of condolence though they had been reduced to a mere trickle. Many of the officers with the command had started sending their observations, experiences or opinions. All were of interest, though most were painful to read. One letter was particularly agonizing. It had been sent to Lieutenant Fred Calhoun, Second Infantry, brother of Jim Calhoun, and had been written by his brother-in-law Myles Moylan a week after the battle, while camped at the mouth of the Little Big Horn. Fred had sent the letter on to Monroe so that the Reed family could have an eyewitness account of what had transpired. Moylan wrote:

"Having traveled most of the night of the 14th until the village was discovered about ten miles in front of us. It could be seen from the bluff of the creek. Gen. Custer then decided to halt his command until night and make the march during the night of the 25th so as to strike them on the morning of the 26th, but during the morning of the 25th it was ascertained that we were discovered, then Custer decided to go forward and attack them at once. . . .[13]

"You will naturally ask where was Custer with the other nine companies all this time. It seems that when Custer reached the Little Big Horn where we crossed (Moylan was with Reno), instead of crossing there he kept down the right bank of the stream with five companies leaving Benteen back with his companies and McDougall's Co. B to bring up the pack train. Custer underrated the number of Indians so much that I know he thought that Reno's command could drive them before them, and in order to cut off the retreat of the Indians he marched his command down the right bank of the river to a crossing some seven or eight miles below, but before he could reach a point half the distance we were driven across the river and the Indians were ready for him. Of his fight the truth will never be known unless indeed the Indians themselves tell it as there can be no question that every officer and man in his command was killed.

"All officers were found stiff in death, stripped naked, and all were more or less cut to pieces by the Indians, excepting Lts. Porter, Sturgis, Harrington and Dr. Lord. There was no doubt of the death of Porter and Sturgis as their clothing was found in the village covered with blood after the Indians left. No trace of any kind of Harrington or Dr. Lord have been found but the bodies were disfigured so much when we buried them it was impossible to recognize the greatest number of them. Jim and young Crittenden of the 20th Infantry, son of Gen. Crittenden of the 17th Infantry, who was on duty with Jim in L Company were found behind L Company. Gen. Custer, Tom, Cook and Smith were found upon a small hill where the last stand was evidently made. Gen. Custer was shot through the ear and not scalped or disfigured in the least. He looked as natural as if sleeping. All the rest of the officers and men, all over the field, were badly cut up and their heads knocked in. I was present when Jim was buried and recognized him at a glance. Bos Custer and the General's nephew were killed some little distance from the General. Both were recognized. Altogether 206 officers and men were found. Some few may have been killed further off whose bodies were not found but they could not have been many as 206 nearly made up the number of the command. . . .

"The Indians did not continue the fight with us after we crossed the river but turned their attention to Custer's command. We could hear the fighting with Custer several miles away; soon after reaching the bluff we were joined by Benteen with four companies. . . .

"There can be no question that Custer's men made a terrible fight. The last line occupied by some of Jim's men as high as 40 cartridge shells were found around some of his men. We had one Crow Indian that was with Custer who says that Custer's men killed more Indians than there was white men altogether. This same Indian describes Cooke as among the last few killed. Up to that time the Indian says Cooke was on horseback all the time fighting in the most terrible manner and all covered with blood. The Sioux fought Custer dismounted all the way through. . . . I would like to write your Mother but can't."[14]

Maggie Calhoun knew that Myles Moylan could provide her with answers to several questions that tormented her. On the 17th of December she wrote to him while he was visiting in Madison, Indiana. Moylan's reply was prompt. He divulged that he could write to her much better than tell her of the burial details on the battlefield.

His company was the rear guard, hence did not arrive on the field until some of the burying had begun. It was assigned the place nearest the river with the exception of McDougall's, which had the extreme left. Moylan went on to describe the scene:

"Positive orders that officers should not leave their respective companies unless special permission was granted them to do so in order that none of the bodies should be overlooked. An accurate count was made of all of the bodies buried and all marks on the bodies that would in any way tend towards identification were carefully noted."[15]

A half hour or more later Moylan was informed that Jim Calhoun's body had been found:

"When I arrived the body was partially covered with earth (from the neck to the waist was covered). I examined the exposed parts of the body carefully. It was all that remained of your husband. The face was not disfigured nor were his limbs mutilated but like all the bodies I saw, except Genl. Custer, he was scalped. I could not tell where he was shot on account of the body being covered up.

"Mr. Crittenden and Jim were not buried in the same grave. . . . I think most of what you have heard of the mutilation of Tom's body, except perhaps cutting out his heart, was true. His body was cut up very much, so much indeed, that it was almost impossible to tell whether or not he had received any shots in the body. Bos was shot in the body several times, was mutilated some. Autie Reed was also shot in the body. I could not tell so much of the manner of his death, however, owing to the fact that most of his clothes had been left on the body. The bodies of all looked quite natural considering that they had lain in the hot June sun two days.

"The distances I give in the diagram are as near correct as I can remember, and of course I cannot give them exact. . . . For the purposes of covering the whole ground the companies were placed in position in about the order indicated in the diagram enclosed. The diagram will give you some idea of the field and the position of the bodies when found."[16]

Many conflicting accounts of the disaster had been printed by the press, resulting in considerable confusion and some anguish. One story was circulated that Custer had been killed early in the engagement near the river, his body having been carried up to the position where he was found. Lieutenant John Carland, Sixth Infantry, wrote to his friends in Detroit that he was standing by General Custer when General Terry came up: "As he looked down upon the noble general the tears coursed down his face as he exclaimed: 'The flower of the army is gone at last.' Custer was supposed to be the first one who died; though he fell first we found 17 cartridge shells by his side, where he kept them off until the last moment."[17]

First Sergeant John Ryan of the Seventh Cavalry was charged with burying the General and Tom Custer. He was assisted by Privates Davis, Harrison, Frank Neeley and James Severs. Ryan had found four or five brass cartridge shells under Custer's body that had been used in Custer's Remington rifle. He had Severs cut off a lock of Custer's hair which he sent to Mrs. Custer with some of the cartridge cases. Ryan related:

"Not over 20 feet away lay the body of his brother Captain Tom Custer. His body when found lay on its face and hands and was so terribly mutilated that it was not recognized until I recalled that I had seen the letters *T.W.C.* in India ink on Captain Custer's arm when he was the 1st Lieut. of M troop. He was split down thro the center of his body, his throat cut, his head smashed flat and he was also split thro the muscles of his arms and thighs.

"A grave about 18 inches deep was dug a little further down the ridge from where Custer fell as it was softer ground, and the two bodies, General Custer and Capt. T. W. Custer, were placed in it side by side. Some pieces of shelter tent, and I think some pieces of blanket were laid over them and covered with earth and on top of all was placed a basket-like affair from an Indian travoy which was spiked down with wooden pins, and some stones laid around the edge to keep the wolves from digging it up."[18]

The finding of the shell cases from Custer's rifle under and around his body precludes the possibility he was killed early in the engagement and his body then carried to Custer Hill.

Indian Agent James McLaughlin asserted that the Sioux were not certain they were fighting Custer since they were unable to recognize him during the battle. In searching for him after the last shot had been fired, he mentioned:

"They knew him only by his long hair, and they could find no body that might possibly be identified in that way.

"They found a man dressed in buckskin, and in the pockets of the blouse they found parchment maps, from which they concluded that the body was that of an officer in command; and their respect for the chief—always marked with the Sioux—impelled them to hold the body inviolate. The body was that of Custer, and it was not mutilated."[19]

McLaughlin's long tenure at the Standing Rock Agency had made him many friends among the Sioux. Mrs. Spotted Horn Bull was one of them and she had been in the Indian village at the time Reno had attacked it. Though there is not room for her entire eyewitness account, portions of it are quite revealing. She states:

"I have seen my people prepare for battle many times, and this I know; that the Sioux that morning (June 25, 1876) had no thought of fighting. We expected no attack, and our young men did not watch for the coming of Long Hair (Custer) and his soldiers.[20]

"The soldiers (Reno's) had been sent by Long Hair to surprise the village of my people. Silently had they moved off around the hills, and kept out of sight of the young men of our people, had crept in, south of what men now call Reno Hill.[21]

"If the soldiers had not fired until all of them were ready for the attack; if they had brought their horses and rode into the camp of the Sioux, the power of the Dakota nation might have been broken, and our young men killed in the surprise, for they were watching Long Hair only and had no thought of an attack anywhere while they could see the soldiers traveling along parallel with the river on the opposite side. . . . Long Hair had planned cunningly that Reno should attack in the rear while he rode down and give battle from the front of the village looking on the river."[22]

Mrs. Spotted Horn Bull was the wife of a Hunkpapa Sioux chief who had been killed with Sitting Bull. She, like many others who had been camping that day on the Little Big Horn, were there to prepare meat and robes and to be present for the Sun Dance. As she stated above, the Sioux "had no thought of fighting."

Major General Hugh L. Scott had interrogated many Indians who had been in the fight. He remarked that they were perfectly frank with him about their part in it. "I never saw one," he proclaimed, "who admitted that he had gone out there to fight. . . . The Indians were attacked at the instance of the Interior Department while they were peaceaby attending to their own business, with no desire to fight."[23]

Present day comment regarding the Indian viewpoint of Custer is principally based on misconceptions and misinformation. The pseudo-intellectuals who place little value on courage are anti-Custer; those who rate courage high are pro-Custer.[24] Those who knew the most about his views of the Indians—his Indian contemporaries—respected him.

The Epsicopalian minister, Reverend Aaron Beede, living among the Sioux for many years, knew them intimately and was highly respected by them. From them he learned: "Custer knew the Indian sign language, was fond of Indians, as they were also of him. Indians throughout the Northwest revere the name of Custer. They keenly saw his flaws and cared nothing for them in the face of what they considered his true manliness. . . . Sitting Bull did not refer to him as a 'soldier.' He referred to him as a 'man,' which is their loftiest term of approbation, while 'not-man' is the meanest term to apply to a human being."[25]

Libbie had made another important decision following her Saturday interview with Mrs. David Lane. She accepted Mrs. Lane's offer to become the secretary of the Society of Decorative Arts. The salary was modest but a most acceptable supplement to the $30-a-month pension she received from a grateful government. And the short work week—three days—would permit her time to work at another labor of love—the story of her life on the plains with Autie.

Candace Wheeler had originated the idea of the Society of Decorative Arts. Recognizing that there was little opportunity for able, educated women, she proposed an organization whose purpose was to "encourage profitable industries among women who possess artistic talent."[26]

Equal opportunity was unheard of, for all women were expected to be dependent upon the wage-earning capabilities of the male. There was no difficulty for women in obtaining employment as a domestic. They were grudgingly compensated for teaching. The world wasn't waiting for the liberation of women for any move of this kind would be frowned upon by most men. These courageous and daring women took matters into their own hand. Like the army, they intended to take care of their own.

Mrs. Lane, who had been president of the financially successful Sanitary Fair of New York, became the first president of the Society. From the very beginning the Society received considerable publicity which resulted in its secretary, Mrs. Sheeler, becoming overwhelmed with correspondence. It became necessary to obtain a fulltime secretary.

The aims of the Society were (1) to induce art workers to master thoroughly the details of one kind of decoration; (2) to assist those who have worked unsuccessfully some practical and popular direction for their labor; (3) to open classes in various kinds of decorative work; (4) to establish a lending library of handibooks on subjects of decorative art and design; (5) to form connections with manufacturers and importers; (6) to develop the art of needlework.[27]

Mrs. Lane, having heard that General Custer's widow was in New York attempting to secure employment since her government pension was too small to live on, suggested that the secretaryship be offered to her. Candace Wheeler reacted with: "Oh, don't! I am sorry for her as can be, but we must have a businesslike and useful secretary."

Mrs. Lane replied that her name would be invaluable at this time, and that she had asked her to come for an interview. As Mrs. Wheeler continues to relate the incident: "She came, the pathetic figure in widow's weeds. . . . so modest in her estimate of herself, so earnest in her desire to do something for our enterprise, and so fixed in her determination to do something practical for her own needs!"[28]

Mrs. Wheeler's jealous protectiveness for this embryonic organization was swept aside once she had met Libbie, and so began a deep friendship. Libbie's sympathy for others and her great capacity to handle and adapt to new situations confronting her made her a valuable asset to the Society. She held deep feeling for this early movement of women's lib.

Libbie entered upon her new duties at once. Traveling back and forth from the William D. Russell residence in Newark soon became a problem and would prove to be more so in the winter months ahead. About the first of July she moved into a few furnished rooms at 122 Madison Avenue in New York City, just a short walk to the Society's headquarters at 67 Madison Avenue.[29] She had pleasant memories of New Jersey. The Russells had been kind to her when she needed it the most. And just ten miles away at Paterson was her cousin Almira Wells, whose husband, Postmaster Darius Wells, had died two years earlier. Darius was the nephew of Libbie's step-mother. The Wells and the Russels had been hosts to the Custers several times during the war.[30]

Things were looking up. The large volume of mail kept Libbie very busy. There were displays to be arranged and classes in the arts to be promoted. The days were long and the work was arduous but Libbie was happy. She was happy in the thought that she was extending a helping hand where none had been offered before.

The rooms she had been occupying were not quite to her liking. They were a bit far from the new quarters of the Society at 4 East 20th Street so she moved. Four months later she was residing in the Glenham Hotel on Fifth Avenue, remaining there about a year.

The Society was having growing pains. Burgeoning and now bulging, it moved to 34 East 19th Street, remaining there until 1881, then moving to 28 East 21st Street.[31]

Attorney John Rauch had been working for more than ten years attempting to rectify the injustice done the estate of the late Judge Bacon. Bacon had posted a surety bond on his old partner and friend Levi Humphrey at the time Humphrey was U.S. Marshal for the District of Michigan. In 1868, nearly two years after Bacon had died, the District Attorney filed a claim against the D.S. Bacon estate, claiming that Humphrey had "misappropriated funds" in October, 1845, to the amount of $3,383, and was in default to that amount.

An examination of Humphrey's account in the office of the Comptroller of the Treasury Department revealed that $2,130 of the claim was a "suspended account," and the balance of $1,253 had been disallowed.

This unsettled account remained open for nearly 22 years with no attempt at settlement, "when it was raked up by the District Attorney, and the estate of Bacon harassed by it until the compromise, as above stated, was effected."[32] In the meantime all those involved had died and their estates settled so none could contribute.

The Committee of Claims was of the opinion that "by reason of the extraordinary delay of the Government in bringing this account to settlement, the petitioner ought to be reimbursed by granting the relief prayed for, and accordingly report a bill for that purpose and recommends its passage."[33]

About the time John Rauch had advised her to be in readiness to travel to Washington in case she was needed there on the matter of her claim, Libbie received a letter from a Philadelphia artist by the name of Weilenback. He announced that he had spent six months and $160 in expenses painting a sensational "battle of the Big Horn," which had hung for two months with no purchases. He still owed $90 for the framing, and had a family to support.

He concluded: "Consequently the deceased General had at least *here* in this City no friends otherwise a painting like this would have been sold long ago. I would like to ask from you the direction of one or more of the General's best friends who would perhaps yield to my wishes." He asked $450 for the work of art.[34]

Frederick Whittaker seemed determined to have Major Marcus A. Reno tried on charges of cowardice and disobedience, contending that Reno's failure to obey orders was the cause of Custer's defeat. Addressing a letter to Delegate William W. Corlett of Wyoming Territory on May 19, 1878, he requested an official investigation by a Congressional committee into what he claimed was Reno's cowardice and Captain Benteen's willful neglect of duty in the battle.[35]

Corlett forwarded the letter to General Banning, chairman of the House Committee on Military Affairs, with a letter stating: "I also desire to say that in the West there is strong suspicion that the facts and circumstances attending the battle referred to have never been made known; on the contrary, that the facts to that affair have been concealed by those interested, and who were in a greater or less degree responsible for the disaster."[36]

When Reno learned of the request he too addressed a communication to the committee urging it to investigate his conduct in the battle. Congress adjourned without taking any action. Reno than addressed a letter to the President asking that a Court of Inquiry be ordered for the purpose.[37]

On November 25th the President authorized a Court of Inquiry to convene in Chicago on January 13, 1879. Twenty-three witnesses were examined over a period of a month in the Palmer House. What began as a front page story ended in 1,300 pages of official testimony.

Reno's testimony under oath conflicted with remarks he had made soon after the battle some 30 months earlier. He stated in his official report that he expected Custer to support him on his flank while at the inquiry he said that Custer was expected to support him from the rear.

In further defense of himself he blamed Custer for not informing him of any battle plans. He knew that Benteen had been ordered to the left to bottle up the valley while he charged the village, and that Custer had led his battalion down the right side of the river parallel to his own advance, this after Custer had told him to charge the village and he would support him with his whole outfit. He knew, as all the officers knew, what Custer's plan was. All were famliar with Custer's tactic of engaging his enemy on one front, then using a charge on the flank when his adversary was off balance.

Though the conclusions absolved Benteen and Reno they did not supply the answer to thc question that had been on everyone's mind—What really happened to Custer and his command?

When the Court adjourned, Libbie was disturbed. She had followed the newspaper accounts of the Court of Inquiry and had received numerous letters from friends commenting about it. There was solace in her work and in a remark Autie once had made: "I assume nothing that I know not to be true." She had read the sworn statements of the men she knew had hated her husband, statements she knew to be untrue. How was she to respond? Then she recalled that Autie had said to John Bulkley when they were discussing President Grant's treatment of Autie: "I don't believe a man ever perpetrated a rank injustice knowingly upon his fellow man but that he suffered for it before he died." It was reassurance for Libbie. She would live to see the prognostication come true.

It is interesting to learn of an effort toward recantation on the part of Lieutenant Jesse M. Lee some 18 years after the Court of Inquiry was held. Lee had been the Recorder of the Court. In a letter written to Libbie in 1897 he admitted to having been influenced to some degree "by the prejudicial opinions of those whose motive I did not then understand, and whose sources of information I then had no means of testing."[38]

Libbie had waited a long time for words like these. There was vindication for Autie in the letter of this fair minded, Christian officer. If only all the nation could know his thoughts. If only the disparagers could read his letter with an open mind.

NOTES — CHAPTER 29

1Nelson A. Miles: *Personal Recollections of General Nelson A. Miles*, N.Y., 1896, p. 151.
2Virginia W. Johnson: *The Unregimented General*, Cambridge, 1962, p. 96.
3*Ibid*, p. 87.
4*Report, General of the Army, 1876*, Crook's report, pp. 144-49.
5*Ibid*, p. 145.
6Johnson: *Unregimented General*, p. 102.
7Nelson Miles to W. T. Sherman, June 15, 1876, W. T. Sherman Papers, Library of Congress.
8Nelson Miles to Libbie, November 3, 1876, BCWC collection.
9Nelson Miles to Libbie, March 16, 1877. EBC-CBNM.
10Nelson Miles: *Serving The Republic*, N.Y., 1911, p. 191.
11*Ibid.*
12*Ibid.* Miles had an illustrious military career. He drove Sitting Bull into Canada, broke up the bands led by him and Crazy Horse, captured the Nez Perces under Chief Joseph, compelled Geronimo and his Apaches to surrender. He became general-in-chief of the army in 1895.
13Lieutenant I. W. Watson (Indian Agent) wrote to Libbie, July 7, 1897 that John Burkman "was with General Custer *just a few hours before the fight.* Burkman has told me several times that Gen. Custer, on the morning of the fight, said to his officers, among other things, '*I did not want to have this fight today, but find I cannot put it off any longer. . . .*'"
14Myles Moylan to Fred Calhoun, July 6, 1876, BCWC collection.
15Myies Moylan to Maggie (Custer) Calhoun, December 21, 1876, BCWC collection.
16*Ibid.*
17Bismarck *Tribune*, July 29, 1876.
18John Ryan: *Burial of Custer*, Coe collection, Yale University Library.
19James McLaughlin: *My Friend The Indian*, Boston, 1910, p. 155.
20*Ibid*, p. 167.
21*Ibid*, p. 169.
22*Ibid*, p. 170.
23Rapid City (S.D.) *Daily Journal*, November 1, 1939.
24Norman Maclean: "Custer's Lost Fight A Ritual Drama," *Chicago Westerners Brand Book*, October, 1958, p. 57.
25Aaron M. Beede: *Sitting Bull and Custer*, Bismarck, 1913, p. 34.
26Candace Wheeler: *Yesterdays In A Busy Life*, N.Y., 1918, pp. 210-216.
27New York Historical Society.
28Wheeler: *Yesterdays*, p. 218.
29Laura Oremieulx to Libbie, May 23, 1877, author's collection.
30Newark *Daily Advertiser*, October 24, (1864?); Communication from Gordon Corbett, Waldwick, N.J.; Merington, pp. 125-26. The Wells had many relatives in Clinton, Michigan, just 30 miles west of Monroe. It was in Clinton that Libbie's mother was residing at this time.
31New York City Directories, Museum of the City of New York; New York Historical Society.
32*Committee of Claims*, Report, H.R. bill #3120, Elizabeth B. Custer, February 8, 1878.
33*Ibid.*
34Fred R. Weilenbeck to Libbie, December 1, 1877, author's collection.
35*Reno Court of Inquiry*, 1879, Exhibit No. 1.
36New York *Times*, June 16, 1878.
37W. A. Graham: *The Reno Court of Inquiry*, Harrisburg, 1954, pp. IV-V.
A Court of Inquiry is purely an investigative body. It has no power to sentence, though it may, if so ordered, make recommendations.
38J. M. Lee to Libbie, June 27, 1897, EBC—CBNM.

CHAPTER 30
HIDE THAT STATUE

John Gordon Bennett's committee had engaged J. Wilson MacDonald to sculpt a statue of General Custer. It would be erected at West Point. When an announcement had been made inviting designs for a monument, the only one submitted was that of MacDonald. It was agreed that the bronze figure would cost but $10,000 if condemned cannon were furnished for the metal needed.

On August 24, 1878, MacDonald gave a private exhibition of his model to a group of artists, connoisseurs, members of the press and guests at his studio in Booth's Theatre Building in New York. The model was described as heroic in size and resting upon a pedestal of granite displaying *bas relief* panels of aspects of Custer's life.[1]

When it was learned that Bennett's committee had progressed to that extent, the Custer Monument Association in Monroe forwarded its subscriptions to August Belmont, treasurer of the *Herald* fund, then advised its own contributors of this action. What really brought this matter to a head was the statement in some newspapers that Custer had once expressed the wish that he be interred at West Point. This gave the impression that if his body was to rest there, the monument would be there too. This killed the Monroe interest in a measure though the announcement that Mrs. Custer preferred to have the monument at West Point or in New York was conclusive. The latter announcement ended the possibility of having a monument in Monroe.[2]

It is interesting to note that Libbie was never, at any time, consulted about the monument or its location. Obviously, with all the attendant publicity, she was aware of the funds being raised and of the intention of the *Herald* committee to place the statue at West Point. It appears that she was not invited to see the model, perhaps evidence of the male unconcern for the female point of view in that era. Yet the well-known actress Clara Morris gave a benefit at Wallack's Theatre in New York, raising nearly $2,000 for the effort.

Some of the gifts to the Herald fund from people of importance were: Theodore Roosevelt—$100; J. A. Roosevelt—$100; John Jacob Astor—$500; Judge Hilton—$500; William Libby—$500; William M. Evarts—$50; William Orton—$50; A. Bierstadt—$50; Henry Parish—$50; Catherine L. Wolfe—$200.

At the point $6,000 had been raised, Congressman McCook introduced House Bill No. 5532, requesting 20 condemned bronze cannon to aid in the erection of the monument. On December 13, 1878, the bill passed the House, and on December 18th, passed the Senate.[3]

Autie's old friend John Bulkley, knowing Libbie's concern for anything relating to her husband, maintained a contact with General Winfield S. Hancock, chairman of the New York monument fund. Near the end of July, 1879, Bulkley was informed by Hancock that the model of Custer had been approved by the committee. It was hoped to be ready for July but General J. M. Schofield preferred August.[4] This was the extent to which Libbie had been informed as to the progress on the proposed monument.

There were 4,000 people gathered at West Point that August 30th for the unveiling of the Custer statue. Visitors began pouring in from 10 A.M. on, arriving on steamers and trains gaily decorated with flags and bunting. Many arrived on the huge New York steamers, the New York and Albany day boat *Vibbard* and other boats from Poughkeepsie, Newburgh and other upper Hudson River towns. The ferryboat *Highlander* kept a continuous stream of train passengers moving between Garrison's and the Point.

As one moved up the steep road from the landing the statue draped in flags could be seen above in the center of a grassy area bordered by the mess hall and the officers' quarters.

At 11 A.M. 13 guns were fired in recognition of Major General Hancock's arrival. The program began shortly after 2 P.M. The guests on the speakers' platform were Major General Schofield,

Major General Hancock, Hon. N. P. Banks, Hon. Hamilton Fish, Dr. Agnew of New York, Hon. Demas Barnes, Judge Wickham of St. Louis, General John Robinson, Chaplain Forsyth, Adjutant General W. M. Wherry, Algernon S. Sullivan, Thomas LeClear, Ex-Governor Morgan, Rufus F. Andrews, Rev. Wendell Prime, John McCullough, Philip Hamilton and Clara Morris. Libbie Custer's absence was noted.

At 2 P.M. the cadets, headed by the Academy band, marched to a postion in front of the mess hall, forming a line just behind the monument to face the river. After the band played a few numbers, including a dirge, the Hon. A. S. Sullivan presented the statue to the Military Academy in behalf of the committee. The sculptor MacDonald pulled the cord that released the flags draping the figure of Custer. The band played "Garry Owen" while the crowd cheered. A salute of 13 guns followed.

General Schofield, as Superintendent of the Academy, accepted the statue, the band played another number, followed by a 30-minute oration of tribute to Custer. John McCullough the tragedian read the poem "Custer's Last Charge," then the Detroit tenor Charles Thompson and his quintette sang "Hail! And Farewell to Custer." Chaplain Forsyth offered the benediction after which 13 guns were fired.

After the ceremony there was considerable discussion over the statue. The cadets were quite enthusiastic over it and, in fact, cheered it. Some of the officers at the Academy ridiculed it. It was asserted that no soldier held a sword or pistol in that manner, and Custer wouldn't have fought in a coat of that kind or died in a colonel's uniform.[5]

The statue represented Custer as he stood on foot facing the enemy in a full dress uniform, a saber in his right hand as if to raise it, and a cocked revolver clutched in his left hand and thrown across his chest. The marble pedestal on which he stood was about six feet high. On both the north and south sides of this base protruded a single bronze buffalo head; the east or front side portrayed Custer on horseback; and on the west side was the inscription:

GEORGE A. CUSTER
Lt. Col., Seventh Cavalry
Bvt. Maj. Gen'l., U.S. Army
BORN
December 5th, 1839, Harrison, Co., Ohio
KILLED
With His Entire Command
In The
BATTLE
OF
"LITTLE BIG HORN"
June 25th, 1876.

Faithful John Bulkley, attending the ceremony, wrote to Libbie a description of it and the statue, ending by telling her there had not been sufficient

NO CAVALRYMAN FOUGHT LIKE THIS, said Mrs. Custer, for cavalrymen fought on horseback using one weapon at a time. The granite base was to her liking. She had it placed on her husband's grave. Monroe *Democrat*, April 29, 1910.

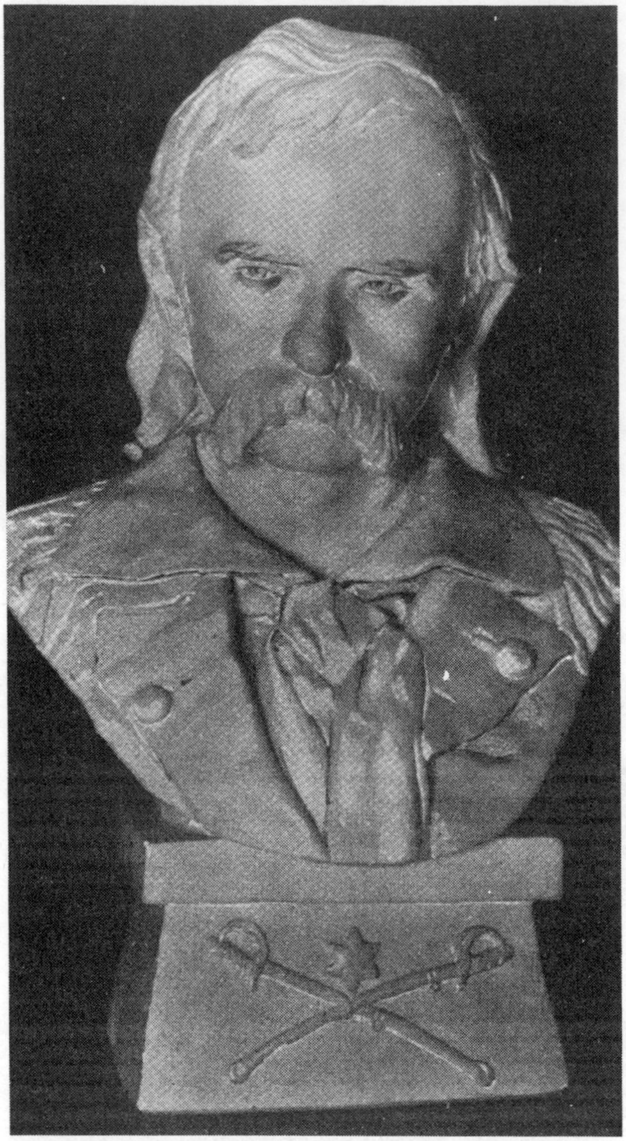

PLASTER BUST OF GENERAL CUSTER by Vinnie Ream Hoxie. Libbie could not convince Vinnie to sell her the original. She settled for a plaster copy. Cosmopolitan Magazine, p. 301, July, 1891.

funds for an equestrian monument as planned, which was why Autie had been placed on foot.[6]

Libbie was upset. If her mission in life was to perpetuate her husband's name and standing in Civil War and frontier history, the statue at West Point was a poor start. She was already heartsick from the accusations and allegations the anti-Custerites had uttered during and following the Reno Court of Inquiry, and the statue seemed to be the last straw.

On a visit to her husband's grave she had an opportunity to view the statue and concluded that it was worse than she had supposed. Her friends had tried to shield her in their descriptions. There was some consolation in Algernon Sullivan's remark made at the unveiling:

"It is the good fortune of some soldiers that, with their death stroke, they are swept along at once into the land of legend, and their names are enveloped in the purple mist of song." A little thought and a little time and the legend would grow. And a legend could mean perpetuity.

Apparently Autie's mentor, Congressman John Bingham, had learned of Libbie's distress for on December 4, 1879, he introduced a joint resolution to authorize the erection of a statue to Custer.[7] There was no mention of location.

Then on March 1st, Congressman John B. Clark of Missouri introduced a bill for the erection of a monument in the city of Washington to the memory of General Custer and the officers and men killed with him at the Little Big Horn. An appropriation of $12,000 was asked and the Secretary of War requested to contract with Wilson MacDonald to duplicate his equestrian and pedestrian figure.[8] Senator Edmunds introduced a companion bill in the Senate on March 9th.[9]

This was just too much for Libbie. One MacDonald atrocity was bad enough. A duplicate of it was doubling up a public display of poor research and a resultant example of bad sculpture. Her strong letter of protest was read to the Committee on Public Buildings and Grounds on April 21st and the matter died in committee. When E. W. Whitaker learned of her protest he advised her that he heartily endorsed her expressed views on the MacDonald statue.[10] He was of the opinion that there were many better artists. At the Clark Mills foundry he had seen a small equestrian statue of the General he wished Libbie could see. He understood that there were many young artists throughout the country designing models of Custer in the hope they would get the order for a monument that would be erected in Washington. Whitaker advised her not to give any hasty written approval to anyone.[11]

All this talk of monuments and statues brought to mind Autie's visit to Vinnie Ream Hoxie's Washington studio some years before when he sat for a bust. Libbie had maintained a correspondence with the talented and vivacious Vinnie but had never asked to purchase the bust of Autie. She had the live original so why try to purchase Vinnie's cold copy? Now the copy held a different value.

In the fall of 1879, learning from Vinnie Ream that the marble bust could be purchased, Libbie sent Vinnie $100 she had earned since going East. Another $50 would be sent later.

The wily Vinnie knew what she was about. She had never intended parting with the bust, but she was after bigger game. It was better to allow Libbie the small item and obtain her support in an endeavor that could mean a commission for a Custer statue in bronze. She had seen an aroused Libbie, a dissatisfied Libbie, and had concluded that Libbie would be the deciding factor in any Custer monuments in the future.

Not long afterward—in June of 1880—Vinnie wrote Libbie:

"Senator Voorhees and Senator Morgan together have prepared a resolution for a statue to Genl. Custer and are watching for an opportunity to bring it up. . . . If this resolution should pass the House and Senate, it would be open to competition, and I would not have a fear of winning it. . . . I feel as if no one could possibly make any statue of him to suit you so well as I could."[12]

Senator Voorhees and Morgan were close friends of the Hoxies. And now Vinnie had made a friend out of Libbie by allowing her to buy the marble bust. She was playing her cards well, in fact, she was stacking the deck.

General Montgomery C. Meigs had been keeping Libbie informed of his proposal to create a National Cemetery and erect a memorial on the Custer Battlefield. He had submitted plans and specifications on October 16, 1878. The estimated cost was $1,000.[13]

The contract to supply the stone shaft of the monument was let to Alexander McDonald of Cambridge, Mass., on February 21, 1879, but it was not until 1881 that the shaft was erected. In the interim, a monument pyramidal in shape and made of cordwood was erected at the site of the present stone shaft. Captain George K. Sanderson and a detail of soldiers from nearby Fort Custer had policed the area by gathering up all of the horse bones strewn over the Battlefield and placing them within the cordwood shaft. This was done to stop the sensational stories circulated in the newspapers that the bones of the soldiers had not been properly interred.[14]

Transporting the 18-ton memorial was quite a task. It was shipped by water to Duluth, by rail to Bismarck, then by river steamer to the mouth of the Big Horn River. In July, 1881, Lieut. Charles F. Roe and Troop C, Second Cavalry, took charge of the erection of the truncated pyramid.

The New York *Times,* on October 6, 1881, announced that the Vermont granite monument had just been erected.In describing the three pieces as weighing 10,000, 12,000 and 14,000 pounds respectively, the base being six feet square and the total height as 13½ feet, the paper indicated that the stone blocks had to be hauled over the snow on sleds from the mouth of the Little Big Horn River to the site, 24 mules being used to haul each block. The skeletons of Custer's men were reinterred in a trench around the foot of the shaft.

It was in the fall of 1881 that Libbie made her trip to Washington to obtain the precious bust of Autie it had taken her two years to pay for. Realizing that her meager income was not obtaining much more than the necessities of life, she called upon General Sherman to ask his aid in obtaining a pension increase of $20 a month. She was then drawing $30 a month. When she came fact to face with the grizzled veteran she lost her nerve and the conversation dwelled on lesser matters.[15]

Libbie interested Senator Ferry of Michigan in her plight. In the spring of 1882 he introduced a bill that would, if passed, increase her pittance to $50 a month.[16] After three months of jockeying around the committees, and after several amendments that were fly-specking in nature, the bill was passed and signed by the President. Libbie now had a guaranteed income of $50 a month.[17]

As Libbie sat at her desk to answer the letters she received each day, her eyes would wander upward to that magnificent bust of her beloved. As she gazed at it herthoughts would turn to the repulsive statue she had seen of him on her Memorial Day visit to West Point. Something had to be done about it. It had to be removed and destroyed. The monstrosity would have a bad impression upon American youth, especially those attending the Academy.

She was not politically naive for hadn't she observed the grass roots politics her father participated in back in Monroe? And hadn't she observed the political processes first hand in Washington while the nation was engaged in a civil war? The removal of the statue would require a touch of politics, of that she was well aware.

Initially she had written to General Sherman a letter of protest. She had objected to the sculptor MacDonald because he had not given the subject adequate research. No qualified artist in his right mind would portray a cavalryman as charging the enemy with a revolver in one hand and a saber in the other. As well show him with the reins in his teeth. Libbie simply could not accept this misrepresentation of the cavalry service and of her husband.[18]

Sherman was surprised to learn that Libbie had not been informed of the design of the statue and that it had not even been submitted to competent judges for their observations. His sympathetic letter suggested that she express her wishes to the Secretary of War, Robert Lincoln. This she did, receiving sympathetic responses from him but no indication that he would press the matter. Then she learned something new about politics. She described her experience in a letter to General Sherman.

A week earlier she accidentally met Secretary Lincoln on which occasion he brought up the subject of her correspondence with him. He told her he was in sympathy with the removal of the statue but the West Point Commandant, General Howard, was not, and now that a new Commandant was appointed "he would again bring up the subject and do what he could."

Libbie then continued:

"I was amazed to find that the Secretary of War looked for assistance from the Commandant at

West Point. I had an idea he would direct what he wished and the commandant would obey.

"I have little hope. But what hope I now have rests in you the kindest and truest of friends to me, when I so need all that they can do to make my sad life endurable.

"I tell you frankly I do not believe that General Merritt (the new Commandant at West Point) will interest himself or aid the Secretary in hiding the statue unless *you* ask him to do it dear General Sherman.

"A wife's love sharpens her eyes and quickens her instinct and years ago I knew (not from my husband) that General Merritt was his enemy. On the plains we entertained him and he seemed to have conquered his enmity and jealousy that was so bitter in the Army of the Potomac. But when he was placed at the head of the Court of Inquiry that met to investigate Col. Reno's conduct at Chicago, I saw all through the trial how General Merritt *still* felt toward his dead comrade. This is the reason I have but little hope from him, in my heart's wish regarding the statue. . . .

"I do not want the statue removed to any part of the Point and set up again. I want the figure taken down and stored somewhere temporarily. If the figure is removed out of site I can do what I told you I wanted to do, place on the pedestal a granite shaft with the battles cut in the sides. If the whole thing is put further back, still I should be compelled to go over the ground again and get the figure out of the way in some manner. I *cannot* live in peace and know that such a blot is before the people."[19]

Two weeks later she would be on the *Adriatic* with Mrs. General Gibbs on their way to London. There would be no traveling other than to Paris. Friends associated with a steamship line had provided her with passes, otherwise she would have had to stay at home for the rest she could "no longer go without." Five and a half years of intensive work in the Society had used her up.

The settlement the Government had reimbursed Libbie with in the matter of the unjust charge made against her father's estate was a windfall. The $3,000 enabled her to buy a small home which she rented furnished during her stay abroad.

She told General Sherman she knew that Autie would not approve of her comments about General Merritt "but this is a desperately intense sort of a matter to me and I have violated his wishes in order to make clear to you what impediments seem to block my way."[20]

On the following day General Sherman replied:

"Mr. Lincoln is kind and good, but not as firm and positive as you or I would wish. He could have ordered the removal of Custer's statue to a storehouse and allowed you to replace it by a shaft as you propose, and he may do so still, but he also knows that MacDonald the artist considers that statue as the heroic creation of his genius.

"He also knows that Mac Donald is backed by the subscribers and he would make a direct issue of it. The Sec. of War is only the custodian of West Point, Congress having exclusive jurisdiction over it, though the Sec. may do almost anything not prohibited by Congress or which does not impair the values of the property.

"I advise you to limit your efforts to the Sec. of War, who has in his heart a warm place for you who have been so brave so true to Custer and his memory that every man who is a man must respond to your appeal.

"I advise you to see some monument maker and make a *conditional* bargain for an obelisk or shaft over Custer's grave like Anderson's or Audenreid—*provided* the MacDonald Statue be removed, boxed and stored, remaining in the warehouse at West Point. Send me a copy of the contract, and accompany it with a short, strong letter *demanding* as the widow of Custer, the *sole and exclusive* right to mark the grave of your husband.

"Your first admirable letter is still on file but it is in the nature of an appeal. The one I want is an emphatic demand of your right; possessed of such a letter from you I will present it to the Secretary endorsed with my judgment that the widow had this unqualified right and that I advise that the statue be taken down and stored away subject only to the order of the Secretary of War, and not of the artist who has been paid for his work and who has parted with all title. If you prefer that shaft on the site of the present statue, well be it. I should suppose it better to put the obelisk or shaft at the grave the same as Genl. Scott.

"I am almost sure that if Merritt was jealous of Custer living, he cannot but admire his plucky widow.

"You may always write to me in absolute frankness for I sympathize with every pulsation of your wounded heart."[21]

As a word of caution he advised her to do all this before she went abroad since there could be rapid changes in politics.

Even though the General of the Army, Sherman, had given the green light to Libbie, the principals were slow to act. In matters involving the displacement of people or the interests of important people, Washington policitians were extremely cautious. Secretary Lincoln recognized this when he replied to the Hon. Leonard Swett of Chicago on April 24, 1884, that there would have been no difficulty if the statue had been put up by the Government, but having been erected by contributions of prominent citizens created difficulties. He hoped to accomplish the

CUSTER MONUMENT AT HIS BIRTHPLACE, New Rumley, Ohio, was unveiled June 22, 1932, the State of Ohio having appropriated $15,000 to honor a native son. Cadiz *Republican.*

CUSTER MONUMENT ONCE AT CUSTER CITY, COLORADO. Erected in 1902, it was intended to be the central theme for attracting investors to a silver mining development. Mrs. E. B. Custer collection, Custer Battlefield National Monument.

removal before leaving office. He concluded: "Perhaps the best way would be to make it one of my last acts of administration. . . . Possibly a gradual removal might be begun which would result in making it difficult to find the statue."[22]

It is apparent that Libbie, on receipt of this letter from Swett (for the original is in her files), contacted her friend and protector Sherman. With his aid and that of Swett, Lincoln was forced to move. It was now obvious that General Merritt was all Libbie had thought. He had exerted no effort in behalf of her pleas. It took an order from Lincoln to force Merritt to accomplish the desired result.

On November 28th Secretary Lincoln advised Swett of the receipt of Libbie's "urgent application." He informed Swett that he had directed General Merritt as Superintendent of the Military Academy "to cause the statue to be removed from its pedestal and to be securely boxed and stored at the Post."[23]

He noted that Mrs. Custer had requested that the statue be removed to the Little Big Horn battlefield, an act he thought to be impractical to comply with for two reasons:

"1) Basis of removal 'is that it is devoid of artistic merit and is offensive to the eye.' (This) would be inconsistent with an order to set it up in a public place.

"2) In 1878, Congress made an appropriation of a number of bronze cannon to assist in the erection of a statue to Gen. Custer at West Point. No doubt these cannon went into the statue."

Lincoln concluded that since the location was fixed by Congress it would be improper for him to change the location.[24]

Merritt, of course, complied with Secretary Lincoln's orders. The statue was taken down and stored in the equipment shed and the spot where it stood was leveled and seeded.[25] The somewhat redoubtable Merritt had been bested, thanks to Sherman's intervention. Libbie had succeeded in obtaining her wish though she admitted that she had "literally cried it off its pedestal."[26]

It was not, however, until the summer of 1906 that the Academy Superintendent General Anson Mills fulfilled her request by having the head and shoulders cut from the statue. This portion was preserved for a time, then disappeared. Mills promised that the bust would be permanently placed though there is no record to show it ever was.[27]

Life for Libbie never remained tranquil. Civil War veterans began banding together around the country in a common bond to promote their interests. They had come home from the wars expecting recognition and some assistance when needed but had found that you get this only when you go after it. It was customary to name each G.A.R. post after some distinguished comrade in arms. Custer was not without his ardent followers. Grant and Merritt might not honor his name but the men who fought under him did, and they organized and named G.A.R. posts after him—from Maine to New Orleans, from St. Joseph, Missouri, to New York City.[28]

Each asked Libbie for some memento and a picture of the General to display in their meeting place. To the best of her ability she complied, at least to the extent of a large Brady portrait of him with a description of the uniform he was wearing at the time the photograph was made.

No post was named after him in Monroe though his townsfolk named a street and country roads, and later schools and business places.

In 1883, Joe C. Sterling of Monroe, in an effort to honor Custer, managed to encourage John Mulvany to bring a large oil painting to Monroe that was receiving considerable publicity.

Artist Mulvany, in keeping with countless other Americans, had been shocked by the Custer tragedy. After a visit to the Custer Battlefield in 1879 he began a two-year project he named "Custer's Last Rally." The 11x22 foot canvas depicting the Custer battle was first exhibited in Kansas City in March, 1881. It was exhibited in Monroe for several days.[29]

The Detroit *Evening Journal* obtained a statement from Libbie that she had twice attempted to view it while it was on display in Chicago in 1882. The first glance had revealed such a realistic scene that everything became blurred before her eyes. She felt that she would never be able to look upon the painting again.

At this time Libbie was spending every spare moment working on the manuscript for her proposed book. Maggie Calhoun would visit her from time to time and, as the two reminisced, Libbie would write down a key sentence or two on a scratch pad which would enable her when alone to recall the occasions they had discussed, then write about them.

Early one morning in September, 1884, shortly before daybreak, Libbie's maid was aroused by a roaring noise in the air shaft. Discovering that the shaft was a mass of flames, she awakened Libbie and Maggie. The three immediately ran into the hall screaming an alarm to everyone in the apartment building. Many of the occupants hurried to the roof. Though it was a fierce fire the firemen soon extinguished it.

At the height of the blaze both Maggie and Libbie tried to return to the apartment but were prevented by the police because of the potential danger. Libbie insisted that she wanted to return to see if an iron safe containing General Custer's letters was intact but was compelled to wait until the fireman announced that the fire had been put out.

When the two women were permitted to return, Libbie discovered a purse was missing that contained a small sum of money. Maggie discovered missing a gold watch and chain that had belonged to her brother Tom and which he had given to her just before his last expedition. Both women refused any comment as to who they suspected might have done the stealing. Fortunately, two marble busts of the General, one by Vinnie Ream, were not harmed.[30]

NOTES—CHAPTER 30

1New York *Times,* August 25, 1878.
2Clipping dated August 31, 1879, in Rebecca Richmond's scrapbook, Grand Rapids Public Library.
3*Congressional Record,* December 13, 1878, House of Representatives; December 18, 1878, Senate.
4J. M. Bulkley to Libbie, July 28, 1879, EBC-CBNM.
5New York *Times,* August 31, 1879; Detroit *Free Press,* August 31, 1879.
6John Bulkley to Libbie, September 3, 1879, EBC-CBNM.
7H.R. Bill No. 130, 46th Congress, 2d Sess., December 4, 1879.
8H.R. Bill No. 4841, 46th Congress, 2d Sess., March 1, 1880, EBC-CBNM.
9Senate Bill No. 1443, March 9, 1880.
10E. W. Whitaker to Libbie, April 24, 1880, EBC-CBNM.
11*Ibid,* December 18, 1880, EBC-CBNM.
12Vinnie R. Hoxie to Libbie, June 5, 1880, author's collection.
13Don Rickey Jr.: *History of Custer Battlefield,* Washington, 1967, pp. 60-63.
14*Ibid.*
15Monaghan: *Life of General Custer,* p. 403.
16May 2, 1882, D.B. No. 1819, 46 Cong., 1st Sess; June 26, 27, 1882 (amendments); July 14, 15, 17, 26, 28, 1882 (amendments).
17July 31, 1882, *Congressional Record,* Senate, p. 6733.
18Merington, p. 327.
19Eliz. B. Custer to Gen. W. T. Sherman, October 16, 1882, W. T. Sherman papers, Library of Congress.
20*Ibid.*
21W. T. Sherman to Libbie, October 17, 1882, EBC-CBNM.
22Secretary of War Robert Lincoln to Hon. Leonard Swett, April 24, 1884, EBC-CBNM.
Swett, an attorney and an intimate friend of Abraham Lincoln, carried considerable weight in political circles.
23Robert Lincoln to Hon. Leonard Swett, November 28, 1884, EBC-CBNM.
24*Ibid.*
25*Army and Navy Register,* May 30, 1885, p. 340.
26Merington, p. 327.
27Brig. Gen. A. L. Mills to Libbie, June 20, 1905, and Eliz. B. Custer to General Mills, June 18, 1906, U.S. Military Academy Library; John Byers: "Custer's Last Stand," *The Pointer,* June 1, 1951.
28Custer Post #7, St. Joseph, Mo.; Gen. George A. Custer Command No. 3, New York, N.Y. (Dec. 5, 1885); Custer Post No. 5, New Orleans (Nov. 2, 1885); Custer Post No. 1, Washington, D.C.; Custer Post No. 7, Dept. of Maine; Gen. Geo. A. Custer Post. No. 40, Chicago (Sept. 18, 1884); etc., EBC-CBNM.
29Monroe *Democrat,* October 18, 1883; Robert Taft: *Artist And Illustrators Of The Old West,* N.Y., 1953, pp. 134-42; Frost: *Custer Album,* p. 9; Don Russell: *Custer's Last,* Fort Worth, 1968, pp. 28-29.
30Monroe *Democrat,* September 11, 1884.

CHAPTER 31
A BOOK IS BORN

Nine years had passed and Libbie's tribute was complete and in print. She dedicated *Boots and Saddles* to her husband with "the echo of whose voice has been my inspiration." The small volume released in March, 1885, received immediate acceptance. The first printing of 2,000 copies quickly sold. By November its sale exceeded 15,000 copies, ultimately surpassing 31,000. The publishers, Harper & Brothers, obtained widespread publicity for it, receiving sympathetic and laudatory reviews literally from coast to coast.

The last year had been a trying one, though the actual writing had not been as hard on her as the depressing and painful experience of rereading Autie's letters to make extracts, particularly for the pages in the final chapter. The anguish she experienced would have made most people cease, but Libbie was of the woof of a stronger cloth. This was to her a tribute to the man she loved.

To a friend she wrote: "I was always looking back in my waking hours and dreaming the most unsatisfactory dreams of my beloved one at night. And of what intense anxiety I felt for fear my crude, inexperienced pen could not so frame a little story of his home life that anyone would be willing to read."[1]

The prepublication fears Libbie endured were washed away once the reviewers received their copies of *Boots and Saddles*. They and the public were astounded yet charmed with the story this genteel woman told. If she had any doubts about her ability to "frame a little story" of her husband's life one of the first reviews, appearing in the Albany *Times* on April 4th, must have pacified them. It stated:

"There is no affectation in striving for elegant words; no exaggerations which, when discovered, would make one doubt the truthfulness of the whole, but descriptions are vivid, and thoughts are expressed clearly.

"Of Mrs. Custer's sweet womanly nature the book gives testimony in every page, a loving wife and true companion, willing to share all dangers with him to whom her heart belonged.

"Had good old Horace Greeley lived to read Mrs. Custer's book, he would have exclaimed, no doubt, 'Stay East, young man, stay East!'"

The commendatory reviews were profuse, filling Libbie with gratitude. She had a feeling that God had answered her prayers and that she had done her duty after years of silence; silence because she felt she had no right to bear his honored name as long as she "could not pay tribute to him from whom it came."[2]

Her reaction to the public acceptance of her efforts overwhelmed her. She was flooded with letters from many friends and admirers, and the marked acceptance caused her to all but collapse. A sense of duty kept her from it.

Harper's Bazaar referred to her autobiography as being unlike any ever before given the public. It observed: "It shows the writer's own strong personality, while she herself is trying most to bring out that of her hero-husband; it is unnecessary to add that she succeeds in doing both."

The St. Paul *Pioneer Press* considered the book worth reading "if only for the way it makes one understand how a woman can love her husband. . . . that he (Gen. Custer) was worthy of the affection he inspired, the whole book convincingly attests."

Lengthier than most reviews, *Harper's Monthly* was of the opinion that "the book is franker than any trained literary hand would or could have made it, and therein lie both its fascination and the secret of its worth. . . . Nothing that her hero did was ignoble or unworthy or of doubtful propriety; nothing that pertains to him is, in her eyes, too trivial to be recorded; nothing needs suppression, apology or explanation."

On April 30th, the Philadelphia *Press* combined its book review with an interview. The reporter, Miss Gilder, gathered from Libbie that her poverty seemed to distress her friends more than it did her, that they made up any deficiency in her income by their practical attention. She received more invitations to spend weeks here and there and to go on long trips from Mexico to England than she could accept. "My friends," she added, "are kindness itself and seem to feel that I am their special care."

Libbie's book stimulated a number of people formerly associated with the Custers to reminisce.

One, S. J. Barrows, wrote for the Boston *Christian Register:*

"That was a narrow escape in 1873, when he (General Custer) was corraled by the Indians on the Yellowstone River, and only fought his way out by a charge against a force of Indians four times as large. In a second sharp battle which he had with the Indians on the Big Horn, his horse was shot under him, the eleventh horse that, during his experience, had been stricken under him this way. He seemed to bear a charmed life.

"Fear was not an element in his nature. He exposed himself freely and even recklessly. In our campaign on the Yellowstone, with his bright red shirt, he was the most conspicuous mark in the command. I protested against soliciting Indian bullets in this way, but found an appeal to his wife more effective, and the next year the red shirt was exchanged for a buckskin suit.

"Custer was a born soldier but not a closet soldier. His place was in the field. He could not compare with many others in knowledge of military theories. He was not the man to sit down, like Sherman or Grant, and plan a great campaign. But, if not the man to plan, he was terrible in execution. He had all the dash, fire, energy, endurance and perseverance which a leader of cavalry requires. . . .

"In crossing new country, he had the instincts of an Indian. His sense of location was remarkable. . . . He was not cruel or vindictive. He did not find pleasure in inflicting death and destruction for its own sake. But whatever he undertook he determined to make successful. . . . He could not bear to have the idea of failure with anything he undertook. Like everyone else, he had his faults."

One reviewer wrote: "Where Mrs. Custer alludes to her married life it seems like a recital of a beautiful poem—a familiar poem, because it grew into shape and loveliness under my own eyes. . . . One finds himself not thinking so much of the fact that Mrs. Custer wrote this book as of the thought that Mrs. Custer lived this life."

And another in the *Review* of April 6th had this to say:

"Those who know Mrs. Custer at all well are aware that it has been her sacred hope since her brave husband died to have some fit monument and tribute erected to his memory. Unintentionally perhaps, the hope of her heart has formed a beautiful realization in this production *(Boots and Saddles)*, far more expressive than bronze or marble and glowing with colors exceeding the richness of the painted portrait."[3]

Though Libbie's book had been selling well it had not been on the market long enough for her to have received any royalties. Her $50 a month pension and the small salary from the Society was barely adequate for routine expenses and rent on her flat in the Stuyvesant Apartments at the corner of Third Ave. and 18th Street. The rental of her small house at 148 East 18th Street was sufficient to cover the payments of the mortgage that encumbered it. In order to augment her small income she had been writing for a number of newspapers, principally Western. Her column dealt with public affairs, art and peoples of interest and in the news. Though many of her articles carried her name at the head, most of them were signed at the end in facsimile, *Elizabeth B. Custer.*

Some of her husband's Michigan Civil War veterans, having learned of the financial plight she was in, and having been informed that a pension agent was about to be appointed for the Detroit Pension Agency, started a movement to secure the appointment for her.

Michigan's Governor Russell A. Alger, in answer to a Detroit *Tribune* reporter, said: "This was done without consulting her, and when she heard of it she wrote she did not want the office herself, but that she would like to have her sister-in-law, Mrs. Calhoun, get it."[4]

Alger had endorsed General John G. Parkhurst, believing that if a Democrat was to be appointed, he was the best that could be selected. The Governor was of the opinion that Parkhurst would waive any claim in Mrs. Custer's favor.

Because of the attendant publicity, Alger released Libbie's letter to the reporter. She indicated:

"Though the salary would have been so acceptable to me, I would rather be poor than lose my chance of putting my husband before his country while the interest is awakened by the 30,000 people who have read of him in 'Boots and Saddles.' I believe 15,000 copies of my book have been sold and I try to think doubling the number would not be overestimating the numbers. Bookmaking, however, is not paying and I know the salary of pension agent would enable me to buy a home in the East among those who encourage me and incite me to work in a literary way. However the movement in my behalf might interest someone to purchase my old home, about which I wrote you, and since I am before the people can I ask you to again suggest it to someone who might be willing to locate in Monroe, or buy the place for some relative who would wish to live reasonably where the schools are good."[5]

Governor Alger, as a result of this letter, wrote to General Spaulding in Monroe, suggesting that the Bacon homestead be purchased by public subscription since "Mrs. Gen. Custer seems to be in pressing need of money."

Libbie, meanwhile, had gone to Washington to see what could be done to get the appointment of Maggie Calhoun. In a special column in the Chicago *Inter Ocean* after her return to New York, she voiced her displeasure with the Administration and the way she was treated both by President Grover Cleveland and General Black, Commissioner of Pensions. She said: "I could not get one member of the Cabinet to talk with me, and the Commissioner of Pensions was so busy he asked to be excused when I called upon him. I am very grateful for the kindness of my friends in Michigan in urging my appointment as pension agent at Detroit, but I did not want the office for myself."[6] Again she indicated that her sister-in-law Mrs. Margaret Calhoun, living with Lieutenant Fred Calhoun, her brother-in-law, at Vancouver Barracks, Wyoming, could use the employment.

Several days later the Chicago *Tribune* carried an article over her signature that struck a blow for women's lib. Under a heading "Office Seeking As It Is," she opened the article with a few lines that had met her eye in a Washington Sunday paper which read: "The President does not consider it consistent with the dignity of true womanhood to come here to seek appointments." She agreed to this, then continued:

> "But when your native State asks you to make a special pilgrimage to solicit something for your family, and when you feel every attempt to honor the family of a soldier should be encouraged and abetted, why there is nothing to do but swallow your pride and come.
>
> "The Senator who wrote me to come disappeared. I do not blame him. I would have taken refuge in flight too, had I been he."[7]

Humorously she described her long wait in the anterooms and final presentation to the various undersecretaires who gave her, along with many others, the run-around.

Over her first fears now that she had received no satisfaction, and realizing it was not for herself she was there, Libbie entered for a second time, determined to see the Secretary of Interior. When given the same rejection she reacted with: "Someone has told an awful fib here," then added that she knew there were to be interviews by appointment. This did the trick. She was given an appointment to see the Secretary. A while later she was ushered into his office by the back way. He was kind but firm in a negative way. She left with the feeling she could send word back to Michigan that "I came, I saw, but I have not conquered."

In conclusion she advised: "If any woman contemplates coming, there is just one word I would like to appropriate that Lord Chesterfield quotes from *Punch* in reply to his son appealing to him for advice about getting married—'Don't.'"[8]

In the fall of 1885 Libbie wrote an article describing a trip to the Catskill Mountains entitled "A Catskill Cabin."[9] An invitation written to her on birchbark by Candace Wheeler began: "Lotus Land, Careaway Cottage, Catskills—Come up and rest, little woman. We all want you."

Leaving New York City and its sweltering 96 degrees, Libbie took the train to Tannersville. It was a two-mile drive from there to the Wheeler cottage where the thermometer registered 50 degrees in the sun.

Libbie described Mrs. Wheeler's cottage in detail, drawing attention to its economy of construction and furnishing, then told of the delightful time everyone had listening to Samuel Clemens' "genial flow of characteristic speech."

Other guests she mentions were General (Adam) Badeau, Consul General to England and author of *"Life of General Grant;"* Mr. and Mrs. Sage, descendent of Henry Sage the founder of Cornell's Women's College; Mr. and Mrs. Frank Thurber, philanthropist and prominent businessman; Mrs. Samuel Clemens and Dunham Wheeler, author.

Now that Libbie had received some reknown as an author there was a demand for articles from her pen. Following her return from the Catskills two newspapers received a series of articles expressing her observations as she traveled to Washington, Boston and Chicago during the balance of the year.

Her trip to Mount Vernon drew attention to the vandalism there.[10] In early December she reported on a wide range of subjects encompassing sketches of prominent New York personalities, the opera, prima donnas, the ballet, lectures for children, a Japanese village on display at the Madison Square Garden, an ice carnival in Macy's store window and a three-day exhibition of the Society of Decorative Art shown in Nickerbocker Hall. This latter exhibition was very successful, realizing several thousand dollars in entrance fees and sales. She indicated: "The proceeds of this exhibition are to be used for free classes to develop children into successful artisans, not artists."[11]

As Libbie admitted to a friend her column in the two newspapers "is remuneration and just now it is bread and butter as my income, aside from my pension, suddenly stopped temporarily. Next spring, if I am strong enough in nerve, I mean to drop the letters to my western papers and begin the book. But I know beforehand it will cost me a year of exhaustion for I feel the moment I take my pen to speak of him, that I am a different being."[12]

By this time she had received several hundred letters from all over the country in response to her book. Each letter, when read, brought tears. Answering them was even more unnerving. Ultimately the task of answering became such an upsetting experience she was forced to give up any attempts to do so. Emotionally drained, she was compelled to put aside her plans to write a second book about her husband for juvenile readers. Her plans for such a volume never came to fruition though she was warmed by the efforts of Mary E. Burt who interested Charles Scribner's Sons in publishing *"THE BOY GENERAL"* in 1901. Frederick S. Dellenbaugh contracted with the Macmillan Company to publish his biography *"George Armstrong Custer"* in 1917. This biography of her husband was so much to her liking she wrote an introduction for it. It became popular reading for the teen-age boys of that decade.

The strain of overwork had affected Libbie's eyes. Now nearing her 44th birthday, she was forced to the wearing of spectacles. She had been proud of her previously perfect vision but had to give way to "the slavery of spectacles" she believed she had hurried onto herself by overwork. Following orders to obtain more rest, her calm returned and her eyesight improved. She arrived at a point she could "write several hours a day, *if it is of subjects that do not* tax my feelings. But letters, except on business, I am only able to undertake with caution."[13]

But to the invalided and dying Mrs. Kingsley, Libbie continued to write and to open her heart:

"I left my Michigan home at the earnest desire of a noble woman who tried to inspire me with a wish to do something with my wrecked life, and entered a philanthropic society here modelled after the Kensington School of Needlework. It was a blessed haven for me and I found a place where I was needed. But after five years and a half of overtaxing and the confinement of a basement room which was especially trying to my strength because I had lived out of doors so long, I was done for and had to leave. I went with tears. . . .

"But some faithful English friends of my husband's, Mr. Graves, who is a partner in Ismer, Irwin Co. in the White Star Line, and whom we entertained on the plains, sent me passes and I went to Europe for nine months and again my life was spared. I know it was for this work. I feel sure that our Heavenly Father will use me yet to do further honor to a man sacrificed by his country. For Dear Mrs. Kingsley, the Indian Policy of our Government has spilled some of its best blood without being necessary."[14]

Libbie told of her tiny little flat and how she had borrowed the mother of one of her friends to take care of her for which she could not be thankful enough. Newspaper work she did not consider taxing "because it is only chit-chat but I need drilling and practice in writing for my whole soul is fixed in putting my husband in the heart of the boys who will be men of the day soon. Then she continued:

"I have such interesting volunteer hospital work also. I am on the Board of the Training School for Nurses and have a ward assigned me which I visit weekly at Bellevue Hospital. I am a trustee in an Infirmary for Women and Children. These two hospitals I hope to be associated with the rest of my days. Most of the ladies on the Boards are older than I am but I was asked because I was so absorbed in the Society of Decorative Arts.

"Do not speak of leaving this earth when you can shed such comfort on sorrowing souls. Do I not *know* how you long to join him you adore but such women are needed on earth, for who can speak the soothing, helpful word to bruised hearts like those who *know* into what depts of anguish a soul can descend."[15]

June, 1886, brought a welcome letter from Eliza. Eliza, now living in Athens, Ohio, had married an attorney there by the name of Denison. Though very happy she, like Libbie, missed the old days. Having received a copy of the book from Libbie, her pride in having participated in the events related in it caused her to ask the price of a copy so that everyone in town could obtain one.[16]

On August 4th, Rhoda Bacon, Libbie's stepmother, suddenly passed away. A short time after her husband, the Judge, had died she took up her residence near Tecumseh, Michigan, making her home with her nephew, Cyrus W. Wells. A year earlier she had noticed that her strength was waning. In the hope that the brisk New England air would restore her health, she had visited her niece, Mrs. Ellen Coggeshall at New Bedford, Mass., planning to remain there through the summer of 1886.

The remains were conveyed to Tecumseh accompanied by her stepdaughter Libbie, Walter Bacon of Northfield, Minn., who had been her friend and counselor for years, C. W. Dixson of Canandaigua, N.Y., and her niece Mrs. Coggeshall.

Rhoda Wells Bacon, the daughter of Cyrus and Rhoda Wells of Richmond, N.Y., was born June 29, 1809. Her seven brothers and one sister had preceded her in death. In October, 1828, she had married Samuel Pitts of Richmond. Pitts, while proprietor of a hotel in Canandaigua, N.Y., responded to the administrations of an evangelist by the name of Finney, and emptied all of his liquor into the street. Thereafter he managed his hotel along temperance principles. It was just a matter of time until his business failed.

His deep religious feelings caused him to study for the ministry. In failing health, he moved to New York City to become a missionary in the Tabernacle Church. The increasing severity of ill health compelled him to move to Tecumseh in 1852. He died from Tuberculosis in 1855. His widow married Libbie's father in 1859.[17]

Considerable difficulty was encountered in the attempt to locate her grave. The Bacon lot in Monroe's Woodland Cemetery displays the markers for both Judge Bacon and his first wife Sophia, but none for Rhoda. A search of Brookside Cemetery in Tecumseh revealed the Pitts lot and on it the marker for Samuel Pitts. Next to it was a marker on which had been chiseled: "Rhoda P. wife of Daniel S. Bacon, Formerly wife of Samuel Pitts, Born June 29, 1809, Died Aug. 4, 1886." Just across the driveway from the Pitt lot was that of Stillman Blanchard, the judge who had introduced Judge Bacon to the widow Pitts. There Judge Blanchard had been buried with his two wives.

When Libbie returned from the funeral she found a letter awaiting her from an old acquaintance, Buffalo Bill Cody. Cody, writing from Staten Island, told her of his success on Staten Island that summer and his intention of duplicating the Wild West success at Madison Square Gardens that winter. He advised her:

"It is my design to illustrate to the public this winter a series of episodes in military life on the frontier that will be a revelation to the unthinking people who know nothing of the valor and heroism of the men who have made civilization possible on this continent. To that end I have decided to make a supreme effort in reproducing in historic accuracy and with great fidelity to detail that memorable field where the nation lost an honored son when the black shadows of widowhood was cast across your life and hopes.

"I shall spare no expense to do credit to our exhibition and deepen the lustre of your glorious husband's reputation as a soldier and a man. May I hope that you will give your sanction to the plan and by your presence endorse my effort to perpetuate his memory. If it should become known that you were to be present on the first occasion of the illustration of the battle of the Little Big Horn it would attract the attention of all the good women in America who would share your pride and my triumph."[18]

Then he asked her if she would keep this information as a confidence until they could talk it over at her appointed time.

On Wednesday, November 27th, Buffalo Bill's Wild West Show opened at Madison Square Garden. The boxes were filled with such notables as General W. T. Sherman, General Phil Sheridan, Henry Ward Beecher, August Belmont, Pierre Lorillard and a radiant and expectant Libbie Custer.[19]

Buffalo Bill and his partner Nate Salsbury had a good thing going. The Wild West Show had brought the thrill of western adventure to the East. It was the sort of show everyone talked about and everyone wanted to see for it was entertainment for young and old. In an era where horses played a role in everyday life, the horse took a part in every act.

The program proved to be so successful there was little variation in it from year to year. Opening with a Grand Review with the entire cast on horseback, the acts followed in quick and thrilling succession. Cowboys racing and roping, Indian boys racing on horseback, cavalry drills, a prairie immigrant train attacked by Indians, the capture of the Deadwood Stage, Buffalo Bill and little Annie Oakley in a demonstration of trick shooting, then finally—the Battle of the Little Big Horn.[20]

Libbie sat through it all and enjoyed it. It brought back memories, some painful, but the kaleidoscopic scenes changed so rapidly she had little time to dwell on any. An unexpected dividend she received was the stimulus to work on the next book she had planned. She soon became a familiar figure backstage as she moved about in her short, tailored jacket and her feathered hat, for she attended many performances after that opening night.

Annie Oakley and Libbie were drawn to each other from the very first meeting. Their mutual interest in the West resulted in frequent visits together either at Annie Oakley's brownstone house or in Libbie's Greenwich Village flat.[21]

That same fall Eliza came to New York. She hadn't been there since she had accompanied the newlywedded Custers to the Fifth Avenue Hotel in 1864. New York had changed and so had Eliza. The Brooklyn bridge, the elevated, the Statue of Liberty, the harbor's activity, the many new buildings and the crowded streets opened Eliza's eyes to a stare. It was a broadening experience for Eliza though she had broadened somewhat since Libbie had last seen her. She was not the slender woman who had once cooked over the Custer campfire.

Libbie experienced a great delight in going about New York with her. Her droll, humorous comments and unique criticisms gave Libbie a spiritual lift. Her many recollections of the past provided Libbie with a host of ideas for the book she was working on.

It was Libbie's wish that Eliza could see Buffalo Bill's Wild West show "because we had lived through so many of the scenes depicted, and I felt sure that nothing would recall so vividly the life on the frontier as the most realistic and faithful representation of a western life that has ceased to be, with advancing civilization."[22]

After the performance Eliza went to Cody's tent to present the card of introduction Libbie had provided her with. The two had not met before, Eliza having left the General before Cody had become one of the General's scouts.

Eliza's delight with the show knew no bounds. The sight of the live buffalo and the horsemanship excited her to a point she could hardly refrain from shouting. Her meeting with Cody just had to be told, so she began, "Well, Miss Libbie, when Mr. Cody come up, I see at once his back and hips was built precisely like the Ginnel, and when I come on to his tent, I jest said to him: 'Mr. Buffalo Bill, when you cum up to the stand and wheeled around, I said to myself, "*Well,* if he ain't the 'spress image of Ginnel Custer in battle, I never seed any one that was."'"[23]

The writing continued, paragraph by paragraph, page by page, then finally, a chapter. It was pleasant enough writing when covering life in Texas after the war since it had not been a period of anxieties and separations. Writing of her experiences in Kansas was different. There was an element of agony in every page that left her exhausted. She was anxious to complete the volume, hoping her health would hold out until she did. Her new publisher, C. L. Webster & Co., had promised to publish simultaneously in England. Bill Cody and his Wild West Show was touring there and arousing great interest in the American West. The prospects in the British market looked good.

One book reviewer had anticipated the release of Libbie's new book in his column, having obtained a false lead from one of Libbie's friends. In a letter of explanation to a Webster editor she indicated that her book was not half done and needed a summer's work to complete it.[24] Webster & Co., which had published Grant's *Memoirs, McClellan's Own Story,* and many of Mark Twain's books, had a clause in Libbie's contract prohibiting her from publishing anything for two years after September.

She had, at the suggestion of her friend, Mrs. Kingsley, dropped a portion of her hospital work to lessen her pressures and give her nerves a chance to recuperate. If her timetable kept her on schedule, a trip to England after the first of the year would provide a rest of at least six months.[25]

Letters continued to arrive and all had to be answered. There were numerous requests for pictures and autographs of the General. When the request for a photograph was made by an organization, institution or well-known personage, the wish was granted. Autographs were never given for, as Libbie replied to one such collector: "If I had attempted to send his writing to the constant applicants for over ten years, I would not possess a single item."[26]

By dint of hard labor that summer she completed her manuscript, and on December 13, 1887, Webster & Co. had *"Tenting On The Plains"* ready for Christmas sale. The large type and its 702 pages made an impressive volume that readily sold. The London edition published by Sampson Low, Marston, Searle & Rivington came out soon after the first of the year. It was reprinted by Webster in 1889, then in a reduced edition of 403 pages by them in 1893. On March 11, 1895, Webster assigned the copyright to Harper & Brothers for the benefit of its creditors. On May 3, 1895, and again in 1915, Harper & Brothers issued editions.[27]

On February 15, 1888, George G. Briggs of Grand Rapids, Michigan, wrote to Libbie advising her that he and his two fellow members of the Michigan At Gettysburg Monuments Commission had allocated $5,400 for a monument to the Michigan Cavalry Brigade. Colonel Briggs stated that they planned to place on the monument a bronze medallion of General Custer together with the Custer badge. They had approved of it and requested her approval. The 80-ton monument was dedicated on June 12th, 1889, displaying the medallion of the General.[28] It was erected on the Cavalry Battlefield near the Rummel farmhouse.

The spring of 1888 saw the first English review of *"Tenting On The Plains." The Spectator* noted that "despite its length and bulk, it is interesting from beginning to end, and is closed with a wish there were more. The reason is not far to seek. It is all expressed in one word—Mrs Custer. . . . we must repeat that the charm of the volume is Mrs. Custer herself, who is ever both sweetness and light."[29]

The laudatory reviews would seem reward enough for the great effort and energy expended on the volume but unsolicited letters of commendation from those who had experienced what Libbie was expressing gave her intense satisfaction. One such letter from Captain Charles King, an author of many volumes dealing with military life, she valued highly. King told her that on the receipt of *Tenting On The Plains* "I knocked off all work until I had read it through and was cross as a bear if anyone came into my den. Even more than *Boots And Saddles* will it tell people what a life our Army women led in those frontier days you knew so well. Mrs. Merritt wrote me from Leavenworth that she too had read and read because she could not lay it down."[30] One wonders what General Merritt thought as he read his wife's copy. Later, in 1892, King dedicated a book—*A Soldier's Secret*—to Libbie.[31]

That September, the *Atlantic Monthly* reviewer of *Tenting On The Plains* said: "What gives peculiar interest to these reminiscences . . . is the personality of the popular hero who is the center of all that goes on . . . here he is seen . . . frank, brave and humane, quick-witted and self-controlled, he was the beau-ideal of a soldier. . . . he was born and trained to his career."[32]

While Custer was receiving plaudits from Libbie's reviewers, Phil Sheridan had a few critics. Thomas Rosser, who had fought against both Custer and Sheridan time and again, was one who was not hesitant to praise or defend Custer. He was equally quick to give his views of Sheridan. In answer to some questions about the latter he remarked:

> "You politely ask me to name the "Predominant military characteristic' of the late Gen. P. H. Sheridan. Gen. Sheridan is now dead—Peace to his ashes—but as I disliked him very much, I fear that I failed to see any high military virtues in him. To me he always appeared vulgar and coarse.
>
> "I often met him while I was connected with the Northern Pacific Railroad, and I saw that he was very intemperate and barbarously profane and was neither great nor good."[33]

Maggie Custer Calhoun, like all of those brave women made widows by the battle on the Little Big Horn, had been struggling along on the monthly pittance from the government pension fund. In a determined bid for the better things in life, she decided to study dramatic elocution in Detroit. She had displayed an interest in dramatics while attending the Boyd Seminary for Young Ladies. Her brother Autie had arranged for her piano and voice lessons for it was his wish that his only sister have some of the educational advantages he had received.

While stationed at Fort Lincoln with her husband Lieutenant James Calhoun, she had taken an active part in the winter theatricals. In each of them she had manifested a flair for the dramatic. It was her greatest pleasure in presenting interpretive readings.

At the completion of her dramatic courses in Detroit she began a career as a professional elocutionist. In the fall season of 1887 she started on the road to make a series of appearances. In Columbus, Ohio, she appeared at Lyndon Hall. There the *Ohio State Journal* said that she "may justly be called the brightest star of the evening." *The Daily Press,* not to be outdone, made any reader feel he had missed something by not having attended the performance. It said: "One of the most delightful features was the elocutionary contributions of Mrs. Margaret Custer Calhoun. . . . Her graceful bearing and commanding presence, her entire self-possession, her masterly interpretation of her subjects, and her impersonation of the characters she assumed, combined to claim her master, or rather mistress, of the situation."

The Detroit *Free Press* indicated that it was her first public appearance in that city. It was a "standing room only" audience, and the program ranged from "grave to gay, from lively to severe," with a diversity of authors which included Whittier, Dickens, Browning and George Elliot.

According to the Flint *Journal* she filled the Music Hall. Perhaps the presence of Libbie played a part, though that is unlikely for wherever Maggie went the crowd was sure to go. In Pittsburgh the *Dispatch* reported she drew a large audience. It described her as "strikingly like her brother, General Custer, in action, gesture and expression. She has an interesting face, lovely figure and graceful movement. . . . She may be said to be a little above medium height, with light brown hair, clear, dark blue eyes, a fresh complexion, vivacity of manner and plenty of fire and force of character. . . . Humor and pathos she admirably interprets, while in childhood dialect, her style is inimitable."

Following a successful tour in New England, Maggie's thoughts turned to the West. Perhaps she was impelled by a desire to be near the grave of her husband. She began her tour in Kansas, stopping at Emporia, Lawrence, Atchison and Topeka, then moved on to Portland and Seattle. In each city her elocutionary ability was lauded in the press reports.[34]

Lured by the thought of an occupation that required little or no traveling, Maggie accepted an appointment as State Librarian in Michigan from 1891 to 1893, while Governor Edwin B. Winans, a Democrat, was in office. On February 28, 1893, she wrote to Governor Rich—Governor Winans' successor—declining reappointment so she could return to her "chosen profession—that of dramatic reading."[35]

Libbie had loved the plains but she loved the mountains even more. Candace Wheeler had lured her to Onteora in the Catskills. One visit there convinced Libbie that, when if ever her circumstances permitted, that would be her site for a summer home. In the summer of 1888 Candace sought her presence there for the week of July 4th. The newly formed Catskill Mountains Camp and Cottage Co., organized by Candace Wheeler and her brother Francis B. Thurber, had four cottages and an inn to start with. The inn was being reserved for guests, most of whom had literary or artistic backgrounds. As Candace wrote Libbie: "We want you to be one of them."[36]

The serious and enervating work on her third book had to be undertaken where there was quiet and ample fresh air. Stroudsburg, Pennsylvania, just a few miles from the Delaware Water Gap, and with a view of the Kittatinny Mountains, was about 75 miles west of New York. It was an ideal place in which to write, so it was there she resided during the summer of 1889.

She had camped for two previous summers on the Paret farm along the Pocono River "and it ended up in my buying a little strip of land each side of the stream," she wrote Mrs. Kingsley, "and having a rough little cabin covered with bark, with four rooms. My adopted Aunt and I sleep in the tent and I work there and the maid sleeps in the cabin. It is off from a private road that leads to the Paret's house and factory, so we rarely see a strange face. There are no noises, odors, or nuisances to disturb. . . ."[37]

The new book was to be called *"Following The Guidon."* No publisher had been contracted with but it was hoped that Harpers would again be the one. Her experience with Webster had been disastrous. On advice she had attempted to buy *Tenting On The Plains* back from it so she could place it with another firm. This experience with a subscription house had quite cured her of dealing with anything other than a trade publisher.

Samuel Clemens, the head of the Webster firm, explained to her the problems that had defeated the chance for success. He wanted another opportunity but Libbie wouldn't agree to it. Her eyes were on the old publishing firms with their steady returns.

As a bit of relaxation from the writing of her book she had undertaken writing of some fiction for a magazine, the first such attempt on her part. Seven publishers had asked her to try her hand at fiction. She had no prior thoughts of writing along such lines. With so much encouragement she thought she ought to give it a try. She completed "To The Victor, The Spoils," and sent it to the *Home Maker,* maintaining a feeling of uncertainty as to its success. Ultimately it was published.

She observed that the public was very interested in frontier life now that it had disappeared. The impact of Buffalo Bill on the boys of that time with his colorful, exciting portrayal of frontier and cowboy life was having its effects upon them. She noted that the newspapers constantly reported runaway boys responding to the glamor of the West. She believed she should do her part in preventing these runaways by writing a boys' story that would "show up cowboy and frontier life in its true colors" so they would realize the terrible trials in such a life.[38]

When first she had gone to Stroudsburg she had written to Lieutenant Charles Braden, who was teaching at the Military Academy, asking him if he would write down any of the rhymes or jingles the soldiers sang with the various bugle calls. She could recall only two: "Go to the stable all you are able," and "Poor old soldier," for the Rogues' March.[39]

The stay out of doors all of that summer had done her a great deal of good. Her strength restored and her nerves back to normal, she dreaded the return to New York November 1st. The book had not been completed but there was a long dreary winter for that. Three invitations to go to Europe that summer had been turned down for this labor of love but it had been worth it. Perhaps she could go next summer, for she did want to go badly.

The following May she was back at Stroudsburg instead, completing the final touches to her manuscript. At the end of the month she sent Harpers the words and music of the Seventh's regimental tune "Garry Owen," asking that it be placed first in the book since "it was the tune to which the regiment went out to battle." Irish born Colonel John J. Coppinger had searched long and hard for the words she was sending which she preferred to those in Lever's *Charles O'Malley*. Near the end of the book she wished to have the other regimental tune the Seventh Cavalry played when it returned to camp from a campaign—"The Girl I Left Behind Me."[40]

By fall Libbie was back at 41 East 10th Street. She had left a cold cabin for a warm flat. *Following The Guidon,* the third book in her trilogy of cavalry life, was in print and well on its way to a large sale. But turning in the manuscript did not mean an end to her writing. She had been receiving more than 100 letters a month, all of which she had been trying to reply to, each response being written by hand. With the release of this new volume the letters increased to a point she could not keep up with them.[41]

Libbie had another pressure applied to her. The Redpath Lyceum Bureau had asked her to lecture in its Melrose lecture course. The thought appealed to her so she accepted an engagement to read a paper at Concord. After learning that a larger number of people were expected than she had bargained for—it had been understood the audience would be not over 400—she feared to undertake it because her voice was not trained to reach so many people.[42] Convinced by the Redpath people she could handle the challenge, she went to Concord.

NOTES — CHAPTER 31

[1]Eliz. B. Custer to Mrs. Kingsley (ca. 1886), Yale University Library.
[2]*Ibid.*
[3]*Boots And Saddles Scrapbook,* once belonging to Libbie Custer and now in the library of the Monroe County Historical Museum. It contains 125 reviews.
[4]Detroit *Tribune,* November 21, 1885.
[5]*Ibid.*
[6]Chicago *Inter Ocean,* November 14, 1885.
[7]Chicago *Tribune,* November 18, 1885.
[8]*Ibid.*
[9]September 19, 1885, Libbie's Scrapbook, Monroe County Historical Museum Library.
[10]*Ibid,* November 24, 1885.
[11]*Ibid,* December 3, 11, 17, 19, 25, 1885.
[12]Eliz. B. Custer to Mrs. Kingsley, February 13, 1886, Yale University Library.
[13]*Ibid.*
[14]*Ibid.*
[15]*Ibid.*
[16]Mrs. Eliza Denison to Libbie, June 6, 1886, EBC-CBNM.
[17]Tecumseh *News,* August 19, 1886. At Rhoda's death the $5,000 Judge Bacon placed in trust, so its interest supported Rhoda, reverted to Libbie.
[18]W. F. Cody to Libbie, August 13, 1886, BCWC collection.
[19]Walter Harighurst: *Annie Oakley Of The West,* London, 1955, p. 93.
[20]Russell: *Buffalo Bill,* pp. 376-77.
[21]Harighurst, p. 98. General Custer's nephew, James C. Custer of Monroe, once told me that when Buffalo Bill's West Show came to Monroe, Buffalo Bill and Annie Oakley would drive a horse and buggy the three miles from the show grounds out to the Custer Farm just to see Custer's horse *Dandy.* When Bill approached *Dandy* the horse would whinny and nuzzle up to him in recognition. Bill then asked the General's father, Emanuel, if he would ride the horse at the head of his parade. The old gentleman, fine horseman that he was, rode the horse at the head of the parade, great pride evident in his every move.
[22]Eliz. B. Custer: *Tenting,* p. 46.
[23]*Ibid,* p. 47.
[24]Libbie to Mr. Bowker, January 28, 1887, New York Public Library, Manuscript Division.
[25]Libbie to Mrs. Kingsley, January 6, 1887, Yale University Library.
[26]Libbie to Mrs. Strickland, January 14, 1887, author's collection.
[27]National Union Catalogue, Library of Congress; Jane R. Stewart, p. X, 1971. University of Oklahoma reprint of *Tenting On The Plains.*
[28]George A. Briggs to Libbie, February 15, 1888, EBC-CBNM; *Michigan At Gettysburg,* Detroit, 1889, p. 5.
[29]The *Spectator,* June 30, 1888.
[30]Charles King to Libbie, July 1, 1888, BCWC collection.
[31]*Ibid,* January 18, 1892, BCWC collection; C. E. Dornbusch: *Charles King,* Cornwallville, 1963, No. 4, p. 12.
[32]The *Atlantic Monthly,* September 1888, p. 426.
[33]Thomas Rosser to Mr. E. F. Gladwin, September 3, 1888, Chicago Historical Society.
[34]All newspaper references were taken from a series of undated clippings that only indicated the years 1887 and 1888.
[35]Information supplied by John C. Larsen, Department of Library Science, University of Michigan. Mrs. Margaret Custer Calhoun resided at 314 Ottawa W., Lansing, in 1892, Lansing City Directory. (See *Portrait And Biographical Album Of Ingham And Livingston Counties,* Chicago, 1891.)
[36]Candace Wheeler to Libbie, May 25, 1888, BCWC collection.
[37]Libbie to Mrs. Kingsley, September 7, 1889, Yale University Library. Her adopted Aunt remains unknown.
[38]*Ibid.*
[39]Libbie to Charles Braden, May 19, 1889, Lisle Reedstrom collection. Braden, a Michigan man, had served in the Seventh under Custer, later becoming Professor of Military Science at the Military Academy.
[40]Libbie to Harper and Brothers, May 31, 1890, Lisle Reedstrom collection.
[41]Libbie to Mr. Brown, February 19, 1898, Lisle Reedstrom collection.
[42]Libbie to Redpath Lyceum Bureau, August 10, 1890, Lisle Reedstrom collection.

Chapter 32
FAITHFUL WIDOW

The press had done its bit to record the campaign leading to the Little Big Horn. Libbie had glamorized the cavalry even more in her three volumes just published. To this she was beginning to create more interest by lecturing on various aspects of life with the cavalry in the field and in the garrison.

Several artists, either sensing opportunity or feeling the need to express themselves, rendered their interpretations of Custer's last fight shortly after the battle.

In 1888 a staff of artists headed by E. Pierpont painted a *Cyclorama of Custer's Last Fight* for the Boston Cyclorama Company.[1] Probably 27 feet high and perhaps 400 feet in circumference—since this was somewhat a standardized size for other traveling cycloramas—the painting consisted of ten large panels depicting the action of that battle.[2]

The painting was first displayed in Boston and was then shown in Detroit and Chicago. That is about all that is known of it other than it was last seen in Hollywood.

Libbie had been asked to loan the Cyclorama Company several articles of Custer's to be displayed in its traveling museum. The most important of these was his service saber, one he had taken from a Confederate officer, and now on display at the Custer Battlefield Museum.[3]

The booklet distributed at the display of the Cyclorama contained several interesting letters. One written by Libbie on January 25, 1889, advised the Cyclorama Company she could not summon the courage to visit the painting so could give no opinion as to its correctness of detail. She considered it impossible for her to write an account of the battle. In recalling the criticism of the battle, she said that one distinguished Indian fighter had commented he would rather fight the whole Sioux nation than the critics and enemies in his rear.[4]

Soon after, Anheuser-Busch, Inc. purchased Cassilly Adam's oil painting, "Custer's Last Fight," and had it made into a lithograph by Otto Becker of Milwaukee.[5] Copies of it were distributed to saloons all over the nation. The 150,000 lithographs were the foundation of millions of discussions and arguments and became the basis for the statement that the painting was seen by more people than any other piece of art in the world. It helped keep the Custer story alive and it certainly assisted in selling Libbie's books for they continued going into other editions.

FOLLOWING THE GUIDON had been dedicated "To ONE WHO HAD FOLLOWED THE GUIDON

Into That Realm Where 'The war-drum throbs no longer and the battleflags are furled.' " For fourteen years Libbie had avoided the West. Chicago had been her limit. A desire coupled with fear had halted her. She had followed an unfurled guidon in time of war; why not one in time of peace?

By the middle of July she was in Helena, Montana, visiting Major and Mrs. Martin Maginnis at 221 Adams Street. The Helena *Herald* noted her arrival.

It had been years since Libbie made daily entries in a diary. Her father had advised her several times to follow the practice of making daily entries and it was not until she began writing her reminiscences that she really valued his advice. Her negligence in that respect during Autie's lifetime had some relief because of her habit of saving all of his letters. They provided information otherwise forgotten.

On her trip West she began a new diary; the first entry—July 16, 1890—was at Fort Sherman, Idaho. Located in northern Idaho on the north shore of Lake Coeur d'Alene, the small post had been established to maintain peace in northern Idaho, guard the Canadian border and supply protection for railroad and telegraph crews[6]

She became acquainted with a Miss Rogers who had met a woman on the boat to Coeur d'Alene. The woman had been a victim of the Nez Perce war some 12 years earlier. She had fled from the Indians at night "pressing her baby to her bosom to still its cries for fear the Indians would hear it," to quote Libbie's diary.

In climbing a steep hill the woman used her free hand to grasp branches to support her. Descending through soft shale and loose stones, she tore her dress and cut her shoes. In the morning she reached a cabin occupied by a settler, his wife and his cousin.

Soon afterward a party of Nez Perces attacked the barricaded cabin, killing the two men. Upon breaking down the door the Indians found the two women under the bed. As Libbie reports in her diary:

"The Indians told them to come out. They said, 'You will kill us.' 'No," said they, 'We are Nez Perce and Chief Joseph said kill white men but no white squaw, children or gray-haired men.' The women then came out and when Miss Rogers asked her if anything else happened the woman turned her head away and the silence meant volumes to Miss Rogers."[7]

On the following evening, as Libbie watched a dress parade, a queer old tramp shambled along the outskirts of the crowd of observers. The contrast between the well-formed uniformed men and the shabby character in his ill-fitting clothes was obvious. Standing back where he thought he was unseen, the forlorn figure suddenly became as erect and military in movement as any of the men before him.

On inquiry it was learned that he had been a valiant officer during the Civil War but in time of peace had "encountered John Barleycorn who finally vanquished him." He was finally court-martialed for drunkenness and discharged. His trial had been in Washington but the frontier beckoned to him. He wandered from frontier post to post begging wherever he went. The officers occasionally gave him money which he quickly converted to liquor. Most of them avoided him because he was such a bore, always endeavoring to show them his papers containing endorsement obtained in his days of sobriety.

Almost as if seeing military protocol for the first time, Libbie wrote:

"All this saluting, addressing in the third person, never speaking unless spoken to, and so many little observances that go to enhance the dignity that hedges around a King seems *now* tremendously like some play being acted. It is not in the least real to me now. The salaams and obsequiousness, the gulf that yawns between an officer and a soldier is something that now only strikes my humorous side. It does me such good to know that nothing is required of me as wife of the commanding officer. It used to be oppressive sometimes."[8]

During Libbie's association with Western garrisons it was common practice to punish enlisted men by tying them up by their thumbs with their toes barely touching the ground for an hour or more, or making them walk a certain beat carrying a full pack or a heavy log for a given number of hours, often during the heat of a summer day. She observed that the policy of the army had changed, the Government trying to prevent men from deserting by indulgence.

"Taps is now at eleven. No punishment except confinement to guardhouse is permitted except as the sentence of court-martial. Logs are carried no longer and men tied up by the thumbs or told to walk a certain beat for certain number of hours. The canteen has replaced the sutler's bar. It is conducted by an officer, and a soldier as bartender. The profits go into company funds and are used to buy luxuries for the mess tables. The canteen has a lunch counter where the pies and cakes are prepared by certain camp women. The order forbidding wine has lately come but there are cigars, nuts, fruits, beer, etc., for sale."[9]

The diary was filled with anecdotes about military and frontier life heard during her stay at the post, the last entry being made on August 23d, 1890. There was little of what happened each day in the garrison. The exciting days of the Indian war were a thing of the past.

When she arrived back in New York there were a number of letters awaiting her, the kind of letters she would preserve. One that warmed her heart was the letter Henry Capehart had written to her friend Charles King who, knowing she would treasure it, had forwarded it to her. Capehart had been an intimate of Custer, having served with him in the third Brigade from Winchester to Appomattox. He had written to King:

"I could never join in the popular belief of his (Custer's) utter rashness and want of judgment at the time. . . . He was the most lovable man it has ever been my fortune to meet. . . . I have seen him under the most varying and critical circumstances, and never without ample resources of mind and body to meet the most trying contingency. He was counted by some rash; it was because he dared, while they dared not. There can be no doubt that he had a positive genius for war, while Merritt, Devin, Wilson, Crook, etc., were comparatively but mediocrities. If I were to begin giving instances of his daring, brilliancy and skill, I should never stop. Sheridan was under obligations to him that he could never have repaid had he tried, and that he should in his memoirs condescendingly praise him on a plane with the others was not a little irritating to me; and that he appropriated success of Custer's with which he himself had nothing whatever to do."[10]

One letter on the stationary of the Civil Service Commission in Washington was from Theodore Roosevelt in reference to her letter commenting about something Teddy had written about the General. He informed her he was "enroute for the West and I have only time to write a line of acknowledgment. I am delighted you liked it; it was written from the heart. I need not tell you that General Custer has always been a favorite of mine."[11]

Another letter from Washington, this one from Mrs. John A. Logan, asked her to write for the magazine she conducted a serial story in. It would pay well and Libbie would be able to retain the copyright on her material for any book planned. Then too, she reminded Libbie that as a writer for a magazine with more than 100,000 subscribers she would be keeping her name before the public.[12]

Mrs. Logan may have been aware of Libbie's propensity for publicity. She must have known of Libbie's desire to perpetuate and memorialize Autie's military accomplishments. Money had its attractions, for memorials cost money, but publicity had its place. Book sales had added considerably to Libbie's income and the papers she had been reading were quite remunerative. Her newspaper column had been worth the effort, but her pension had remained at $600 a year.

The widows of a number of the general officers had increases in their pensions. Mrs. Crook, Mrs. Kilpatrick, Mrs. Logan, Mrs. Blair, Mrs. Fremont and several others were receiving $1,200 a year. Libbie's Western friends had urged her repeatedly to ask the Government for the same amount but she had refused to do so. These friends appealed to Judge Chipman, Congressman from Michigan, and he introduced successfully a bill to increase her annual pension to $1,200.[13]

An Ohioan, Captain Edward S. Godfrey, had been making waves. The paper he had written and had been reading about the battle of the Little Big Horn had created considerable comment. Godfrey had been a participant in the battle, having served under Reno. His fearless and uninfluenced testimony at the Reno Court of Inquiry gave him an uncommon distinction in the proceedings. In a like manner his paper on the battle "called them as he saw them." He was one person who could say he had participated.

He had been asked by Libbie to submit his paper to the *Century Magazine,* to which he assented. Libbie then wrote to her friend Mr. Buel at *Century* that Captain Godfrey "would be glad to submit his paper to the *Century* for examination." She added that she would like to see a short supplemental article by General James B. Fry follow that of Godfrey.[14]

Because of illnese Godfrey delayed sending in his paper. In February, 1891, Mr. Buel advised her and Maggie, who was visiting Libbie at the time, that Godfrey was ready to submit his article.[15] This was a happy moment for Libbie. She was satisfied that *Century* would publish the Godfrey article for she had read it and found it not at all distasteful. If *Century* would publish Godfrey's objective observations, Fry would provide the spice to the main course that would precede him.

But happiness is often tempered with pain, and so it was with Libbie. On March 20th the bad news arrived. Lawrence Barrett was dead! Lawrence Barrett, dear, true friend of Autie's. The details soon arrived. He had been suffering from a severe cold for several days, yet on Wednesday night (the 18th) had taken his stage role in *Richelieu.* In the third act he was seized with a chill and had to give up his part. It was discovered that he had pneumonia. His temperature of 103 soon passed 105 and the consultants gave up hope. It was Libbie's good fortune to be in New York at the time of his passing, enabling her to be at the side of Mrs. Barrett in her time of need.

Several weeks later, not long before she sailed to England for a much needed rest, she wrote Mr. Buel giving her reason for not reading Captain Godfrey's revised article:

> "The reason I did not read it was because I feared to trust my own much biased judgment. I feel that Gen. Fry could read so much more dispassionately and I am sure that Capt. Godfrey has taken the right course. His paper is history and not eulogy. It is all I ask. Eulogies came thick and fast from my husband admirers but a man who calmly writes of what he knows because he was an actor in the drama will have far more weight with the public than a wife could possibly have."[16]

After her return from England that fall she and Buel discussed the illustrations that were planned for the Godfrey article. Buel wanted to use a Brady photograph of Custer standing with his arms folded across his chest. Libbie previously had not cared for it but considered it a characteristic pose she now looked on favorably.

Another photo of Autie in buckskin and low boots bothered her because high troop boots had been more commonly used by him. He "was rarely seen without them while campaigning or hunting for fifteen years." Having been suddenly called by General Sheridan to join the Grand Duke Alexis, he did not have all of his luggage available during the buffalo hunt.[17] Libbie considered low boots to be uncommon attire for Autie in 1872.

On October 24th Libbie left on a tour to read her paper on the plains before various women's clubs and girls' schools. She had sent Fry important authenticated facts about the battle with the hope they would be of some use to him. She had been waiting a long time for articles such as Godfrey and Fry had to offer. There had been published entirely too much material unsupported by facts offered by individuals who were at best Monday morning quarterbacks. "This is an hour that I have been waiting for, for fifteen years my dear Mr. Buel," she wrote, "and you know that my earnestness is great in my anxiety to have every fact brought to light."[18]

Libbie was a realist. There was no doubt in her mind that Autie displayed unusual characteristics as a cavalry leader during the Civil War and, in doing so, had incurred the animosity of many superior officers over whom he had jumped in rank. They, unable to win battles, resented anyone younger who did. Many in staff positions, with no occasion to display any ability they might possess to lead men in the field, used every chance to downgrade Custer. Custer had little time to write reports of his accomplishments in the field. Necessity forced him to forego writing grandiose reports, instead utilizing his time to pound the retreating forces of a defeated adversary. The cavalry defeat of Stuart on the third day at Gettysburg by Custer leading the Michigan Cavalry Brigade is a case in point.

Libbie used every device in her power to equalize the harm done by these armchair officers who, behind the lines and safe from all harm, used every dirty trick in the book to hurt her husband. As she told Buel: "Oh if you knew how I think and think and plan at night in the still hours to have the world see my husband as he should be known."[19]

Libbie's "Garrison Life On The Plains" reading had been much in demand that winter. She had read it 64 times by the middle of September which exhausted her to the point she took a month of rest at Onteora at Tannersville. She explained to her friend Mrs. Andrew Carnegie that she went to "women's clubs, girls' schools, missionary societies and philanthropies that need money and tho' of course, I am much interested in my own earnings I am also very glad to be the means of filling up the empty coffers of the societies."[20] Indeed, lecturing had been found to be much more profitable than writing.

On November 7th the New York *Times* reported a talk she had given before a large audience in the Grace Reformed Church on Seventh Avenue. The talk was principally on the life of the cavalryman. She cited instances of the trooper's love for his horse, declaring that in moving regiments of cavalry to another post, the horses are often alloted to the new regiment. It was not unusual for a man to transfer to the new garrison, severing his connection with his old comrades, just "for the sake of retaining his old mount."

"At our last post," she told her audience, "none of the ladies went outside the post without an escort for three years. It was hard to believe that the bluffs that looked so inviting were filled with Indians. . . . When we all went out for a picnic one day, an entire troop of cavalry, completely armed, accompanied us. We were so accustomed to it that we thought nothing of it."

Money was of no great concern since there was little of it. They always had enough to eat and something to wear and "were contented and happy." She thought, "that army marriages, to be happy, should be for love, for there was nothing else in it to marry for."[21]

Most women who are continually exposed to the business commentary and activities of their husbands acquire an insight and knowledge of that specialty that is surprising to the uninformed. Though Libbie was never invited to discuss military affairs, wisely leaving that for the male guests who constantly frequented their quarters, she listened intently and drew her own conclusions.

She had been discussing with Mr. Buel Captain Godfrey's assertion that the disaster at the Little Big Horn had been due to the dividing of the regiment. She had learned of his viewpoint with somewhat of a start for she had concluded that the mistake in dividing the main force rested on the shoulders of those who planned the overall strategy in Washington for they were the ones who sent out the three large columns independent of each other with no means of communication. She felt that Godfrey was not logical in saying the disaster was due to dividing the regiment under her husband's command and hoped Mr. Buel could convince him of his error.

What bothered her aching heart most was the thought that "the other portion of the command did not at least attempt to save the lives of some of their beleaguered comrades."[22]

Then, right after the first of the New Year, a bomb burst. The *New York Times* under a heading "Did Custer Disobey Orders?" in a dispatch from New Haven, printed disturbing comments from the memorial service given by the Reverend Theodore T. Munger at the funeral of Major General Alfred H. Terry.

Referring to the Battle of the Little Big Horn in 1876, he said:

> "Custer's fatal movement was in direct violation of both verbal and written orders. When his rashness and disobedience ended in the total destruction of his command, Gen. Terry withheld the fact of the disobeyed orders and suffered a disputation hurtful to his own military reputation rather than subject a brave but indiscreet subordinate to a charge of disobedience."[23]

In an interview of the Rev. Dr. Munger by a *Times* correspondent reference was made to an article in the January, 1892, issue of *Century Magazine* that had been written by General James B. Fry. Fry had given supportive comments to an article printed in the same issue written by Captain Edward S. Godfrey. Colonel R. P. Hughes, Terry's brother-in-law, took exception to the comments. It was from Hughes that Rev. Munger obtained his information, as he explained to the correspondent:

> "Prior to the funeral, Col. Hughes, in conversation about Gen. Terry and of his connection with the illfated Indian wars, said that Custer had disobeyed both written and verbal orders. He (Hughes) had listened to the verbal orders and knew what they were. Col. Hughes, however, did not state to me the nature of the orders. He simply stated that Custer had disobeyed orders. Col. Hughes stated that he had several times urged Gen. Terry to tell the whole story of the affair, as it was due him that the whole affair was cleared up. Terry replied that he did not care to disclose the

facts as he, living, could stand it better than Gen. Custer, who was dead. Col. Hughes suggested that in my remarks I should refer to the statement as it was. That is the reason I did so. That is all there is to it, so far as I am concerned."[24]

Fry, in his article, asserted that Colonel Hughes denied giving Rev. Munger authority to make the statement though admitting he was the source of Munger's information.

The Fry letter in *Century* made Hughes squirm. Sometime later he offered *Century* a response to Fry's article but was told it would be published only if it was of equal length. This was not acceptable to him. Obviously he did not believe in equal time. Eventually he had his article printed in a periodical that gave him all the space he wished.[25]

The gist of Hughes' published rebuttal centered on his contention that Custer had disobeyed Terry's orders on his march to the Little Big Horn. He bolstered his conclusion with a number of obvious falsehoods, which the noted Custer Scholar Dr. Charles Kuhlman disclosed in a study published in 1957.[26] Hughes, like so many others, in an effort to elevate his own cause, had to downgrade Custer. The attempt to smear Custer's record is a discredit to Hughes.

Once again Libbie had to come to the defense of her husband. She had dedicated her life to keeping his name lustrous, his honor unsullied. The Hughes article had been called to her attention innumerable times, so much so she felt obliged to answer it. Believing that a detailed reply would just prolong a discussion that would end up in various tangents rather than with a conclusion on the central question of disobedience, she resolved on a simple course of action. On June 21, 1897, she had printed for distribution to her friends a three-page pamphlet reproducing a portion of a letter an army officer had written to her.[27]

The officer, who was unnamed, made the observation that Hughes failed to produce the order "as evidence to sustain his charge." He went on to say: "Did General Custer disobey General Terry's orders? If he did, where is and what was the order he disobeyed? It has not been produced. Its existence has never been shown. General Terry never affirmed it. His papers have never shown any reference to it. The only known order in the case is General Terry's well-known written order of June 22, 1876."

The letter continued:

"He was sending against an enemy of unknown numbers and in an uncertain location in a column of troops which for a time must be entirely self-sufficient and liable to come in hostile contact before support could be had. General Terry himself was out of reach for instructions in an emergency."

Terry, in his order of June 22, directed Custer to take his regiment and pursue the Indians up the Rosebud River, then it went on to say:

"It is, of course, impossible to give you any definite instructions in regard to this movement, and were it is not impossible to do so, the department commander places too much confidence in your zeal, energy, and ability to impose upon you precise orders which might hamper your action when nearly in contact with the enemy. He will, however, indicate to you his own views of what your action should be, and he desires that you should conform to them unless you shall see sufficient reasons for departing from them."

". . . . These were Custer's orders up to the moment of his coming 'nearly in contact with the enemy.' Then did he disobey them? When he came nearly in such contact all things were at his discretion, and unless he failed to play the soldier and the man at that moment there is no longer a question of disobedience of orders."

Godfrey turned out to be one of the stalwarts. He was assailed by some for daring to tell the truth as he saw it. One who took him to task was General James S. Brisbin, a retired officer who had been a major in command of a battalion of the Second Cavalry that was with Gibbon's column at the Little Big Horn. On January 1, 1892, Brisbin wrote Godfrey a lengthy letter that was critical of Godfrey's article in *Century Magazine*.

Brisbin accused Godfrey of reproducing an order dissimilar to the copy in Terry's order books. Godfrey had no chance to reply for Brisbin died just a few days after Godfrey received his letter. Years later—about 1923—Custer battle authority Colonel William Graham unearthed Terry's order books and compared both the Brisbin and the Godfrey copies with the original. Terry's records proved that Godfrey had been correct and that Brisbin had deleted a sentence from his copy which in effect made Custer appear to have disobeyed Terry. Brisbin distinctly disliked Custer, Custer apparently having little confidence in Brisbin and his Second Cavalry at the time of the battle. At this distance it is apparent that Brisbin deliberately deleted that last line in an effort to tarnish the Custer image.

The Custer detractors received another setback. It occurred when General Nelson A. Miles published his memoirs in 1896. He had made an intensive study of the battlefield, being commander of the district encompassing the Little Big Horn, and had interviewed many of the red and white participants. In describing his findings he gave considerable space to praising Custer, laying the blame for his death on Reno and Benteen.[28] Miles also let it be known that he had the affidavit of a witness to a conversation between Terry and Custer in the latter's tent after the final orders had been issued to him at the mouth of the Rosebud. Terry, according to the witness, advised Custer to use his own judgment and do what he thought best if he struck the trail of the Indians.[29]

The witness in question was Mary Adams, well-known colored servant of the Custers who, Colonel Graham states, did not accompany the expedition from Fort Lincoln in 1876, so he was told by General Godfrey.[30]

Colonel Graham also quotes an article presumably written by W. A. Falconer of Bismarck and published in the Bismarck *Capital* June 15, 1925, in which Falconer claims the affidavit to be fraudulent. Falconer related the account of Lieutenant C. L. Gurley who claimed that at seven o'clock on the morning of July 7th (1876) he "went to the rear of the Custer house, woke up Maria, Mrs. Custer's housemaid, and requested her to rap on Mrs. Custer's door. . . ."[31] Received at face value, one would think Maria (Mary Adams) was at Fort Lincoln and not with General Custer as General Miles states.

Colonel Graham, excellent researcher and judge advocate that he was, undoubtedly would be the first to question a witness who drew an account of an event that had happened many years previous. In this case he accepted that sort of an account and from a secondary source rather than from the actual participant.

The late Colonel Brice C. W. Custer, grandnephew of General Custer, threw new light on the question when he displayed a letter in his collection written by Autie Reed to his mother and father in Monroe from Camp No. 24, June 21, 1876:

"Uncle Autie is now in full command. . . . Everybody is sure of success for the Indians are moving very slowly, not over 4 or 5 miles a day. At that rate we can soon catch them.

"We have all kinds of pets. . . . the latest is a tame Jack rabbit which Mary thinks all the world of. *Mary is staying on the boat.*" (italics are mine)[32]

Unquestionably the Mary Autie Reed refers to is Mary Adams. Quite naturally she was with General Custer to do his cooking and, as usual, she was left behind when it came time to strike the enemy. There should be no doubt in the reader's mind that Lieutenant Gurley was disturbed in mind when he approached the Custer residence to break that terrible news to the widows within. It is surprising that he could even be certain which end of the house he approached when thinking back almost 50 years to that nerve shattering experience.

Matters were taking on a better shape. The Godfrey and the Fry articles had increased the public interest in the West, all of which promoted the sale of Libbie's books. Her lectures on "Buffaloes And Buffalo Hunting" and "Garrison Life On The Plains" were becoming increasingly popular. Though mainly intended for women, they were given before mixed groups invited by clubs, schools and church societies.

An article in the New York *Sun* at this time revealed that "the great secret of Mrs. Custer's popularity is her gracious cordiality, sincerity of manner, rare tact, straighforwardness of address," and that she has "the happy faculty of taking things as they are in the world."

In interviewing women associated with Libbie during her garrison life, the correspondent learned that Libbie's constant thought as the wife of the commandant was to smooth over the rough places for those below her in rank. When the new orderly, unacquainted with General Custer's voice and rapidity of speech, stood dazed and perplexed, trying to understand his orders, it was she who slipped past her husband unobserved and translated the words for him.

When the young wife of an officer fearfully faced the prospect of maternity in a snowbound post away from all nurses, with only an inexperienced young army surgeon available, it was Mrs. Custer who welcomed and cared for the newborn and comforted the unhappy mother. Even dogs took refuge in her tent.

After the news of the Battle of the Little Big Horn it was Libbie who gave special attention to "my widows" as she called them, taking three of them (Mrs. Calhoun, Smith and Yates) back to Monroe with her. It was she who counseled them and aided them and other widows in getting their pensions and cash awards.

As secretary for the Society of Decorative Arts Libbie spent several years consoling and advising thousands of women who were bereaved and burdened with family responsibilities. As time passed she came to realize that the yellow journals and sensational dramas were portraying her husband falsely. As a means of counteracting this trend she resolved to write a book that would show him as he really was. She went on to tell the correspondent:

"It took me several years to make up my mind to write the book. My grammer was, well—peculiar; my sentences odd in construction. I didn't know anything about writing a book. I counted the words and pages in other books, and the pages in a chapter to see how to divide it. I didn't want to ask anybody because I knew the book would be declined, and I didn't want to subject myself to the ignominy of having people know it. In writing I had no thought or idea of the literary qualities of the style. My one purpose was to have the world know my husband's great beauty of character, his chivalry to women, his devotion to his parents, his kindness to the men under him, his love of books and of his home.

"So it was not for glory that I wrote. It was simply a woman's heart full of her husband and the desire to set before the world his valor and chivalry and tenderness that inspired me to write, and I think that is why the book has been kindly received by the people."

The correspondent observed that Libbie was actively engaged in hospital and nursery work but "is not actively engaged with any of the great reforms of the day, and belongs to none of the organizations of women devoted to either political, social or dress agitation. Her chief ambition in life is to honor her husband's memory through her books and lectures."

Early in the spring of 1892, Laurence Hutton, who conducted a popular column in *Harper's Weekly,* felt his readers would like to know what Libbie did during the summer months. Under the heading "The Summer Home of Gen. Custer's Faithful Widow" he began by comparing her books commemorating her gallant husband to the efforts of Queen Victoria who scattered memorials to her Albert all over England, though he thought the comparison advantageous to Libbie.

He advised his readers that Libbie spent her summer at her cabin near the Delaware Water Gap living with an elderly lady companion from May till October, "roughing it almost as much as when she lived on the plains." He observed:

"Her home is two miles from a lemon, but is near enough to a farmhouse where butter, eggs, milk and chickens are to be had in abundance. Twice a day mechanics going to their work at a factory in the nearest town stop at her door—in the morning to take her mail and in the evening to bring it. Her cabin is rudely furnished—that is, its equipments might seem rude to you or me, but Mrs. Custer, who likes luxury in her city apartment, despises it in her woodland cabin."[33]

Unknown to Hutton was the heavy lecture schedule Libbie faced that year. The short rest obtained at the cabin by the faithful widow barely prepared her for the rigors of travel ahead.

NOTES — CHAPTER 32

[1]Don Russell: *Custer's Last,* Fort Worth, 1968, p. 37. Russell's research revealed 1,000 sketches and paintings on the Custer subject.

[2]National Archives.

[3]Pamphlet, *Cyclorama of Custer's Last Fight,* Boston, 1889, author's collection.

[4]*Ibid,* p. 13.

[5]Russell: *Custer's Last,* pp. 33-34; Frost: *Custer Album,* p. 11.

[6]Herbert M. Hart: *Old Forts Of The Northwest,* Seattle, 1963, pp. 171-72.

[7]Elizabeth Bacon Custer Diary, 1890, Monroe County Historical Museum Library.

[8]*Ibid.*

[9]*Ibid.*

[10]Charles Capehart to Gen. Charles King, August 16, 1890, EBC-CBNM.

[11]Theodore Roosevelt to Libbie, August 22, 1890, BCWC collection.

[12]Mrs. John A. Logan to Libbie, August 26, 1890, BCWC collection.

[13]New York *Times,* December 6, 1890.

[14]Libbie to Mr. Buel, November 28, 1890, New York Public Library.

[15]Libbie to Mr. Buel, February 26, 1891, New York Public Library.

[16]Libbie to Mr. Buel, April 27, 1891, New York Public Library.

[17]Libbie to Mr. Buel, August 26, 1891, Century collection, New York Public Library.

[18]Libbie to Mr. Buel, October 21, 1891, Century collection, New York Public Library.

[19]Libbie to Mr. Buel, October 23, 1891, Century collection, New York Public Library.

[20]Libbie to Mrs. Andrew Carnegie, November 27, 1891, Carnegie collection, New York Public Library.

[21]A speech Libbie gave in Detroit in early 1926, when she was 84 years of age, follows. From the collection of her great grand nephew Colonel George Artmstrong Custer III, it is representative of the many popular lectures she gave in the late eighties and early nineties.

Introduction.

May I ask you not to consider this a formal lecture: the sketches that I have written of military life on the frontier or our country . . . in 1867—It was then an unmapped wilderness a great part of the way from the Missouri river to the Rocky mountains.

General Custer was mustered out of service as a Major General of Volunteers in 1866 and appointed as Lieut. Colonel of one of the five new regiments that were added to the five original cavalry regiments of the regular army.

The Seventh Cavalry patrolled the frontier from the Indian Territory south to the border of the British possessions North—We began our marches and campaigns in Texas, then went to Kansas.

The regiment was detailed to guard the engineers and builders of the Kansas Pacific Railroad to Denver. There was at that time only the Union Pacific, farther north, that President Lincoln had fought for so valiantly, seeing with his rare vision, the possibility of the separation of the States and the Territories of the Pacific coast,—into a new Republic of its own.

The trail of the 7th Cavalry could be found all over that disturbed desert. The Indians were of course opposed to any railroad that was to invade their country. An expedition into the Indian territory after a year or two of fruitless efforts to suppress their lawlessness, was finally made when the tribes were in winter camp and wholly unprepared for attack.

It is accorded that there was no greater achievement in frontier history than the battle of the "Washita", which was fought by our regiment.

The 7th, which is now, and has been for a long time on the Mexican border, narrates their achievements and praise their predecessors in a little magazine *lately* published—that fills my heart with gratitude. They sing, and the band plays, the *tune* that General Custer selected as a regimental air when the regiment was formed,—the inspiring old Scottish Air, "Garry Owen". It rang out even under the walls of the old Moro Castle in the Spanish War! They go on to say that for fifteen years the 7th fought Sioux and Cheyenne Indians, collectively, *days, nights,* and *in their sleep.* And again they do not forget their fallen comrades and write thus of the battle of the Little Big Horn in 1876:

"To the 212 men who were surrounded, overwhelmed and annihilated by the Sioux—at once the most heroic and tragic episode of the United States Army."

Second Part.

The command of a regiment was in a measure patriarchal. The Colonel, no matter how young, was really the Father. United as they were there was a certain aloofness necessary and expected by the Government, of the Colonel in order to better enforce discipline and carry out the innumerable rules of the book of regulations.

There were from the first a sufficient number of officers of the 7th that agreed with the commander that *all* joining should be of a high type of manhood. Before this decision was finally acted upon the regiment had been officered *three times over.* Many were merely political appointments given with the hope that the voting of families of those appointed, would be given to them in the coming campaigns. In some instances an offending officer was tried by courtmartial and dismissed. In other cases the conduct was so unbearable from the first, that a meeting of the officers was called and a resignation was requested.

BAND

If I could only picture to you the desolateness of the desert and the monotony of camp when not on a campaign, you would realize what a regimental *band* was to us! The Officers decided to buy instruments and support one. A leader was hired, and trained musicians found in the ranks were detailed for special duty. One of the officers who was on recruiting duty in the States einlisted two who were in a street band. When they arrived with their instruments there were shouts of delight, for we all instantly realized that the recruiting officer had in mind *Winter Nights* in Garrison, when we had longed previously for stringed instruments for dancing music. But the absurdity of the *harp,* which suggests luxury, appealed to us who were living almost as primitive a life as the Indians. The owner, an Italian, of course had another instrument when assigned to the band.

It was difficult of course to keep the instruments in any kind of order, carried as they were on a trooper's horse, (with all his accoutrements) over rough roads, and banged about a good deal in camp. But in the winter, in Garrison, the hat went round and a check was forwarded to the East to replace our Summer's losses in Instruments.

Once we rented from a distant town, a *piano*—It was from the first common property. Our doors were never locked, as the sentinel walked his beat before our quarters nightly; and the youngsters of the regiment were thrumming the ancient wreck even before breakfast,—"picking out a tune!" as the Commander put it!

I had one waltz—or portions of one—all that was left of an attempted musical education. Our chaffing brother called it my "five thousand dollar" waltz, for the struggles to make me a musician had of course cost that and more—on and on went the bars of this one dance tune, the officers and girls—*if we had them*—quite indifferent to *monotony*.

Third part—

HORSES

And now may I tell you at once of our horses? They came first in our list of blessings and if anyone was ordered away on temporary duty, the first question on his return after the greeting, would be for his horse.

The Government gives the use of a horse to each officer and enlisted man. They are bought from contractors, for soundness and endurance, and answered very well for long marches. But our regiment became the best mounted in the service, owing to a great piece of good luck. General Custer was sent to Kentucky on temporary duty and made many friends among the planters. He had opportunities to buy pedigreed horses *reasonably* in case the animals failed to reach the high standards of those famous experts who had racing stables. He wrote once to our officers—and *such* saving up ensued among the usually prodigal men!

These horses not only had such endurance, such speed, such spirit; but they were so intelligent.

One of the most delightful pictures that I recall was at evening parade. The last order, after the evolutions, is for the officers all to meet and advance in a long line to salute the commanding officer. It was always an hour of pride to him! The young officers of whom he was so proud, at last mounted on steeds that were worthy of the knights of old!

The officers at the time of which I speak, had become by outdoor life and campaigning almost physically perfect.

And they had learned to have great seasons of economy,—(when these times were announced it was known that a military tailor's bill clouded the air)—after having once worn the troop boots of a famous Philadelphia firm, nothing else could be tolerated. Sometimes they were sent, one at a time, by mail to our distant stations. The whole regiment was in a state of trepidation if their was delay in the arrival of the second boot!

The riding jackets and breeches also made great inroads in the pay; and it was revealed at the time by subtle devices to those who *always borrowed,* and were always hard up that it was best to *defer* the usual request.

Riding: I must not forget to mention one of the agonies of our early military family. Only a few knew how to ride when the regiment was formed. But they were fine manly fellows not in the least afraid to acknowledge their failures.

I recall one great six-footer going off by himself one day to practice mounting and dismounting. It was evidently mostly the *latter,* for he said when he returned that he had been thrown twenty-seven times, (and produced the fine, his basket of champaigne, at once.)

I was keenly sympathetic with each struggler, for I recalled vividly my own chagrin when I first went to camp in Virginia. I had only ridden the gentle ponies that the father of an only child had selected—A quiet animal was found for me, but most of the staff had elected to *accompany* the bride. The impatient horses chomping the bit, snorting with rage, at being held in, aggravated my own steed and made me *limp* with terror and *mortification* that I could ride no better.

However I will not leave myself in the valley of humiliation. I *did* learn to ride in the midst of all the spirited horses that the Staff finally owned, and I had a swift intelligent animal that could, when it was desired, outdistance many of them.

Fourth Part—

MARCHING

And now I come to another phase of our life *marching on the plains.*

Sometimes the Indians were very daring and troublesome and left their reservations to follow and murder the pioneers who were making overland journeys to the Rockies; or raiding the little settlements of those who had ventured too far in the desert.

Our regiment was scouting all summer at different times. The marches were usually at the rate of four miles an hour so as not to over-work the horses, or the mules of the supply wagons. The question of water on the arid plains regulated most marches. We approached the streams in the middle of summer, seeing, long in advance, the deeper tinge of green of the turf, but *often* found no water.

One memorable march (we started before dawn of course) and passed only dry beds of streams for *forty miles*—At the rate of four miles an hour it was a long, *long* day.

No shooting on the march was permitted of course. Herds of deer and antelope *flew* before us. The usual tranquil buffalo were in sight most of the way, quietly grazing and moving slowly as we advanced.

When our march ended our camp was stretched along the stream for a good way, on account of the water which was usually shallow. *Our* tents were pitched some distance from the rest. My husband lifted me from the saddle and I lost no time in clamoring into the traveling wagon, for it was my *fortress* and for this reason—

The rattle snakes were rampant! The soldiers beat the ground before the tent was pitched. The snakes were *always* near, but the banner record was *forty* killed in the small space needed for our headquarter camp. I need not tell any woman kindly listening to me, that after the tent was pitched in running to my *other* safety zone, *the camp bed*—I did not stand upon the order of my going—and who ever came to the tent I received a la turk for a time, but I assure you that I was ready for the march the next morning. I was afraid to acknowledge to *myself* even that I was *hungry, thirsty,* or *tired,* for fear I would not be permitted to go again. Of course our most ambitious officers were working to get medals for bravery.

I was told by the commanding officer—(with a twinkle in his eye), that if I was *never late* and that if I didn't *whimper* when I was frightened, that *possibly* I might be decorated with a "leather" medal at the end of the summer!

HUNTING AND DOGS

We had what was called a permanent camp one summer near Ft. Hays, a small army post in Kansas—no fortifications of course, only the sentinels walking their beats night and day.

Indians were always watching, hidden behind irregularities in the soil or in gulleys outside the camp. They could remain almost motionless from dawn till dark. One reason there was no attack at Hays by the foe was because of the severe punishment given them in the battle of the "Washita", and another powerful one was that three of their greatest chiefs that had been taken prisoners in the battle were with their families imprisoned in a wooden stockade, strongly guarded by the sentinels at the little Fort Hays. The Indians believed that their chiefs would be *shot* if any attempt was made on their part to rescue them.

The Indians protested the building of the Kansas Pacific railroad to Denver and the engineers had to have guards always. The officers feared that *we* women might wander outside the beat of the sentinel and they warned us constantly—the Indians never *shot* women captives. They left them alive to a fate far worse than death. The officers made us sure that if at any time our troops were outnumbered and defeated they would shoot us at once rather than have us fall into the hands of savages - - - - - - - - We sometimes had interesting visitors in our summer camps, (if the Indians were not too troublesome) and we gave them buffalo hunts. Some were Scotch, English, and Russian tourists doing *round the world* journey. They were veteran hunters; having shot game in many lands. But pursuing and shooting our *enormous* buffaloes was a sensation to *them.* I have since seen those of India and they are beasts of burden, tame and cow-like. And never hunted.

Some of our guests sent us pedigreed *dogs* after they returned to their homes. The pack was started in Texas with deer hounds that hospitable planters gave us. Some English officers stationed in Canada sent us on their return, superb stag hounds that could do what *we* thought impossible—catch the fleet jack rabbit. Two English peers sent two Scotch stag hounds, rough-haired vigorous dogs, that as they leaped over the prairie appeared only to be a long brown line so closely did they gather their legs to their bodies! Our pack thus started gave the regiment delight *for years;* and in due time we were able to give dogs to other regiments. The Mother dogs exercised no discretion in presenting us with large families, even on the march; and there was always a soft place in the corner of the tent for any mother who wished to claim it. The puppies were *always* under foot. If I was doing by back hair and spearing it with countless hairpins (for the wind blew furiously most of the time) and trying to see what I was doing with a little hand glass fastened to the wabbling tent pole, it would perhaps happen that I would step on one of the progeny of *exalted birth!* The *Mother* rose in wrath and the owner of the highborn expostulated in a very onesided manner, for an officer wants to see fair play usually.

There was one lordly hound that had accomplished the great feat of the year, pulling down a buffalo by running his powerful jaws in the animal's mouth and holding on like a vise. After that he was given by the commander what might be termed a yearly pass for my half of the camp bed, (growling when I even came near) and always a place in the traveling wagon which was also temporarily a dog hospital if he was torn or cut, when hunting on the march. When the dogs gathered around the camp dining table, this great assertive beast had always especial tender bits thrown to him. And when I tell you that he seized everything given to the rest of the pack, you will be sure that his name—Blucher—after a German General, was most appropriate. Our cook Eliza agreed with me that he was the most spoiled and dominant animal. She would come up the bank from the cook tent, fire in her usually merry eye. The meat was kept in one of the scrubby little trees along the creek fastened by a rope that could be pulled at will. "Miss Libby", she said, "That onery scamp Blucher leaped as you know he can jump, and dragged down the venison and tore off before I got a *lick* at him. Now Miss Libby the General can go on about the dog's high birth, but you can't make me believe that he ain't a direct *des*cendant of a pack of thieving, sassy, onery dogs, with no *good* blood *in* him."

I hardly know where to stop when I think of all the delight we had with out pack that, when I count the never failing family of puppies, reached fifty in all. It was the only pack in the army and the regiment always on duty in a barren desert had none of the diversions of troops stationed near cities, consequently we knew *well* how to value our dogs.

One more tale of the family idol who stole from Eliza and tried to rank me out of the tent, but I acknowledge his prowess—in one hunt he seized an elk by the nose and hung on even after the animal had taken to the water. The General was afraid to fire for fear he would kill the dog, but finally he shot. He went with an officer into the water, they attached a lariat to their saddles and then to the animal, and hauled him ashore. He weighed 800 pounds. My husband had the fine taxidermist in St. Paul set him up and then presented him to the Audubon Society of Detroit where he knew a number of members.

BUFFALOES

I hardly know, even after these many years, how to speak guardedly of the buffaloes. Whatever one says of the immense numbers and the final annihilation, seems such an exaggerated story. May I quote an unquestionable authority of that distant day: "After the subjugation of the Indians, making the country safe for civilians, great numbers of professional hunters and others came to the grazing ground of the buffalo and hunted as a *business*. A single herd of buffalo was reported so large that they would have provided meat for every woman and child in the United States!"

"Carcasses stripped of their hides were lying so close together a man could walk a hundred miles in a line without stepping off from them. There were not cars enough to ship the hides. Two hundred thousand skins were left to decay along the Missouri River because there were not enough boats to carry them to market."

Once on the march an officer of long experience and accustomed to estimating numbers of men called my attention to the horizon—It was completely encirculed with *black* and he said that we were looking upon a hundred thousand animals—They were grazing slowly, moving out of our way, the cows and calves surrounded by a guard, as *intelligently* as *our* wagon trains of supplies was defended by our soldiers from Indian attack on our marches.

A great deal of the time that our army was on the frontier there *was* no hunting, for it was too dangerous, as the Indians were in vastly superior numbers. And when we *did* hunt the shooting was done with discretion and the fresh meat given to the soldiers who so much of the time, had only salt pork with their rations. The buffaloes were *seemingly* so dull, but they were terrible creatures when brought to bay. There were fearful fights among *rivals* also the "eternal triangle" was there in the wilderness, as it is everywhere.

At first I misjudged the great lumbering beast, but if driven into a rage by pursuit, if one bore down upon *me,* his huge head and horns lowered, his eyes balls of fire, I rushed to the traveling wagon and clamored in.

Really, when enraged, they were like the Spanish bull, infuriated by the javelin in his side. Sometimes when stampeded by fright, great numbers would charge blindly on and apparently not *heeding our camp.* The sentinels, always on guard, would be doubled to ward them off.

Of course the officers wanted three girls who were once visiting in camp, to have a hunt. Fortunately they were courageous and knew how to ride; and they had been drilled before by their escorts to shoot low at the only vulnerable spot in the buffalo—*Under the shoulder.* Naturally each officer boasted, after the day ended, of the superior riding and marksmanship of his enamorata. And through the wild scramble, I took note of their charm and femininity and wished that our men could revert to the primitive days when knights in armor carried off their lady loves—asking no permission of opposing parents. And *I* did my best when I *saw* "opposing parents" in the East, to assert that there were no husbands like military men, for they never *ceased* to appreciate the sacrifices a woman made who followed the bugle.

As this is a personal tale I have to confess that *I* went to the hunts in a wagon, urged to do so by my husband. (I suppose, as he knew that I was not a fearless rider, he feared that I might take a tumble while he was engaged in leading the hunt.)

The ground was honeycombed with gopher and prairie dog holes and terrible accidents were constantly occurring.

Our colored servant Henry drove superbly and we often came in at the death, for his pride was up in conducting me, even in a wagon!

Henry would assure me in the start that "I wouldn't lose nothing by *driving* and that he had sat up half the night oilin' and mendin' the harness and that he had an extra wagon tongue beside, and whiffletrees." He kept his word and we arrived on the gallop cheered by the officers, in time to see the enormous beast with head down pawing ground and putting up a magnificent fight.

SCOUTS

A little town moved along with the builders of the railroad. The section at Hays City near our camp was completed. All the desperados and fugitives from justice located there temporarily. Their coming in was a feature of Western travel. When the tracks of each section were laid they pulled down the canvas and slab shacks, piled them with their scant belongings, (mostly saloon furnishings and faro tables,) on the flat cars. In no time after the arrival of the construction train, a street with rows of huts, tents, and dugouts stretched along the track with flaming signs of home construction. A dull place by day but all night there were shouts of hilarity, or the rage of fights or the fury of pursuit, when some cheat at cards or murderer was driven out into the desert. We could hear these brawls in our camp when they "Shot up the town."

The past tempestuous history of most of these men made it necessary for them to keep moving beyond the pale of civilization. The etiquette of the temporary towns was never to ask a question regarding one's *past,* or try to find out the *real* name of any of the citizens. In this collection of incognitos were some of the valuable Scouts employed by the Government—Wild Bill, Buffalo Bill, and California Joe. A portion of our camp was assigned to them but they were under no strict regulations except on the march. One scout rode at the head of the column with the commanding officer as guide. I am quite sure that my husband knew their histories but no question from others sufficiently adroit to betray them into any confidence. Their names were *all* assumed or given for some particular point in their career. My husband valued several of them very highly and wanted me to know them; but when they came to our tent for orders they were so shy nothing could induce them to talk of themselves.

Still I knew several of them slightly, and when they looked at the women in camp with such reverence, I was *moved* by their silent homage and realized in a measure what it must be to these fearless, strong characters never to be thrown with any woman save those pitiful wrecks of humanity who followed the *desperados* and lived always beyond the pale of the law.

Of course the finer men among these scouts could have chosen a domestic life in the States but there was something so alluring in the perilous and exciting existence of the frontier it would have been almost impossible for them to go back to civilization. Buffalo Bill was an exception.

Among the Scouts that served the Government so well and so faithfully none succeeded as well as did he after the Indian wars were ended. But I must mention his great feat first where he risked his life for his country. When the Government had *two* expeditions in the field in the unmapped unknown desert, in the worst of the Indian troubles, and it was of vital importance that they should communicate, Buffalo Bill crossed the desert hundreds of miles alone, hiding his intelligent horse and himself in the thick chaparral bushes or in a gully by day, traveling at night guided by the stars and his compass. When he reached his destination and handed his dispatches to the commanding officer he was speechless, his tongue so swollen from want of water that he could not articulate. He was eminently a leader and would have made a great and successful general. His "Wild West" exhibition was genuine representation of phases of our history. He had the gift of controlling men. He led with order and dignity a large number of people and Indians who had never submitted to the laws of a civilized country nor been subject to any kind of discipline.

He considered that his representation of our country in its primitive days was worthy even of the great colosseum at Rome. He took the invitation of the then Prince of Wales to give a performance at Sandringham to Queen Victoria with due modesty, but with a feeling of certainty that *nothing like it could ever* be produced.

CONCLUSION

Where so many of the gallant 7th fell in battle (and are so carefully guarded in a national cemetery) the Little Big Horn River near the great battle field is to have a huge dam, like the famous Roosevelt one, that will redeem thousands and thousands of acres of arid land that now is almost worthless, and prepare the way for the homes of countless numbers who are struggling for a livelihood in the crowded east. And may I ask you not to forget that it was our little army that helped to bring all this about.

Since I have this privilege of speaking to those of my own State and also General Custer's by adoption—for he went to school in Monroe when a boy and moved his family to Monroe as soon as he graduated from West Point. I want to tell you what gratitude I feel for the gift of our State of the beautiful Equestrian Statue in my home Monroe. The General commanded the Michigan Cavalry Brigade in the Civil War and these dauntless Michigan men followed this boy of 23 to many victories and finally after he had given up his life on our frontier they paid him tribute.

The battlefield of the Little Big Horn in Montana near the town of Hardin is now a National Cemetery and the soldiers of our late war decorate the graves of those who fell so long ago.

Where Custer Avenue crosses Custer Battle Field Highway the people of Hardin are erecting a monument to General Custer with a bronze relief portrait on one side and a tablet with his record on the other.

The Little Big Horn River near the battlefield is soon to have the highest dam in the world that will redeem thousands of acres of arid land and open the way for countless numbers who are struggling for livelihood in the crowded East.

In South Dakota where General Custer and his regiment opened the Black Hills to settlers (which had always been protested by the Indians) there is a government reservation of 30,000 acres for the protection of game named for the General and this past session of Congress has passed a bill for thirty thousand more to be called the Custer Sanctuary where it is planned that animals that are almost extinct will be raised for parks and museums.

The Custer Battlefield Highway of fifteen hundred miles from Omaha to Glacier National Park on the Canadian border is now to be extended to St. Louis and further North.

These energetic and loyal people take my breath away with their plans and I need not tell you how my heart warms to them for many are the third generation since the way was opened to that wonderful Montana.

[22] Libbie to Mr. Buel, November 25, 1891, Century collection, New York Public Library.

[23] New York *Times,* January 5, 1892.

[24] *Ibid.*

[25] Robert P. Hughes: "The Campaign Against The Sioux in 1876," *Journal of the Military Service Institution,* January, 1896.

[26] Charles Kuhlman: *Did Custer Disobey Orders,* Harrisburg, 1957, pp. 53-54.

[27] Elizabeth B. Custer: *General Custer At The Battle Of The Little Big Horn,* N.Y., 1897. The cover of this rare pamphlet displays: *"Printed, Not Published."* Further information may be obtained by reading: Utley: *Custer And The Great Controversy;* Graham: *Story of The Little Big Horn;* Graham: *The Custer Myth;* Lawrence Frost: "Custer's Lost Orders—Found!" *Westerner Magazine,* March, 1971.

[28] Nelson A. Miles: *Personal Recollections,* Chicago, 1896, pp. 197-210; 286-293.

[29] *Ibid,* pp. 205-206.

[30] Graham: *Custer Myth,* p. 280. Mary Adams was the oft referred to Maria in Mrs. Custer's writings and lectures.

[31] *Ibid,* pp. 281-82.

[32] Autie Reed to Mr. and Mrs. David Reed, June 21, 1876, BCWC collection.

[33] Laurence Hutton: "Mrs. Custer's Loyalty," *Harper's Weekly,* May 20, 1892.

Chapter 33
LET THE TRUTH BE KNOWN

Libbie loved reading to appreciative audiences. There was a bit of the ham in her for she did well in the presence of a cordial welcome. Her tour began that May of 1892 in Chicago. It was at Mrs. Arthur Caton's residence at 1910 Calumet Avenue she gave her address on "Garrison Life." Libbie was completely at ease. The audience was large, attentive and familiar, for it was the second time she had appeared before most of them.[1]

During her reading many remarks were directed to various friends in the audience. Mrs. Miles and her mother would smile when Libbie directed a remark toward them. Mrs. McKeever's eyes would cloud with tears when some familiar scene was described. Libbie noticed the reaction among the army people present and it gave her a pleasant feeling to know they were satisfied with her comments.

After the reading the women crowded around and said many delightful things about her magnetism. Several embraced and praised her. One woman said she hated the lectures of men and women but hers was so informal it could not be considered a lecture.

Three soldiers waited to meet her afterward to ask for a picture of her and Autie to hang in the lodge of the Veterans' League named after Autie. One of them had served in the Seventh at Fort Hays while the Custers were there.

Her old friend Emma Schwartz told her she felt herself living over the old days and had been alternately hot, cold and shivery all through the reading. After the reception Libbie went home with Emma to spend an evening with her and her husband for they had much to talk about of the old days. It was not until she was back in her quarters that evening that she had an opportunity to get out the roll of bills that had been given to her earlier for her share of the endeavor and to count it. To her amazement she had earned $388.[2]

On the following afternoon at 4 P.M. she presented her paper on "Buffalo Hunting" at the residence of Mrs. Charles Swartz, 1824 Prairie Avenue. She appreciated Professor Swing's introduction because he "did not take all the tucker out of me by referring to the tragedy of my life nor by anticipating what I was going to say and overlauding me." Libbie had experienced all the tribulations of professional speakers and had become quite appreciative of the simpler forms of introduction.

She was terribly frightened at first. Chicago held some of her best friends and she longed to please them; and Emma had done so very much to organize the reading. Mrs. McKeever, "who knew and loved Autie," was there again, and so was Mrs. Dunlap and dear Mrs. John Clark who told her she looked so pretty. She liked that for such words were seldom said to her.

Mr. Pullman "was delightful in his praise." His famous cars were used to transport the Grand Duke Alexis in 1872. He told Libbie that when the Grand Duke Alexis shot his first buffalo he picked General Sheridan up and carried him the whole length of the car.

It was Emma Schwartz who capped the day. With tears in her eyes she squeezed Libbie's arm and chokingly told her she was satisfied, and so proud.[3]

Three days later Libbie was in Cincinnati talking at the home of Mrs. McDonald for the benefit of the Woman's Exchange. The exquisitely beautiful house held 200 attentive listeners. From the start Libbie felt in sympathy with her audience. It appears she was a surprise to them. They had expected something heavy and instructive—a typical lecture. In response they applauded, laughed, cried and whispered their approval. Some could not understand Libbie's enthusiasm that carried them along with her as she relived the life. Mrs. Capt. O'Connell said the talk was photographic in its depiction with a fidelity to all sides of the life. She indicated that she was relieved to know Libbie presented all sides of the story.

Many spoke of her expression and her distinctness of voice, wondering where she had learned to use it so. She answered: "But I never learned; it came to me." When asked her opinion of the East as compared to the West she exclaimed: "I can see the difference in the East and West in so many ways. For instance, *looks* count so here."[4]

On may 20th she gave a reading in Detroit before 200 people in Mrs. Stearns' home. Don Dickenson, in introducing her, said that since she was so well known for her BOOTS AND SADDLES he would not present her to the audience but would present the audience to her.

In the audience were many of her old friends and schoolmates but she soon lost her tension. Afterward she received many compliments. At the dinner table Mr. Stearns quietly showed her a scrap of paper indicating she had earned $354.[5]

A particularly pleasurable moment occurred when she talked in Cleveland June 3, 1892, for Colonel Albert Barnitz, one of Autie's finest officers, presented her to the audience. Barnitz, serving as a captain in the Seventh Cavalry, had been wounded in the Battle of the Washita in 1868. Libbie always enjoyed meeting Autie's old comrades though she suffered some pain from the memories recalled. In his introductory remarks he recalled:

"I had the fortune to serve under him throughout the whole period when, at the head of his flaming division, he led the charge whenever the enemy in force, was assembled in front of him; and I well remember how when, after the closing review in Washington, he massed his division in an open field, and surrounded by the 37 captured battleflags, trophies of the last campaign, his own standard well advanced, bade us farewell. . . . that tears came into my eyes. . . ."[6]

When tendered a commission in the regular army afterward, Barnitz became associated with Custer again during his Indian campaigns, receiving one of the original appointments to the Seventh Cavalry at its organization in 1866. He remembered, so he told the audience:

"When we first caught gladdening glimpses of the winsome bride, as the headquarters ambulance especially fitted up for the occasion, bore her through the fenceless fields and through the broom sedge and sweet June grass of Virginia—over the gentle undulations, paralleled with and at times near to our marching columns . . . when her ambulance paused for a moment on some swelling knoll, and gallant cavaliers surrounded her conveyance and were made glad by her smiling glance of recognition. . . . "

He recalled "that dreadful night on Big Creek, Kansas, when during the absence of the General and most of the command, a cloudburst inundated the valley where we were encamped and a raging torrent surrounded us and swept everything before it . . . eight soldiers being caught in the seething flood and drowned. I remember the fortitude with which Mrs. Custer awaited in an ambulance with mules attached, while I rode, swam and floundered through water, sometimes submerged in buffalo wallows with tentpoles and a sledgehammer as I endeavored to explore and stake out a safe or reasonably practical route for escape to the distant hills. . . . The lightning poured down in rivers, great balls of fire rolled down the hills, while the crashes of thunder were terrific and appalling beyond description."[7]

It was back to the summer cabin for Libbie. She had been through a busy winter, a trying winter. She had presented the story of her husband to many people and had received considerable attention in the newspapers. Slowly she was making inroads, counteracting the malicious stories concocted by her husband's enemies. After hearing the straightforward story of this little bundle of sweetness, who could believe the whisper campaigns of the military malcontents?

Some have claimed that Custer's enemies and antagonists, in deference to Libbie, made no statements or charges against the General. Nothing is further from the truth. Hughes hadn't hesitated in using Terry's funeral to get his point across. Benteen, a malicious antagonist from his first meeting with Custer, carried his campaign through the Reno Court of Inquiry and beyond. General Merritt had blocked her request for the removal of the atrocious monument of Autie at West Point. None would meet her face to face for none could face the truth. Her books and her lectures had evolved into a campaign of truth. She would see to it that the truth would be known; if only the Lord would spare her, give her health and longevity.

The summer passed quickly enough. In October she opened at Montclair, New Jersey, by reading a paper in the chapel of the Congregational Church.[8] On the following day she read—it was her second visit there—at the Benford Academy in Massachusetts. After the reading the Academy girls dressed in pink, white, yellow, blue and pale green frocks lined up on each side of the dull hall while one of them presented her with a vase of white roses they had purchased with their pin money. They crowded around and ran down the steps in front of her as she made her way to the waiting hack. As she drove away she saw the waving hands and handkerchiefs, the crowded windows filled with waving hands as they called their goodbyes.[9]

On the 19th she was in Glen Ridge. She considered it a milestone that winter since the Reverend and Mrs. Frank Goodwin were her hosts. Mrs. Goodwin was a Duffield from Detroit, one of Michigan's pioneer families.

The bunting-draped church was filled to capacity, chairs having to be brought in to take care of the overflow. Libbie opened her remarks by telling the audience how fearless officers were in carrying bundles. Then she told how her husband used to call himself a model New Jersey husband when he came laden with parcels for her, for "he had sat in the ferry house and watched the miles of New Jersey husbands who tramped by us laden with parcels unmistakably for their wives." The ladies in the audience cheered. After her reading everyone came up to shake hands with her. One old soldier held up the line while he showed her his discharge papers marked "excellent." He was bound to talk about the frontier.[10]

At Elizabethtown, New Jersey, on the 20th, she read for the City Library. She was welcomed by the Williamsons and taken to their home for dinner. They used some of the fixtures their family had used there when they had a feast for Lafayette. The house was filled with the ancestral heirlooms of this illustrious old family.

Libbie had appeared in Elizabethtown the previous winter but this time she was afraid. She hardly had time to hurry through her manuscript the "Buffalo Hunt," which she had not looked at since spring. The lighting in the chapel was poor so she was fearful of losing her place. Nervously she bit her lip until it was disabled the next day. Mrs. Williamson told her not to be anxious, that she could make a "go" of anything with her personality. After an unusually able introduction by Mrs. Williamson, Libbie came through with flying colors. She reached the door of her New York apartment at midnight, tired but happy.[11]

A day of rest followed, then up to Saratoga to give a reading for the benefit of the Emergency Hospital Fund. Libbie enjoyed aiding anything charitable but assisting hospitals gave her a special pleasure. The guiding light was Dr. Strong who had been in sanitarium work for more than 30 years assisted by his lovely wife and unselfish daughter. Libbie took an instant liking to all three of them. She observed that he was "one of those rare men who inspires even women of the world with his sympathy, his strength, his dignity of character. The very shake of his hand gives a woman who lacks faith in men's fidelity—confidence."

The reading was in the dining room of the sanitarium. It was very warm in the room. Midway through her paper Libbie stopped to tell her audience it would not hurt her feelings in the least if they wanted to leave. Not a soul budged, so she continued to the end. So pleased was everyone that the managers asked for an immediate return engagement. She was obliged to inform them she was scheduled until February at which time she would present her paper on buffalo hunting.[12]

She dreaded her next talk which had been set for October 29th in Hartford, Connecticut, for the benefit of the Working Girls Guild. She had been there twice before. Having given the two papers there she was forced to prepare a new one so she wouldn't be repeating herself. Carrie Greene met her at the station and took her to meet Mr. and Mrs. Charles Dudley Warner at their residence. Mr. Warner, in making the introduction that afternoon, told the audience that the world had heard much of war from soldiers but few women told it as well as Libbie did in her books and talks.

A professor there very earnestly gave her a lecture on elocution. He felt that a voice like hers ought to be cultivated, that she should attend the Emerson School of Oratory in Boston. She told him she knew her defects and, since she did not expect to keep up this work very long, she didn't think it worthwhile to take the training. She added that she read only in small rooms since her papers were conversational in nature.

Though Libbie felt honestly indebted to the professor, the Warners thought such training would make her conscious and spoil her naturalness, that she would be so anxious as to her manner of saying things she would forget the earnestness and enthusiasm she now had. The sincerity with which this advice was given made Libbie quite happy.[13]

On Friday, November 5th, she read at a benefit for the Messiah Home For Babies. Just before she began her reading, 33 little waifs, clean, fat and happy looking, marched in two-by-two. All but the two-year-olds recited the 25th Psalm, then knelt and said their prayers. Libbie was quite touched by "this little white aproned band of nobodies."[14]

Engagement followed engagement, each tiring her a bit more and making her conclude "there is no royal way to earn one's living and the way of the 'show woman' is not easy."[15] She had learned a few of the tricks of the trade. Now she selected some person in the audience unconsciously, reading and talking to him. She had a fear that people in the larger rooms would not be able to hear her. By selecting someone near the rear she would try to push her voice so that person could hear her. She never seemed able to conquer her fear of audiences, yet once she observed the audience's interest in her remarks, her calm always returned.

Then Libbie received sad news. Father Custer was dead! He had passed away quite suddenly on November 27, 1892, just two weeks before his 86th birthday. He had been living with his son Nevin on the farm three miles west of Monroe on the north side of the River Raisin. His wife Maria had preceded him in death by ten years.

Emanuel had been a stalwart character, firm in his convictions on two subjects—religion and politics. His deep religious feelings were never challenged by his boys for they had absorbed his reverence. With politics it was a different matter. Their constant chafing on other subjects led quite naturally into politics. Libbie had seen them concoct schemes well in advance in an effort to outwit the old gentleman in a political argument.

To fire him up they would present extremist views of the Republicans. Completely deceived into believing they had wandered into the wrong camp while away from his home, he would answer them vehemently and well. When he was through presenting his counter-argument he would end with "Oh, that I should have lived to raise such scamps," his blue eyes sparkling as he said it.

With that the boys would change their tone and come over to his side in full realization that his argument was valid. Then he would laugh heartily at the joke they had played on him.

Politics had been talked to the boys since babyhood. Emanuel had taken them to many political caucuses, instilling in them an interest in the country and its causes. This old patriot who was to give to his country three sons, a son-in-law and a nephew draped his house in black at the time of the assassination of Lincoln.

One of the townspeople said: "Don't it shake your faith in Democracy in general, Father Custer, to know that most clergymen are Republicans?" "No," he replied, "it don't shake my faith in Democracy, but it does make me rather suspicious of their religion."

Libbie, in an interview by the Detroit *Free Press* shortly after his passing, said:

"His warmest friends, his genuine admirers, were half of them opposed to him in politics, but he loved dearly to have them oppose him; he challenged their thrusts and then invited them to a country dinner of fatted turkey after Michigan went Democratic two years ago, in order to show them how he valued their society in spite of what he thought their mistaken views."[16]

Returning East after a brief visit with old Monroe friends following Father Custer's funeral, Libbie returned to her speaking schedule. Starting in Connecticut she toured the New England states for the balance of the year. In January, 1893, she made a highly successful appearance in Detroit. The subzero weather did not diminish the attendance to the several readings she gave nor the enthusiasm with which she was received. She was able to meet several former schoolmates and a childhood sweetheart. The sight of the latter caused her to write in her diary: "Henry Thurber's fine head and handsome face (for the little carroty headed freckled boy I used to love is now a fine and distinguished white-haired man) really took my courage. I did not dare look at him for an instant for I knew he expected so much."[17]

In early January Libbie answered Mrs. Mendenhall's request that she read her new "Marching On The Plains" at Lincoln Hall in Cincinnati. Libbie's response indicated she could do so on one of the afternoons of January 17, 18, 19, 21, 25, 26, 27 or 30 for $50 and $10 for train expenses "as a proportion of my carfare that I divide with the other western engagements."[18]

On her way to Cincinnati she spoke before the Travelers' Club in Springfield, Ohio. After her paper on "Garrison Life" had been read she went up to an old soldier who had been eagerly, though shyly, watching her. She discovered he was one of those who had been first to reach the Custer battlefield. Tears rolled down his face, Libbie soon following suit. She asked him if he liked civilian life and he said he was compelled to. "Ah, you were wounded?" "Yes," he replied, "Sitting Bull made it impossible for me to go back several times." Then he gave her a look of modesty.

Changing the subject, he told her he was satisfied with her paper and proud of her. He had wanted to see her before she read it but had heard she would become unnerved by seeing old soldiers, then couldn't speak or read. She thought this was considerate of him and told him so.[19]

She was a bit anxious before her 2:30 reading in Cincinnati because "my paper and I were not friends yet as it is still new and had only been read once before in Hartford." She was introduced by the retired ex-volunteer General James Cox before a flag-draped picture of Autie thoughtfully placed there by Major Lloyd.

General Cox referred to what "our men" had done in opening up the West to settlers and progress. Libbie responded to this reference by closing her paper with a tribute to the dead in unknown graves over the plains, reminding the audience that "in ten years on the frontier more lives had been given up than in all the Crimean war."

Major Lloyd told her that "an old soldier who knows what a trouble and nuisance women are on a march said to him after her paper was finished: 'I don't wonder they let that woman go with the column.'"[20]

From Richmond, Indiana, to Toledo and then on to Providence, Rhode Island, where she read at Pawtucket for a day nursery. There she was introduced by a Unitarian minister who gave her a "beautiful send off" by saying:

"All know General Custer because of the service he rendered his country and they know Mrs. Custer also not only for her service to her country in following her husband in the field but from the eloquence of her pen which had given the country the first true knowledge of the life of an army women on the frontier—a life hitherto unknown."

Afterward Mr. Fenner asked how she could stand such introductory remarks—they had brought a lump to his throat and tears to his eyes. She replied: "I was obliged to for often and often the words of those introducing me made all the first lines of my paper blurred like a veil of mist before my eyes."[21]

After she lectured the next day for the benefit of the Women's Alliance in Cambridge, Massachusetts, several people asked where she was born in order to trace her Virginia accent. "The darkey dialect came from being months at a time with Eliza and Henry," she replied.[22]

On February 23rd she was in West Newton reading for the benefit of a church society. Her previous engagement there had been preempted by Father Custer's funeral. The delay was expected to affect the attendance but even the standing room was filled.

One gentleman told her that it was a surprise to him to know what people on the frontier had endured; that he thought her description was as good and better than a sermon to bring home to the people a sense of what others were enduring while they in their luxury never realized what our officers and families were living through.[23]

The following day she was to read in the town hall at Harvard. Forty years earlier the town had declined the railroad, wanting no innovations or outsiders. There was no other means of transportation other than the cutter of the stage driver. On the way over a deeply drifted road through a pretty valley, a four-horse team kept for opening the road turned out for them. Libbie mentioned that they were very accommodating. The old driver said: "Oh, don't they know well enough who I've got here!" She was the event of the winter.

People came as far as five miles over the drifted roads, having to walk their horses all of the way. Babies and children came to the town hall because the hired girl had to come, and no one was left at home to care for the infants. Twenty-five of 50 old vets came in uniform and sat in the front row.

The entertainments were free through the generosity of a citizen (Mr. Warner) who gave money the interest of which was more than enough to secure the best of entertainment. Libbie had been preceded by Governor Long and Mr. Riddle.[24]

The balance of spring and early summer kept Libbie busy enough. Albany, Portland, Camden, Woonsocket, Middletown, Morristown, Bridgeport, Brooklyn and Germantown, and many places in between until she reached Pittsfield, Massachusetts, on June 29th. That was the end of the line for that year. Fittingly enough she was introduced by General Morris Schaff, a West Point classmate of Custer who was the author of several books and of Custer's biography in *Cullum's Biographical Register of the Officers and Graduates of the United States Military Academy.*[25]

The summer of 1894 saw Libbie make a change. Restless soul that she was, she had outgrown her cabin near Stroudsville. It had served its purpose while she was utilizing the summer months to write, for it had provided the necessary seclusion. But her gregarious disposition required the stimulus of people of like interests. Previous visits to Onteora in the Catskills, where many of her friends rested during the summer months to escape the heat of the city, were recalled.

The summer colony at Onteora had grown considerably since its founding in 1887, its serenity, beauty and isolation from the trials and turmoil of city life offering advantages to those with literary interests. The summer sojourners would rent sleeping rooms in the log cabins, taking their meals at the Bear Inn.

Most of these original residents were artists, musicians and writers seeking a life in "a community of interests and a way of life consonant with the best American tradition."[26] It attracted Samuel B. Clemens, Henry Stimson, John Burroughs, Louise Homer, Laurence Hutton, Jeannette Gilder, Kate Field, Ruth McEnery Stuart, Edward A. Blashfield, Maude Adams, Frank Stockton and Mary Mapes Dodge. William T. Tilden Jr., tennis champion and actor, learned his first tennis at Onteora and Carr Van Anda relaxed there from his labors as managing editor of the New York *Times.*[27] Mr. Carroll Beckwith was the first of the resident painters.

Cottages were soon built on the eastern and southern sides of the Onteora Mountain by those selected few who had come to visit at the Inn and then chose to stay. Candace Wheeler, the sister of Francis S. Thurber, built a sawed lumber house the east wall of which was a picture gallery of portraits painted directly on the plaster. One of these was that of Libbie in a charming sunbonnet.

John Burroughs owned one he called "Slabsides." The Clemenses took a cottage named "The Balsam" just across from the Inn. Jeannette Gilder built "Cloud Cabin" on the south side of the mountain.

Libbie became a property owning member in 1898, moving into her new brown shingled cottage in the summer of 1899 which she promptly named "The Flags." She owned it until 1924.[28]

Libbie maintained a close friendship with Candace Wheeler; Mary Mapes Dodge, author of "Hans Brinker and the Silver Skates"; author Susan Coolidge; Jeannette Gilder; Ruth McEnery Stuart, and playwright Marguerite Merington who later became Libbie's literary executrix and author of THE CUSTER STORY.[29]

Marguerite Merington, who first met Libbie in 1894 while taking a room at Onteora Park, had been troubled with insomnia. On such occasions she slept late. Mrs. Maggie Calhoun and Libbie had made a place for her at their table. Noting that Miss Merington had not arrived, Libbie "would come trotting up the hill with a laden tray, salvaged from the breakfast room (at the Bear Inn) before its close," Miss Merington recalled. "That was characteristic of her. She was kind and practical, a real friend."[30]

The discussions in that summer colony were not necessarily centered upon literature and art. Ofttimes, perhaps because women predominated, the subject turned to a discussion of women. Candace Wheeler, free spirit and free thinker, espoused a philosophy that "it should be a matter of course for women to be educated with reference to a profession. . . . Every woman as well as man should have special training in some craft or profession."

At a luncheon one day at Mrs. Wheeler's house attended by a dozen women authors, editors, writers and artists such as Mary Mapes Dodge, Kate Field and Kate Douglas Wiggin, Libbie exclaimed: "Why, we are all working women; *not a lady among us!*"[31] A bit of a shock to all for each realized there was no need to work, no one expected them to work and most men would have disapproved of their work. It was a man's world.

Libbie had ample time to reflect upon the social and economic status of the female. She had observed the manner in which the soldiers and the pioneers had treated their spouses on the western frontier. The contrast between those men and the men in the East in their attitude toward women was obvious to her. Soldiers in the West placed their wives on pedestals whereas the men of the East, other than a select few, tended to treat women as inferiors. Libbie was not hesitant to draw attention to the plight of women. When the opportunity presented itself she would offer suggestions and present observations in a manner so delicately and with such tact that even the most sensitive and resentful male chauvinist would not be annoyed. For charm and poise she had few peers. When she "turned it on," the males present listened. In her low, musical voice a statement was made which, for its logic and reasonableness, was difficult to reject.

An instance is related in Chalmers' "The Penny Piper of Saranac,"[32] which occurred at a December dinner party attended by Libbie, Dr. Trudeau and Robert Louis Stevenson. Chalmer observed: "After the soup, Mrs. Custer opened fire upon the Penny Piper."

"Mrs. Custer: 'Now, why is it, Mr. Stevenson, that you never put a real woman in your stories?'

"Stevenson (with twinkling gravity): 'Madam, I have little knowledge of Greek.'

"Mrs. Custer: 'But you have some knowledge of women, surely! Why, you have been a married man these seven years!'

"Stevenson: 'With the result, Mrs. Custer, that I have forgotten all the Greek I knew.'

"Mrs. Custer: 'But the public expects it of you, and the feminine portion demands it. Come! When are we to be introduced to the Stevenson woman in fiction?'

"Stevenson (with sudden enthusiasm): 'Mrs. Custer! I promise you there shall be a woman in my next book.'

The Penny Piper regretted his rash gallantry before the close of the evening. Later, he confided his fears to Dr. Trudeau.

"Trudeau: 'I've often wondered, Stevenson, but never thought to ask: Why do you never put a real woman in a story?'

"Stevenson: 'Good heavens! Trudeau, when I have tried I find she talks like a grenadier!'

"Nevertheless, he kept his promise to Mrs. Custer, and the result is that wooden effigy in 'The Master of Ballantrae,' who is called, for identification's sake, Alison Durie.

"But the ice was broken, and from this point the evolution of the real Stevenson woman in fiction is interesting to trace. . . ."

Robert U. Johnson, who was editor of *Century Magazine* for 40 years and knew Libbie well, related a few stories about her that are revealing.[33] *Century* was giving a dinner party in honor of Rudyard Kipling in about 1895. When he became ill from typhoid all invitations were recalled. By chance, Libbie had not been informed of the cancellation. She arrived in her finest gown and prettiest smile "radiant with expectation of an enchanting evening with the prince of storytellers." A few others, in the same predicament, made up a dinner party, accepting conditions as they found them. After the dinner Libbie gave them a graphic account of cowboy life in the West.

While in London during the Durbar, the gentle but adventurous Libbie thought she would like to witness the spectacle. Visiting the War Office, she sent in her card. After being received by a fine young officer she made known her wish, then added the request that she be permitted to go to India on a British transport.

"There are army ships going out, are there not?" inquired the little lady with the soft gray curls and the winning smile.

"Oh, yes, madam," was the reply, "but these are only for families of the British officers. I take it you are an American, madam. What makes you think you might be included?"

"Oh, nothing," she answered, adding wistfully, "I just thought there might be room and that there would be no harm in trying."

"Not the least harm in the world, madam. I am only very sorry that it is quite out of the question to forward your wish—quite so. It would be entirely unheard of."

"Well, I thank you for your politeness. But I should really like to go," she said like a child who had to stay home from a party. "Good morning," and she rose to leave.

"Good morning, madam," said the officer, bringing his heels together and making his best bow. Then, at the door, glancing at her card, he caught the name again and said, "Oh, one moment, madam! May I ask you a question? Are you, by any chance, related to General Custer, the famous Indian fighter?"

"Oh, yes, I am his widow."

"His widow! Oh, permit me madam. Pray be good enough to sit down and excuse me a moment," and off he went on the tangent of a new idea.

Very soon he returned with the chief of the bureau and several other members of the staff, all of whom desired very particularly to be presented to the widow of General Custer, the famous Indian fighter.

And the upshot of it all was that Mrs. Custer went to the Durbar in a British transport with every comfort.[14]

Libbie's propensity for making friends increased her circle of influence in the drive to perpetuate her husband's name. Some, like General Miles, aided her cause by the permanency of their writings. One of these friends was the poetess Ella Wheeler Wilcox. In 1896 a small volume of her poems was published under the title of *Custer And Other Poems*. Several

MRS. ELIZABETH B. CUSTER in 1900. C. W. Hill photos.

years later she missed Libbie when she called upon her at Onteora. So impressed was she with the view she wrote to Libbie:

"THE CATSKILL MOUNTAINS
FROM ONTEORA

Along the green primeval paths
By mature feet untrod
The Dromedary Mountains wind
Out from the tents of God."[35]

Libbie's books, lectures and friends produced a huge volume of mail that intruded upon her time to such a degree she had little time to write. In the back of her mind was a plan to write a book about Autie's exploits in the Civil War. To her way of thinking entirely too much emphasis had been placed on the battle at the Little Big Horn. The younger generation thought of the General as an Indian fighter, hardly knowing that he had been a veteran of the Civil War. She had tried to encourage others to write along that channel but without success. The dramatic ending to Autie's career captured the imagination of most writers. That was the scope of their interests.

The continued interest of writers in the last stand had some advantages. From time to time the stories published about the affair seemed to root out a recollection of some participant who responded to the stimulus by writing Libbie a letter or talking to a correspondent revealing information that helped fill out the jigsaw puzzle. Not all of such letters or accounts could be relied upon for some laid claims to have been survivors. One letter of particular interest was that written to Libbie by General Jesse M. Lee, who had been the Recorder at the Reno Court of Inquiry in 1879.

Lee opened his letter by referring to Libbie's letter of June 19, 1897. Her letter had been the result of having read a letter Lee had sent to General Miles in December, 1896. Lee admitted that at one time he had been in some degree "influenced by the prejudicial opinions of those whose motives I did not understand, and whose sources of information I then had no means of testing." Soon afterward he had been brought in contact with thousands of Sioux, Cheyennes and other Indians, and had an opportunity to visit the Custer battlefield. He went on to write:

"Now, I tried to be honest and fair minded and allow nothing but *facts* to make an impression on my mind. So it came about in the light of long and confidential talks to me by witnesses *before* they went on the stand, and in light of much of the testimony *on the stand;* and finally in the light of my visit to the field,my judgment could no more escape the conclusion of *facts* than to deny that I am penning these lines. That conclusion I referred to in my letter to General Miles and I am glad you consider it 'generous and fair.' *It is true!* I do not believe an unprejudiced mind—anyone whose heart is free from the contact of jealousy—could, with a knowledge of all the facts, come to any other conclusion. When I got at the facts it was easy to understand how *self interest* influenced opinions; how jealousy being unopposed could unmask its horrid power and loosen its tongue of calumny—with none to answer; how the living could extol themselves for *prudence* and *delay*—and condemn the dead as *rash* and *impetuous;* how authority through inexperience, sought to evade responsibility through a loophole of escape. Had some one blundered? Then how easy to censure those who could not answer. It was both cruel and unjust for *anyone* to send that dispatch: 'Orders were disobeyed but the penalty paid.'

"This dispatch reveals both weakness and incompetency. The sender, as I believe, knew but little if anything of Indians, but he did know General Custer, and it verges on imbecility to suppose that anyone would expect those Indians to be held in position several days by one column waiting and making it convenient for another column to attack them.

"My opinion, as such, is of but little account one way or the other, but I believe as an unprejudiced person I have had better opportunities to get at the *facts* than almost any other person. These facts show beyond successful contradiction:

"1st: Major General Custer was *not* disobeying General Terry's orders in attacking the Indians. Any other course under the circumstances would have been ridiculous and absurd.

"2nd: Major Reno, according to General Gibbon's testimony—left, *abandoned,* a splended position where he threatened the entire village and thus enabled the entire force of Indians to concentrate on General Custer, who was thus compelled to meet them with *less* than 2/5 of the effective force of his regiment.

"3rd: Major Reno's disastrous retreat in *keeping out of the battle at a critical period fully 3/5 of the effective force,* and in doing this all chance for victory over the Indians was lost.

"I had not the honor of a personal acquaintance with General Custer; I saw him but once in my life; but I feel that I would be remiss to Truth were I to fail to say and write on appropriate occasions that which I know is in accord with his great reputation."[36]

This gem was not all that Libbie received in the mail to make 1897 a memorable year, but it certainly was a key letter. For who could be more objective and who could have had greater access to Indians and whites who fought in the Custer battle?

General Charles King, the prolific and popular author of military and adventure stories, dedicated a book—"A Soldier's Secret And An Army Portia"—"To ELIZABETH BACON CUSTER, whose devotion as wife, whose desolation as widow, and whose bravery and patience through long years 'In The Shadow' have touched all hearts, this story is *INSCRIBED.*"[37]

BACON-CUSTER HOME IN MONROE in 1910 during the time of the unveiling of the Custer Monument. Monroe County Historical Museum Library.

NOTES—CHAPTER 33

[1]Elizabeth Bacon Custer Diary of 1892, Monroe County Historical Museum Library, hereinafter called EBC Diary—1892.
[2]EBC Diary—1892, May 9, 1892.
[3]*Ibid,* May, 1892.
[4]*Ibid,* May 13, 1892.
[5]*Ibid,* May 20, 1892. It is presumed—though not recorded—Libbie visited the Custers in Monroe on her way to Cleveland.
[6]Albert Barnitz: "Remarks of Introduction," Cleveland, Ohio, June 3, 1892, BCWC collection.
[7]*Ibid.*
[8]EBC Diary—1892, October 15, 1892.
[9]*Ibid,* October 16, 1892.
[10]*Ibid,* October 19, 1892.
[11]*Ibid,* October 20, 1892.
[12]*Ibid,* October 22, 1892.
[13]*Ibid,* October 29, 1892.
[14]*Ibid,* November 5, 1892.
[15]*Ibid,* November 14, 1892.
[16]Detroit *Free Press,* December 11, 1892.
[17]Elizabeth B. Custer Diary of 1893, Monroe County Historical Museum Library, hereinafter called EBC Diary—1893.
[18]Libbie to Mrs. Mendenhall, January 6, 1893, New York Historical Society.
[19]EBC Diary—1893, January 21, 1893.
[20]EBC Diary—1893, Cincinnati, no date.
[21]*Ibid,* February 19, 1893.
[22]*Ibid, February 22, 1893.*
[23]*Ibid,* February 23, 1893.
[24]*Ibid,* February 24, 1893.
[25]EBC Diary—1893.
[26]The Onteora Club, a booklet in the files of the Haines Falls (N.Y.) Free Library.
[27]*Ibid.*
[28]Wheeler: *Yesterdays,* pp. 279, 287, 302, 307, 312.
[29]Correspondence with Mrs. Frederick T. Cumerford, Onteora Club, Tannersville, N.Y.
[30]Karl Zeisler: "The Observor," Monroe *Evening News,* February 11, 1950.
[31]Wheeler: *Yesterdays,* p. 422.
[32]Stephen Chalmers: *The Penny Piper of Saranac,* Boston, 1916, p. 41.
[33]Robert U. Johnson: *Remembered Yesterdays,* Boston, 1923, p. 398.
[34]*Ibid,* pp. 498-99.
[35]Ella Wheeler Wilcox to Libbie, February 5, 1900, BCWC collection.
[36]General Jesse M. Lee to Libbie, from Madison Barracks, Sackett's Harbor, June 27, 1897, EBC-CBNM.
[37]Charles King: *A Soldier's Secret and an Army Portia,* Philadelphia, 1897.

CHAPTER 34
TELL ME WHAT TO DO

William Van Duzer Lawrence, at the age of eight, moved with his family from New York state to Monroe, Michigan. At the age of 15 he had matriculated at the State Normal School in nearby Ypsilanti, attending classes there for three years. Teaching held little interest.

The Bates family in Monroe had made quite an impression on him, or at least one member — Sarah — had. On August 22, 1867, they were married. In 1889 they moved to Bronxville, New York, terminating a successful career in the drug business.

Bronxville was a charming village just north of New York City. Lawrence had been attracted there by his brother-in-law Arthur M. Wellington. An astute businessman, Lawrence purchased 85 acres of rolling, rocky hills for $500 an acre, then began the development of Lawrence Park. This exclusive residential area was soon exhibiting a variety of charming homes representing all of the major architectural styles in fashion at the turn of the century. Though the Romanesque Revival architecture with its high roofs and high gables and its stone construction predominated, the shingle style was quite evident. William A. Bates was the architect for a majority of the houses.[1]

In acquiring the property Lawrence became the owner of the Manor House, a home built in the 1840s by the Bronxville pioneer James Minot Prescott. It was quickly converted into an inn for the convenience of those who awaited the completion of their homes in the newly developing Lawrence Park.

The Park had all the charm of a small community and all of the advantages but none of the disadvantages of nearby New York City. No wonder it attracted artists William H. Howe, Will Hicok Low, Mary Fairchild and William T. Smedley, poet Edmund Clarence Stedman, playwright Zona Gale, authors Kate Douglas Wiggin and Alice Wellington Rollins, architect William H. Kent, lawyer-artist-poet Tudor Jenks, portraitist William T. Smedley, mural painter Herman T. Schladermundt and etcher and illustrator Otto Bacher.[2]

To a great extent Bronxville has been able to maintain the charm of its origin. The romantic and fanciful architecture that prevails throughout Lawrence Park provides an atmosphere conducive to reflection and leisurely living. The lovely tower houses, the "shingle style" and the rambling wood and stone habitations, many of which are perched on rocky prominences, set back from the narrow winding roads, offer the occupants privacy surrounded by rustic beauty. It was to this attractive setting Libbie first came to visit Sarah Lawrence in 1892.

Bronxville had a certain magnetism for the Bates family of Monroe. Agnes Bates Wellington had been the first to settle there with her husband Arthur, her sister Sarah and husband William Lawrence soon following. Later, a sister, Mrs. Burk (Adelle Bates) Stone moved there to be followed by her brother John S. Bates. Another brother, Major Alfred E. Bates, a West Point graduate in 1865 and later paymaster of the Army, visited there often. George Custer Christiancy of Monroe, though no relative of the Bates or of Libbie, also came there to live.[3]

The imaginative though realistic Lawrence saw advantages others had not seen. He established a weekly newspaper, the Bronxville *Review,* and in 1897 built the Hotel Gramatan atop Sunset Hill. Its architect was William A. Bates. Though he is said to be from Monroe, he was not related to the other Bates at Bronxville.[4]

Two years after the Hotel Gramatan opened, it all but burned to the ground. The inadequate fire equipment of that period was not equal to the task of a fire of that magnitude high up on that hill.

In 1904 Lawrence rebuilt the hotel on the same site, making it much larger. It was a fashionable spot for New Yorkers and soon boasted of such guests as Greta Garbo, Theodore Dreiser, Theodore Roosevelt and Mrs. Elizabeth B. Custer.[5]

By 1913, Lawrence Park had grown to 500 acres. In 1921, Lawrence built the Osceola Inn at Daytona Beach, Florida, where Libbie spent many winters in her late years to inhibit the ravages of arthritis.[6]

BACON-CUSTER HOME about 1912. Libbie was born in this house. Emanuel Custer and his wife lived in it after Judge Bacon died in 1866. Author's collection.

About 1892 Libbie built a large brown-shingled residence in Lawrence Park at 20 Park Avenue. She lived in this tower-type residence until she had built a house at 6 Chester Avenue, just a short distance away. It too was a tower-type covered with brown shingles though the first floor was of native cut stone construction. This imposing house was built on the crest of an outcropping of rock on a hillside. The attractive fortresslike residence must have provided Libbie with a feeling of security she had yearned for during her life on the plains.

One cold, rainy evening in December of 1892, Libbie supplied a full house with one of her pleasant readings.[7] She was to provide her neighbors and friends with many such readings, delighting them with her experiences with her husband[8]

Lecturing was more remunerative than she had ever expected. Though difficulties had been encountered in the renting of the New York cottage, she had managed to pay off the mortgage with money to spare. Encouraged by the real estate successes of the Lawrences, she purchased property in Lawrence Park both in 1901 and in 1904. One section of the village had been named Custer Place and an apartment house at Parkview and Palmer avenues had been named the Custer Arms in her honor.

Libbie maintained a deep and continuous interest in hospitals. She had seen the inadequate and inefficient care the wounded and sick received when she traveled with the Army of the Potomac. She had observed the benefits derived from the ministration of the Sanitary Commission when it furnished medical and surgical aid to soldiers in the camps and field hospitals. When asked to help compose the material for the Westchester Historical Pageant, the proceeds from which would be used to benefit the new Lawrence Hospital, she was quick to accept.[9]

On May 28 and 31, 1909, the benefit was given in Bronxville on the grounds of the DeWitt estate. New York Governor Charles Evans Hughes, after reviewing the Memorial Day Parade in New York City, drove to Bronxville to visit the Pageant grounds. Libbie with Ellis Gladwin and William Lawrence were the reception committee.[10]

During the 1890s Libbie did little writing of magazine articles. Her last such article had been published in the July 18, 1891, issue of *Harper's Weekly* under the title of "An Out-of-the-Way Outing," in which she described her trip into the Northwest.

Then in 1900 she evidenced a renewed interest in writing magazine articles. Her first article that year dealt with the distaff problems at an army post. It was an occasion to give the quartermaster his due. And she gave it to him.

It was the quartermaster's assignment to build the posts. Too often he placed the officers quarters, which usually faced one of the four sides of the parade ground, so that the rooms would not be warmed by the sun. His excuse that "the strategic position must be considered" was unacceptable to these women seasoned in military affairs. In their opinion any child could have selected a spot on the prairie that would ward off the approach of an enemy.

The quartermaster, usually a bachelor, avoided consultation with the wives. This was an oversight he rarely repeated. The women would descend upon him and plague him daily as long as he was unfortunate enough to remain at that post.

Libbie recalled that the kitchen of her best quarters "had no sink, drain or pump. The cook hurled everything out of the door. In place of a cistern, there were two or three barrels at the rear filled daily with river water, hard for washing and muddy for drinking." There were no shelves, no closets, no wall paper, just rough plastered walls and huge rooms with little furniture to fill them.[11]

Another magazine article related experiences while traveling with a cavalry on the move. "We were fortunate if we had half a wagon for our belongings," she wrote. Antlers were fastened to the wagon tops which in the dimness of dawn, made them look like prehistoric monsters peering at them.[12]

Eliza frequently went on tirades, though only when the wood was wet or the wind and blowing sand made cooking difficult. Eliza would tie up her tent and tussle with the meal, taking time to take a stick to the tip of the nose of any dog that dared thrust it under the tent wall. It was at just such a time that the "dog-robber" made himself scarce.

One of the editors had been encouraging Libbie to write a novel. Her first attempt was in the form of an adventure story for children, which was published in *St. Nicholas Magazine.*[13] Since there was no pressing need for funds at this time and since she found the narrative style more natural for her, this story was the last such attempt.

In the spring of 1877, the State of Colorado had acted to honor General Custer. On March 9, the southern part of Fremont County was formed into Custer County by an act of the 1st Colorado State Legislature.

When traces of silver and other valuable deposits became evident toward the end of the century, Francis I. Meston of Pueblo decided to organize a mining company. The best site for such an office was in the center of the mining country 75 miles from Pueblo. A mining company office needed people to sell stock to and, since there were few people in that area, Meston thought of a venture that could be remunerative in two ways. Why not lay out a town and sell the real estate?

The site selected was a hilltop a mile south of Querida. There the newly created Custer Mining and Realty Company opened its offices. Seeking publicity that would draw prospects to their flytrap, Meston and his collaborators decided to organize a christening day for the future metropolis they would call Custer City.

Since General Custer could not be present at this gala event, another luminary would serve the purpose. Why not invite Mrs. Custer? To make the invitation difficult to reject, they proposed to erect a statue of the General to be unveiled on the occasion of the civic christening. On April 18, 1902, a letter was sent to Libbie embodying such an invitation.[14] The writer mentioned that Col. W. F. Cody had also been invited. They would be willing to bear all of her expenses if she could be present that day. The proposed date of dedication was tentatively set for June 15th.

CUSTER CITY, COLORADO. The Custer monument, which has since disappeared, may be seen near the center of the picture not far from three of the city's earliest structures, 1902. Denver Public Library Western Collection.

Three weeks later another letter of invitation was sent to Libbie to advise her that ex-Governor Alva Adams would deliver the address at the unveiling of the Custer statue. Apparently Libbie saw through the humbuggery and never responded for she never attended.[15]

The christening of Custer City took place on June 10th, some 3,000 people witnessing the affair. Governor Orman and his staff were welcomed by a 21-gun salute. At 2:30 P.M. "Boots and Saddles" was sounded followed a few minutes later by "Assembly."

After Governor Orman made the usual appropriate remarks as to the great potential of this embryonic community, ex-Governor Alva Adams paid tribute to General Custer. The unveiling of the Custer statue was the work of Myrtle Rants of Querida. That evening the town was brightly illuminated by electricity and fireworks while some 300 people made their way to the dance at the new hotel.[16]

A newspaper aptly named the *Custer Guidon* had been established and a score of houses had been built along the streets in the meadows. The Custer Mining and Realty Company had hopefully engaged in the selling of stock in their two mines, the "Toledo" and the First Colorado."[17]

Like the Custer statue once at West Point, this one too at Custer City mysteriously disappeared. The *Wet Mountain Tribune,* in an effort to explain what had happened to the monument, indicated there were several stories extant. "The most likely seems the one that says the statue was sold for metal during World War I"[18]

Then an event occurred that brought a certain amount of satisfaction and joy to Libbie. Her sister-in-law Maggie, as restless as Libbie, had traveled constantly around the country. Other than the few years spent as the State Librarian in Michigan she had been on the go constantly, endeavoring to meet her wellfilled scheduled of readings. It was inevitable that the vivacious Maggie Calhoun would meet someone who would sweep her off her feet. Proud Libbie sent out engraved cards that read:

> "Mrs. Custer announces the marriage of her sister, Mrs. Margaret Custer Calhoun, to Mr. John Halbert Maugham, at Onteora Park, Catskill Mountains, on Thursday the second of July, One Thousand Nine Hundred And Three. At Home after July the Twentieth, Hotel Iturbide, Mexico, Mexico."[19]

Following the wedding, Libbie took passage for the Far East, stopping at Egypt and Turkey on the way.

The Literary Section of the April 19, 1903, issue of the New York *Herald* published a story that kicked up a storm in the world of art. Native born though Munich trained Charles Schreyvogel resided in Hoboken, New Jersey. His enthusiastic interest in the West was such that he spent some time there collecting firearms, Indian clothing, cavalry equipment and ideas for future pictures. In 1889 his painting "My Bunkie" brought him considerable acclaim.[20] Early in April, Knoedler Art Galleries in New York unveiled his latest painting "Custer's Demand." The *Herald,* in its Sunday edition, carried a laudatory feature article fully illustrated. The scene portrayed General Custer and his staff parleying with Lone Wolf, King Bird and Satanta during the Plains Indian campaign of 1869.

Schreyvogel had extensively researched his subject. He had obtained copies of Custer's and Sheridan's reports of their 1868-1869 campaigns, had interviewed numerous officers and men of the Seventh Cavalry and had purchased and borrowed uniforms and equipment used by them.[21]

The April 28th issue of the *Herald* published an article on page three headed, "Finds Flaws in Custer's Demand." In it the noted artist and illustrator Frederic Remington referred to the painting as "a so-called historical picture," and "half-baked stuff," then criticized it point by point. His

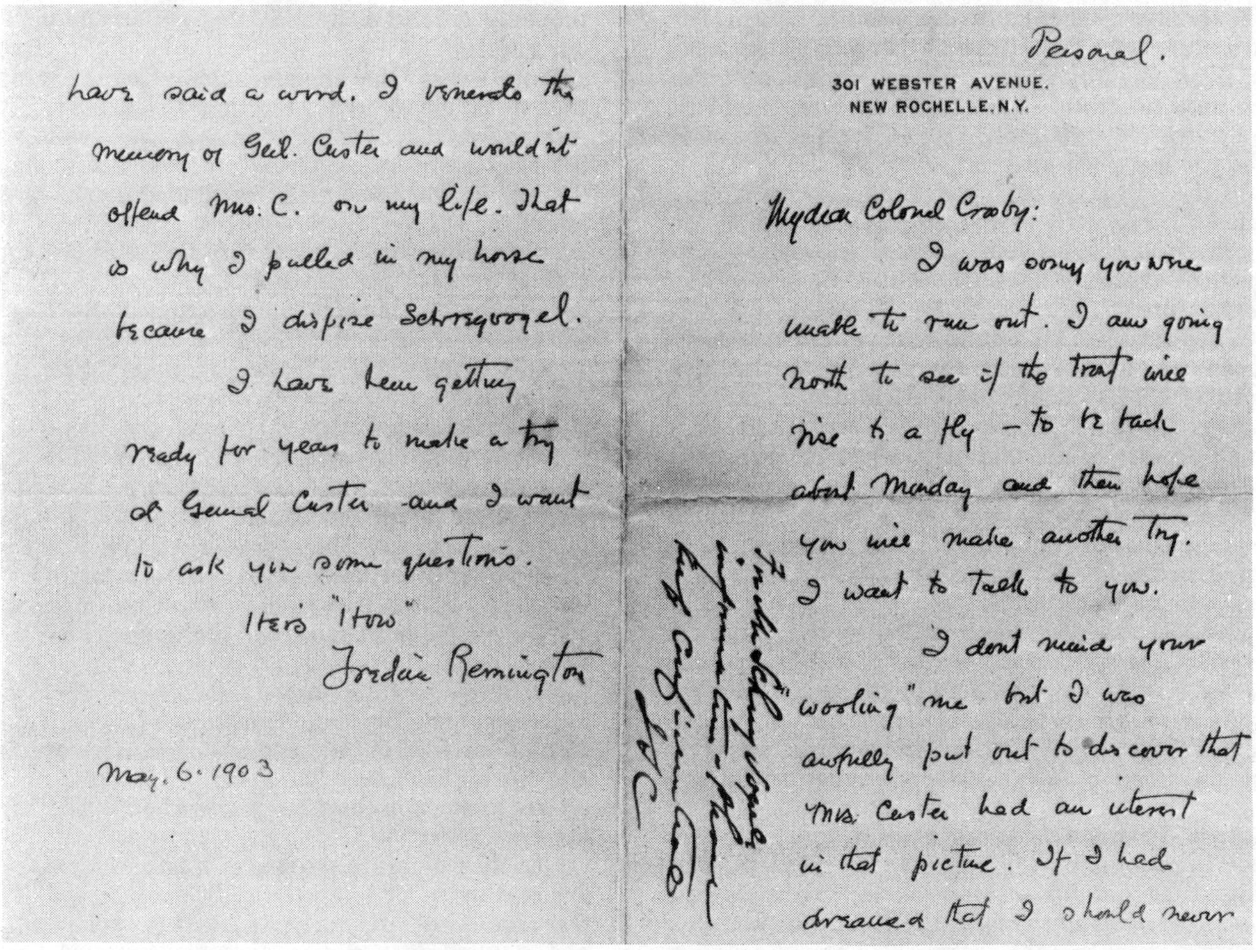
Personal.
301 WEBSTER AVENUE.
NEW ROCHELLE, N.Y.

My dear Colonel Crosby:

I was sorry you were unable to run out. I am going north to see if the trout will rise to a fly — to be back about Monday and then hope you will make another try. I want to talk to you.

I dont mind your "wooling" me but I was awfully put out to discover that Mrs. Custer had an interest in that picture. If I had dreamed that I should never have said a word. I venerate the memory of Gen. Custer and wouldn't offend Mrs. C. on my life. That is why I pulled in my horse because I despise Schreyvogel.

I have been getting ready for years to make a try at General Custer and I want to ask you some questions.

Here's "How"

Frederic Remington

May. 6. 1903

REMINGTON TO COLONEL SCHUYLER CROSBY. May 6, 1903. National Cowboy Hall of Fame.

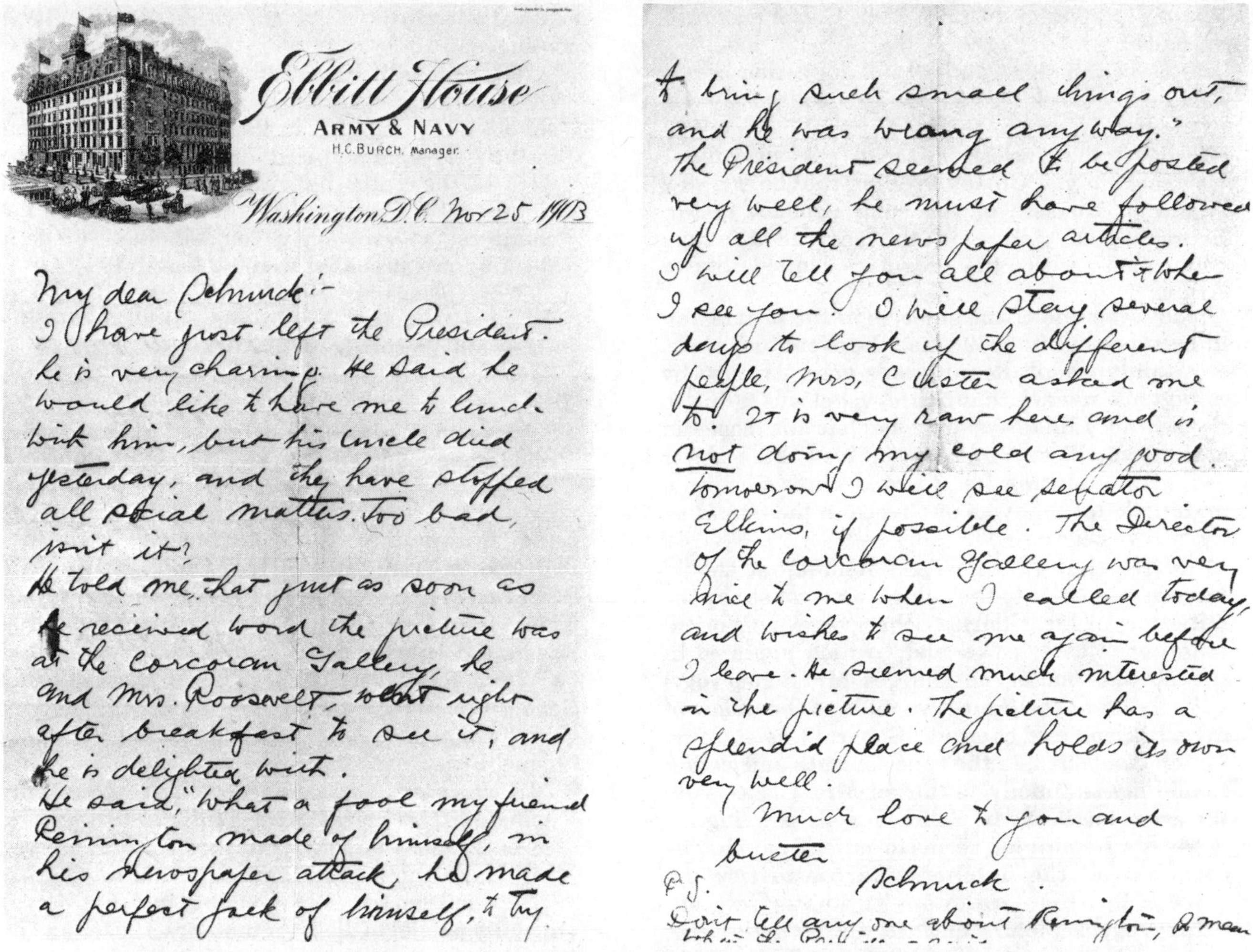

Ebbitt House
ARMY & NAVY
H.C. BURCH, Manager.

Washington D.C. Nov 25 1903

My dear Schmuck:-
I have just left the President. he is very charming. He said he would like to have me to lunch with him, but his uncle died yesterday, and they have stopped all social matters. Too bad, isn't it?
He told me that just as soon as he received word the picture was at the Corcoran Gallery, he and Mrs. Roosevelt, went right after breakfast to see it, and he is delighted with.
He said, "What a fool my friend Remington made of himself, in his newspaper attack, he made a perfect jack of himself, to try to bring such small things out, and he was wrong anyway."
The President seemed to be posted very well, he must have followed up all the newspaper articles. I will tell you all about it when I see you. I will stay several days to look up the different people, Mrs. Custer asked me to. It is very raw here, and is not doing my cold any good. Tomorrow I will see Senator Elkins, if possible. The Director of the Corcoran Gallery was very nice to me when I called today and wishes to see me again before I leave. He seemed much interested in the picture. The picture has a splendid place and holds its own very well.
Much love to you and buster
Schmuck.
P.S.
Don't tell any one about Remington, a man

CHARLES SCHREYVOGEL TO HIS WIFE. November 25, 1903. National Cowboy Hall of Fame.

principal criticism was directed toward clothing and equipment he claimed were not used in 1869 but were of a later period. Because both he and Schreyvogel were so well-known, his comments created national interest.

News reporters attempted to obtain a retort from Schreyvogel. The remark he had made two years earlier about Remington was: "He is the greatest of all." He refused to make any other statement.

Schreyvogel had received a letter Libbie had written to him from Bronxville on April 24, 1902, which began:

"I have been out of town for some time and have not seen your painting of *Custer's Demand* until today. I think the likeness excellent, the composition of the picture and harmony of color admirable. It all shows how familiar the plains and the frontier life are to you. An artist who had not lived West would have painted officers and horses as if they had only known the luxury of the East, while in those days of privation and hard riding there was no superfluous flesh on man or beast, nor was there glitter or pomp in the clothes they wore.

"Though the regulations were so strict as to uniform in garrison, on a campaign great freedom was allowed. The red necktie, buckskins and wide felt hat were the unvarying outfit of my husband on a campaign, while the troop's boots, as they were then called, were those made by the Philadelphia bootmaker who shod so many distinguished feet in our service. This freedom with regard to costume and equipment adds much to the picturesqueness of the column on the march.

"I was impressed with the fidelity of the likeness and the costume of the Indians, with whom I was familiar, especially with war bonnet and shield, for my husband had both presented to him by chiefs at that time. The whole picture is so free from sensationalism, and yet so spirited, that I want to commend your skill."[22]

Libbie had written this letter before the laudatory article had appeared in the *Herald,* and Schreyvogel had shown it to the reporters pressing him for a response to Remington's uncalled-for criticism. When it was shown to Remington just before it was published in the *Herald,* he responded with a letter to the paper charging that Schreyvogel was "going to fly to the protective folds of Mrs. Custer's skirts," then added:

"But to rob this comment of its seriousness I enclose my check for one hundred dollars payable to the *Herald,* and to be given by that paper to any charity it may select if it can get the gallant Colonel Schuyler Crosby to admit that he ever saw a pair of trousers of the color depicted in Mr. Schreyvogel's picture in the year 1869 in any connection with the regular United States Army."[23]

Crosby was one of the subjects in the picture and had been present in 1869 when the event took place. He certainly wasn't Remington's man. Angered by Remington's remark that Schreyvogel was trying to hide behind Libbie's skirts, he left his home in Charlestown, West Virginia, for New York. After viewing the painting he returned home to write a scorching letter that was published in the *Herald* on May 2d. He began:

"I regret that Mr. Frederic Remington should have drawn me into the controversy caused by the criticisms of Mr. Charles Schreyvogel's historical painting, 'Custer's Demand," which appeared in the *Herald,* but as he charges Mr. Schreyvogel with flying to the protective folds of the widow of my old friend and comrade, General Custer, I find myself compelled, in the cause of truth and justice, to add my testimony to that of Mrs. Custer as to the great merit of Mr. Schreyvogel's painting.

"As Mr. Remington seems to suffer from what he describes as the 'interminable controversy' involved by his gratuitous criticism of Mr. Schreyvogel's picture entitled *Custer's Demand,* perhaps it would be as well, so far as it lies within my power, to put him out of his pain — always presupposing that his fellow artist and Mrs. Custer's reputation and endorsement have not already done so. . . .

"Of course, if I were criticizing this picture as a work of art, I should bow to the superior knowledge and well known ability of Mr. Remington as an artist who has spent so many recent years on the plains, but I am not; I am only referring to certain facts that I know, and Mr. Remington could not, because I was present at the moment Mr. Schreyvogel depicts on canvas. . . ."

Colonel Crosby then proceeded to counter each of Remington's criticisms point by point. He pointed out that he had seen many war bonnets on the day depicted; that the leggings Remington said were not in general use until 1890 he had worn as early as 1863; that he and Tom Custer had worn light colored hats and not black ones; that the stirrup leathers were often of varying sizes and shapes. He did agree with Remington that the trousers worn on that occasion were not that shade of blue though they were blue. As to the exact shade of blue, he could not recall, as Remington couldn't enlighten him as to the exact shade since he was not there. Caustically he continued:

"Of course it must be very annoying to a conscientious artist that we were not dressed as we should have been, but in those days our uniforms in the field were not according to regulations and were of the 'catch as catch can' order, and our clothes were few and far between, and were not changed as regularly as Master Frederic Remington's probably were at that date.

"Now, please Mr. Editor, understand I have no feeling either way. I only know that Dr. Boteler once said of strawberries: — 'Doubtless God could have made a better berry, but doubtless God never did,' and so I, to be more than gracious, say of the Schreyvogel painting, doubtless Mr. Remington could have made a better picture, but doubtless he never did."

Crosby had said in his letter that he had regretted being drawn into the controversy. Remington regretted it even more. He hadn't known that Schreyvogel had obtained many of the details for his picture from Crosby. And Crosby hadn't known that Remington nurtured a hatred for Schreyvogel because he had been first to paint a painting of General Custer at an historic moment. This was quite evident in a letter Remington had written to Colonel Crosby on May 6th:

"I was sorry you were unable to run out. I am going north to see if the trout will rise to a fly — to be back about Monday and then hope to see you will make another try. I want to talk to you.

"I don't mind your 'wooling me' but I was awfully put out to discover that Mrs. Custer had an interest in that picture. If I had dreamed that I should never have said a word. I venerate the memory of Genl. Custer and wouldn't offend Mrs. C. on my life. That is why I pulled in my horse because I despise Schreyvogel.

"I have been getting ready for years to make a try of General Custer and I want to ask you some questions."[24]

Remington had been in touch with Libbie in early 1891 requesting the loan of some photographs. Libbie had been in Europe all summer and unable to comply with his request. On her return she wrote to advise him that she had been unable to get anyone to her chest in the storehouse for the pictures he wanted but wondered: "Is it too late now and was it California Joe and Charley Reynolds that you wanted?"[25]

In the early fall of 1903 the Corcoran Gallery in Washington displayed *"Custer's Demand."* There as in New York crowds gathered and studied it in humble silence. Many were veteran cavalrymen.

That November Schreyvogel was the guest of President Theodore Roosevelt. As soon as Schreyvogel got back to the Ebbitt House where he was lodging he wrote to his wife Lulu, addressing her by his pet name, "Schnuck":

"I have just left the President. He is very charming. He said he would like me to have lunch with him, but his uncle died yesterday, and they stopped all social matters. Too bad, isn't it?

"He told me that just as soon as he received word the picture was at the Corcoran Gallery, he and Mrs. Roosevelt went right after breakfast to see it, and he is delighted with it.

"He said, 'What a fool my friend Remington made of himself, in his newspaper attack; he made a perfect jack of himself, to bring such small things out, and he was wrong anyways.'

"The President seemed to be posted very well; he must have followed all of the newspaper articles. I will tell you all about it when I see you. I will stay several days to look up the different people Mrs. Custer asked me to. . . ."[26]

"P.S. Don't tell anyone about Remington, I mean what the President said."[26]

Pearson's Magazine was a slick paper publication offering articles and stories for those whose literary taste ran slightly higher than those who purchased the popular pulp magazines. In early summer of 1904 it began a series of articles by a clergyman-author Cyrus Townsend Brady. Each dealt with a western Indian engagement of Custer. The last article covered Custer's final battle. When it was announced that Brady's book, *"Indian Fights and Fighters,"* soon to be released, would contain an appendix presenting Custer's alleged disobedience of orders as discussed by various military authorities, Libbie was disturbed.

When Brady petitioned Libbie to answer his opinions by appearing in the appendix of this book, she had certain misgivings. Turning to her old friend Jacob Greene, who was now the president of the Connecticut Mutual Life Insurance Company at Hartford, Conn., she asked for his counsel, as she had done many times before. Greene never let her down.

He began by assuring her that: *"Pearson's* is not of the highest type and its articles will not control the judgment of the impartial historian of the future. Nor is Mr. Brady especially fitted in any way to discuss the questions he affects to decide. He is a professional journalist, the maker of copy that will make a sensation and so will sell well."[27]

Greene seriously questioned the propriety of appearing in the appendix. He thought she was "right in thinking that it would be just so much advertising to his (Brady's) book. He would be assuming the office of judge."

After writing to Libbie, Greene read Brady's article in *Pearson's* dealing with Custer's last battle. It was his opinion that Brady had changed nothing, that in quoting Terry's last order to Custer he had taken the life out of his opinion. He advised Libbie to let the matter rest. "The world can never know what led the General to the actual exercise of that discretion." Then he said: "My dear Libbie, I know — even by my own feeling — how much more satisfactory it would be to say something and not let this thing, weak as it is, pass in silence. . . ."[28]

Impatiently Libbie had been sitting by the sideline awaiting an opportunity to make her play. Wisely she refrained from offering any public statement for she knew there were champions on her side who were masters in the art of warfare. She might suggest or direct, but never openly participate. Greene and other fine friends had given her this sound advice. She had followed their guidance.

The side she supported could always rely upon her as a cheer leader though they hardly needed one. More useful to them was her ability as a research assistant. When questions remained unanswered she knew in which direction to turn to obtain correct answers. With champions on her side such as Greene, Godfrey, Forsyth, Miles and Fry, her first team usually won the confrontations though they did not always hold the opposition scoreless. In a sense they lined up as debating teams though there was much more at stake. It was a matter of defending Custer's honor.

Brady managed to extract considerable controversial comment from each faction, cleverly pitting them against each other. Greene, rather than allowing Libbie to expose herself to the jackals, took them on himself. Hughes, Brisbin and Woodruff with the support of Brady did their best but it was not good enough.

Greene had advised Libbie to let it pass in silence. After having read some of Brady's appendix he was stirred to action. He wrote Libbie that he had made up his mind to say something. The ground covered by the others would not be traversed by him for that would simply add to the confusion. A different approach was needed and he thought he had one. It would be better this way rather than for either Margaret or Libbie to speak.[29]

Greene let Brady know from the very beginning of his letter just which side he was firing from. He wrote:

"Let me say that General Custer was my intimate friend. . . . I know his virtues and his defects, which were the defects of his virtues. He was born a soldier, and specifically a born cavalryman. The true end of warfare was to him not only a professional theory, it was instinct. When he set out to destroy an enemy, he laid hands on him as soon as possible, and never left off. He knew the whole art of war.

"Did this man, this soldier, whose service throughout the Civil War and a long career of Frontier warfare was for 18 years unequalled for efficiency and brilliancy within the range of its opportunities and responsibilities, who never failed his commanders, who never disobeyed an order, nor disappointed an expectation, nor deceived a friend, did this man, at the last, deny his whole life history, his whole mental and moral habit, his whole character, and wilfully disobey an understood order, or fail of its right execution according to his best judgment, within the limits of his ability under the conditions of the event. . . ?[30]

"To charge disobedience is to say that he wilfully and with a wrong motive and intent did that which his own military judgment forbade; for it was his own military judgment, right or wrong, that was to govern his own actions under the terms of that order. The quality of his judgment does not touch the question of obedience. If he disobeyed that order, it was by going contrary to his own judgment. That was the only way he could disobey it. If men differ as to whether he did that, they will differ."[31]

When Libbie had read Jacob Greene's letter to Brady, she immediately wrote him a letter expressing her gratitude. He, in turn, said to her: "If it serves the purpose I shall be thankful," then mentioned that his son Humphrey had "a little bunch of three buttons tied with a string which was Nettie's (Nettie Humphrey): one the General gave her, one was from me & the other from Elliot Bates—one of his cadet buttons." Libbie had just received a visit from Agnes and Sallie Bates — both acquaintances of Colonel Greene—at her Bronxville home.[32]

Then Brady's *"Indian Fights And Fighters"* was released. When Libbie had read it she could hold in no longer. Taking her pen in hand, she addressed a letter to "The Book Review" section of the New York *Times* objecting to its review statement of the book, that "the appendix relates the account of Custer's defeat and shows that Custer himself was responsible for it by ignoring to a certain degree orders."

The book had caused her such anguish. She was fearful that the reviewers and the public would not take time to read Terry's orders "which gave my husband such latitude and trusted his judgment so entirely." Then she added, "Among the enemies of my husband none has ever made such a terrible accusation. It remains for him (Brady) to say that Gen. Custer deliberately planned disobedience."[33]

There was some consolation in a letter she received from R. W. Barkley several days after her letter in the *Times* was published. Barkley, who was an Annapolis classmate of Brady, said of him: "He is not a deep water sailor. He is not always accurate, even where his knowledge is first hand. . . . Getting down to the bottom of a thing is not Dr. Brady's forte. . . ."[34]

Brady had little concern for getting to the bottom of anything. As a promoter of his own interests he had few peers. He was not interested in the truth, only in the sale of his book. To obtain top sales he would go to any extreme. Libbie had thought the charge of "disobedience of orders" had been dropped. Generals Miles and Godfrey had seen to that. It took Reverend Brady to dig up the dead where most other preachers would be satisfied with officiating at the burial.

NOTES—CHAPTER 34

1. William VanDuzer Lawrence: *A Diary,* Poughkeepsie, 1922, pp. 21, 64-65.
2. Alice W. Rollins: *The Story of Lawrence Park,* N.Y., 1894.
3. Wing: *History of Monroe County,* pp. 157-59.
According to Wing, William V. Lawrence had been a wholesale merchant in Montreal, Canada; Burk Stone had been a wholesale merchant in Chicago; Arthur W. Wellington had been a civil engineer and editor of *Engineering News* of New York City.
4. Lawrence: *Diary,* pp. 65, 78.
5. Victor Mays: *Pathway To A Village,* Bronxville, 1904, p. 106.
6. Lawrence: *Diary,* p. 141.
7. Alexander Masterson Jr.: *Diary,* 1891-92, December 18, Bronxville Village Hall.
8. Julia M. Howe: *Reminiscences,* Bronxville, December 5, 1916, read by her before the Nondescript Club.
9. Eastchester *Citizens Bulletin,* May 28, 1909.
10. Bronxville *Review,* May 28, 1909, June 4, 1909.
11. Elizabeth B. Custer: "Where The Heart Is—A Sketch of Woman's Life on The Fronter," *Lippincott's Monthly Magazine,* January, 1900.
12. Elizabeth B. Custer: "Home Making in The American Army," *Harper's Bazaar,* September 22, 1900.
13. Elizabeth B. Custer: "The Kid," *St. Nicholas Magazine,* September, 1900.
14. John J. Burns to Libbie, from Pueblo, Colorado, April 18, 1902, EBC-CBNM.
15. Geo. D. Weston to Libbie, May 13, 1902, EBC-CBNM.
16. *Wet Mountain Tribune,* June 14, 1902.
17. *Pueblo Chieftain,* June 11, 1902; Robert L. Brown: *Ghost Towns of the Colorado Rockies,* Denver, 1968.
18. *Wet Mountain Tribune,* Silver City, Colorado, November 12, 1971.
19. Monroe County Historical Museum Library.
20. Robert Taft: *Artists And Illustrators Of The West,* N.Y., 1953, pp. 226-27.
21. James D. Horan: *The Life and Art of Charles Schreyvogel,* N.Y., 1969.
22. New York *Herald,* April 30, 1903.
23. *Ibid.*
24. Frederic Remington to Col. S. Crosby, New Rochelle, N.Y., May 6, 1903, National Cowboy Hall of Fame and Western Heritage Center.
25. Libbie to Frederick Remington, August 31, 1891, Remington Art Gallery, Ogdensburg, N.Y.
26. Charles Schreyvogel to his wife, November 25, 1903, National Cowboy Hall of Fame and Western Heritage Center.
27. Jacob Greene to Libbie, August 16, 1904, EBC-CBNM.
28. Jacob Greene to Libbie, August 18, 1904, ECB-CBNM.
29. Jacob Greene to Libbie, September 1, 1904, EBC-CBNM.
30. Jacob Greene to Cyrus T. Brady, September 1, 1904; Cyrus T. Brady: *Indian Fights and Fighters,* N.Y., 1904, p. 391.
31. *Ibid,* p. 395.
32. Jacob Greene to Libbie, September 23, 1904, EBC-CBNM.
33. New York *Times,* December 10, 1904.
34. R. W. Barkley to Libbie, December 12, 1904, EBC-CBNM.

Chapter 35
SHE NEVER SURRENDERED

The thought of a fitting monument as an enduring memorial to Autie had preyed on Libbie's mind for some time. The experience with the MacDonald statue at West Point had taught her a great deal. By biding her time and awaiting the proper moment she believed she would obtain the kind of memorial worthy of her husband.

In the summer of 1906, while resting at Onteora, she learned that the superintendent of the Military Academy Albert L. Mills would soon be leaving his post. Mills had been sympathetic to her cause and she thought he might respond to her final request. So she wrote:

"I want to ask if you will give the order before you leave to have the head and shoulders cut from the statue of my husband. I am so afraid that someone may sometime, when I am no longer here, attempt to erect the figure to another pedestal. As you have said, the bust is not so offensive as the whole figure and a place may be found for it at the Academy that my husband so dearly loved."[1]

Mills' response was pacifying:

"You need give yourself no further concern about your gallant husband's statue being erected in its original form. The head and shoulders have been cut from the statue, and as soon as an appropriate place is available the bust will be permanently placed."[2]

Libbie was content.

Success at West Point stirred Libbie to further action. She had learned that the Michigan Cavalry Brigade Association had discussed the erection of a monument upon the Capitol grounds in Lansing. In early July of 1906 she received a reply from Colonel George Briggs of Grand Rapids indicating that the Brigade Association had adopted a resolution at its annual reunion that year to ask the Legislature at its January session to erect a suitable monument to the memory of General Custer.

Briggs admitted that the "work ought to have been undertaken long ago" since the numbers were growing smaller and were unable to fight like they once could. He promised they would work for success but cautioned:

"I deem it proper to advise being prepared for disappointment. The obstacle I fear is that General Custer was not a native son of Michigan; that he never held a commission from this state. Against this we have the other fact of his having taken four Michigan regiments and made them into the most famous cavalry brigade of the war."

He suggested a personal letter to General Alger, General Kidd and General Trowbridge, expressing her wishes and asking for their cooperation.[3]

One of Monroe's leading citizens had a similar idea. Since there is no evidence that the idea had been obtained from Libbie or Colonel Briggs, some might conclude that this was a case of extrasensory perception. The Monroe citizen was nurseryman Charles E. Greening.

At the annual banquet of the M & M Club of Monroe on November 22, in response to a toast given to the Civic Improvement Association, he suggested that a worthy project would be the erection "of a monument in the memory of General George Armstrong Custer."[4]

At its regular meeting of November 26th, the M & M Club covered the subject in a general discussion led by Greening. Among those taking an active part in the discussion were Fred A. Nims who had been an aide on Custer's staff, news publisher A. B. Bragdon Jr. and State Representative Flagget Trabbic. Nims gave some interesting reminiscences after which Trabbic "pledged his heartiest support in the matter of any Bill that would be presented before the Legislature of the State for an appropriation of this kind."[5]

Carl Franke, president of the club, appointed a committee of Fred Nims, Charles Greening and Captain Irving Harrington, suggesting that they take the matter up with the City Council and the

Ladies Civic Improvement Association. A joint meeting of the committee, the City Council and the Civic Improvement Association was held in the Council chambers on the evening of January 3, 1907.

The weather was extremely bad that evening with the result that Greening was rewarded with the presence of four women. No others attended. This did not deter Greening. Long experience in committee affairs had taught him the wisdom of small committees. He outlined for the women a plan of action to approach the Legislature for an appropriation. It was his belief that a general committee should be appointed of prominent people outside the city of Monroe in order to give the project more prominence and to arouse the people of the state. This was approved.

Then, with the common cause before them, they appointed: Hon. J. C. Burrows of Kalamazoo; Hon. Wm. Alden Smith of Grand Rapids; Hon. Russell A. Alger of Detroit; Hon. James E. Townsend of Jackson; Hon. James B. Angel of Ann Arbor; Hon. Flagget Trabbic of Erie; General C. W. Harrah of Detroit; General Wm. G. McGurrin of Grand Rapids; Rt. Rev. John S. Foley of Detroit; Hon. James V. Barry of Lansing; Hon. Harry A. Conant of Monroe; Hon. Burton Parker of Monroe; John M. Bulkley of Monroe; Mayor George F. Heath, A. B. Bragdon and Rev. M. J. Crowley of Monroe.[6]

Two days before this meeting convened the Michigan Cavalry Brigade Association sent out a letter urging its members to write their representatives asking for aid and support for the Brigade Association's formal resolution presented to the Legislature "favoring the erection of an Equestrian Monument upon the Capitol Grounds at Lansing to commemorate the military services of General George A. Custer."[7]

Whether Greening was aware of this letter we are not able to determine. Had he known, it probably would not have discouraged him. Within a few days he had mailed 3,000 pamphlets throughtout the state to members of the clergy and to GAR posts in particular. Petitions were enclosed with letters urging that the recipient write directly to members of the Legislature asking their support of the Custer Monument bill introduced by the Michigan Custer Memorial Association. One copy reached the desk of President Roosevelt who replied to its sender:

"My dear Mr. Conant:

I have your letter of the 14th instant. I of course wish you all success in your efforts to erect a monument to General Custer. He has become, in a peculiar sense, the typical representative of the American regular officer who fought for the extension of our frontier, and it is eminently fitting that such a memorial as is proposed should be raised to him.

"Sincerely yours, Theodore Roosevelt."[8]

Governor Fred Warner, on receiving notice of the activity in Monroe, wrote Greening that he had no idea what the Legislature might do about the propose monument but gave as his opinion that "if the monument is erected, the proper place for it is at his (Custer's) home city, Monroe."[9]

The Monroe group saw in this the need for additional action. The Cavalry Brigade Association wielded a lot of political power and just might get the monument placed on the Capitol grounds. With this thought in mind a bill was introduced on January 22 by Senator Fred B. Kline requesting an appropriation of $40,000 for a Custer Monument in Monroe, and a commission of three be appointed by the Governor. The bill was referred to the Committee on Military Affairs.

On the evening of January 28th the Custer Memorial Committee met in the M & M Clubrooms. Charles Greening was elected secretary of the committee, an office he had been holding unofficially. Mayor Heath, who had been unable to attend previous meetings, was present. To show official community support he appointed Councilmen Charles Hoyt, Fred Strong and Dr. H. C. Orvis to act in conjuction with this committee.[10]

Greening exhibited a form letter he had been mailing which requested financial support to defray current expenses and to indicate to everyone that the people of Monroe were behind the project. As an inducement, a "Custer Portrait Souvenir" was being printed on which the name of every donor of $5.00 or more would be placed which would entitle the holder to a reserved seat at the Custer Benefit Entertainment to be given at the Opera House on February 11, 1907.

After advising that the bill Senator Kline introduced would be acted upon by the Committee of Military Affairs in two weeks, he implored the recipient of the letter to assist in doing "honor to our brave and gallant soldier-citizen, Gen. George Armstrong Custer, who gave his life for his country and rendered valuable service during the Civil War and until his death. His sacrifices, courage and services were not fully appreciated by the people while in life, and it is but fitting for us to make acknowledgment of our esteem for him by erecting a testimonial of love and respect to perpetuate his memory."[11]

On January 30th the Custer Memorial Committee reconvened in the City Clerk's office where it adopted the name "The Michigan Custer Memorial Association." Fred Nims was elected president, Mayor Heath vice-president, Charles Greening secretary and Irving Harrington treasurer. They finally resolved that "the purpose of the Association will be to take honorable means to raise funds for the erection of a monument to Gen. Geo. A. Custer in the city of Monroe."[12]

The Association met again on February 5th at which time Alderman Strong reported that the City Council had voted at its last meeting to furnish a site for the Custer Monument if the State came through with an appropriation for it.

Also discussed was the need for unity in the move to secure favorable action from the Legislature. After considerable discussion it was decided that the Association should merge its interests with the Michigan Cavalry Brigade Association on the condition that they amend their Bill (Fyfe Bill), naming $50,000 as the amount to be requested, and the monument be erected in Monroe. It was agreed that if these conditions were complied with, the Bill introduced by Senator Kline in behalf of the Association would be withdrawn.[13]

William O. Lee of Port Huron had written to Libbie informing her that the citizens of Monroe had a bill before the Legislature asking for a monument to the memory of her husband as did the Cavalry Brigade Association in another bill introduced through his committee's efforts. His bill asked that the monument be erected in Lansing.

Lee wanted her to know that the Monroe Association had asked the Brigade Association to amend its bill so that the monument would be located in Monroe in which case they would withdraw their bill and give all of their support to the Brigade's. He believed she should express her feeling on the matter: "The question arises at which point you prefer to have it located. With both bills in the field we both will fail so I favor a compromise. If possible express your views to my committee also the Monroe people."[14]

Greening wrote Libbie a similar letter though going more into the details of organization and the need to avoid friction between the two associations. He hoped she would write an expression favoring Monroe as the location for the proposed monument. Libbie responded immediately to both communications, setting forth her belief that the monument should repose in Monroe, thereby removing the last possible objection that could prevent a consolidation of efforts.

On February 16th the Monroe Association passed a resolution to the Michigan Cavalry Brigade Association for "friendly and patriotic spirit manifested in their action of amending the Fyfe Bill naming Monroe, Michigan, as the place for the erection of an equestrian statue in honor of the brave and gallant soldier, Gen. George A. Custer."[15]

A Seminary classmate of Libbie living in Albany, New York—Josephine Van Miller—wrote asking Libbie if she was aware of the proposed project to raise a monument "for our dear hero." She wanted Libbie to know that the guiding light behind the effort was that bundle of energy Charles E. Greening and thought she should write a letter of appreciation since "this man is to be credited with the success which is sure to follow. He has worked, and written, and traveled, has originated schemes for paying expenses, and has sent out 29,000 stamps."[16]

A letter followed from Greening, who had just returned from Lansing where his committee had a successful meeting with the Military Affairs Committee. He reported that the bill was moving to the Ways and Means Committee with a request for $50,000 though that sum might be cut to a certain extent. They had proposed an equestrian monument. He thought she would be interested to know that his Association had mailed out about 5,000 communications and had received petitions from almost every city in the state.[17]

While the enthusiastic Greening had the bill all but passed, Harry Conant wrote to Libbie in a more conservative vein. He thought the prospect of passage "fair" since the joint committee of the Legislature was unanimous in its approval. Then, too, he thought the President's letter to him endorsing the project aided considerably in strengthening sentiment in its favor. He thought that the enthusiastic and energetic home committee deserved great praise.[18]

Greening was delighted with the congratulatory letter he received from Libbie. He acknowledged its receipt and assured her nothing would be left undone within his committee's power to accomplish. Then he briefly outlined the course of his project from its origination when he presented the idea to the M & M Club. The thought had occurred to him while he was in the offices of the Greening Nursery in the old Morris house across the street from the Bacon-Emanuel Custer-home.

There was one more thing Libbie could do to assist them, Greening urged. Would she "communicate at once with the Hon. Charles E. Ward, Lansing, chairman of the Ways and Means Committee, and urge upon him an early and favorable consideration of the Custer Memorial Bill?"[19]

The correspondence in and out of Libbie's Bronxville home had been heavy. With the development of the Monroe plan, it was increasing. It was no burden to her now. She had prayed for a moment like this.

Most of the correspondence relating to the project she saved. One such letter came from Fred Nims in response to a letter from her. He was appreciative of her thoughtful letter and wondered: "If we are successful . . . please grant me the favor of standing by your side at its unveiling. As I grow older, I appreciated more and more his kindness to me, and his masterly ability as a leader of men."[20]

Two and a half months later he was able to write to her: "I have just been informed that the bill to appropriate $25,000 for the General's Monument has passed both houses and will be signed by the Governor. I can hardly find words to express my satisfaction."[21]

Libbie was quick to respond. She wrote commendatory letters to everyone she knew had been actively supporting the project but she did not know who had provided political assistance. William Lee advised her that their Congressman was not entitled to much consideration, that "Charles Townsend of

Jackson interested himself a little. Senators Fred B. Kline, Addison, and Burt D. Cady, Port Huron, did the best work at Lansing. Charles E. Greening of Monroe is entitled to much credit. I suggested to the Governor that he appoint him on the committee and I would be pleased to be one. . . ."[22]

An additional pleasure came in the form of a letter from the noted bandmaster John Philip Sousa. Sousa told her he was renaming Gustave Luder's "A Cavalry Charge," to "Custer's Last Charge," which he had been playing for the past twelve years.[23]

A letter from Vinnie Ream Hoxie arrived at this time. Vinnie, who had made the bust of Autie from life that Libbie viewed each time she passed her desk, had not been heard of for the past two years. Vinnie had been recuperating from a heart attack but was now back at her sculptoring. She was making a ten foot statue of Ezra Cornell for Cornell University and a heroic-size statue of Governor Kirkwood in bronze which the State of Iowa was to place in the Capitol at Washington.

Vinnie wanted to make the equestrian statue of Custer for the State of Michigan and wished Libbie would "lend her voice in the selection of her." She reminded Libbie of the bust and how she had appreciated it, then recalled, "Yes, he even worked on it himself and helped with the wide hat, the shoulder straps, necktie and all. . . . I feel that no one can produce him in bronze more carefully, more faithfully than I can. Will you write and ask them to allow me to make the statue?"[24]

Nims had learned from the newspapers that the Governor thought the members of the Monument Commission should be selected from the Michigan Cavalry Brigade. Nims was in accord with this thinking and advised Libbie accordingly. He told her that Mr. Lee, as president of the Brigade Association, had worked long and hard for the appropriation so should be one of the commissioners. And General Kidd, a colonel of the Seventh Michigan Cavalry and presently Quartermaster General of the State, would make a good one. As for himself:

"While I feel another could be found more competent, as it is your wish I would accept, and do all in my power to please you.

"I see no reason why you should not make your preferences known to the Governor, and through him thank the State for the appropriation as the work has been too general for you to specialize.

"I know that the West Point statue had been a disappointment but have never learned the circumstances."[25]

Vinnie Ream was champing at the bit. She wanted the commission to do the monument so badly she became a bit obnoxious. Vinnie had written to both Father Crowley and Governor Warner asking them to place Libbie on the Commission "as the Government had placed Mrs. Farragut on a similar commission and as Iowa had been influenced by the wife of Governor Kirkwood." She had read that mainly through Father Crowley's efforts the Custer Monument was to be erected.

Putting pressure on Libbie, she wrote:

"When your answer came to my letter — so conventional—so unsympathetic, with no kind words even, no mention of my likeness of the brave Genl. Custer, I felt sorely hurt, but I do not think I would ever importune you to be my friend or write—or ask you to write such a letter in my behalf as you wrote years ago for even if it would give me the order, I would not want even to make the statue unless you—his wife—were not anxious for me to do so. Then indeed it would be a pleasure for I feel Genl. Custer would like to have me make it, for *no other* sculptor could be inspired as I would be. . . . I felt that God intended that I should make it."[26]

Libbie had advised Governor Warner who she would like to see appointed to the Commission but her letter arrived too late. Two of the three she had suggested had been appointed.[27] Kidd got in touch with Libbie immediately, voicing his approval of Colonel George Briggs as chairman. "He is a gentleman of leisure," he wrote, "Of means, and a connoisseur of art. . . . He was with him when he came to us as 'the boy general' in June, 1863, and he was with him at Sailors Creek, Five Forks and Appomattox."[28]

The appointments were pleasing to Fred Nims. He was proud to be associated with Briggs and Kidd and told Libbie so. He wanted her to know that the City Fathers had given permission to place the monument on Loranger Square at the intersection of Washington and First streets which would provide a view of it the entire length of both streets.[29]

Libbie had understood from a remark Nims made that the other members of the Commission would listen to her every wish. Nims had suggested that she must have in her mind's eye a picture of the statue as she wanted it. He had reminded her of the $25,000 limit and suggested that she communicate with various artists as it would be of great assistance to the Commission.[30]

Libbie went right to work. She had Nims' approval to proceed in the search for a sculptor and a tacit agreement to do so with the other two members of the Commission. Elliot Bates agreed to visit the widow of General Phil Sheridan, who was living at Nonquitt, Mass., to learn what he could of her experiences with a monument that had been in the process of construction for 13 years. Mrs. Sheridan advised to "have nothing to do with the artist whoever may be selected; make no suggestions as to the statue. Tell him: 'Study the life of the General then design your statue and when I see it I'll tell you whether I like it or not'."

Mrs. Sheridan's experience revolved around J.Q.A. Ward who apparently was too old when he took on the project and had been engaged in it for 13 years. Mrs. Sheridan claimed that Ward made her husband look older than at the time of his death. Ward had begun a suit for damages at this time.[31]

Then began the long process of sifting through prospective sculptors. Libbie had forwarded Vinnie Ream's two letters to Colonel Briggs. He had suggested that she do so, and also send letters from any other applicants who might write in the future. Briggs feared that $25,000 would not give them what they wanted and that men like Daniel French and J.Q.A. Ward might ask for all of the sum for simply supplying a model.

Henry C. Beeman, the chief of Canandaigua, New York's police department had an idea. As a teenage private—he enlisted in the Union army in 1862 at the age of 15—he had served under General Custer in the 15th New York Cavalry. Though he had never met Custer while in the service he had admired him at a distance. It was not until 1866 when Custer came to Canandaigua with President Andrew Johnson's party on his famous "swing around the circle" that he had an opportunity to meet and shake hands with his former commander. It was a bad day for Beeman when he learned of Custer's death at the hands of the Indians in 1876.

Beeman's idea was to hold a reunion of Custer's comrades in Canandaigua. Though the veterans were widely scattered the idea was received with eagerness. This "First Custer Reunion" was set for August 21 and 22, 1907. Of the 21 regimental organizations serving under Custer that were invited about 300 representatives of 19 regiments attended, coming from 17 states and Canada. Libbie attended the event as the guest of honor, staying at the home of her cousin Miss H. Etta Smith of Gorham Street.

On August 21 there was a dinner at Flanagan's restaurant and a campfire at the Union School afterward. Senator John Raines of Canandaigua and Father Crowley of Monroe spoke. Appropriately, Father Crowley related incidents in Custer's boyhood.

The highlight of the reunion was the parade the next day. Governor Charles Evans Hughes was to be the guest of honor that day but was unable to attend because of the arrival of a baby son. In the parade of 2,000 were 26 regimental units and five bands. Libbie reviewed the parade at the Court House after having met with many veterans of her husband's Third Cavalry Division at the Smith residence.

Four survivors of the old Seventh Cavalry were present: John M. Ryan, Co. M, Chief of police of West Newton, Mass.; Benjamin Bech of Buffalo, N.Y., who was left with the regimental band at the mouth of the Powder River; Sergeant Thomas W. Harrison of Philadelphia, who remembered Libbie waving her handkerchief as they marched off in 1876, and John Martin who brought his trumpet and moistened many old eyes as he blew the various calls.[32]

Some plans had been made by Libbie to spend four months in India with friends. Colonel Briggs had advised her to go; the preliminary work would go slowly, allowing her to be home in time to pass judgment on the models and sketches. By mid-September she had canceled plans for the trip. Apparently her arthritis was acting up again. It had a habit of doing that whenever she made any extensive plans to travel.

By remaining at home she was able to keep in touch with members of the Commission. Colonel Briggs informed her that their first meeting was held in Grand Rapids on September 11 at which time he was elected both chairman and secretary. They had voted to serve without compensation though actual expenses such as rail fare, hotel bills, etc., would be paid for. $1,000 was set aside for expenses, leaving $24,000 for the monument. Senator Smith assured them he could obtain some old cannon to be resmelted which would save them $1,000.[33]

Maggie (Calhoun) Maughan had been invited by Libbie to give her views. Libbie had used her as a sounding board and Maggie responded in the straightforward manner good friends use. Maggie believed that the statue "should represent Autie at the age and period when *he* represented Michigan. I agree with you that the long hair should not be the extreme but simply long enough to justify the description always associated with his personal appearance."[34]

Briggs was seeking Libbie's impression as to the sort of representation she had in mind for the statue. The Commission had concluded that it should portray General Custer as he appeared while in command of the Michigan Cavalry Brigade. The men were pleased to learn that she approved of their suggestion.

Briggs cautioned her about artists: "You will certainly have many trials in listening to all the whims and suggestions of the artists whom you meet. As a rule they are a visionary set and inhabit the mountain tops. . . . What we require is a faithful representation of Gen. Custer as he appeared in actual warfare, mounted upon a splendid specimen of a horse, and where both horse and rider are alive to the important and dangerous duty in which they are engaged. . . . At any rate, before any man is awarded the contract for the work, his model of same will have to receive the approval of the Commission as well as yourself."[35]

One month later Briggs thought it well to review the results of two months work. He sent Libbie a list of 20 sculptors with a synopsis of the capabilities and accomplishments under each name, asking her to draw a blue line around each one she wished eliminated so that they could be notified accordingly.

He thought that the appropriate size of the statue at the site chosen should be one and one-third size, known as "heroic" size. "As the General was six feet, if we add a third, the figure would be eight feet. With horse of the same proportions and base of suitable size for same, the effect would be all that could be desired," he wrote.[36]

Libbie needed more time to examine the work of several New York sculptors, so she asked for it. The Commission met at Grand Rapids on November 13 to discuss her request and other matters. The members agreed that she should take all of the time necessary. She was jocularly advised by Briggs: "Back of you are three stalwart veterans who are loyal to their leader; who will follow the banner of their Joan of Arc to victory, and when her work is completed will see that no 'burning at the stake' takes place."[37]

At this point Libbie was quite sold on Solon Borglum who impressed her not only with his ability but with his generous and unselfish nature. James Fraser had impressed Briggs though he shared Libbie's feelings about Borglum. Briggs had noted Borglum's suggestion to select three or four to compete and to pay the unsuccessful of them. Briggs thought they had no funds to pay for rejected models but did believe the man they decide upon should submit a model one-third life size.[38]

Vinnie Ream would not take no for an answer. Apparently the commission had informed her that she lacked experience with equestrian monuments for which reason they were not considering her. On November 25 she wrote to them: "I have never erected an equestrian statue—neither has any other sculptor who has not received an order . . ." She told how Mrs. Custer had urged her to sell the bust of General Custer to her but her husband, Mr. Hoxie, would not allow it though he permitted her to give Libbie a copy. In conclusion she wrote: "It would pain me very much if you should give the order for Custer without being willing to examine my likeness of him, and I would not ask the least consideration if I did not present the best model."[39]

Edward C. Potter of Greenwich, Connecticut, had made a deep impression upon Libbie. His previous experience with equestrian statues, practical ideas, ability and former successes were qualities she appreciated but the final touch was his proposal to visit the site where the statue was to be placed so it could be given the best point of view. He was the only one to make such a suggestion. Briggs thought he was the right man.[40]

Several weeks later Libbie received another pleasant surprise. She was staying at the Hotel Gramatan in Bronxville when she received a letter from Gifford Pinchot. Pinchot told her he had decided to name a National Forest in Montana, not far from Custer's battlefield, after her husband. He had wanted her to know that he had made this decision prior to having received knowledge that she had written, or was about to write, to the President about naming some National Forest after the General.[1]

By this time Libbie had narrowed down the contestants to five: Edward Potter, Alexander Proctor, Henry Shrady, Solon Borglum and Henry Brush-Brown. Briggs suffered no doubts about Libbie's selections and thought there was little to gain by a search for additional sculptors. He held that no order should be placed until the artists selected should have submitted a working model of some three feet in height which would first be approved by the Commission and Libbie.

Briggs had changed his mind about the qualities that should be evident in the monument. While he once thought the plunging horse and the uplifted hand of the rider arrested attention and caught the eye, he now believed that a figure in repose possessed a dignity, and often a dramatic quality, that was not found where action was represented. He had reached a point of thinking that they would "be more sure of satisfactory results if our choice of sculptor is made from the list of older men; men who have done great things and whose reputation is a guarantee of success. The young speaker may please the fancy by his flights of oratory but the words of the older man, strong and convincing by reason of his wisdom and experience, are the ones we carry home and remember."[42]

Previously Libbie had expressed an interest in the younger sculptors. From this point on that interest seemed to have been abandoned. She had not abandoned her thoughts of a trip abroad. Briggs, knowing she had been invited by the Lawrences of Bronxville to make such a trip with them, asked her not to think of it until after the choice of a sculptor had been made and his working model approved. "You must not desert us," he wrote. "When our work so far as making choice of sculptor and approving his design, is finished, you will be able to go aboard the outgoing steamer comfortable in the knowledge that all is well."[43]

Briggs was pleased to learn that the Lawrences had postponed their trip abroad until April. He had arranged to be in New York by the end of January to meet Potter and see his model. On his return to Grand Rapids a meeting of the Commission was held on February 21 at which time the contract was awarded to Potter.[44] Briggs had arranged with his fellow commissioners to meet Potter in Monroe on March 10. The meeting was postponed until the end of the week—March 13—because of severe flood conditions in downtown Monroe. An ice jam near the mouth of the River Raisin was the malfactor. Briggs had been delighted with Libbie's suggestion of having Nevin Custer meet Potter and had invited Nevin to do so.[45]

When it was announced that Potter had been awarded the contract Libbie received several letters from contestants thanking her for the pleasure of her friendship. Another letter arrived on the stationary of the *Hotel Irma* in Cody, Wyoming, in the familiar hand of Buffalo Bill Cody in response to her letter asking for a copy of a lecture he had been making about General Custer. He informed her he couldn't send a copy of his lecture because he used no manuscript. "I just get up," he said, "and rattle it off. It's no trouble for me to talk two hours on General Custer. . . . When I hear anyone say that the General disobeyed orders I can't stand for it, and they have got to show me which they can't. For General Terry told me himself that General Custer did *not* disobey any order he gave them."[46]

On March 2, 1908, George Briggs felt inclined to present Libbie with some thoughts he had finalized regarding Potter's sketch models. He was taken with one showing the horse brought to a sudden halt. "This because it shows the General to better advantage," he wrote, "is more original and dramatic, and the horse is less conspicuous than the one with heads up. I feel that the controlling and central idea of our statue should be 'General Custer.' That which detracts from such an idea should be eliminated."[47]

Briggs, in looking at the sketch, felt the situation and the occasion in which Custer had sighted the enemy. He had pulled his horse to a temporary halt as if to plan a course of action. There was only one conclusion he could arrive at: "that in Mr. Potter, we gave the biggest man in the lot."[48]

The time had arrived for Libbie and her friends the Lawrences to leave for Europe. She sailed in an atmosphere of blessed relief, equipped with the knowledge that the major part of the task was over, the burden now in the capable hands of Edward Potter. Leaving New York on the *S.S. Oceanic* May 6, and headed for Plymouth and Cherbourg, she sat in a deck chair, a red leather covered notebook in her hand. On its cover was printed "My Ocean Voyage."

She was relaxed now and was able to view those who trod the deck as others sat nearby in groups talking or watched the flight of the ever present gulls. Opening her notebook, she wrote in it the first thought that crossed her mind: "Doctor Parkhurst says that when one goes abroad they had better leave their morals behind—morals need a rest just as one needs a rest physically." Brave words from the little widow. Hardly the advice she would give or take.[49] The very thought provoked her into writing beneath it: "when there's a widow there's a way—when there's a *will* there's a widow."

LIBBIE AS SHE APPEARED IN 1910 at the time of the dedication of the Custer Equestrian Monument in Monroe. Gus Beck photo. Custer Battlefield National Monument.

NOTES — CHAPTER 35

[1]Libbie to General Albert L. Mills, June, 1906, West Point Museum files.
[2]General Albert L. Mills to Libbie, June 20, 1906, EBC-CBNM.
[3]Colonel George G. Briggs to Libbie, July 2, 1906, author's collection. Briggs had served under Custer in the Michigan Cavalry Brigade and had been chairman of the Michigan at Gettysburg Monument Commission.
[4]Michigan Custer Memorial Association minutes, Ed Greening Collection. Hereinafter referred to as *Custer Minutes.* M & M meant Merchant & Manufacturers.
[5]*Ibid.*
[6]*Ibid.*
[7]Port Huron, Michigan, January 1, 1907, BCWC collection.
[8]President Theodore Roosevelt to Hon. H. A. Conant, American Consul, Windsor, Ontario, Canada, January 16, 1907, *Custer Minutes.*
[9]*Ibid,* January 17, 1907.
[10]*Ibid.*
[11]BCWC collection.
[12]*Custer Minutes,* January 30, 1907.
[13]*Ibid,* February 5, 1907.
[14]William O. Lee, Port Huron, Michigan, to Libbie, February 5, 1907, BCWC collection.
[15]*Custer Minutes,* February 16, 1907.
[16]Josephine Van Miller to Libbie, February 23, 1907, BCWC collection.
[17]Charles E. Greening to Libbie, March 2, 1907, BCWC collection.
[18]Harry B. Conant to Libbie, March 10, 1907, BCWC collection.
[19]Charles E. Greening to Libbie, March 20, 1907, BCWC collection.
[20]Frederic A. Nims to Libbie, March 24, 1907, BCWC collection.
[21]Frederic A. Nims to Libbie, June 19, 1907, BCWC collection.
[22]William O. Lee to Libbie, July 6, 1907, BCWC collection.
[23]John Philip Sousa to Libbie, July 11, 1907, EBC-CBNM.
[24]Vinnie Ream Hoxie, Iowa City, Iowa, to Libbie, July 12, 1907, BCWC collection.
[25]Frederic A. Nims to Libbie, July 15, 1907, BCWC collection.
[26]Vinnie Ream Hoxie to Libbie, July 25, 1907, BCWC collection.
[27]Governor Fred M. Warner to Libbie at Onteora, August 8, 1907, BCWC collection. The appointees were: Col. George G. Briggs, General James H. Kidd, and Lieutenant Frederic A. Nims.
[28]James A. Kidd to Libbie, July 26, 1907, BCWC collection.
[29]Frederic A. Nims to Libbie, July 29, 1907, BCWC collection.
[30]*Ibid.*
[31]Elliot Bates to Libbie, August 1, 1907, BCWC collection.
[32]John S. Manion: "The Day A Private Led Custer's Commands," *Little Big Horn Associates Newsletter,* Fall, 1969, pp. 1-5.
[33]George G. Briggs to Libbie, September 17, 1907, BCWC collection.
[34]Margaret Custer Maughan to Libbie, September 20, 1907, BCWC collection.
[35]George G. Briggs to Libbie, September 27, 1907, BCWC collection.
[36]George G. Briggs to Libbie, October 28, 1907, BCWC collection.
[37]George G. Briggs to Libbie, November 20, 1907, BCWC collection.
[38]Ibid.
[39]Vinnie Ream Hoxie to Commissioners Briggs, Kidd and Nims, November 25, 1907, BCWC collection.
[40]George G. Briggs to Libbie, December 2, 1907, BCWC collection.
[41]Gifford Pinchot, Washington, D.C., to Libbie, December 19, 1907, BCWC collection.
[42]George G. Briggs to Libbie, December 21, 1907, BCWC collection.
[43]*Ibid.*
[44]Frederic Nims to Libbie, February 23, 1908, BCWC collection; George Briggs to Libbie, February 24, 1908, BCWC collection.
[45]George Briggs to Libbie, March 9, 1908, BCWC collection; Monroe *Democrat,* March 13, 1908.
[46]W. F. Cody to Libbie, January 5, 1908, EBC-CBNM.
[47]George Briggs to Libbie, March 2, 1908, BCWC collection.
[48]*Ibid.*
[49]*My Ocean Voyage,* 1908, BCWC collection. In June, 1908, according to passports in the BCWC collection, Libbie visited Germany and Russia.

CHAPTER THIRTY-SIX INSPIRATION IN BRONZE

Edward Potter had a deadline. In the contractual agreement signed February 21, 1908, he had agreed to have the statue ready for dedication by October 1, 1909. The completion date agreed upon seemed ample at the time but the sculptor's ill-health following the contract signing was not anticipated. There were other problems that added to the delay. When Potter's physicians ordered complete rest that spring an extension of time had to be granted. It was agreed that May 1, 1910, would be an acceptable completion date if the sculptor could begin a full-sized model.

Originally it was planned to unveil the monument on a day commemorating a battle won by the Michigan Cavalry Brigade when led by General Custer. May 6 was the anniversary of the Wilderness; May 11 the battle of Yellow Tavern; May 28, Haw's Shop; June 11, Trevilian Station, and June 30th was the day he assumed command of the Brigade. June 4 was the day finally selected for the simple reason that it was the only day President Taft could be present.[1]

In early March, 1909, the Custer Memorial Association had been called together for a report from Fred Nims on the 34-foot high statue. He drew attention to the fact there had been no committees appointed as yet to take charge of the Custer unveiling celebration. Committees were promptly appointed.[2]

A few days later General William O. Lee appeared before a meeting of all interested parties to give some war reminiscences. He told those assembled that the Brigade Association would hold its annual meeting at the unveiling, then suggested that preparations be made to receive members by "providing halls for their meetings, and lodging for one night."[3]

It was reported that the pose selected was as Custer appeared leading the Michigan Brigade against Stuart and his cavalry at Gettsburg July 3, 1863. Potter's conception was called "Sighting The Enemy." Custer was 24 years old at the time.[4]

These were exciting times for Libbie. Her trip abroad had been restful and had supplied her with peace of mind. The great day of her life was rapidly approaching. There were decisions to be made, letters to be written, clothing to select. She planned to leave New York in the company of a dozen guests, arriving in Monroe about May 31st. She would be accompanied by Edward C. Potter, the sculptor, and by the widow of General John "Black Jack" Logan. The two widows would be the guests of honor of the women of Monroe, the Civic Improvement Association of which Mrs. William Van Miller had been the president since its organization in 1902.[5]

One sad note crept into the plans. Libbie's sister-in-law Maggie (Custer) Maugham had been ill in New York City for some time with cancer. If Libbie could have selected but one person to accompany her to the dedication it surely would have been Maggie. Maggie who had been through so much and had triumphed, had been given no hope. Physicians had suggested surgical intervention several years back so she could pass the remaining time in reasonable comfort. A steadfast fear of ether caused her to embrace Christian Science. As her condition grew worse her husband unsuccessfully tried to obtain her consent to call a physician. She preferred the Christian Science practitioner Wentworth Bryan Winslow and his nurses.

On the day she died—Tuesday, March 22, 1910—her husband and her niece Mrs. May Custer Elmer had been informed she was improving. The shock of not being with her in her dying moments so upset Mr. Maugham he did not accompany the remains to Monroe.[6]

Governor Warner had appointed a Custer Dedication Commission and instructed it to cooperate fully with the Monroe committee. In a joint meeting with the Monroe committee and officers of the Brigade Association in Detroit on April 19th a program was finalized for the Brigade Association for June 3. It was decided that the Regimental reunions would convene at 1:30 P.M., the Brigade reunion at 4 P.M. followed by the Association banquet, with campfire entertainment in the Opera House afterward.[7]

The presiding chairman, William Lee, announced that the "Red Necktie" would be the Association members' badge for the unveiling day. He then asked that the Monroe Cornet Band lead the march of the Brigade Association that June 4th. It was decided that the Association would occupy the position of honor on the right of the statue where the members would sing the song, "The Old Brigade," accompanied by the band.[8]

It was estimated there would be 400 members of the Brigade Association in Monroe for the occasion. A drive to solicit accomodations for them was under way. The Mother Superior at St. Mary Academy had promised lodging for 32 and many citizens had offered extra rooms in their homes. An unforeseen stumbling block in the drive to obtain accommodations was the great number of friends and visitors expected by the citizens.

On May 10th Fred Nims announced that the 7,500-pound statue had been shipped from the foundry and would arrive in a few days. In his report of May 31st he stated there would be 800 seats on each side of the statue and a grandstand in front of it that would accommodate 500. A means for eradicating the need for housing the veterans was the rental of 150 cots to be placed in various Monroe homes offered for that purpose.[9]

The release of the information around the country aroused considerable interest. In Monroe there were some street-corner discussions. One question was asked by many and finally raised in a local paper—Who was the first Custer Monument man? The editor thought that John M. Bulkley, Autie's old friend and deskmate at the Stebbins Academy for Boys, was the first to make the suggestion that a monument to Custer should be erected in Monroe.

Bulkley, in a letter to the editors, cleared the air. He stated that he shared the honor with Harry A. Conant and the late Hon. C. G. Johnson. He recalled that it was first discussed in July, 1876, in the Director's Room of the First National Bank of Monroe, shortly after the Battle of the Little Big Horn. It was decided to call a meeting in the Court House on Thursday evening, July 13. At this meeting a committee was formed and Lieutenant General Phil Sheridan, as "Custer's most cherished friend," was elected president. Forty-five vice presidents were named; all accepted.[10]

Subscriptions came in slowly; the country was still recovering from the severe business depression of 1873. To this was added the interference, shortly afterward, of James Gordon Bennett's drive to obtain funds for a Custer statue at West Point. The sum he raised made Monroe's effort seem small in comparison. The Monroe effort bogged down further when it appeared that Libbie favored the West Point location.

It was finally decided, with the consent of the donors, to transfer this fund to that of the New York *Herald*. When this statue was dedicated at West Point on August 30, 1879, no mention was made of the transfer of funds, of the work done to raise them or of the distinguished personnel aiding the effort. It was quite obvious that John Bulkley was disgusted with the handling of the West Point monument.[11]

One of the Detroit newspapers featured an article under Libbie's byline. At some length she treated the events that had led to the day she was awaiting. She commented about cavalry officers who, thinking they might be commemorated, fear that their likeness might be placed on a bronze horse of a kind they would never consent to ride during their lifetime. They had seen horses modeled by sculptors that looked like no horses they had ever encountered.

"There is a bronze horse in Washington," she wrote, "whose modeling is such that were his rider to return to earth he would be justified in dismounting, and even changing his branch of service to the infantry to escape further memorials of the kind.

"Gen. Sheridan, walking by this statue with a friend a short time before his death, referred pathetically to his invalidism and said: 'I have a mortal disease. After I die there may be some tribute to my memory, but, for my sake, don't let them put me on a horse like that!'"[12]

She mentioned that Potter made all of the horses for Daniel French's equestrian statues. On a visit she made to his studio to see the model of Custer he was preparing, he showed her three sketches of models about two feet high. He asked for suggestions about the General's dress. The committee had decided upon the picturesque dress Custer had adopted after his promotion to brigadier general. She mentioned this and described the uniform, then he proceeded to alter his sketches. In explanation of her husband's unusual uniform at this time she announced:

"He (Custer) made a study of a costume which, in spite of the accusation of 'foppery' from a few who only knew him as a daring boy, he wore as long as he commanded the brigade. He did not explain the purpose of his dress to his soldiers, but to one or two of his imtimate friends he said that it was deliberately planned in order that his soldiers would never fail to distinguish him in the field."[13]

Over the years Libbie had encouraged Autie's boyhood friend and seatmate, attorney John Bulkley, to write a biography of his old classmate. Though Bulkley wrote a short sketch of him in his two-volume *"History of Monroe County"* in 1913, the nearest to a biography was an article he prepared for a New York newspaper at this time. He recalled that:

"Professor Stebbins would steal from the aisle of the study hall in his felt slippers, and suddenly detect Custer, his head buried under the raised desk lid, poring over the pages of 'Ivanhoe,' 'Harry Lorrequer' or 'Charles O'Mally, the Irish Dragoon.'

"'Armstrong,' he would mildly say, 'as you seem to prefer romance to grammar, you may stay an hour after the morning session and we will have an interview on the subject—or some other!'

"Custer loved adventure and excitement; he craved it, and withall had the keenest sense of humor. . . . He loved his fellowmen, and he loved animals; of these he was always surrounded by magnificent specimens of both horses and dogs.

"The popular idea of Gen. Custer as a soldier is to some extent a misconception. . . he was not reckless. He was not regardless of human life. . . . Likewise is there a misconception of Custer's private life, the life that comparatively few shared. Nothing, perhaps, is more illustrative of the real nature of the man than his devotion to his aged mother and father. His tenderness and solicitude for their comfort and enjoyment, which was his first consideration.

"Custer had not the flight of oratory of a public speaker at all, neither was he a great conversationalist, but he was a good, clear, agreeable writer. . . . While in Detroit together entertained by K. C. Barker, then Mayor, who was a friend and admirer of the General, he opened a letter from his publishers, requesting an installment of copy for the story then running. Custer laughed and said, 'This is pretty short notice, when my authorship is done by my wife, who is far away; however, I will just write a chapter or two, if you will excuse me.' He wrote for half an hour, enclosed the MS to the magazine, and exclaimed with a laugh, 'Well, you fellows know I wrote this, anyhow.' When this particular chapter was printed, all agreed, with all deference to Mrs. Custer, it was one of the best things he had written."[14]

Bulkley went on to relate the story of Custer's last evening in Monroe. Custer spent most of it in the Bulkley home with a number of friends who had called to wish him farewell. After they had left, the two sat down to talk of events in the years past. There were no regrets. Custer's only sore spot was the unjust manner in which he had been treated by Grant while he was in Washington. Grant had believed that Custer was instrumental in the expose′ of Belknap's post tradership frauds. Even though Custer had made no severe criticisms of the President, he had made a statement that was considered by Grant to be harmful to his friend Belknap. Grant never forgave anyone who was supposed to have done Belknap an injury. Custer believed that if Grant would have understood his position more fully he would not have humiliated him. Custer had not, at the moment of his visit with Bulkley, received his most humiliating experience from Grant—his arrest and detention in Chicago the day after he left Monroe for Fort Lincoln.

Custer told Bulkley: "Never mind. It is a long lane that has no turning. I don't believe that a man ever perpetrated a rank injustice, knowingly, upon his fellow man but that he suffered for it before he died."

As if writing Custer's epitaph, Bulkley wrote:

"Brave as a lion, he fought as few men fought, but he did not for the love of it, but from a high sense of duty which always obsessed him. Fighting was his profession, his business, and he knew that through this means and by this instrumentality only, could peace be conquered."[15]

Responses to the invitations to attend the unveiling ceremony were beginning to arrive. It was disappointing to learn that the chairman of the monument commission would not be there. An injury Colonel Briggs had sustained several months earlier prevented him from traveling.[16] Edward S. Godfrey left his station at Jefferson Barracks on June 2 to stay at the Boody House in Toledo with his daughter so they would be on hand to witness the honors to his old commander.[17] Another officer of the old Seventh, John F. Weston, advised Libbie he was unable to attend because of his rheumatism, then went on to say: "You were always my friend and while the General gave me inspiration, opportunity, example and high praise, your graciousness to all the officers and the ladies did much to give the regiment a tone and reputation that made it so conspicuous and helped to shape our conduct." He regretted he could not pay his share of honors "due the gallant, generous and modest General Custer."[18]

Then Charles Greening let Libbie read a letter written to him by her old friend General Edward Whittaker of Washington. After stating his inability to attend, it read:

"You all know my admiration for his (Custer's) sterling character and the opportunity I had to witness his great coolness in battle, bravery as well as his genius for inspiring his command. . . . In the Grand Army of the Potomac, General Custer, through his magical power was able to turn the tide of battle to victory at the critical moment on the most important movements.

"If Meade had been Sheridan the war would have ended with the Gettysburg campaign. You have not forgotten the failure to support our command, when we held the Hagerstown Pike in Lee's rear. You have not forgotten Yellow Tavern, Meadow Bridge, Winchester, Cedar Creek, Waynesboro, Five Forks, Sailor's Creek and Appomattox Station and how much depended upon each success won by our young leader.

"His great success over his rivals may have caused envy and criticism which never disturbed him. His whole soul was inspired with a patriotic desire to end the rebellion with never an unkind feeling for our midguided friends of the south."[19]

He concluded by telling Greening that a bill was before the present Congress providing for a statue of General Custer in the Capitol.

Did she get married for love, a reporter asked Libbie. "There is nothing else to marry for," she replied. "Army men are proverbially poor, and the life is full of hardships, separation and danger. It was the chief reason my father, who knew military life so well, opposed my marriage to the General. Judge Talcott Wing, executor of my father, told me long years after: 'Your father looked forward and saw your fate.' "[20]

When asked if she had any future plans, now that the monument was an actuality, she answered in the affirmative. "You see, the General always felt that girls, no matter how brave they were, needed so much help and protection, and since I lived in New York, I have seen so much of the suffering of poor girls living in hall bedrooms, subsisting on tea and crackers, and going out to work. . . . It is such girls I want to help and if I should die tomorrow the money will be ready and the place picked out in Bronxville, where a house stands that will serve the purpose as a beginning. I have earned the money myself through lecturing and writing for this and I do not want it called a home, but just 'Custer's club,' and I know that no memories I could build to him would please him half as much."[21]

Another reporter, Charles D. Cameron, pressed her for any future plans of writing. She told him: "I expect to write a book about our Civil War days and if I do I shall present General Sherman's letter in which he said: 'General Custer died that homes might be built and civilization extended.' "[22]

On her arrival in Monroe June 2, Libbie went directly to the quiet home of her niece, Mrs. Clara Custer Vivian, on East Third Street.[23] That afternoon it rained heavily but it did not deter nine of her schoolmates from visiting her.

Word soon reached the veterans as to where Libbie was staying. John Burkman (Old Neutriment) was one of the first to see her the following day. A stream of visitors followed. Veterans would come to the house with wives, children and grandchildren and argue why they should be seen. Some would stand there and argue for 15 minutes offering reasons they thought would bring her out of her room.

There were frontiersmen, scouts, newspapermen, former servants. Libbie could not remember any of them. The soldier's reunion at Canandaigua, which was the only one she had ever attended, had left her unnerved for six months afterward. She had decided on this occasion not to meet them individually. She had Clara tell each of them she would see them all at the Armory that evening and at the Park Hotel the next afternoon.[24]

At the Armory that night a large crowd packed around the door. Squeezing through, she met General William O. Lee at the far end of the hall. He and Father Crowley were too excited at the banquet to eat. The veterans ate like 20-year olds.

After the meal Libbie was taken up onto the stage. The hall was packed with veterans in their red neckties, and the galleries with their families and their hosts.

General George Spaulding introduced her to the people present and after eulogizing General Custer he said: "We loved him but we adore her." There was such a burst of applause she gasped. All that from those veterans with their missing teeth, snowy or

GOVERNOR FRED M. WARNER, PRESIDENT HOWARD TAFT, MRS. CUSTER, left to right, June 4, 1910, Monroe, Michigan, at the time of the unveiling of the Custer Equestrian Monument. Everette Payette collection.

shiny heads, dim eyes and wrinkles. There was nothing wrong with their lungs. Their cheers gave her the courage to face an ordeal on the morrow she thought she could not endure.

There were speeches, recitations and music keyed to stir the emotions of this willing audience. An extremely lengthy recitation of the Battle of the Little Big Horn followed. Almost as lengthy was a song that covered distressing details of the battle.

The composer who led the orchestra had written to her for the name of the General's favorite songs, which touched her deeply. "Then You'll Remember Me"—the first piece of music Autie had given her—was sung quite beautifully by a woman. Every note went through Libbie like a stilleto.

Speech after speech followed, all dwelling on the period they were together on the Potomac, and ending in some form of eulogy for "the wife of their beloved commander." They indicated that the statue was due greatly to her writings and her vigilance in keeping before the country the laurels he had won but could not enjoy before he passed on and the disputes of his critics had subsided.

One officer in particular pleased Libbie with his humor. The tenor of the evening had been rather doleful up to his appearance. The humorous officer, who had been in the infantry, lifted the pall of gloom that prevailed by describing how desolate the country was after the cavalry had marched in advance of them. No fence rails for a fire, no pigs or chickens, and all the smoke houses empty. Libbie had heard all of this when she was with the army for the infantry officers had irately raged about it.

He laughingly referred to the crowd of veterans waiting at the door for a place at the banquet tables, saying there must be some mistake about the reportedly high record of casualties in the Michigan Cavalry Brigade or there wouldn't be as many survivors as he saw this evening.

Feeling remorseful because she had not received the veterans who thronged at her niece's door that afternoon, Libbie asked General Lee to find out if

CUSTER EQUESTRIAN MONUMENT in the intersection of the Court House (Loranger Square) square as it appeared about 1915. Gus Beck photo. Author's collection.

SENATOR WILLIAM ALDEN SMITH ORATES while Libbie, seated to the extreme left in the front row, peers into the crowd. The framed guidon is that of the 7th Michigan Volunteer Infantry, a Monroe County Civil War unit. The wreath in the same case was made of sage brush obtained from Custer Hill on the Little Big Horn. June 4, 1910. Everette Payette collection.

they would like her to receive them after the evening program was over. They responded with vigorous cheers.

Libbie was inclined to agree as to the number that survived when she went among them to greet them.

"There were legions of them" she wrote. "Their horny, rheumatic hands appealed to me so, and when at last the children came I took their soft little hands in mine. They seemed like petals of flowers. But tho' many of the veterans were unable to speak at all, swallowing the lump in their throat, wiping their eyes or choking at the first words they tried to utter, I did get many a heartfelt 'God bless you' spoken softly in my ear, and I told them how I needed such words, and it was a sincere rejoinder for the inevitable result of those who try always to go smiling through life, and put up a bluff of perpetual content, that only a few ever know that the hours one sees people and keeps up the farce of perpetaul happiness are few compared with the never ending hours when one is alone with the past. . . . "[25]

She who had traveled the world unattended for 34 years got a chuckle out of a citizen who, when he saw her vain attempt to penetrate the crowd blocking the way into the Armory, called out repeatedly in commanding tones: "Make way for Mrs. Custer! Make way for Mrs. Custer!" Libbie hated publicity or parade as all of her friends were well aware.

It was 10 o'clock before the handshaking was complete and she had crept into bed. The evening had been occupied by the company of genuine soldiers.

President Taft arrived in Monroe on June 4 at 9 A.M. Mayor Jacob Martin and Dr. H. C. Orvis received the President at the Lake Shore railroad station. From there they motored to St. Mary Academy escorted by B Troop of the Michigan Cavalry. In the auditorium of the Academy 250 girls dressed in white and holding the Stars and Stripes stood at attention. After a brief musical ceremony the party re-entered its automobiles and carriages, moving to a position across from Libbie's old home on Monroe Street,[26] there to review the veterans of the Michigan Cavalry Brigade, the Third Cavalry Division and the Seventh U.S. Cavalry, all part of Custer's old commands. The parade continued past that point to the monument two blocks away, the President following after the streets were cleared of all vehicles.

The President was seated in the grandstand between Governor Fred Warner and Mayor Martin. Charles Greening and three women from the Civic Improvement Society led by Mrs. Van Miller had called for Libbie to escort her. When Libbie arrived at the grandstand she was breathless from fright and became moreso when a tremendous cheer sprang from the huge throng assembled there.[27]

She was immediately presented to the President, who sat in the front row, and then seated on his left between Mrs. Otto Kirschner and Mrs. Van Miller, her old friend and schoolmate. Her heart sank when she saw the long line of reporters and photographers in front of her. Just before leaving New York she had seen a horrible photograph of her friend the suffragist, Dr. Mary Anna Smith. The photographers had caught her mouth open which gave the appearance of her lower jaw leaving her head. She resolved to remember the photograph and not open her mouth except carefully.

The President's comments to her made her forget her intent, and she was snapped again and again. When she saw the finished prints she realized that her dentist's gold crowns and bridgework had been given wide publicity.

The President made her happy with his comments but her fright wiped away all recollection of them. She did remember that he said he had read her books. She thanked him for honoring them but felt afterwards that she had not exactly covered herself with glory. She did remember to thank the Governor for appointing old comrades of the General to select the sculptor rather than citizens who had known him.[28]

Restoring her self-assurance and confidence was the knowledge that Nellie and William Taylor, Will and Sallie and Louise Lawrence, Burke Stone, John and Ada Bates, Will Bates and the Custer family were in sight.

She was amazed at almost everything for she had not foreseen the immensity of the event. "It was so much more of a function than I anticipated," she recalled. The main streets were a mass of color, garlands of flags and bunting made the town look, at a distance, like the gardens of a giant. Porch pillars were wound with red, white and blue bunting; flags hung from every window. Some 25,000 people had poured into the town by rail, trolley and horse-and-buggy. The courthouse square and the two streets intersecting in it were a solid mass of humanity. There were army bands, civilian bands, artillery, infantry and cavalry from nearby forts. The State militia and the Monroe Guard formed a khaki wall around the statue. To her left was the church in which she had been married, and to her right was the Court House where her father had his office in her youth.[29]

An added touch of the Old West was a wreath of sagebrush and short buffalo grass that had been brought from the battleground of the Little Big Horn and placed in a frame below the speakers' stand.

The preliminaries moved along smoothly. The absence of the Monument Commission Chairman, Colonel Briggs, was regretted. He had been on crutches for some months as a semi-invalid, the result of an accident. He had worked untiringly and managed to save $200 of the $1,000 intended for the committee's expenses. As one New Yorker said to Libbie when he heard of it: "Would any committee in this city (New York) ever come out $200 ahead of an appropriation of $1,000 for expenses? Most of the money voted by the Legislature would have been consumed in expenses and graft before the statue was ever completed."[30]

Libbie was overwhelmed with the manner in which each speaker turned to address her and speak earnestly to her. She resolved to "arise from this bench and go hence to aim to be as *near* what they evidently believe I am and what husband would *say* I was in a measure."[31]

Edward Potter was asked to speak, something he had never been asked to do before. Modestly he explained that he had faced the statue south because the face would always be in the shade if it faced north. "On the field at Gettysburg, it is usual to face a statue toward the line of the enemy, and I think it is very appropriate that the statue of Custer should face south," he said laughingly, "for whoever heard of Custer showing the tail of his horse to a Southerner."[32]

Then Mr. Kirschner had everyone arise while Libbie unveiled the monument. Her breath quickened and her pulse raced at the thought. She recalled what her husband's friend, John Bulkley, had said that morning: "Libbie, I hope the ribbon won't break as it did at West Point when the first statue of Armstrong was unveiled. The old sculptor wouldn't let anyone help him but sent for a ladder and unveiled the statue himself and there was a long and awkward wait." To add to her "calm" he said there had been an accident before they arrived at the statue site in Monroe. Someone had brushed against the controlling ribbon that had been fastened to the speakers' stand and down came the flags. The ladders used to reposition the flags had been removed just as she arrived.[33]

Standing just in front of the President, Libbie turned to him and said: "This is indeed a very anxious moment for me. It is quite an honor for me to supercede you for a short time, President Taft. I should much prefer that you should do it, Mr. President."

President Taft replied: "We are all here to pay honor to you and yours."

"Do I have to pull very hard?" she asked. "And the ribbon is yellow; the cavalry colors. I wanted it to be in the cavalry colors."[34]

Ever so gently she pulled on the ribbon with both hands. It was 10:50 A.M. As the ribbons untied, the huge flags swung apart smoothly, floating off on either side of the copper colored hero. Libbie was astonished at the ease with which it was accomplished, then alarmed, for she thought the ribbon had broken loose. Mr. Kirschner instantly assured her all was well.

A great shout arose. The bands played "The Star Spangled Banner" while the battery fired a salute of 17 guns. The moment of anxiety was over. A. B. Bragdon, Jr. gathered up the yellow ribbon and handed it to Mr. Kirchner who in turn handed it to Libbie.

The eyes of the crowd now shifted from the monument to Libbie, for they saw on her face a new expression. There was a mixture of adoration, wonderment, thoughtfulness, satisfaction and relaxation.[35]

Senator William Allen Smith gave the oration. He followed Custer's career, using various highlights to make his point that youth should use him as an example for both his patriotism and his character.

The President recounted Custer's military services especially in the West and complimented Libbie on being a conspicious example of an officer's wife.

Governor Warner presented the statue, "not to Monroe, but to the world." Mayor Martin accepted it in behalf of Monroe.

Libbie told her friends: "All of the ceremonial was so well done, so dignified, so deliberate, so earnest, and with the solemnity that should attend any memorial to the dead. . . . It was such a surprise and such a source of inexpressible gratitude to me that it was made such a function, for New York or Boston could not have done better nor could they have done more."[36]

As the ceremony drew to a close the chorus of 75 young ladies sang impressively "The Old Brigade," in honor of the veterans of the Michigan Cavalry Brigade. The veterans, obviously so by their red neckties, bowed their heads, many shedding tears as they were reminded of old comrades and old times under Custer.

The special train that was to bear President Taft and his party to Jackson moved slowly through the crowd during the last day of the program, stopping just west of the statue. Khaki-clad troops bordered a lane from the grandstand to the last car of the train through which the President walked. Slowly, the train moved out, the President standing on the observation platform waving farewell to the cheering crowd.[37]

That afternoon, after dining at the Park Hotel, Libbie attended the final reception. She soon discovered there were frauds present. Some had been "bummers" during the Civil War; others were bogus scouts and frontiersmen who made a practice of attending veterans' functions, using the opportunity to beg transportation of the committees, or to borrow.

From a distance, Libbie saw such a fake in a buckskin suit with "devices to proclaim his prowess as a hunter." He was very conspicuous in the crowd. She knew him for what he was, since a genuine scout was too modest to decorate his person as this one did.

He worked his way through the crowd toward her and addressed her familiarly as "Elizabeth" and asked if she remembered seeing him in Cheyenne. She took his hand but did not inform him or those nearby who resented his familiarity she had never seen Cheyenne.[38]

She had often thought how she would conduct herself "on the great day of my life; the very proudest day." Agnes Wellington had insisted that there be no economies or carelessness in selecting clothes. Libbie showed a greater interest in selecting a veil "that would conceal the wrinkles and gray locks from the peering eyes of the veterans who expect me to look just as I did 40 years ago."

She had managed to elude the persistent questions of these veterans as to her age. In their frankness they would say: "You ain't so young as you onct was." They remembered her as a red-cheeked girl with long, flying hair in a very long riding habit the hem of which had been loaded with shot to keep it down. Then about 118 pounds, the sleeves of her blouse having gold braid loops well above the elbow, her hat sporting a drooping red feather; quite a contrast to the clothes she wore that day.

So many of them confronted her with: "You don't remember who I am?" She would have had a phenomenal memory had she remembered anyone except those who had served on her husband's staff for all dressed in the same uniform during the war.

John Burkman had called upon her three times; John who had been the General's groom and had taken care of *Dandy*. On that day he said to her slowly, ponderously, as was his custom: "*Miss* Custer! The men detail me to come and ask a question, but you ain't to answer it unless you want to. They want to know just how old you be."[39]

NOTES—CHAPTER 36

1 *Unveiling Ceremonies*—Custer Equestrian Monument, Monroe, Michigan, June 4, 1910, p. 5.
2 *Custer Minutes,* March 6, 1909.
3 *Ibid,* March 9, 1909.
4 *Unveiling Ceremonies,* pp. 8, 21.
5 Toledo *Blade,* May 28, 1910.
6 Monroe *Democrat,* April 1, 1910. It had been said (See Monghan: *Custer Biogra-hy,* p. 409) that Libbie had disapproved of Maggie's marriage to Maugham and insisted that his name not appear on her headstone. Monaghan's source for this statement was unreliable in this regard. Libbie had sponsored the marriage. It was a Custer family custom to use only first names on the headstones in the Custer plot. Margaret's conformed and, according to the Custer family, Libbie approved.
John Maugham was vice president of the Ferguson Construction Company of New York.
7 *Custer Minutes,* April 12, 1910.
8 *Ibid,* April 19, 1910.
9 *Ibid,* May 31, 1910.
10 Monroe *Democrat,* April 29, 1910. Bulkley erred on the date the meeting having been held on Monday, July 17, 1876.
11 *Ibid.*
12 Detroit *News,* May 15, 1910.
13 *Ibid;* A clipping from a Monroe paper of unknown date revealed there were only 83 equestrian statues in the world of which Potter had erected three. General Custer's was his fourth.
14 John M. Bulkley: "As A Classmate Saw Custer," New York *Post,* May 28, 1910.
15 *Ibid.*
16 George G. Briggs to Libbie, May 30, 1910, BCWC collection.
17 E. S. Godfrey to Libbie, June 1, 1910, BCWC collection.
18 John F. Weston to Libbie, June 2, 1910, BCWC collection.
19 Edward W. Whitaker to Charles Greening, June 2, 1910, BCWC collection.
20 Detroit *Free Press,* June 3, 1910.
21 *Ibid.*
22 Hugh Winkworth (Monroe) informed me that the Vivians lived in a small house on the North side of East Third Street on the alley between Washington and Monroe Streets. Andrew Vivian managed the Lotus Dairy on East Front Street across from the Sawyer Memorial Building.
24 Elizabeth B. Custer: "Account of the Monument Unveiling," June 8, 1910. Written by Libbie for several of her friends who could not attend the ceremony. Original in author's collection. Hereinafter referred to as *Monument Account.*
25 *Ibid.*
26 Monroe *Record Commercial,* June 9, 1910.
27 *Monument Account.*
28 *Ibid.*
29 *Ibid.*
30 *Ibid.*
31 *Ibid.*
32 *Unveiling Ceremonies,* p. 26.
33 *Monument Account.*
34 Monroe *Record Commercial,* June 9, 1910.
35 *Ibid; Monument Account; Unveiling Ceremony,* p. 27.
37 *Ibid; Unveiling Ceremonies,* p. 60. By coincidence President Andrew Johnson addressed the citizens of Monroe from the rear platform of a railroad coach in 1866, within a few feet of where President Taft boarded his train for Jackson, Michigan.
38 *Monument Account.*
39 *Ibid.*

Chapter 37
PRESS AGENT FOR AUTIE

As if in a dream she arose on Sunday. The feeling of tension she had maintained for many months, years, had left her. Slowly she dressed as she recalled the events of yesterday. A feeling of satisfaction, of accomplishment, enveloped her. She had experienced this sensation before but never to this degree. She hoped it would last but knew it would not.

There were too many things to accomplish. Just the day before she had told a reporter: "I feel now, so inspired, that it will be easy to write a book which I had planned, dealing with the General's life and our experiences during the Civil War."[1] Then too, there was the Custer club for girls she had planned.

She sat down to add a few thoughts to the notes she had been making to use when she prepared a resumé of Saturday's events for several dear friends who could not be with her. What better moment to jot down a thought she would use as her concluding paragraph. So she wrote:

"I acknowledge to a relief that I can now hide again from the newspaper people, the cameras, the kodaks, the gaze of the public; but it is something to feel that the day made it well worthwhile to endure the painful subjection to publicity."[2]

It was a day to get together. There were some last farewells, then the big turkey dinner out at Nevin's place. Cousin Rebecca Richmond and her sister Mary Kendall were there. It was a day of total happiness given to humorous stories and Custer pranks.

The next day was spent in meeting old friends at the home of Miss Emily Lewis on Fifth and Washington streets. Libbie, as the guest of honor, had agreed to read a paper on "The Passion Play of Oberomergau."

Chairs were arranged in the parlors as if for a lecture. At 3 o'clock Libbie entered looking fresh and sweet in her dainty black messaline, showing no evidence of the three strenuous days she had undergone. Her only ornament was a string of pearls suspending an amethyst pendant close to the high black lace collar she wore.[3]

Mrs. Van Miller introduced Libbie to the 60 women present, then Libbie addressed them informally before she read her paper. She said she had had many things to do that kept her away from Monroe but that if her friends had kept faith in her, as she was now sure they had, she would try to do better by visiting them oftener in the future.

On the following day Miss Carrie Boyd entertained 40 former pupils of the Young Ladies Seminary in her home across from the Lewis residence, giving Libbie another opportunity of meeting her former classmates.

Oscar Sieb is uncertain as to which day following the unveiling ceremony the following incident occurred:

"I was ten years old when Mrs. Custer called at my house. I went to the door and when I saw her I said: 'I didn't mean any harm.' She said: 'I know you didn't. Do you know, I never have known of an instance where a bouquet was used on a monument in this way so I've brought you a picture of the General and a piece of the ribbon that unveiled his monument.' "

Oscar had told his father (who was a very short man) that the General looked so lonely he wanted to put some flowers in his arms. His father agreed so Oscar cut a large bouquet of pink peonies the day before the unveiling and let them soak in a pail of cold water, as his father had advised.

They drove a horse and wagon loaded with a 14 foot ladder down to the courthouse square at 4 A.M. Pulling up along side the monument and using the ladder from the wagon, Oscar crawled under the flags that draped Custer and placed the peonies in his arms. And there they were to the amazement of all when Mrs. Custer pulled the yellow ribbon and unveiled the statue.[4]

Back in Bronxville Libbie was able to relax and reflect while replying to the many letters that arrived each day. There were people to be thanked for what they had done in her behalf.

Bill Roeder, a reporter for the Monroe *Record Commercial,* was one of the first she wrote to. Thanking him and his editor, Mr. Compton, for urging her to release her picture to the press, she told him he was right in saying that some newspapers would publish something they would label as her if they had no others. She wished she had decided sooner for, to her chagrin, a picture of Mother Custer had been charged to her. She told Bill: "I hope when I do wear caps and spectacles I shall look as well as she did."[5]

In turn she wrote a letter of thanks to Mayor Martin and Governor Warner, thanking each for his part in the success of the day and presenting each with a piece of the yellow ribbon.[6]

Attracted as she was to uniforms, she had taken particular note of the khaki uniforms that had formed a frame around the monument and a brown lane through which the President had walked in safety to his car. She did not know until later that they were Monroe Spanish American War veterans commanded by Captain Irving S. Harrington. In reliving daily that delightful day, she was becoming increasingly aware of its joy and more grateful to those who had participated in its grand success. In appreciation to Captain Harrington she wrote a short letter thanking him and his men for the perfect manner in which they filled their roles.[7]

Libbie continued to work on her Civil War reminiscences. There had been some controversy as to which of two tables had been the one in which General Grant had signed the terms of capitulation at Appomattox Court House. She, in an effort to clear the air once and for all time, wrote an explanatory article for *Harper's Weekly*.[8]

With the signing of Lee's surrender at Appomattox, the war came virtually to a close. A week earlier Richmond had fallen, President Davis and his Cabinet were in full flight and General Sherman's thrust into Georgia was eminently successful.

Nineteen years later—March 16, 1884, to be exact—Grant wrote to Mrs. General Ord, whose husband paid $40 for the table at which General Lee sat, that he (Grant) had written the terms of surrender on that marble-topped table and that he and Lee had signed them on it.

Libbie, in writing of this episode, excuses Grant's inaccuracy of recall by saying he "was preoccupied, with the preparation of his momentous letter. He was not the sort of man to think much of essential details at the time. It is not surprising therefore, that he who would have seemed to be the best possible witness in the case, should have proved to be an unworthy one, and that his memory should have played him a trick so long afterward on a point which, at best, must have seemed to him unimportant, save an opportunity of doing kindness to a friend in need."

Grant had stated that he and Lee both had signed it which is of course incorrect. Each general signed a separate agreement.

Sheridan, who had purchased the small pine table from Wilmer McLean on which Grant had written the terms of surrender, had paid him 20 dollars in gold which he had carried for years in case he was captured. Sheridan promptly presented it to Libbie with a letter.[9]

Sheridan re-emphasized his observations in a paper he read before the Illinois Commandery of the Loyal Legion on February 7, 1883.

On April 15, 1895, Colonel Charles Marshall, Lee's military secretary, who was the only other Confederate officer present at the signing of the surrender, wrote to Libbie:

> "Gen. Grant is certainly mistaken in saying that the terms of the surrender were written on the marble-topped table referred to in his letter to Mrs. Ord. Gen. Grant wrote nothing on the marble-topped table next to which Gen. Lee was sitting."

Marshall had conversed both with General Orville Babcock and General Horace Porter, who were there at the time, and both remembered the details as he did.[10]

By nature Libbie was restless. In her childhood she had moved oftener than the average child. Making her home in Onondaga, Howlett Hill and Auburn, New York, then at the Boyd Seminary, all after the death of her mother, had accustomed her to moving. Her life with Autie had nurtured this to a point it had become a fixed habit. Never did she remain long in one place. Seemingly she was seeking solace for an aching heart. Constantly on the move, no place was home without her Autie, even though she carried him in her heart.

In the 25 years since her husband's death she had had no fewer than 20 different residences, not taking into account her trips abroad which now had become an annual occurrence. At one time, she maintained an apartment in New York, a large house in Bronxville and a large "cabin" in Onteora Park. She also owned a house in New York that she rented and, until 1890, had owned her birthplace home in Monroe which had been lived in by Father Custer until near that time.

She never lived alone. Gregariously she clung to the big city or its immediate environs so she could be near people. Though she sought a quiet rural atmosphere when writing during the summer, she required a companion, and ofttimes a housekeeper, to maintain her touch with society. Libbie had her fears. Perhaps one of them was solitude though she never gave any such indication in words.

A club woman by instinct, it was natural enough that she became a founding member of the Cosmopolitan Club in New York when it became housed on West 40th Street.[11] It was her habit for many years to spend each Thursday evening at the club. That she was held in high esteem by its membership was evidenced by a reception given in her honor by its Board of Governors on April 28, 1927. On that occasion, a motion picture, "The Pottery Maker," was shown. It had been made at the Metropolitan Museum of Art by Grace Olmstead

Clarke. The film was directed by Maude Adams and photographed by Robert Flaherty. Libbie played the part of "Grandma."[12]

In traveling abroad it is well to go prepared. Passport, letters of credit and letters of introduction, all were a part of Libbie's portfolio. Wisely she carried a letter from the State Department addressed to all its diplmoatic and consular officers recommending that all courtesies and assistance be extended to her.[13]

India held a fascination for her. She left London on the R.M.S. *Dunottar Castle* November 8, 1911. The Indian Empire Cruise conveyed her to Marseilles, Port Said, Suez, Bombay, Calcutta, Rangoon, Madras and back to Marseilles by January 1. While in Delhi she was admitted to the Coronation Durbar of the King-Emperor and Queen-Empress on December 12, 1911.[14]

From Rome on February 12, 1912, she wrote to John Bulkley advising him that though she would be home in March she did not feel equal to visiting Monroe on "Custer Day." Physically she felt fine, being able to outwalk and tire almost everyone near her age, but she did not think she should tax her nerves by attending such an affair. She felt inclined to do some wandering for a bit longer "among people whom I cannot venture to tax by talking of the one who is ever on my mind. I know that I have several things to do for him I love."[15] Instead of leaving Naples as planned she returned to New York via Southampton on the *S.S. Oceanic,* arriving on February 28.[16]

Prior to leaving for England in November, Libbie had written Secretary of War Henry L. Stimson at his offices in Washington asking him if the model of General Custer's equestrian monument could be suitably housed at West Point.

Twice he responded to her letter, both of his letters going astray. He finally resorted to writing to Mrs. Boudinot Keith, a friend of Libbie, advising her there was no building at West Point "of sufficient size to hold and show off a heroic size equestrian statue. I was therefore obliged to tell her that they had decided to tell her that it was impossible to accept the gift."[17]

John Bulkley had been spending a great deal of time out of his busy law practice obtaining primary source material for the two-volume history of Monroe County he was in the process of writing. On a visit to the Monroe Light Guard Armory in a search for military history, he used the opportunity to examine General Custer's relics that Libbie had loaned for display there. He was so upset by the condition of these historic items that he sent Libbie a letter advising her that he was "deeply impressed with the fact that they must at no distant day become of very little value through ignorance, neglect and inattention. The great pelt of the grizzly and the head have already disappeared having been the victim of moths and neglect, and the other trophies apparently following in its wake, from the same cause. Captain Harrington was very much chagrined that I should see these evidences of lack of appreciation and care, and I am afraid I showed my disapproval quite plainly. In my opinion these should be removed to the Capitol in Lansing and placed in the Military Museum in charge of the State."[18]

Bulkley explained that the museum was located in the Rotunda of the Capitol Building where any one of the panels would be large enough to house the General's entire collection with ample room in glass cases for all of the smaller articles "now *hidden* in the *dusty drawers* of *desks* in the *Armory* here."

Mrs. M. Ferry, in behalf of the Michigan Pioneer and Historical Society, asked the Hon. James Barry to persuade Libbie to write to the State Board of Auditors offering the Custer relics to the State Pioneer Society on the condition that they should be properly cased, catalogued and cared for in the Rotunda. She insisted that "no small local body can properly care for these exhibits. General Custer was too big a man with a national reputation to be represented in a private corporation."[19]

Libbie must have acquiesced for a letter in her collection indicated that, through lack of space in the Rotunda, "the Board finds it impossible to accept the collection. . . ."[20] She had reached another point of decision. It was obvious that the collection of relics should not remain in Monroe, and what had appeared to be a display area in Lansing retaining an element of perpetuity was but a dream. But why not another state institution that would exist for all time? Well, why not the University of Michigan? It had welcomed the specimen Custer had sent them from his Black Hills Expedition in 1874. Wasn't John Bulkley's son Harry on its Board of Regents?

She wrote to John Bulkley as to the change of sentiment in Lansing and that she first had thought of offering the relics to the Agricultural College there but thought better of it when thinking of the University of Michigan. What did he think? John agreed that the University of Michigan would be the better place. He would have Harry bring about plans for the collection to be placed there.[21] Ultimately, Libbie retained all of the collection. At a later date, a portion of it was willed to a museum to be built at the Custer Battlefield, and the balance was left to members of the Custer family.

Nevin had a matter on his mind he had decided to take up with Libbie now that the threshers had left his farm. Some Monroe citizens had written the Postmaster General in Washington proposing that a bronze tablet be placed on the new post office building that had just been completed on the site of Libbie's old home. They wanted the tablet to indicate that General Custer had lived on the site. The Postmaster General had requested a picture and a copy of the proposed inscription to inspect.

Knowing that Libbie had told him she wanted to put a tablet on the building as a memorial to Autie,

Nevin wrote to advise her of the circumstances, suggesting that she "let the City see to the Post Office affair." He knew they were progressing quietly and that Postmaster Compton would write to her regarding the kind of inscription she preferred.[22]

He had advised a man from Lansing that she would be in Monroe that fall. The man in question, Nevin informed Libbie, "was very anxious to have the relics brought to Lansing" where they would fit up a room for their display.

When Libbie received her copy of John Bulkley's *History of Monroe County, Michigan* in the spring of 1913, it had just been issued. She responded by writing Bulkley a letter of congratulations, for his comments about Autie pleased her immensely. She indicated concern for the way Monroe might feel because she had not returned to Monroe on its Custer Day last June.

Nevin had written to her once again reminding her of the urgent need to be there to commemorate Autie. He reacted as if he had not realized she had been watching and taking advantages of such opportunities for the past 35 years. She had planned a tour of India, China and Japan with three friends in September and had concluded that, even though her flat was rented while she would be traveling, she could not afford the expense of a trip to Monroe. She hoped she would not be hurting Monroe's feelings.

Libbie, who once before had written of her constant effort to memorialize Autie, now told John Bulkley:

> "I have my hands full this summer of schemes or plans to keep him (Autie) before the public. I never want to let an opportunity to go by to write and thank whoever writes an article or book, a play or a poem—or whoever paints him."[23]

A change in the plans of two of her companions, Mrs. Wild and her daughter, narrowed the sailing date to the latter part of August. Mrs. Wild was the daughter of Richard Dana, author of "Two Years Before The Mast." Libbie's fourth companion was Dr. Eleanor Kilhem, an associate in her philanthropies.[24]

About July 2nd or 3rd, 1914, while Libbie was traveling in Germany, news came of the assassination of Francis Ferdinand, heir to the Austrian throne. She was staying in a pension at Bad Manheim at the time, the hostess informing them of the shocking news at dinner.

Her party migrated to the Black Forest by automobile. At Freiberg, about July 28th, the German newspapers published an ultimatum to Serbia. Libbie's account indicated that Serbia's answer the next day "seemed very conciliatory," which made everyone think war had been averted.

On the 31st she left Freiberg for Lucerne, Switzerland. It was while on this trip that she learned the Austrians had declared war on Serbia.

At Zurich her money problems began. The discount rate was $23 in exchange for $25, only paper money being given in return.

On August 1 the streets of Lucerne were filled with people. The Swiss troops were being mobilized with the result the hotel service was disrupted. That afternoon official bulletins were issued by the Chamber of Deputies stating that Switzerland would remain neutral.

All tourists had but one thought, and that was to return home at once. The motorists seemed to have the only means of escape until gasoline was seized by the Swiss Government since all of it was imported.

On August 6 two meetings were held by all of the American visitors to discuss the unprecedented situation. Most of the banks declared they had inadequate funds to handle all of the American claims. Running paramount in the minds of everyone was the fear that little Switzerland would be swallowed up by Germany any day.

It was not until August 8 that word was received from Washington asking how many people wished to return home. The bankers met with the hotel managers that day and decided to honor only letters of credit to pay hotel bills. That helped for the moment but did not solve the question of a way out of Europe. Everyone hoped Italy would remain neutral so it would be a possible route home.

By the middle of August word was received that all funds deposited with the Secretary of the Treasury to the credit of individuals would be paid at the Swiss banks. On the following day there was a mad rush to arrange transportation home.[25]

In a diary Libbie kept at this time she mentioned, in particular, the 280,000 soldiers in little Switzerland who "seemed to spring up from the ground. No bugle calls or barracks are evident. The moment war is declared no one owns his horses, cattle, motor vehicles; everyone is subject to the grasp of the Government. . . . Then, as there is no volunteering there are no tramps in the ranks. They are all men taken from active business, from farms, from shops and factories. . . . These are columns of dignified, solemn men."

Two notations in her diary are worth repeating. On August 4—"The bulletins saying France would remain neutral have been taken down and it was called a false report. Each morning these appalling bulletins meet us. The few days seem like months, and really, it is to us as if the end of the world was coming."

August 8—"The sinking of the English ship by the explosion of a mine with 130 drowned of the passengers has grieved everyone and sent another thrill thro the excited crowd and but more of today's news regarding the Lusitania followed by an enemy's ship and the radiogram call for help."[26]

It had been quite a year for Libbie. Earlier in it she

had been to the Far East, visiting India again and spending some time in Singapore, Hong Kong and Shanghai. Now 72, she still retained her dread of publicity. Dr. Joseph K. Dixon, American Indian authority and author of *"The Vanishing Race,"* had invited her to see his exhibit of the Rodman Wanamaker Indian photographs on "Custer Day." Because of the attendant publicity she was obliged to refuse but promised Dr. Dixon she would visit the exhibit soon and bring her copy of his book for him to write in it. She thanked him for his interest in the American Indian and his understanding of them and their needs.[27]

Nevin Custer, the General's surviving brother, passed away suddenly on February 25, 1915. Nev had been shopping for some hardware in downtown Monroe when he was seized by a sudden attack of gastritis. He was taken to the home of his daughter, Mrs. Andrew Vivian, where he died a short time later. Libbie arrived in time to attend the funeral services of the 72-year-old Nevin on Saturday, February 27th. She remained in Monroe for several days and spoke to a number of small gatherings, telling of her recent experiences in war-torn Europe and of her earlier trip to India.

From all information available this was Libbie's last trip to Monroe. She had well-intentioned plans to visit her birthplace each year following the dedication of the equestrian monument but had been compelled to relinquish any such thoughts because of schemes she was promoting to perpetuate Autie's memory. Several years earlier she had to decline an invitation from John Bulkley to be present at the centennial anniversary of the Battle of the River Raisin. In response to Bulkley's lettter she had told him of the renovation and remodeling of a Bronxville property she had purchased several years before as a memorial to Autie. She planned to leave it for a home for the daughters of Army and Navy officers. She just could not leave the project for even a short trip home.[28]

She had been working, as time permitted, on her Civil War reminiscences. In a search for letters she had written while living in Washington and with the army of the Potomac she had asked her cousin Rebecca to look for any she might have retained through the years. Rebecca had found some she promised to send on.[29]

The matter of finding a suitable repository for her husband's relics continued to prey on her mind. The Michigan State Museum of Relics had solicited General William Lee to aid it in obtaining this historic material for its museum. Lee had written to Charles Greening asking about those he recalled seeing in the Monroe Armory. Greening informed him that they were now in Libbie's possession.[30]

At this time, Professor Ward W. Sullivan, head of the Department of History at the Fort Hays Kansas Normal School, wrote to her requesting permission to pursue an interesting project. It was his plan to place a copy of *"My Life On The Plains"* in "every home between the Washita and the Platte." He considered "this book the best source book of Western life, especially the Plains Indians and his relation to the frontiersman and the soldier, in existence." To place a copy in every home he planned to reprint a portion of the book, eliminating personal and incidental parts, add footnotes to explain places, terms and persons mentioned, and add two chapters, one a biography and the other on the Plains Indians.[31]

A few months later the President of the Normal School, William A. Lewis, wrote Libbie a letter informing her that the senior class had raised funds to build a memorial "on the spot where your tent stood" on "Custer's Island" where she had spent several months. He noted that the students held many picnics there. And he knew she would be interested to learn that "in two years we shall ask the State of Kansas for $100,000 for a library building and it is our purpose to name the building 'Custer Library'."[32]

Ten years later the librarian of the Kansas State Teachers College, Floyd B. Streeter, wrote Libbie reminding her that "Custer Hall," a dormitory for women, was named in her honor and that it was located about two miles from "Custer Island" where "one of the classes has erected a monument in memory of General Custer." Streeter suggested that their new Forsyth Library was available to house her manuscript collection of documents and letters written to or by General Custer. They would be, he said, "Designated as the Custer Collection and will be housed in our room for special libraries."[33] There is no explanation why the library that President Lewis had indicated earlier would be named "Custer Library" had been christened "Forsythe Library." Perhaps the politicians who appropriated the money had the final say. It certainly wasn't the way to encourage Libbie to bequeath her valuable manuscript collection. Hays, certainly, held pleasant memories for Libbie.

She did send Streeter a portrait of Autie and autographed copies of her books. He, in turn, asked for "a flag, medal or other memento of yourself or the General," and hoped she could locate the manuscripts and deposit them in their library.[34]

June 25, 1916, was the 40th anniversary of the Custer Battle. Until this year, observances of the anniversaries of the battle had been rather insignificant affairs. Interested citizens from Billings, Hardin and Sheridan met and formed a committee to lay plans for properly commemorating the occasion. General Edward S. Godfrey, one of the few surviving officers, was invited with all of the other survivors who could be located. Libbie was especially invited but declined. Instead she sent interesting material for printing in the Custer Battle Number of *"The Tepee Book"* and a letter thanking the people involved for "the thought that planned this coming memorial to our brave 7th Cavalry." In her way she reminded the reader that history could repeat itself. Pancho Villa and his followers had been making trouble along the Mexican border. Libbie noted that: "In a late newspaper report from the Mexican border, on the unpreparedness of our troops for such a difficult campaign, mention was made of my husband. It was a warning that 'if there were not more troops and better outfitting there would be another sacrifice as there was of Custer'."[35]

The Anniversary commemoration was a huge success. About 5,000 people arrived on everything from special trains to automobiles, the 300 automobiles in 1916 being news enough to make the front page. General Godfrey led a procession of mounted veterans to the memorial, there to meet a delegation of former hostile warriors led by Two Moon, a Cheyenne chief. The two solemnly shook hands and made statements of friendship. Following several speeches, three volleys were fired over the mass grave of the memorial, and a band played "Garry Owen."[36]

There was more time for charitable endeavors now that Libbie had discontinued her practice of giving readings. More time was devoted to visiting hospitals and more thought was given to the development of a home for officers' daughters at Bronxville. One of her friends, a Mrs. Stuart,[37] broke her wrist in April, 1917. Libbie, in conjunction with Mrs. Clemens, obtained an advance of $200 from the Authors Club for Mrs. Stuart so she could be sent to a sanitarium until she had fully recovered. Mrs. Stuart had a book of verse nearly ready for publication. A short stay at the sanitarium, in Libbie's opinion, would ready Mrs. Stuart for her work.

There was news that a bill had been introduced in the 65th Congress to provide for the appropriation of $50,000 for the erection of a statue to General Custer at his birthplace in New Rumley, Ohio.[38] There was news also that a tract of land near Battle Creek, Michigan, was to be named Camp Custer.

The day of dedication at Battle Creek was a rainy one. Owing to the bad weather that October 23rd it became necessary to hold the ceremonies in the auditorium of the new Battle Creek YMCA. Fred Gage of Battle Creek introduced Governor Albert E. Sleeper who paid tribute to General Custer after acknowledging the presence of Libbie. After Michigan's Senator William Alden Smith—who had been the orator at the Custer Monument dedication in Monroe in 1910—had paid tribute to Custer, Libbie was introduced to present the flag for the flag raising ceremony. "So deep was the feeling of the audience, everyone in the house arose also." Libbie was so affected by this tribute she was unable to speak, Senator Smith having to say for her that she appreciated the honor done her husband.[39]

Winter months were beginning to have some bad effects on Libbie. The time that she could resist the winter cold had passed for she was now 77. The freezing winters of Fargo and Bismarck came at a time her resistance was high and blood was warm. In 1919 she was confined to her apartment most of the winter with severe bronchitis. She missed the speeches at the Authors Club. They provided her with stimulation her gregarious nature needed.

The winter of 1920 saw her housed and confined to bed a good share of the time with a cold. She had been to Europe again for a change and rest only to come back to the task of answering 800 letters in the first six months of her return. She tried to answer those of the veterans by hand though she had mastered the use of a typewriter. Ofttimes a neuritis would afflict her right hand to the point she was forced to write with her left.[40]

Libbie's efforts to keep her husband's name before the public continued to pay off. As a press agent she had few equals. In her quiet way she could report progress at almost every turn. In April, 1920, she received notice from the Detroit Board of Education it was building a new school at the southwest corner of Midland and Linwood avenues it planned to name the General George A. Custer School.[41] In September, 1921, the $800,000 school was opened.[42]

Harry Conant continued to search for a repository for Libbie's relics and trophies. He realized that time was growing short and she had made no final determination for their placement. Governor Sleeper had told him "the State (of Michigan) would be very glad to receive these relics and place them in a safe and conspicuous place. . . ."[43] There were no details to pin the offer down.

Meanwhile, the Detroit Museum of Art had contacted her. Its director, Clyde Burroughs hoped that by the time of her fall visit to Monroe, she would decide on presenting the museum with the General's trophies of the chase.[44]

The Director of the Field Museum in Chicago had learned of the Indian relic collection and had requested Libbie to give it some consideration.[45] Apparently Libbie shipped many of Autie's trophies there, for in her files was a letter from the Director stating: "The heads are not so desirable, as they are, as you say, trophies and not of particular scientific interest." He preferred just the Indian collection.[46] On July 1, 1920, a Chicago taxidermist by the name of Louis Eppinger advised her he had ready for shipping:

1. Antelope Head
2. Antelope Head
3. Brown Bear
4. Rocky Mountain Sheep Head
5. One 14 x 14 pt. Virginia Deer Head
6. Buffalo Head[47]

By this time she had received welcome news of a Congressional Act (H.R. 11398) that had passed both houses creating "the Custer State Park Game Sanctuary in the State of South Dakota." It was not to exceed 30,000 acres of the Harney National Forest in the State of South Dakota adjoining or in the vicinity of Custer State Park.[48] This was in keeping with Autie's views on conservation.

Following the dedication of the Custer Equestrian monument in Monroe, Potter, the sculptor, had given Libbie the plaster cast from which the monument was molded. With the approach of the first World War no disposition could be made of it though the Gorham Manufacturing Company permitted Libbie to leave it in its storehouse indefinitely but at her own risk. Libbie had offered it to West Point but there was no space or facilities in which to display it.

Libbie had given a mirror to the State of Ohio for placement in the Rotunda of the Capitol. Since Michigan had the original bronze equestrian monument of General Custer, she offered the State of Ohio this plaster replica of it if it could be favorably exhibited and protected from the elements. While awaiting an answer from Ohio officials she received notification from William A. Day of the Gorham Manufacturing Co. that "owing to war activities . . . we found it necessary to move a large number of plaster models and, unfortunately, quite a number of them were ruined, and among the lot, we regret to say, was the one of Gen. Custer."[49]

Libbie couldn't get on the phone but she did get a letter out to Harry Conant informing him of the destruction of the statue. General I.R. Sherwood, Congressman from Toledo, Ohio, who had been acting as an intermediary in effecting the transfer of the statue to the State of Ohio, was contacted at once by Conant to inform him that there was no use to pursue the matter further.[50]

NOTES — CHAPTER 37

1Detroit *Journal,* June 6, 1910.
2*Monument Account.*
3Monroe *Democrat,* June 10, 1910; Carrie L. Boyd: "Elizabeth Bacon Custer," written and read by her September 17, 1938 at the unveiling of the mural painting "Romance of Monroe" in the Post Office building; Monroe *Evening News,* March 5, 1933.
4Personal communication from Oscar Sieb who is president of the Sieb Plumbing & Heating Company in Monroe.
5Libbie to William Roeder, June 27, 1910, Monroe County Historical Museum files.
6Libbie to Mayor Jacob Martin, July 18, 1910, Monroe County Historical Museum files; Governor F. M. Warner to Libbie, July 29, 1910, BCWC collection.
7Libbie to Captain Irving S. Harrington, July 20, 1910, Monroe County Historical Museum files.
8Elizabeth B. Custer: "Where Grant Wrote Peace," *Harper's Weekly,* June 24, 1911.
9Frost: *Custer Album,* pp. 61, 67; Frost: *Grant Album,* pp. 130-33.
10Eliz. B. Custer: "Where Grant Wrote Peace." Libbie bequeathed the table to the Smithsonian Institution in Washington so that "the sight of it may awaken in the youth of today a lively interest in the times when their fathers and grandfathers gave themselves so freely in the services of their country."
11Monroe *Evening News,* February 11, 1950 as told to Karl Zeisler by Marguerite Merington.
12Communication from Mrs. William H. Griggs, Archivist for the Cosmopolitan Club, June 16, 1968.
13U.S. Department of State, May 18, 1911, BCWC collection.
14Admission ticket issued to Libbie, BCWC collection.
15Libbie to John Bulkley, February 12, 1912, Charles Verhoeven collection.
16Passenger list of *S.S. Oceanic,* BCWC collection.
17H. L. Stimson to Mrs. Boudinot Keith, March 11, 1912, EBC-CBNM.
18John M. Bulkley to Libbie, June 8, 1912, EBC-CBNM.
19Mrs. M. Ferry of the Michigan Pioneer & Historical Society, to Hon. James Barry, July 3, 1912, EBC-CBNM.
20John B. Mathews, clerk, Board of Auditors, to Libbie, August 1, 1912, EBC-CBNM.
21John Bulkley to Libbie in an undated letter, #2302 in EBC-CBNM.
22Nevin J. Custer to Libbie, August 25, 1912, BCWC collection. Libbie advised the Monroe postmaster that she wanted the names of her father and mother on the tablet and suggested that it read:

1845
On this site lived
Judge Daniel Stanton Bacon
and his wife
Eleanor Sophia Page
1864
Major General
George Armstrong Custer
and his wife
Elizabeth Clift Bacon

Several of Libbie's friends did not think the inscription clear enough. The bronze tablet, now on the south wall of the post office foyer, reads:

**This Building
Is Erected On The
Old Homestead Of
Major General
George A. Custer
Monroe's Tribute To Her Brave Son**

23Libbie to John Bulkley, April 15, 1913, Charles Verhoeven collection.
24*Ibid,* May 25, 1913.
25Manuscript written by Libbie in 1914, BCWC collection.
26Elizabeth B. Custer Diary, Lucerne, Switzerland, 1914, BCWC collection.

It is interesting to note the following discrepancies on Libbie's passports in the BCWC collection:

1. Passport to Egypt—Turkey, September 24, 1903.

Age—62 (she was 61)	Height—5 feet 4 inches
Hair—grey and brown	Face—oval
Eyes—grey	Chin—oval
Mouth—medium	Nose—normal Forehead—normal

2. Passport to Berlin and Russia, June 30, 1908.

Age—66	Height—5 feet six inches
Hair—grey	Eyes—Blue-grey

3. Passport at Zurich, Switzerland, August 18, 1914.

Age—71	Height—5 feet 5 inches
Hair—grey	Complexion—blond
Eyes—grey	Chin—firm with a rise

27Libbie to Dr. J. K. Dixon, November 14, 1914, Lisle Reedstrom collection.
28Libbie to John Bulkley, May 28, 1912, letter in Charles Verhoeven collection.
29Rebecca Richmond to Libbie, September 19, 1915, BCWC collection.
30W. O. Lee to Libbie, December 10, 1915, EBC-CBNM.
31W. W. Sullivan to Libbie, December 4, 1915, BCWC collection.
32William A. Lewis to Libbie, April 28, 1916, BCWC collection.
33Floyd B. Streeter to Libbie, September 14, 1926, BCWC collection.
34F. B. Streeter to Libbie, September 20, 1927, BCWC collection; D. L. Wooster: "Fort Hays State College—An Historical Story," Hays, 1961, pp. 75-76.
35Libbie to Mr. H. H. Thompson, *The Teepee Book,* June, 1916, p. 23.
36Don Rickey Jr.: *History of Custer Battlefield,* Washington, 1967, pp. 77-78.
37Libbie to Rossiter, April 12, 13, 1917, New York Public Library. Mrs. Stuart is presumed to be Ruth McEnery Stuart.
38H. R. Bill No. 4006, 65th Cong., 1st Sess., May 1, 1917, introduced by Representative David A. Hollingsworth of Ohio.
39Camp Custer *Bulletin,* October 25, 1917.
40Libbie to W. W. Shilling, July 5, 1919; Libbie to friend Ernest, March 20, 1920, New York Public Library.
41Mr. H. L. Reeves to Libbie, April 22, 1920, EBC-CBNM.
42Detroit Board of Education.
43Governor Albert E. Sleeper to Harry Conant, August 14, 1919, EBC-CBNM.
44Clyde Burroughs to Libbie, September 5, 1919, EBC-CBNM.
45Letter from Chicago Field Museum of Natural History, May 14, 1920, EBC-CBNM.
46*Ibid,* July 7, 1920, EBC-CBNM.
47Louis Eppinger, taxidermist, to Libbie, July 1, 1920, EBC-CBNM.
48H.R. Bill No. 11398, 66th Congress, approved, June 5, 1920.
49Gorham Mfg. Co. to Libbie, August 13, 1919, EBC-CBNM.
50Harry Conant to Libbie, August 20, 1919, EBC-CBNM.

Chapter Thirty-Eight
FIFTY YEARS OF DEFENSE

The efforts of concentration and hard labor were paying off. A group of Hardin, Montana, citizens were laying plans to commemorate the forty-fifth anniversary of the Custer Battle on June 25, 1921. Cooperating in the planning were members of the Crow Indian Agency and several residents of Billings.

The program would open that day with a sham battle at the Custer Battlefield between members of the Hardin American Legion Post and 500 Indians from the Crow reservation. Three roundups were planned to run concurrently starting at 2 o'clock at Hardin, at the Crow Agency and on the Fort Custer branch.[1]

Libbie was delighted with the thoughtfulness and gratitude of the Hardin townfolk in their plan to erect a monument to General Custer in their city park and dedicate it on that day. Learning that the Hardin Library had established a permanent display case of items relating to the Custer Battle, she wrote to the librarian, Miss E. Fearis, that she was sending the General's bucksins "that he wore in the campaigns in Montana and Dakota," and added that she would be glad to pay for a pine box with a glass front to protect the suit.[2] Nothing had been done to the buckskins to remove the evidence of the hard riding they encountered on the western plains.

Consistent with her desire to avoid any public appearances, Libbie refused the invitation to attend the ceremonies. Behind her rejection was the fear of renewing the agony she had suffered 45 years earlier. Seeing the hillside where Autie had perished would tear open the old wound.

Though she would not be there for the dedication of the Custer monument in Hardin, there was no reason why she couldn't send a representative. A letter to her cousin John Bronson Case of Kansas City settled that. Case, who had gone to Kansas to visit the Custers in 1870, stayed to become a businessman in Abilene, later becoming president of the Farmers Loan & Trust Company of Kansas City.[3]

General Godfrey's article published in *Century Magazine* in 1892 had made a deep impression on Libbie as it had on countless others. Anxious that Godfrey's eyewitness account reach the hands of those who would be witnessing the anniversary proceedings, she contacted the Century Company and arranged to have 1,000 copies printed in soft covers.[4]

In its original form the booklet was planned to contain an article Libbie thought had been written by General W. S. Edgerly. Edgerly too, had been a participant in the battle, serving with Godfrey in Reno's attachment.

Libbie had written to John Burkman's mentor in Billings, Mr. I. D. O'Donnell, that she was glad he was on the list of those making June 25th a success. She informed him of the printing of the booklet containing Godfrey's article and that Godfrey "had added to it from time to time, after seeing the Indians who took part in the fight and talking with them. . . . Gen. W. S. Edgerly's article will be a part of the pamphlet and I am adding General Custer's record from the Appleton Encyclopedia."[5]

The pamphlet Libbie referred to became a booklet of 38 pages. It contained Custer's record, and a single page preface by Libbie. It contained no article by Edgerly. There was an obvious mixup in determining who had written the article purported to have been written by Edgerly. When Edgerly got the proofs of the article from Century—Edgerly was in the Hot Springs Hospital at the time—he advised Godfrey he was not the author. Godfrey asked for a copy of the article since it included some data and arguments he would like "to use in refuting the disobedience of orders."[6]

On the day before the ceremony 1,000 copies of the booklet arrived in Hardin. They were placed on sale for one dollar, 55 cents of which went to Libbie to defray the expense of publishing.

The preface Libbie had written indicated that she had published Godfrey's authoritative account so that "the people of the Northwest, particularly those who will assemble at Hardin, Montana . . . could become fully and accurately informed as to the *facts* of the campaign and the battle." Her other purpose, so she indicated, was her "wish to set at rest some of the fictions that were broadcast by the enemies of General Custer, or by friends of General Terry, who thought the latter needed protection from blame or censure."[7]

Godfrey had first presented his account in the form of a paper at the Lyceum at West Point in 1879. He had revisited the battlefield afterward and interviewed Chief Gall and Mrs. Spotted Horn Bull and her husband, with a map of the field before them. Still later he visited the field with Gall, going over the story once more. For the more than 30 years following its publication in *Century Magazine*—in January, 1892—it had received acclaim by those who had served with Godfrey in that campaign as an authoritative and truthful account that showed no prejudice.

As an afterthought Libbie had printed a short introduction that was attached to the inside of a very limited number of the booklets. She stated, in part:

"The lesson of the tragedy of the battle of the Little Big Horn in Montana, 1876, was one to arouse the public to insist upon our Government sending out in 1877 (what proved to be the last Indian campaign) fully equipped to combat the foe on what was then our western frontier. In this campaign, following the battle of the Little Big Horn, there was a sufficient number of troops to meet the enemy, there were modern arms and light artillery in place of the antiquated short-range guns that fouled often after the first firing; these were modern rifles such as the Indians had received heretofore as gifts from the Government."[8]

Custer's Last Stand was re-enacted on the morning of June 25th before approximately 5,000 people. Three of Custer's scouts, Curley, White-Man-Runs-Him and Hairy Moccasin, members of the Crow Agency Post of the American Legion, and many Indian warriors took part in the sham battle. More than 1,200 warriors took part in the scenes captured by the Pathe Film cameramen.[9]

Governor Joseph M. Dixon gave the principal address at the unveiling of the Custer monument at Hardin, the ceremony beginning at 5 P.M.

Among the notables present were the cowboy artist Charlie Russell, photographer D. F. Barry, Seventh Cavalry veterans W. C. Slaper, Daniel J. Newell, Theodore Goldin, Gharles Chesterwood, L. A. Moore, W. E. Lewis, A. C. Rallya, Colonel Fitzhugh Lee, commander of the Seventh Cavalry, Peter Thompson, J. M. Snipes, John Myers, Russell White Bear, General E. S. Godfrey and former mayor Jacob Martin of Monroe.[10]

Speaking for his cousin Libbie at the monument unveiling, Mr. Case indicated that she displayed a deep interest in the observance but had never visited the battlefield and had always refused to do so. Of her he said, "No woman is her peer in American History."[11]

The granite monument that was unveiled in Hardin's City Park had a bronze tablet on one side bearing Custer's military record; on the other side was a bronze medallion displaying his likeness The parksite is at the intersection of Custer Avenue and the Custer Battlefield Highway which originates at Omaha and continues on to Glacier National Park.[12]

When John Case got back to Kansas City, "home from witnessing the most imposing spectacle in America," the press asked him if there were any survivors to the battle. "Not a man was left, history says, although Rain-in-the-Face contends one trooper raced through the lines to safety. Frank Finkel of Dayton, Washington, says he is that man. But Finkel is a fake," Case asserted.[13]

While Hardin was eulogizing General Custer, Monroe was doing its bit to further Libbie's wishes. For quite some time she had thought that future generations might not be as familiar with her husband's accomplishments as his contemporaries were. The monument at Hardin had a bronze plate attached that was inscribed with his record. Why not place a similar one on the equestrian monument in Monroe?

Her offer to the Mayor and City Council to provide one was accepted. Mayor C. B. Southworth arranged for its unveiling on the same day the monument in Hardin was unveiled. Judge Jesse H. Root and the Hon. Burton Parker were the speakers, for no politician would let this opportunity go by. With the assistance of the Girl Scouts, the Boy Scouts, the Joseph R. Smith Post of the G.A.R. and the Monroe Band, the event was properly celebrated.[14]

On the doctor's orders Libbie migrated to Daytona Beach for the winter of 1922. He didn't want her exposed to another severe northern winter after having observed her lengthy convalescence from the bronchitis of the previous one. Before going she made certain that a pair of General Custer's cavalry boots were forwarded to the Kansas Historical Society.[16]. Though she had a kindly feeling for Kansas it is probable that her cousin, Mary Richmond Kendall, living in Topeka, influenced her to part with such a valued possession.

In searching for the boots she came upon a coat Autie had captured from his friend General Rosser during the Civil War. Now realizing more than ever before the historical value of and sentimental attachment to such items, she wrote to General K. M. Van Zandt, commanding the Society of the Confederate Army, asking for the correct address of the Virginia Historical Society. She explained that she wished to give the coat for its museum along with an explanatory letter telling of the unbroken friendship that existed between these two West Pointers during all their encounters as cavalrymen in the Shenandoah Valley in 1863 and 1864.[16]

In May while in New York she received an invitation from the president of the Bacon Society of America to attend an organization meeting at the National Arts Club on May 15th. The main purpose of the meeting was to determine whether it should carry on as an incorporated or unincorporated society. Libbie took no active role but did pay her annual dues of $5.[17]

That fall Libbie made a realistic decision. To her friend of the frontier days, Mrs. Frank Gibson, she confessed that she had made a new will. She had determined there would not be enough money left to build and equip a home for army girls. "I have left what I have for scholarships," she wrote, "and preparatory courses at Vassar College for daughters of officers."[18] This would satisfy Autie but did not entirely satisfy Libbie.

A new movie—"The Covered Wagon"—was stirring the country. Libbie had seen it and it had stirred her imagination. She had been impressed with the wonderful collection of frontier relics used in it. It entered her mind that if there were so many relics in a movie there must be enough left in the West and among the families of the officers who served on the plains to put into some simple, inexpensive building near a military museum that the Government might erect on the battlefield.[19] The thought could rest for the moment. She was following the birds south to escape the ravages of another attack of bronchitis. There would be time enough to round out a plan.

Another uncertainty had been settled. She had long wanted to own an apartment "but the drawbacks seemed to outnumber the advantages." Since the obstacles had been conquered, and the drawbacks could be met, she had purchased an apartment on Park Ave. near 38th Street (71 Park Avenue). As she related to Kate Gibson (Mrs. Frank Gibson): "It is not much more than a hole in the ground. It is so near the club I can count on my dinners if the hoity-toity maids of today march off. I'll have to *rent* winters if I must go South to escape bronchitis, but I am used to that."[20]

Trouble had brewed to a boil back in Monroe. One of the local gentry, more than politely inebriated, had claimed the center of the intersection at the Courthouse Square. He had made the claim while driving his new car. An equestrian blocked his way and there was a collision. Whether the street lighting momentarily dimmed or the horseman failed to respond to the driver's frantic horn is not known. Once sober the uninjured driver was embarrassed to learn that the equestrian was mounted on a bronze horse. The equestrian was General Custer.

When the City Commission learned of the accident an assessment was made of the damages to the monument. The damages were negligible. Some citizens thought the monument was a traffic hazard. Others thought the foundation was weakening from the passage of the weekly freight deliveries on the track some 100 feet away. An element in the community long jealous of the German boy who towered over them historically, and as a bronze actuality as they passed by him to their various places of business each day, took it from there. The sight of him had irked their English blood. They had a natural champion in a position of some consequence in the being of Welsh-born State Representative Dr. Denias D. Dawe.

Pressure was brought to bear upon the City Commission. On March 19, 1923, a resolution was passed by that body to authorized the mayor to appoint a committee to request the State of Michigan to make the necessary repairs on the Custer Monument. Mr. Charles Greening was made chairman of the committee.[21]

The committee under Greening acted promptly but something new was added to the request, for on June 9th Dr. Dawe announced that the State had appropriated $3,000 "for repairs *and removal*" (italics mine). Governor Alex J. Groesbeck had appointed a commission vested with the authority to remove the monument. The City Commission, predominantly German, seemed to have been led by an English halter or nose ring and voted unanimously for a resolution to move the Custer monument to Riverside Park (now called Soldiers and Sailors Park.[22]

In a crash effort to ram the program through, the City Commission awarded a contract to Lloyd Brothers of Toledo to move the monument to Riverside Park for $2,700. Mayor Gilmore passed a resolution to have it placed in the park at the foot of Navarre Street, since it was the Governor's request that the State's monument be placed in a park.[23]

Then all hell broke loose. Letters of wrath poured in from every part of the county. The City Commission, apparently thinking some positive action on its part might mollify some of the complainants met, on the day after its regular meeting in which it had taken the drastic action to move the monument, and passed a resolution to change the name of Riverside Park to Soldiers and Sailors Memorial Park.[24] This action, so obviously political, did nothing but stir the anger of irate citizens. It did, as planned, obtain the support of Spanish American and World War I veterans who had been requesting a memorial to their comrades.[25]

The real reaction was just around the corner. Libbie had been informed of this effort by her old friend Kate Landon Dansard. Kate stated her preference of location and that of many others as being the center of town in one of the public squares. It was her belief that "selfish motives on the part of one who is part owner of property at the corner of Monroe Street and Elm Avenue accounts for, or is responsible for, the suggestion to have the statue placed there."[26] In any event, the location was changed to that of the park, as the Governor had directed that it be located in one.

It did not take Libbie long to act. She directed her telegram to the strongest influence in the county, The Monroe *Evening News,* indicating that she had regretfully learned of the proposed removal of the Statue from its "present excellent location to the river bank," and that she "shall feel very great regret if the change is made."[27]

The *Evening News* was quick to size up the situation. Reporters were ordered out to interview principal citizens. Jacob Martin, Mayor at the time of the dedication, wished they would "leave it where it is or move it approximately 25 feet south. They might as well move it to the lighthouse as to place it in the park on East Front Street."

William F. Haas, president of the Exchange Club, favored the Courthouse Square. Boyez Dansard, president of the Dansard State Bank, agreed that the Square was the place, "where it can be seen." A former City Commissioner, Sidney N. Eaton, was convinced that "the proper place for it is either the Park adjoining the Park Hotel or in the one adjoining the Presbyterian Church."

The oldest Monroe citizen was Thurlow Strong, age 92. When asked, he said, "I favor the park on the east side of Washington Street."

To be different, Circuit Court Commissioner C. J. McCormick favored Soldiers and Sailors Park. Shoe merchant John Erfurt thought the park would be a nice place for it if the park was beautified. Dr. James Humphrey, who was a captain of the Ambulance Company of the Michigan State Guard, favored the Soldiers and Sailors Park, "it being historical ground."

When the president of the First National Bank, William G. Guttman, was interviewed, he said: "The park on East Front Street is alright, but the proper place for it would be the post office site if the Government would allow it."

Ed. G. Lauer, dry goods merchant, advised the city to "put it where it will be seen by visitors to our city. The Park on East Front Street is too far away." Yet County Clerk William C. Cron believed that "if Soldiers and Sailors Park is beautiful and East Front Street is paved, this would be a desirable place."

Former Mayor C. B. Southworth, who was the proprietor of the Park Hotel, advised, "Leave it where it is." Postmaster Sidney Younglove said: "Place it in the park adjoining the Park Hotel where it will be seen." An undertaker, F. H. Humphrey, responded: "It should be placed on one of the public squares; either the Park Hotel side or the church side." Col. Ira J. Humphrey said he favored the park adjoining the Park Hotel. Attorney George Wright concluded that "the monument should be removed from the street. I favor Soldiers and Sailors Park."[28]

This was just getting too far out of hand for the womenfolk. They had labored long and hard for civic improvements and the monument was one of them. Had it not been for the women, Monroe would still have been pasturing cows on the Courthouse Square and the streets would have remained unpaved. Aroused by the disregard for Libbie's entreaty and enraged because of the total absence of interviews of members of their sex, they requested a voice in the matter.

On June 18th the *Evening News* gave the distaff views. Mrs. George M. Landon voiced the opinion of many when she said: "In deference to the wishes of Mrs. Custer and to many citizens it should retain a central and prominent position. . . ." Mrs. John M. Bulkley added her voice in protest. "In honor to Gen. Custer," she stated, "it ought to occupy a prominent place in the heart of the city."

Mrs. James G. Little offered logic few men could compete with when she remarked:

> "Scores of women in our city and surrounding country wish to join in a plea not to remove the Custer Monument from the center of our city. The suggestion that the foundation has been injured by the jarring of the railroad hardly seems reasonable as the residence of Mrs. Hogarth and Mrs. Phinney have stood nearly 100 years without injury. The resident of Mrs. George Armitage, very near the track, has stood 80 years or more in perfect order."

She advised that the monument could be moved a number of feet southward and the curb set back.

Mary G. Little wondered why a new foundation could not be build just south of the present one, while Lulu Weiss, Carrie Boyd and Mrs. K. G. Bumpus favored leaving the monument alone.

The lone male voice that accompanied these women on the warpath was that of the Hon. Harry Conant who let it be known he believed that the wishes of Mrs. Custer in this matter should be respected.[29] They hardly would argue with him about that.

Shortly afterward, Samuel Duvall, who was the local contractor for Lloyd Brothers, received a telegram from them to stop all work of the removal of the monument. The monument committee was quite puzzled by this action and could only conclude that the protest of the women was the cause of the order.[30]

Then on June 22, Chairman Greening received the notification from Governor Groesbeck: "I personally feel that if Mrs. Custer objects to the removal of the monument to the site selected by the committee, her wishes ought to be considered." It was thought that the monument might be moved to Lansing.[31]

At a meeting of the committee the next day, Greening strongly opposed moving the monument, saying he had received many letters, telephone calls, telegrams and petitions asking that it remain where it is. Mayor James Gilmore said he received many calls from Monroe citizens endorsing the removal. He said the Spanish and World War veterans endorsed the removal. Dr. Dawe in a motion proposed that the previous action of the City Commission be sustained. The monument committee voted four to two to move the monument to Soldiers and Sailors Park as originally planned. Judge Jesse Root, Capt. William Luft, Dr. Dawe and Mayor James Gilmore approved. Charles Greening and Col. Burton Parker opposed, with Capt. Oliver Golden and General William O. Lee not being present.[32]

It was a strange conclusion to very strong community opposition. There was Representative Denias Dawe opposing the wish of the Governor of the state in which he served in its Legislature. Acting as the ringleader and fomenter in this action that obviously was contrary to the wishes of the leaders of the community, he appears, at this distance and time, to be regardless of the wishes of the electors. The Walesborn Dawe was a man of strong feelings, quite determined in his ways.

On July 5th, the monument was loaded on a truck and taken to Soldiers and Sailors Park, a large crowd assembling to observe its removal. And on July 31, 1923, there was a public announcement that the monument was in place. There was no ceremony of any kind.[33]

In an effort to pacify the irate citizens, City Commissioner Marx, on August 13, offered a resolution requesting Congressman Earl C. Michener to use his best endeavors in procuring "such cannon or other articles of armament . . . for the appropriate architectural arrangement of the Park." It was passed. Michener — a canny politician — was unable to obtain the requested articles.

Libbie lost all faith in Monroe. Though she kept in constant touch with her friends and relatives in Monroe, she never returned.

In December of 1923, Libbie made a trip to Washington with a purpose. She had given considerable thought to a modest museum at the Custer Battlefield so she had some plans drawn of a mission or pueblo-type structure to house Indian Wars exhibits. On a visit to Senator Walsh of Montana she learned that he had introduced a bill that would provide $15,000 for a building at the Custer Battlefield National Cemetery "for use as an office for the custodian and for the convenience and comfort of the public."[34]

This comfort station was not quite what Libbie had planned, nor did it satisfy General Nelson Miles. Miles addressed a letter to the senators and various members of Congress on December 19, recommending that a museum building be constructed at the Custer Battlefield and that $40,000 be appropriated.[35] The Walsh effort died presumably because Libbie was dissatisfied with his plans. Several other efforts to obtain a museum on the battlefield followed as the years passed but none were successful until a drive led by Major Edward S. Luce saw fruition in a museum dedication there in 1952.[36]

Things were going a bit smoother for Libbie now that she was settled in the cooperative apartment she had purchased. She would have placed her business affairs in the hands of her closest kin, cousin Bronson Case, but Kansas City was too distant to make this a practical arrangement. The feasible solution was to place her affairs in the hands of a trust company. This she did.

It was her custom each Thursday after lunch to have her maid, Margaret Flood, escort her to the Cosmopolitan Club on East 40th Street. Margaret would then call for her at half-past nine and see her to her apartment.

Margaret Flood had been Libbie's devoted maid for some years. Margaret's husband Patrick lived there too, having continued his work as a truck driver after he had served in World War I. Libbie referred to him as "our permanent guest."[37]

Though Libbie lived in comfortable seclusion her old friends called on her frequently. Ever before her was the thought of "keeping her hero's sword untarnished, his shield burnished bright." Her friends tried to convince her that her husband's course had been fully vindicated by General Miles and General Godfrey. But she was realistic. Autie had been the object of envy during his lifetime and was becoming a source of profitable income to writers who made their reputations by besmirching and defaming the famous. Once she was gone there would be no survivors to take up the sword and defend her hero. As author Marguerite Merington said: "Mrs. Custer was not afraid of death or dying, but she was afraid of being dead, for she feared that his reputation would be assailed by misrepresentations which she from her arsenal of carefully collected facts, could easily refute."[38]

Now age 82, for it was 1924, Libbie had found another champion. Colonel Charles Francis Bates had taken up the Custer guidon. Bates, who knew Libbie well, became a deep student of the man, Custer, and of his engagements. He, like many others, resented the new trend among some writers who insisted on producing material that was derogatory and disparaging to Custer. Unlike most military men who believed that the best defense was an offense, Bates avoided personalities. In a number of articles and booklets he presented facts these writers could not controvert.

One of his first articles was published in the July, 1924, issue of the *Cavalry Journal.* In it he drew attention to a meeting held in Bronxville for the purpose of organizing the "Westchester Horse." This organization was formed to encourage horseback riding and the development of additional bridle paths throughout Westchester County. It was suggested that the Park authorities name one of the bridle paths the "Custer Trail." The trail would begin at Bronxville and end at West Point.

This seemed appropriate since Mrs. Custer had made her summer home in Bronxville where she voted and had done much of her literary work. "Such a trail as proposed," he wrote, "would lead from Mrs. Custer's long-time home to General Custer's final resting place." He went on to say: "The large and enthusiastic Monroe colony in Bronxville are wont to attribute much of Mrs. Custer's mental acumen and intellectual brilliancy to her long horseback rides with her cavalry husband. . . . Only a few years ago Mrs. Custer's love of travel led her to India where she rode through the Khyber Pass, the Afghanistan Gateway to India. . . ."[39]

Later, Bates wrote two significant articles. The first was in the New York *Times* in June, 1926, just prior to the 50th anniversary celebration of the Custer Battle.[40] Ten years later, and after considerable research, he published *Custer's Indian Battles.*[41]

The year of 1925 began with a shock. On January 17th, Libbie was informed that her cousin Rebecca Richmond had passed away the evening before. Rebecca, who had been a resident of Grand Rapids all of her 84 years, had seen the city from its infancy. Her father, William Almy Richmond, had come from Aurora, N.Y. He had served as a member of the first board of village trustees and had been cashier of the first bank established in Grand Rapids. His successful effort in developing the first plank road between Grand Rapids and Kalamazoo, and the construction of the first lattice bridge across the Grand River, were well-known. Active in politics, he had served as a delegate in 1836 to the first "Convention of Assent," which rejected Congress' conditions for the admission of Michigan into the Union. He served in the State Legislature and was active in Indian Affairs. In 1837, Michigan's year of admission to statehood, he married Libbie's aunt, Lorraine Page, the daughter of Deacon Abel Page. Libbie had lost a dear friend.[42]

At the Gramatan Inn at Daytona Beach, Florida, she had received a letter from Mr. J. A. Shoemaker of Billings, Montana, inviting her to be a guest at the 50th anniversary of the Custer Battle in June, 1926. Neuritis had hindered an earlier reply, her desk being heaped with unanswered letters. "If I am ill again," she continued, "I wll dictate and *not* let the letters heap up on my desk as within the last fortnight. . . . I am sorry not to have the courage to face the ordeal of publicity. I have lived a retired life for so long I would not know how to suppress the *day,* the *ceremonies,* the *place,* would surely call forth."[43] She was more than interested in the proposed plans and the thought of a commemorative coin being issued. She had told Miss Merington she had declined going West because of her failing health and because she believed her presence would be inexpedient.

Libbie had been maintaining a correspondence with David F. Barry for some years. He was one of her few remaining contacts with the old West, for Barry had been a photographer at Fort Lincoln when Autie was alive. Confident that he would give her an honest answer, she had asked him whether she should accept the invitation to the 50th anniversary celebration. In his straightforward manner he said: "You want me to be honest. I think it would be a great mental strain to be shown — certain points on that Field that I am quite familiar with — let them use your name — and you use your good judgment. This I say to *you only.*"[44]

Libbie's friends had been urging her acceptance of the invitation to attend the ceremony which resulted in its being her first thought on awakening and her last thought each night.[45] It was only after she had returned to her Fifth Avenue apartment that she had made her final decision to stay home. Undoubtedly Barry had firmed her resolution. She advised Shoemaker that the General's niece and her husband, Mr. and Mrs. Charles W. Elmer of Brooklyn, would attend the ceremonies and represent her "so that you will have a Custer for the great day."[46]

A movement had been started to raise a fund to unveil a monument to Major Reno during the Semi-Centennial. General Godfrey, who retained many reservations about Reno, was not hesitant in voicing his objections. On March 2 he let Mr. Shoemaker know in no uncertain terms, and sent Libbie a copy of his letter to inform her of his action.[47]

Libbie wrote Shoemaker a remarkable letter. It was the one instance in which she said what she had felt about Reno but had kept hidden for 50 years. She began:

"General Godfrey has sent me a copy of his letter to you and I join him in appealing to you not to permit any memorial of any kind to be placed on that sacred battlefield to so great a coward as Col. Reno. Please use your influence in preventing any and thus pay tribute to so unworthy a man. He had used influence to be placed on duty in the East when our regiment of battle scarred heroes were campaigning from almost the Mexican to the Canadian border. The battle of the Little Big Horn was his first battle and he seemed not to *try* to hide his cowardice. I beg you to try and arrest any move in Congress that would glorify so faithless a soldier.

"In writing this I feel almost my husband's hand taking the pen away from me. He was so opposed to my taking up regimental or official affairs but in this instance I cannot refrain from making an appeal. I beg that you consider what I have written as confidential. Of course you are at liberty to say that I am opposed and have *unquestionable reasons* for opposition but this letter is for your consideration. . . . I *long* for a memorial to our heroes on the battlefield of the Little Big Horn but not to *single out* for honor, the one coward of the regiment."[48]

NOTES — CHAPTER 38

[1]Billings *Gazette*, June 22, 1921.
[2]Libbie to Miss E. Fearis, May 30, 1921. The buckskins were, in later years, transferred to the museum of the Custer Battlefield National Monument.
[3]Billings *Gazette*, June 23, 1921.
[4]Mr. Fayal to Libbie, May 25, 1921, EBC-CBNM.
Fayal stated that the Century Co. "for a thousand copies of the Godfrey article alone, the cost would be about $336. Adding Gen. Edgerly's paper would total about $454."
[5]Libbie to Mr. I. D. O'Donnell, May 26, 1921, EBC-CBNM.
[6]Gen. E. S. Godfrey to Libbie, June 21, 1921, BCWC collection.
[7]Elizabeth B. Custer (editor): *"General George A. Custer and The Battle of The Little Big Horn,* N.Y., 1926.
[8]Author's collection.
[9]Billings *Gazette*, June 26,1926.
[10]*Ibid*, June 25, 1926.
[11]*Ibid*, June 25, 1921.
[12]New York *Times*, June 19, 1921.
[13]Updated clipping from the Kansas City *Post* (Ca. July, 1921).
[14]Harry Conant to Libbie, June 9, 25, 1921, BCWC collection; Monroe *Evening News*, June 27, 1921.
[15]Libbie to Mr. Fisher, January 2, 1922, EBC-CBNM.
[16]Libbie to Gen. K. M. VanZandt, February 7, 1922, EBC-CBNM.
[17]Willard Parker to Libbie, May 9, 1922, letter in author's collection.
Mrs. Elizabeth W. Wrigley, Claremont, Calif., president of The Francis Bacon Foundation, kindly pored through all issues of *American Baconiana* from February, 1923, through January, 1931, but could find no mention of Libbie.
[18]Libbie to Mrs. Francis Gibson, September 16, 1923, EBC-CBNM.
[19]*Ibid*.
[20]*Ibid*. Libbie failed to list her "drawbacks" and "obstacles."
[21]Monroe City Commission minutes, Monday,March 19, 1923.
[22]*Ibid*, June 11, 1923.
[23]Monroe *Evening News*, June 11, 1923.
[24]*Ibid*, June 13, 1923.
[25]*Ibid*, June 23, 1923.
[26]Kate Landon Dansard to Libbie, Ca. June, 1923, BCWC collection.
[27]Monroe *Evening News*, June 16, 1923.
[28]*Ibid*.
[29]*Ibid*, June 18, 1923.
[30]*Ibid*, June 20, 1923.
[31]*Ibid*, June 22, 1923.
[32]*Ibid*, June 23, 1923.
[33]There are a few interesting side notes. Walter Gesell, whose barber shop was about 50 yards from the Custer monument at the time of its removal, said to me when I asked him about the alleged weakness of the foundation under the monument: "Hell, Doc, they dynamited it for two days before they got it loose."
In 1955 it was my privilege to head a movement for removing the Custer monument from its site in Soldiers and Sailors Park to its present position at the corner of Monroe and Elm streets. The City had permitted trees to surround the monument in rather close proximity at its park site. So much so that it became a challenge to Monroe Camera Club members. The best opportunity for photographs was in the winter when all the leaves had fallen.
When it came time to lift the monument off its base a Detroit contractor was obtained for the purpose. His mobile crane passed down Front Street within 50 feet of it where it remained hidden in the foliage of the trees. Two blocks beyond it the operator reversed his course before he saw it. As he told me later that day: "We knew we were on the right street but wondered how in hell we could lose a monument."
When the Custer Monument was rededicated by the First Cavalry Division Association on September 3, 1955, the General's grandnephew, Colonel Brice C. W. Custer, in addressing the 2,000 persons assembled, said: "The Custer family deeply appreciates the statue being brought out of the wilderness and up here in sight again."
His brother Colonel Charles Custer, declared: "General Custer's widow, Elizabeth Bacon Custer of Monroe, who unveiled the monument in Courthouse Square here in 1910, was deeply hurt when it was moved in 1923 to Soldiers and Sailors Park on East Front Street. She considered that too obscure a site and until her death wished it might have been a better one. The City of Monroe today keeps faith with the devoted wife and widow of General Custer."
The last known effort to erect a statue to General Custer was that of Eugene McAuliffe of Omaha, Nebraska. In 1954 he began a drive to erect an equestrian monument of Custer at the Custer Battlefield National Monument. Dr. Avard Fairbanks, well-known sculptor of Salt Lake City, prepared the model. Resisted in his efforts by the Park Service, McAuliffe directed his energies to launching a drive for its erection at Fort Abraham Lincoln near Bismarck, North Dakota. A recession at this time destroyed all plans.
[34]Senate Bill No. 323, 68th Cong., 1st sess., December 6, 1923.
[35]Gen. Nelson A. Miles to "The Honorable Senators and Members of Congress, December 19, 1923, EBC-CBNM.
[36]Harry B. Robinson: "Guide To The Custer Battlefield Museum," *Montana Magazine of History*, July, 1952, pp. 42-47; Don Rickey Jr.: *History Of The Custer Battlefield,* Washington, 1967, pp. 31-36.
[37]Zeisler, Monroe *Evening News*, February 11, 1950.
[38]*Ibid*.
[39]Charles F. Bates: "The Westchester Horse And The "Custer Trail," *Cavalry Journal*, July 1924, p. 312. This article was expanded upon in a booklet entitled, "Westchester — Hudson River — West Point."
[40]Charles F. Bates: "Lost And Won; Custer's Last Battle," New York *Times*, June 20, 1926. It was reprinted in a booklet.
[41]Charles F. Bates: *Custer's Indian Battles*, Bronxville, 1936.
[42]Grand Rapids *Press*, January 17, 1925.
[43]Libbie to Mr. J. A. Shoemaker, December 19, 1925, Billings Public Library. Libbie now wintered at the Gramatan Inn at Daytona Beach, Florida.
[44]D. F. Barry to Libbie, March 4, 1926, BCWC collection.
[45]Libbie to J. A. Shoemaker, January 8, 1926, Billings Public Library.
[46]*Ibid*, March 12, 1926.
[47]Gen. E. S. Godfrey to Mr. J. A. Shoemaker, March 2, 1926, EBC-CBNM.
[48]Libbie to J. A. Shoemaker, March 19, 1926, Billings Public Library.

Chapter 39
COMPANION FOR ETERNITY

The heroes of Custer Hill would receive national recognition. This was the plan of the National Custer Memorial Association. Its members, presided over by General Godfrey, planned a three-day recognition of this 50th anniversary beginning on June 24, 1926. The Seventh Cavalry then stationed at Fort Bliss, Texas, was ordered to the Custer Battlefield to participate in the ceremonies and a reenactment of Reno's retreat from the valley.

Thousands of people arrived from all parts of the country to view the observance. The National Indian War Veterans were invited to attend and invitations were sent to the Crows, Sioux and Cheyennes.

An impressive ceremony on June 24th was the meeting of Seventh cavalrymen and Indian warriors at the memorial shaft on Custer Hill where White Bull, a nephew of Sitting Bull, presented General Godfrey with an Indian blanket, Godfrey reciprocating with an American flag. After the speeches a salute was fired and taps blown over the mass grave of the 220 Seventh cavalrymen.[1]

A few weeks before the observance the skeleton of a cavalryman was found in the valley below, along the line of Reno's pickets. A concrete tomb was prepared to receive the bones of the unknown soldier at the nearby town of Garryowen, where an interment ceremony was planned for June 26th. The services were held that morning followed by a ceremonial burying of the hatchet. The Seventh Cavalry then reenacted Reno's retreat from Garryowen across the river up to the Reno-Benteen battlefield.[2]

While the red men and the white men smoked a pipe of peace that June 25th, Libbie remained in seclusion. Except for a brief trip to a nearby hotel to hear a radio re-enactment of her husband's last battle, she spent the day quietly in her apartment. The thought of the great demonstration in honor of her husband thrilled her.

On the day before, a reporter for the New York *Herald* had interviewed her. He asked questions of the days gone by as her "blue eyes sparkled and her gentle face,in its frame of soft white curls, flushed with pleasure at the thought of the praise coming to her hero-husband. "One sees," he wrote, "after fifty years he is still her hero. . . . The last fifty years have offered her nothing so precious as her memories."[3]

Her recollections contained no bitterness, no hatred for the Indians. "I do not resent their part in the celebration," she said. "They were only defending their country as they thought. The only thing that I cannot ever feel right about is the fact that my husband had too few troops and too little ammunition. It was the common complaint throughout the West in those days the army was given old worn-out rifles, while the 'good' Indians were always getting the best modern firearms from the Indian Department.

"It was a terrible tragedy—so many wonderful lives lost. But perhaps it was necessary in the scheme of things, for the public clamor that rose after the battle resulted in better equipment for the soldiers everywhere, and very soon the Indian warfare came to an end."[4]

Though Libbie was not destined to have a son, she did have a godson. George L. Yates, the son of Captain George Walter Yates who had seen service with Autie during the Civil War and died with him on the Little Big Horn, ably served as her godson. He was the first-born of George and Annie Yates, and the Custers had been his godparents at the christening. Dutifully over the years George made frequent calls on Libbie, seeing to her comfort, performing errands for her and reminding her of the past. Though he lived just across the river in Jersey, it was not always easy to visit her for he had a family of his own.

George had gone out to Montana to observe the anniversary celebration at the Custer Battlefield. Nothing he could have done would have pleased her more. She wrote to his wife Suzanne that she was "so touched because George went." The 50th anniversary had left her "millions of letters to be answered," at a time her neuritis was torturing her. Hot sea baths piped into the Gramatan Hotel, and followed by Swedish massage, was making her trip to Florida worthwhile. It had taken "the *tucker*" out of her so, she hadn't been able to write on her war book.[5]

Life was a bit lonely in Florida. Unable to cope with all of the unanswered letters because of her affliction, and away from her Cosmopolitan Club and many dear friends, she yearned for companionship. On her desk was a small picture of George and Suzanne Yates sitting on a bench in a garden. She prized it highly. Wistfully she wrote to them: "Oh how I wish that you two were where we could 'neighbor'."[6]

George Yates' mother, Annie, had ample opportunity to observe General Custer and Libbie under every manner of condition except on the battlefield. She had first met the Custers at Fort Hays, Kansas, when, as a girl, she visited her uncle, Col. George Gibson. She recalled that:

"In later years it was again my privilege to have seen the home life of the Custers pass like a panorama before my eyes from day to day. The remembrance of the last three years of their life together when, in his devotion to his wife, General Custer rarely left her side except when called upon by the exigencies of the service, must be to Mrs. Custer now the richest gift that memory could bestow.

"One never to be fogotten afternoon, the hammock was swung between some trees in a romantic nook on the sloping bank of Big Creek, sunbeams slipping through, played upon the sweet face and the brown hair, the white dress and blue ribbons of General Custer's girl wife as she reclined in the hammock. The General stood rocking the hammock to and fro, and as he moved back and forth, the sunshine flashed the gold of his hair above the blue of his uniform. Bronzed and manly though he was and looking every inch a born fighter, there was something gentle and tender in his attitude and expression that proclaimed him an ideal lover. Every now and then leaning over her he would murmur something in her ear that seemed to call an answering blush to her cheek and then they would look towards me and smile as if to say: 'This is love,' and I smiling back, said to myself: 'Will it ever come to me like this?' Suddenly the General glanced towards me, his face illuminated with enthusiasm, and exclaimed: 'Annie, I am the happiest man in the world. I envy no one. With my dear little wife whom I adore and the 7th Cavalry, the proudest command in the world, I would not change places with a king'."[7]

David F. Barry must have been facing some lean times at his studio in Superior, Wisconsin, or perhaps it was his reaction to a business opportunity. The Buffalo Bill Museum at Cody, Wyoming, was in its fledgling years and many friends of Bill Cody were extending every effort to build a fine collection. David Barry thought the museum should have a large picture of General Custer to hang in the exhibits. "If I were on easy street and could afford to," he wrote Libbie, "it simply would be a pleasure for me to furnish one with my compliments." He could, however, provide such a photo completely framed—a 16 x 20—for $25.[8]

Libbie's reaction was negative, for some unknown reason. It was over two years later Barry informed her that Henry F. Seitz of Duluth had presented the portrait of General Custer to the Buffalo Bill Museum. Barry suggested that she drop him a line.[9]

In August of 1927, Libbie had to make a hard decision. A family reunion was being held at Howlett Hill, the scene of her childhood vacations and the birthplace of her father. Reluctantly, but with a painful reminder of her infirmities, she wrote: "When I was a motherless and lonely little girl my father took me—vacation time from boarding school in our Michigan home to Howlett Hill, Onondaga County where his sisters lived—Aunt Mary and Uncle John Case, Aunt Eliza and Denison Sabin."

She recalled the stage station near there and the impressive stage coach with its large springs, its sway from side to side and its folding steps that gave it a touch reminiscent of royalty. It took the steep Camillus Hill to wipe away the feeling of grandeur for it caused her to hold her breath as she buried her head in Aunt Mary's seven breadths of petticoats.

A pleasant memory was the patience of Uncle John allowing them to milk an old cow whose permissiveness extended to approaches from either side. Young Bronson Case extended this liberty by crawling between old Bessie's hind legs and dodging her swishing tail as he sought to fill his small pail. These were her pleasant memories and there would be more rekindled at the family gathering she would be unable to attend.[10]

General Godfrey and Libbie had voiced strong objections when a monument was proposed to honor Major Reno in 1926. When the subject was discussed again some three years later, Godfrey took it upon himself to make a vehement protest against the use of any names on a marker on the Benteen-Reno Battlefield site. Godfrey first heard of the plan from Agent C. H. Asbury at the Crow Agency early in 1929. In his protest he wrote Asbury:

"1st—Because I have always felt that Major Reno failed in his part in the valley attack in the disposition of his command when he fell back in the old stream bed; that he failed to exercise any fire control; that he *could* and *should* have held his position.

"2nd—Having made the decision to retreat, he made no disposition to cover that retreat or to properly inform the command of such decision; that he in person led a panic, straggling retreat, thereby sacrificing many lives and the morale of his command. The shock from the killing of Bloody Knife at his side or near him seems to have

LIBBIE WAITS FOR A FRIEND. Ca. 1916. Mrs. E. B. Custer collection. Custer Battlefield National Monument.

bereft him of the sense of official responsibility and to impel him to seek safety in flight.

"3rd—After the command had taken the position, when we were besieged he seemed resigned to inactivity except when urged by Captain Benteen. After all firing had ceased the night of June 25th, he planned to abandon the position, destroy property that could not be transported, mount all men who could ride and retreat to the supply camp at the mouth of Powder River. When asked what he proposed to do with the wounded who could not ride, he said they would have to be *abandoned* and Benteen then told him he would not do it. This I had from Captain Benteen himself.

"I protest the name of Major Reno on the marker and as the titulary commander's name should not be engraved thereon, therefore no individual names of survivors should appear and I suggest the following inscription:

"This area was occupied by Companies A, B, D, H, K and M, 7th U.S. Cavalry, and the pack train where they were beseiged, June 25th & 26th, 1876."

This inscription was used on the marker with very slight change, the marker being dedicated on August 14, 1929.[12] No names were used.

It had become an annual custom for New York newspapers to interview Libbie just prior to each anniversary of the battle. On the 53rd anniversary—June 25th, 1929—the New York *Herald Tribune* referred to her as "Murray Hill's most prized pedestrian," and that it was "a dull day on which Mrs. Custer does not give lower Park Avenue a glimpse of her stately figure crossing the street."[13] In the following year the New York *Times* captioned its article with a "Day Of Memories For Custer's Widow," then went on to say: "Because of her advanced age—Mrs. Custer is 76 (sic) years old—she has told her friends she wishes to spend the day quietly, alone with her memories and her war relics. She will take no part in any public observance of the event. . . ."[14]

Libbie did take time to admire the flowers and to read the many messages sent to her. She had curtailed her daily walk along Park Avenue of late so she could spend more time on her Civil War book. Her niece, Mrs. Elmer, explained to the press that "considering her declining years and occasional attacks of neuritis," she was in good health and showed a keen interest in current events.

The 55th anniversary of the Little Big Horn was unmarked by any observance. The New York *Times* said: "It was an uneventful day also for the General's widow."[15] Libbie had just passed her 90th birthday when the anniversary of 1932 arrived. The *Times* noted: "Usually Mrs. Custer marks the observance of the 'Last Stand' with an interview, recounting the perils of a pioneer life in the Western wilderness of the '70s which she encountered with her husband, but yesterday she declined to make any comment. 'I am not feeling up to the mark,' she announced through her companion Mrs. Margaret Flood."[16]

LIBBIE'S FRIEND ARRIVES. Ca. 1916. Mrs. E. B. Custer collection. Custer Battlefield National Monument.

Several days earlier she had been listening to a radio broadcast of the ceremonies in New Rumley, Ohio, where a statue of her husband was unveiled as Ohio's belated tribute to one of its most colorful soldiers. The Ohio General Assembly had appropriated $15,000 three years earlier.[17] Libbie had been informed that Lown F. Slater had initiated a move to have a monument to Autie placed in New Rumley as early as 1929. The news drew forth the comment from Libbie that her husband "and his family loved that little town and always talked of it when there was a family gathering."[18]

With Custer monuments in Pennsylvania, Montana, Michigan, Colorado and Ohio, it was natural enough to think in terms of Kansas and the Dakotas. She wished there could be a memorial at Bismarck, she suggested it wistfully to David Barry.[19]

Soon after the first of the year, Barry sent her an editorial from the Miles City (Montana) *Star* that contained complimentary remarks of General Custer. Barry had sent such articles to Libbie from time to time knowing she had little opportunity to learn of them.

His response to her suggestion was to inform her that Joe Scanlan of the *Star* had been promoting a monument for General Miles on the Milk River. Barry thought a bill introduced by Senators Walsh and Wheeler might be introduced in the Senate for a monument to be erected at Bismarck. He wouldn't suggest a monument to Custer at Fort Lincoln since there was "nothing there but a field."[20] He suggested, as he had in several previous letters, that she give something of her husband's to the Buffalo Bill Museum at Cody. Colonel Hare had died December 22, 1929, in Washington, he noted, leaving only General Godfrey and Colonel Varnum of the Old Seventh.

John S. McMillan, Monroe's entrepreneur, had been stirring the decadent community to action. A former newspaperman, he had the unique quality of viewing his birthplace objectively. Almost single-handedly he had obtained Federal funds to enlarge and deepen Monroe's port on Lake Erie. He had stirred the State Highway Department to widening the Dixie Highway through the heart of the business district. With the abandonment of the Detroit United Railway, McMillan had arranged for the purchase of its old power house and freight sheds on the northeast corner of Monroe and Elm Streets.

McMillan's next plan was to raze the D.U.R. buildings and prepare a large area he would name Custer Square. He already had acquired the southeast corner property which ran south along Monroe Street to the bank of the River Raisin. On this piece of property he planned to build a half-million-dollar 120-room hotel that would be named the Hotel General Custer. In it would be a room off the lobby devoted to a display of Custer mementoes.

Presumably McMillan had contacted Libbie and members of the Custer family and obtained from them promises of material for display.[21]

It was proposed to move the Custer monument from Soldiers and Sailors Park to a terrace in front of St. Mary's Church, diagonally from the hotel. A theatre—the Lennox Theatre—would be constructed on the northeast corner.

When Libbie learned of the projects she became quite excited as evidenced in a letter to David Barry. She told him:

> "I am just now so interested in my own town, Monroe. It is very old and behind the times, with Toledo so successful on one side and Detroit on the other. But some energetic people with money, have invested in real estate and are making an addition across the river with a Hotel General Custer and with avenues and parks. It is well laid out and a new bridge crossing the River Raisin is very handsomely constructed. Our old town is closely built up and without much life."[22]

Libbie continued her fight against the gnawing discomfort and disability from her neuritis. Her knee had been bothering her for several years but seemed not to be painful. As she told George Yates' wife: "If it was painful I *would* rebel. It is a trial never to go out alone except perhaps the three blocks to the club. But think of it dear ones, that I escape pain. . . . I could do little away from home because of the ailing knee. It is gaining. No violent pain but cannot trust it on the street."[23]

Ten days later she told Suzanne she had given up going South for the winter in her effort to fight neuritis. She had become so lame she could not walk alone so was eager to stay home near her doctor who lived in the same apartment building and had been treating her satisfactorily with *"electricity, violet rays, massage,* etc. with all this I ought to dance the Can Can very soon."[24]

Time was having its effect on her. Her memory was failing. Searching her mind for thoughts, she often found it threadbare. Miss Merington often saved her embarrassment "when she forgot a name or failed to recognize an acquaintance."[25]

In April of 1930 she had told Suzanne Yates she had "finished, after two years, writing answers to over 300 letters following the 50th anniversary."[26] The Yates had sent her a birthday card and a handkerchief. Libbie had written in response, then, forgetfully, had laid the letter aside among others she had previously answered. For a second time she acknowledged the card and kerchief, then finally, a third time.[27] Two days earlier, her letter to Suzanne Yates referred to the kerchief and to the anniversary of the battle of the Little Big Horn as having occurred in the year just passed. Her letters now evidenced frequent lapses of memory as to the year, and there was a repetition of thought. The Yates, recognizing that Aunt Libbie was failing, tenderly administered to her wants.

Libbie was going to the club on Sundays now for it was Margaret's day out.[28] One of the maids there recalled that she looked "like a beautiful picture."

Those were lonely days. So many of her friends had gone. She had a radio now. She hadn't known the solace of music until this gift from some of her acquaintances at the trust department had introduced her to it. Her relatives, the Custers, lived far away in Michigan. Most of Nevin's children were alive but were not affluent enough to travel East for those were depression days. May—Maria Custer—lived with her husband Charles Elmer (of Monroe) in Brooklyn. The Elmers saw her frequently as did George Yates but that was not as often as the lonely Libbie would have liked for she knew there was not too much time left.

Hopelessly she continued to struggle with her mail. Her method of placing her unanswered letters in one pile and the answered ones in another had worked successfully over the years. Now it was beginning to boomerang. She would mark those she answered with *ack* (acknowledged) or *ans* (answered) but often placed her letter of reply in this heap.

In 1931, Melvin Hollinshead of Detroit arranged to have Medal of Honor winner Corporal Leander Herron meet Mrs. Custer again. Hollinshead escorted the 85 year old veteran from his home in Omaha, Nebraska. When they arrived at 71 Park Avenue, Miss Merington let them in.

Libbie, with all her great charm, seated the old scout beside her on a davenport. As Hollinshead recalled that meeting:

> "They launched into an animated conversation that sought to bridge a lapse of 60 years. . . . They talked of those they knew 60 years before—of Grant and Sheridan, of Wild Bill Hickok and California Joe, of Sitting Bull and Crazy Horse; they argued who rode the bay horse and who the black, that time they had to run for the fort when the Indians chased them. . . . And they talked of General Custer and how they rode with him at the head of the column on the long patrols. But finally they seemed talked out, two very old people, tiring from the excitement of reliving other days."[29]

As they rose to leave, the old Corporal sagged and tears came to his eyes. He could not let go of Libbie's hand. She, retaining her poise, smiled at him and said in the way of encouragement: "Now, remember, Corporal, I expect you to keep those letters coming. Don't disappoint me." He kept the letters coming for he outlived her four years.[30]

Another visitor from the West that year was I. D. O'Donnell of Billings. Libbie's maid refused him admittance until he sent in his card with the message that he was John Burkman's friend.

Burkman's name was the magic word. He was immediately admitted.

As he entered the apartment a little, frail, white-haired old lady advanced slowly to meet him. Except for the brightness of her blue eyes there was nothing remaining of the Libble John had known 60 years before. Her alert mind was still clinging to precious memories. Were John's last days happy ones? Did he continue to talk to the last of the General and of *Vic* and *Dandy?* Was there much interest in Montana of the museum building proposed for the Custer Battlefield?[31]

On the eve of the 55th anniversary of the Custer Battle there was some discussion in her apartment of a recent order to dismantle some of the old frontier forts as an economy measure. "It does seem as if some of the old forts ought to be saved," she said a bit wistfully. "We ought not to allow every vestige of that period to die. After all, this country has very little history, considering how big it is, and we should preserve what we have."

She recalled some of the forts that were made of logs, others that were dugouts. Of the scarcity of water she recalled:

> "Often we lived under the shelving bank of some river when it was low in the dry season, and we brought water carefully up the crumbling path in meager utensils for our daily use. I can remember holding a glass of water in my hands, waiting for the sand to settle, and the natural history to be hidden, so that an inch or two would be clear enough to drink. It was great discipline for us. Afterwards, when I returned to communities where there was plenty of water, I would still pour it out savingly.
>
> "With all that dust and sun, it was 'goodbye complexion.' We knew our husbands wouldn't notice, for it was one nice thing about men; if they get it into their heads that they have married a pretty girl they never see anything to the contrary."[32]

General Edward S. Godfrey, on his retirement in 1907, after 40 years of service, had moved into a family home at Cookstown, New Jersey. He spent his retirement gardening, writing about the Battle of the Little Big Horn and dispelling allegations that discredited General Custer. At various times he had been commander of the Department of Arizona G.A.R.; commander and historian of the Military Order of Indian Wars; senior vice commander of the Military Order of the Loyal Legion, and commander of the Army and Navy Legion of Valor. He and Colonel Charles Varnum were the surviving officers of the Custer Battle.[33]

On April 1, 1932, after an illness of two weeks, Godfrey died. Three weeks after the funeral David Barry wrote Libbie disconsolately. He told her that B. B. Brooks of Casper, Wyoming, and R. S. Ellison of Tulsa, Oklahoma, both had written "asking who we have to take General Godfrey's place in keeping that famous battle the Custer fight alive and before the world. There isn't any one living who could take his place. The old 7th Cavalry have all passed on but Col. Varnum and he never took any interest. . . . I often think I will take my plates of the West—break them up—throw them in the scrap. Over 50 years of hard work simply lost. Why should I leave them to any one. . . . What a loss, Gen. Godfrey going."[34]

That year, for Libbie, had started badly. With the stalwart Godfrey gone there was only one man left who was capable of carrying the guidon and that was Colonel Charles Francis Bates. Colonel Bates, though retired from the Army and practicing law in Bronxville, was preparing a booklet on General Custer's Indian battles in readiness for the 60th anniversary of the Custer Battle. He had observed the need for it when attending the 55th commemoration.[35]

June tempered the feeling of regret that attended Godfrey's passing. Ohio, belatedly, was recognizing Custer's accomplishments. On June 22, 1932, a bronze figure of Custer was unveiled by Mrs. May Custer Elmer who acted in Libbie's behalf. The eight and a half foot figure of Custer was placed in Custer Memorial Park, New Rumley, Ohio, which comprises about an acre of ground on which stood the house in which Custer had been born. The Custer home was torn down in 1898.[36]

$15,000 had been appropriated by the State of Ohio, the monument being erected by the Ohio Archaeological and Historical Society. The sculptor was Erwin F. Frey of Ohio State University.

Governor George White, in a eulogy to General Custer, said: "Until the day of his death, failure was a word which Custer never knew. His talents required room for individual action and his superiors soon learned to trust him on his own resources. . . . wherever man loves courage and honor and high-souled devotion to duty, there you will find his monument. . . . in the hour of his country's need he counted not himself but placed his need beyond his love of life."[37]

Late that year Libbie received a letter addressed to "My Sweet young Aunt Elizabeth" advising Libbie that a group of residents at Southold, Long Island, had met on December 2 and organized as The Custer Institute.[38] Charles Elmer, husband of May Custer, had a longtime interest in astronomy. On moving to Southold from Brooklyn he found many others sharing his interest. They first met in the Custer residence, then later constructed The Custer Observatory as a portion of the Custer Institute.

Libbie, who once thought she would be separated from her Autie when life ended, wrote to a friend: "I was at West Point recently. Autie lies in such a lovely spot, quite alone in that exquisite place. To my relief I found wives with their husbands."[39]

Another relief for Libbie was the knowledge that her affairs were in order. In 1926 she had signed a will bequeathing all of her husband's arms, uniforms, accoutrements and personal property to a public museum or memorial that might be erected on the Custer Battlefield during her lifetime or that of Elizabeth E. Wellington or May Custer Elmer. If not, "then to any historical museum or museums anywhere which may be selected by my Executor, or said Executor can deliver such articles as it may seem proper as souvenirs to my personal friends or to any relative of General George Armstrong Custer."[40]

The remainder of her property, including the proceeds of the sale of her real estate, was bequeathed to Vassar College with the provision that it be invested in securities, the income from which would be used "for the support and education of the daughters of commissioned officers in the regular army." There was some discretion allowed in the use of the fund. The fund would be known as the "GENERAL GEORGE ARMSTRONG CUSTER AND ELIZABETH BACON CUSTER SCHOLARSHIP FUND FOR DAUGHTERS OF ARMY OFFICERS." The National City Bank of New York was named the executor. The terms of the will were such that one had little doubt Libbie was well aware of the employment and education problems of her sex. There had been little equality during her lifetime and, though the trend to change this untenable situation was on its way, she would not live long enough to see it through, but she could influence it in her small way.[41]

Three years later—1929—for some unaccountable reason Libbie had a change of mind. In a codicil, that portion of the original will that had designated Vassar College and a scholarship fund as the recipients of a large share of her estate was removed. Her assets were divided equally between Agnes Bates Wellington and May Custer Elmer. The City Bank Farmers Trust Company was named as the new executor.[42]

Her last illness was brief. When it became apparent that it was her last, her niece, Lula Custer in Monroe, was summoned for Lula was a nurse.

On Sunday, April 2, 1933, Libbie suffered a heart attack, and on Tuesday afternoon she passed away. At her bedside were her two nieces, Lula Custer and Mrs. Charles Elmer, and Mr. Elmer.[43] Miss Merington arrived soon after and when asked what dress Libbie should wear for her last journey, she answered, "White and her best." At long last she was going to her "Autie." He had been waiting while she did what she had to do. Now they could be together at West Point.

A brief, informal service was held in her Park Avenue apartment on Wednesday, attended by a few close friends. It consisted of a prayer and the reading of a psalm by her old friend the Reverend H. P. Silver, who had been the West Point chaplain from 1913 to 1918.[44]

On Thursday, April 6, funeral services were held at West Point in the afternoon. Reverend Arthur B. Kinsolving, chaplain of the Military Academy, conducted the service. The funeral cortege, on its arrival from New York, was escorted from the Academy gate to the cemetery by a military police detail. Six pallbearers drawn from noncommissioned officers of the regular army garrison there joined the detail. It was not a military funeral.[45]

Just two days later Libbie would have been 92. Her mission accomplished, she and Autie could now celebrate her birthday together.[46]

NOTES—CHAPTER 39

1Rickey: *History of C.B.*, pp. 80-82. The bones of the cavalry men lie around the base of the stone shaft.
2*Ibid*, p. 82.
3New York *Herald*, June 25, 1926.
4*Ibid*.
5Libbie to Mrs. George (Suzanne) Yates, January 30, 1927, Mrs. Ethel Yates Gray collection.
6*Ibid*, February 10, 1927.
7Annie Yates: *General Custer*. An unpublished manuscript among Libbie's papers, author's collection. It is obvious Annie was describing a scene on Big Creek near Fort Hays, Kansas, in 1867.
8D. F. Barry to Libbie, January 22, 1927, BCWC collection.
9*Ibid*, April 6, 1929, BCWC collection.
10Libbie to "Dear Friends and Kinsmen," August 16, 1927, John Manion collection.
11E. S. Godfrey to C. H. Asbury, January 18, 1929, EBC-CBNM.
12Rickey: *History of C.B.*, p. 64.
13New York *Herald Tribune*, June 25, 1929.
14New York *Times*, June 25, 1930.
15New York *Times*, June 26, 1931.
16*Ibid*, June 25, 1932.
17*Ibid*.
18Libbie to D. F. Barry, July 3, 15, 1929, EBC-CBNM.
19*Ibid*, November 26, 1929.
20D. F. Barry to Libbie, February 1, 1930, BCWC collection.
21Monroe *Evening News*, May 21, 1929; Detroit *Free Press*, February 9, 1930. Additional information was obtained from Hugh Winkworth, Mrs. Elizabeth Meyers, Kathleen Lohr, and Arthur Lesow, Monroe, Michigan.
22Libbie to David Barry, December 12, 1929, EBC-CBNM.
23Libbie to Mrs. Suzanne Yates, February 7, 1930, Mrs. Ethel Yates Gray collection.
24*Ibid*, February 18, 1930.
25Monroe *Evening News*, February 11, 1950.
26Libbie to Mrs. George Yates, April 23, 1930, Mrs. Ethel Yates Gray collection. The anniversary had been celebrated *four* years earlier.
27*Ibid*, May 12, 1930.
28*Ibid*, May 20, 1930.
29Melvin Hollinshead: *The General Custer Story—From The Distaff Side;* unpublished manuscript courtesy of Mr. Hollinshead.
30*Ibid*.
31Wagner: *Old Neutriment*, pp. 218-20.

The late Colonel Brice C. W. Custer recalled his first visit to Libbie's New York apartment for it was in the Christmas season of 1918. Seated on her davenport with her hands folded in her lap, she enjoyed talking about her life with Brice's Uncle Autie. She smiled but never laughed. She appeared quite relaxed and while talking she never used her hands. An air of seriousness overcame her when talking about General Grant; when talking of Lincoln or other generals she would beam. At all times her voice was low and sweet.

32New York *Sun*, 1931,Ca. June 26.
33Newark *Evening News*, April 2, 1932; Kenneth Hammer: *Men With Custer*, Fort Collins, 1972, pp. 207-208.
34David Barry to Libbie, April 24, 1932, BCWC collection.
35Charles Francis Bates: *Custer's Indian Battles*, Bronxville, 1936. Bates' extensive research culminated in this well-written and scarce booklet. On page 22 he asserts that:

"Custer's career had few parallels in the history of any war in any country. His success was no more the result of luck than are the rewards of any human effort, for if there is any calling in life where the fruits are gathered in accordance with real merit it is in

MONROE BUSINESS SECTION about 1863. View is north side of East Front Street. C. W. Hill photo.

the profession of arms, where patient study, sleepless vigilance, laborious toil and iron nerve are requisite in order to reap the harvest of glory. 'Custer's luck' was the result of judgment to do the right thing at the right time, and to his devotion to his profession and to his great energy and persistency."

Then in a preface to the booklet he quoted Custer's explanation of his method of meeting a military situation as follows:

"I am not impetuous or impulsive. I resent that. Everything that I have ever done has been the result of the study that I have made of imaginary military situations that might arise. When I became engaged in campaign or battle and a great emergency arose, everything that I had ever read or studied focused in my mind as if the situation were under a magnifying glass and my decision was the instantaneous result. My mind worked instantaneously, but always as the result of everything I had ever studied being brought to bear on the situation."

[36]Cadiz (Ohio) *Republican,* June 23, 1932; Monroe *Evening News,* June 23, 1932.

[37]*Ibid.*

[38]Charles Elmer to Libbie, December 5, 1932, EBC-CBNM.

[39]Merington: *Custer Story,* p. 329.

[40]Last Will and Testament of Elizabeth B. Custer, November 18, 1926, EBC-CBNM.

[41]*Ibid.*

[42]Codicil to Libbie's Last Will and Testament, August 23, 1929, EBC-CBNM.

At Libbie's death, and because of the revocation in her codicil, Vassar College was beneficiary of a $5,000 trust fund. The estate was appraised at $113,581 gross and $101,491 net which included securities worth $93,774. There was $344 in cash deposited in the Bronxville Trust Co. to the credit of the "Custer Monument Fund," Charles S. Bates treasurer, having turned it over to Mrs. Custer's estate.

A white towel certified to be the flag of truce used by the Confederate forces, and a white linen handkerchief used by Gen. Custer as a flag of truce at Appomattox, were valued at $100. Both were bequeathed to the War Department.

A pine table used by Grant and Lee at the surrender ceremony, with a letter presenting it to Mrs. Custer by Phil Sheridan, and sword and scabbard of Gen. Custer's all valued at $100, were left to the Smithsonian Institution.

A button from the uniform of George Washington was left to West Point but could not be found. (From Monroe *Evening News,* March 2, 1934 and New York *Times,* March 1, 1934.)

[43]Monroe *Evening News,* April 5, 1933.

[44]Billings *Gazette,* April 5, 1933.

[45]New York *Times,* April 7, 1933.

[46]*Ibid,* April 9, 1933 (Editorial):

"To read of the death of GENERAL CUSTER'S widow is to be once more reminded how very near this country stands to its epic past. Less than 60 years ago the Indian tribes of the Far West were still a problem." And little progress has been evident in the 40 years since.

Widow of General Custer Dies at Age Of 92 in New York; Is Remembered Here

By United Press

New York, April 5.—Mrs. Elizabeth Bacon Custer, who accompanied her husband, Gen. George A. Custer, on many of his Indian campaigns, died late yesterday after a heart attack.

General Custer

She was 91. Mrs. Custer was born in Monroe, Mich. She married the "boy general with the golden locks" in 1864.

A few are left in Bismarck who remember the days when the old frontier town rang with the news of the battle of the Little Big Horn, and heard the tragic news of the annihilation of General George A. Custer and his command.

Among them are Mrs. J. P. Dunn, Mrs. Joe Dietrich, Mr. and Mrs. Jacob Horner, W. A. Falconer, Mr. and Mrs. J. D. Wakeman, Mrs. W. O. Ward, and others.

Mrs. Custer and 25 wives of other men in Custer's command were quartered at Fort Abraham Lincoln, near Bismarck, and from there bade their husbands farewell as the Seventh cavalry started on its last expedition.

On June 25, the 200 men marched forth to meet a force they thought would number 1,200. Instead, 5,000 Indians swarmed about the fated regiment and not a man lived to tell the tale. Three weeks later the Missouri river steamer Far West bore Capt. Grant Marsh to the fort with the first news of the annihilation, one of the most tragic incidents in American history. The story flashed like wildfire along the frontier, once it reached the fort. Business men left their stores and pioneer farmers came from their fields to hear more of the news. Housewives forgot their duties as they heard word of the catastrophe.

Mrs. Custer

As she appeared during her short stay at old Fort Lincoln near Bismarck.

PRESS CLIPPINGS of April 5th and 6th, 1933, announcing the passing of Elizabeth B. Custer. Note the disagreement about her age, 90, 91, and 92! From the collection of Albert P. Salisbury.

Rites Held for Mrs. Custer

NEW YORK, Thursday, April 6.—(AP)—A brief informal funeral service was held yesterday for Mrs. Elizabeth Bacon Custer, 90 years old, widow of Gen. George A. Custer, the Cavalry leader who was killed with his entire command at the Battle of the Little Big Horn in 1876.

Mrs. Custer's body will be sent to West Point today for burial in the cemetery where her husband lies.

Hold Informal Rites For Widow of Custer

New York, April 6.—(AP)—A brief informal funeral service was held Wednesday for Mrs. Elizabeth Bacon Custer, 90, widow of General George A. Custer, the cavalry leader who was killed with his entire command at the battle of the Little Big Horn in 1876.

The service was held in the Park Avenue apartment where Mrs. Custer died Tuesday and was attended by a few close friends. It consisted of a prayer and the reading of a psalm by the Rev. H. P. Silver, chaplain at West Point from 1913 to 1918 and an old friend of Mrs. Custer.

Mrs. Custer's body will be sent to West Point Thursday for burial in the cemetery where her husband lies. Services will be conducted in the chapel there by the chaplain the Rev. Arthur Kinsolving

WEDNESD

Widow of General Custer, His Loyal Defender, Is Dead

By Associated Press.

NEW YORK, Wednesday, April 5.—Mrs. Elizabeth Bacon Custer, widow of Gen. George A. Custer, who made his last stand at the battle of Little Big Horn, Mont., in 1876, died in her Park Avenue apartment today of heart disease. She was 91 years old.

Herself a veteran of the prairie schooner trails and the Indian campaigns led by her young soldier husband in the era following the Civil War, Mrs. Custer spent much of her later life recording the glamour, hardship and romance of those stirring days on the western plains.

Her first book, "Boots and Saddles," was published nine years after General Custer and his squadron of the 7th Cavalry were annihilated by the Sioux Indians. In it she detailed the adventure and tragedy of her campaigning days with "the boy general of the golden locks."

Burial May Be West Point

Until stricken Sunday night, Mrs. Custer had been in her usual health and had continued her habit of taking occasional drives and short walks through the Murray Hill section of Park Avenue.

Two nieces, Mrs. Charles W. Elmer of Brooklyn and Miss Lula Custer, summoned from her home on the old Custer farm at Monroe, Mich., were with her when she died. Burial probably will be at West Point, where General Custer lies interred.

BILLINGS, Mont., Wednesday, April 5.—(AP)—With the death of Mrs. Elizabeth Custer the West loses one of its last links between the era of her late warrior-husband and the late Gen. George A. Custer loses his most steadfast champion.

For fifty-six years after Custer and 205 of his men went to their deaths on the banks of the Little Big Horn, near Crow Agency, Mont., Mrs. Custer vigorously defended her husband's actions and motives in precipitating the last major Indian battle.

Controversy Raged for Years

A controversy raged for years in these parts after the battle itself. Whether additional revelations at this late date will be of value is doubted by students of Custer's last campaign.

Old soliders and pioneers who were in contact with Custer and his famous 7th Cavalry when it took the field in 1876 to subdue the Sioux and Cheyennes have always maintained the "full truth" of the battle of the Little Big Horn would never be told while the white-haired, gentle-voiced widow lived.

At the time of the fight Mrs. Custer, with the wives of other officers and soldiers of the regiment was at Fort Abraham Lincoln, near Bismarck, N. D. It was there they learned the heart-breaking news.

PORTRAIT OF LIBBIE, age 79, by Dora Wheeler Keith. 1921. Courtesy of the Monroe County Historical Museum.

INDEX

The frequency with which Libbie and her husband appear on these pages has necessitated eliminating the page numbers except as they apply to certain activities and events.